Why Do You Need This New Edition?

If you're wondering why you should buy this new edition of *Conversations*, here are six great reasons!

1. **Sixty new reading selections** provide students with an entry point to an extraordinary variety of authors, genres, voices, and viewpoints on important contemporary civic issues. This edition includes a larger number of texts that directly reference and respond to one another, demonstrating how public conversations develop in electronic and published writings.

2. **New and revised topics** make the issues discussed in this edition more timely—and closer to students' experience of the world. Included are: sustainable food; environmental sustainability; public education and the value of college; new media; the role of gender and ethnicity in identity; and the changing nature of romantic relationships.

3. **Five new "Conversations in Context" sections** help students see current issues against a rich historical backdrop. A wide range of brief textual and visual arguments expand the context of each debate.

4. **Expanded attention to new media and multi-modal texts** illustrates the ways that even conversations that start in traditional publication venues are extended into electronic environments like Facebook, Twitter, blogs, and visual media where students increasingly direct their time and attention.

5. **A revised Introduction** showcases the "conversation model" of research and writing. Successful academic writers employ this model to illustrate various points of view while developing and defending their own claims.

6. *Conversations* is available with **MyCompLab**—the gateway to a world of online resources developed specifically for students!

PEARSON

IMPORTANT

1. TEXTBOOKS MUST BE RETURNED BY DESIGNATED SEMESTER/TERM DEADLINES OR BE SUBJECT TO A   PER BOOK LATE FINE.

2. LATE BOOKS/FINES ONLY ACCEPTED FOR 5 SPECIFIED DAYS FOLLOWING ESTABLISHED DEADLINES.

3. YOU WILL BE REQUIRED TO PURCHASE THIS TEXTBOOK IF YOU HAVE WRITTEN IN, UNDERLINED, HIGHLIGHTED OR IF THERE ARE ANY VISIBLE SIGNS OF WATER DAMAGE OR UNUSUAL WEAR.

CHECK OUR WEBSITE AT:
www.eiu.edu/~textbks/

NAME
_____
_____
_____

PLEASE RETURN THIS TEXTBOOK TO:
TEXTBOOK RENTAL SERVICE
'30 E.   AVENUE
EASTERN ILLINOIS UNIVERSITY
CHARLESTON, IL 61920

Conversations
Readings for Writing

Eighth Edition

Dominic DelliCarpini
York College of Pennsylvania

Jack Selzer
The Pennsylvania State University

Longman
is an imprint of

Boston   Columbus   Indianapolis   New York   San Francisco
Upper Saddle River   Amsterdam   Cape Town   Dubai   London   Madrid
Milan   Munich   Paris   Montreal   Toronto   Delhi   Mexico City
Sao Paulo   Sydney   Hong Kong   Seoul   Singapore   Taipei   Tokyo

Senior Acquisitions Editor: Brad Potthoff
Development Editor: Karen Mauk
Senior Marketing Manager: Sandra McGuire
Production Manager: Stacey Kulig
Project Coordination, Text Design, and Electronic Page Makeup:
    Electronic Publishing Services Inc., NYC
Senior Cover Design Manager: Nancy Danahy
Cover Designer: Nancy Sacks
Cover Image: © A-Digit/iStockphoto
Photo Researcher: Jullie Chung
Senior Manufacturing Buyer: Dennis J. Para
Printer and Binder: Edwards Brothers
Cover Printer: Lehigh-Phoenix

For permission to use copyrighted material, grateful acknowledgment is
made to the copyright holders on p. 701, which are hereby made part of
this copyright page.

Library of Congress Cataloging-in-Publication Data
Conversations: readings for writing / [compiled by] Dominic Dellicarpini,
Jack Selzer.
    p.cm.
    Includes bibliographical references and index.
    ISBN 978–0–205–83511–9
 1. College readers.   2. Report writing—Problems, exercises, etc.
3. English—language—Rhetoric—Problems, exercises, etc.
I. DelliCarpini, Dominic.   II. Selzer, Jack.   III. Title
    PE1417.C6545 2012
    808'.0427—dc22

1 2 3 4 5 6 7 8 9 10—EDW—15 14 13 12 11

Longman
is an imprint of

www.pearsonhighered.com

ISBN-13: 978-0-205-83511-9
ISBN-10: 0-205-83511-2

Contents

In this part of *Conversations*, writers explore questions about one of the most fundamental of American values: the goal of effectively educating our citizens. Conversation topics include the purposes of education, how well we are succeeding in fulfilling those purposes (and how we measure success), the level of access to higher education citizens are given, and whether higher education is the best (or only) route to success for all Americans.

PART 2   Conversations About Information and Technology   167

In this part of *Conversations*, writers discuss the ways that new technologies are affecting the flow of information, its reliability and biases, and the ways that we think and communicate. Specific questions explored include the effect of new media on journalism, on what we treat as authoritative information, and on our brains as we interact with current technological tools such as Google and PowerPoint.

PART 3   Conversations About Identity: Gender, Race, and Ethnicity   275

In this part of *Conversations*, writers explore the ways that our personal and public identities are affected by two key facets of our humanity: our gender and our ethnic/racial backgrounds. This conversation also features discussions about whether our attention to these issues has changed the ways we interact with one another and whether those changes have been productive or divisive.

PART 4   Conversations About Love Relationships and Marriage   387

In this part of *Conversations*, writers examine one of the most central facets of our humanity: how we relate to one another in love relationships. The conversations range from the effects of technology on love relationships, to the effects of casual sexual relationships in our "hookup culture," to changes in the ways we think about marriage in the 21st century.

PART 5   Conversations About Sustainability   527

In this part of *Conversations*, writers converse about how our culture's growing interest in sustainability has affected attitudes toward the production of food and energy. It also explores questions about who is best equipped to move sustainability agendas forward—and how far we should go in defense of a sustainable world environment.

Rhetorical Contents

As noted in the General Introduction of this book, one reason why writers read is to learn the techniques for developing arguments that fit the needs of a specific situation. This table of contents can help you to find pieces that employ some commonly used rhetorical techniques, styles, and approaches that writers use to explore topics, present information, and build arguments. Reading them analytically—with an eye to the techniques used—can greatly enrich your own writing. Since rhetorical techniques are often used in combination with one another, many of the pieces fall into several different categories; the categories into which they have been placed suggests that a particular technique is one of its dominant methods.

Exploratory Writing: Exploratory writing shows writers working out complex ideas through the writing itself; as a result, these pieces give readers insight into the process by which an idea develops in the writer's mind.

Journal, Personal Report, Weblogs: These pieces demonstrate the various ways that authors use personal experiences to engage an audience—in both traditional and electronic venues.

Description and Narration: These techniques rely upon storytelling and vivid details as a central form of evidence and argument.

Process, Methods: These techniques help readers to understand a concept and/or advance their argument by explaining how something works or by describing a set of steps involved in a complex process.

Illustration, Example: These techniques make use of typical examples to make abstract concepts or arguments more specific and concrete.

Comparison and Contrast: This classic technique
helps readers to see similarities and differences in key
concepts, examples, or situations, in order to build an

argument and/or help readers better understand a complex idea or case.

Analysis: This technique breaks down a complex topic or object into constituent parts, helping the reader to better understand the underlying parts and their relationship to the whole.

Cause and Effect: This technique draws a line of logic between some action or situation and the results of that action or situation.

Definition: This technique helps readers to better understand meanings of key concepts that are specific to a given case, thus establishing or changing the terms of an argument.

Argument, Categorical Proposition: This technique is related to definition; more specifically, it redefines something in a way that the reader may not have otherwise considered, in effect, suggesting that "X is in fact Y."

Argument, Evaluation: This technique is used to argue for the value of some situation, concept, or thing based upon a specific set of criteria—criteria that must first be established and agreed upon by writer and reader.

Argument, Proposal: This technique suggests a course of
action that the writer believes is worth taking (or at least

exploring)—usually because it will lead to positive effects in the future or because it will alleviate or solve a present or past problem.

Argument, Refutation: This technique is used to show the deficiencies in an argument that runs counter to the writer's own beliefs. It can be used to take on the whole of another's argument, or just smaller components of it.

Writing from Sources: Though all writing, to a degree, relies upon previous learning, writing from sources relies heavily upon specific citations and references to other experts on a topic—and so is the hallmark of academic and other forms of researched writing.

Preface

The *Conversations* Model of Reading, Research, and Writing

There is little doubt that our nation and the world are facing unprecedented challenges, challenges that require the cooperation, collaboration, and public support of a wide range of informed citizens. Now, more than ever, students need to find a voice in crucial public conversations through their writing. To stimulate participation in these dialogues, students need not only interesting and timely topics, but also rhetorical models for how productive public conversations take place. What makes this anthology unique is that instead of merely grouping readings by topic, it demonstrates the ways that writers respond to one another—in many cases, quite directly.

This anthology encourages students to adopt a social and rhetorical model—a "conversation model"—for their own writing. Instead of seeing argument merely as private or as a point-counterpoint debate, students will learn from *Conversations* the moves that writers make to argue productively. While some of these discussions get quite heated, students will also learn that writers cooperate as well as compete with others, that they raise and address subissues and ignore side effects related to the topic in order to enrich the dialogue, and that they often seek consensus and new syntheses more so than victory. That is, they will learn that thoughtful writing is usually part of an ongoing conversation, not the last word.

For these reasons, *Conversations* is organized around areas of both private and public debates: the state and purpose of education, the effect of new media and information technologies, the ways our identity is influenced by gender, race, and ethnicity, the status of love relationships in the 21st century, and issues related to building a sustainable environment. Some pieces speak directly and explicitly to each other, as with the debates over whether college is for everybody, whether technologies like Google and PowerPoint are "making us stupid," or whether feminism is harming men.

Although this edition provides a larger percentage of readings that directly reference or respond to one another, it is also important that students learn how to construct dialogues among authors across time and space by imagining how they might respond to one another. Thus, other pieces refer only indirectly to others, as in whether "hook-up" culture is a sign of growing personal freedom or of declining morality, or whether eating locally is an effective way to create a sustainable food supply while protecting the environment. Also, the book provides many opportunities for instructors to create dialogues across sections of the book: how educational opportunities are affected by gender, whether human relationships are affected by new technologies, and whether ideals of beauty are influenced by cultural or racial norms.

The range of texts included helps make the book work within a wide range of writing courses. Although the book is organized topically, there is certainly no reason why the selections could not be read in some other order to fit the curriculum plan of individual teachers. In fact, *Conversations* is intentionally planned in ways that allow individual classroom teachers to use and build upon the topics included based on their course focus. If, for example, you choose to develop your course around the modes of exposition or inquiry, the rhetorical table of contents can help you do so. Also, the Instructor's Manual offers further suggestions on customizing the book's use to your course.

Conversations will also accommodate courses with an argumentative approach. As this book presents the writings of a wide variety of stakeholders in the public debate, it treats argument not as a polemical act, but rather as a dialogical one. It is not about the harangue or the monologue in isolation, the sole voice at the bully pulpit or upon a soapbox, but instead about the dialogue that ensues as writers respond to one another. In that sense, the goal is to give students an ear for both the text and context. The readings ask students to see the world not in black and white, but in shades and tints and colors. It asks them to hear other speakers who, rather than merely saying, "You are wrong," might also say, "I see your point, but have you considered this as well?" In this way, the book provides a model of "argument" that leads to civil conversation about issues, not shrillness and refusal to listen. (Even though some of the pieces here *do* get shrill, the full context of the conversation tends to be more even-tempered.)

The pieces included here also will remind students that arguments have many shapes—that is, many genres that represent as fully as possible the "universe of discourse" as it exists in the 21st century. Teachers who design their courses around genre will find much to work with here. True, essays are most prominent in *Conversations* because the essay is a common and important genre and because the form has important correspondences with other genres (for example, the letter, the sermon, the report, and the news story). But essays are not so prominent here as to exclude other genres. Students will find other ways of engaging in public discourse as well: through letters of various kinds, blogs, public oratory, websites, reports and legal documents, sociological studies, cartoons, and advertisements. The occasions for public discourse provided here are equally diverse and various. Students and their teachers will find weblog musings and arguments, narratives and analyses of cultural phenomena, professional writing, and citizen journalism.

In sum, *Conversations* encourages students to engage in civic, public discourses. At the same time, this book encourages students to remember that entering an ongoing discussion does not preclude the possibility for personal inventiveness—to cross genres, blend alphabetic and visual rhetoric, to bring a personal voice to academic research, and to apply private beliefs to the public forum (and vice versa). Indeed, *Conversations* is committed to the proposition that there are many possible rhetorical stances, that there is no one "correct" way to address a reader. Through this rich diversity of authors and contexts, mainstream authors and radical outliers, traditionally "published" works and electronic statements that say "I am here, too," students will learn many conventional rhetorical maneuvers as well as many new ones afforded by recent times. Through this diversity of participants, *Conversations* gives students a better chance to find their own voices because they have experienced a full range of possible voices in their reading.

"A rhetorician," says Kenneth Burke in his essay "Rhetoric—Old and New," "is like one voice in a dialogue. Put several such voices together, with each voicing its own special assertion, let them act upon one another in cooperative competition, and you get a dialectic that properly developed, can lead to views transcending the limitations of each." Fostering that "cooperative competition" is the aim of *Conversations*.

Features of this Edition

Although the eighth edition of this anthology remains true to *Conversations*' time-tested approach of inviting students into important civic dialogues, this edition also acknowledges two types of changes in those dialogues. First, many new issues have entered and/or gained new prominence in the public forum during these eventful times; second, electronic communication, changes in media and genre, and the development of new literacy skills continue to expand the ways that public conversations are carried out. Both sets of changes are acknowledged in this edition. This edition also includes some new pedagogical features that can help teachers make use of this textbook in a wide variety of classes.

More specifically, this edition includes

1. ***Conversations in Context***: This new feature of the Eighth edition helps students see a current issue against a richer historical backdrop—to better understand that even seemingly new topics did not arise in a vacuum. As such, each of these five *Conversations in Context* sections provides historical background on the issue considered, one or more anchor essays that set up the larger context of the debate and positions held on the issue, and then brief snippets of arguments made by a wide range of individuals who have weighed in on this topic, drawing upon both verbal and visual techniques. Each section concludes with some ideas and advice for student writers to help them find their way into the conversation with their own perspectives on these issues.

2. **A new introduction focusing on the "conversation model" of research:** The revised introduction helps students see the connection between active, critical reading and the production of thoughtful writing. In order to do so, it helps students read in ways that seek synthesis of the varied views on any given topic as well as expose stasis points that will allow them to find their entry point into the dialogue. It provides advice on annotating texts carefully and using those annotations to organize their own thoughts. It also helps them widen their perspectives on these topics by seeing the surrounding social and historical contexts that inform the opinions of other writers.

3. **Questions for prompting discussion and writing:** Although the reading selections remain central, this edition also includes some guides that can assist students in reading well, challenge them to synthesize the various texts into coherent dialogues on each topic, and help them find their way into these conversations.
   - Each reading headnote supplies context on the topic, the author, and the original place of publication. It then provides some facets of the text to consider as they read, preparing them to read actively.

- "Getting Into the Conversation" questions following each chapter of the book help students bring together the key arguments that inform the conversation on any given topic.
- "Extending the Conversation" suggestions following each part of the book help students find connections in the conversation *across the issues throughout the book,* making it easier to customize course design.

4. **Expanded attention to new media and multimodal texts:** Because public conversations are greatly expanded and enhanced by new media, this book illustrates the ways that even conversations that start in traditional publication venues are extended through blog postings, citizen journalism, Facebook and Twitter, and in visual media. Part 2 directly addresses the topic of new media in ways that will help students see the advantages and limitations of these new genres in fostering public dialogues.

5. **New topics and updated texts make the issues discussed more timely and closer to students' experience of the world—including**
   - A serious questioning of the goals and methods of public education, and the predisposition that college is necessary for all Americans in order to be successful, in Part 1.
   - An examination of the effects of new technologies upon the ways we think and share information in Part 2.
   - An updated examination of identity issues in Part 3, including conversations about how feminism has affected *both women and men* and how race and ethnicity influence one's view of the world.
   - A serious and personal look at the ways that human love relationships have changed in our "hookup" culture and its effects upon the institution of marriage, in Part 4.
   - A look at the growing importance of sustainability issues in both the realm of food production and consumption and in the realm of environmental protection and activism in Part 5.

6. **More texts and authors who truly "speak to one another":** This edition includes a larger number of texts that directly reference and respond to one another, demonstrating how real public conversations develop in electronic and published writings.

Instructor's Manual

Teachers who do want additional background on unfamiliar readings or specific suggestions for making the most of *Conversations* will find plenty of help in the extensive Instructor's Manual that we have compiled. The manual contains further information on writers, overviews of the parts, discussions of each selection, some suggestions for further reading, and ideas for discussion and writing. It also offers pointers for teaching each "conversation"—for how particular selections can be used with other selections. Together, the editorial apparatus and the Instructor's Manual are designed with the conversation model of public discourse in mind and to engage the intelligence and passion of students and teachers without getting in the way of either.

MyCompLab™

MyCompLab empowers student writers and facilitates writing instruction by uniquely integrating a composing space and assessment tools with market-leading instruction, multimedia tutorials, and exercises for writing, grammar, and research.

Students can use MyCompLab on their own, benefiting from self-paced diagnostics and a personal study plan that recommends the instruction and practice that each student needs to improve his or her writing skills. The composing space and its integrated resources, tools, and services (such as online tutoring) are also available to each student as he or she writes.

MyCompLab is an eminently flexible application that instructors can use in ways that best complement their course and teaching style. They can recommend it to students for self-study, set up courses to track student progress, or leverage the power of administrative features to be more effective and save time. The assignment builder and commenting tools, developed specifically for writing instruction, bring instructors closer to their student writers, make managing assignments and evaluating papers more efficient, and put powerful assessment within reach.

Students receive feedback within the context of their own writing, which encourages critical thinking and revision and helps them develop skills based on their individual needs.

Learn more at www.mycomplab.com.

Acknowledgments

This book, true to its concept, is the product of many, many conversations between its two editors and among the many colleagues who have influenced our work as writing teachers (and teachers of writing teachers). This conversation began when we were teaching composition years ago at Penn State, and those conversations—about the connections between teaching writing and the advancement of democratic dialogue—have deepened for nearly two decades. Still, as we work together on this edition of *Conversations,* we know our work has always been in the context of the wider conversation surrounding the teaching of writing.

The present edition represents the work of numerous individuals, including those who reviewed the many drafts of its many editions. In particular, we would like to thank the reviewers of this edition:

- Mark Addison Amos, Southern Illinois University-Carbondale
- Albert J. DeFazio III, George Mason University
- Curtis Harrell, NorthWest Arkansas Community College
- Kim Jacobs-Beck, University of Cincinnati-Clermont
- Gary McIlroy, Henry Ford Community College
- Sylvia Newman, Weber State University
- Justin St. Clair, University of South Alabama

Further, many other colleagues from Penn State and York College of Pennsylvania—as well as those from the Conference on College Composition and Communication and the Council of Writing Program Administrators—continue to inform our understanding of how students learn to read, write, and engage in civic dialogue.

Thanks, too, to those involved in the production of this book. Development Editor Karen Mauk has worked closely with us throughout the project to bring it to fruition; her thoughtful suggestions and hard work are evident throughout this book. Karen has also revised the Instructor's manual for this edition, with the able assistance of editor Teresa Ward. Julie Chung worked diligently to find appropriate visuals and secure permissions for their use. Melinda Durham and the staff at Electronic Publishing Services Inc., and Stacey Kulig at Pearson Education watched over the details of turning our manuscript into a polished product.

Finally, we owe a debt of gratitude to our editors at Longman. Eben Ludlow was from the start a driving force behind each edition of this project and has deeply influenced us both, not only in the production of this book, but also in the shape of our careers. Also, the vision and thoughtful critique of our new editor Brad Potthoff has helped us find the proper balance between sustaining the features of this book that have assisted so many young writers over its eight editions and developing ways to reach out to a new generation of students.

DOMINIC DELLICARPINI

JACK SELZER

Joining the Conversation: Reading, Research, and Writing

Writing to Join the Conversation

Why do people write? For many reasons, of course. Sometimes the impulse to write comes from a desire to express ourselves. Everyone needs to sort out feelings at one time or another or to make some personal sense of the world—and writing is a good way to do so. If you have a Facebook page which you update with your current status, or if you've kept track of your most intimate feelings in a journal, or if you've written poems or stories in order to sort out your beliefs and feelings, then you know what it means to write for personal reasons.

But on most occasions, we write for others. We write because we want to be part of important conversations with those who are concerned with similar topics. And while some people identify themselves primarily as writers—essayists, news reporters, novelists, technical writers, screenwriters— the truth is, we are *all* writers. As students and as professionals, no matter our field, we write as part of our daily work. So, while we might not think of ourselves as writers, we do a great deal of our most important work *being* writers. Students, police officers, engineers, college professors, lawyers, physicians, corporate managers, teachers, and so forth all write a great deal. (You'd be surprised at how much time such people spend on the writing required by their jobs—just ask them! Or just keep track of the many hours you spend writing for school, writing emails, writing texts or Facebook messages, jotting down notes, and you'll see how much of your connection to the world comes through writing.)

Since writing is one of the most important ways that we engage in conversations with others, and since we write for so many purposes and audiences, we must learn to write in many different ways. Each role we play—as a student, a friend, a worker, a citizen, and so forth—calls for a particular kind of writing or *genre*: Scientists write up lab reports and experiment protocols; journalists write news stories, feature stories, or editorials; business people write both internal correspondences (memos, reports) and external documents (advertising, letters to clients, reports to stockholders, business plans and grant applications); engineers or police officers spend time composing reports that record their activities or events; citizens write arguments to convince others to join their cause; lawyers write to produce those legal briefs that are due to the judge next week. Each of those types of writing, or *genres*, are expected by others in the conversations they are entering. And speaking the expected language is extremely important in specific fields; though there is still room for one's own voice and purposes, there are expectations of form and style that you will need to learn to be taken seriously in those communities.

As a student, you have a particularly challenging set of writing tasks. You go from community to community in the course of a single day. When you move from psychology class to economics class to philosophy class, you are challenged with a different set of topics and a different set of expectations about how people in that community communicate with one another. If you pay attention to similarities and differences in the way those groups communicate, you'll learn many different styles or genres in the process.

When we think of writers and writing in this expanded way—as encompassing all who write—we also learn that writers are anything but self-absorbed. Indeed, all kinds of writing are social and (to a degree) acts of persuasion. The engineer who is designing an alternative fuel engine must write a report to gain approval from project managers. A physician's report on a patient is used by other caregivers. A teacher's curriculum proposal is meant to influence the educational system. The lawyer's brief is meant to sway a judge. The movie reviewer's account is designed to direct people to (or away from) a film. Even "private" writing is often quite public in its uses. The letters in which you pour out your feelings are read by sympathetic and responsive friends. Your thoughts on love relationships or gender become essays that help others see your way of thinking. Your Facebook status reports or Twitter tweets communicate your current state of mind to others in your network of friends. Even private journal entries are shaped to an extent by the society around you, the things you experience, and the words that you hear. (And part of us is always aware that someone, someday, might read those entries.) In all these ways, writing is always a kind of "social networking."

Understanding the context of each of our social, citizen, educational, and professional networks—electronic or otherwise—is crucial. It reminds us that when we write, we are entering a conversation that has been going on for some time before we arrived. That is why the title of this book is *Conversations*. It assumes that your writing is a response to the words or actions of others, part of a dialogue. And by reading the wide array of selections here, you can learn a great deal about how the conversation works in each of those communities.

The Conversation Model of Reading, Writing, and Research

> Imagine that you enter a parlor. You come late. When you arrive, others have long preceded you, and they are engaged in a heated discussion, a discussion too heated for them to pause and tell you exactly what it is about. In fact, the discussion had already begun long before any of them got there, so that no one present is qualified to retrace for you all the steps that had gone before. You listen for a while, until you decide that you have caught the tenor of the argument; then you put in your oar. Someone answers; you answer him; another comes to your defense; another aligns himself against you, to either the embarrassment or gratification of your opponent, depending upon the quality of your ally's assistance.

This well-known passage from Kenneth Burke's *Philosophy of Literary Form* introduces us to a place where people meet for open (but sometimes contentious) conversations on topics of shared interest. Burke's metaphorical parlor is much like the world you are entering as a college student—a place where you will come upon ongoing conversations about all sorts of topics. At first, those conversations—both real ones and ones you encounter as you read in new subject areas—will seem a bit daunting. But like the newest entrants into that parlor, you will find that if you listen for a while, you will start to understand the contexts of those conversations better and better—and will soon be a participant in them. And in college, one of the most frequent ways one enters these ongoing conversations is through writing and reading.

Of course, to get in on that conversation, you have to know what others have said about the matter at hand, and you must be able to anticipate possible responses to that which you have to say. That's where this book, in combination with your own research and writing, can help. This collection of readings comprises *public* conversations—conversations on issues that concern educated and concerned individuals. Not every burning issue is represented here, of course; that would be impossible (and new ones come up every day). But this book does include conversations—give-and-take discussions—on many matters that concern you and others in your networks, some of which interact with one another. Is public education serving students in the best way possible? How is technology affecting what, and how, we learn—or our social and love relationships? Is college really a necessity to get ahead in today's world? How important is our gender, our ethnicity, or our race in determining our identity? Are standardized tests the most effective way we have of assessing learning? Have love relationships changed significantly, or are love and marriage still central components of a good life? How can we best sustain our natural resources and our food supply? Questions like these are all around us, and affect our day-to-day lives; so people are talking about them and writing about them. This book assumes that you'll want to get in on some of those conversations, both nationally and locally.

Surrounded as we are by a "world wide web" of dialogue, it is more important than ever that we have the appropriate reading skills to sort through those conversations in order to find what we want, what we need, and what we can trust. The term that is often used to describe those necessary skills of reading is called *literacy*. While literacy was once a simpler concept—the ability to read and write paper texts—it has more recently been applied to multiple abilities. Information literacy requires the ability to find, evaluate, and use information. Civic literacy requires knowing how to act as a member of our democratic culture. Quantitative literacy requires the ability to understand and use numbers and statistics. And technological literacy can give you the ability to compose in many media. What it means to publish something has also changed. The good news is that you all have the ability to *publish* (i.e., make public) your own thoughts instantaneously through digital writing. The challenge is that you need the ability to read, analyze, and compose in all sorts of communication styles, from traditional texts like articles and books, to graphics, videos, websites, blogs, wikis, and so forth. And you also need ways to get your writing noticed amidst all the others that exist out there.

So how do you learn those multiple literacies? The same way we learn most things: by being good listeners and good readers first. As you read the pieces in this book, you'll experience a broad range of strategies and stylistic decisions that represent the possible ways of engaging in *public discourse*— writing meant to be read by whole groups of people. You'll encounter a wide variety of approaches writers take to the public audiences for whom they are writing, and various modes of composing—from formal reports and essays to informal blogs and commentaries. You'll find conventional presentations and startlingly inventive ones. You'll see how famous professional writers earned their fame, and you'll hear from anonymous but just-as-eloquent fellow citizens.

You'll hear from women as well as men, from majority as well as minority voices. Listening to these many voices can give you a better chance of finding your voice in any given circumstance, exposing you to a range of possible voices in your reading. The idea is to empower you to engage in the ongoing conversations that concern you and your community by first being an analytical reader.

Two Kinds of Reading

In our information age, there is certainly no shortage of reading material on any given topic; it can, however, be challenging to sort through the huge amount of information available to determine its relevance to your topic and its credibility (a topic discussed in the readings in Part 2 of this book). This book can help you learn how to read many kinds of writing composed for many different types of occasions. To do so effectively, you will need to develop two kinds of reading strategies.

In the first kind of reading, think of yourself as part of each writer's intended audience—someone who the writer actually hoped would read and respond to his or her message. In this kind of reading, you read as you normally read the things that are directed at you every day: as you would read a newspaper or an article in your favorite magazine or a personal email from a friend. Read the piece as if the writer had written it just for, and to, you, and react accordingly. In most cases, this will be quite easy to do, since most of the items in *Conversations* are directed to the public—people like you—and were written quite recently to address topics of interest to us all. In some cases, you'll feel more remote from an article because it is addressing a topic about which you don't feel particularly well-versed, or because it seems directed at a community of which you are not necessarily a member; but even then, you can behave as (and so become) a member of the writer's intended audience by reading the headnote that provides you with context on the writer and when, and why, the piece was originally written.

But to become a better writer, a second kind of reading is equally important—let's call it *critical reading* or *rhetorical reading*. In this kind of reading, you approach a document not only as the intended reader but *as a writer*, as someone studying it to appreciate its style, its strategies, and its techniques. This time you are reading in a way similar to how a car enthusiast looks at a car or how a musician hears a symphony or how an engineer looks at a machine: though you still appreciate the harmony of the whole thing, you also mentally take it apart to see what's under the hood or to hear how the individual notes and chords fit together. When you read rhetorically, you not only react to the message, but you also appreciate *how* the writing gets the job done—the craft, and sometimes the beauty, of the writer's presentation. And sometimes, you will also discover flaws in logic or deceptive writing practices. In any case, you are reading like a writer—learning new strategies by admiring or criticizing those used by others.

Being a thoughtful and analytical reader can teach us a great deal about how writers compose and frame their messages. Using the conversation model—that is, reading as a potential participant in those conversations—requires you to pay attention to not only what a piece says, but *how* it says it. You'll need to consider not only the topic, but the styles that are used by participants in these conversations so that you can join in. Are they formal, less formal, or downright intimate with their reader? Do they present themselves as something of an expert on the matter or question, or as someone on the same level as the readers? Do they speak dispassionately, or do they let their feelings show? Are they explicit in stating their purpose, or less direct? Are their sentences careful and complex, or direct and emphatic? If you apply these analytical skills not only to the reading you do from this book, but also to the reading you do in other courses, you will also be able to learn a range of communication styles that can be applied within a wide range of written conversations.

Of course, the two types of reading are not completely separate—we always do a bit of each. But assuming that you are reading this book as part of a course in writing, thinking consciously about that second kind of reading can help you to discover the way writers do business. Reading in that way asks you to pay attention to the same things that concerned the writer: shaping an idea to an audience in a particular form for a particular purpose. If you keep those things in mind, reading can help make you a better writer.

Developing an Expert Ear and Voice: Critical Reading Techniques

Both kinds of reading—reading for content and reading to learn new stylistic techniques—are necessary to enter into the conversation on any given topic. The first kind of reading—reading as a member of the audience—is a necessary step for you to "get up on" the various arguments that people have offered on a given topic. That's the listening part, the necessary first step toward knowing the terms of the debate, the information that is available, and the various ways that people have used that information toward drawing conclusions. Reading in this way asks you not only to collect "facts" (or to assume that the facts are accurate), but to assess their validity—to become a critical reader that evaluates the support for each argument that is offered.

The word "critical" might make it sound like we are always looking for the flaws in someone else's arguments; and to a degree, we are. But critical reading also requires us to find that which seems valid, useful, and interesting. But how can we know that? When we enter a conversation, how can we feel comfortable in making the kinds of judgments necessary to weigh the value of what we read? One answer is to keep on "listening" (i.e., reading) until we begin to learn the agreed-upon—and the disputed—points in the varied arguments being made. Those points of dispute are sometimes called *stasis points,* or points of contention among various writers. If you identify the points upon which people disagree, you will have come a long way toward finding your own entry point into the conversation, allowing you to weigh in on those stasis points. As a critical reader, you should consistently be looking for what is at issue, what specific elements of a topic seem to be the crux of the ongoing conversation. This text offers you a number of those conversations. Sometimes, a series of pieces you'll read will directly respond to one another. In other cases, it is up to you to construct a conversation by reading creatively, bringing together specific facets of the readings—sometimes just small parts—that can help you to hear the ongoing conversation among the various experts, to find the stasis points, and then to write in a way that engages in those points of contention.

Creating a Focused Conversation: Annotating and Synthesizing Arguments

Being an informed writer in any field or on any topic involves piecing together the various voices in a conversation. By using this book, you can practice two well-accepted and useful methods for helping you to really understand the ongoing conversation: annotating a text and then using those annotations to synthesize (or bring together) the key points of discussion. In academic writing, that synthesis is often called a *review of the literature*—a summary of the state of the conversation that you are entering. But no matter the kind of writing, seeing how various arguments speak to one another is crucial to finding your own place in the conversation.

Let's start with the process of reading. *Writers are writers even when they are reading.* They approach each new text with a pencil in hand, ready to add their own thoughts, questions, and responses to everything they read. Those written responses, placed in the margins of that which we read, are often called *annotations*. Let's look at this process of active reading, examining the ways that reading as a writer can help you to enter a conversation on any given topic. To do so, let's examine the ways that active, cumulative reading—consecutively examining the relationship among the ideas within a conversation—can help you to focus your own thoughts and lead toward your own contributions to that conversation.

Chapter 2 of *Conversations*, for example, will ask you to consider a question that is likely very much on your mind as you begin your college career: What, and who, is college for? That broad question, of course, has many individual facets, along with an array of opinions on that topic. Your job as an active reader is to tease out those *stasis points*—points of debate—and to carefully consider the validity of each writer's thoughts on that topic. Ultimately, you are seeking to bring some order to this conversation and to locate the most important issues that are at play in that dialogue.

As a reader enters this conversation, she will encounter two pieces that suggest that the idea that college is for everyone is wrongheaded, even detrimental. For example, W. J. Reeves begins his essay with the following assertion:

> In America today, there exists a goal that the majority of the nation's youth should go to college and that access should be the byword for higher education. On the surface, this sounds like a great idea; in reality, it is not.

What reaction might the reader have to this assertion? What response might she write in the margin of this essay? One possibility might look like this:

> In America today, there exists a
>
> goal that the majority of the

nation's youth should go to college

and that access should be the

byword for higher education. On

the surface, this sounds like a

great idea; in reality, it is not.

> This author is questioning the assumption that going to college is the best choice for most people. What leads him to question this?

This annotation allows the reader, as she first enters this conversation, to demand good reasons for this assertion. The reader also expresses some surprise that something that is usually seen as a universal good—a college education—would be questioned. Already, the annotations are making her an inquisitive reader. As she continues reading, she can start to collect the reasons for what might first seem like an unusual claim. For example, W. J. Reeves continues like this:

Access in its most-extreme form—

open admissions—was instituted

at The City University of New York

during the turmoil of the 1960s.

Any student who had graduated

from high school, with no regard

given to grade point average (GPA)

and/or the SAT scores, was allowed

> Suggests open access has lowered standards.

into one of the CUNY schools.

Today, while that policy is officially

off the books, many of its aspects

remain. CUNY is not alone in its

attitude toward access. In every

state, midrange colleges exist by

some form of easy access, for

access=numbers, and low num-

bers=low funding, and really low

numbers=no college. Connected

with access is retention, which

means that, once inside the col-

lege, the students are more or less

guaranteed graduation.

> Reeves seems to be suggesting that *keeping* students, not *educating* them, has become the priority.

> Reeves seems to suggest that open access has lowered the value of education, making a degree "guaranteed" rather than earned.

   Already, the reader has found many possible topics for further examination and for comparison with other pieces she reads. This process, of course, is cumulative. That is, when she moves from W. J. Reeves' essay to another essay on this topic, the reader is increasingly equipped to find points of contact between the pieces—and so her annotations can help her to cross-reference similar or different arguments on the topic—to find stasis points. For example, let's say the reader now moves on to an essay by Thomas Reeves, also included in Chapter 2 of *Conversations*. In his piece, Thomas Reeves writes this:

The impact on college and univer-

sity campuses of legions of unpre-

pared freshmen is never positive.

Millions of dollars must be spent

annually in remedial education.

And the rate of failure is still

extraordinarily high. The ACT esti-

mates that one in four fail or drop

out after one year. A third of the

freshmen at the relatively select

University of Wisconsin-Madison

do not return for a second year.

> This seems to conflict with W.J. Reeves' claim that open access = guaranteed graduation. I need to investigate the statistics on this.

This annotation shows how the attentive reader has found a "fact" that is in dispute—whether colleges are retaining students to keep their enrollments up, or whether unprepared students are simply dropping out, causing a waste of resources. Now the reader is starting to find the stasis points that can be further investigated and considered in her own writing. More will accumulate as she continues reading. For example, Thomas Reeves goes on to write this:

Even more important is the impact

of intellectually unprepared people

on the educational process itself.

Anti-intellectualism is the Great

Enemy of the educator, and with a

classroom full of people who do

not read, study, or think, academic

standards inevitably suffer. In an

> Here the author suggests that admitting unprepared students lowers the quality of education for those who really want to learn.

article titled "The Classroom

Game," (_Academic Questions,_

Spring, 2001), I described my own

tribulations with students in an

> I should read this piece, too, to get more details on this argument.

open-admissions environment. The
most well-intentioned professor
cannot educate those who refuse to
be educated. All too often, such students demand that they be passed
through the system and awarded a
diploma, as they were in high
school.

> This brings in another dimension: is the problem being unprepared, or is it that the students are not really engaged in being educated?

Several things take place in these annotations. The reader notices that another issue has been raised—how unprepared students affect the education of other students and the ability of teachers to do their job. She also notices that not only preparedness, but willingness to learn, is an issue to consider. And she has found a source of further information, another article by this author. In her reading, she will also discover this passage:

Minorities too are getting into the
act, being wooed and financially
rewarded by campus administrators to meet institutional racial
quotas. But is this crush for
diplomas necessarily a good
thing? Is it always a prudent
investment, for the individual and
for society, to be sending junior
off to the dorm?

> The writer seems to suggest that minority enrollments are based upon "quotas" and then, through his questions, seems to express doubt that this is good for the college or the students. Note the words "wooed" and "financially rewarded." Sounds like the author is suggesting that colleges are not being ethical in attracting minority students.

Here, the reader has found a new dimension within the conversation—whether colleges should work so hard to attract a diverse student body, and whether their motives are reasonable and ethical, or just financial. She also notes the style and tone of the piece, drawing attention to the word choice of the author and its effect. If this reader were to continue listening to this debate, reading the passage from Paul Attewell and David E. Lavin's *Passing the Torch: Does Higher Education for the Disadvantaged Pay Off,* she would find a different take on this question. In that book, the authors suggest that complaints by "critics of 'college for all'" are a form of "nostalgia," and that

Unfortunately, it is a short step

from nostalgia to condemning the

new, and another short step to

blaming educational changes on

the kinds of students now attend-

ing college. A widespread com-

plaint is that the college

curriculum has been "dumbed

down" because colleges have

admitted students who lack the

skills or intelligence to cope with a

rigorous curriculum (Gray and

Herr   1996;   Harwood   1997;

MacDonald   1997,   1998,   1999;

Stanfield 1997; Traub 1995). In our

opinion,   blaming   disadvantaged

> This sounds like the arguments made by both W. J. Reeves and Thomas Reeves, both of whom suggest students are underprepared and just filling quotas.

> I should check these sources.

students for educational changes is unfair. Many of the developments that traditionalists decry—from modifications in the canon of "great books" to the spread of preprofessional majors and majors in the social and behavioral sciences to the deemphasis on moral education and the spread of postmodernism—were pioneered at elite colleges.

Clearly, these authors take a different perspective than Thomas Reeves and W. J. Reeves. In fact, this piece seems to address and contradict claims just like theirs.

This claim suggests that the problem isn't just because of open access colleges, as W. J. Reeves suggests.

Can you hear the conversation points starting to emerge here? Through the annotations, the reader is accumulating the key points of contention that are worth considering and possible areas for further research. She is also able to consider which of these various subpoints seem most interesting to her, and so which she might choose to write about herself.

Another set of arguments on this topic surrounds the question of whether college education can help students to advance economically. Just the title of Clive Crook's "A Matter of Degrees: Why College Is Not an Economic Cure-all," suggests that this question is anything but settled. Other pieces in this section, including that by Paul Attewell and David E. Lavin, also address the economics of obtaining a college degree.

In these ways, annotating a text can help you to read actively—that is, as a writer who will eventually enter these conversations. This process develops slowly, with each new piece adding a new dimension. So you'll need to be patient. And in some cases, you may need to go back and re-read some of the pieces you read early in the process, now that you have a wider perspective on the topic, and add more annotations. But it is well worth the effort, because this running commentary will then allow you to find a focused topic that most concerns and interests you, and so to develop your own summary of the key points in the conversation that you are entering. Your next task is to reconstruct or "synthesize" this conversation into a *review of the literature* that will help others—your readers—enter that conversation as well.

The first thing to keep in mind about a review of the literature is that the word *literature,* in this case, is not limited to creative writing. All fields and all topics have a *literature,* which in this case means the body of writing on a given topic. When we create a bibliography, we are really creating a list of the pertinent literature on a given topic. A review of the literature is more than just a list; it shows how the various pieces interact with one another, what particular sub-topics on that topic emerge, and what stasis points exist in the dialogue on the topic. The annotations that we add to each reading we encounter can be used to recreate the ongoing conversation. If we go back and read our own annotations, trends and sub-topics will emerge that then can be put into dialogue with one another. Let's use the sample annotations above to see how the beginnings of a review of the literature might be constructed from them.

Just the few annotations above (you will have many more when you do a full investigation of a topic) have already begun to give shape to what might be a review of the literature on the questions of what, and who, college is for. Some of the stasis points that have emerged are:

- Whether college should be available to all;
- Whether making college available to all "dumbs down" higher education;
- Whether making college available to all is meant to help students, or simply to allow colleges to have what amounts to more paying customers;
- Whether college for all is making the job of teachers (both Thomas and W.J. Reeves are college teachers) too difficult;
- Whether going to college ensures economic success— and whether that ought to be the purpose of college (which is also addressed by some of the other readings in Chapter 2 of *Conversations*); and
- Whether college should be treated as a way for minorities and underprivileged students to gain access to more economic success.

The list could continue, but you can already hear how this brief stint of critical reading has exposed a great many directions for further research and which can be the focus as we read more. So, a synthesis or review of the literature on this topic might start something like this:

> While the ideal of granting access to college to as many Americans as possible may seem to fit well with our democratic values, experts disagree about the effect of open access policies in higher education. Writers on this topic question the effect of open access upon the quality of education and teaching, about the chances of underprepared students succeeding in college, about whether some students might be better served—both personally and economically—by taking a different path to their careers. Writers also seem to question the motives of colleges in granting wider access to college—whether it is meant to benefit the students or the colleges.

This sample opening demonstrates how a review of the literature can help a writer—and his readers—to see not only the general topic, but to synthesize specific points of conversation about this topic. This introductory paragraph both sets up the general question being examined—access to college—and lays out the debate points that have been gleaned from the various sources. Each of those debate points can then be examined in the paragraphs that follow, giving your review of the literature a clear organization and structure. Also, you should note that this organization is not created by merely summarizing each piece individually. To the contrary, this structure allows you to show the conversation among the various authors on similar points of discussion—and so helps you (and your reader) *synthesize* the work of those authors— to see how the various pieces create a dialogue among the writers. Thus, a later paragraph in this review of the literature might look something like this:

> There is some dispute about whether granting wider access to college has the potential to increase social mobility of Americans—whether it can help underprivileged groups and individuals to become more economically successful. Thomas Reeves argues that attending college may not be economically "prudent" for all students, suggesting that there are many other ways for students to succeed financially. Likewise, Clive Crook suggests that "the necessary intellectual assets are acquired long before college, or not at

all," arguing that the tendency to require a college education for too many careers is the real problem, as is a growing illiteracy in more "basic" skills that can be learned before college. W. J. Reeves offers alternatives other than college, noting that "possibly the best course of action during senior year" for many students might be "job cooperative programs that link high schools to the worlds of work." However, Kathleen Waldron draws our attention to economic statistics that suggest that students who complete college are likely to earn $900,000 more than those who do not have college degrees, suggesting that providing access to less privileged individuals remains crucial. Paul Attewell and David Lavin use similar statistics to demonstrate the ways that open access has boosted earnings for underserved populations, while acknowledging that the correlation is anything but simple.

This paragraph demonstrates the ways that a review of the literature can help both the writer and reader to see the key points of debate and the varied arguments on that debate. This synthesis of arguments on a given topic can then focus the writer's research around specific sub-issues rather than general claims, and so to eventually help the writer judge which of the arguments seems most viable—and, in some cases, which arguments do not hold water. A synthesis, in effect, allows the writer to get into this conversation in more developed, more informed ways.

A review of the literature can also open up what is sometimes called the "gap statement" or "gap in the literature." By examining what has already been said on a given topic, we can also determine what has *not* been said, or what has not yet been examined adequately. When we find those gaps in the conversation thus far, we are ready to seek further information that can help to fill those gaps. For example, in this case, one might do further research on whether the expenditures for college—and the debt that students accrue—are offset by later earnings. They might also examine trends in jobs, noting if growth in careers that do not require a college degree suggests that open access is becoming more or less necessary. Or they might study dropout rates to see if expenditures for college are in fact "prudent"—or if the completion rate of underprepared students might suggest that tuition is often wasted. And those are just areas of research that relate directly to economic issues. One might also choose to examine whether the need to "remediate" underprepared students is reducing the rigor of a college curriculum and so creating a deleterious effect upon students with a stronger preparation. It also may lead to questions about whether we are creating a two-tiered system of higher education, one for students with strong educational preparation and one for those who have weaker backgrounds. By listening to the various stasis points, and noting how they interact, the writer has started to find a number of angles from which to approach the broader question, and so to focus his own writing. As you read the pieces in this book, which are designed to converse with one another, you too can find focused ways to examine a specific facet of a topic.

Thus, *annotating* what we read and *synthesizing* the literature we review on any given issue involves more than compiling past ideas; the goal should be to create a structured dialogue among those whose ideas are pertinent to the question we are examining. To construct such a dialogue, we must find points of connection among the various authors whose work we read, represent the ideas of those authors fairly, and help our readers to understand the crucial terms and disputed points surrounding that particular question. In a sense, we are re-creating the conversation on the topic for our readers, so they can hear the dialogue before we—and our readers—enter in. In this way, reviewing the literature serves several purposes. It helps us, and our readers, to better understand the nature of the disagreement on any given topic. It can help us to focus the wide range of questions we have at the beginning of our research. And it also helps us better understand the disputes that we must negotiate if we are to become a credible participant in this conversation.

These active reading techniques not only help your reader understand what is at issue, but they help *you* to ask critical questions that can lead to further research. This process keeps us from simply accepting every argument we read and helps us to find our own voice on the given topic. The above examples also show how annotations and a review of the literature can help us to enter other possible areas of inquiry—and honest, open inquiry is really what research is about. This close reading helps us to get a sense of the biases of each writer, as well as our own (and we all have biases of one sort or another). And no matter what we believe as we start, we should be willing to listen. But we must also be ready to be skeptical, demanding solid proof and well-reasoned arguments from the published sources we read, rather than assume that they are accurate just because they are in print.

There is another benefit to this process as well. Real research is *recursive*, not linear. That means that rather than just accepting the validity of what we find, we keep asking questions throughout the process, and do further research to test out what we find in our initial searches. After identifying more specific facets of the topic, we can focus our search in ways that go beyond the very broad searches for articles about "college access" or "benefits for college" that the original question might have prompted. Those search terms would breed so many hits as to be unproductive—and would make synthesizing the wide range of results very difficult. On the other hand, the more focused searches that come from initial, active reading can help us to find secondary sources on the specific line of inquiry that we are following (or, if you are so inclined, to do some primary research by designing surveys, interviews, or other forms of case studies that can add *new* information to the literature you have reviewed). But before we discuss those processes in more detail, let's discuss a third form of reading that you will need to be a careful reader.

A Third Kind of Reading: Conversations in Context

While there are many topics that seem perennial to human beings, new topics of conversation arise all the time—and even those perennial topics (like love and marriage, human and gender rights, how to best educate our citizens, and so forth) take on new dimensions depending upon the surrounding contexts. For example, though our country continues to discuss the role of marriage in our lives, the frequency of divorce and the growing number of people who choose to remain single does change that dialogue. And though our country no longer supports racial segregation, there are still discussions about other, more subtle discrepancies in the opportunities afforded to what are sometimes called "underrepresented groups." (See how even that name, "underrepresented," as opposed to "minority" changes the conversation.) And though we have always believed in environmental protection, new fears about food supplies and sustainable energies now raise questions about how to best treat our natural resources—and who to trust with that task. That is, every conversation, new or old, has *contexts* based on the times and the surrounding social conditions.

Another change in the way we participate in, or "read," conversations comes from the increasingly visual world in which we live. Advertisements and political ads, the CNN news screen and the Web sites we visit, YouTube and blogs, and film and graphic novel adaptations of books, all do their work through a combination of words and images; not long ago, in many of these cases, words might have had to do the job on their own. And some would even say that images now have a greater effect than words. Even music has become visual: "I don't like the way that song looks," a young girl listening to the radio blurted out, referring to the music video she had in her head. Times change.

In such a world, where music *looks* a certain way and where images have messages that are at least as strong as words, being a critical reader and an effective writer—the things we've been discussing in this introduction—requires another related skill: the ability to "read" in many media. Like the idea of *looking at* music, *reading* images or videos might seem like an odd concept. But you do it all the time, really. Just as you react, both viscerally (on a gut level) and analytically, to that which you read, you also have gut reactions to other media, reactions that can then be made more rich and thoughtful through critical "reading." Reading any medium—writing, picture, video, sound—requires you to first acknowledge that each is in fact a kind of text. A text need not be just words on a page; it is anything that can be interpreted (whether it be speaking, writing, or a visual image) because it presents a point of view or a way of seeing the world. Defined in those ways, all media can be read critically using techniques similar to how we "read" written texts (as discussed in the previous section).

To give you practice with understanding the larger social and historical context of specific conversations as well as the variety of ways that arguments are made—both in words and in other media—this edition of *Conversations* includes six sections called "Conversations in Context." These sections are a collection of text and images that speak to audiences—and to each other—about a particular issue, at a particular time, and for a particular purpose. Sometimes that purpose is very obvious; on other occasions, that purpose might be a bit more submerged, and require your careful analysis to find it. But as with all forms of analysis, expending the energy can make you a clearer thinker, and so a better writer as well.

By acknowledging these two kinds of contexts—social and historical contexts, as well as the surrounding visual context supplied by the medium—writers are able to offer fresh perspectives even on topics that seem well-worn. These sections of the book, then, invite you to consider the context of a set of arguments—some old and some new, some verbal and some visual, as a way of developing your own writing. They each supply you with some basic history and context, and then offer you one or two longer pieces to read along with a number of other snippets of conversations (in multiple media) that can help spur your own further research, reading, and writing. These details will help you to better understand the importance of considering *exigency* as you write. Exigency is a sense of immediacy, a reason why a particular topic is of importance right now (and/or was important at some point in the past); it also helps to explain why a particular medium or mode of presentation was chosen in order to best address that topic at that time, with a particular audience, and with a particular set of circumstances. Keep in mind that exigencies change dramatically over time, so part of your job in reading about such topics is to determine how the changes in context change our perspective on those topics. Do current economic struggles change the way we view class structures, or the need for higher education, in America? Do they change our perspective on how much attention we pay to environmental issues? Do they change our perspectives on the interactions among races, ethnicities, or genders? And how do they change the media within which the messages are best presented?

Our arguments are enriched by our attention to current exigencies and surrounding contexts. During times of a heightened attention to potential terrorism, one might build an argument against illegal immigration and tight border control around that context. Or during times of economic crisis, one might build that argument around the need to maintain jobs for legal U. S. citizens. Or one might suggest that, in such times, engaging all those who live in the U.S. and making them feel a sense of belonging should be valued. Gauging the surrounding contexts—and so arguing why a topic is timely or exigent—can help us to gain the attention of our audience. By studying the issues raised in the *Conversations in Context* sections, you can better understand how arguments of exigency are built.

Since the arguments in these sections are both verbal and visual, you can also think more about the ways that images and design—the context on a page or a screen—can help to make an argument. For example, you might consider the arguments that have been made opposing standardized testing that characterize it as a less than effective measure of student success, as a source of student stress, as unfair to underrepresented groups and non-native speakers. Those arguments are often built around statistics, anecdotes from teachers and students, expert testimony, and so forth. But visuals can also make strong arguments. Consider, for example, the image that opens Part 1 of this book.

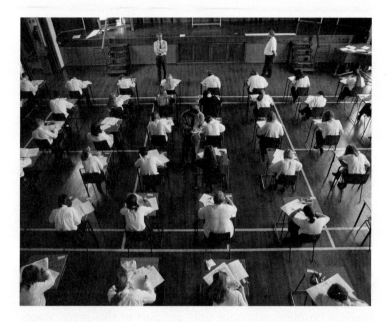

On the surface, we might see this picture as just a group of students in rows of desks. But if we look deeper, and read this image rhetorically, we can see many other elements. Does it make an argument about the effects of standardized testing or about our educational system more generally? Will it affect different audiences differently?

In order to answer questions such as those, as with critical reading of written texts, we need to look at the details and consider how they are likely to affect an audience. So, for example, we might note some of the more obvious features first. The students are in precise rows, a picture of order. They all face the same way, supervised by two test proctors in the front of the room. There is no interaction (indeed, interaction in such a setting would be considered a violation), and in front of each is a test booklet, which has the sole attention of each student. Of course, one might read that order in different ways; is this to be considered a sign of school discipline, or does it suggest the suppression of creativity? Is it a depiction of hard work and diligence, or is it to be seen as creating a leveling effect? In order to draw some conclusions—or at least some discussion points—from these questions, we might need to know more about the context. If this visual accompanied an article that was praising the way a school had helped its students achieve positive outcomes through discipline, then some of the details (like the diligence and order, which is further highlighted by the lines on the floor that also speak to order) would stand out. You might also want to know when the photograph was taken and the social contexts surrounding the image: If you learned that this image was from the 1950s, or from 2008, would that make a difference? What effect does the way the students are dressed have upon your impressions? What about the setting, which appears to be a gymnasium?

Your critical analysis, as with written texts, might also extend from your reading of the image as part of the audience to your reading of the image as a potential composer. That is, rather than just think about what the image does to you as a viewer, you might consider how you might *use* the image as part of your own arguments. So, let's imagine that you are writing a piece that suggests that standardized testing tends to undermine individual student creativity and uniqueness. This photograph could certainly show the way that students are (quite literally) inscribed within a box by the system. You might also note the way that this piece is cropped; since we only see part of this huge space, an illusion is created that the rows extend to both sides and further back, making the mass of students seem almost limitless. As a writer/composer, you might also consider how cropping the picture differently, focusing more on individual students or upon the proctors in the front of the room or on the papers in front of the students, might create a different effect.

You might also consider how words and images interact. A caption could help direct the viewers to experience the photograph in a different way. Give that a try: what caption might you add to stress the way standardized tests encourage conformity? What about if you wanted to stress the positive discipline that could come from such tests? What about if your goal was to demonstrate how outdated standardized testing is, or if you wanted to stress that teachers are put in the position of surveillance? The words that accompany the image work together with the image itself to literally "frame" the message—and the response of an audience. And audience is a crucial concept here. Imagine showing this picture to different groups, and what their likely response would be. Might an older audience see this nostalgically? What about a younger audience? What if you were to pair this with a picture of students interacting or of a group of students sitting in desks sending text messages from their cell phones? Or in rows of computer terminals? Those internal contexts interact with external elements to make of that same image a very different set of likely responses.

Thinking about images such as this one can help you to consider not only the external context (the times and current conversations about education or standardized testing) but the internal one (the way that image is presented, how it is cropped, and its interaction with a caption). It can also help you apply the two kinds of reading—reading as part of the audience and reading as a writer—to images as well as to text. These techniques can likewise be applied to video and audio "texts."

Using this form of reading or analysis can benefit you as a twenty-first-century writer in many ways. It can help you to become a better reader of the vast array of "texts" that exist in multiple media, giving you a better understanding of how conversations are influenced by those media. It can also help you as a writer in our multi-media world, asking you to consider the media that you now have at your disposal as you write in a world that relies upon many forms of composing. All of these techniques can be applied as you read the selections in this book.

Using This Book to Enter and Extend the Conversation

Looked at as a whole, then, the conversation model of reading and writing has some distinct characteristics, characteristics that go beyond ways that you may have approached research in the past. In the model we're suggesting, careful reading and reflection (driven by annotation and synthesis) are ways to find your place in the conversation about any given topic. By asking questions of both written and visual texts, by using active, critical reading, and by considering the contexts of any text, you can then find good reasons to respond with your own writing. It is hard to overestimate how important this process of finding a focus can be for your own writing.

If you peruse the table of contents of this book, you'll find that the editors have started this process for you. The methods we used to compile this book mirror the research process that you might use to enter and extend the conversation, building upon points of inquiry that people are discussing. Just as we're suggesting for you, the editors of this volume began with broad categories on inquiry—education, gender and race, marriage and family, sustainability, and so forth.

And just as we're suggesting for you, we tried to create an array of texts—books, journals, letters, Web sites, Weblogs, visuals, and so forth—that concern themselves, more or less, with questions one might ask on each topic.

But just *collecting* readings under those broad categories would not have been particularly useful. What we sought, rather, was an array of readings under each topic area that spoke to one another. In some cases, as for example with the debate between John Taylor Gatto and Ron Miller on public education in Chapter 1, Jeff Jarvis's response to Frank Partsch in Chapter 3, or the debate surrounding environmental activism between Patrick Moore (one of the founders of Greenpeace) and current members of Greenpeace in Chapter 12, we find direct conversations. But even readings that range across a wide expanse of time, or writers who have no knowledge of one another, can speak to one another, and in ways that they perhaps never anticipated. The conversation model of reading is meant to emphasize specific, focused questions, even if the reading originally addressed many questions. For example, by placing the readings on gender, race, and ethnicity in a section on "identity," we have already suggested the ways in which we are asking you to think about those categories. And by placing the issues of race, gender, and ethnicity together, we are also suggesting that there are similarities and important points of contrast among them. They could just as easily have been framed as a question of civil rights, of biological difference, of education, of history, and so forth.

What you can learn from the ways in which we have contextualized the debate (as an identity issue) illustrates the various ways that writers use secondary sources, ways that were sometimes not imagined by the original authors. Writers use that which they find in their research to create vivid new conversations, arranging reading materials in ways that bring out new facets of a conversation among other writers—a dialogue that we then will enter as well. Not only do these conversations take on new meaning as we reconfigure them (while, of course, always being careful not to use secondary sources in ways that betray the author's ideas), but the conversations also proceed across time. Though "currency" (how recent a work is) is important—and more important in some fields than others—we can also gain a great deal of perspective as an argument moves through various social contexts. That is, we can bring the ideas of writers from one context into dialogue with those from another. For example, in the section on marriage, the work of a current social scientist, Stephanie Coontz, has intriguing parallels with a more popular press study by Jillian Straus on the growing number of women who choose to remain single. That perspective, in turn, informs the views on current love relationships suggested by the conversation about "hooking up" in Chapter 7. In each case, the accumulation of voices helps us to examine the questions surrounding human love relationships in its due complexity, and to find a central line of discussion—and eventually, a thesis that we will argue. This should also remind us that while our research need not be limited to those things that have been written most recently, connections to our current society's questions and issues are eminently important in valuing past writings. By thinking about your reading and writing in this way, you can extend the conversations in this book, using the stasis points you discover to search for other readings that are also part of these conversations, and so to expand and develop your own review of the literature on your own focused area of interest. At the end of each part of the book, you'll find some guiding questions to get you started on this process.

Let's return then, to Kenneth Burke's parlor metaphor one last time. As you begin your college career, you are the latest comer to a set of conversations that has begun without you—and which has in some cases been going on for years, decades, even centuries. It is no doubt a daunting task to find your voice in such a world. But we all were newcomers at some point, and you'll be surprised how some focused research and careful reading can make you feel ready to, as Burke suggests, "put in your oar" and start paddling. If you learn the terms of the conversation by paying attention to both the content and the ways that people talk about that content, and you're willing to listen to the feedback that comes from continuing to read even *after* you've started to write, your writing will become sharper, more confident, more expert. We learn by doing, and writing is doing.

10 Strategies for Using the Conversation Model of Reading and Writing

1. *Enter a conversation looking for a specific purpose and audience.* Being clear on what your focused purpose is, what readers comprise your core audience, and what that audience already thinks, knows (and think they

know) can help you to decide what you need to learn to speak intelligently and effectively on a topic. As you read, don't do so passively, just accepting what you read. Ask questions about the contexts and implications of the conversation, and how your own interests can help you to use the material you read toward your own purposes and to affect your own audiences. *Remember, too—and this is crucial—that your understanding of the audience and purpose will keep changing as you learn more.*

TRY THIS: As you read the selections in a given chapter, keep a *reading journal* that chronicles the development of your own thoughts on a given topic and those of the authors in that chapter. Analyze the ways that other writers have approached a topic, what seems to matter most to them, and the key points of contention (or stasis points) that emerge in the conversation. With each new reading you encounter, react to the main points that the writer makes and how they make you feel, what they make you consider (or re-consider), and where you tend to agree and disagree. Then, go back and read your own journal entries, trying to determine the facets of the conversation that most matter to you, the perspectives on the topic that you'd like to add, and the ideas that you'd like to change in your own readers. From this summary, attempt to articulate your purpose for writing—what you'd like your writing to accomplish. Then, summarize the things that seem most to matter to your potential audience, and how you can frame your own argument in ways that are most likely to persuade your readers to approach your writing with an open mind. What points made by other authors can you accept? What points do you question? What more information will you need in order to support or contest those points? This early process will help you to invent approaches to the conversation that you hope to enter.

2. *Enter the conversation with an open mind: Be sure not to begin with the answer, but with questions.* Rather than state from the start that your purpose is to "prove to others that college should be open to all," you might instead delay that conclusion, asking instead "What is the purpose of college?" and "Does college really serve that purpose?" That is, you do not start with a thesis, but instead see what thesis develops as you read critically.

TRY THIS: One of the traditional ways that people have been trained in forming good arguments is an exercise called *dissoi logoi* ("different words"). The idea is to tease out the intricacies of an issue by forcing yourself to see multiple perspectives of it. So, rather than start from a firm position on a topic, try writing the best argument you can for the opposite perspective from that which you tend to feel or believe. For example, let's say that you tend to believe that marriage is the cornerstone of our culture. In order to investigate whether that belief is sound, try forming as many good arguments as you can *against* marriage: its effect upon independence, its history of male dominance, its high failure rate, and so forth. Add to your own thoughts the arguments made by other writers on the topic. The key to using this technique successfully is to try your hardest to build sound arguments that *contradict* the position that you tend to believe. What this will allow you to do is to formulate and assess the possible counterarguments on this topic, and so give you some specific questions that you can examine further as you formulate the stance you choose to take. Doing so can help you to widen your perspective, and, in some cases, to change your mind on at least some facets of the issue. And even if you continue to believe your original position, this can help you to address those counterarguments in your writing.

3. *Read cumulatively, noting the ways that your ideas develop as you encounter new arguments.* The process of invention, gathering ideas for our own writing, involves two kinds of methods. *Introspective* methods for gathering ideas—looking into yourself through techniques like brainstorming and freewriting—can be useful to help you generate ideas and articulate what you already know. But those techniques are not adequate. You also need to invent—get ideas—by *careful and analytical reading.* As you read on a topic, new ideas will continually emerge, and you'll start to come to terms with the ongoing conversation. To do so, you'll need to continuously trace the progress of your own ideas, accumulating new ones and asking how they change your own thinking on a topic.

   TRY THIS: Before beginning your reading, *brainstorm* or *freewrite* to consider what you think about a topic. Brainstorming can be done alone or in groups. The idea is to generate as many ideas on a topic as you can, without yet worrying about the value of each idea—just list whatever ideas come out in your writing or discussion. You can decide later which seem to have the most potential. These ideas can be in sentences, phrases, or even just words, and usually end up as a list. Freewriting is similar in that it also encourages you to simply write whatever comes to mind. But unlike brainstorming, which tends to generate a list of separate ideas, freewriting is more developmental. That is, you write the first thing about a topic that you think about, then build upon it, writing quickly and without stopping. This can allow you to follow ideas forward to see where they lead you. Try to write on the topic for a sustained 10 or 15 minutes, and you'll be surprised how many ideas you can generate. So, for example, before reading the selections in Chapter 4 on whether technology is a help or a hindrance to one's learning, you might brainstorm or freewrite on your own thoughts about the topic. In what ways might the Internet have made us lazy or less likely to question the validity of sources? What are the reasons why Wikipedia is a poor (or good) source of information? Should we only trust academic journals? What do you find to be the best technologies for finding, or presenting, your ideas? Is text-messaging harming our ability to write using proper conventions of the language, or are you able to move from one style to another as appropriate? Then, keep a log of how your ideas change as you read the arguments of other writers. Each time you encounter a new reading, go back to your original thoughts and make notes of how those original ideas have changed, been reinforced, developed, or created new questions for you to examine. In this way, you'll develop a personal intellectual history of your own thinking on a given topic. These informal writings can then be used as you begin the process of writing your way into the conversation.

4. *To read actively, write as you read.* It is not possible to read actively without a pen—so feel free to write in this book! As you read, you should be making a text your own by underlining key passages and creating a running account in the margins of what you find important in a text, what the authors' stance in that text is, and how you are reacting to that text. As you continue to read, you'll also be creating a dialogue in the margin that includes not only you and the author, but other authors whose work you have read.

TRY THIS: As you read the selections in this book, make notes in the margin as you discover new ideas and contributions to your own thinking on a topic. As you read each new piece, make a conscious effort to compare the ideas of the author with those of previous authors. That is, ask yourself what one author would be likely to say to another author, and note that too in the margins. You might even attempt to construct an actual dialogue among the authors, imagining how a debate among those authors might go. Start with one statement which captures the main idea of one author's essay; then, ask yourself what the other authors you have read might say to that, and let the conversation begin. What you construct might look something like this:

> *W.J. Reeves:* College is not for everyone; it is a waste of time for students who aren't intellectually prepared.
>
> *Paul Attewell:* But if we restrict college to only those who are prepared, how will any underprepared group ever make progress?
>
> *Clive Crook:* There are many ways for a group to make progress—it doesn't need to be college. The problem really is that employers are requiring college for jobs that don't need it.
>
> *Ellen Lagemann:* But it doesn't have to be one or the other, does it? Can't a liberal arts education also serve career interests?
>
> *Thomas Reeves:* Sure, if the students are prepared, and if we don't dumb down the curriculum to make it open to all.

By creating this fictional conversation, you can come to grips with the ideas of each author, and so find the stasis points—the points of debate—that inform this conversation. You can also get a feel for which perspectives you most support, and why.

5. *Note the terminology that is used frequently, not only to learn the lingo surrounding a topic (such as "sustainability," "civil rights," "hooking up," "underrepresented groups," "literacy," and so forth), but also to develop search strings that are likely to breed the information you need.* Learning the vocabulary surrounding a topic will make you more capable of reading more specialized texts (found through more specialized search engines), and will do a great deal to lead you to important new sources of information. It will also train you in the language of that discipline and that subject area, so that you can write (comfortably) like an expert.

TRY THIS: As you annotate a text, circle or write in the margin terms that seem to come up again and again, paying special attention to those terms that seem to be used by multiple authors. Then, make a list of the key terms used by authors in this conversation. Use those terms to do searches for further readings on the topic. If the terms are unfamiliar, start by looking for several definitions of the term. Create a glossary of key terms that you can then use in your own writing on the topic. In doing so, you'll be better equipped with the tools used by experts on this issue.

6. *Follow the references from articles that you read.* For many years, you've been asked to create Reference pages (APA style) or Works Cited pages (MLA style). Published authors do this as well. Though part of the reason to do this is to help your own credibility and to give credit where it is due, there is an even more important reason for this: to leave a roadmap to the information that each researcher used for future researchers. Even pieces that don't have a Works Cited or Reference list do make internal references to other authors who have written on this topic. So, if you find a recent article on a topic, its reference page is an excellent place for you to look for other pieces of information that might serve your purposes as well. Take special note of those names and sources that seem to come up again and again within a particular conversation, and take the time to seek them in their work in its original form. You can also use the titles of those references to suggest new ways to look at your topic.

   TRY THIS: As you annotate, keep track of the names of other writers that are mentioned, and pay special attention to authors whose names seem to come up again and again. Where specific works by those authors are named, either internally or in the reference page, note those titles as well. Keep an electronic "working bibliography" of sources on the topic, adding a sentence or two that describes why this author or source might be important to your further research and, where available, the publication information. By doing this, by the end of your reading, you'll have an excellent start toward becoming more informed on the topic, should you decide to enter into that conversation.

7. *Don't neglect how important actual conversations can be—with your classmates, with your teachers, with other experts you know.* One of the unique joys of being in a college environment is that you are surrounded by people with a vast array of expertise. Get advice from those experts whenever possible, not only on specific sources of information, but on the ways one might approach the questions you have. As you talk to others, you will also be learning how to talk about those topics, something that will be reflected in the writing you do as well.

TRY THIS: As you read, keep a list of "human resources" on the topic with whom you'd like to talk further. So, for example, as you read the pieces on the past and current state of marriage, you might recall that you talked about this issue in a sociology or literature class. Take a minute to send out an email to a past or current teacher, asking his or her thoughts on the issue. Or call your grandmother, and get her perspective on how marriage has changed. Or post a question to your Facebook page or Twitter to gather the opinions of your "friends." Or pose a question to a listserv on the topic. You might even try to find the webpage of the author him or herself, and send an email. Think widely about whose perspectives on any given topic might be useful, and inquire about those perspectives. You, of course, will need to weigh the value of those opinions individually, but each new voice you hear from will help you to enrich your own thinking on the topic.

8. *Remember that visuals make arguments, too, and so need to be "read" like any other text.* When you encounter not only photographs or drawings, but graphs, charts, and other visual aids, you are encountering an argument—a case someone is making for a particular way of seeing. It is important that you use the same analytical skills for interpreting the credibility, relevance, and rhetorical (persuasive) stance that visual is making. Likewise, you should consider how using visual arguments can sometimes be stronger than using words alone.

TRY THIS: Page through a newspaper or magazine, or watch a YouTube video, paying special attention to the ways that arguments are made visually. First, make note of your initial impression of what you see—how it makes you feel, what it makes you think about, and so forth. Then, ask yourself why you had that reaction, looking more closely at some of the visual (and, in the case of a video, the auditory) elements of the piece. What specific features of this multi-media text seem to be most effective? How does the composition of the piece reinforce a specific point of view or argument? Is it deceptive in any way? How is color used? Contrasts? How do small details contribute to the overall effect? Make note of these features, and write an analysis of the visual persuasion you find there. You might also show the piece to others to see what they notice. Doing this will help you to gauge the ways that visual arguments work, and how you might incorporate them into your own writing. It can also help you to be a more careful reader of these visual arguments, and so keep you from being drawn in to arguments that are deceptive and not substantial enough.

9. *Consider contexts for that which you read.* Every argument has a set of surrounding contexts. Those contexts include both external elements (the time in which it was written and what was going on locally, nationally, and internationally during the time period) and internal elements (the surrounding visuals, the place where it was published and the audience for that publication, the responses to the piece through letters to the editor or blog posts, and so forth). In order to read well, we need to take into account those surrounding circumstances. For example, if we want to understand Naomi Wolf's landmark book, *The Beauty Myth*, we also need to consider the current state of feminism at the time, the expectations of women then, the advertisements of the time period that suggested what a woman should look like, and so on. Likewise, to understand Martin Luther King's "Letter from a Birmingham Jail," we need to not only understand the state of the civil rights movement at the time, but also the letter from 8 Alabama clergymen to which it was responding (which is why both are included in this book). If we don't account for the surrounding context, we may not fully understand the origins of a past—or current—conversation.

   TRY THIS: Using information from the headnote of one of the selections in this text that you are reading, find the original date and place of publication of a piece. Then, do some background reading. Try to find out what news events were gaining attention during that time. Consider what was in fashion. Consider the music or films that were popular or what political events or debates were concerning us in the months or years leading up to this time of publication. And if you can find the original publication, you might even look at the other stories in that issue of the publication (or in the months preceding it). Then, write your own extended headnote, explaining the contexts of the piece as you now understand them, and how those contexts might have influenced the publication of this piece. You can use the introductions to the *Conversations in Context* sections of this book as a model.

10. *Apply these techniques to reading you do in other courses and in your daily life.* One of the most important ways to assure that your college education is useful is to extend what you learn in one class to that which you learn in others—and to your life outside of college. To get the

most of the techniques of reading and writing that are suggested in this book, it is important that you find their applicability to other facets of your life and education. Don't delay that process until after the course is done, or you may lose some of that learning. The best way to assure that you'll be able to transfer what you learn from this book or this course is to start applying that learning right now.

TRY THIS: Use the techniques of conversation-based reading to the reading you are doing in another course or in your private life. That is, as you read a textbook or article from another class, annotate it using the techniques above, or create a reading journal or working bibliography of key experts on the topic, or a glossary of key terms. You might even try writing a dialogue among the various experts on a topic from a psychology or history class, or analyzing the visuals used in a chemistry article, or considering the context of a new engineering trend. Any one of the nine techniques summarized above can apply to the work you are doing in other classes or to your reading in your day-to-day life. Doing so will not only help you better see how these techniques work, but they will help you succeed in your other classes and become more thoughtful citizens.

Conversations About Education

Introduction

Americans have always been passionate about issues related
to education. Why? For one, education issues affect every
American in a personal way. True, there is a strong anti-
intellectual strain in our national culture (that is, although
we respect education, many also value common sense over
book learning). But it is also true that most Americans pursue with a passion the ideal of "education for all," as a means
of self-improvement and as the source of the enlightened citizenry required by democratic institutions. That ideal forms
the theoretical basis for our public education system, which
is meant to provide schooling to all Americans. As a larger
percentage and a more diverse demographic of Americans
seek a college education—and indeed have started to consider
college attendance a necessity for advancement—discussions
about access to, and the quality of, higher education have
also become more frequent. But despite a great deal of agreement that education is a good thing, there is a good deal of
disagreement about the goals, methods, and delivery of the
education that we provide at both levels. Those disagree-
ments form the basis of the conversations about education
featured in this part of the book. Also, as a student, you are
clearly a stakeholder in those conversations.

The readings in Chapter 1 examine two related, but separate, facets of our system of public education: its goals and
its condition. After all, it is difficult to gauge the "condition"
of public education if we do not first agree, at least partially,
upon its goals. Questions about the purposes and quality of
our public education are not new; the history of public education in this country, it sometimes seems, is a story told as
one crisis after another. The most recent set of debates was
stirred by the 1983 report entitled, "A Nation at Risk." Since
then, a number of committees and commissions have
launched well-publicized reform efforts aimed at everything
from teacher education and accountability to classroom climate and curriculum, asking things like: What elements of
the curriculum are most crucial? Should we emphasize
learning skills—problem solving, critical thinking, flexibility, independent decision-making—or a body of knowledge
that all educated folks should know? Or should we focus
upon vocationalism—preparing students for their future
work? Should the way that schools are funded be reconsid-
ered, to even out differences between the "haves" and the
"have-nots"? Or would that undermine a cornerstone of our
educational tradition, local control? Are teachers trained

adequately, paid adequately, kept current in their fields, given enough autonomy over their classrooms? Are they held accountable? Also, what are the students themselves thinking about their educational experiences? The list seems endless, as are the available conversations. The readings in this section allow you to listen in to this conversation about the goals of education and how they might best be achieved. You will hear from those who feel that the system itself is the problem and from those who believe that standards have been lowered too far. You will hear from teachers, from students, and from parents. You will hear from those who believe that education is about discipline and those who believe it is about freedom. You will also hear the ongoing discussions as they are portrayed in narratives, blogs, research-based essays, and diatribes. If you listen closely, you will find many places for you to join in this conversation that involves you so personally.

One specific debate about our public education system involves the use of frequent and high-stakes testing, driven partially by the "No Child Left Behind" legislation. This debate asks a number of questions: Do we test too much and educate too little, or is testing necessary to assess students and schools? Do standardized tests really measure the outcomes we most want for students? Do they cause too much stress on students? Are they more about making money for testing companies than they are about education? Do they provide a valuable, standard measure, by which we can be sure that students nationally are receiving access to the same quality education? Do teachers teach to the test instead of to students? All of these questions make for important and current discussions. The *Conversations in Context* section of this chapter will provide you with some background on the recent history of this debate and an array of voices and images on the topic that you can read, discuss, and—if you choose—use as a starting point for your own further research and writing.

The second set of readings addresses the questions "What, and who, is college for?" In a country where growing numbers of students go to college (although many do not complete college), and where we are hearing more and more references to "K–16 education," these are questions that have some exigency. (The questions likely have a great deal of personal exigency for you as well, as you begin college.) In broad terms, the questions can be posed this way: Is college an opportunity for personal growth and general intellectual development? Or is college a means to economic advancement? If college should foster both general education and professional specialization, then in what proportions should it do so, and through what means? Is there still a role for a "liberal arts" education? Is formal education less necessary in an Internet age, when information is so readily available at every computer terminal? Should college be designed for the intellectual elite who are sophisticated enough to pursue truly advanced learning, or is college something that ought to be within reach of most high school graduates? If so, what effect do "open access" policies—which make college admission more available to underprepared students—have upon college standards? Also, what are the obligations of educators to develop college courses within the ability range of the wider array of students? Should all students be encouraged to go to college? Or are there other, more suitable paths for some? Or would that tend to divide the intellectual class from the working class and the wealthy from the lower classes? That is, are colleges the gatekeepers of economic success? Also, what should we make of the growing percentage of girls and the shrinking percentage of boys who are attending college? As you read the selections, you will no doubt also reflect upon your own choices and experiences; the combination can lead to some nicely balanced writing.

Taken as a whole, the first part of *Conversations* invites you into a wide-ranging set of individual, but related, discussions—discussions with which you have a great deal of knowledge and experience, having been students for a large percentage of your life. If you bring those experiences to those that you read, you will no doubt have a great deal to add to this crucial set of conversations.

CHAPTER 1

The Goals and Condition of Public Education

John Taylor Gatto

How Public Education Cripples Our Kids, and Why

John Taylor Gatto was a school teacher in the New York public schools for 29 years, after also working in a number of other diverse professions, including scriptwriter in the film business, jewelry designer, songwriter, and hot dog vendor. It was his very public retirement from the public schools (after having been named teacher of the year three times) that brought him into the public eye as a leader in the debate about public education. That retirement announcement came in the form of a *Wall Street Journal* editorial, in which he not only asserted his reasons for quitting—because he could no longer "hurt kids to make a living"—but also vowed to "start a conversation among those who've been silent up until now" about the problems with mandatory schooling and the purposes of public education. His books include *Dumbing Us Down: The Hidden Curriculum of Compulsory Schooling* (1992, from which this excerpt is taken); *The Exhausted School* (1993); *A Different Kind of Teacher* (2000); and *The Underground History Of American Education* (2001). As you read, you might consider the degree to which the features of public education that are discussed here still apply to public education—and to your own experiences as a student.

taught for thirty years in some of the worst schools in   1
Manhattan, and in some of the best, and during that time I
became an expert in boredom. Boredom was everywhere in

my world, and if you asked the kids, as I often did, *why* they felt so bored, they always gave the same answers: They said the work was stupid, that it made no sense, that they already knew it. They said they wanted to be doing something real, not just sitting around. They said teachers didn't seem to know much about their subjects and clearly weren't interested in learning more. And the kids were right: their teachers were every bit as bored as they were.

2   Boredom is the common condition of schoolteachers, and anyone who has spent time in a teachers' lounge can vouch for the low energy, the whining, the dispirited attitudes, to be found there. When asked why *they* feel bored, the teachers tend to blame the kids, as you might expect. Who wouldn't get bored teaching students who are rude and interested only in grades? If even that. Of course, teachers are themselves products of the same twelve-year compulsory school programs that so thoroughly bore their students, and as school personnel they are trapped inside structures even more rigid than those imposed upon the children. Who, then, is to blame?

3   We all are. My grandfather taught me that. One afternoon when I was seven I complained to him of boredom, and he batted me hard on the head. He told me that I was never to use that term in his presence again, that if I was bored it was my fault and no one else's. The obligation to amuse and instruct myself was entirely my own, and people who didn't know that were childish people, to be avoided if possible. Certainly not to be trusted. That episode cured me of boredom forever, and here and there over the years I was able to pass on the lesson to some remarkable student. For the most part, however, I found it futile to challenge the official notion that boredom and childishness were the natural state of affairs in the classroom. Often I had to defy custom, and even bend the law, to help kids break out of this trap.

4   The empire struck back, of course; childish adults regularly conflate opposition with disloyalty. I once returned from a medical leave to discover that all evidence of my having been granted the leave had been purposely destroyed, that my job had been terminated, and that I no longer possessed even a teaching license. After nine months of tormented effort I was able to retrieve the license when a school secretary testified to witnessing the plot unfold. In the meantime my family suffered more than I care to remember. By the time I finally retired in 1991, I had more than enough reason to think of our schools—with their long-term, cell-block-style, forced confinement of both students and teachers—as virtual factories of childishness. Yet I honestly could not see why they had to be that way. My own experience had revealed to me what many other teachers must learn along the way, too, yet keep to themselves for fear of

reprisal: if we wanted to we could easily and inexpensively jettison the old, stupid structures and help kids take an education rather than merely receive a schooling. We could encourage the best qualities of youthfulness—curiosity, adventure, resilience, the capacity for surprising insight—simply by being more flexible about time, texts, and tests, by introducing kids to truly competent adults, and by giving each student what autonomy he or she needs in order to take a risk every now and then.

But we don't do that. And the more I asked why not, and persisted in thinking about the "problem" of schooling as an engineer might, the more I missed the point: What if there is no "problem" with our schools? What if they are the way they are, so expensively flying in the face of common sense and long experience in how children learn things, not because they are doing something wrong but because they are doing something right? Is it possible that George W. Bush accidentally spoke the truth when he said we would "leave no child behind"? Could it be that our schools are designed to make sure not one of them ever really grows up? 5

Do we really need school? I don't mean education, just forced schooling: six classes a day, five days a week, nine months a year, for twelve years. Is this deadly routine really necessary? And if so, for what? Don't hide behind reading, writing, and arithmetic as a rationale, because 2 million happy homeschoolers have surely put that banal justification to rest. Even if they hadn't, a considerable number of well-known Americans never went through the twelve-year wringer our kids currently go through, and they turned out all right. George Washington, Benjamin Franklin, Thomas Jefferson, Abraham Lincoln? Someone taught them, to be sure, but they were not products of a school system, and not one of them was ever "graduated" from a secondary school. Throughout most of American history, kids generally didn't go to high school, yet the unschooled rose to be admirals, like Farragut; inventors, like Edison; captains of industry, like Carnegie and Rockefeller; writers, like Melville and Twain and Conrad; and even scholars, like Margaret Mead. In fact, until pretty recently people who reached the age of thirteen weren't looked upon as children at all. Ariel Durant, who co-wrote an enormous, and very good, multivolume history of the world with her husband, Will, was happily married at fifteen, and who could reasonably claim that Ariel Durant was an uneducated person? Unschooled, perhaps, but not uneducated. 6

We have been taught (that is, schooled) in this country to think of "success" as synonymous with, or at least dependent upon, "schooling," but historically that isn't true in either an intellectual or a financial sense. And plenty of people throughout the world today find a way to educate themselves without resorting to a system of compulsory secondary schools that all 7 too often resemble prisons. Why, then, do Americans confuse education with just such a system? What exactly is the purpose of our public schools?

8   Mass schooling of a compulsory nature really got its teeth into the United States between 1905 and 1915, though it was conceived of much earlier and pushed for throughout most of the nineteenth century. The reason given for this enormous upheaval of family life and cultural traditions was, roughly speaking, threefold:

1. To make good people.
2. To make good citizens.
3. To make each person his or her personal best.

9   These goals are still trotted out today on a regular basis, and most of us accept them in one form or another as a decent definition of public education's mission, however short schools actually fall in achieving them. But we are dead wrong. Compounding our error is the fact that the national literature holds numerous and surprisingly consistent statements of compulsory schooling's true purpose. We have, for example, the great H. L. Mencken, who wrote in *The American Mercury* for April 1924 that the aim of public education is

> not to fill the young of the species with knowledge and awaken their intelligence . . . Nothing could be further from the truth. The aim . . . is simply to reduce as many individuals as possible to the same safe level, to breed and train a standardized citizenry, to put down dissent and originality. That is its aim in the United States . . . and that is its aim everywhere else.

10   Because of Mencken's reputation as a satirist, we might be tempted to dismiss this passage as a bit of hyperbolic sarcasm. His article, however, goes on to trace the template for our own educational system back to the now vanished, though never to be forgotten, military state of Prussia. And although he was certainly aware of the irony that we had recently been at war with Germany, the heir to Prussian thought and culture, Mencken was being perfectly serious here. Our educational system really is Prussian in origin, and that really is cause for concern.

11   The odd fact of a Prussian provenance for our schools pops up again and again once you know to look for it. William James alluded to it many times at the turn of the century. Orestes Brownson, the hero of Christopher Lasch's 1991 book, *The True and Only Heaven*, was publicly denouncing the Prussianization

of American schools back in the 1840s. Horace Mann's "Seventh Annual Report" to the Massachusetts State Board of Education in 1843 is essentially a paean to the land of Frederick the Great and a call for its schooling to be brought here. That Prussian culture loomed large in America is hardly surprising, given our early association with that utopian state. A Prussian served as Washington's aide during the Revolutionary War, and so many German-speaking people had settled here by 1795 that Congress considered publishing a German-language edition of the federal laws. But what shocks is that we should so eagerly have adopted one of the very worst aspects of Prussian culture: an educational system deliberately designed to produce mediocre intellects, to hamstring the inner life, to deny students appreciable leadership skills, and to ensure docile and incomplete citizens—all in order to render the populace "manageable."

It was from James Bryant Conant—president of Harvard for   12
twenty years, WWI poison-gas specialist, WWII executive on the atomic-bomb project, high commissioner of the American zone in Germany after WWII, and truly one of the most influential figures of the twentieth century—that I first got wind of the real purposes of American schooling. Without Conant, we would probably not have the same style and degree of standardized testing that we enjoy today, nor would we be blessed with gargantuan high schools that warehouse 2,000 to 4,000 students at a time, like the famous Columbine High in Littleton, Colorado. Shortly after I retired from teaching I picked up Conant's 1959 book-length essay, *The Child the Parent and the State*, and was more than a little intrigued to see him mention in passing that the modern schools we attend were the result of a "revolution" engineered between 1905 and 1930. A revolution? He declines to elaborate, but he does direct the curious and the uninformed to Alexander Inglis's 1918 book, *Principles of Secondary Education*, in which "one saw this revolution through the eyes of a revolutionary."

Inglis, for whom a lecture in education at Harvard is named,   13
makes it perfectly clear that compulsory schooling on this continent was intended to be just what it had been for Prussia in the 1820s: a fifth column into the burgeoning democratic movement that threatened to give the peasants and the proletarians a voice at the bargaining table. Modern, industrialized, compulsory schooling was to make a sort of surgical incision into the prospective unity of these underclasses. Divide children by subject, by age-grading, by constant rankings on tests, and by many other more subtle means, and it was unlikely that the ignorant mass of mankind, separated in childhood, would ever reintegrate into a dangerous whole.

Inglis breaks down the purpose—the actual purpose—of   14
modem schooling into six basic functions, any one of which is

enough to curl the hair of those innocent enough to believe the three traditional goals listed earlier:

1. The *adjustive* or *adaptive* function. Schools are to establish fixed habits of reaction to authority. This, of course, precludes critical judgment completely. It also pretty much destroys the idea that useful or interesting material should be taught, because you can't test for reflexive obedience until you know whether you can make kids learn, and do, foolish and boring things.

2. The *integrating* function. This might well be called "the conformity function," because its intention is to make children as alike as possible. People who conform are predictable, and this is of great use to those who wish to harness and manipulate a large labor force.

3. The *diagnostic and directive* function. School is meant to determine each student's proper social role. This is done by logging evidence mathematically and anecdotally on cumulative records. As in "your permanent record." Yes, you do have one.

4. The *differentiating* function. Once their social role has been "diagnosed," children are to be sorted by role and trained only so far as their destination in the social machine merits—and not one step further. So much for making kids their personal best.

5. The *selective* function. This refers not to human choice at all but to Darwin's theory of natural selection as applied to what he called "the favored races." In short, the idea is to help things along by consciously attempting to improve the breeding stock. Schools are meant to tag the unfit—with poor grades, remedial placement, and other punishments—clearly enough that their peers will accept them as inferior and effectively bar them from the reproductive sweepstakes. That's what all those little humiliations from first grade onward were intended to do: wash the dirt down the drain.

6. The *propaedeutic* function. The societal system implied by these rules will require an elite group of caretakers. To that end, a small fraction of the kids will quietly be taught how to manage this continuing project, how to watch over and control a population deliberately dumbed down and declawed in order that government might proceed unchallenged and corporations might never want for obedient labor.

15   That, unfortunately, is the purpose of mandatory public education in this country. And lest you take Inglis for an isolated crank with a rather too cynical take on the educational enter-

prise, you should know that he was hardly alone in championing these ideas. Conant himself, building on the ideas of Horace Mann and others, campaigned tirelessly for an American school system designed along the same lines. Men like George Peabody, who funded the cause of mandatory schooling throughout the South, surely understood that the Prussian system was useful in creating not only a harmless electorate and a servile labor force but also a virtual herd of mindless consumers. In time a great number of industrial titans came to recognize the enormous profits to be had by cultivating and tending just such a herd via public education, among them Andrew Carnegie and John D. Rockefeller.

There you have it. Now you know. We don't need Karl Marx's 16
conception of a grand warfare between the classes to see that it is in the interest of complex management, economic or political, to dumb people down, to demoralize them, to divide them from one another, and to discard them if they don't conform. Class may frame the proposition, as when Woodrow Wilson, then president of Princeton University, said the following to the New York City School Teachers Association in 1909: "We want one class of persons to have a liberal education, and we want another class of persons, a very much larger class, of necessity, in every society, to forgo the privileges of a liberal education and fit themselves to perform specific difficult manual tasks." But the motives behind the disgusting decisions that bring about these ends need not be class-based at all. They can stem purely from fear, or from the by now familiar belief that "efficiency" is the paramount virtue, rather than love, liberty, laughter, or hope. Above all, they can stem from simple greed.

There were vast fortunes to be made, after all, in an economy 17
based on mass production and organized to favor the large corporation rather than the small business or the family farm. But mass production required mass consumption, and at the turn of the twentieth century most Americans considered it both unnatural and unwise to buy things they didn't actually need. Mandatory schooling was a godsend on that count. School didn't have to train kids in any direct sense to think they should consume nonstop, because it did something even better: it encouraged them not to think at all. And that left them sitting ducks for another great invention of the modem era—marketing.

Now, you needn't have studied marketing to know that there 18
are two groups of people who can always be convinced to consume more than they need to: addicts and children. School has done a pretty good job of turning our children into addicts, but it has done a spectacular job of turning our children into children. Again, this is no accident. Theorists from Plato to Rousseau to our own Dr. Inglis knew that if children could be

cloistered with other children, stripped of responsibility and independence, encouraged to develop only the trivializing emotions of greed, envy, jealousy, and fear, they would grow older but never truly grow up. In the 1934 edition of his once well-known book *Public Education in the United States*, Ellwood P. Cubberley detailed and praised the way the strategy of successive school enlargements had extended childhood by two to six years, and forced schooling was at the point still quite new. This same Cubberley—who was dean of Stanford's School of Education, a textbook editor at Houghton Mifflin, and Conant's friend and correspondent at Harvard—had written the following in the 1922 edition of his book *Public School Administration*: "Our schools are . . . factories in which the raw products (children) are to be shaped and fashioned . . . And it is the business of the school to build its pupils according to the specifications laid down."

19   It's perfectly obvious from our society today what those specifications were. Maturity has by now been banished from nearly every aspect of our lives. Easy divorce laws have removed the need to work at relationships; easy credit has removed the need for fiscal self-control; easy entertainment has removed the need to learn to entertain oneself; easy answers have removed the need to ask questions. We have become a nation of children, happy to surrender our judgments and our wills to political exhortations and commercial blandishments that would insult actual adults. We buy televisions, and then we buy the things we see on the television. We buy computers, and then we buy the things we see on the computer. We buy $150 sneakers whether we need them or not, and when they fall apart too soon we buy another pair. We drive SUVs and believe the lie that they constitute a kind of life insurance, even when we're upside-down in them. And, worst of all, we don't bat an eye when Ari Fleischer tells us to "be careful what you say," even if we remember having been told somewhere back in school that America is the land of the free. We simply buy that one too. Our schooling, as intended, has seen to it.

20   Now for the good news. Once you understand the logic behind modern schooling, its tricks and traps are fairly easy to avoid. School trains children to be employees and consumers; teach your own to be leaders and adventurers. School trains children to obey reflexively; teach your own to think critically and independently. Well-schooled kids have a low threshold for boredom; help your own to develop an inner life so that they'll never be bored. Urge them to take on the serious material, the *grown-up* material, in history, literature, philosophy, music, art, economics, theology—all the stuff schoolteachers know well enough to avoid. Challenge your kids with plenty of solitude so that they

can learn to enjoy their own company, to conduct inner dialogues. Well-schooled people are conditioned to dread being alone, and they seek constant companionship through the TV, the computer, the cell phone, and through shallow friendships quickly acquired and quickly abandoned. Your children should have a more meaningful life, and they can.

First, though, we must wake up to what our schools really are: 21 laboratories of experimentation on young minds, drill centers for the habits and attitudes that corporate society demands. Mandatory education serves children only incidentally; its real purpose is to turn them into servants. Don't let your own have their childhoods extended, not even for a day. If David Farragut could take command of a captured British warship as a preteen, if Thomas Edison could publish a broadsheet at the age of twelve, if Ben Franklin could apprentice himself to a printer at the same age (then put himself through a course of study that would choke a Yale senior today), there's no telling what your own kids could do. After a long life, and thirty years in the public school trenches, I've concluded that genius is as common as dirt. We suppress our genius only because we haven't yet figured out how to manage a population of educated men and women. The solution, I think, is simple and glorious. Let them manage themselves.

Ron Miller

Review of *Dumbing Us Down*: The Hidden Curriculum of Compulsory Schooling

Ron Miller, who holds a master's degree in Humanistic Psychology and a Ph.D. in American Studies, is a leader in the holistic education movement. Holistic education seeks to educate the whole person rather than just focus upon traditional curriculum elements. It begins from the premise that education should flow from those things that an individual truly needs to learn in order to be happy, healthy, and—as social psychologist Abrahan Maslow suggested—"self-actualized." Miller established an independent journal, *Holistic Education Review* (where this piece was first published, and which is now called *Encounter: Education for Meaning and Social Justice*) in order to spur research and conversations on this topic. He has also authored nine books, inlcuding *What Are Schools For? Holistic Education in American Culture* (1990) and *Free Schools, Free People: Education and Democracy After the 1960s* (2002). As you read Miller's review of John Taylor Gatto's book, *Dumbing Us Down* (which is excerpted in the previous selection), you might consider what theories on education these two writers share and where they diverge. You might also note that this author uses the occasion of a book review to offer subtle critique, present his own views, and so spur a conversation with Gatto—which is continued through Gatto's response in the next selection.

1   John Taylor Gatto's fiery speech to the New York legislature, upon being named the state teacher of the year, was reprinted in several publications and widely circulated among alternative and radical educators, making Gatto an immediate hero within the alternative education movement. That speech, along with four other essays, are brought together in *Dumbing Us Down*, a book that should further establish Gatto as the most visible contemporary critic of public schooling. Like Paul Goodman, John Holt, Herb Kohl, Jim Herndon, and Jonathan Kozol in the 1960s, Gatto is a morally sensitive and passionate teacher who is thoroughly disgusted by the spirit-crushing regimen of mass schooling, and unafraid to say so. Both Kohl and Kozol are still writing important books that present a progressive/radical critique of schools, but Gatto (like the late John Holt) gives voice to a growing populist rebellion against schooling as such. Whether this rebellion will support or counteract the holistic education movement is an open question, to which *Dumbing Us Down* may offer some clues.

2   One thing must be said up front: Gatto is a superb essayist. His writing is not academic or pedantic, but a model of harnessed passion. He builds his argument carefully and smoothly and then unleashes bold attacks that cut right to the core of many problems of modern education. He clearly has a solid understanding of the historical foundations of modern education, but generally makes his own personal interpretations rather than citing sources or scholars. Indeed, his essay "The Green Monongahela" is an intimate account of his own life and how he became a teacher. He tells a simple story from early in his career, of rescuing a young Hispanic girl from the "stupid" injustice of the system (she later went on to become an award-

winning teacher herself), that captures the essence of his moral crusade against institutional schooling.

Gatto summarizes his argument in an introductory chapter: 3

> Was it possible I had been hired not to enlarge children's power, but to diminish it? That seemed crazy on the face of it, but slowly I began to realize that the bells and the confinement, the crazy sequences, the age-segregation, the lack of privacy, the constant surveillance, and all the rest of the national curriculum of schooling were designed exactly as if someone had set out to prevent children from learning how to think and act, to coax them into addiction and dependent behavior. (p. xii)

In his speech to the legislature, he makes this charge explicit,   4 describing seven "lessons" that form the heart of the compulsory curriculum.

"These are the things you pay me to teach":

1. *Confusion.* "Everything I teach is out of context. I teach the unrelating of everything." (p. 2)
2. *Class position.* "That's the real lesson of any rigged competition like school. You come to know your place." (p. 3)
3. *Indifference.* "Indeed, the lesson of bells is that no work is worth finishing, so why care too deeply about anything?" (p. 6)
4. *Emotional dependency.* "By stars and red checks, smiles and frowns, prizes, honors, and disgraces, I teach kids to surrender their will to the predestined chain of command." (p. 7)
5. *Intellectual dependency.* "Of the millions of things of value to study, I decide what few we have time for, or actually it is decided by my faceless employers . . . Curiosity has no important place in my work, only conformity" (p. 8). Gatto says this is "the most important lesson, that we must wait for other people, better trained than ourselves, to make the meanings of our lives." (p. 8)
6. *Provisional self-esteem.* "The lesson of report cards, grades and tests is that children should not trust themselves or their parents but should rely on the evaluation of certified officials. People need to be told what they are worth." (p. 11)
7. *One can't hide.* "Surveillance is an ancient imperative, espoused by certain influential thinkers (such as Plato, Augustine, Calvin, Bacon, and Hobbes). All these childless men . . . discovered the same thing: children must be closely watched if you want to keep a society under tight central control." (pp. 11-12)

5 And here is the crux of Gatto's critique: in the past 125 years, social engineers have sought to keep American life under tight central control. Compulsory schooling is a deliberate effort to establish intellectual, economic, and political conformity so that society can be managed efficiently by a technocratic elite. "School," claims Gatto, "is an artifice that makes . . . a pyramidal social order seem inevitable, although such a premise is a fundamental betrayal of the American Revolution" (p. 13). Along with the media—especially television, which Gatto criticizes harshly in another essay—schooling removes young people from any genuine experience of community, any genuine engagement with the world or immersion in lasting relationships. It robs them of solitude and privacy. Yet these experiences are what enable us to develop self-knowledge and to grow up "fully human," argues Gatto, and he asserts that our most troubling social pathologies, such as drug abuse and violence, are the natural reaction of human lives subjected to mechanical, abstract discipline.

6 Gatto insistently calls for a return to genuine family and community life by rejecting the social engineering of experts and institutions. In a particularly powerful passage, he rejects the notion that a "life-and-death international competition" threatens our national existence, as *A Nation at Risk* (National Commission on Excellence in Education, 1983) warned. Such a notion is "based on a definition of productivity and the good life" that is "alienated from common human reality." "True meaning is genuinely found," Gatto writes:

> in families, in friends, in the passage of seasons, in nature, in simple ceremonies and rituals, in curiosity, generosity, compassion, and service to others, in a decent in-dependence and privacy, in all the free and inexpensive things out of which real families, real friends, and real communities are built . . . (pp. 16-17)

7 And these are the things we have lost in our hierarchically managed, global empire-building society.

8 In the essay "We Need Less School, Not More," Gatto draws a sharp distinction between true community (in which there is open communication and shared participation) and institutional networks (which value the individual in terms of only the institution's particular goals). A network cannot be a healthy substitute for family or community, Gatto argues; it is mechanical, impersonal, and overly rational. Schooling is a prime example of this:

> If, for instance, an A average is accounted the central purpose of adolescent life—the requirements for which take

most of the time and attention of the aspirant—and the worth of the individual is reckoned by victory or defeat in this abstract pursuit, then a social machine has been constructed which, by attaching purpose and meaning to essentially meaningless and fantastic behavior, will certainly dehumanize students, alienate them from their own human nature, and break the natural connection between them and their parents, to whom they would otherwise look for significant affirmations. (p. 62)

This is a brilliant, radical critique of the nature of modern 9
schooling. Gatto has certainly earned his heroic stature with his deeply insightful observations into the very essence of what public education has become. His writings deserve to be pondered seriously by holistic teachers and can contribute a great deal of insight and energy to our work.

Nevertheless, there is a fundamental issue at stake here, 10
which could end up sharply dividing the holistic education movement if we do not sensitively address it. Gatto, like John Holt and a great many homeschoolers, holds and defends a libertarian social philosophy. In the John Locke/Adam Smith tradition. Gatto argues that a common (social) good arises only out of the free interaction of individuals and intimate communities pursuing their own local good. Individuals and families are seen as the primary human reality, while social forces are generally treated as a distressing nuisance. (The term "social engineers" seems to include anyone who seriously addresses social issues.)

In the spirit of dialectical discourse (honest disagreement 11
leading to a more inclusive synthesis), which Gatto admires and knows to be the heart of genuine education, I wish to oppose the libertarian position with one that is more socially conscious. I am especially sensitive to the nuances of this question, since I spent several of my intellectual formative years as an enthusiastic student of libertarian philosophy and political theory, and still have a great deal of sympathy for it. Gatto is justified in calling for a genuine community life, to replace the stultifying power of the state, huge corporations, self-serving experts and professionals, and all impersonal institutions. Like other libertarians and homeschool advocates, however, Gatto throws the baby out with the bathwater by categorically defining school as an impersonal network and virtually equating educators and activists with "social engineers."

The problem is illustrated vividly in the book's closing essay, 12
"The Congregational Principle." Here, Gatto lauds the Puritan settlers of Massachusetts Bay for organizing their churches and

towns largely free of higher authority, thereby bringing about local solutions to social and political questions.

13   He explicitly recognizes the parochialism inherent in such radical localism: He discusses the towns' practice of banishing people whose religious views or personal qualities were discomfiting to the community, and he even acknowledges that dissidents (such as Quakers) were publicly humiliated and whipped (a few were also executed). Gatto's main point in relating this story is to celebrate the fact that New Englanders eventually evolved to a more open, liberal worldview without compulsory schooling or social engineering.

14   But Gatto's historical interpretation is flawed by his libertarian bias and is quite unconvincing: He asserts that the colonists enjoyed "nearly unconditional local choice" in a social "free market" (pp. 90-91), a strange claim to make for a rigidly moralistic society with a single established church!

15   Gatto claims that New England culture was transformed by "something mysterious inside the structure of Congregationalism" (p. 90). (Read Adam Smith's "invisible hand" that magically turns self-interest into common good.) But this utterly ignores the distinctly social events that forced New Englanders to alter their parochial culture in the early decades of the 19th century—the nationalistic impulses released by the War of 1812 (which New Englanders had bitterly and futilely opposed); Irish Catholic immigration; enlightenment and romantic movements; the rise of science, industrialism, and urban centers; and the growing tensions between North and South over trade, tariffs, and slavery. More important, it doesn't bother Gatto in the least that the liberalization of New England culture took two hundred years and probably would have taken far longer had these crucial societal events not intervened.

16   Libertarian thinking is a much-needed antidote to the hierarchical, mechanical power that has been amassed by social institutions in the 20th century. We surely do need to pull the plug on these monstrous organizations. But that is not all we need to do. We live in a society that is poisoned by inequality, racism, and grossly materialistic values. We live on a planet that is threatened with biocide within the next decade or two. We simply do not have two hundred years to wait for some "invisible hand" to lead individuals and families and self-satisfied little communities to begin addressing these tremendous issues! We must find a way to incorporate personal and communal independence into a social movement that recognizes our interdependence.

17   As I see it, this is exactly what holistic thinking attempts to do. Holistic educators are not "social engineers." We reject the compulsion and fragmentation and alienation of public schooling as earnestly as Gatto, but we recognize that the modern

crisis demands a concrete response grounded in certain moral, philosophical, and spiritual principles. Holistic politics, otherwise known as the Green movement, explicitly embraces decentralization and personal empowerment but within the context of severe social and ecological problems that need to be addressed. In a society of blatant inequality, how will the free market provide quality educational opportunity for poor children? In a society driven by addicted consumerism, how will families, on their own, deal with environmental devastation, media brainwashing, or corporate control of resources and jobs? These are problems of a social dimension, not solely a personal one. Getting rid of compulsory regimentation in school is an important part of our task, but by no means is it a panacea that will restore our society to some golden age of free people and whole families. A holistic response, not an atomistic one, is required.

John Taylor Gatto

Reply to Ron Miller

Biographical information on John Taylor Gatto can be found in the headnote to "How Public Education Cripples our Kids, and Why," included earlier in this chapter of Conversations (see page 41). In the selection, Gatto uses the Letter to the Editor format in order to respond to Ron Miller's review of Gatto's *Dumbing Us Down*. As you read, you might consider the ways that Gatto, while using a civil tone, refutes some of Miller's contentions, and so continues this dialogue about the status of public education in this country. Note particularly the ways that Gatto uses quotations from Miller's review in order to develop his own argument—an important technique for writers as they incorporate material from outside sources.

D ear Editor: 1
    I thank Ron Miller for the generous words of praise in the review of my book *Dumbing Us Down: the Hidden Curriculum of Compulsory Schooling* and at the same time am sending along some brief comments, in the spirit of the dialectic, about the "fundamental issue" (Ron's characterization) he finds at stake in my perspective.

2   To begin, some amendments are necessary. Ron says I hold and defend a libertarian social philosophy. While I have an approximate idea what he means by that, I live in horror of any labels (including, to be frank, "holistic") that box people in. My own observation of reality is that classification systems should not be taken seriously—they interfere with clear thought and virtually prevent discovery when they go beyond casual convenience. Having said that, let me classify myself more accurately than Ron did: The social philosophy I hold is a hybrid of Scotch-Irish folkways, Italian Presbyterian iconoclasm, some aristocratic seasoning (we were Lords of the Straits of Messina in the 13th century), a certain amount of classical training, a year spent with the Jesuits, a spell as altar boy for a wonderful priest who drank sacramental wine and played baseball (the Catholic strain through my Irish/German grandmother), and three decades of constant experimentation as a junior high teacher of both the near-rich and the dirt poor. Those are the external influences of substance; internally I've tried to push beyond the conditioned circuitry to discover the perimeter of my own singularity.

3   [I'm] still finding things out at 57. Calling me a libertarian would eventually mislead you. On the other hand, I like most libertarians I know of (Robert Ringer being one exception, Ayn Rand another), but I could say the same of most capital "C" conservatives, too.

4   In an understandable urge to establish the poles of dialectic, Ron accidentally sets me up as inhabiting a location I don't live in, and misstates some of my positions. I understand the realities of book reviewing and take no offense (in his position I would hardly have done as well) but in a contest of ideas it's crucial that all parties agree what ideas are actually being contested.

5   In his first assertion, that I argue common social good arises only out of free interaction of individuals and intimate communities he's about 95% accurate but the premise is an exceedingly complicated one requiring years of Jesuitical reflection to come to terms with. I expect argument, of course, but in its nature it isn't a debating point but a tool designed to help people challenge their own assumptions. Challenge, that is, not necessarily discard. In the coda of this assertion Ron makes that I believe individuals and families are the primary human reality—he is only a bit better than half right. The largest omission is the importance of nature and location. I regard the fabric of the natural world, unaltered, as a central part of sanity. Not a minor part, not a dismissable part, not an exchangeable part, not an amenity, but one of the few primary essences. In my codebook people without places are incompletely human; to move frequently is to display derangement. That accounts for the essay, "The Green Monongahela." It's in my book to demonstrate the role of place as a teacher. I am who I am because of Monongahela. If my

place had been Erie I would not be who I am. I won't belabor what must seem to most "well-schooled" Americans an eccentricity, but most of human history including the best part honored this very conservative idea and lived it. The tale of Jews in history is inexplicable unless it is seen in some important part as the story of a people deprived of their place; the tale of America and its strangely Procrustean institutions is another story from the same genre.

However if Ron had said individual and families and 6
rocks/trees/water/air/places are the primary human reality, he'd have been nearly right. If he'd have added our mortality and relation to the mystery we call God, completely right. But in his leap to a guess [that] I think something he calls "social forces" are a "distressing nuisance," he falls far short of where I really am. It's my turn now to guess, and if I guess correctly what he means by social forces, then "nuisance" doesn't begin to describe the distaste I feel. Substitute "horrifying psychopathology" and we'll be closer to the truth. People who mind other people's business, materially, in any arbitrary way are always bad news. It's the movers and shakers; I mean, the "great" names of history. It would be impossible for me, in a short compass, to explain adequately how damaging the Pasteurs, the Copernicuses, the Columbus's, the Newtons, the Horace Manns, and all the rest of the Egyptian hierarchy has really been, but the mechanism is not hard to see—each of these men (and of course they are all men, mostly childless men) short circuits the human dialectic, arrogating to themselves a false and morally corrosive authority that creates the dependent human mass it then "illuminates." I would follow Paul Valery's M. le Teste in throwing the mass of prominent men in the ocean. The brilliant, and as yet largely unseen, American homeschooling movement is brilliant precisely because it is leaderless, lacking canonical texts, experts, and laws. At the moment true leadership emerges—which I pray will not happen—it will be co-opted, and the movement regimented, routinized, drained of its life.

I despair in the short time I have with you of explaining ade- 7
quately these contentions but let me go at least a part of the distance: short of preserving your immediate world the only justification possible, moral justification, that is, for interfering in someone else's life is that you know more than the other fellow does and are "intervening" (that's the "helping profession" jargon, isn't it?) "for his own good."

I reject that view in the overwhelming percentage of cases, 8
believing with cause that the mathematical bell curve in human intelligence is a bald lie, albeit an exceedingly profitable one. What is good or bad is either a religious question or a philosophical one and not easily addressed—never by creating a demonology that relegates any individual into a mass that is managed for its

own good. It might shed some light on that last conclusion by confessing I was deeply depressed by Jonathan Kozol's contention that money would improve the schools of the poor. It would not, any more than money has improved the schools of the middle class. What money has done is to dehumanize most of the lives it touches, not least those in the sinecures of academia; nor could it be expected to do better in the hands of any other group than the present government gang. What Kozol accomplished is truly depressing—by transmuting his wonderful rage into a nasty, envious petulance, he has called attention away from his hard-won, and well-deserved, role as a biographer of human justice. All synthetic mobilizations must similarly be exercises in pen and pencil abstraction, or cynical exercises in manipulation, or display a fatal gulf between fecund natural reality and the reductionism inherent in collectivizing it.

9   This is a subtle thing to consider: on one hand, the best way is hands off anything outside a local reach (the architects of "global community," who date back before Plato, are the single great manifestation of Evil in human affairs), but not minds-off. I think we have an absolute obligation to preach to each other, chide each other, praise and condemn each other, take hold of hands held out for help—in Vonnegut's words, if you are no use you must be useless. I believe that, I taught that, and as a toll for associating with my classes through much of my teaching career I demanded a full day's community service work each week. If kids freely chose to associate with me, the price of our association was community service (which I encouraged kids to self-design). I hope you can see the difference between this kind of compulsion and the kind that social engineers effect.

10   The immense danger which inevitably comes to pass when you set up social machinery compelling people to be "better" is that that machinery will be inherited by people whose "better" is your own "worse." Jefferson saw that in imploring our original legislators to give us a weak central government. Were it not for the unholy and largely unexamined close relationships between Germany (especially the synthetic state of Prussia) and the colonial and federal leadership classes, we might have followed Jefferson's prescription. Certainly it was the overwhelming choice of the common people here. But the curious company of Deists and Unitarians who pulled (pull?) the national strings were too enchanted with Adam Weishaupt's vision, and too intoxicated with victory and prosperity; too vicariously identified with the lessons of Frederick the Great, Prussian compulsion schools, research universities, and ultimately the deadly world view of Wilhelm Wundt to allow the nascent urges of freedom and democracy to develop. By 1850 both were stone cold dead. We have only a memory of our stillborn democracy.

There is no way to avoid the passage of effective social   11
machinery into dirty hands; that is what history teaches to anyone with eyes. The only way to avoid this, the best defense, is to
strike down ambitious organization before it grows (Cassius was
right) or once grown, to combat it through relentless sabotage.
That is what I did on a daily basis as a government schoolteacher, I broke the machine, I threw sand in the gears, I falsified papers, spread dissension among new recruits so subtly it
was undetectable, broke laws regularly, destroyed records,
undermined the confidence of the young in the institution and
replaced it with confidence in self, in friends, in family, in neighborhood. I taught kids how to cheat their destiny so successfully
that they created an astonishing record of successes; it is this
latter course of silent warfare that much of our country's population has unconsciously chosen. It explains why few things
work very well here, least of all schools. Nothing that John Gardner or Ted Sizer or (so far) Chris Whittle has done will change
that need to sabotage the web that is strangling us. They ask the
wrong questions and in any case would be unwilling to accept
their own large contribution to the persistence of schooling
problems. All sane solutions would eliminate them!

The only acceptable way to make people "better," your own   12
children or strangers, is by your own personal living example to
make a better way. The only curricular arrangements worth
arranging are those that help an individual, not a class: (1) to
know himself, (2) to love responsibility, (3) to feel obligation as
a joy, (4) to need very little in a material sense, (5) to express
love, (6) to love truth, (7) to hate tyranny, (8) to gain useful
knowledge, (9) to be involved in loving families at work, (10) to
be involved in communities at work, and (11) to be humble in
the face of the great mysteries, and to keep them constantly in
mind because only from that wellhead does the meaning of life
flow.

As a schoolteacher/saboteur I was able to help poor kids come   13
to see such things just as easily as I was able to help prosperous
ones; with a modest income I was able to finance all my classroom
enterprises without assistance from foundations, universities,
the business community, or the school administration—and so
could anyone else so disposed.

Now to turn to a charge Ron makes honestly, but which, upon   14
examination, dissolves into smoke:

> Gatto throws the baby out with the bathwater by categori-
> cally defining "school" as an impersonal network and virtu-
> ally equating educators and activists with social engineers.

There's a lot of slipperiness here. Does "education" mean school-   15
teacher? Do the activists Ron refers to have an agenda to

eventually gain control of our compulsion-schools? If both guesses are correct, then he is right, I do believe they are social engineers of the worst stripe. But perhaps he means something different.

16   How in Heaven's name can "school," in any of the varieties of definition possible for mass employment by a central government, NOT be an impersonal network? Can you school anything "personally?" I know you can fake it, most "good" schools do, but I find the really dangerous places to be the ones that preempt the family role, pretending to be families instead of networks; that's the horrible lesson I try to read in the chapter "We Need Less School, Not More." We're all dying of networks. Networks are not families. Pseudo-family schools confuse the rising gorge of their student prisoners for a long time (although never permanently, the disguise wears through). If you find my "prisoner" to be infamous rhetoric, then you're going to have to explain to me the social logic that allows you to use the police power of the state to command children's presence and respect, to preempt their daylight hours, to prescribe what they will think about, to judge them constantly and rank them.

17   It makes no sense to me to drain children from a living community and confine them with strangers for all of their natural youth. No sense from a human community perspective, that is. It seems to make great sense, of course, to minds that wallow in dreams of human life as an anthill or a beehive, the great world society crowd. And of course, too, though we seldom talk about it because the prospect leaves us dumbfounded, it makes great sense to those still free, if mean-spirited, minds who benefit substantially from the docile, confused population that central planning leaves in its wake. That great, timeless families, who follow a different directive than the progressive one, have taken advantage of—indeed are imperfectly in charge of—the movement toward the nightmare of a global society seems to me not only beyond question, but the only conservative explanation of a crescendo of anomalies. For those who read these words who might be intrigued by this admission of madness, a little research into the utterly central role of family foundations in giving us the schools we have—a role curiously overlooked by school histories, or dealt with en passant—will, I guarantee, reward the time spent with numerous marvels.

18   Back to business. Once you claim for your cause the sweeping power of compelling mass behavior, you have forfeited any claim at all to moral ground in my book. This is the rock on which all holistic ships founder, Rousseau's, Froebel's, Fichte's et al. You are practicing religion, then, and you are engaged in a holy war. I would imagine that nobody in 1992 is so naive as not to recognize that the religion of our schools, since their inception, has been the Unitarian faith—but I am constantly disappointed.

I may be misreading the conclusion of Ron's review: if you publicly disavow any right to assume control of the compulsion machinery, Ron, including those exquisite controls Jacques Ellul discusses in his wonderful book, *Propaganda,* I hope God smiles on your undertakings; but keep compulsion and it's hard for me not to regard cynically any justification which might be offered. Convincing me to accept your religion is legitimate and dialectical, forcing me to do so or tricking me into it is so vile that disdain or violence is the proper response.

There's much more at stake here than a little old-fashioned coercion—one-party systems are always corrupt; that is a fundamental truth of human nature. Eric Hoffer's *True Believer* was a turning point in my own life, however invested I seem to be here in my screed. In my view the only consensus ever valid is that consensus that arises slowly, painfully, naturally from millennial combats. Such consensus at its heart is a challenge to the premises of rationality. It cannot be hurried, cannot be hastened by Mind or Directives, by the Associations that John Dewey so loved. It contradicts the premises of the academic life as Francis Bacon conceived it, in service to the Central State. Such a belief calls for the destruction of Salomon's House as an unsurpassed agency of harm. Again, if you regard this as airy rhetoric, look about you at the cities and the natural world that Salomon's House, the haunt of the social engineers, has given us. I don't need to recite the dreary catalogue; use your own eyes and ears. What got us into the mess won't get us out, in the immortal words of Nixon's "Checkers" speech.

Such consensus assumes a timeless wisdom that realizes a scale of historical process much vaster than the scale of human life. One of the instrumental advantages of a belief in Family, God and immortality is that it allows such a stepping back from the social arena that spans one's life. It's not hard for me to understand that Ron—or any other activist interested in collective action—wants to see substantial change in the span of his own years. But from my view, all such forced changes are doomed to cause harm, regardless of how beneficently they are conceived.

Such consensus at its heart is *sui generis,* exclusionary in the early part of the going, relatively local, slow spreading. The revolution that produced the Chinese peasantry or American native cultures is an example of the historical process in action at its finest—the human solutions in both cases are transcendentally brilliant, inspiring, funny, wonderful. Neither was fully worked out when they were destroyed by the demon of Western homelessness which sent European pirates and their slaves intervening in every laboratory of human life on the planet. That thousand-year destructive swath, currently managed by an academic service class, a secular priesthood, and protected by

19

20

21

compulsion schooling, is what I write about in *Dumbing Us Down*, however indirectly. To dispossess the magical human possibilities underlying the appearance of Indians and Chinese, Queeg-Queeg and Dagoo, and replace these infinitely complex processes with a monochrome utopia is the act of a lunatic or a desperate man. All remote assignments of children's time and attention must, as I've said, be grounded in a vision of the good life, by its nature unprovable, by its nature religious at the core.

22   To the extent Puritan vision was that of a world order, it was diseased and murderous, but genius implicit in the Congregational mechanism, by a wonderful irony (which unfortunately became obvious over time to Unitarians) is so relentlessly local, so unmistakably personal, it sabotaged the global vision of Calvinism right from the beginning. It is a fascinating paradox never examined to my knowledge by academic scholarship and it is the real point I explore in "The Congregational Principle" (first published in *Maine Scholar*).

23   It wasn't "something mysterious" inside the structure of Congregationalism in any sense like Adam Smith's "magic hand" to use Ron's phrases in the area where he goes farthest astray, it was one of the great fundamental discoveries of human social genius. What is mysterious is how it ever came into being—and sustained itself until the Unitarians destroyed it right under the noses of the very social engineers who were giving New England its global economic mission. In Marx's felicitous locution, it illustrates strikingly the ignorant perfection of ordinary people, a perfection which is really the guiding inspiration of my teaching, my book, and my life. I learned the lesson from Monongahela, a town of ordinary people who perfected a community and the secret of meaning.

24   I was not "asserting" that colonists enjoyed nearly unconditional local choice. In point of fact that truth is built right into the structure of Congregationalism which demands that no two communities be alike, that all be rigorously tuned to that single congregation. *Mirabile dictu*. I grow weak with the joy of merely saying it! You have choice because there are choices to have under a Congregational system—under a Unitarian system there are none. The confusion here arose, I would guess, because Ron misread individual choice where specifically I meant local choice. Choice by local consensus. However, it isn't too long a reach to argue that individual choice had to be there, too, because of the boundless dark woods, the many different states available, (each independent in its culture), and always, too, the frontier. The sarcastic among you will say, "Some choice if I have to move out!" but consider first that even that option isn't available today in the Theocracy of Unitarianism, and consider, too, that moving out is as just a choice as human affairs offers: would that we still had it. If the global people get their way we're

not even going to be able to move abroad—every place will be here. Then we will have arrived at the Utopia of social engineering, where everyone has to be "adjusted" to fit the pre-conceived model. Naturally a liberal interpretation will allow a 10% deviation either way from True North to accommodate human error economically.

For a wonderful example of human courage in just such a   25
rigidly moralistic society as Ron characterizes New England to be, and what individual human courage can accomplish, see Hawthorne's *Scarlet Letter* where the elders plan to take little Pearl from her mother, the letter-bearer, and she—alone and friendless, poor and ignorant—says starkly, ". . . over my dead body!" So much for that batch of social engineers with the power of the state behind them.

My point is that only by trusting ordinary people thoroughly   26
and only by emphasizing the individual, the family, the neighborhood, the local economy, can we slowly win through to a better life. All synthetic schemes radically distort the only slightly plastic material of humanity; all of them are impious, all rob the future in many ways, none work for very long—see official human history for evidence. All leave the world worse at their dissolution than before they found it. The Progressives are right, there has been a progression through recorded history, but it has been a progression backwards—just as Plato said it had been. We might mark the decline symbolically from the time the invisible labor engine was fabricated to build the Great Pyramid, an event strangely commemorated on the back of our dollar bill, though no one can produce an adequate explanation why. Disraeli knew, I think, but he spoke about it in riddles.

So what to do with the strong human impulse to meddle, to   27
tinker, to dominate, to improve, to not accept destiny? Well, my own answer is to do what you personally can, and suffer what you personally must. Accept the punishment of Prometheus if you want to play the part. And do I think you should play the part? Yes, of course, I've tried to myself all my adult life, but the other side of that dialectic is that I also believe that brilliant and beautiful lives are possible everywhere, under any duress or deprivation, as long as you see clearly what really matters.

Now what scares me a little about Ron's conclusion is that he,   28
toward the end, seems to be calling some sort of invisible army together for mass social engineering projects. He says, "we simply do not have 200 years to wait for some "invisible hand" to begin addressing these tremendous issues, "to lead" individuals and families and "self-satisfied" little communities, etc. OK, there seem to be two lines leading out from that one, that we act locally with like-minded people and try to convince the rest, and two, that we seize control of the apparatus and do it differently. I'd be with him on number one, and I'd cheer him on on number

two if he led a small guerilla band in some boldly suicidal stroke. But change one master for another? Nope. Ron asks how the free market would provide educational opportunity for poor children, and the answer is that that is the wrong question. Of course the "market" can't do anything but act as a field for action; its a necessary pre-condition for solutions but in and of itself it's neutral. But government action is never neutral and cannot be—it must impose one or another religious view of the good life on everybody. And that is a pre-condition for bad things to happen, most often immediately, but also frequently when the second generation of zealots inherit the compulsion machinery and the police force. And even zealots are preferable to bureaucrats, who are the likeliest heirs.

29   This response has been a quick, spontaneous draft. I wish there were time to spend on creating a careful answer to some of the points Ron raises but there isn't, so this is the best can do. I'd ask him and all your readers to carefully examine one huge unstated assumption that deeply disturbs me, namely that government schools have ever merited the term "public," implying a service to the commonality. This is based on such specious reasoning, and such a peculiar definition of what the public is, that it won't bear scrutiny. These are not public schools we are talking about, they are government schools—as much different from public as flowers are from weeds.

30   Indeed, that there is a "public" at all except in the bizarre fantasy of utopians and Deweyists and positivists of all stripes is something that merits careful consideration before reflexively accepting its existence. As a western Pennsylvanian I find the term more than mildly insulting. A cartoon of reality. The forces that oppress the public, to borrow some of Ron's language, are the forces that rob it of its right of self-determination—without which people cannot be principals, but only agents (or "educators").

31   Anyway, the dishes aren't washed, the shirts aren't ironed, a colony of ants has taken up residence in my bedroom, and I've got to fly to Spokane tomorrow morning to tell people why I think a schooling, any flavor, can't be an education. Deconstruct these synthetic institutions, the machinery is a constant temptation to the worst people on the planet to scheme for its control. As I read history, they always win in the long run. But ah, if we broke the machinery.

Sign me,
John Taylor Gatto

Kathleen Anderson

Reflections in Education: Considering the Impact of Schooling on the Learner

Kathleen Anderson, before attending medical school, taught for 2 years in elementary school. This paper combines her hands-on experience as a teacher with her reading in educational theory (and specifically from the field of alternative education, including the work of John Taylor Gatto). As you read Anderson's essay, pay attention not only to her ideas—and how they interact with other selections in this chapter—but also to the ways that she blends her personal narrative with her research sources. Doing so can help you consider ways that you, too, may find links between personal observation, primary research, and secondary sources. Note also the ways that she structures her piece, considering the organizational choices she made in order to develop a coherent essay and her use of the "reflection" genre.

Abstract:

Each child has unique gifts waiting to be discovered and cul-   1
tivated. Unfortunately, our current school system does not
always provide children with the opportunity to develop
their special interests. The following article is a personal narrative structured as a series of reflections, and aims to reconsider
schooling's role in assisting the crucial development of creativity. Drawing from ideas of researchers in the field of alternative
education, I present reflections on my role as an elementary
school teacher, and I examine the impact of teaching, curriculum and our current evaluation system on the development of
children's creativity.

Introduction:

2

"The predicament is simple: A great deal of energy is expended
by those in power to craft an illusory world designed to benefit
only a very small percentage of the population"

—*The Institute of Unlearning*

3   Although the above statement may have an alarmist overtone, it also captures the entrenched essence of the classic North American education system. This semester, in *Principals of Curriculum and Instruction*, an M.Ed. course taught by Dr. C. Ricci, I was introduced to alternative ideologies that reshaped my personal philosophy of education, and affected the manner in which I interact with students.

4   This paper is structured as a series of reflections on material presented and discussed over the course of the term. I chose topics that inspired and deepened my understanding towards students, my role as a teacher, and the overall purpose of education.

5   I begin by reflecting on the thoughts of Ken Robinson in his presentation "Do Schools Today Kill Creativity?" Next, I focus on ideas from John Holt in an interview for the magazine *Mothering*, titled "*Mothering* Interviews John Holt" and reflect on his words in relation to my role as a teacher and the demands of our language and math programs. And finally, I reflect on the purpose of public education as John Taylor Gatto presents it in his article "Against School: How Public Education Cripples Our Kids, and Why."

Reflection One

The Importance of Creativity in School

6   Ken Robinson's presentation "Do Schools Today Kill Creativity?" highlighted in the TEDTalks lecture series, touched on many points that as an educator I feel are necessary to consider. He discusses the importance of human creativity and says that "children who we believe possess exceptional talents, aren't necessarily exceptional, but were simply able to discover their talents" (Robinson, 2006). He explains that children have the capacity for creativity but school prevents them from finding and developing it (Robinson, 2006).

7   As a teacher, I believe that we do not provide children with nearly enough opportunity to discover and develop their talents. My students cannot realize their abilities because my lessons and the curriculum content do not necessarily reflect their interests and allow for any creativity. Instead, I tell students how to do everything from a science experiment to creating a piece of art. Their time to explore, be creative and choose activities is very limited or even nonexistent most days.

8   I am beginning to change the way I handle students' disinterest towards classroom work. I find myself becoming more lenient in regards to how and when they choose to complete assignments. I realize when students seem disengaged; it is probably because *I* have chosen the activities for the day. I basically give

instructions and they follow them, always responding the way they are taught. There is no creativity involved. Robinson (2006) also believes:

> Kids take chances because they are not scared of being wrong. However, as they get older, teachers and the school system continuously tell them that there is no room for mistakes. If they aren't prepared to be wrong, then they will never come up with anything original.

In the classroom, even when students are given the opportunity to be creative within subject areas, such as to create and present plays, we evaluate the work. We grade everything students do throughout the day from socializing and participating to their attendance and the work they produce. They are constantly being evaluated.   9

Evaluating will always limit their creativity and prevent them from producing original work, no matter how flexible teachers are in our classrooms. As a result, students often go through the system liking subjects they are good at in school and sticking with them because they become afraid to fail or be judged when they attempt something new (C. Ricci, personal communication, November 30, 2007).   10

As a teacher, part of my job is to teach children that there are certain ways to do our work. There are expectations in art, dance, writing a paragraph, reading a book and even behaving. Students learn to rely on marks and seek approval from teachers to know if what they have produced is acceptable. In class I try to give less direction and more choice in how my students do their work. However, I am still very limited in the ways I can let them be creative.   11

Ken Robinson goes on to point out that the most useful subjects are valued in schools. He says "children are told not to take music because they will never be a musician, or art because they will not be an artist. Children are pushed away from this because they are told that they will not get a job" (Robinson, 2006). This is another way the school system prevents students from finding and developing their talents. Teachers fit in drama, dance, art and even science and social studies whenever they can be integrated into the language and math programs. Along the way, "highly talented people think they aren't [talented] because they were told that what they are good at isn't important and isn't valuable" (Robinson, 2006). They then get older and find a regular job instead of creating a life for themselves around their talents and interests.   12

In addition to limiting our focus to teaching math and language, we discourage children from developing talents that are   13 not taught in school because they are not valued. We even place subjects in order of importance with the highest ranking being on language and math, then science and social studies and then the arts (Robinson, 2006). So if students are talented in areas other than those which are valued, they may put aside a possible brilliant career because they fear they will not get a "real job" (Robinson, 2006).

14   Also, many of our students possess talents that are not taught in school at all. I remember Dr. Ricci showing a video in class of a person who made shadow puppets and was able to turn this skill into a successful career (personal communication, November 30, 2007). This is a great example of a talent and career that was not developed in or by our school system. Many students are taught to put talents like this aside. This made me wonder, how many wonderful talents have been squandered by our education system?

15   I think that we get so busy trying to make sure our students are reading, writing and understanding math that we forget that they need to play, be creative and learn on their own. When I have yard duty, I often watch the students play and I notice how creative they can be. As an example, I can think of a student who loves acting and creating plays. He will do this at recess time even if no one else wants to join him. The expressions he uses, the characters he invents and the life he brings to his plays is amazing. However, he was in my class last year and never had the chance to do this. I did touch on plays in class, and we even created one, but never to the extent required by his talent. I think this is just one example of how limiting the curriculum can be for children with unique interests.

16   Another part that I really enjoyed in Ted Robinson's talk was about Gillian Lynne, the choreographer of the Broadway musical CATS, and how she discovered her talent for dance. Robinson (2006) explains:

As a young girl, she was disruptive and was not doing well in school so her mother brought her to see a specialist. He told her mother that there was nothing wrong with Gillian but that she was a dancer. She soon after went to dance school and was happy because there were people just like her there who had to move to think. Someone else may have put her on medication and told her to calm down.

17   This part of his presentation made me consider the impact we as teachers have on our students when we label them as struggling or needing to be identified. Teachers fill out checklists from doctors in order for students to be diagnosed as having ADHD, we spend time researching possible reasons why

students are not meeting our expectations and diagnose them with learning disabilities.

I think about the example of Ms. Lynne and the way she dis- 19
covered her talent. How often we must misdiagnose students in our school and steer them away from what they are really meant to do. As educators we are quick to label and blame children for their unwillingness to learn in ways that we demand. If a child does not fit into the mold we create, then something is wrong with the child and we label it as a learning problem. We then spend countless hours trying to find ways to help them attain our expectations.

I look at my students this year and recognize that they each 20
possess special talents. I often wonder if they will have the chance to develop them. I know that because of the topics covered in this presentation and classroom discussions with Dr. Ricci, the way that I interact with my students has changed and so have my expectations. In my classroom, I try to provide opportunities for creative thinking and choice of activities. I also try to talk about grades and evaluations as little as possible and not judge their daily work. However, I also understand that in today's system, no matter what I decide to do in the classroom, my program will never allow students to develop their talents and interests the way they would on their own. There must be a better way.

Reflection Two

Ideas on Teaching and Learning

Throughout the term, we discussed some of John Holt's ideas. 21
I was inspired by his theories so I began reading some of his material and past interviews. The following are his responses from an interview conducted in 1981 with Dr. Marlene Bumgarner for the magazine *Mothering*. The responses I found of particular interest touch on the topics of learning, home schooling, teaching, and language and math programs.

In this interview, John Holt comments, "We like to learn; we 22
need to learn; we are good at it; we don't need to be shown how or be made to do it. What kills the processes are the people interfering with it or trying to regulate it or control it" (1981). Reading his ideas on how teachers impact student learning has reshaped my view of my role as an educator.

When I began teaching, I believed my job was to guide stu- 23
dents to learn new skills, encourage them to develop their talents, and provide opportunities that allow them to appreciate our world. I desperately wanted to get them hooked on all of the subjects. I thought that if I made lessons fun, they would learn

to like everything. I am now realizing, that unwittingly, I am still forcing curriculum onto my students and I am actually impeding their true learning.

24   Do we (the education system) have to decide for all children what they will learn? Is it worth spending the effort trying to inspire students, or will they inspire themselves if given the proper forum? Children know better than teachers what they want and need to discover at each step of the way. If humans are creatures that naturally like, want, and need to learn, then my students will do so when the need arises, in their own way and at their own pace. This is difficult, if not impossible, to accomplish in our school system where there exists curricular demands and prescribed ways of learning.

25   I now understand that great lessons will not make all students more curious about the subject and they will not make them remember the material taught. John Holt (1981) says, "If we try to make students learn something other than what they want to learn, they probably will not learn it, or they will soon forget most of what they have learned, or worst of all, they will lose their desire to learn anything." Teachers teach and students have no choice but to listen and learn. We are therefore part of the reason that students are often bored and uninterested in learning.

26   In this interview, John Holt also highlights the advantages of home schooling. He states that "The great advantage [of home schooling] is intimacy, control of your time, flexibility of schedule, and the ability to respond to the needs of the child and to the inclinations" (Holt 1981). If a child is feeling tired, sick, or unhappy, then home schooling allows them to take it easy. When the child is full of energy, then they can tackle bigger projects (Holt 1981). We do not offer this type of flexibility. School seems very artificial when compared to home schooling. We do not allow children the option to feel like not working. We expect them to give their best performance each day, no matter how they are feeling. As teachers, is this a realistic expectation?

27   When it comes to correcting students and grading their work, John Holt (1981) believes that teachers don't always have to immediately correct their students' mistakes. Instead, he says, "We can afford to give them time to notice and correct them themselves. And the more they do this, the better they will become at doing it, and the less they will need and depend on us to do it for them" (Holt 1981). He goes on to say that tests and evaluations are ways of telling learners that we have no confidence in them. The fact that teachers even check on what the students have learned proves to students that we fear they have not learned the material (Holt 1981).

28   This quote made me conscious of the impact I have on my students when I grade them, tag a reading level to them, and correct their mistakes. By doing so, I am making my students

dependent on me to provide them with the right answers. They will not take chances and problem solve to find their own solutions. They become afraid of being wrong and learn to play it safe by doing work that gets them good marks. They learn that taking chances may lead to bad marks and therefore stop taking chances, discovering, and being creative.

Furthermore, the grading we do is not standardized and therefore the marks we give students are not a true reflection of what they can do. I remember discussing in Dr. Ricci's class that it can be just as damaging to assign a good mark to a child as it is to assign a bad mark to a child. The child with the good mark will continue to do work they have been told they are good at instead of taking chances and discovering other talents. The student who receives a bad mark may not pursue interests in those areas because they were told it was not their strength (C. Ricci, personal communication, November 30, 2007). As a result, I am experiencing difficulty marking and completing report cards without thinking of the effects I am having on these children. I try not to discourage students in any way through marking. I talk about it as little as possible in class, and I always tell them they did a great job, no matter what they hand in. However, this part of my job is unavoidable.

In the interview, John Holt also discusses his beliefs on reading programs. He explains that teaching reading is actually what prevents children from reading because children learn in different ways (Holt 1981). He says, "Reading aloud is fun, but I would never read aloud to a kid so that the kid would learn to read. You read aloud because it's fun and companionable" (Holt 1981). He also says that when children see adults read books with lots of print, they realize that to find out what is in them, they will have to learn how to read (Holt 1981). This reminds me of a discussion in Dr. Ricci's class about how children will learn to do something when the need arises. If children choose to learn something like reading, they will learn it because it is relevant to their lives (C. Ricci, personal communication, November 30, 2007). If we force them to read when they have no use for it or do not want to learn it, they will not remember what we teach, they will not meet those expectations we set for them, and they will not enjoy reading.

I think that there are many problems with our literacy program. As an example, part of the EQAO questionnaire that students fill out in grade six asks if they enjoy reading. Most of our students responded that they do not like reading. Our solution to this problem involves applying for grants to get newer and more interesting books. We also try to make reading fun by setting up reading buddy programs, trips to the public library, book bag programs, and daily independent, guided, and modeled and shared readings. In addition, we track children's progress in reading on a monthly basis and worry that they will not succeed in life if they can't read up to a certain leveled book by the end of their primary years. Children have no choice when it comes to reading. They must learn to like it. The school system puts pressure on teachers to get students hooked on reading, but by the end of grade six most of them still don't enjoy it.

32   If we took away the pressure, then learning to read would become more pleasurable. Children would be more curious about books and learn the skill because the need would eventually arise. However, our school system would never allow this. We will therefore always have many students disinterested in reading despite our continued efforts to engage them.

33   On the topic of teaching mathematics to children, John Holt (1981) says that the best way to be introduced to numbers is in real life. He explains that "numbers are embedded in the context of reality" (Holt 1981). Numbers are found everywhere. They are found in building, construction, business, photography, music, and even cooking. However, schools take everything out of the context of reality (Holt 1981). By doing so, "everything appears like some little thing floating around in space" (Holt 1981). Instead, Holt (1981) suggests that we should learn to work with numbers in real life.

34   There is such a big focus on math in our schools that I thought John Holt's opinion of how we should learn it was interesting. We teach children how to take numbers, learn and use equations, but we do not focus on the importance of it in the real world. Students don't understand why they are learning math. This makes learning math less interesting and more difficult to learn. Even though teachers are supposed to try to relate math to real life situations, it is still done in the classroom, at their desks using manipulatives like fake money, and pretending to do things like buy items at a store.

35   All in all, John Holt presents many interesting points about our education system. His views on how teaching, evaluating, reading, and math helped me redefine my role as an educator. I realize I have little choice when it comes to how I teach. I am expected to teach math and reading in a certain way and follow the programs provided. I am also expected to evaluate my students. I can understand how I am interfering with the natural process of learning.

Reflection Three

The Purpose of Education

36   John Taylor Gatto participated in *Harper's Magazine* forum "School on a Hill," that appeared in the September 2003 issue. I read his article entitled, "How Public Education Cripples Our

Kids, and Why," and it brought about some very interesting points concerning the primary purpose of schooling. Briefly, Gatto (2003) explains that the purpose of public education is to make people into employees and consumers, and the root of this problem is embedded in the history of education (p. 37).

Gatto begins by using examples of famous Americans that 37 never graduated from secondary school to support his view that schooling is not necessary to be successful. He states:

> Throughout history, most children did not go to school and still the unschooled rose to be admirals, like Farragut; inventors, like Edison; captains of industry, like Carnegie and Rockefeller; writers, like Melville and Twain and Conrad; and even scholars, like Margaret Mead (Gatto 2003, p. 34).

Though they may have learned skills from others, we cannot 38 credit formal education for their success. He then explains that our educational system was designed to produce citizens, who are passive, have average intelligence, and a lack of leadership skills (Gatto 2003, p. 36). It was believed to be necessary in order to maintain a "manageable" population (Gatto 2003, p. 36).

When I considered these points, I thought about how we teach 39 our children and whether it supports this view. We do not teach children to think critically or to question, especially authority. We do not teach them to be leaders because they just follow instructions at school and respond in the way that will get them the best marks. We also do not provide students with the opportunity to be creative and discover their talents. We make them learn strictly curriculum content, which is very limiting. I was shocked to think that could really be the purpose of education. I kept on reading.

Gatto (2003) then explains that with industrialization the econ- 40 omy moved toward mass production (p. 37). However, mass production could only be successful if there was mass consumption. Schooling was a way of ensuring both. Its main goal was to educate people into being employees and consumers (Gatto 2003, p. 37). Gatto (2003) states, "School encouraged [students] not to think at all and that left them sitting ducks for another great invention of the modem era—marketing" (p. 37). The idea was to group children by subject, age-grading, and test scores and strip them of their responsibility and independence, so "they would grow older but never truly grow up" (Gatto 2003, p. 38).

Today, in our schools, teachers encourage this behavior. We 41 group children, take away responsibility and independence, and we spoon-feed them knowledge. As a result, in today's society, according to Gatto (2003), maturity is not part of our lives because everything comes to us so easily (p. 38). For example, we no longer have a need to learn to entertain ourselves (Gatto

2003, p. 38). Gatto (2003) states, "We have become a nation of children, happy to surrender our judgments and our wills to political exhortations and commercial blandishments that would insult actual adults" (p. 38). Over the years, adults have learned from years of schooling to abandon their ability to be creative, to think, and to develop true talents. As teachers, are we doing the same to our students, without being aware of it?

42   However, according to Gatto (2003), if we understand the history and purpose of schooling, then we can teach our children differently (p. 38). We can teach them useful skills. Gatto lists many of these skills in his article. For instance, he says that we could help children develop "an inner life so that they'll never be bored" since our students presently have a low tolerance for boredom (Gatto 2003, p. 38). We could also teach them to think critically and independently instead of simply obeying authority and learning the curriculum that has been decided for them (Gatto 2003, p. 38). Furthermore, we could let them have solitude so they learn to enjoy their own company (Gatto 2003, p. 38).

43   Gatto (2003) says that children who are schooled "are conditioned to dread being alone, and they seek constant companionship through the TV, the computer, the cell phone, and through shallow friendships" (p. 38). I must agree that there is much evidence of this sort of behavior found in students and adults, including myself. It is true that we tend to get bored easily, look to external sources for companionship, and do not always think critically toward marketing. When you grow up this way, it seems perfectly normal. Now that I am aware of this view, I am more conscious of it in my classroom and in my own life. While teaching, I can provide my students with opportunities, like the ones suggested in Gatto's article, but schooling is still very limiting. I feel that home schooling or free schooling would definitely offer children the opportunity to develop these skills. All in all, if education is not necessary to be successful, as shown through Gatto's examples, then its purpose is something other than this.

Conclusion

44 The ideas of Ken Robinson, John Holt, and John Taylor Gatto, along with the many interesting discussions held in Dr. Ricci's course, have impacted my personal philosophy of education. They have reshaped my interactions with my students, and I am starting to redefine my role as a teacher. I am much more relaxed during the day. I find myself laughing and having fun with them and being more flexible in daily routines than ever before. The past couple months have been much more enjoyable for me and my students. I realize that I will never be able to let them choose their own activities, but I feel that I can still make

adjustments and let them be creative in how they decide to do their work. It is frustrating to learn about views on education that are so influential and not be able to make any significant changes in my classroom. Nevertheless, I enjoy learning about these topics, and I look forward to digging deeper into them.

Throughout the term, I also began to reflect on my own 45 schooling and how it has shaped me. When I think about it, I did not learn much that really interested me in school. Also, I overlooked many of my interests because I had to focus most of my time on my studies. I started thinking about all of the things I wanted to learn but pushed aside. I then decided to try a couple of them each term. This term, I decided to learn to play the piano. It worked out well because the school where I teach offers lessons. My students think this is funny because they are much better players than I am. They enjoy teaching me notes and correct finger placement. I also started doing yoga. I really enjoyed this in high school but stopped because there was just never enough time to do everything. I enjoy it so much now that I know it will remain part of my weekly routine. It calms me and I feel more present when I am at work. I also started learning to sew. I have always wanted to do this, and I am learning from my grandmother. I think these efforts are small steps in the direction of learning everything I have never made the time for before. It is a great feeling to be excited about learning. As a teacher, I think it is important to acknowledge that I can also in some ways help my students "*take* an education rather than simply *receive* a schooling" too (Gatto 2003, p. 34).

I am glad my Master of Education started with Dr. Ricci's 46 course. It has helped me redefine my role as a teacher and think about schooling from a whole other perspective that I was not familiar with. I am eager to learn more about these ideas of the education system and to see how they will continue to influence me at work, home, and in other courses I take.

References

1. Gatto, J. T. (2003). "How Public Education Cripples Our Kids, and Why." *Harper's Magazine*. Retrieved December 13, 2007, from http://www.harpers.org.
2. Holt, J. (1981). "*Mothering* interviews John Holt." *Mothering* 19. Retrieved December 10, 2007, from http://www.naturalchild.org.
3. Mooney, P. (1998). "The Institute of Unlearning." Retrieved December 10, 2007, from http://www.unlearning.org/home.htm.
4. Robinson, K. Lecture. "Do Schools Today Kill Creativity?" *Monterey*, February 2006. As referenced from TEDTalks, http://www.ted.com/talks.

Dennis Fermoyle and Respondents to the Blog,

From the Trenches of Public Education

Dennis Fermoyle, a graduate of Bemidji State University, also holds a master's degree from the College of St. Scholastica. He has been a high school teacher in Minnesota for over 30 years, where he teaches American history, government, economics, and sociology. He has served as a school union president and was named his school district's Teacher of the Year. Fermoyle is the author of *In the Trenches: A Teacher's Defense of Public Education* (2005), and for three years, administered an active blog called *From the Trenches of Public Education* that conducted a public discussion of education among many teachers and parents. What follows is a post by Fermoyle from March 2008, in which he critiques John Taylor Gatto's work, followed by responses to other bloggers to Fermoyle's post. As you read this series of well thought-out and, at times, contentious blog entries, consider the ways in which each of the writers constructs his or her own argument by responding to some element of a previous post. Doing so can help you better understand the ways that public conversations are developed not only in this medium, but also in a variety of genres. You might also consider the unique facets of the conversations that are conducted in blogs. What are the advantages of this genre? What are its challenges and problems? What techniques do bloggers tend to use in order to respond to other writers?

Arrogance

1   In a comment on my last post, Charley, whose views on public education differs a tad bit from my own, recommended that I read a couple of pieces by John Taylor Gatto, a former New York City teacher of the year. One was called "Why Schools Don't Educate," and the other one was "Against School: How Public Education Cripples Our Kids, and Why." I came away impressed with Gatto's intelligence, and I assume he was probably a pretty good teacher. But I feel strongly that the picture he paints of our pubic education system is horribly inaccurate, and quite frankly, I resented most of what he had to say.

In "Why Schools Don't Educate," which I assume is the speech   2
he gave in accepting his teacher of the year award, Gatto started
out graciously enough:

> I accept this award on behalf of all the fine teachers I've
> known over the years who've struggled to make their trans-
> actions with children honorable ones, men and women who
> are never complacent, always questioning, always wrestling
> to define and redefine endlessly what the word "education"
> should mean. A Teacher of the Year is not the best teacher
> around, those people are too quiet to be easily uncovered,
> but he is a standard-bearer, symbolic of these private people
> who spend their lives gladly in the service of children. This is
> their award as well as mine.

I'm not sure which teachers he's talking about there, but I   3
assume it's not many of us, because that's the last positive thing
he has to say about anything in public education. I would imagine that people like my friend Daniel Simms are thrilled that
Gatto basically argues that the entire purpose of public education has been a plot by some nameless entities above us all to
keep the masses in their place:

> We don't need Karl Marx's conception of a grand warfare be-
> tween the classes to see that it is in the interest of complex
> management, economic or political, to dumb people down,
> to demoralize them, to divide them from one another, and to
> discard them if they don't conform . . . But the motives be-
> hind the disgusting decisions that bring about these ends
> need not be class-based at all. They can stem purely from
> fear, or from the by now familiar belief that "efficiency" is
> the paramount virtue, rather than love, liberty, laughter, or
> hope. Above all, they can stem from simple greed . . .
>
> We must wake up to what our schools really are: laborato-
> ries of experimentation on young minds, drill centers for
> the habits and attitudes that corporate society demands.
> Mandatory education serves children only incidentally; its
> real purpose is to turn them into servants.

Now, I just finished Diane Ravitch's history on public educa-   4
tion, and I got the impression that there had been a lot of
mistakes made, but I completely missed the idea that Gatto is
selling in his history. I don't know how anyone could spend any
time in a public school these days and come to the conclusion

that we are making kids too compliant. And as if it isn't bad enough that public education is simply there to turn young people into servants.

5   Gatto also blames public education for nearly all of society's ills:

> Think of the things that are killing us as a nation—narcotic drugs, brainless competition, recreational sex, the pornography of violence, gambling, alcohol, and the worst pornography of all—lives devoted to buying things, accumulation as a philosophy—all of them are addictions of dependent personalities, and that is what our brand of schooling must inevitably produce . . .
>
> Maturity has by now been banished from nearly every aspect of our lives. Easy divorce laws have removed the need to work at relationships; easy credit has removed the need for fiscal self-control; easy entertainment has removed the need to learn to entertain oneself; easy answers have removed the need to ask questions. We have become a nation of children, happy to surrender our judgments and our wills to political exhortations and commercial blandishments that would insult actual adults. We buy televisions, and then we buy the things we see on the television. We buy computers, and then we buy the things we see on the computer. We buy $150 sneakers whether we need them or not, and when they fall apart too soon we buy another pair. We drive SUVs and believe the lie that they constitute a kind of life insurance, even when we're upside-down in them. And, worst of all, we don't bat an eye when Ari Fleischer tells us to "be careful what you say," even if we remember having been told somewhere back in school that America is the land of the free. We simply buy that one too. Our schooling, as intended, has seen to it.

6   My first question regarding Gatto's point of view is this: If that was the way he felt, why did he stay in the field for thirty years? Wouldn't the honorable thing to do have been to resign and find something else to do?

7   There is only one answer that I can think of, and it is that Gatto saw himself as having a messianic duty to save as many kids as possible from those of us who are unwitting saps and simply cogs in the machine. I have read books by "progressive" educators before who have the same mentality, and I am turned off by it. The arrogance of Gatto and other "expert" teachers like him make me want to vomit. They seem to be saying, "Those few teachers who do things like me are wonderful and caring and

saving kids from the system. The rest of you are all uncaring, inept, educational Neanderthals." Gatto gives a couple of examples of things we should be doing as teachers, but I didn't exactly get how I'm supposed to apply his ideas. I think maybe we're just supposed to wing it.

During my career as a teacher I have seen educators with 8 greatly varying styles be successful with them. Quite frankly, the ones who have most consistently been successful have been the ones with the most order and discipline in their classes, and by the end of the year they are often the most popular with their students. Unless I am completely misreading him, these are the teachers that Gatto seems to have the most disdain for. But, on the other hand, I've also seen teachers who use so-called progressive methods be very successful. If there is one thing I have learned, it is that one size does not fit all.

Unlike Gatto, I do not see public schools as prisons. Do I 9 ever get frustrated? You betcha! But nearly every day that I leave my house and head for school, I feel pretty good about it. I see our school as a place of fantastic opportunity for young people. I have seen and continue to see wonderful kids excel in academics, sports, and the arts. I have seen and continue to see kids in our hallways with a spring in their step, and smiles on their faces. Is that true for all kids in public schools? Obviously not. In fact, it's not true for enough of them. But it is true for most of the kids who come to school with the right attitude—the kids who have the desire to take advantage of the opportunity in front of them. If that's a prison, then it's one helluva nice one, and despite all the complaining I do and the frustrations that I feel, there's no place I'd rather be. The good kids we have make it more than worth it. I don't see myself as the educational messiah, but the hope that I'm making a small difference in some of their lives gives me a pretty good feeling.

Corygon Trail **said . . .**

Gatto does make outstanding points on the non-educational side of life. Constant entertainment from TV, computers, cell phones, etc. I think are the real bane of contemporary education. It's a constant struggle to keep kids motivated on work, paying attention in class, taking notes, etc. when the only reward some are seeking (if they're seeking any) is a grade. The rest of their lives, whether real or lived vicariously through entertainment—is much more gratifying.

That being said, I disagree with pretty much everything else he writes about here. He mentions individuals (Edison, Franklin, etc.) that rose to greatness despite being forced into compulsory education. He—like everyone else who completely disparages publication education—gives no honor to the countless people who have made amazing progress in every field of science, arts, and business in every decade of American History. Did America's wheels fall off when compulsory education came into play? Quite the contrary. I'm not smart (or to use your word, Dennis, arrogant) to say that the US became a superpower because of pub ed, but our place in the world certainly didn't suffer from it.

It really all comes down to something that you preach all the time, Dennis, and which I whole-heartedly agree on: a desire to learn. I'm a high school teacher, so I'm not wizened in the when or how people lose a love of learning in the early years. But I do know that children come to school at different levels, and that when a child enters first grade already knowing how to read because of their parents' teachings, odds are that they're going to do better in the rest of their schooling than their classmate who isn't at that level. Fundamentally, it's not the walls or the memorization or anything else that causes most problems—it's simply behind behind at the beginning. To take Gatto to task, there are millions of publicly educated adults who are not bored, who don't feel confined by the walls of a school, because they used school to heighten their own desire for discovery.

Of course, all his philosophical flim-flam carries no weight without logical ideas for improvements. And the fact that schools do nothing but breed the idea to not question the authority is quite laughable, and I would be interested to see how he, as a former inner-city teacher, came to that conclusion.

3/29/2008, 2:22 PM

Dennis Fermoyle **said . . .**

Schools do nothing but breed the idea to not question the authority is quite laughable, and I would be interested to see how he, as a former inner-city teacher, came to that conclusion.

A big "Amen!" to that, Corygon!

3/29/2008, 3:24 PM

din819go **said . . .**

As a parent who has read both Gatto's book "the underground history . . .," got half-way through Charlotte Iserbyt's book "the deliberate dumbing down . . ." and have been actively involved in public education . . . I have to state I believe the monopoly of public education is its own worse enemy.

Lack of quality/qualified teachers. The biggest problem in our district is with its math teachers. This starts in third grade when the more advanced math concepts are starting to be introduced. We have teachers in the classroom with a horrible general ed degree that have never taken a math class or more than one in their lives. If children in third grade do not have a qualified math teacher they will be lost once they get to middle school and high school (same concept if they cannot read by third grade). I do believe ed schools have finally woken to the fact that they need to raise the standards for entering students and require they get a degree in liberal arts with an education minor. I do believe some ed schools are following the trend to make getting an education degree a five year program where the fifth year is spent in the classroom as the lead teacher. The student is then critiqued before they are licensed to teach. This is great. However, what to do about the ill-trained teachers in the schools now that you cannot terminate or top-grade? (Other comments on this below)

Discipline . . . what discipline? Kids at all ages need boundries (yes, they loosen as they age and prove themselves trustworthy) yet discipline in almost every form except ISS and OSS are sorely lacking in many if not most schools in my district starting with elementary schools. Teachers need to know how to maintain discipline in a way that keeps kids excited about learning.

Kids are born curious and want to learn, explore, grow, etc (the number of why questions I have received over the past 19 years have been incredible!). However, I believe education and educators destroy this natural curiosity in our kids. Why do you think the drop out rate is so high? The kids are no engage in what should be an active learning environment ("The Courage to Teach"—wow, what an idea!!) My kids understand the importance of education but they have become very cynical because of the bad teachers they have had primarily in their middle school and high school years. I believe involved parents do more to keep their kids dreams alive and help them understand the supposed importance of a formal education (I am truly having my doubts) than most teachers/ educators.

Educators for the most part and the vast majority of the people in the field have been in education all their lives. They do not know how the real world operates. They are protected by a horribly damaging and unreal system of tenure (it takes years I mean 3, 4, 5 years to fire a teacher in my district—think about the damage to the kids—(and morale of others in the same building) while that teacher is allowed to stay in the classroom!)

The quality of textbooks—what quality? So many of them are out of date. Heck, there are not enough for all students at the start of the school year.

Teachers—the quality is sorely lacking even in my younger son's top 100 public academic magnet high school! They do not know how to teach (i.e. engage the student in the topic at hand, make it understandable for kids at different levels of interest and abilities, etc), they are publicly stating to the kids how they better "get it" because they want to keep their job (since when has it been all about the adults?)

It does seem that public education is all about the adults— from the school board to the classroom (in most cases) the students and their families are an after thought. I have never seen a group of people jump blindly from one fad to the next following the money rather than stepping back and truly assessing what is wrong, what is right and what is needed to improve before accepting the next grant to do the latest and greatest fad which will be proven in three years NOT to work . . . Geez how blind can one group be?

Solution? Get all the crap that is not related to education out of the schools. What is this? The fact that in urban districts the schools are mother, father, chief bottle washer, cook and baby-sitter. This is the role of the family, church and community.

Engage in an active learning environment. Yes, rote memorizaton and multiplication drills are critical, too. Stop the use of calculators (whose hair brain idea was this?) Open more voc/tech opportunities for the students so those that do not want to go to college exit school with marketable skills. (We do not need as many kids going to college as the public is being force fed. Education has become a huge money racket and again the needs of the kids are missing!) Hire quality teachers including those from the real world with real world skills in the subject being taught—all of them! These people (yes, they need to be the right people) can actively engage and connect with the kids.

Remember to put the needs of the kids first! After all, the students and their families are the clients of education, right???

Maybe my views are skewed in the opinion of most. I was ready to drop out of school at age 13. An incredible private high school turned me on to learning. I spent two years in "formal/normal" college and then was ready to drop out until I went full time with my current employer of 34 years.

I learned they would pay for my education and I knew I needed a degree to advance. So . . . I spent four years in college while working full time to comlete my degree. I have advanced and we are constantly being asked to learn new things and lead our teams through the changes. None of these skills were learned in college!

I stumbled across your blog when I was cleaning out my education blogs. I will save yours and read it with interest.

Just wanted to share an engaged parent's point of view. Thank you—

3/30/2008, 5:15 AM

Dennis Fermoyle **said** . . .

Wow, DIN819GO, that was quite a comment! Thank you for the time and thought you put into it. You might be surprised by the fact that I agree with much of what you said. We DO have problems in public schools, and although I'm going strictly by what you say, it sounds like they are pretty bad in your district.

Since you've just come across my blog, I want you to know that there are two changes that I am constantly promoting. The first one is that I think we must make it easier for principals to keep their best teachers and get rid of the worst ones. I am opposed to our tenure and seniority systems. Although, you seem to think there are a lot more bad teachers than I do, I know they exist, and I believe it should be a lot easier to get rid of them. I'm only one person, but I'm doing what I can.

I also believe we must make it easier for teachers to remove disruptive kids and kids who refuse to work from our classes. Your concern about discipline is well-founded, and the basic problem is that we have no "bottom line" in dealing with kids who don't care. Something must be done to separate them from kids who actually want to learn. I know you have some other ideas, but I firmly believe that if we did these two things, public education would improve dramatically.

3/30/2008, 6:10 AM

Charley **said** . . .

OK . . . Gatto's a New Yorker and we *all* know that *all* New Yorkers are rude, arrogant, blatant, and in-your-face! ;-)

Maybe those weren't the best of his writings to start you out on . . . sorry. But since you read a history of public education from one source, maybe you should read the one from his. It's on his website and available for free. Arrogance and pronouncements aside, I have a hard time arguing with his sources . . .

As for a compliant populace . . .

Have you looked at your students lately as a group? They all dress alike! Hollister, American Eagle, Abercrombie and Fitch. They are walking billboards! Why? Several years ago my eldest joined the high school alpine ski team. After she went to the first meeting, she remarked, "Dad, I'm SO glad I'm homeschooled. Even though the girls were nice, they were all cookie-cutters of each other. They dressed the same, they talked of the same subjects (boys, makeup, and shopping), they spoke alike, and they acted alike. I'm glad I'm free to be myself . . ."

While you live in a small town, how many would be mall rats if they could? How carefully is the consumer mentality cultivated in their lives? How important is it for them to have the "latest" in fashion and technology . . . just because that is what it is: the latest?—

Granted, that is outward expression.

But what about attitudes and ideas? How much REAL individuality is there? The few exceptions aside, how many of the majority seriously have clear, individual thought? How many understand what it means to be statist? How many understand what liberty really is? How many understand what their responsibilities under the American form of government are?

How many think they should turn to the government to solve any problem that comes up in life?

How many are individual enough to acquire true wisdom and to muse upon what kind of adult they are aiming to become? Have they even thought about it?

Or . . . how many are so peer-dependent they can't get beyond today and the requirements of being "cool" in the eyes of the other fools (Bible's word, not mine) they hang with each and every day?

Dennis, I will grant you that you teach in a smaller town and thus it might not be this bad. But trust me when I say it is this bad in the larger schools . . .

3/30/2008, 8:29 PM

Dennis Fermoyle **said** . . .

Charley, I read your comment this morning, but I didn't have time to reply. I just got home from school, and my last class is Sociology. Guess what subject we started on today? Education. It's a relatively small class, so there is a lot of discussion. When we talked about trends in education today, one of the trends I brought up is homeschooling. You said that your daughter said she was very happy that she was homeschooled, and I believe you. This group had very different attitudes. One student said, "Why would anyone ever do that?" You probably won't believe this, but I actually tried to deal with this as fairly as I could. I started to say that the reputation of public education had been taking some pretty heavy hits for the past several years, and that a lot of people do it for religious reasons, but then I was interrupted by one young man sitting in the front. He said he was homeschooled for two years, and he absolutely hated it. I say this only to point out that not everyone who has been homeschooled has been enthralled with the experience.

When you say that public school kids have no individuality, I think you unfairly putting them all in the same pot. My students actually started to do the same thing. One of the students said that homeschooled kids have absolutely no social skills, and at first there was agreement. But then other students started to name homeschooled friends of theirs who do perfectly well socially.

In any case, many people who homeschool their kids are Christian fundamentalists. Public school kids all think alike? Let he who is without sin cast the first stone.

3/31/2008, 2:54 PM

Charley **said . . .**

Dennis,

The point of the story about my daughter wasn't that she was happy being educated at home, but that she recognized the uniformity of the other girls and was happy she was free to be herself.

Given that these kids have (all but one) been in public schools their whole lives, they consider that "normal." So I would consider their response to the homeschooling question to be uniform . . . and uniformly ignorant to what educating at home actually entails. (And I believe you when you say you tried to treat it as fairly as you could . . . but I'm willing to bet the overall consensus at the end of the discussion was that public school was "normal" and "superior.")

Obviously I don't know the young man who had been homeschooled, but I'm willing to guess he had most of his time in public school. Then his parents pulled him out and made the typical mistake of most new homeschoolers . . . they brought "school" home. In other words, they attempted to recreate what was happening in the group classroom at home. That never works. The mom burns out and the kids hate it. Been there; done that, to include whiteboard, desks, flag, and Pledge of Allegiance! On top of that, he was probably peer-dependent and hated being away from his peers. No wonder it was a bad experience for him.

I didn't say the kids have no individuality. I said, **for the most part,** they are uniform in their thinking and in their peer-dominated culture. I'm not talking about opinions (you know the old saying about opinions . . . too crude to repeat here), but rather about actual deep thought. For instance, the comment about social skills is a parroting of the typical adult concern about homeschooled kids. It reflects no thought as to what actual socialization is nor to its goal.

(I'm going to use the word "all" in the next paragraph. Please take it for what I mean . . . "the vast majority.")

I'm willing to bet that if you go beyond opinions, you will find uniformity of thought on a basic level. They will all be well informed on all aspects of pop culture. They will all think the global warming debate is settled. (How many times have they been required to see Gore's propaganda movie without any critical thought to what was presented??) They will all have similar opinions on sex. They will all think "tolerance" is the ultimate virtue. They will reject any idea that there is absolute truth, except that it is absolutely right to excoriate anyone who believes in absolutes! They will all think government is there to solve societal problems (this is a problem on BOTH the left and the right these days). None will have a clue to what liberty means or what responsibilities it demands from them.

While there is a large contingent of Christians who educate at home, the backgrounds and beliefs of homeschooling families crosses all social, economic, and cultural boundaries.

And yes, I still hold that, opinions aside, the deeply held beliefs of most public schooled kids are fairly uniform.

Charley
HomeDiscipling Dad Blog
3/31/2008, 8:05 PM

Daniel Simms **said . . .**

The central purpose of public education IS to make children into obedient servants of the state. Perhaps that's not your goal, Dennis, but in the big picture that is the way it is. And it's working. (It may not be your goal, Dennis, but you're not in charge. The elite are in charge. They call the shots and you must obey.)

To me, one of the worst forms of arrogance is holding that one has the right to use the police power of the state to impose their way of life on other individuals. Such people always use reasons such as "it's for your own good" or "it's in the best interests of society", or other like nonsense. And, of course, these ideas are always funded through government confiscation. People who oppose these ideas are called selfish or mean-spirited (or arrogant). This is how democracy works. It is felt that we must all sacrifice ourselves for the good of society. The idea that individuals have a right to live for their own happiness doesn't have much support these days.

You probably get the idea that I don't think much of democracy. Well, I don't. The best description I ever heard of democracy is that it's "three wolves and a sheep deciding what's for dinner." Democracy is just another form of might makes right. It turns people into slaves.

3/31/2008, 8:23 PM

Conversations 2.0: Is Public Education Is Failing?

In the current environment, many public conversations take place in a virtual, online space. And while calling these conversations "virtual conversations" might make them seem less real or less important, that is not the case. In fact, online conversations have become one of the central locations for public debate on key issues, including the issues that are included in this book. To enrich your understanding of public conversations, you can make use of the array of online discussion boards, listservs, blogs, Facebook pages, and Twitter sites that are available via the web. The Conversations 2.0 *pages in this book suggest some possible ways to do so, and point out some particularly useful and credible online conversations; you of course can use your own online forums and communities to add to these suggestions—or even to start your own.*

Discussions about the state of public education abound on the web. If you search using an array of terms like "public education" and "condition," "crisis," "failing," "status," and so forth, you will find many, many such conversations. As you search, pay attention not only to the conversations themselves, but the surrounding contexts. Who is sponsoring this blog and what is their motivation? Does the blog present the views of people with diverse opinions, or do the participants tend to agree and validate one another? Are the main contributors teachers, students, parents, or taxpayers? What are the key issues that seem to be debated and the main stasis points? If you approach your reading on the web as carefully as you do the reading you do in your classes—and in ways discussed in the introduction to this book—you will be able to sort valid arguments from those that have less credibility.

Consider one particularly useful set of discussions, found in a blog called "Betrayed: Why Public Education is Failing," maintained by Laurie H. Rogers. (You can find this by searching some of the terms in the title and the author's name.) Consider the context of this site: Rogers holds a bachelors degree in Mass Communications and a masters degree in Interpersonal Communications. She is founder and president of Safer Child, Inc., which is a nonprofit agency that describes its mission as "providing parents, caregivers and educators worldwide with the resources and information they need in order to help all children grow up healthy, safe and happy." She has also volunteered in elementary schools as a tutor in literacy and mathematics. Her blog attempts to develop a conversation among parents, teachers and community members "to offer their thoughts on what's wrong with public education and how to make it work better for the students." Contributors to this blog discuss what they take to be the most central goals of public education and how those goals might be achieved. In the March 2009 postings, for example, bloggers debate whether attempts at providing equity and tolerance have overshadowed the need for a "coherent and rigorous education." As you read these posts, consider the problem posed by Rogers, and the potential solutions offered by respondents. On what principles do they seem to agree? On what do they most disagree? Does an answer to the title question emerge from these responses?

By examining and following the conversations on sites like this one (and others you can find)—and doing so with a keen critical eye—you can stay up to date with, and participate in, the debate on this important public issue.

Larry Cuban

Making Public Schools Business-Like . . . Again

Though most of us would agree that one of the tasks of public education is to prepare students for their role in the workforce, there are many other purposes for education as well. Larry Cuban, an education specialist who brings 14 years of public school teaching experience to his position at Stanford University, explores the relationship between the use of schools to prepare students for work and the many other goals of public education. This essay was first published in 2004 in PSOnline, the American Political Science Association's online journal. Note the way that it uses an academic format and background research to make its argument. How do the purposes of education suggested by Cuban square with those offered by other writers in this chapter?

A contracting firm in New York City employed 4,900 skilled mechanics direct from Europe, paying them fifty cents per day above the union rate, because it was impossible to secure such valuable workmen in our greatest industrial center. We must not depend on Europe for our skill; *we must educate our own boys* [original italics]—Report of the Committee on Industrial Education, National Association of Manufacturers, 1905.

"Education . . . is a major economic issue," wrote John Akers, chairman of IBM, in an advertisement in the *New York Times Magazine* (1991). "If our students can't compete today, how will our companies compete tomorrow?" he asked.

Throughout the 20th century, business-inspired reform coalitions, driven by a deep belief that strong public schools produce a strong economy, have changed school goals, governance, management, organization, and curriculum. In doing so, the traditional and primary collective goal of public schools building literate citizens able to engage in democratic practices has been replaced by the goal of social efficiency, that is, preparing students for a competitive labor market anchored in a swiftly changing economy.

2   Akers and other business leaders, past and present, have not been alone in their new emphasis. In August of 2001, for example, then Chancellor of the New York City Public Schools Harold Levy—himself a corporate lawyer—had this to say about his goals for the public schools:

> That's the bottom line. Business has profit and loss. The school system has students and . . . there is nothing more important than our getting the children up to the levels of reading and math so that they can get through these exams and go on to successful careers. That's what this system is about. The minute we take our eyes off that we begin doing something wrong.
>
> (*New York Times* 2001)

3   As a teacher and local superintendent as well as a researcher, I have worked in schools for more than four decades and, recently, have studied this past century's business-inspired reforms. Pushed by a broad coalition of business executives since the late 1970s, public officials, union leaders, and educators, the policies, mirrored in an array of reports and commentaries as well as legislation, are chiefly rooted in the following assumptions:[1]

a. According to national and international test results, American students have insufficient knowledge and skills, and this mediocre performance imperils U.S. economic performance;

b. These student deficits have occurred because local school boards and practitioners are hostile to competition, have been unaccountable for student outcomes, have little managerial expertise, and have relaxed academic standards. They lack both the political will and a grasp of the larger economic situation to solve these problems;

c. More authority over schools must therefore be shifted to state and federal agencies, to develop uniform academic standards, require more tests, and hold local schools accountable while promoting parental choice and school competition.[2]

4   The trouble with these assumptions, advanced by the business-inspired reformers who have dominated education policy since the 1970s, is that they are mostly mistaken.

5   That students from other countries outstrip U.S. students at certain ages on particular tests is well known. The results for the last three international tests in mathematics and science, though, were mixed: U.S. students were ahead of both European

and Asian counterparts in some areas and in some grades. For the past three decades, moreover, results on the National Assessment of Educational Progress also have been mixed, with alternating gains and losses in reading and mathematics performance (National Assessment of Education 2003; Amrein and Berliner 2002). These test scores suggest, however, that U.S. students do have a spotty record on school-learned knowledge and skills as compared with pupils in other industrialized nations.

The problems begin, however, when public school critics link   6
test scores to worker productivity and the national economy. In 1991, for example, a U.S. Assistant Secretary of Education said that "faltering academic achievement between 1967 and 1980 sliced billions of dollars from the U.S. gross national product." Support for such a linkage is conspicuously underwhelming (Finn 1991).

Consider the lack of substantial evidence in three areas: (1)   7
the assumed connection between test scores and productivity; (2) the reliance on a theory of mismatched worker skills and employer demands to explain wage differentials among jobs and youth unemployment as well as labor productivity; and (3) the tie between workers' supposed skill deficits and America's global competitiveness.

1. Test Scores and Wages

Economists connect standardized test scores to hourly wages   8
by taking gains in the scores and computing corresponding increases in dollars earned. They also use broad supervisory ratings of employees (high, medium, and low) to estimate worker productivity. Both measures are, of course, proxies for actual productivity, and they certainly stretch reality. Using standardized achievement tests, for example, assumes that these instruments measure the analytic, creative, and practical skills and positive attitudes valued by employers. Gauging the results against hourly wages assumes that pay is set by equals, by employer and worker negotiating in fully competitive markets. Furthermore, the measures require complex manipulation of data and substantial interpretation and contain many methodological problems. Little wonder that experts disagree on the worth of such data in estimating worker productivity. Yet conclusions are put forward as unadorned facts.[3]

2. Skills Deficits

In this argument, not only low worker productivity and decreas-   9
ing global competitiveness but also youth unemployment and a widening gap between high-salary and low-wage jobs all stem

from inadequate knowledge and skills that high school graduates bring to the workplace. The skills-deficit argument first appeared in the late 19th century, when industrial leaders also were deeply concerned about global competition, at that time from German and British manufacturers. In 1898, for example, the president of the National Association of Manufacturers told members at the group's annual conference:

> There is hardly any work we can do or any expenditures we can make that will yield so large a return to our industries as would come from the establishment of educational institutions which would give us skilled hands and trained minds for the conduct of our industries and our commerce (Kliebard 1999).

10   As a result, a broad coalition of civic, business, labor, and education leaders pressed district, state, and federal policy makers to introduce vocational curricula so U.S. students would be better prepared for the industrial workplace. By 1917, federal policy makers decided to subsidize high school industrial arts and home economics courses, while states and districts adopted vocational education and guidance in all schools (Kantor 1982; Lazerson and Grubb 1974).

11   Through the Great Depression, World War II, the Cold War, and Vietnam, moreover, vocational education received enormous political and economic support from business and civic elites. Yet youth unemployment, of course, still rose and fell, remaining especially high among minority populations—and even in flush times, employers grumbled that high school graduates were unprepared for the workplace (Kliebard 1988).

12   Unfortunately, those who complain of skills deficits rarely specify what knowledge and skills are needed to succeed in an information-based economy, and they generally overlook the wealth of evidence showing that employers are far more concerned about applicants' attitudes and behavior than about their school-based knowledge in math or science. In fact, the supposed mismatch between worker skills and employer desires has little evidence to support it other than sturdy popular and media-amplified assertions. It is thus simply rash to suggest that students who are pressed by centralized, standards-based reforms to take more math and science courses or who do well on standardized achievement tests will succeed in entry-level jobs or in college.[4]

3. Global Competitiveness

13 Finally, the prior claims snowball into the assertion that insufficiently educated workers have slowed U.S. productivity and threatened America's position in global markets. This assertion

is flawed. For one, it ignores how the United States enjoyed nearly a decade of unbroken prosperity in the 1990s. For another, U.S. productivity rates have increased (not decreased) over the past decade. For a third, even with the weaker U.S. economy of 2000–2002, the World Economic Forum found that the United States had the world's second most competitive economy, after Finland. In short, few economists or public officials doubt the predominance of the U.S. economy today.[5]

In light of such prosperity and competitiveness and the piv- 14
otal role that student achievement is supposed to play in U.S. economic performance, one might reasonably have expected public schools to be commended for producing graduates who contributed so much to this remarkable record. Yet no such praise has been uttered by corporate leaders, governors, policy analysts, or Oval Office occupants. Perhaps economic gains do not depend so heavily on student test scores as public school critics contend. This has, indeed, dawned on various observers. As economist Kevin Hollenbeck of the W. E. Upjohn Institute for Employment Research has put it, "The evidence seems to suggest that mediocre educational results do not threaten economic performance" (Hollenbeck 2001). In this regard, note what historian Lawrence Cremin wrote in 1990 about where responsibility does lie for economic challenges:

> American economic competitiveness with Japan and other nations is to a considerable degree a function of monetary, trade and industrial policy, and of decisions made by the President and Congress, the Federal Reserve Board, and the federal Departments of the Treasury and Commerce and Labor. Therefore, to contend that problems of international competitiveness can be solved by education reform, especially education reform defined solely as school reform, is not merely utopian and millennialist, it is at best foolish and at worst a crass effort to direct attention away from those truly responsible for doing something about competitiveness and to lay the burden instead on the schools (Cremin 1990).

To the list of those responsible for economic performance one 15
should add inventors of technologies that contribute significantly to improved productivity and managers (or mismanagers) of U.S. businesses, including CEOs who have been issuing so many fanciful numbers in recent years.

Competing with the list of those who directly influence 16
national economic performance, however, is another list of those business-inspired reformers drawn from civic and economic elites, educators, union officials, and others who, for the past 30 years, helped shape the current purpose: insuring that public schools are little more than boot camps for future

employees. Well-intentioned civic and business leaders have done what so many other reformers have been accused of in past decades: they have experimented on teachers and students for over three decades without showing much evidence of success.

17   The issue is *not* whether schools should prepare students for productive labor. They should. The issue is that the single-minded pursuit of preparing all students for college and high-paying jobs has narrowed the far broader and historic mission of civic engagement. Historically and presently, schools have been and are still expected to instill civic, social, and humanitarian attitudes and skills that will shape our democracy and influence how graduates lead their lives in their communities. Schools are expected to build student respect for differences in ideas and cultures. Schools are expected to be decent and livable places for the young to spend a large portion of their waking time. These historic and contemporary aims of public schools often have been neglected in the mistaken rush to turn schools into engines for the larger economy (Labaree 1997; Goodlad 1984).

18   Even more damning are the questions that have been omitted from the current economic and political agendas shaped by business-inspired reformers.

Consider a few of the missing questions:

- Do schools geared toward preparing workers also build literate, active, and morally sensitive citizens who carry out their civic duties?
- How can schools develop independently thinking citizens who earn their living in corporate workplaces?
- When the economy hiccups, unemployment increases, and graduates have little money to secure higher education or find a job matched to their skills, will public schools, now an arm of the economy, get blamed—as they have in the past—for creating the mismatch?

19   These basic questions, unasked by business-inspired reform coalitions in the past three decades, go unanswered today.

Notes

1. For details of the formation of this business-inspired coalition concentrating on school reform, see Thomas Toch, *In The Name of Excellence* (New York: Oxford University Press, 1991); Larry Cuban, *Why Are Good Schools So Hard To Get?* (New York: Teachers College Press, 2003). Gordon Lafer maps a sequence of events in the same quarter-century where employers focused on workers' lack of skills and the need for more training and education to equip employees for the future workplace. See *The Job Training Charade* (Ithaca, NY: Cornell University Press, 2002). Economists and widely respected analysts also produced best sellers in these years that judged schools as failures in teaching students to think and

solve problems. See Ray Marshall and Marc Tucker, *Thinking for a Living: Education and the Wealth of Nations* (New York: Basic Books, 1992); Robert Reich, *The Work of Nations* (New York: Alfred Knopf, 1991); and Lester Thurow, *Head to Head: The Coming Economic Battle among Japan, Europe, and America* (New York: Morrow, 1992).

2. For a brief history of the movement towards standards-based reform with its accountability and testing, see Richard Elmore, "Building a New Structure for School Leadership," winter (Washington, D.C.: Albert Shanker Institute, 2000).

3. An example of connecting tests to wages and productivity is John Bishop, "Is The Test Score Decline Responsible for the Productivity Growth Decline?" *American Economic Review,* 1989, 74(1), 178–197. Bishop's answer to his question is "yes." For those who doubt these assumptions of test scores and worker productivity, see Henry Levin, "High-Stakes Testing and Economic Productivity," in Gary Orfield and Mindy Kornhaber (Eds.), *Raising Standards or Raising Barriers? Inequality and High-Stakes Testing in Public Education* (New York: The Century Foundation Press, 2001), 39–49; Robert Balfanz, "Local Knowledge, Academic Skills, and Individual Productivity: An Alternative View," *Educational Policy,* 5(4), 1991, 343–370.

4. Levin, "High Stakes Tests and Economic Productivity"; John P. Smith, III, "Tracking the Mathematics of Automobile Production: Are Schools Failing To Prepare Students for Work?" (1999), 835–878. Also see Lafer, *The Job Training Charade,* chapters 2 and 3, for a comprehensive summary of evidence revealing how workplace demands are inconsistent with the theory and beliefs of those who argue for more well-trained graduates from high school and college. Critics of using standardized test scores as the only or best indicator of improved teaching and learning have often referred to other important measures that are either ignored or missing because of measurement difficulties. These include the quality of intellectual work in school, the linkages between classroom teaching and assessment, and other measures of student performance. The work of Lorrie Shepard is best in this regard. See "The Role of Assessment in a Learning Culture" (2000), 4–14.

5. For growth in productivity in the 1990s, see Louis Uchitelle, "Big Increases in Productivity by Workers," *New York Times,* November 13, 1999, B1; Hal Varian, "The Economic Scene," *New York Times,* June 6, 2002, C2; Michael Porter, Jeffrey Sachs, and John McArthur, *Global Competitiveness Report 2001–2002* (New York: World Economic Forum, 2002).

References

Amrein, Audrey, and David Berliner. 2002. "High Stakes Testing, Uncertainty, and Student Learning." *Education Policy Analysis Archives* 10(18).

Balfanz, Robert. 1991. "Local Knowledge, Academic Skills, and Individual Productivity: An Alternative View." *Educational Policy* 5(4): 343–370.

Bishop, John. 1989. "Is The Test Score Decline Responsible for the Productivity Growth Decline?" *American Economic Review* 74(1): 178–197.

Cremin, Lawrence. 1990. *Popular Education and Its Discontents.* New York: Harper & Row.

Cuban, Larry. 2004. "A Solution That Lost Its Problem: Why Centralized Policymaking Is Unlikely To Yield Many Classroom Gains." Denver, CO: Education Commission of States.

___. 2005. *The Blackboard and the Bottom Line: Why Can't Schools Be Like Businesses?* Cambridge, MA: Harvard University Press.

___. 2003. *Why Are Good Schools So Hard To Get?* New York: Teachers College Press.

Elmore, Richard. 2000. "Building a New Structure for School Leadership." Washington, D.C.: Albert Shanker Institute.

Finn, Chester, Jr. 1991. *We Must Take Charge.* New York: Free Press.

Goodlad, John. 1984. *A Place Called School.* New York: MacMillan.

Hollenbeck, Kevin. 2001. *Education and the Economy.* W. E. Upjohn Institute for Employment Research.

Kantor, Harvey. 1982. "Vocationalism in American Education: The Economic and Political Context, 1880–1930." In *Work, Youth, and Schooling,* eds. H. Kantor and D. Tyack. Stanford: Stanford University Press, 14–44.

___. 1988. *Learning to Earn: School, Work, and Vocational Reform in California, 1880–1930.* Madison: University of Wisconsin Press.

Herb Childress

A Subtractive Education

Herb Childress directs the liberal studies program at the Boston Architectural College. His background in architecture gives him a unique perspective on how the physical design of a place influences what actually happens there. For example, in his study of the lives of teenagers, *Landscapes of Betrayal* (2000), he shows how the community planning has failed to provide challenging growth opportunities for our youth. He maintains a blog called Vita Activa, which is "about architectural theory, and more importantly about architectural purpose" at http://thevitaactiva.blogspot.com. In the essay below, published in the educational journal *Phi Delta Kappan* in 2006, Childress asks how the shape of our schools affects secondary education. What new dimensions does this essay bring into the conversation on the goals of education? Are there other authors in this section that might tend to agree, or disagree, with his premises?

1   I am a meandering kind of thinker. Something comes up for me, and that reminds me of something else, and then I remember a third thing, and pretty soon I'm talking about something brand new. Let me take you on a little tour of how that works for me.

2   I'm walking to Albertson's because Ben & Jerry's Frozen Yogurt is on sale—two pints for five dollars. I get to the store, it's about seven o'clock at night, and the parking lot is jammed;

people are weaving around with their shopping carts through the stream of incoming cars trying to get their groceries to their own cars and go home.

And I'm looking at all of these hundreds of people and all of these cars, and I suddenly think, "I wonder how many of these people could resolve a trigonometric identity." Honest to God, that's what came into my head. Well, from there, this meandering thinker was off to the races. "I wonder how many of these people could tell you about the origins of the French Revolution. I wonder how many can still diagram a sentence."

And then I thought, "Well, why would I care if they could or not? They all have enough money to afford their cars and their groceries; they're getting by. Would they get by any better if they remembered how to construct the perpendicular bisector of a line segment using only a straightedge and a compass?"

Well, that of course took me right back to the high school that I wrote my book about and to all the kids who ever asked why they should bother learning something. "Why are we doing this?" That was the plaintive cry from the back corners of the room. "Why are we doing this?" It never came from the front: up front were the kids to whom it never occurred to ask that question or who had given up asking it. And the arguments that came back from the teachers were never very compelling to me. They said things like, "There's *lots* of careers that use algebra," though they never offered a specific example. Or, when the question came up with regard to conjugating French verbs, it would be met with, "Well, you might travel to France someday." For these kids from rural Northern California, even the City of Lights was neither a likely nor an especially desirable destination. Their picture of France amounted to the Eiffel Tower, the Arc de Triomphe, and a language that made them say things like, "Hello, I name myself Stacy. How do you name yourself?"

"Why are we doing this?" the kids ask. So let's ask ourselves why we have them doing all of these crazy things. When I think about what high school is for, I remember that John Ogbu, the educational anthropologist, wrote that, "whatever else education may be, from the standpoint of society it is a preparation of children for adult life as adults in their society conceive it."

Well, I don't know, John. Here I am in the Albertson's parking lot, willing to bet my Ben & Jerry's and most of my paycheck that not one of the next three people I see could name the first European to sail around the Cape of Good Hope. "Adult life as adults in our society conceive it" doesn't typically include answering trivia questions like that, unless we're standing on a stage across from Alex Trebek. (By the way, it was Vasco da Gama in 1497, and yes, I had to look it up.)

But let's give John Ogbu another reading and another chance: "Whatever else education may be, from the standpoint of society

it is a preparation of children for adult life as adults in their society conceive it." I think that's true, but the problem we have, in
our very diverse society, is that Ogbu's phrase "preparation for
adulthood" has many different meanings, based on a lot of
potential adulthoods. I think we need to make those adulthoods
explicit so that we're not working at cross-purposes. So I'm
going to do two things here. I'm going to start out by telling you
what I think a successful adulthood is, and then I'm going to tell
you—based on the evidence of my own and other people's
research—what our education system says that a successful
adulthood is.

9   Here's a definition I hold of strong adulthood. I've cast it in
the form of a list of my ideal outcome measures for a high
school, the characteristics I hope that graduates have as they
prepare to move toward adulthood.

- *Graduates of my ideal high school should love to read.*
  This is not at all the same as saying that they can read.
  There's an enormous middle ground between illiterate
  and literate, which has sometimes been called alliter-
  ate—a term for people who can read but choose not to,
  who see little value or reward in it. People who love to
  read are people who are open to new ideas, who are
  engaged in constant reinvention.
- *Graduates of my ideal high school should enjoy numbers.*
  I'm no mathematician, but I can do arithmetic in my
  head very well. It's a skill I developed before I was 8 by
  playing cribbage and rummy and pinochle and by keeping score at bowling. It's a skill that has served me well all
  the way through calculus and physics, it's a skill that
  helps me navigate the everyday world of taxes and budg-
  eting, of saving and knowing when I can indulge in an
  extravagance, and it's a skill that helps me evaluate the
  accuracy and pertinence of information that's offered to
  me.
- *Graduates of my ideal high school should enjoy physical
  exertion and activity.* And that activity should take several forms, from team sports to hiking across town to playing hacky sack. Anything that gets you sweaty is a damn
  sight better than television, and we should encourage
  young people to regard physical activity as a lifelong pursuit, rather than as something to look back on fondly
  once high school football has ended.
- *Graduates of my ideal high school should have some well-
  developed outlet for their creative desires.* This will also take
  all kinds of forms, from writing to visual arts to music to
  physics, but the quest for putting ideas together in a
  unique way is part of what makes us really human.

- *Graduates of my ideal high school should know how to work in groups, and they should know how to teach a skill to someone else.* Kids are going to be working with groups for the rest of their lives, from work to marriage and parenthood to community service. We are social animals, and we need to quit pretending that individual performance is the only thing that really matters.
- *Graduates of my ideal high school should be brave and take risks.* This means that they must be exposed to failure and supported through the other side. They need to know that it's possible to fall down and still get up again. They must know that, if a magazine rejects their article, there are hundreds more to try. They need to know that anything really worth doing will be scary and intimidating—and that they have to do it anyway.
- *Graduates of my ideal high school should understand and take an interest in their community.* They should know something about real estate, local government and services, major local industries, and the natural landscape and climate. Even if they move away, knowing *how* to find out about these things is a skill that will serve them wherever they go.
- *Graduates of my ideal high school should be compassionate and care about people they don't know.* They should understand that a lot of what happens in people's lives isn't their fault—and that even things that *are* someone's fault usually are mistakes that can be recovered from rather than a sign of a core moral failing that leaves people irredeemable and so dismissible.

For me, this list presents a compelling model of an attractive 10 adulthood. It is a set of characteristics that I don't encounter all that often in the adults I know. In fact, it is a set of characteristics that I strive for but sometimes fail to live up to myself. The list outlines adulthood as a rigorous, ongoing practice rather than a state to be obtained and then mounted on the wall with the high school diploma. And such an adulthood is one that will serve as the foundation for an infinite number of careers, in an ever-shifting economic world.

Now, this may not be the same definition that *you* would cre- 11 ate for an attractive, complete adulthood. And that's fine, so long as you actually go through the exercise and create a definition that you can really stand behind and don't just accept the default version.

And believe me, there is a default version. Our institutions— 12 maintained and shepherded as they are by white-collar people who understand complex organizations—promote as the norm their own white-collar, managerial, hierarchical, certified view of adulthood. That's what schools attempt to perpetuate, and it's the model of adulthood for which they prepare young people. Half a century ago, the sociologist C. Wright Mills had the same impression and described the high school as "the seed-bed of white-collar skills." Like the early Spanish in California and Mexico, the white-collar, information-laden school takes on the missionary role of civilizing the uncivilized and converting the heathens. Even the most benevolent of the conquerors are preparing the natives for what they see as a materially and morally superior way of life. We are "helping," "developing," or "training," or whatever term we might use to mean making someone else be more like us.

13   This has led to a model of secondary education that I call an "additive education," in which each certified specialist takes an assembly under construction and screws on a particular component and then passes the material along to the next specialist. One person takes 150 kids and screws on some algebra, and another person takes those same kids and screws on some world history, and a third person takes those same kids and screws on some Hemingway. Over the course of four years, each successful kid gets more than 20 components screwed on. And in the end, they're screwed, indeed. They're encased in this educational armor and have no experience in encountering and challenging their own communities, futures, or desires, because all of that has been sublimated to the repetitive and mechanical structures that they endured.

14   In the high school I've studied most thoroughly, which is a tragically normal high school, I found six underlying principles of the school, principles that were never stated overtly but that were repeated over and over in the rules that were laid, in the spaces that were created, in the furniture that was used, in the lessons that were taught, and in the lessons that were avoided. And these were the six principles:

1. Kids and adults should be physically separated.
2. Teaching should be active, and learning should be passive.
3. Abstraction is beneficial, and uniqueness should be avoided.
4. Economies of scale are necessary and beneficial.
5. Objective evaluation and peer competition are necessary and beneficial.
6. Students should be prepared for a life of geographic and organizational mobility.

15   And, after all, the world educators endure is governed by these same rules. So let's look at them as educators suffer them.

1. *Kids and adults should be physically separated.* Certainly, teachers, administrators, and education policy makers

are all physically (and conceptually) separated from one another.

2. *Teaching should be active, and learning should be passive.* The school that most completely follows the guidelines is considered the best school by those who write the guidelines, which become more prescriptive all the time.

3. *Abstraction is beneficial, and uniqueness should be avoided.* Unique local outcomes and desires are less important than test scores and standings on other indices of achievement—and certainly less important than the number of AP courses offered.

4. *Economies of scale are necessary and beneficial.* Every single school must be immersed in district, state, and federal systems that ensure completeness and correctness and that avoid duplication of services.

5. *Objective evaluation and peer competition are necessary and beneficial.* Schools themselves are forced to compete with one another on grossly abstract terms that have little to do with the life of learning and citizenship.

6. *Students should be prepared for a life of geographic and organizational mobility.* Teachers and administrators, if they are successful, also move upward or outward from their classrooms and into larger communities or educational structures.

So schools, to their credit, don't ask kids to deal with anything   16
that adults don't have to face as well. Our white-collar organizational biases, in our modern economic circumstances, lead toward an education in which kids are trained primarily to endure what educators themselves endure. Remember again Ogbu's quote: "Whatever else education may be, from the standpoint of society it is a preparation of children for adult life as adults in their society conceive it." The main lessons of the "hidden curriculum" are to compete with your peers, to be compliant with your superiors, and to refrain from asking awkward questions. And those lessons are there on purpose! That's what makes the safest economic life in a culture in which capital is mobile and a company can leave Michigan for Georgia and then leave Georgia for Indonesia. In such a world, you have to demonstrate superiority over other workers and unquestioning loyalty to your supervisors and their world view.

This additive education is an education of fear. It's an effort   17
to avoid disaster rather than to reach for a dream, to avoid a career at McDonald's rather than to pursue a deep personal mission. It's an effort to ensure that kids will have the tools necessary to survive in the similarly white-collar colleges and workplaces they will move on to. It's an effort to keep them from being sorted out of the pool for advancement before they ever

really get under way. It's a recognition that our modern economic terrain allows employers to use the desperation of labor as a resource anywhere in the world, that every American who might formerly have done physical work is competing with someone in another country who is willing to work for less, in worse conditions, and for longer hours than our nation allows. It's a recognition that we have educated ourselves into a society in which information is the only material we have left to manipulate.

18   I understand this education of fear, and I think I know why it exists. But I have no patience for it, because I see how cold and empty it leaves its products—both the kids and the adults. They learn to avoid pain instead of to seek love. They learn to avoid commitment, because they might have to leave. They're never asked to engage who they really are, but rather to be more and more like their masters.

19   When I encounter students in a high school like that—which is to say, almost all the time—my immediate urge is to help them escape, to get them into the lifeboats before they drown. I'm not entirely sure what we'd be moving toward, but that's not a question that you ask in a time of crisis. You just get people out of the wreckage and away from the danger. This is my own fearful response to the education of fear.

20   When I was talking to the folks at Duke about the possibility of my coming there to teach their first-year students, I told them that I was fascinated by people who were between about 15 and 25 years old, standing on the brink of adulthood, peering over the edge in simultaneous fear and anticipation. I told them that I thought high school was something that had to be recovered from and that I thought I could aid in that recovery.

21   And I talked about my friend Pete. Pete is a young man; he'll be 29 soon. He's a wonderful writer, a great friend to those of us blessed to know him well, a great son and brother to his family, and, possibly, the best illustrator that I've ever had the chance to watch at work. He draws like an angel.

22   Pete has no idea what he wants from an adult life. Both of his parents are teachers, and he enjoyed school all the way up through sixth grade. But when he moved from elementary school to junior high school, began to move from one teacher and 25 classmates to six teachers and 150 classmates who shifted all day long, he didn't survive the change. He told me that he could recognize instantly that those adults weren't really there for him, that they didn't even know him. And about halfway through seventh grade, he tested his hypothesis, as any good scientist would. In the middle of an assigned five-page essay, he wrote the third page in an imaginary alphabet that he'd drawn, to see if anyone would read it. No one did, and his hypothesis was confirmed.

23   Pete had a naturally occurring social life in elementary school; in a class of 25 kids who are together all year long, people make

allowances for eccentricity and learn to appreciate one another's gifts. When you're shoved into an anonymous crowd of 600
kids you don't know, you tend to seek out people who are the
most like you in order to have some safety and stability. But Pete
wasn't in any of those natural safety groups. His eccentricity and
artistic mind, assets through sixth grade, became social and academic liabilities three months later.

By the time I met him in high school, Pete had two lives: exu-   24
berant and creative with his small circle of friends and in the
theater and completely alienated in the classroom and in the
larger social life of the school. He maintained his mathematically precise 2.0 grade-point average so that he could graduate,
but there was never even one entire course that reliably captured
his attention. There were *days*, there were *topics*, there were
moments when you could see him come alive and watch the
gears turn, but mostly Pete was that kid in the back right corner
who you'd never guess was six feet tall because he sat so low in
his chair. He saw nothing in the adult world that he trusted, that
he wanted, or that he was adequately guided toward. And that
distrust of and distaste for adult life persist for him to this day.

So I was talking to the folks at Duke about Pete in the context   25
of helping kids recover from high school, and the director of the
writing program said, "Our kids don't come here with 2.0s. We
help kids recover from getting 4.3s." And then I began to think
in a different way about the scars left by our education system.
The rebellious get their 40 lashes on a regular basis, but the silent
and compliant have wounds of their own, harder to see but no
less real and no less deep. We rightfully strive to eliminate a system of schooling in which there are winners and losers, but we
don't think to eliminate a system of schooling in which even the
winners have lost their curiosity, have lost their passion, have lost
the willingness to ask, "Why are we doing this?"

We are deeply familiar with this screwed-on model of high   26
school, this additive education in which each professional adds
his or her component onto the raw material that comes down the
line. But I've been wondering: What would a subtractive model
of education look like? And I'm beginning to think it might look
something like what a sculptor does. When Michelangelo wrote
about the experience of sculpting, he said that the stone itself told
him what to do, that the figure was waiting inside that stone and
that his task as an artist was to take away what wasn't essential.
"I saw the angel in the marble and carved until I set him free."

And that's what I do with Pete—informally but very purpose-   27
fully. And it's what I hoped to be able to do with my Duke students. I think I have to sit with a person and be with him or her
for a quite a while before I can expect to have much of an effect.
And then I think I can ask for permission to pick off some of the
armor and maybe find out who's under all of those uniform
shells. I trust that there is a core person there, and my belief is

that it's probably the same person who was there at 10 years old, before the specialists got to him or her. Once I know who that is, I am able to see some things that excite this student, and I can introduce him or her to a wider range of such things. There will be some natural skills, and I can help the student hone and develop and expand and challenge those.

28   And each person will have his or her own visions of success-ful adult life, collected by being a part of a family and immersed in the media and knowing a larger group of friends. I can show a young person my own model of adulthood as another poten-tial way of living to examine, but I can't expect that he or she will choose it, and I can't personalize a response—when he or she *doesn't* choose it—as a rejection of me.

29   I realize that this is a hazy vision. I can't tell you what the struc-ture of a subtractive education looks like on a day-to-day basis. I know that it looks small and attentive, somewhat passive on the part of the educator, slow, inexpert, and out of control, and that it requires the time and the inclination to listen to and believe young people. But I think it also looks different for every practi-tioner and with every student, and probably on every day.

30   Even if you agree with me that a subtractive education would be a humane and powerful experience, I cannot offer you a cur-riculum that you could all follow to get there with every student. That kind of static curriculum would automatically lead us back toward nonresponsive, nonseeing, automatic, additive ways of being. All I can do is tell you what I see in the world, tell you what I think it means, tell you about some of the lives that are hindered by our common practices, and sit together with you to see if there's something different that we can do.

31   Here's the vision that drives me, and *this* vision is very clear. I'm 48 years old, and I'm optimistically assuming that I have another 35 years or so to work with teenagers and young adults. My dream is that I will live to see the day that the modern high school will be considered the counterpart of the mission, the orphanage, and the poor farm—an institution that was taken for granted and considered beneficial in its time but has since been judged to be inhumane and unthinkable. High school is taken for granted, and it was and is still considered beneficial. But I believe that we have outgrown the institution's usefulness. I believe that we have different ways of service—different ways of *being*—that we can employ on behalf of young people. And I believe that we are fundamentally not the kind of people who want to make our least powerful citizens endure this four-year sentence of disrespect and invisibility.

32   We are better than our systems. We are better than our struc-tures. We can be brave, help our kids discover who they are, help them go where they want to go, and wish them Godspeed as they leave us behind.

getting into the conversation •••1

The Goals and Condition of Public Education

1. One of the central debates in this chapter is spurred by John Taylor Gatto, who goes beyond suggesting that public education needs reform to argue that the system itself is a large part of the problem. As you can tell from several of the other pieces in this section, this contentious point has drawn a great deal of attention, including that of Ron Miller, Kathleen Anderson, and Dennis Fermoyle. Using the model of Kathleen Anderson's ."Reflections in Education," construct a personal narrative that demonstrates your agreement, disagreement, or partial agreement with one specific part of Gatto's argument. If you choose, you might either include the ideas of other authors in this section, or do some further research, and blend that research into your narrative in the ways used by Anderson.

2. Although Larry Cuban does take issue with some facets of the current educational system, he does seem to accept that preparing students for their vocation is at least *one* of the central purposes of public education. Herb Childress, on the other hand, objects to the notion that public education should take as its mission the prepara-tion of students for a "white-collar hierarchy." Where do you stand on this issue? Is preparation for the work world a major concern for our educational system? Should it be? Drawing upon your own ex-perience, respond to these three authors' main arguments and points of evidence.

3. One frequent critique of the "blogosphere" is that individual blogs tend to attract only like-minded individuals, and so the discussion on any given blog tends to amount to group-think—one person posting and others agreeing or building similar arguments. Two sets of blog posts, Dennis Fermoyle's *From the Trenches of Public Education* (included in this chapter) and Laurie. H. Rogers' *Betrayed—Why Public Education is Failing* (which can be accessed by searching the title and author on the internet) feature rather lengthy and thoughtful pieces of writing. But is there a wide array of perspectives? What community or communities does each blog most seem to represent? Does it seem open to ideas from outside the community? Using the entries included in this chapter, and per-haps going to the blogs themselves (just search them by title using an Internet search engine, and you will find them easily), write an analysis of one of these online communities—or a comparative analysis of both of them. What characteristics do the users seem to share? Does there seem to be a common set of principles or beliefs? What types of tone, language, and attitude seem to be most appro-priate on this site? Does it lend itself more to civil debate or to more contentious forms of argument? Do the opinions seem to be in-formed and reliable—and how can you tell? How informed do the

writers seem to be on the topic? After you have made notes on these questions, write an analysis of the site, its users, and its usefulness to both participants and people who might simply use it as a site of facts and opinions about this topic by lurking on the blog. Would you consider it to be a reliable source for a research paper on educational philosophies or methods?

conversations in context ...1

Debating Standardized Testing

I. The Context

As students in 21st century America, you are no strangers to the standardized test. In fact, such tests—SATs, ACTs, yearly progress tests, and so forth—may have become so much a part of your regular pattern of education that you have not thought much about their value, their shortcomings, and the reasons why these tests have become so ingrained in our educational culture. But many conversations about those issues and many details of standardized testing are ongoing among government officials, school boards, teachers, parents, and students. As a veteran of our testing-based system, you can bring a great deal of personal experience to thinking and writing about the topic.

This section of *Conversations,* then, allows you to get some of the back story about standardized testing as well as to hear some of the current debate points that can help you enter the conversation. Let's begin with a brief overview of 3 key moments to consider how we got where we are now.

In 1965, President Lyndon Johnson signed the Elementary and Secondary Education Act (ESEA) as part of his "Great Society" and "War on Poverty" initiatives. In effect, what this bill did was authorize the federal government to take an active role in funding public education and to demand accountability of schools to assure that students are meeting standards for educational effectiveness. How to best measure that effectiveness is, of course, the detail that has bred a great deal of conversation.

In 1983, at the request of President Ronald Reagan, a National Commission on Excellence in Education was formed, chaired by David Pierpont Gardner. This commission issued one of the most influential reports in American history entitled "A Nation at Risk: The Imperative for National Reform." This report began with a short, but extremely effective sentence: "Our Nation is at risk." It went on to assert that "our once unchallenged preeminence in commerce, industry, science, and technological innovation is being overtaken by competitors throughout the world," even suggesting that "if an unfriendly power had attempted to impose on America the mediocre educational performance that exists today, we might well have viewed it as an act of war." This clarion call gave rise to another active national conversation on how to best battle this achievement gap, and as you'll see by the excerpts included, frequently pointed to achievement tests as "indicators of the risk."

Then, in early 2002, President George W. Bush signed into law the No Child Left Behind Act of 2001. This act, which was named for President Bush's campaign assertion that "no child should be left behind," reauthorized and revised the 1965 ESEA. Though there are many complexities to this law, it was based upon what the administration called "four pillars" of providing a better educational system for America, which were formulated as follows: "*No Child Left Behind* is based on stronger accountability for results, more freedom for states and communities, proven education methods, and more choices for parents." The first of those pillars, "Stronger Accountability for Results," is crucial to our growing reliance upon standardized tests:

> *Under* No Child Left Behind, *states are working to close the achievement gap and make sure all students, including those who are disadvantaged, achieve academic proficiency. Annual state and school district report cards inform parents and communities about state and school progress. Schools that do not make progress must provide supplemental services, such as free tutoring or after-school assistance; take corrective actions; and, if still not making adequate yearly progress after five years, make dramatic changes to the way the school is run.*

As you can see, the goals of the program were based in *accountability,* making sure that "adequate yearly progress" is made by students in each American school—requiring measures to assess that progress and adding very high stakes for schools, students, and parents. The standardized test, seen as an objective measure of success that could maintain consistency of assessment nationwide, was thus reinforced as the central tool for determining educational success.

Considering Contexts: from *A Nation At Risk, April 1983*

> *Since this 1983 report is seen by many as a key catalyst for our current testing culture, it is important that you treat this document as a major context for your own thoughts on standardized testing. As you read the introductory sections of this landmark report, consider how the "indicators of risk" are frequently based upon standardized testing data. Consider also the implied purposes of public education upon which the authors of this report base their conclusions; that is, what is the standard of successful education that is assumed here, and which informs the conclusion that our nation is at risk?*

All, regardless of race or class or economic status, are entitled to a fair chance and to the tools for developing their individual powers of mind and spirit to the utmost. This promise means that all children by virtue of their own efforts, competently guided, can hope to attain the mature and informed judgment needed to secure gainful employment, and to manage their own lives, thereby serving not only their own interests but also the progress of society itself.

Our Nation is at risk. Our once unchallenged preeminence in commerce, industry, science, and technological innovation is being overtaken by competitors throughout the world. This report is concerned with only one of the many causes and dimensions of the problem, but it is the one that undergirds American prosperity, security, and civility. We report to the American people that while we can take justifiable pride in what our schools and colleges have historically accomplished and contributed to the United States and the well-being of its people, the educational foundations of our society are presently being eroded by a rising tide of mediocrity that threatens our very future as a Nation and a people. What was unimaginable a generation ago has begun to occur—others are matching and surpassing our educational attainments.

If an unfriendly foreign power had attempted to impose on America the mediocre educational performance that exists today, we might well have viewed it as an act of war. As it stands, we have allowed this to happen to ourselves. We have even squandered the gains in student achievement made in the wake of the Sputnik challenge. Moreover, we have dismantled essential support systems which helped make those gains possible. We have, in effect, been committing an act of unthinking, unilateral educational disarmament.

Our society and its educational institutions seem to have lost sight of the basic purposes of schooling, and of the high expectations and disciplined effort needed to attain them. This report, the result of 18 months of study, seeks to generate reform of our educational system in fundamental ways and to renew the Nation's commitment to schools and colleges of high quality throughout the length and breadth of our land.

That we have compromised this commitment is, upon reflection, hardly surprising, given the multitude of often conflicting demands we have placed on our Nation's schools and colleges. They are routinely called on to provide solutions to personal, social, and political problems that the home and other institutions either will not or cannot resolve. We must understand that these demands on our schools and colleges often exact an educational cost as well as a financial one.

On the occasion of the Commission's first meeting, President Reagan noted the central importance of education in American life when he said: "Certainly there are few areas of American life as important to our society, to our people, and to our families as our schools and colleges." This report, therefore, is as much an open letter to the American people as it is a report to the Secretary of Education. We are confident that the American people, properly informed, will do what is right for their children and for the generations to come.

The Risk

History is not kind to idlers. The time is long past when American's destiny was assured simply by an abundance of natural resources and inexhaustible human enthusiasm, and by our relative isolation from the malignant problems of older civilizations. The world is indeed one global village. We live among determined, well-educated, and strongly motivated competitors. We compete with them for international standing and markets, not only with products but also with the ideas of our laboratories and neighborhood workshops.

America's position in the world may once have been reasonably secure with only a few exceptionally well-trained men and women. It is no longer.

The risk is not only that the Japanese make automobiles more efficiently than Americans and have government subsidies for development and export. It is not just that the South Koreans recently built the world's most efficient steel mill, or that American machine tools, once the pride of the world, are being displaced by German products. It is also that these developments signify a redistribution of trained capability throughout the globe. Knowledge, learning, information, and skilled intelligence are the new raw materials of international commerce and are today spreading throughout the world as vigorously as miracle drugs, synthetic fertilizers, and blue jeans did earlier. If only to keep and improve on the slim competitive edge we still retain in world markets, we must dedicate ourselves to the reform of our educational system for the benefit of all—old and young alike, affluent and poor, majority and minority. Learning is the indispensable investment required for success in the "information age" we are entering.

Our concern, however, goes well beyond matters such as industry and commerce. It also includes the intellectual, moral, and spiritual strengths of our people which knit together the very fabric of our society. The people of the United States need to know that individuals in our society who do not possess the levels of skill, literacy, and training essential to this new era will be effectively disenfranchised, not simply from the material rewards that accompany competent performance, but also from the chance to participate fully in our national life. A high level of shared education is essential to a free, democratic society and to the fostering of a common culture, especially in a country that prides itself on pluralism and individual freedom.

For our country to function, citizens must be able to reach some common understandings on complex issues, often on short notice and on the basis of conflicting or incomplete evidence. Education helps form these common understandings, a point Thomas Jefferson made long ago in his justly famous dictum:

I know no safe depository of the ultimate powers of the society but the people themselves; and if we think them not enlightened enough to exercise their control with a wholesome discretion, the remedy is not to take it from them but to inform their discretion.

Part of what is at risk is the promise first made on this continent: All, regardless of race or class or economic status, are entitled to a fair chance and to the tools for developing their individual powers of mind and spirit to the utmost. This promise means that all children by virtue of their own efforts, competently guided, can hope to attain the mature and informed judgment needed to secure gainful employment, and to manage their own lives, thereby serving not only their own interests but also the progress of society itself.

Indicators of the Risk

The educational dimensions of the risk before us have been amply documented in testimony received by the Commission. For example:

- International comparisons of student achievement, completed a decade ago, reveal that on 19 academic tests American students were never first or second and, in comparison with other industrialized nations, were last seven times.

- Some 23 million American adults are functionally illiterate by the simplest tests of everyday reading, writing, and comprehension.

- About 13 percent of all 17-year-olds in the United States can be considered functionally illiterate. Functional illiteracy among minority youth may run as high as 40 percent.

- Average achievement of high school students on most standardized tests is now lower than 26 years ago when Sputnik was launched.

- Over half the population of gifted students do not match their tested ability with comparable achievement in school.

- The College Board's Scholastic Aptitude Tests (SAT) demonstrate a virtually unbroken decline from 1963 to 1980. Average verbal scores fell over 50 points and average mathematics scores dropped nearly 40 points.

- College Board achievement tests also reveal consistent declines in recent years in such subjects as physics and English.

- Both the number and proportion of students demonstrating superior achievement on the SATs (i.e., those with scores of 650 or higher) have also dramatically declined.

- Many 17-year-olds do not possess the "higher order" intellectual skills we should expect of them. Nearly 40 percent cannot draw inferences from written material; only one-fifth can write a persuasive essay; and only one-third can solve a mathematics problem requiring several steps.

- There was a steady decline in science achievement scores of U.S. 17-year-olds as measured by national assessments of science in 1969, 1973, and 1977.

- Between 1975 and 1980, remedial mathematics courses in public 4-year colleges increased by 72 percent and now constitute one-quarter of all mathematics courses taught in those institutions.

- Average tested achievement of students graduating from college is also lower.

- Business and military leaders complain that they are required to spend millions of dollars on costly remedial education and training programs in such basic skills as reading, writing, spelling, and computation. The Department of the Navy, for example, reported to the Commission that one-quarter of its recent recruits cannot read at the ninth grade level, the minimum needed simply to understand written safety instructions. Without remedial work they cannot even begin, much less complete, the sophisticated training essential in much of the modern military.

These deficiencies come at a time when the demand for highly skilled workers in new fields is accelerating rapidly. For example:

- Computers and computer-controlled equipment are penetrating every aspect of our lives—homes, factories, and offices.

- One estimate indicates that by the turn of the century millions of jobs will involve laser technology and robotics.

- Technology is radically transforming a host of other occupations. They include health care, medical science, energy production, food processing, construction, and the building, repair, and maintenance of sophisticated scientific, educational, military, and industrial equipment.

Analysts examining these indicators of student performance and the demands for new skills have made some chilling observations. Educational researcher Paul Hurd concluded at the end of a thorough national survey of student achievement that within the context of the modern scientific revolution, "We are raising a new generation of Americans that is scientifically and technologically illiterate." In a similar vein, John Slaughter, a former Director of the National Science Foundation, warned of "a growing chasm between a small scientific and technological elite and a citizenry ill-informed, indeed uninformed, on issues with a science component."

But the problem does not stop there, nor do all observers see it the same way. Some worry that schools may emphasize such rudiments as reading and computation at the expense of other essential skills such as comprehension, analysis, solving problems, and drawing conclusions. Still others are concerned that an over-emphasis on technical and occupational skills will leave little time for studying the arts and humanities that so enrich daily life, help maintain civility, and develop a sense of community. Knowledge of the humanities, they maintain, must be harnessed to science and technology if the latter are to remain creative and humane, just as the humanities need to be informed by science and technology if they are to remain relevant to the human condition. Another analyst, Paul Copperman, has drawn a sobering conclusion. Until now, he has noted:

Each generation of Americans has outstripped its parents in education, in literacy, and in economic attainment. For the first time in the history of our country, the educational skills of one generation will not surpass, will not equal, will not even approach, those of their parents.

It is important, of course, to recognize that *the average citizen* today is better educated and more knowledgeable than the average citizen of a generation ago—more literate, and exposed to more mathematics, literature, and science. The positive impact of this fact on the well-being of our country and the lives of our people cannot be overstated. Nevertheless, *the average graduate* of our schools and colleges today is not as well-educated as the average graduate of 25 or 35 years ago, when a much smaller proportion of our population completed high school and college. The negative impact of this fact likewise cannot be overstated.

II. The Conversation

The effects of the ESEA and of A Nation at Risk are clear; drawing upon American values, which promise equal opportunity for all, they argue for efforts to bring that promise to fruition. And while few would disagree that assuring educational opportunities for all Americans is essential to our belief system, the crux of this debate has been about how to best achieve that goal, and to measure whether we are living up to it. The excerpts and images that follow give you a sampling of the conversations surrounding this shared national goal. These snippets of the conversation in this section will allow you to listen in as this national conversation plays out through assertions by a wide range of citizens and in visual representations of this conversation as well. Each of these participants in the conversation has something to say, and each raises another element in this ongoing conversation. Your job, as a new entrant into this conversation, is to listen for a while in order to see what is at issue and where folks agree and disagree. Drawing upon the conversation model of reading and writing discussed in the Introduction of this book, you can use active, critical reading to bring these various voices into dialogue—and so to find the *stasis points* (points of contention) in that dialogue. Then, you'll be ready to join in. Look for those facets of the conversation that most interest and affect you, and for an audience of stakeholders, a group with a vested interest in the topic, to whom you might write. Your ultimate job is to move the conversation forward with your own further research, thoughts, and writing.

conversations in context ••• 1

What does this image's use of the flag and child, and other features of layout, suggest about its message?

https://www.ocps.net/lc/southeast/mja/parents/ Pages/NCLB.aspx

"Majorities of teachers were telling us that NCLB was badly affecting teacher morale," but majorities "also said it was having a good effect on coordination in the schools. Teachers are particularly bugged by NCLB's measurement standard for schools—called Average Yearly Progress, or AYP— because it "doesn't reflect what they're really doing," Hamilton says. The AYP compares, for example, achievement by this year's fourth-grade class to last year's, and many teachers and education analysts point out that the two classes may not be comparable." [SOURCE: Testing the Tests from CQ Researcher, July 13, 2007 • Volume 17, Issue 25]

Q. What's your reaction to the news that thousands of New York City school-children were denied a summer vacation because somebody read their test scores wrong?

A. It's simply outrageous. They didn't care about the consequences for kids. It's a clear misuse of tests.

Q. How so?

A. The misuse comes when testing is in effect the sole criteria. In Chicago right now it doesn't matter what your attendance and grades are. Testing alone determines promotion. And even the people who make the tests say that's a test misuse. But standards get ignored when there's money to be made.

An Interview with Monty Neil, executive director of FairTest National Center for Fair & Open Testing

SOURCE: Katy Abel, *The Standardized Testing Debate [http://school.familyeducation.com/ college-tests/educational-testing/38358.html]*

"Our students are tested to an extent that is unprecedented in American history and unparalleled anywhere in the world. Politicians and businesspeople, determined to get tough with students and teachers, have increased the pressure to raise standardized test scores. Unfortunately, the effort to do so typically comes at the expense of more meaningful forms of learning."

SOURCE: Book jacket cover, Alfie Kohn, The Case Against Standardized Testing: Raising the Scores, Ruining the Schools *(Portsmouth, NH: Heinemann, 2000)*

Book Cover: Alfie Kohn, *The Case Against Standardized Testing*

What does this cover image say about standardized testing? Upon what iconic images does it draw? What is your emotional reaction to this image?

I am not criticizing *standardized* tests, because standardization is the key to fairness. When a test is standardized, it simply means that everyone has to take it under the same conditions. That is, you and I have to answer the same questions, in the same amount of time. As H. D. Hoover of Iowa notes, "It would not be fair to make comparisons if one student has three days to complete the test, and another has only ten minutes. Or if one student has the test questions read to him, while the other does not." Properly used, standardized tests are a source of useful information that helps teachers do a better job.

Excerpted from *Choosing Excellence: "Good Enough" Schools Are Not Good Enough* (Scarecrow Press, 2001) by John Merrow. [© 2001 by John Merrow. All rights reserved. Reprinted by permission of the author. Reprinted by PBS at: http://www.pbs.org/wgbh/pages/frontline/shows/schools/testing/merrow.html]

SOURCE: *http://family.go.com/parenting/pkg-learning/article-205674-what-every-parent-should-know-about-standardized-testing-t/*

"Kids get tested and labeled as soon as they get into kindergarten," said Lee, who runs the state-certified Alternative Preschool Solutions in Accokeek . . . "They have to pass a standardized test from the second they get in. I saw kindergartners who weren't used to taking a test, and they fell apart, crying, saying they couldn't do it. "The child who can sit and answer the questions correctly is identified as talented," Lee said. "It hurts me to have to do this, but it hurts the kids if I don't."

SOURCE: *"The Rise of the Testing Culture As Exam-Takers Get Younger, Some Say Value Is Overblown,"* by Valerie Strauss, Washington Post Staff Writer, Tuesday, October 10, 2006

These two images present differing depictions about the effect of test-taking on young children. What is the message of each? What specific details of each image suggest the argument of the image?

conversations in context ...1

"I think we have probably, as a culture and as a society, gone too far," said Michael A. Morehead, associate dean of the College of Education at New Mexico State University. "We need to really reflect on what these tests imply. They don't really evaluate character. They don't really evaluate persistence of an individual."

SOURCE: *"The Rise of the Testing Culture As Exam-Takers Get Younger, Some Say Value Is Overblown,"* By Valerie Strauss, Washington Post *Staff Writer, Tuesday, October 10, 2006*

How do the words in this cartoon reinforce the image? What does it suggest about the role of parents in the standardized testing debate?

SOURCE: DAVE COVERLY http://www.speedbump.com/ and IMAGE AT: http://images. google.com /imgres?imgurl=http://www.creators.com/comics/2/10650_thumb.gif&imgrefurl=http: //schansblog.blogspot.com/2007/10/i-wonder-what-their-mascot-would-look.html &usg=__ wtxxthYvWJbx82-0uQY1HtUKkrk= &h=349&w=315&sz=65&hl=en&start=10&um=1&itbs=1&tb-nid=PWuu2vU7vJbbHM:&tbnh=120&tbnw=108&prev=/images%3Fq%3Dstandardized%2Btesting %26um%3D1%26hl%3Den%26sa%3DN%26tbs%3Disch:1

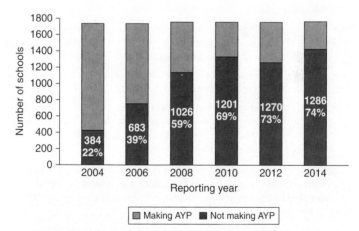

How do graphs and charts reinforce claims to objectivity in standardized testing? What does this graph suggest about the ways data from standardized tests are used?

SOURCE: http://images.google.com/imgres?imgurl=http://www.massteacher.org/ news/images/ayp_web_graph.jpg&imgrefurl=http://www.schoolsmatter.info/ 2006_08_01_ archive.html&usg=__zywVvKfqt_EHZvU_48mL0GGJ8Z0=&h= 329&w=500&sz=56&hl=en&start=16&itbs=1&tbnid=ECkujHZHWbEQUM: &tbnh=86&tbnw=130&prev=/images%3Fq%3Dannual%2Byearly%2Bprogress %2Bgraph%26hl%3Den%26gbv%3D2%26tbs%3Disch:1

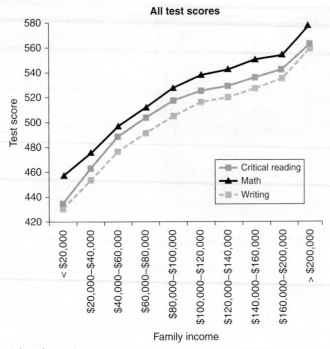

A few observations

- There's a very strong positive correlation between income and test scores. (For the math geeks out there, the R^2 for each test *average*/income range chart is about 0.95.)

- On every test section, moving up an income category was associated with an average score boost of over 12 points.

- Moving from the second-highest income group and the highest income group seemed to show the biggest score boost. However, keep in mind the top income category is uncapped, so it includes a much broader spectrum of families by wealth.

How does this image graphically represent the correlation—the relationship—between two sets of data? What argument does it seem to support regarding standardized testing, or the educational system more generally? How do the "few observations" interact with the graph?

SOURCE: http://economix.blogs.nytimes.com/2009/08/27/sat-scores-and-family-income/

What does this image suggest about the effects of No Child Left Behind? In favor of what specific facets of education does this seem to be arguing? What groups might use such an image to build their argument?

SOURCE: http://www.seattlepi.com/dayart/20040403/spin20040403.gif

III. Entering the Conversation

Now that you have some background on this important civic conversation, and have heard and seen sampling of the perspectives on the topic, it's your turn to enter the conversation. If you've been using the conversation model of reading and writing, you have kept track of the key points of debate or stasis points; you have noted the arguments being made about the value and detriments of standardized testing; and you have learned about who some of the key players in this debate are, as well as the views of other stakeholders in this dialogue.

So, while you probably have a great many personal opinions from your own experience with testing, in order to think and write in informed ways, you also need to go *beyond* personal experience. Knowing the contexts that led to the omnipresence of testing can help you better understand the reasoning behind it. That allows you to ask if those original purposes are being served—or even whether those original purposes were good ones. You can also better understand the sometimes hidden rationales for, and effects of, the use of standardized tests. There are many such reasons and many related effects, including but not limited to:

- whether standardized tests make faculty and students accountable for the learning that goes on in school, or if they take away from actual learning time;
- whether such tests provide direct measures of what students learn and retain, or if they only show a snapshot of what one knows on a given day;
- whether such tests challenge students to achieve, or if they cause undue stress upon students;

- whether tests set a standard that is important for all Americans to achieve, or if they are biased toward specific groups;

- whether the multiple-choice format of standardized tests helps to quantify knowledge in useful ways, or if it really measures the kinds of learning we value;

- whether without standardized testing we would be able to assess the consistency of education nationally (does an A at your school mean the same as an A at another school in another city?);

- whether there are other, better measures of learning; and

- whether high-stakes testing (testing that has a large influence on funding for schools and the future education and career paths of students) can develop a positive meritocracy—where hard work is rewarded—or causes teachers to "teach to the test" and/or students to focus more on testing well, and less on education for education's sake.

The list, of course, could go on; indeed, you would find many other conversations on this topic should you do more research. In any case, as you weigh in on this topic, be sure to draw upon what you have learned by seeing this conversation within the larger contexts here and to consider what other information you need to write in more informed ways on this topic. Below are a few ways for you to get started on extending the conversation about standardized testing through your own reading and research. You can use them as jumping off points. Feel free to take them in whatever directions your interests and your research take you, or to develop related topics on your own.

1. While multiple choice tests have taken a great deal of criticism over the years, one might also ask if perhaps they do have some value. In order to study this topic, you might do some research on the origins and theory behind standardized testing, asking questions like: How long have we been using multiple choice testing? Where did these tests originate, and when did they become popular? Are they accurate measures of specific kinds of learning, or are they merely used as a convenience—for easy assessment? How well do students retain the information they learn in preparing for such a test? What methods do the experts who write the tests use to insure that they are fair, challenging, and breed reliable results? What do psychologists say about the cognition that they create? What do statisticians say about the reliability of such results in measuring learning? Is there an optimum number of choices that work best on multiple choice tests? Is the multiple choice format more applicable to certain disciplines or subject areas than others? Beginning with such questions might lead you in a number of directions, allowing you to learn enough to make good judgments about the value of these tests—judgments that go beyond just your emotional reactions—and so help an audience better understand why such tests are used. Then, think about the types of research you can do, and the types of experts

that might best weigh in on this: Education specialists, statisticians, psychologists, legislators, experts at organizations like the Educational Testing Service, students, parents, and so forth, might have a good deal to say on the topic. Either focus on one of those groups (perhaps those in the field that you are studying), or try to get a range of ideas and compare their thinking on the topic. Also consider the kinds of secondary research you might do (reading the studies conducted by others) and primary research you could do (interviewing experts, parents, teachers, legislators, and so forth).

2. There has been a great deal of discussion lately about the stress put upon students, from elementary school to college, because of standardized testing. But while some studies have shown that school is one of the largest causes of student stress, others have suggested that some degree of stress can actually improve student performance. To better understand this topic, and to prepare to write about it, you might research the current thinking on this topic by experts—as well as by parents, teachers, and students—about the relationship between frequent high-stakes testing and student stress levels. Clearly, this is an issue that would be discussed by psychologists and counselors, but think about all the questions you could ask about this as well as the sources of information that you could find in other areas as well. Have teachers found that standardized testing has affected students' mental well-being? Has "test anxiety" increased over the years? Are there programs to help such anxiety? Are there strategies for reducing stress for students? Does the testing culture actually help students to cope better with tests—and succeed more—or does it build anxiety? Is it a preparation for future stresses? Does it affect certain groups more than others (consider, for example, age, ethnicity/race, gender, urban versus suburban or rural, and so forth). The more specific you are in asking these questions, the more likely that you will find a focused and specific topic about which you can garner expertise.

3. "Teaching to the test" has become a well-worn phrase that suggests that teachers—under the pressure of accountability for student success—have begun to spend more time and energy on helping students achieve high test scores and less time on helping students learn material in richer ways or develop critical thinking skills. Is this true? In order to examine this question, there are many possible lines of inquiry. First, you might ask if teaching to the test is itself a problem, or if teaching to *the right kind of test* might be beneficial. You might ask not just if, but how, teaching methods have changed due to standardized testing—and if certain kinds of content (like music or art education) have suffered, since most tests focus upon math, science, and reading. You might consider if test-taking strategies are applicable to other forms of problem-solving. And think of all the experts and stakeholders to whom you might turn to do your research, both through reading

conversations in context ...1

and primary research: the teachers and students themselves, developmental psychologists, college professors (to ask if students are more or less prepared for college learning), employers (to see if the skills learned in standardized tests are applicable, or if they've noticed a change in workers' thinking), and so forth. In order to contextualize this, you might study specifically how reports like *A Nation at Risk* or initiatives like No Child Left Behind have affected teaching methods at a particular time.

CHAPTER 2

What and Who Is College For?

W. J. Reeves

College Isn't for Everyone

W. J. Reeves is an English Professor at Brooklyn College, City University of New York. His essay draws on his experiences with students at this traditionally open-enrollment college—a college that accepts all students who apply. Reeves's essay raises questions not only about access to college, but also about whether college is the best path for all students. It was originally published in May 2003 in *USA Today Magazine*— not the newspaper of the same name, but a general-interest magazine that presents, among other things, opinion pieces on American culture. As you read, you might consider your own choice to attend college and that of others you know. Has the culture made college too much of a necessity? Are other paths better for some?

Approximately 15,000,000 Americans are enrolled in college, although about half of them probably *shouldn't be*!

During the junior year of high school, students and, to a greater extent, their parents start to fret about getting the teenager into a college. Most of these students are unable to be admitted to first-rate schools like Williams College or the Ivy League institutions, but they and their parents believe that a college education, from any school, is necessary to succeed in the 21st century. However, Edward E. Gordon reports in an article entitled "Creating Tomorrow's Work Force" (*The Futurist*, August, 2000) that 70% of the workers in the coming decades will not need a four-year college degree, but, rather, an associate degree from a community college or some type of technical certificate. Thus, moms and dads, who foot the bill, delude themselves that going to any four-year college will make their sons and daughters literate, analytical, culturally aware, technologically advanced, and therefore employable.

3   In America today, there exists a goal that the majority of the nation's youth should go to college and that access should be the byword for higher education. On the surface, this sounds like a great idea; in reality, it is not.

4   Access in its most-extreme form—open admissions—was instituted at The City University of New York during the turmoil of the 1960s. Any student who had graduated from high school, with no regard given to grade point average (GPA) and/or the SAT scores, was allowed into one of the CUNY schools. Today, while that policy is officially off the books, many of its aspects remain. CUNY is not alone in its attitude toward access. In every state, midrange colleges exist by some form of easy access, for access=numbers, and low numbers=low funding, and really low numbers=no college. Connected with access is *retention,* which means that, once inside the college, the students are more or less guaranteed graduation.

5   An examination of the relationship among access and retention and preparation for the 21st-century workplace is illuminating:

6   ***Being there.*** It is hard to be a productive worker if one appears occasionally, yet token appearances, sometimes just cameos, are tolerated in college. Jennifer Jacobson in "Rookies in the Classroom" (*The Chronicle: Career Network,* July 18, 2002) details a professor's experience with attendance: "Some of them have amazingly intricate excuses, such as one student who explained that his parent's credit card had been canceled and by the time he'd driven home to get a new card, the bookstore had sold out the texts he'd needed." In the meantime, the student had simply not come to class. One solution to this problem is to use "click-and-brick courses" (classes which combine online and in-class instruction), for being absent online is not possible.

7   ***On time.*** With regard to punctuality, Jacobson's article also tells of a fledgling professor's encounter with a student who arrived late for class with the excuse that she'd been "caught in a traffic jam after visiting a sick grandmother." After she lamented "What was I to do?," the young professor learned after class from another student that the reason for lateness was a lie and that the person being visited was the late-to-class student's "out-of-town boyfriend."

8   After four years, the bad habits of not being on time and attending sporadically have become second nature. Such habits are unlikely to make for a very productive worker.

Cultural awareness. Most liberal arts colleges tout the virtues   9
of a well-rounded education. Becoming aware of a culture usually involves reading. In my Core Literature class that covers
Western and non-Western works, the major problem is the
refusal to read the assigned texts.

Teaching can be a lonely profession when the only person in   10
the classroom who has read all of *The Scarlet Letter* is the professor. In their handbooks, many moderately difficult-to-enter
colleges state certain requirements, but many students spend
most of their time trying to get around the requirement of reading. Their methods include shortcuts (*Cliff Notes*) and cheating
(buying a paper online about an assigned work of literature).
Such evasions of becoming learned are not the hallmark of the
well-rounded.

Becoming culturally aware involves change, and change is   11
frightening. Faced with a dilemma in a play, poem, or novel,
many students become angry if pressed to offer a point of view.
Expansion of vistas is not on their agenda. They want me to provide some notes, which they, or someone, will copy or record,
and they expect me to produce a test, which, when graded,
will produce a range of grades from A to B+. An article in *The
Chronicle* (July 12, 2002), "Reports of Grade Inflation May Be
Inflated," by Catherine E. Shoichet, states that "one-third of college students receive grades of C or below" and offers this number as evidence to attack the concept of grade inflation. This is
skewed reasoning, for those students receiving C's in reality
deserve F's, and the C is given to keep them in the college. Further, of what value is a degree with a C average from a mediocre
college?

The end result is that students emerge from college with a   12
diploma which the Victorian sage Matthew Arnold would characterize as "The Grand Thing without the Grand Meaning"—*i.e.,*
merely a piece of paper.

Literacy. One would expect that, at the very least, colleges   13
would not graduate students whose writing would be gener-
ously regarded as poor. One would be wrong.

Learning to write is supposed to be taken seriously. Sean   14
Cavanagh, in an article entitled "Overhauled SAT Could Shake
up School Curriculum" (*Education Week,* July 10, 2002),
announces that the SATs will now include a writing test. Such a
requirement sounds rigorous, but appearances are deceiving.

At one time, I scored the essay section of the GMAT, the   15
required test for entrance into graduate schools of business
where one would acquire an MBA. The test-takers were college
graduates from every state and from countries around the
world. Fully two-thirds of the essays I scored would not have
passed my freshman composition class, yet I was expected to

give a score of 4 (Passing) to such writing and, apparently, the graduate schools of business accepted such students. Access again had reared its ugly head. No graduate students=no graduate school.

16 **Diversity.** Since diversity is desired, many English-as-a-second-language (ESL) students are admitted to colleges. Once there, they must take an English composition class. In my experience, the majority of these students speak English only when compelled to. They sit in my classes, all together, in self-imposed segregation, speaking in their native language.

17 Outside the class, at home, and everywhere in their existence, they converse in a language other than English. These students need to spend several years in an adult education program focused on the basics of the English language before applying to an institution of higher learning. Some of these ESL students work quite hard, but lack a basic understanding of the language. There is pressure put on professors to pass on to the world of work college graduates whose grasp of the English language is, to be kind, "shaky."

18 This is not to say that the ESL students are worse than the homegrown functional illiterates whose command of their own language is less than commanding. During the 1960s, I taught seventh-grade English in an inner-city junior high school. Now, I offer lessons on syntax and diction which I created for that junior high class to my present college classes, and I encounter failure in excess of 50%. Failing more than half of my class at the end of the semester would be asking for a public flogging. A recent case at Temple University, reported by Robin Wilson in her article, "The Teaching Equation Didn't Add Up" (*The Chronicle*, March 29, 2002), involved a tenured professor of mathematics who was fired for being an "extremely harsh grader" who was "rude" to his students. Another professor at the university remarked that "he noticed that if somebody flunks a lot of people then the administration doesn't like that, and I do what I think will not put me out on the street without a job." Translation? The inmates are running the asylum.

Solutions

19 What can be done? A college administrator could have the courage to let the word go forth that the college has admission standards and that access does not guarantee graduation. One of the state schools in New Jersey—The College of New Jersey, formerly Trenton State University—did exactly that, transforming itself from a college where admittance was rather easy into

a true institution of higher learning with high admission standards. An initial dip in enrollment occurred, but today the college is listed as one of the top bargains for a quality education in the country.

I would not count on the above scenario sweeping the country. Most administrators keep their ships of education afloat by scrounging for the few dollars that come their way from full-time equivalent students. FTEs are generated by easy access and retention.   20

A more-practical solution is for parents to find a cheap apartment some distance from the family home, deposit their son or daughter in it, along with the considerable clutter accumulated during a brief lifetime, and secure enrollment in a community college. The teachers at a community college earn a living by teaching. Therefore, the students are more likely to be taught by a full-time, professional teacher.   21

In addition, community colleges offer training in the technical fields where there are jobs. In the county in New Jersey where I live, students can obtain an associate degree in radiography and get a job. It has been estimated that 1,000,000 workers in the technical fields will be needed in the coming decades. How many job offers will come the way of a graduate of a moderately difficult-to-enter, four-year college with a 2.75 GPA in English, women's studies, or history?   22

Possibly the best course of action during senior year is to participate in one of the job cooperative programs that link high schools to the world of work. One such initiative at Allentown High School in central New Jersey is entitled the Senior Practicum. It is a for-credit class in which a student explores an interest in the workplace. The program's mission is to create an opportunity for high school seniors to learn to function as responsible, contributing adults. Serving as a rite of passage, it "provides a bridge from the traditional school structure to the self-directed, self-initiated world of adults." Participation in jobs ranging from work in retail sales to positions in a pain management clinic, the local police department, law offices, and architectural firms, students learn what is expected of them by the worth of work. After graduation, some of these students gain employment in the very business where they interned and find out that the employer will pay for their further education. However, the major benefit of such school-to-work programs is the personal growth as teenagers shed their childish ways and take a major step toward becoming adults.   23

Higher education is very expensive, taxing the resources of the already overtaxed, middle-class family. In addition to the cost, the college years are a moment in time that will never return. Again and again, in my night classes, I encounter adults, now   24 burdened with kids and dead-end jobs, who, 10 years ago, wasted their time in college with adolescent behavior. Now, they tell me, "You know, Prof, if I had just listened to you back then, but I . . ." I smile and nod and tune them out by repeating to myself the old saw: "If 'ifs' and 'buts' were ginger and nuts, what a Merry Christmas we'd all have."

25   The 19th-century novelist, and twice Prime Minister, Benjamin Disraeli wrote a book entitled *The Two Nations* which exposed the class gap in Victorian England. In 21st-century America, there is an education gap. Students with brains who have worked hard in high school can go to the top of the academic food chain and attend an Ivy League school, Stanford University, MIT, or Amherst College. Those students will lead this century. Others can receive a technical education at a local community college that will allow them to earn a good living. In his book, *Success Without a College Degree*, John T. Murphy reports that 75% of the American populace does not have a college degree, which means that those possessed of other than academic skills can find a way to succeed financially.

26   Then, there is the great, gray middle. Going to a midrange college is of value only for those students who wish to become educated and accept the fact that attendance, punctuality, and hard work are parts of the process. However, going to a college is an utter waste of time for those students who have emerged from high school neither literate nor numerate, with cultural focuses revolving around hip-hop and body piercing and with zero interest in changing their behavior. Parents should investigate one of the above solutions or invest their hard-earned dollars elsewhere while their offspring find employment in the world of the minimum wage.

Garry B. Trudeau

Doonesbury

Garry B. Trudeau (b. 1948) is one of America's most influential (and controversial) political and social commentators. His vehicle is the comic strip "Doonesbury," which appeared in more than 850 newspapers and whose audience may have exceeded 100 million readers. How does this comic strip use visuals to make its point? In what ways does it converse with the arguments made by W.J. Reeves and Thomas Reeves?

Thomas Reeves

College Isn't for Everybody, and It's a Scandal that We Think It Is

Thomas Reeves is a well-published U.S. historian who has written or edited 13 books, including a number of influential biographies. As he notes in his piece, he is a "veteran of forty years of college teaching," including his work as a Professor of History at the University of Wisconsin-Parkside until his retirement in 2001. This essay was first published by the National Association of Scholars (on whose board Reeves served) and later on the History News Network (for which Reeves wrote a twice-weekly column). Upon its 2003 publication on the History News Network, this piece bred a great deal of conversation in blog responses. As you read the piece and the responses to it which you can access on the internet by following the guidelines in the Conversations 2.0 feature which follows this reading, compare this argument to the similar one by W.J. Reeves earlier in this chapter, looking for areas of agreement and disagreement. Consider also how Reeves' perspectives might reflect changes in higher education over his 40 years of teaching service. Try to place yourself among the bloggers as well, considering how you would respond to the contentions made by Reeves and the others in this online conversation.

1   A billboard I saw recently featured the photograph of a smiling woman and under it, in large letters, the boast that she has sent nineteen young people to college. Whether this was an advertisement for a bank or a charitable organization, the thought occurred to me, a veteran of forty years of college teaching, that the act itself, while on the surface laudable, might not have been a wise investment of time and money.

2   Going to college has become a national fad, a rite of passage, millions hope, into the world of hefty salaries and McMansions. The trek to academia has now spread to the working class, who see sending their kids to college as a sign of respectability, like vacationing in Branson, Missouri, owning an SUV, and having a weed-free lawn with a gazing globe. Minorities too are getting into the act, being wooed and financially rewarded by campus

administrators to meet institutional racial quotas. But is this
crush for diplomas necessarily a good thing? Is it always a prudent investment, for the individual and for society, to be sending junior off to the dorm?

Let us consider our nineteen new college students. In the first   3
place, how many of them have the intellect and the intellectual
preparation to be serious and successful students? ACT scores
continue to decline nationally, and Richard T. Ferguson, ACT's
chief executive, urges better high school preparation. About four
in ten last year scored well enough on the test to suggest that
they could earn at least a C in a college-level math course. On
tenth grade math tests in Wisconsin recently, 76 percent of white
students attained proficiency or better, compared with 40 percent of Hispanics, and 23 percent of blacks. In Michigan, Colorado, Texas, and New York academic tests have been altered or
thrown out because of low scores. The great majority of high
schools continue to require little in exchange for their diplomas.
Hundreds of thousands enter the campus gates without a clue
about the intellectual challenges that are, or at least should be,
awaiting them.

The impact on college and university campuses of legions of   4
unprepared freshmen is never positive. Millions of dollars must
be spent annually in remedial education. And the rate of failure
is still extraordinarily high. The ACT estimates that one in four
fail or drop out after one year. A third of the freshmen at the relatively select University of Wisconsin-Madison do not return for
a second year. I toiled for decades on a Wisconsin campus on
which a mere 18 percent of the entering freshmen ever graduate. The financial costs, let alone the emotional toll on the young
people involved, is scandalous.

Even more important is the impact of intellectually unprepared   5
people on the educational process itself. Anti-intellectualism is the
Great Enemy of the educator, and with a classroom full of people
who do not read, study, or think, academic standards inevitably
suffer. In an article titled "The Classroom Game," (*Academic Questions*, Spring, 2001), I described my own tribulations with students
in an open-admissions environment. The most well-intentioned
professor cannot educate those who refuse to be educated. All too
often, such students demand that they be passed through the system and awarded a diploma, as they were in high school.

The well-documented proliferation of stuff and nonsense for   6
academic credit in large part stems from the admission of masses
of ill-prepared students. Why take a lab science, a foreign language, or (for real diversity) the history of foreign countries if
these courses aren't required? Why take classes with written
examinations and term papers when most do not? That almost
no one cares about the denigration of academic standards in
higher education is also scandalous.

7   And what colleges and universities did our nineteen students on the billboard attend? Did they go where leftist indoctrination is their daily food and drink? Probably. It is difficult to find alternatives these days. When the University of California Academic Assembly recently dropped its requirement for professors to be impartial and dispassionate, it was simply acknowledging the abandonment of efforts to be objective. A San Diego schoolteacher whose son complained about leftist bias in a class he took at the local UC campus, commented, "I'm very concerned about the changes. This gives much greater latitude to those professors who would use the classroom as a personal bully pulpit. UC students and the people of California deserve better." So do young people and taxpayers all over the country.

8   In America and all across the western world, intellectuals are enthralled with the abolition of moral and intellectual standards. In the courts and in the media, as well as the classroom, they are ramming this dogma down the throats of the vast majority. Are our nineteen students better off for being enveloped by the very poison that is slowly killing our civilization? Are we by definition doing them a favor by sending them to college? They may earn more during their lifetimes. But at what cost?

9   Shortages in skilled labor abound. Why not a billboard boasting that, say, eight of our nineteen young people have been sent to tech schools, have learned trades, and are currently in the work force leading productive lives and earning good wages? Is a machinist or a carpenter any less of a respectable American than someone who spent six years studying Mass Communications and Anthropology? In my judgment, we say so at our national peril.

10   I recently read about an auto mechanic whose high school counselor told him that he was ruining his life by opting for vocational training. The young man is now in great demand in the job market, works extremely hard, and makes over $100,000 a year. He is a happy and productive citizen. Did he waste his life? Not in this old professor's book.

Conversations 2.0: Is College for Everyone?

In the current environment, many public conversations take place in a virtual, online space. And while calling these conversations "virtual conversations" might make them seem less real or less important, that is not the case; online discussions have become one of the central locations for public debate on key issues, including the issues that are included in this book. To enrich your understanding of the conversation surrounding these and other public conversations, you can make use of the array of online discussion boards, listservs, blogs, Facebook pages, and Twitter sites that are available via the web. The Conversations 2.0 pages in this book suggest some possible ways to do so, and point out some particularly useful and credible online conversations; you of course can use your own online forums and communities to add to these suggestions.

The articles by W.J. Reeves and Thomas Reeves, as you might imagine, spurred a great deal of public conversation, including those in online forums. If you search using terms like "Is college for everyone" or "college access" or "open enrollment debate," you will find many of those discussions, some by education experts and others by private, but concerned, citizens. As you browse this series of virtual conversations, try to develop a list of the most frequent—and most convincing—arguments for allowing wide access to college or for restricting college to those who are most likely to succeed and benefit from it. You might also try posting to some of these discussion forums to see what kinds of responses that you get.

Since Thomas Reeves is an historian by trade, his article spurred a particularly active blog discussion in 2003 on the History News Network. You can find this discussion by searching "Thomas Reeves college for everyone History News Network." As you read over this conversation—much of which is quite contentious—try to find the stasis points around which this debate revolves, and in the process, sort out your own thoughts on the topic. Consider also the rhetorical situation of this debate, since most participants are other academics. How would that be likely to influence this debate?

Paul Attewell and David E. Lavin

What the Critics of "College for All" Say

Paul Attewell and David E. Lavin are both professors of sociology at the Graduate Center of the City University of New York (CUNY). Both authors have published widely on issues related to educational opportunity and its relationship to social class and mobility. Because CUNY is a pioneering institution in the open enrollment movement—which granted access to higher education to a much wider range of students—their work is clearly related to the contexts within which they work. This excerpt, which responds to the "critics of 'college for all,'" was first published in *Passing the Torch: Does Higher Education for the Disadvantaged Pay Off Across the Generations?* a book that won the Outstanding Book award of the American Educational Research Association in 2009 and also the 2009 Grawemeyer Prize in education. As you read, consider how the evidence used in this piece typifies the work of sociologists, and compare the methods of proof used here with those that are used in other selections in this section. What does the type of evidence used by each tell you about the audience and the disciplinary community of each of these writers? How does it affect the style of each writer?

1   Criticism of mass higher education is far from mono-lithic. All parts of the political spectrum, from the Marxist left to the conservative right, are represented. Nor is politics necessarily the motivation; sometimes nostalgia seems to be the driving force behind criticism. Several commentators, for example, bemoan the erosion of the traditional curriculum. William Bennett (1994) complains about a retreat from the study of ethical and civic virtues, mainstays of the classical liberal arts curriculum. Allan Bloom (1988) decries the decline of the "great books" approach. Both dislike the emergence of new disciplines such as sociology, the spread of vocational majors in college, and the expansion of the literary canon to include what they view as less-distinguished works by women and members of ethnic minorities.

2   Unfortunately, it is a short step from nostalgia to condemning the new, and another short step to blaming educational changes on the kinds of students now attending college. A widespread complaint is that the college curriculum has been "dumbed down" because colleges have admitted students who lack the skills or intelligence to cope with a rigorous curriculum (Gray and Herr 1996; Harwood 1997; MacDonald 1997, 1998, 1999; Stanfield 1997; Traub 1995). In our opinion, blaming disadvantaged students for educational change is unfair. Many of the developments that traditionalists decry—from modifications in the canon of "great books" to the spread of preprofessional majors and majors in the social and behavioral sciences to the deemphasis on moral education and the spread of postmodernism—were pioneered at elite colleges. Several of these innovations emerged during decades when student applications to those institutions were increasing, and when top colleges were becoming more selective, demanding higher intellectual standards from applicants. Those educational changes therefore had nothing to do with a decline in student quality. Nevertheless, in the popular

media, curricular changes, along with grade inflation, high dropout rates, and the prevalence of remedial course work, are all read as symptoms of a malaise in higher education and are often seen to be results of lower intellectual standards caused by wider access to public universities.

If intellectual standards have been debased, and if colleges   3
routinely graduate students who cannot write a coherent sentence, as Stanley Fish (2005) asserts, one would expect the value of a degree to be undermined. That claim was made as early as 1971, when Vice President Spiro Agnew ("Bowker for Berkeley," *Time*, April 26, 1971, 81) talked disparagingly of "100,000 devalued diplomas." Others argued that the expanded production of college graduates exceeded the number of suitable job openings, leading to undervalued and underemployed degree holders (Berg 1970; Freeman 1976). Indeed, economic theory would lead one to expect a fall in the economic value of a degree from oversupply or from a drop in quality. We will examine whether that devaluation actually came to pass in a following section.

As college enrollments climbed, a quite different type of crit-   4
icism from the left focused on equity issues, noting that students from disadvantaged backgrounds were disproportionately found in two-year associate's degree programs at community colleges. Associate's degrees are seen as inferior to bachelor's degrees. Thus, what at first seemed a democratization of higher education was arguably transformed into a kind of academic apartheid, whereby students from poorer backgrounds were relegated to a second-class education (Brint and Karabel 1989; Clark 1960; Dougherty 1994). According to such critics, students enrolled in two-year institutions might not have understood that they might get a lesser education. It takes students several semesters in a community college before some realize that they aren't going to get as far as a B.A. degree. By then, their aspirations have been lowered, in a process that Burton Clark (1960) terms "cooling out."

This notion that educators are systematically misleading dis-   5
advantaged students has been reiterated over the years. In a recent version, scholars charge that poorly prepared students in community colleges don't realize that their remedial courses carry no credit toward a degree, and that college staff members fail to alert them to this fact. Thus, weak students get bogged down taking multiple remedial courses that don't advance them toward a degree, leading many to give up and drop out. Remedial education, in this view, is a hoax perpetrated by educators upon academically weak students who will be unlikely ever to graduate (Deil-Amen and Rosenbaum 2002; Rosenbaum 2001).

One striking complaint about expanded access to college is   6
that it has undermined the work ethic of students still in high school. If any high school graduate can gain admission into

college, no matter how badly he or she performs in high school, then what incentive remains for students to study hard during their school years? "Many low-achieving high school seniors believe they can attain a college degree," James Rosenbaum has written (2001, 58). "Students who believe they can attain a college degree in spite of low achievement . . . exert little effort in high school." According to Heather MacDonald (1998), "But the greatest tragedy of open admissions occurred . . . in the city's public schools. CUNY's decision to admit any breathing human being with a record of occasional high school attendance proved a deathblow to the city's schools. Already underperforming in the 1960s, the schools had no incentive to strive."

7   Some of these criticisms about the expansion of higher education are too subjective or complex to evaluate empirically,[1] but we can extract five hard claims concerning American higher education that can be tested against the factual record:

1. Did the value of a college degree go down as student enrollments increased?
2. Are graduation rates abysmally low, especially for students with poor high school preparation?
3. Are community colleges a dead end, academically and occupationally?
4. Does remedial education imply a lack of academic standards in college?
5. Has increased access to college undermined the work ethic of students in high school?

We will marshal evidence to answer each of these questions in the following sections.

The Changing Payoff from College Attendance

8   There is a broad consensus among social scientists that college degrees have a substantial payoff in terms of annual and life-time earnings (Boesel and Fredland 1999; Card 1999; Day and Newberger 2002). As we saw in chapter 3, college attendance paid off economically for the CUNY and NLSY populations. In this chapter we will document that college pays off for those entering college with weak high school backgrounds in addition to those who enter with straight A's; and for recipients of associate's as well as bachelor's degrees. College even pays off for students who attend but fail to graduate. As one reviewer of the literature put it, "While it is clear that investment in a college degree, especially for those students in the lowest income brackets, is a financial burden, the long-term benefits to individuals as well as to society at large, appear to far outweigh the costs" (Porter 2002).

Mean Income by Educational Attainment for Male and Female
Full-Time Year-Round Workers, 1974 to 2003

Education Level	Percentage Mean Income Change 1974 to 1990 (Inflation-Adjusted)	Percentage Mean Income Change 1991 to 2003 (Inflation-Adjusted)	Mean Income in 2003
Men Twenty-five Years Old and Over			
Less than ninth grade	−12.1	−4.6	$23,972
Ninth to twelfth grade	−16.1	−1.6	$29,100
High school graduate (includes GED)	−8.4	7.8	$38,331
Some college or associate's degree	−0.4	—	—
Some college, no degree	—	9.5	$46,332
Associate's degree	—	6.8	$48,683
Bachelor's degree	6.1	20.9	$69,913
Women Twenty-five Years Old and Over			
Less than ninth grade	3.0	28.6	$20,979
Ninth to twelfth grade	5.2	8.7	$21,426
High school graduate (includes GED)	10.1	13.5	$27,956
Some college or associate's degree	16.0	—	—
Some college, no degree	—	10.5	$31,655
Associate's degree	—	10.8	$36,528
Bachelor's degree	25.6	23.8	$47,910

SOURCES: U.S. Census Bureau, Historical Income Tables P-32, P-33, P-34, and P-35 (Derived from Current Population Survey, Annual Social and Economic Survey) (U.S. Census Bureau 2004b).

Note: Owing to changes in educational attainment questions in 1991, data from 1974 to 1990 are not completely comparable with data from 1991 to 2003.

Despite a steady growth in the proportion of high school stu- 9
dents continuing on to college since the 1960s, and the burgeoning numbers of college students and graduates, the economic value of a B.A. degree has climbed over time. In the table
above we summarize a thirty-year span of education and
income data, drawing upon the U.S. Census Bureau's annual
Current Population Surveys (CPS). The data in this table are

limited to full-time year-round workers, but we also analyzed data for the years 1963 to 2003 that included part-time and part-year employees, and the same patterns prevailed. Between 1974 and 1990 the incomes of men with B.A.s who worked full-time year-round grew by 6.1 percent, adjusted for inflation. Between 1991 and 2003, male B.A. incomes increased by another 20.9 percent. The incomes of full-time working women with B.A.s rose even more dramatically over the same periods, reflecting ever greater numbers of women college graduates who stay in the labor force through their childbearing years and hold professional jobs.

10   College students who enter college but don't go as far as a B.A. have also experienced income growth over the last three decades. Prior to 1990, the surveys classified persons with A.A. degrees along with those who had some college short of a B.A. degree. Between 1974 and 1990, the incomes of full-time year-round male workers in this category stagnated (−0.4 percent in real dollars), although those of women grew by 16 percent. Since 1990, real incomes for men with an A.A. degree and those with some college short of a degree have risen by 9.5 percent and 6.8 percent, respectively.

11   Full-time year-round employees who were high school graduates have fared less well than college goers over the last three decades. Male incomes for these high school graduates dropped by 8.4 percent, adjusted for inflation, between 1974 and 1990, and have risen by 7.8 percent since. However, the mean income for women high school graduates who work full-time year round has grown substantially over this period.

12   The largest drop in income over the last four decades has occurred among men who did *not* complete high school. As table 7.1 shows, the mean income for this group dropped by 16.1 percent in inflation-corrected terms between 1974 and 1990; it has declined another 1.6 percent since then. This plunge in the real income of the least-educated workers means that the gap between college-educated and the least-educated workers has widened considerably over time.

13   In sum, there is little empirical basis for the idea that college credentials have become devalued over the last four decades, either because more people, or less able students, were going to college. That idea emerged around the time the baby boom generation entered the labor market in the early 1970s, and indeed the earnings of college graduates did drop temporarily at that time. However, the incomes of college-educated employees recovered and they have been growing in the decades since then. Employees with college education earn considerably more today than their counterparts did in the 1960s and '70s, and the gap between the economic worth of a degree and that of a high

school diploma has grown steadily wider.[2] Economic theory suggests that this pattern would not have developed if there had been a plunge in the quality of degree holders.

Nevertheless, critics of "college for all" remain convinced that   14
many students currently attending college will not benefit economically from college. Rosenbaum (2001), for example, focuses on students with weak high school achievement, and argues vehemently that they are very unlikely to gain from going to college. As evidence, he reports that the earnings of college graduates with weak high school GPAs trail those of college students who had strong GPAs in high school. That may be true, but this is not a good yardstick for assessing the value of college attendance. A better comparison contrasts weak students who went to college with classmates with identical high school grades who never went beyond high school. Did the weak students who continued into college fare better economically than their counterparts?

In the table on the following page we provide this contrast,   15
analyzing national income data solely for people who graduated high school with a C average or worse. When evaluating the value of going to college, it is important to allow enough time elapse after college for people to establish their careers.[3] Fortunately, the NLSY surveys provide earnings data for full-time workers in the year 2000, by which time the people in the sample were all thirty-five or older.

These analyses assess the effects of college attendance after   16
removing the influence of several confounding factors such as IQ, psychological orientation, race, sex, and family background.[4] In effect, we estimate the earnings of two students, both of whom had a C or below high school average and who were equivalent in intellectual and social respects, except that one went to college and the other did not.

The top panel compares academically weak students who   17
went to college, including those who did not finish college, with otherwise-equivalent students who only completed high school. The ones who went to college earned about 13 percent more per year, on average. The middle panel of table 7.2 compares academically weak students who attended college but failed to obtain a degree with equivalent students who only completed high school. Even these college dropouts earned about 10 percent more than equivalent high school graduates. The bottom panel examines community college attendance separately, because some critics appear especially skeptical about the economic prospects of weak students who enter community college. This contrast includes all C or worse students who attended community college, whether or not they completed a degree. On average, the C or worse students who attended

Long-Term Payoff to College Attendance for Students With a
C Average or Worse During High School

Earnings	Estimated Value from Conventional Regression	Estimated Value from Matched Sample
Effect of college attendance, including nongraduates (log earnings)	.1290***	.1284***
Mean personal earnings (high school only)	$24,851.91	$25,766.75
Mean personal earnings (college)	$28,273.61	$29,297.10
Number of cases	N = 2,598	N = 1,514
Effect of college attendance for nongraduates only (log earnings)	.0992***	.1071***
Mean personal earnings (high school only)	$23,537.97	$26,166.62
Mean personal earnings (incomplete college)	$25,992.66	$29,124.51
Number of cases	N = 1,814	N = 992
Effect of community college attendance, including nongraduates (log earnings)	.1346***	.1550***
Mean personal earnings (high school only)	$24,478.89	$25,900.05
Mean personal earnings (community college)	$28,006.39	$30,243.27
Number of cases	N = 2,027	N = 1,032

SOURCE: NLSY79.
Note: The log coefficients may read as percentage differences, so a
.129 coefficient implies that those attending college earned
on average 12.9 percent more than those who did not attend,
controlling for differences in family background and high school
preparation.
*p < 0.05; **p < .01; ***p < .001

community college were earning between 13 percent and 15
percent more than their counterparts who only finished high
school. All these annual earnings differences are statistically
significant.

These longitudinal analyses that followed students until they   18
were thirty-five or older document that, on average, there is a
substantial economic benefit when students with weak high
school records attend college. This payoff is evident even among
those who failed to graduate with a degree. Critics' claims that
students who are "not college material" would have been better
off economically had they not attended college are contradicted
by these analyses.

In providing these analyses, we do not mean to downplay the   19
problem of poor academic performance in high school. Many
students with low high school GPAs have to struggle to keep up
with college work, and students would progress better in college
if they improved their academic performance in high school.
Nevertheless, academically weak high school students are correct in believing they will gain economically from going to college. Their average income gain is impressive. Thus, contrary to
critics' assertions, career counselors in high school are not doing
weaker students a disservice when they encourage them to
aspire to college.

Some critics argue that our nation should build new sys-   20
tems of vocational education, revive the apprenticeship system, or build bridges from high school to work, to better serve
the career needs of high school graduates who are not academically inclined. Those are sensible proposals. At present,
however, those academically weak high school students who
do go to college are gaining economically by attending college. It makes no sense to discourage them from continuing
to college, and it is incorrect to assert that they are wasting
their time there.

Notes

1. After considering various potential indicators of the quality of undergraduate education, William G. Bowen, Martin Kurzweil, and Eugene
   Tobin (2005, 64) conclude, "We see no reliable way of answering defin-
   itively either of two questions of interest: Is American undergraduate
   education better today than in the past? And is it better than undergraduate education outside the United States?"
2. Notwithstanding the long-term increase in the value of a degree, there
   are fluctuations in the value of a college credential that are linked to
   recessions and expansions. In a recent newspaper article, the economist
   Paul Krugman ("Left Behind Economics," *New York Times*, July 14,
   2006) discusses evidence that except for the very richest strata, almost
   all Americans, including college graduates, have experienced income
   loss in the last year or two.
3. Neither the NELS88, which followed students for about eight and a
   half years after high school graduation in 1992, nor the High School
   and Beyond data, which followed students for ten years after high
   school graduation in 1982, are suitable for assessing the economic
   payoffs to different levels of higher education. Employees whose labor-
   market experience is only three or four years past completing their

degree are usually far from the earning power they will have from age thirty-five on.

4. The table on page 140 reports personal earnings data in the year 2000 for full-time workers for the NLSY data set. Regression models include the following controls: race and gender dummies, age, mother's and father's highest grade completed, family income when respondent was fourteen, mother's and father's occupational prestige when respondent was fourteen, dummies indicating whether or not respondent or parent was foreign-born, dummies indicating whether or not respondent's mother and father were employed when respondent was fourteen, respondent's high school academic GPA, the total number of academic courses respondent took in high school, respondents' self-esteem and self-mastery scale scores, respondents' Armed Forces Qualification Test score, dummies indicating whether or not respondent was married or had a child before his or her eighteenth birthday. The propensity score–matched models include these controls, as well as several interaction terms, quadratics, and dummy variables to capture nonlinear effects of these predictors. In addition, the matched cases are only paired with same-race and same-gender respondents: one who went to college, the other who did not.

Jay Mathews

Multiplying Benefits of College for Everybody

Jay Mathews (b. 1945) is an education reporter and online columnist for the Washington Post. He has also published three books on the American education system, including his 1998 *Class Struggle : What's Wrong (and Right) with America's Best Public High Schools.* In this piece, Mathews discusses Paul Attewell and David E. Lavine's *Passing the Torch* (an excerpt of which is included in this chapter) and its implications for the "college for everyone" debate. Mathews' essay, is a review of that book, but at the same time, an argument for the importance of the book's ideas. As you read, consider the way that Mathews uses the review genre to go beyond just the "thumbs up/thumbs down" stereotype, and instead places the book reviewed within the context of the larger conversation—a conversation about which Mathews himself has frequently written, and which is at the heart of this chapter's selections.

M any intelligent people don't think going to college is so 1 important. They send me emails whenever I vent about the need to prepare more low-income students for higher education. They ask a simple, excellent question: Why should college be for everybody?

They say some kids are not capable of succeeding in college. 2 They say some kids don't want to go to college. They say if everyone went to college, who would do the important non-college jobs, like plumbing and carpentry and auto repair? They say if everyone went to college, we would have a lot of unemployed college graduates—as has happened in some underdeveloped countries—with neither the skills nor the desire to work with their hands.

These are honest statements worthy of debate. My quick 3 response: Maybe there will come a day when we have more college grads than we need, and the smartest high schoolers will compete to get into the best trade schools. But at the moment only about a third of American adults have graduated from college, and the economy appears to have room for many more.

College graduates earn considerably more money over their 4 careers than non-college graduates. They have more choices about what to do with their lives, and much more flexibility if they change their minds about what is best for them. If a Hamilton College graduate with a degree in English literature decides she would prefer to become a fry cook or a midwife or a farmer, she can develop those skills relatively quickly as a paid assistant or apprentice, and still enjoy writing poetry in her spare time. But if that same young woman is told in high school that she just isn't college material, and accepts a more menial job after graduation, a late-blooming desire to earn a degree in English literature from Hamilton is going to be much more difficult, expensive and time-consuming.

But an exceptional new book has reminded me of another 5 important reason for encouraging more students to go to college—the effect that experience will have on their children. Many colleges are worrying, with good reason, about the small portion of low-income students entering their freshman classes. The book "Passing The Torch," by Paul Attewell and David E. Lavin, sociologists at the Graduate Center at the City University of New York, explains that the failure to welcome more such students into college not only reduces their chances for greater income and more choices, but ignores a golden opportunity to raise their children to a higher intellectual and social level, and increase the chances that they also will attend college.

6   Attewell and Lavin examined the impact of one of the most controversial moments in the history of American higher education—the decision in the early 1970s to guarantee all graduates of the New York City high schools admission to the 18-campus City University of New York (CUNY). They followed the low-income students who poured in the city college system and earned degrees, and then looked at what happened to them after they left college, as well as what happened to their children. They also analyzed the impact of college graduation on low-income students and their children nationally during roughly the same period.

7   The opening of CUNY to all New York high schools grads has been criticized as a wrong-headed dumbing-down of a great system with a long history of raising the brightest young people from immigrant families into the middle class. Eventually, then-Mayor Rudolph Guiliani, who objected to the university remedial courses designed to help ill-prepared freshmen, got the decision reversed, and admission became somewhat selective again.

8   But before that happened, many low-income students with inadequate high school educations got into college. Many struggled with the graduation requirements, but many also earned degrees. Attewell and Lavin make three important points about those graduates, based on a sample of about 2,000 of them, plus a much larger national sample.

9   First, the disadvantaged women who are the subject of the Attewell-Lavin study (since it was easiest to follow their children) completed college in far greater numbers than scholars predicted at the time. Half of them received bachelor's degrees, far above the overall college graduation rate of low-income American women. Some of them took a long time to accomplish this, in some cases 10 to 20 years, but they reached their goal.

10   Second, the rewards of college graduation were there for them, despite predictions that letting all these disadvantaged students into the city colleges would degrade the value of their degrees. The women who started at CUNY eventually earned as much as other women of the same age and degree in national studies, and that was considerably above what they would have earned if they had not gone to college.

11   Third, the low-income women who earned the degrees developed parenting skills that encouraged academic achievement in their children to a far greater degree than similar women who did not earn college degrees. Such skills included taking children to museums, including them in conversations and getting involved in their schools. As a consequence, their children were more likely to enroll in college than women of similar background who did not have the advantage of a chance to get to college despite their feeble high school records.

The economic benefits of college for these women, and for   12
their communities, were breathtaking. Attewell and Lavin
looked at 13,338 women whose admission to a four-year college
or to a community college was made possible by opening up the
city university system between 1970 and 1972. In the year 2000
that group made $102.6 million—an average bonus of $7,692
per person—more than researchers calculated they would have
made if they had not been given a chance at college. That extra
money was not only a benefit to them, but to the local
economies where they spent it.

Attewell and Lavin note that not all of the students admitted   13
to the city university system during open enrollment benefited
from the change and that such policies are far from a perfect
solution to the lack of academic opportunity for low-income students. In particular, they said (and I heartily agree), more needs
to be done to improve the high school preparation of disadvantaged high school students.

But they have shown this is not a zero sum game. Millions of   14
low-income Americans, their data demonstrate, have the ability
to use college to acquire new skills and capabilities that improve
their lives, and their children's lives, in a significant way.

We can argue about how many people need or want college.   15
Many do not. But there is no argument that we are not giving
nearly as many of them as we ought to a college experience.
American higher education has many flaws, but it still is one of
the greatest engines of social, economic and intellectual
advancement ever invented. It should be a national goal to give
every American, particularly those who start out in life in last
place, a shot at it. If we do that, Attewell and Lavin prove, all of
us are going to be the better for it.

Ellen Condliffe Lagemann

The Challenge of Liberty

Ellen Condliffe Lagemann is the Dean of the Harvard
University Graduate School of Education and the author of
many books on educational research, including *Private Power
for the Public Good: A History of the Carnegie Foundation for
the Advancement of Teaching* (1983), which won a Critic's
Choice Award, and more recently, *An Elusive Science: The
Troubling History of Education Research* (2000). The essay
below was first published in the Spring 2003 edition of *Liberal*

Education, the journal of the Association of American
Colleges and Universities. It explores ways that the liberal arts
and vocational education might work together, entering the
conversations about the purpose of education found in this
section as well as in the previous section on public schools.
As you read, consider how the question about who college is
for is influenced by the question of what college is for.

1   We live in a world that is fundamentally new—new in
the often fearful interconnectedness of regions,
states, and people; new in both the scope of the challenges we face in finding and sustaining peace and in the consequences we face if we fail to achieve peace; and new, too, in
the heterogeneity of the peoples with whom we live, work, and
communicate. As globalization has changed the world we
know, it has brought great opportunity and challenge and it
has added renewed vigor to old, familiar questions. One such
question is the one I would like to take up: What can we learn
from the past to enliven our thinking about liberal education
in the present and future?

2   Let me begin with two comments on the current situation of
American higher education. The first is simple. According to a
recent report of the Carnegie Corporation of New York, higher
education today is significantly more professional and technical
in orientation than it was thirty years ago. In 1970, 50 percent of
all bachelor's degrees were awarded in a liberal arts subject. In
2000, nearly 60 percent of the degrees were awarded in a preprofessional or technical field. I could multiply the statistics, but
I do not think that is necessary to make the point. Today's college
students do not have time or money to waste. They are careful
consumers. And they are voting with their feet for more vocationally oriented programs of study.

3   My second observation derives from an essay by the journalist Nicholas Lemann, called "The Kids in the Conference Room."
It is about recent college graduates, mostly from highly selective
institutions, who are recruited to work at consulting firms for at
least a few years after graduation. As Lemann put it, working for
McKinsey & Co., or some close approximate, is "the present-day
equivalent of working for the C.I.A. in the nineteen-fifties, or the
Peace Corps in the sixties, or Ralph Nader in the seventies, or
First Boston in the eighties . . . the job that encapsulates the Zeit-
geist of the moment." Lemann goes on to point out that working
for McKinsey for a few years is "an ideal placeholder" for bright
young people, who leave college with heavy debt and no certain
idea of where they want to end up vocationally.

4   To me, there is a disturbing paradox evident in the data presented in the Carnegie Corporation's report and the observation

made by Lemann. On the one hand, student course selection indicates that they want their college education to prepare them for careers. On the other hand, by contrast, those students who attend our most selective institutions—all of which, I might add, consider themselves liberal arts colleges and universities—graduate without a clear sense of vocational direction. At a time of extreme social challenge, we seem to have few alternatives between clear and, inevitably, rather narrow vocational preparation and seemingly directionless programs of liberal study. This makes me wonder whether in the challenge of our moment in history there is not a way to enliven the liberal arts by organizing them around deliberate consideration of what it means to have a vocation.

Having a Calling

The word vocation implies more than earning a living or having   5 a career. The word vocation implies having a calling: knowing who one is, what one believes, what one values, and where one stands in the world. A sense of vocation is not something fully achieved early in life. For those of us who are lucky, it grows over time, becomes more articulate, and deepens. Granting, then, that a sense of vocation develops over time, it is still not unreasonable to suggest that one purpose of a college education, and a central purpose of liberal education, should be to nurture an initial sense of vocation. This might encompass personal dispositions such as awareness of the importance of deliberate choices, individual agency, and social connection as well as recognition, albeit initial, of the ways of thinking and acting that seem most personally congenial. It should also include a capacity for civic intelligence. This requires that one recognize one's personal stake in public problems, global as well as domestic. It also necessitates respect for tolerance, the rights of others, evidence-based decision making, and deliberative judgment—in a word, respect for the values of due process that are essential to a democratic way of life. Vocation is not simply about an individual calling. It is about one's calling within one's society and, increasingly, across different societies around the world.

Historically, it is quite easy to see the power of vocation as a   6 driving force in the education of individual people. One might even venture that vocation, broadly defined, in the terms I have just described, tends usually to be the theme that links the different experiences that define an individual's education. Bearing in mind that I am trying to draw from history to help us think well about the liberal arts today and tomorrow, let me illustrate the importance of vocation by saying a few words about the education of some very well-known people.

Benjamin Franklin

7   The first person is Benjamin Franklin, who left us a wonderful record of his life in his Autobiography. Franklin was born in Puritan Boston in 1706, the tenth son and fifteenth child of Josiah Franklin and his second wife, Abiah. Intended for the ministry by his father, Ben was sent to what is now called the Boston Latin School at the age of eight. He survived only a year. The tuition at Boston Latin was high, and Ben was not sufficiently pious to make a promising candidate for the ministry. His penchant for practical efficiency led him to suggest to his father that he say grace over the family's food once for the entire year rather than before every meal. A struggling candle maker, Josiah quickly realized that Ben was not suited for the church.

8   At that point, a search for vocation began. Nothing appealed to young Ben, so, in desperation, Josiah apprenticed Ben to his older brother James, who was a printer.

9   It was as a printer's apprentice that Ben Franklin began quite self-consciously to find ways to understand who he was as a person. He did this initially by taking on the roles of people he was not. While working for his brother James, Ben wrote fourteen essays describing the complaints of a poor rural widow, whom he named Silence Dogood. In so doing, he initiated a process of self-definition that one can also see in Poor Richard's Almanac, which Franklin wrote as a prosperous printer in Philadelphia, or in reports and portraits of Franklin as a seasoned diplomat, parading around Paris dressed as a rural hick in a coonskin cap. Repeatedly throughout his life, Ben Franklin sought, defined, and clarified who he was in relation to others, by juxtaposing his own persona with those of others different from him.

Knowing Oneself

10   If what might be described as role playing was an important part of Franklin's search for vocation, so were his various deliberate attempts at self-improvement. As a young man, for example, Ben created a chart to measure his progress toward moral perfection. It began with fairly obvious virtues such as "Temperance—Eat not to dullness. Drink not to elevation." And it ended with more adventuresome ones like "Humility—Imitate Jesus and Socrates." As a Philadelphia merchant, Franklin organized the Junto, a discussion group that considered ways to better the city and then sponsored projects to carry out specific reforms and improvements. Whether charting his own progress toward perfection or examining his city's adequacy as a growing urban center, Franklin was studying who he was, what his responsibilities were as a virtuous person or a civic leader, and, especially in the case of the Junto, how actions taken for the public good

advanced not only the well-being of his fellow citizens of Philadelphia, but also his own stature as a first citizen and, increasingly, as a very wealthy printer and statesman.

If Franklin's own education was energized by an extraordinar- 11 ily self-conscious effort constantly to find a congenial, public role for himself—a vocation—so, too, were his writings about education predicated on the importance of vocation. Consider as an example, the "Proposals Relating to the Education of Youth in Pennsylvania," which was a plan for what became the University of Pennsylvania. In this document, Franklin admitted, "It would be well if [the youth of Pennsylvania] could be taught every Thing that is useful and every Thing that is ornamental." But Franklin observed: "Art is long, and [the students'] Time is short. It is therefore propos'd that they learn those Things that are likely to be most useful and most ornamental, regard being had to the Professions for which they are intended." Here, subsequent occupation became an explicit guide in the selection of the subjects to be studied.

In line with his emphasis on vocation, Franklin insisted that 12 the curriculum for the new university be modern. It was to be free of medieval anachronism. Thus, it should include contemporary writers along with the classics. Although all students should study English grammar, instruction in foreign languages should vary by future profession. Franklin did not dispense with all traditional learning, but the curriculum he generated reflected his insistent belief that, by preparing young men for a useful role in the world, advanced learning could have greater meaning for both the individual and the society of which that individual was a part (women, it was then, of course, presumed, did not need advanced education). Having been essential to his own education, vocation became a foundation for the education Franklin recommended for others.

Jane Addams

Jane Addams's life was also inspired by a search for vocation. 13 Growing up in central Illinois, Addams greatly admired her father, a prominent local lawyer and first citizen of Cedarville, Illinois, with whom she had an especially close relationship since her mother died when she was two. She recalled in her autobiography that, as a child, she had spent many hours trying to imitate her father. But, of course, Addams could not imitate her father exactly since as a woman her occupational choices were restricted.

Rather than retreat to a traditional role, Addams instead 14 embraced the fact of gender limitation and defined herself and her generation in opposition to traditional expectations. Speaking of changes in the education offered to women, as a student at

Rockford Seminary in 1881, Addams said: "[Women's education] has passed from accomplishments and the arts of pleasing, to the development of her intellectual force, and capability for direct labor. She wishes not to be a man, nor like a man, but she claims the same right to independent thought and action . . . As young women of the 19th century, we gladly claim these privileges, and proudly assert our independence . . . So we have planned to be 'Breadgivers' throughout our lives; believing . . . that the only true and honorable life is now filled with good works and honest toil . . . [we will] thus happily fulfill Woman's Noblest Mission."

15   The articulate and self-conscious search for vocation that Jane Addams was able to describe in this statement had been shaped by the formal study in which she engaged at Rockford. The curriculum, while Addams was a student there, included Latin, Greek, German, geology, astronomy, botany, medieval history, civil government, music, American literature, and evidence of Christianity. But, as her peers recalled, "the intellectual ozone" that exuded from "her vicinity" came from her unusual determination and purpose. Jane Addams's insistent wish to find a way to express her ideals and talents, despite the limitations imposed on her as a woman, was clearly an extended and successful search for vocation.

16   That search, of course, eventually led her to the West Side of Chicago, where, with Ellen Gates Starr, she founded Hull House, a world-famous social settlement that provided social, educational, and cultural services to the diverse immigrant population of that neighborhood. Hull House's fame came, in part, from the fact that Jane Addams helped to support it by writing constantly for magazines and by lecturing. But it is important to realize that it was not merely economics that drove Jane Addams's public expressions. It was both a desire to educate the educated middle-class public about how their neighbors lived and also to continue to work out for herself what she was doing and why it mattered. Questions of vocation continued to drive Jane Addams's education even after she founded Hull House.

W.E.B. Du Bois

17   As an educated woman, Addams was constrained by the fact of her sex, and yet eager to be effective in the world. One could say that she bore the burden of what her contemporary W.E.B. Du Bois called a "double consciousness." Perhaps a sense of social marginality is always at the root of soul-searching concerning who one is and where one can contribute to the common good. Certainly that was the case for Du Bois, who, throughout his long life struggled to understand whether and how he, as a black man, could be an American. Like Addams, Du Bois turned his

personal anguish about vocation into sometimes stinging, always acute social criticism. His keenest insight was probably the line that introduced the second chapter of Souls of Black Folk: "The problem of the twentieth century is the problem of the color line." However that may be, having learned as a young schoolboy in Great Barrington, Massachusetts, that he was seen as different and "a problem" by his classmates, Du Bois spent most of his ninety-five years writing about what he could and could not do as a Black American. Even at the very end of his life, when he left the United States for Ghana, Du Bois was still figuring out his place in the world.

Searching for vocation is a deep human need that different 18 cultures and different historical eras have treated differently. My suggestion here is that colleges and universities today need to acknowledge the educative drive one can see in the lives of people like W.E.B. Du Bois, Jane Addams, and Benjamin Franklin, and, recognizing the essentially vocational character of that drive, find ways to make vocational exploration central to liberal education.

Vocational Exploration and Faculty Roles

I trust that the difference I assume between vocational and occu- 19 pational exploration is clear already. Vocational exploration is about identity formation within the context of a particular society and a particular time. Occupational exploration, by contrast, is considering one's job alternatives. Vocational exploration is, in my view, the job of the faculty; occupational exploration is a matter for the office of career services.

To make vocational exploration a more important aspect of 20 liberal education, faculty will need to re-think their roles. They will need to take seriously John Dewey's admonition that if one teaches math, history, or science in school, one must remember that it is people that one is really teaching, and not the subject matter. The subject matter is the medium through which one seeks to nurture habits of deliberation and orientations toward inquiry. It is the medium through which one helps people to learn to learn. Hopefully, the subject matter of the school curriculum is also important knowledge that is worth mastering. Still, it is worth acknowledging that teaching is not merely about furnishing the mind. It is equally, if not more importantly, about shaping, energizing, and refining the mind.

This is difficult for teachers in K-12 schools to keep in mind, 21 and it is even more difficult for professors. Virtually all professors are trained as scholars. A number are now also being trained as teachers. Even when teaching is presented to graduate students as an art to be valued and mastered, it is still one's scholarly credentials that tend to get one a job, and it is certainly one's scholarly credentials that determine whether one wins tenure. Hence, it will take determined, steady work to convince faculty members that they are, first, teaching young people, and secondly, teaching some aspect of the field they profess.

22   More important, giving increased primacy to overall student development will also necessitate institutional reform. As we all know, colleges and universities, especially the most selective, are reluctant to modify the model that has helped them to thrive for more than fifty years. As Louis Menand recently observed in the New York Review of Books, from the end of World War II until quite recently, universities flourished if they gave priority to research and publication and increasingly specialized knowledge. This enabled the faculty to view their teaching and advisement responsibilities as less important than their "own work," which was fairly transparent code for going to the library or laboratory to develop new ideas.

23   Giving teaching and advisement equal priority among faculty activities will be necessary to engage faculty more centrally in the lives and vocational concerns of their students. And that is not all that will need to be altered to give more emphasis to matters of vocation.

Humanistic Values

24   Generally, today, core liberal arts subjects are taught in ways that are intended to give students an introduction to characteristic ways of thinking in a discipline, to the essential elements of an area, and, more generally, to what I would call the map of knowledge in some particular domain. All that is important. But the purposes currently most commonly associated with liberal arts study represent an unnecessarily narrow conception of why one should read Shakespeare or consider the ideas of French philosophers.

25   In addition to their canonical value, subjects like these have humanistic value. They can and should encourage thought about oneself and others and about virtue and vice—the good, the bad, and the ugly. They can and should encourage thought about vocation, in the broad sense in which I am using this word. As the philosopher William James once asserted, a liberal education should "help you . . . know a good man when you see him." That is because a liberal education, at least according to James, is not a matter of taking certain specific courses, but rather of viewing any subject in terms of its "humanistic value," its value to illuminate the human condition.

26   Of course, in many liberal arts classes there is discussion of the humanistic side of things. But without neglecting canonical perspectives, which are important for helping students locate knowledge in historical or cultural perspective, the humanistic

side of things could be given greater emphasis if faculty members spent more time talking with students about what they could learn and what they are learning about their own interests, values, and sense of person and place as well as what they are learning about the subject matter in question.

Going "meta" with students, by which I mean helping them 27 realize that they should be learning about themselves while reading *The Tempest* or debating Camus and not merely becoming culturally literate, is not something, at least in my experience, that faculty members tend to do systematically and on a regular basis. They tend not to do this because they tend not to have learned about meta-cognition. They tend not to know that it is pedagogically powerful to help students understand how and why they can learn what they are learning. Being subject-matter specialists as opposed to teachers, they tend not to touch upon the personal because they are instead inclined to focus on insuring an understanding of, say, the play's structure or meaning. Taking this one step further to capture in addition how and why the play connects to particular students is to take a step beyond a faculty member's role at least as traditionally configured. It would require pedagogical knowledge that many professors lack. But doing this would likely enhance a student's interest. It would offer a vital, personal reason for studying Shakespeare beyond knowing that somehow it is good to be "cultured."

Vocational interests can make the liberal arts more compelling 28 to students, and so can tying programs of liberal education quite directly to the world and its problems. This is happening increasingly on college campuses today as more and more institutions offer programs of service learning. More often than not, however, such programs are special courses often linked to community service of one kind or another. What I have in mind is broader.

Emerson observed that without action "thought can never 29 ripen into truth." If that is, indeed, the case, as I believe it is, then, virtually all college classes should have some kind of practicum attached to them. There is a lot of this already going on, but there needs to be more translation of classroom abstractions into action. This would enhance learning because the test of knowledge is in its application and also because constantly having opportunities to act in the world will help students develop a sense of vocation.

Having to help their students apply the models and theories 30 they were presenting in their classes would also present faculty with a salutary challenge. After all, the efficacy of a professor's ideas would be evident in his or her students' worldly competence. That is a high threshold for faculty accountability, but one that is not out of line in our times. The challenges we face domestically and globally are vast. With poverty, disease, and inequity fueling attacks on secular democracies around the world, we cannot allow colleges and universities to be home to what Alfred North Whitehead called "inert ideas." Instead, we need to encourage faculty to become engaged with the problems around us in ways that will at once contribute to our society as well as to their students and their own competence and even wisdom as scholars.

Recalling Our Mission

31   None of what I have said is very new or original. But I believe that the problems facing all of us require recalling what our collective mission is. Colleges and universities grew up across the United States for all sorts of reasons. Many were founded to insure the continuance of a particular religious group. Some were established to increase the land values in a small town. All were intended to educate people who could provide the leadership necessary to improve society. That's why the capstone experience for nineteenth century college students at liberal arts colleges was a course in moral philosophy usually taught by the college's president. The course was intended to insure that graduates would know their responsibilities as college-educated people (actually, with few exceptions, college-educated men). It provided a last chance to inculcate values and a sense of one's self as an educated citizen. It offered a final window on the opportunities and challenges then current in the locality and the region and across the United States.

32   I do not entirely live in the past and I do not think we can revive moral philosophy classes. But I do think we need to re-embrace the logic behind them. Liberal education should establish one's sense of direction, one's knowledge of one's self as an active, effective person and citizen. Liberal education should ready one to participate in the defining issues of our times. Whether it's the AIDS epidemic in southern Africa, the chaos of states like Afghanistan that lack basic civil infrastructures, or the social anomalies we observe in our own country where there are, for example, racial achievement gaps among high school students in both wealthy, racially integrated suburbs and blighted urban areas, social challenges like these should be familiar to graduates of liberal arts colleges. They should have helped to define how graduates see themselves making a difference in the world.

33   By giving renewed emphasis to their vocational purposes, liberal arts colleges and universities can help people live productively, responsibly, and well, amidst all the confusions of the present times. By making matters of vocation central to all they do, liberal arts colleges and universities can play a more direct role in improving the world. This is not to say that detached, seemingly idle speculation and abstract knowledge do not have value—great value—in institutions of liberal learning. They do. My concern is balance and underscoring the educative power of vocational interests. The famed social psychologist Kurt Lewin once said,

"there is nothing so useful as a good theory," and following this logic, I would like to close by saying: There is nothing more liberal or liberating than education approached with matters of vocation foremost in mind. Our students seem to know that. We should give them the kind of education they want and deserve.

Advertisements for The American Indian College Fund and West Hill College

The advertisements for the American Indian College Fund and for West Hill College present two different answers to the question "What and who is college for?" That argument is not only contained in words—though the words are clearly a crucial part of the message—but also in the associated images. As you "read" these advertisements, then, you will need to use several of the skills of analysis discussed in the introduction to this book. You will need to consider the audience for each, the surrounding context, and the use of both verbal and visual persuasion. First try to articulate the message each piece is trying to convey. Then, discuss the ways that the message is geared for that audience and context, describing how that message is supported by specific wordings and images. And finally, try to clarify—both for yourself and others—what each of these advertisements suggests about the reasons for attending college and perhaps where you stand on each advertisement's perspective.

Clive Crook

A Matter of Degrees: Why College Is Not an Economic Cure-All

Born in 1955 and educated at Magdalen College, Oxford and the London School of Economics, Clive Crook served as a deputy editor of *The Economist,* and is currently a senior editor for *The Atlantic Monthly,* where the following piece was published in November 2006. In this essay, Crook looks at the question of higher education with an economist's eye, considering whether the stigma of *not* attending college— more than just the lack of education—has limited the choices for those who do not attend. Has college, as some have argued, become a type of gatekeeper that determines who gets into higher social classes? And, as you read, consider how Crook would answer this section's central questions: What and who is college for?

It is unusual nowadays to venture more than five minutes 1 into any debate about the American economy—about widening income inequality, say, or threats to the country's global competitiveness, or the squeeze on the middle class— without somebody invoking the great economic cure-all: education. We must improve it. For a moment, partisan passions subside and everybody nods.

But only for a moment. How, exactly, do we improve education? 2 Where does the problem reside—in elementary schools, high schools, or colleges? Is the answer to recruit better teachers, or to get more students moving from high school to university? Should we spend more public money? Change the way schools are organized and paid for (supporting charter schools and vouchers, perhaps)? In no time, correctly orthogonal positions are laid down, and the quarreling resumes. But nobody challenges the importance of the issue. The centrality of education as a driver of the nation's economic prospects appears beyond dispute.

Yet the connections between education and economics are not 3 as they seem. To rest the case for improving schools and colleges largely on economic grounds is a mistake. It distorts education policy in unproductive ways. And though getting education right surely matters, more is at stake than a slight increase in economic growth.

4   Everybody understands that, as a rule of thumb, more school means a bigger paycheck. On average, having a college degree, rather than just a high-school degree, increases your earnings by about two-thirds. A problem arises, however, if you try to gross up these gains across the whole population. If an extra year of education equipped students with skills that increased their productivity, then giving everybody another year of school or college would indeed raise everybody's income. But take the extreme case, and suppose that the extra year brought no gain in productive skills. Suppose it merely sorted people, signaling "higher ability" to a would-be employer. Then giving an extra year of school to everybody would raise nobody's income, because nobody's position in the ordering would change. The private benefit of more education would remain, but the social benefit would be zero.

5   Would sending everybody to Harvard raise everybody's future income by the full amount of the "Harvard premium"? Yes, if the value of a degree from Harvard resided in the premium skills you acquired there (and if the college's classrooms could be scaled up a little). Well, ask any Harvard graduate about the teaching. The value of a degree from Harvard lies mainly in the sorting that happens during the application process. So the answer is no: if everybody went to Harvard, the Harvard premium would collapse.

6   In the case of an extra year of education, it need not be all or nothing; another year of study usually does impart *some* productivity-enhancing skill. But how much? A year of extra training in computer programming presumably has a direct material value. An extra year spent learning medieval history might improve a student's intellectual self-discipline and ability to think analytically, but has lower material utility: nobody studies feudal land grants for the boost to lifetime earnings. So aggregated figures such as the proportion of high-school graduates going on to college—a number that is constantly cited and compared internationally—tell you very little.

7   Totting up college matriculations as a way of measuring national success is doubly ill-conceived if the signaling function flips over, so that a college education becomes the norm, and college nonattendance is taken to mean "unfit for most jobs."

8   In 2004, 67 percent of American high-school graduates went straight on to college, compared with just under half in 1972. This is widely applauded. It looks like progress—but is it really? Failing to go to college did not always mark people out as rejects, unfit for any kind of well-paid employment. But now, increasingly, it does. In a cruel paradox, this may be one reason why parental incomes better predict children's incomes in the

United States than they used to—in other words, one reason why America is becoming less meritocratic. A college degree has become an expensive passport to good employment, one for which drive and ability less often can substitute, yet one that looks unaffordable to many poor families.

Many occupations are suffering from chronic entry-requirement   9 inflation. Hotels, for instance, used to appoint junior managers from among the more able, energetic, and presentable people on their support or service staff, and give them on-the-job training. Today, according to the Bureau of Labor Statistics, around 800 community and junior colleges offer two-year associate degrees in hotel management. In hotel chains, the norm now is to require a four-year bachelor's or master's degree in the discipline.

For countless other jobs that once required little or no formal   10 academic training—preschool teacher, medical technician, dental hygienist, physical-therapy assistant, police officer, paralegal, librarian, auditor, surveyor, software engineer, financial manager, sales manager, and on and on—employers now look for a degree. In some of these instances, in some jurisdictions, the law requires one. All of these occupations are, or soon will be, closed to nongraduates. At the very least, some of the public and private investment in additional education needs to be questioned.

To be sure, today's IT-driven world is creating a genuine need   11 for some kinds of better-educated workers. It is the shortage of such people, according to most politicians and many economists, that is causing the well-documented rise in income inequality. Both to spur the economy and to lessen inequality, they argue, the supply of college graduates needs to keep rising.

It seems plausible, but this theory too is often overstated, and   12 does not fit the facts particularly well. The college wage premium rose rapidly for many years, up to the late 1990s. Since then it has flattened off, just when the pace of innovation would have led you to expect a further acceleration. An even more awkward fact is that especially in the past decade or so, rising inequality has been driven by huge income increases at the very top of the distribution. In the wide middle, where differences in educational attainment ought to count, changes in relative earnings have been far more subdued. During the 1990s, CEO salaries roughly doubled in inflation-adjusted terms. But median pay actually went up more slowly than pay at the bottom of the earnings distribution, and even pay at the 90th percentile (highly educated workers, mostly, but not CEOs) increased only a little faster than median wages. Today, shortages of narrowly defined skills *are* apparent in specific industries or parts of industries—but simply pushing more students through any kind of college seems a poorly judged response.

13   The country will continue to need cadres of highly trained specialists in an array of technical fields. In many cases, of course, the best place to learn the necessary skills will be a university. For many and perhaps most of us, however, university education is not mainly for acquiring directly marketable skills that raise the nation's productivity. It is for securing a higher ranking in the labor market, and for cultural and intellectual enrichment. Summed across society, the first of those purposes cancels out. The second does not. That is why enlightenment, not productivity, is the chief social justification for four years at college.

14   Shoving ever more people from high school to college is not only of dubious economic value, it is unlikely to serve the cause of intellectual enrichment if the new students are reluctant or disinclined. Yet there are still large prizes to be had through educational reform—certainly in enlightenment and perhaps in productivity. They simply lurk farther down the educational ladder.

15   The most valuable attribute for young people now entering the work-force is adaptability. This generation must equip itself to change jobs readily, and the ability to retrain, whether on the job or away from the job, will be crucial. The necessary intellectual assets are acquired long before college, or not at all. Aside from self-discipline and the capacity to concentrate, they are preeminently the core-curriculum skills of literacy and numeracy.

16   Illiteracy has always cut people off from the possibility of a prosperous life, from the consolations of culture, and from full civic engagement. In the future, as horizons broaden for everybody else, people lacking these most basic skills will seem even more imprisoned. The most recent National Assessment of Adult Literacy found that 30 million adult Americans have less than basic literacy (meaning, for instance, that they find it difficult to read mail, or address an envelope). Three out of ten seniors in public high schools still fail to reach the basic-literacy standard. Progress on literacy would bring great material benefits, of course, for the people concerned and some benefits for the wider economy—but those benefits are not the main reason to make confronting illiteracy the country's highest educational priority.

17   In addressing the nation's assorted economic anxieties—over rising inequality, the stagnation of middle-class incomes, and the fading American dream of economic opportunity—education is not the longed-for cure-all. Nor is anything else. The debate about these issues will have to range all across the more bitterly disputed terrains of public policy–taxes, public spending, health care, and more. It is a pity, but in the end a consensus that blinds itself to the complexity of the issues is no use to anyone.

getting into the conversation •••2

What and Who Is College For?

1. To an increasing degree, going to college is—at least among middle- and upper-class families—considered to be a necessity. But many of the pieces in this section raise questions about that mindset. W. J. Reeves, Thomas Reeves, and Clive Crook each ask us to consider whether college is, or should be, the only path to economic and personal success. However, others such as Paul Attewell and David Lavin, as well as Ellen Lagemann, suggest that college does indeed provide important life skills, as well as economic ones, to students. Reflect on your own decision to attend college, and, in light of the readings in this section, consider whether you believe that attending college has indeed become a necessity for a secure and rewarding future, whether too much pressure has been put on young people to see college as the only route to success, and/or whether the growing percentage of students who are now attending college is the sign of a positive growth in our educational policies.

2. One of the ways that we are able to better understand a topic is to look at it from multiple perspectives and through the eyes of experts with different life and educational experiences. In this chapter of *Conversations,* you are provided with responses to the title questions ("What and Who Is College For?") from a number of perspectives— that of two college professors, a cartoonist and social critic, the dean of a College of Education, two sociologists at an open-enrollment college, an economist, a journalist, and bloggers on an online history forum. Using the headnotes for each selection to guide you (and seeking further information about the authors and their other publications if you choose to), discuss how at least two of the authors' educational background and/or job might account for the views they are taking on the topic of college education, its purposes, and the importance of granting wide access to it.

3. Not only are the perspectives and life experiences of the various authors in this chapter diverse, but so are the styles and genres within which they write. Reading as a writer (as discussed in the Introduction to this book) invites you to think not only about content, but also about style and form. While a content analysis asks you to consider the quality of the argument and its evidence, a *rhetorical* analysis asks you to consider how the argument is made. To help you focus on this form of reading, write a rhetorical analysis of the methods of persuasion used in one or several of these pieces. To do so, you should consider things like

   ■ *Audience*: To whom does this piece seem to be primarily written? What are the characteristics of that audience to which the piece seems to appeal? What kinds of evidence is this audience likely to expect, and how does the author accommodate those expectations? Even if the piece is likely to have a wide readership, try to avoid seeing it as just having a "general public" audience—there are always some specific characteristics of the intended audience revealed in both the original place of publication, the times, and the style of presentation.

- *Purpose*: What specific things does this author seem to want to accomplish in the piece? How does it hope to change readers' minds?

- *Genre*: What form does the piece take? Does it rely upon narrative (stories)? Is it written for a journalistic publication? For an academic, discipline-based journal or book publisher? Is it meant as a personal essay? Is it a "diatribe" (a bitter or sarcastic attack)? Then consider the reasons why this author would choose that genre for his or her particular audience and purpose—and whether it was a good choice.

- *Tone*: What type of persona or *ethos* (character) does the piece portray? What kind of person does the writer seem to be—and what choices seem to suggest that persona? What word choices create that tone? What point of view is used, and how does that affect the audience? How formal or informal is the writing—and thus the tone of the writer?

- *Appeals:* Three appeals to an audience are generally recognized by those who study rhetoric: (1) *ethos* (appeals to the author's own character and credibility); (2) *pathos* (appeals to the audience's emotions); and (3) *logos* (appeals to the audience's reasoning). While these three appeals usually work in combination with one another, you can sometimes identify the dominant appeal and demonstrate how that appeal makes a piece effective (or ineffective). Doing so can help you better understand the persuasive strategy of the piece and how it can also help you as a writer.

If you begin by asking questions like these and then assess the effectiveness of each of these persuasive strategies, it will help you focus upon and learn from each writer's choices—and thus help you expand your own versatility as a writer.

extending the conversation ...1

Opportunities for Reading, Writing, and Research

Though the readings in *Conversations* are organized into specific topic areas, they can also be used to start your research into other related areas of interest. The following writing opportunities suggested can help you extend the conversations across the various subjects discussed in the book—and beyond the book into research areas you might explore on your own. These examples demonstrate how you might develop the readings from this book into larger projects; you can come up with many more on your own. As you do so, think especially about how your major field of study or other interests you have can inform your research.

1. The readings in Chapter 1 ask you to consider the goals and condition of our public education system and do so in sometimes radical ways. John Taylor Gatto's examination of the fundamental purposes of education leads him to the conclusion that the system is so badly flawed that it, in fact, works counter to those principles. Others agree, in whole or part, while some suggest that the public education system is, at its heart, a successful part of our democratic culture. As a recent (or not-so-recent) graduate of our elementary and secondary education system, you are in a strong position to add your own thoughts to the conversation. You might, then, research and write a proposal that suggests a reorganization or reinforcement of the educational system based upon your own experiences there. Based upon your readings in Chapter 1 and further research that you might do, develop a plan for improving the educational policies of your own school system. Begin by developing a statement about the goals of education as you see them: Is education meant as preparation for college or work? Is it about moral and ethical decision-making? About learning basic literacies or how to become a contributing member of our democracy? Develop a set of what you take to be the most important learning goals or outcomes of education. Then, focus upon changes or enhancements to the system that we now use to build an argument for a few feasible and important changes that could be made in order to engage students in learning that will serve the goals and outcomes that you take to be most important: Would you increase opportunities for experiential learning—learning done outside of the classroom? Would you decrease class or school sizes? Would you give more, or less, freedom to teachers? How would you measure the success of your program? As you consider these questions, develop research methods that will help inform you on this topic. What kinds of primary research (interviews, polls, focus groups) might you use, and with whom? What secondary research might you do, and in what disciplinary fields? In the end, consider not only what you need to learn, but also the information that you will need to persuade those in your own school board to consider your proposals.

2. While education in a country that begins from the principle that "all men are created equal" suggests that all U.S. citizens are given the same access to education, many authors in this section raise questions about whether that is true in practice. Questions about the relationship between educational opportunity and race, ethnicity, and class are especially poignant. In order to ascertain—and write about—whether our educational system has afforded equal opportunity to all, you will need to focus upon a specific facet of our system. So, you might research the legal safeguards that are in place to assure this, including provisions in the No Child Left Behind bill. You might examine the ways that schools are funded to determine whether the same resources are afforded to all schools and their students. You might look more closely at college costs and admissions standards and their effect upon who has access to higher education. You might consider the conversation about bilingual versus English-only education, or whether both genders are being served by our system. (While until recently, the gender issue has focused upon assuring equal opportunity for women, recent conversations have begun to ponder whether men—who are not attending college in the numbers that women are—are now at a disadvantage.) Or you might consider whether assessment measures—discussed in the *Conversations in Context* section—are fair to all groups. Using a combination of primary and secondary research, write a report on the state of educational opportunity as it applies to a particular group. Be sure to support your findings with evidence of achievements, failures, and challenges faced by that group, and highlight what you take to be positive steps or the root causes of current inequities.

3. While Chapter 1 focuses upon elementary and secondary education, and Chapter 2 upon higher education, there is a good deal to be said and written about in the space between the two—how well we prepare students for the transition from one to the other. Because you are currently attempting to negotiate that transition, you might do some research on the ways that educational programs on both sides of this equation help students move from secondary to higher education. There are many ways to investigate and write about this topic. You might, for example, consider curricular issues: Does the secondary school curriculum supply students with the content knowledge to succeed in college? Does it prepare students with the necessary skills and literacies? (Here, you might consider whether the focus in many schools on standardized tests has affected students' abilities in higher order critical thinking, reading, and speaking.) Do the representations of what will be expected in college given to you by high school teachers and guidance counselors correspond with your experience of college thus far? Do children with parents or siblings who have attended college have an advantage over those who do not? You could also focus upon a particular field of study—perhaps your own discipline. So, if you are a biology major, do the scientific methods in

college seem to match those you learned in high school? If you are a business major, have the writing skills you learned in high school matched the skills required in your college classes? Have you been prepared through the high school system for the time management and study skills necessary to be a more independent learner in college? After considering these or related questions, use primary and secondary research to investigate whether the current system encourages this transition well enough and what might be put in place in order to enhance the chances of succeeding in the move from high school to college—or to work.

Conversations About Information and Technology

Introduction

You have probably heard the arguments: Internet search engines are making us reliant upon less-than-credible sources (such as Wikipedia). New media like blogs and YouTube are killing true journalism, allowing anyone with a cell phone and access to the Web to post his or her own version of the "news." Text-messaging is undermining writing skills. Twitter and Facebook are putting the most insignificant details about individuals' lives ahead of the more important civic conversations we should be having. All of these claims are based in a level of discomfort many people feel about the ways we gather and, more importantly, assess the glut of information that is now instantaneously available to most U.S. citizens. The readings in this part of *Conversations* can help you listen in to the dialogue on these important topics, and thus help you form your own thoughts on their accuracy and their significance.

We might start by acknowledging what an important topic this is for a democratic culture like ours. Democracy is largely about talk—but not in the "all talk" or "just talk" sense. A well-functioning democracy, rather, is about *productive* talk—talk that allows citizens to express areas of agreement and disagreement, and thus live within an open and responsive culture. Such a culture requires a public forum within which such conversations can be heard. But in a country as large as ours, creating a public forum to which all citizens have access is difficult.

Before new media, the responsibility for the dissemination of information, ideas, and opinions fell upon journalists, first in print and then in radio and television as well. Journalism, the so-called "fourth branch of government," provided the populace with news and comment. Since the mass media has played such a grave role in the health of our democracy, it has historically not been treated as just any other business, but one that deserves special freedoms—and that requires special ethics on the part of its practitioners. Even the founders, who could not have imagined the speed with which news can travel today, saw fit to include freedom of the press in the first constitutional amendment, but also to put checks upon the regulation of media sources. But what happens when "the "fourth branch of government" is no longer just the role of professionals who call themselves journalists, but now includes individuals who have access to the means to rapidly disseminate information and opinions to the world? Chapter 3 of *Conversations* is an extended dialogue about the changes in what we call journalism in a new media environment.

For those of you who have grown up in an Internet world, it is likely difficult to imagine that this technology, first developed in 1973 by the Defense Advanced Research Projects Agency (DARPA) and limited to uses by researchers, has been accessible to the general public for only less than 30 years. The boom in Internet technologies over the past two decades has provided American citizens with unprecedented access to information and unprecedented methods of rapid communication. Some believe that these alternative or "new" media— personal and institutional websites, e-mail, weblogs, Twitter, YouTube, and so forth—have provided important new freedoms and reenergized grassroots democratic actions. Just about any special interest you can think of is likely to have its own websites, discussion boards, chat rooms, and so forth that bring interested people from all over the country, or world, together. But critics suggest that the Web splinters our citizenry, developing so many private conversations and interest groups that a common discussion fails to take place. Others are concerned that without a critical eye, misinformation is as likely to be accepted as reliable information.

New media technologies, then, have not merely changed the ways that information is disseminated, but also have changed the product itself. Journalists have become bloggers—and bloggers journalists. As those lines are blurred, many new questions have been raised about reliability, validity, and quality of research. Each citizen can become a journalist, but can they be a responsible, informed journalist? Is this media a world of unbridled democracy, or, as one of the writers in this section has suggested, unbounded misrepresentation? Blogs have grown beyond the personal journals they once were, now challenging traditional journalism as a source of news for many Americans and becoming a central tool for political candidates. (Indeed, the election of President Obama is in many ways due to his campaign's ability to use new media technologies through his *Obama for America* site, and his attempts to forward his political agenda, through its use of the *Organizing for America* site that was built upon it.) But how reliable—and how objective—are these individual and political sites? Just as we have standards for judging the reliability and authority of researched materials when we do academic research—based on peer review by other experts—so journalism has traditionally had editors and fact-checkers to be sure that what is published is accurate. The readings in Chapter 3 will engage you in debates and the effects of this widening of access to new technologies.

Among the many sites that have made the dissemination of information more available to individuals, perhaps no other site has had the influence of Wikipedia. With its articles on over three million topics (a number that grows each day), this site has become the center of a debate about reliability of information, especially—but not limited to—the field of education. Wikipedia allows its users to write articles on a huge array of topics and to edit the entries that already exist, using wiki technology. To better participate in this debate, we must first understand this site's original intentions, the technology that drives it, and how the site's information is provided and edited by users of the site. The *Conversations in Context* section in this part of *Conversations* can help you get up to speed on those and other facets of this site's history and the ways that it functions. It will also provide you with arguments made by individuals from many perspectives that you can listen to and assess. In doing so, it can also help make you a more engaged and informed participant in this dialogue, challenging you to weigh in on the effects of Wikipedia upon the ways that we create, exchange, and judge the quality of information.

Chapter 4 focuses upon another topic related to information and technology—the effect of technology upon our minds. Many participants in this discussion fear that the easy access to information provided by technological advances have made us less judicious and less thoughtful in the ways that we process information, going so far as to suggest that search engines like Google and presentation software like PowerPoint have made us "stupid." Others, however, have argued that these technologies have, in fact, advanced our abilities as thinkers, giving us new tools with which we can expand and develop the abilities of the human mind, allowing us to reach unprecedented levels of cognition and providing powerful new ways of making effective arguments. In Chapter 4, those weighing in on this issue make it clear that there are not just two sides in the debate—for or against technology—but that the arguments are more complex and nuanced. By suggesting both the potential and the pitfalls of such technologies, they explore the changes that technology has brought to the ways we think and converse about the world around us.

Information is power, as the proverb goes. As technology expands our ability to find, process, and disseminate information, access to that power has clearly expanded. This part of *Conversations* challenges you to consider the effects of that expansion and to join the discussion about ways to use available technologies in the most thoughtful and effective ways.

CHAPTER 3

Information and Misinformation in New Media Journalism

Caryl Rivers

The New Media Politics of Emotion and Attitude

Caryl Rivers is a professor of journalism in the Boston University College of Communication. She has written a number of books about media issues including *Slick Spins and Fractured Facts: How Cultural Myths Distort the News*. Rivers contributes regularly to *The Boston Globe, Los Angeles Times, Philadelphia Inquirer, Newsday,* and other media outlets, including *The Huffington Post,* where this piece was published in late 2009. In this essay, Rivers discusses the ways that journalism has changed in an era of new media and how those changes have affected the ways that citizens interact about politics as well. As you read this piece, which introduces many topics that are discussed throughout the chapter, consider how civil argument is affected by emotions and whether pathos-laden argument has made us pay less attention to the logical and ethical (character-based) nature of our national conversation on shared issues—and our attention to reliable information. To fully experience this piece, you might also spend some time listening in to the various media outlets that Rivers discusses here.

More and more Americans are moving to "hot," emotion-laden methods of getting news, and away from cool, more objective forms of information, and this fact has already begun to affect our politics.

2   Unlike newspapers, magazines and network newscasts, 24-hour cable, talk radio, the Internet and millions of bloggers bring no hierarchical structure to the news. There is no "page one" staff meeting to determine what's important and what's trivial. The critical issue is what's available now, and what's sexy or sensational. The long term impact of a story matters not in a universe in which everything is forgotten by the next two or three news cycles.

3   With cable, as with talk radio, the medium really is the message, as Marshall McLuhan once famously declaimed. Who remembers what Rush Limbaugh, Keith Olberman, Glenn Beck or Sean Hannity actually said? What lingers is the emotion and the attitude, and at whom these are directed. There is little sense of proportion in the disapproval that results. Did Obama create death squads to kill grannies? Did he bow too low to the president of Japan and thus dishonor America? A bow and a death sentence are approached with a comparable degree of outrage.

4   Both stories leach into the coverage by the mainstream media. The sheer sound and fury generated by the emotional media forces the "objective" media to desert their usual judgments and plunge into the fray, at least to some degree. The pot is continually being stirred, in our living rooms, on our car radios and when we surf the net. Attitudes are being constructed, not from facts, but from feelings.

5   This isn't entirely new. The late Lee Atwater, the Republican consultant who masterminded the media strategy of George HW Bush against Michael Dukakis, understood the power of emotion versus that of rationality. Dukakis, the respected governor of Massachusetts, was a hands-on guy who understood systems and the way they worked. The state was often looked to as a model of the way government programs should be run.

6   But Atwater found one flaw in what was otherwise regarded as an excellent—and fairly tough—criminal justice system. He found Willie Horton, a murderer who had been furloughed, and while out of jail had committed a rape. Atwater said "by the time this election is over, Willie Horton will be a household name." Another consultant, Roger Ailes (now head of Fox news,) added, "the only question is whether we depict Willie Horton with a knife in his hand or without it."

7   Dukakis may have been the first victim of the emotionalizing of the media. The Willie Horton ad—which brought a scowling, bearded black felon into white living rooms—was widely credited with dissolving an early Dukakis lead in the race.

8   Today, with all the instant news media, we could have a Willie Horton every other day—and sometimes it seems that we do. Scandal and scorn have crowded out the news that has real impact on people's lives.

This makes Washington an increasingly toxic place. When I   9
first started out covering national politics, DC was in many ways
an amiable place. The political parties had enormous power and
old bulls ran the congress with an iron hand. "To get along, you
go along," as Sam Rayburn said. Senators and congressmen
brought their families to DC with them, and there was a great
deal of across-the-aisle fraternizing. The press, on the whole,
focused on policy and politics and mainly ignored scandal.
Everyone in Kennedy's press corps knew about the president's
affairs, but would not think of writing about them. The idea that
reporters could bring down a president—as Woodward and
Bernstein would do with Nixon—was unimaginable.

The affable Washington had its major drawbacks—one being   10
that with segregationist Southern senators holding so much
power, civil rights legislation couldn't get passed.

But our system is designed to work by consensus. We do not   11
have a parliamentary system like the Brits have, where the Ins
get to do most of what they want until they are the Outs again.
We seem to do best with two "big tent" parties where enough
legislators can be cobbled together to actually get something
done. Missing that, there's gridlock.

The new emotional media are the friends of the ideological   12
purists, not the go-along-and-get-along types. If you can keep
the base frothing at the mouth, you can also keep legislators
who are inclined to compromise from straying too far from the
fringes. As I write, senator Lindsey Graham of South Carolina
is being attacked by right-wingers for working on a bill with
(gasp!) John Kerry.

Politics and media based on emotion just make people crazier   13
and more vulnerable to manipulation. My daughter-in-law was
asked by a neighbor in Houston to sign a petition directing
Texas to secede from the union. She told the neighbor that the
state could not do that. There was this thing called the Civil War.

"Glen Beck says we can," the neighbor replied.   14

The celebrities of TV news used to be the opposite of Beck,   15
calm and rational types. There was avuncular Walter Cronkite,
the most trusted man in America, Huntley and Brinkley, never
losing their heads in a storm, and others of that ilk. David Hal-
berstam once called the nightly TV news shows "Our national
evening séance." But the audiences for the network news shows
are dropping, just as newspapers rapidly lose circulation. More
and more, audiences are fracturing into smaller pieces where
emotion is the stock in trade.

A media and politics of emotion leave the national agenda in   16
a prolonged stall. Constant invective drives down the approval
rating of presidents, making it harder for them to use the bully
pulpit. If this trend continues, we may see a series of one-term
presidents, and a series of failed initiatives on the national agenda.

This will come at a time when the nation faces urgent issues such as climate change, the loss of jobs from globalization and a major recession, and the growth of terrorism.

17   Once, we prided ourselves on being a "can do" country, able to come together to win World War II, to build a national highway system, to go to the moon. As the media and politics of emotion turn us into squabbling camps, paralysis will soon be our most salient national characteristic.

Matt Welch

Blogworld and Its Gravity

Matt Welch is an American journalist and blogger, and a supporter of the Libertarian movement, which consistently seeks smaller, less intrusive government practices and forwards individual liberty and responsibility. According to the national platform of the Libertarian Party, this group seeks "a world in which all individuals are sovereign over their own lives, and no one is forced to sacrifice his or her values for the benefit of others." Welch is the editor-in-chief of Reason Magazine (which shares the Libertarian agenda), has served as an editorial page editor for *The Los Angeles Times,* and has written for many other publications, including *ESPN, The Los Angeles Daily News, Salon,* and the *Columbia Journalism Review* (where this essay was first published in 2003). As you read Welch's essay, consider the ways in which Welch characterizes and envisions the role of blogging within the larger world of post 9/11 journalism, and whether his predictions seem to have been borne out in the years since. You might also compare his perspectives on the role of bloggers with those in the exchange between Frank Partsch and Jeff Jarvis, included later in the chapter.

1   This February, I attended my first Association of Alternative Newsweeklies conference, in the great media incubator of San Francisco. It's impossible to walk a single block of that storied town without feeling the ghosts of great contrarian media innovators past: Hearst and Twain, Hinckle and Wenner, Rossetto and Talbot. But after twelve hours with the AAN, a much different reality set in: never in my life have I seen a more conformist gathering of journalists.

All the newspapers looked the same—same format, same 2
fonts, same columns complaining about the local daily, same sex
advice, same five-thousand-word hole for the cover story. The
people were largely the same, too: all but maybe 2 percent of the
city-slicker journalists in attendance were white; the vast majority were either Boomer hippies or Gen X slackers. Several asked
me the exact same question with the same suspicious looks on
their faces: "So . . . what's your alternative experience?"

At the bar, I started a discussion about what specific attributes 3
qualified these papers, and the forty-seven-year-old publishing
genre that spawned them, to continue meriting the adjective
"alternative." Alternative to what? To the straight-laced "objectivity" and pyramid-style writing of daily newspapers? New Journalists and other narrative storytellers crashed those gates long
ago. Alternative to society's oppressive intolerance toward
deviant behavior? Tell it to the Osbournes, as they watch *Queer
Eye for the Straight Guy*. Something to do with corporate ownership? Not unless "alternative" no longer applies to *Village Voice
Media* (owned in part by *Goldman Sachs*) or the New Times chain
(which has been involved in some brutal acquisition and liqui-
dation deals). Someone at the table lamely offered up "a sense of
community," but Fox News could easily clear that particular bar.

No, it must have something to do with political slant—or, to 4
be technically accurate, political correctness. Richard Karpel,
the AAN executive director, joined the conversation, so I put him
on the spot: Of all the weeklies his organization had rejected for
membership on political grounds, which one was the best edi-
torially? The *Independent Florida Sun*, he replied. Good-looking
paper, some sharp writing but, well, it was just too friendly
toward the church. "And if there's anything we all agree on,"
Karpel said with a smile, "it's that we're antichurch."

I assumed he was joking—that couldn't be all we have left 5
from the legacy of Norman Mailer, Art Kunkin, Paul Krassner,
and my other childhood heroes, could it? Then later I looked up
the AAN's Web site to read the admission committee's rejection
notes for the *Florida Sun* (which was excluded by a vote of 9–2).
"The right-wing church columnist has no place in AAN,"
explained one judge. "All the God-and-flag shit disturbs me,"
wrote another. "Weirdly right-wing," chimed a third.

The original alternative papers were not at all this politically 6
monochromatic, despite entering the world at a time when
Lenny Bruce was being prosecuted for obscenity, Tom Dooley
was proselytizing for American intervention in Vietnam, and
Republicans ruled the nation's editorial pages. Dan Wolf,
cofounder of the trailblazing *Village Voice*, loved to throw darts
at what he called "the dull pieties of official liberalism," and
founding editors like Mailer were forever trying to tune their
antennae to previously undetected political frequencies.

7   The dull pieties of official progressivism is one of many attributes that show how modern alt weeklies have strayed from what made them alternative in the first place. The papers once embraced amateur writers; now they are firmly established in the journalistic pecking order, with the salaries and professional standards to match. They once championed the slogan "never trust anyone over thirty"; now their average reader is over forty and aging fast. They have become so ubiquitous in cities over a certain size, during decades when so many other new media formats have sprung up (cable television, newsletters, talk radio, business journals, Web sites), that the very notion that they represent a crucial "alternative" to a monolithic journalism establishment now strains credulity.

8   But there still exists a publishing format that manages to embody all these lost qualities, and more—the Weblog. The average blog, needless to say, pales in comparison to a 1957 issue of the *Voice*, or a 1964 *Los Angeles Free Press*, or a 2003 Lexington, Kentucky, *ACE Weekly*, for that matter. But that's missing the point. Blogging technology has, for the first time in history, given the average Jane the ability to write, edit, design, and publish her own editorial product—to be read and responded to by millions of people, potentially—for around $0 to $200 a year. It has begun to deliver on some of the wild promises about the Internet that were heard in the 1990s. Never before have so many passionate outsiders—hundreds of thousands, at minimum—stormed the ramparts of professional journalism.

9   And these amateurs, especially the ones focusing on news and current events, are doing some fascinating things. Many are connecting intimately with readers in a way reminiscent of old-style metro columnists or the liveliest of the New Journalists. Others are staking the narrowest of editorial claims as their own—appellate court rulings, new media proliferation in Tehran, the intersection of hip-hop and libertarianism—and covering them like no one else. They are forever fact-checking the daylights out of truth-fudging ideologues like Ann Coulter and Michael Moore, and sifting through the biases of the *BBC* and Bill O'Reilly, often while cheerfully acknowledging and/or demonstrating their own lopsided political sympathies. At this instant, all over the world, bloggers are busy popularizing under-appreciated print journalists (like *Chicago Sun-Times* columnist Mark Steyn), pumping up stories that should be getting more attention (like the Trent Lott debacle), and perhaps most excitingly of all, committing impressive, spontaneous acts of decentralized journalism.

Blogging's Big Bang

10   Every significant new publishing phenomenon has been mid-wifed by a great leap forward in printing technology. The

movable-type printing press begat the Gutenberg Bible, which begat the Renaissance. Moving from rags to pulp paved the way for Hearst and Pulitzer. The birth of alternative newspapers coincided almost perfectly with the development of the offset press. Laser printers and desktop publishing ushered in the newsletter and the 'zine, and helped spawn the business journal.

When it burst onto the scene just ten years ago, the World   11
Wide Web promised to be an even cheaper version of desktop publishing. And for many people it was, but you still had to learn HTML coding, which was inscrutable enough to make one long for the days of typesetting and paste-up. By the late 1990s, I owned a few Web domains and made a living writing about online journalism, yet if I really needed to publish something on my own, I'd print up a Word file and take it down to the local copy shop. Web publishing was theoretically possible and cheap (if you used a hosting service like Tripod), but it just wasn't easy for people as dull-witted as I.

In August 1999, Pyra Labs changed all that, with a product   12
called Blogger (responsible, as much as anything, for that terrible four-letter word). As much of the world knows by now, "Weblog" is usually defined as a Web site where information is updated frequently and presented in reverse chronological order (newest stuff on top). Typically, each post contains one and often several hyperlinks to other Web sites and stories, and usually there is a standing list of links to the author's favorite bookmarks. Pyra Labs, since bought out by *Google*, had a revolutionary insight that made all this popular: every technological requirement of Web publishing—graphic design, simple coding for things like links, hosting—is a barrier to entry, keeping nontechies out; why not remove them? Blogger gave users a for-dummies choice of templates, an easy-to-navigate five-minute registration process, and (perhaps best of all) Web hosting. All for free. You didn't even need to buy your own domain; simply make sure joesixpack.blogspot.com wasn't taken, pick a template, and off you go.

The concept took off, and new blogging companies like Live-   13
journal, UserLand, and Movable Type scrambled to compete. Blogger cofounders Evan Williams, Paul Bausch, and Meg Hourihan, along with Web designer Jason Kottke, and tech writer Rebecca Blood—these were the stars of the first major mainstream-media feature about blogging, a November 2000 *New Yorker* story by Rebecca Mead, who christened the phenomenon "the CB radio of the Dave Eggers generation."

Like just about everything else, blogging changed forever on   14
September 11, 2001. The destruction of the World Trade Center and the attack on the Pentagon created a huge appetite on the part of the public to be part of *The Conversation*, to vent and analyze and publicly ponder or mourn. Many, too, were unsatisfied

with what they read and saw in the mainstream media. Glenn Reynolds, proprietor of the wildly popular InstaPundit.com blog, thought the mainstream analysis was terrible. "All the talking heads . . . kept saying that 'we're gonna have to grow up, we're gonna have to give up a lot of our freedoms,'" he says. "Or it was the 'Why do they hate us' sort of teeth-gnashing. And I think there was a deep dissatisfaction with that." The daily op-ed diet of Column Left and Column Right often fell way off the mark. "It's time for the United Nations to get the hell out of town. And take with it CNN war-slut Christiane Amanpour," the *New York Post*'s Andrea Peyser seethed on September 21. "We forgive you; we reject vengeance," Colman McCarthy whimpered to the terrorists in the *Los Angeles Times* September 17. September 11 was the impetus for my own blog (mattwelch.com/warblog.html). Jeff Jarvis, who was trapped in the WTC dust cloud on September 11, started his a few days later. "I had a personal story I needed to tell," said Jarvis, a former *San Francisco Examiner* columnist, founding editor of *Entertainment Weekly*, and current president and creative director of Advance.net, which is the Internet wing of the Conde Nast empire. "Then lo and behold! I discovered people were linking to me and talking about my story, so I joined this great conversation."

15   He wasn't alone. Reynolds, a hyper-kinetic University of Tennessee law professor and occasional columnist who produces techno records in his spare time, had launched InstaPundit the month before. On September 11, his traffic jumped from 1,600 visitors to almost 4,200; now it averages 100,000 per weekday. With his prolific posting pace—dozens of links a day, each with comments ranging from a word to several paragraphs—and a deliberate ethic of driving traffic to new blogs from all over the political spectrum, Reynolds quickly became the "Blogfather" of a newly coined genre of sites: the warblogs. "I think people were looking for context, they were looking for stuff that wasn't dumb," he said. "They were looking for stuff that seemed to them to be consistent with how Americans ought to respond to something like this."

16   There had been plenty of news-and-opinion Weblogs previously—from political journalists such as Joshua Micah Marshall, Mickey Kaus, Andrew Sullivan, and Virginia Postrel; not to mention "amateurs" like Matt Drudge. But September 11 drew unpaid nonprofessionals into the current-events fray. And like the first alternative publishers, who eagerly sought out and formed a network with like-minded mavericks across the country, the post-September 11 Webloggers spent considerable energy propping up their new comrades and encouraging their readers to join the fun. I'd guess 90 percent of my most vocal early readers have gone on to start sites of their own. In April 2002 Reynolds asked InstaPundit readers to let him know if he had inspired any of them to start

their own blogs. Nearly two hundred wrote in. (Imagine two hundred people deciding to become a columnist just because Maureen Dowd was so persuasive.) Meanwhile, Blogger alone has more than 1.5 million registered users, and Livejournal reports 1.2 million. No one knows how many active blogs there are worldwide, but Blogcount (yes, a blog that counts blogs) guesses between 2.4 million and 2.9 million. Freedom of the press belongs to nearly 3 million people.

What's the Point?

So what have these people contributed to journalism? Four   17
things: personality, eyewitness testimony, editorial filtering, and uncounted gigabytes of new knowledge.

"Why are Weblogs popular?" asks Jarvis, whose company has   18
launched four dozen of them, ranging from beachcams on the Jersey shore to a temporary blog during the latest Iraq war. "I think it's because they have something to say. In a media world that's otherwise leached of opinions and life, there's so much life in them."

For all the history made by newspapers between 1960 and   19
2000, the profession was also busy contracting, standardizing, and homogenizing. Most cities now have their monopolist daily, their alt weekly or two, their business journal. Journalism is done a certain way, by a certain kind of people. Bloggers are basically oblivious to such traditions, so reading the best of them is like receiving a bracing slap in the face. It's a reminder that America is far more diverse and iconoclastic than its newsrooms.

After two years of reading Weblogs, my short list of favorite   20
news commentators in the world now includes an Air Force mechanic (Paul Palubicki of *sgtstryker.com*), a punk rock singer-songwriter (Dr. Frank of *doktorfrank.com*), a twenty-four-year-old Norwegian programmer (Bjorn Staerk of *http://bearstrong. net/warblog/index.html*), and a cranky libertarian journalist from Alberta, Canada (Colby Cosh). Outsiders with vivid writing styles and unique viewpoints have risen to the top of the blog heap and begun vaulting into mainstream media. Less than two years ago, Elizabeth Spiers was a tech-stock analyst for a hedge fund who at night wrote sharp-tongued observations about Manhattan life on her personal blog; now she's the It Girl of New York media, lancing her colleagues at *Gawker.com*, while doing free-lance work for the *Times*, the *New York Post*, *Radar*, and other publications. Salam Pax, a pseudonymous young gay Iraqi architect who made hearts flutter with his idiosyncratic personal descriptions of Baghdad before and after the war, now writes columns for *The Guardian* and in July signed a book deal with Grove/Atlantic. Steven Den Beste, a middle-aged unemployed software engineer in San Diego, has been spinning out thousands

of words of international analysis most every day for the last two years; recently he has been seen in the online edition of *The Wall Street Journal*.

21   With personality and an online audience, meanwhile, comes a kind of reader interaction far more intense and personal than anything comparable in print. Once, when I had the poor taste to mention in my blog that I was going through a rough financial period, readers sent me more than $1,000 in two days. Far more important, the intimacy and network effects of the blog-world enable you to meet people beyond your typical circle and political affiliation, sometimes with specialized knowledge of interest to you. "It exposes you to worlds that most people, let alone reporters, never interact with," says Jarvis, whose personal blog (*buzzmachine.com*) has morphed into a one-stop shop for catching up on Iranian and Iraqi bloggers, some of whom he has now met online or face to face.

22   Such specialization and filtering is one of the form's key functions. Many bloggers, like the estimable Jim Romenesko, with his popular journalism forum on Poynter's site, focus like a laser beam on one microcategory, and provide simple links to the day's relevant news. There are scores dealing with ever-narrower categories of media alone, from a site that obsesses over the *San Francisco Chronicle (ChronWatch.com)*, to one that keeps the heat on newspaper ombudsmen (*OmbudsGod. blogspot.com*). Charles Johnson, a Los Angeles Web designer, has built a huge and intensely loyal audience by spotting and vilifying venalities in the Arab press (*littlegreenfootballs.com/weblog*). And individual news events, such as the Iraq war, spark their own temporary group blogs, where five or ten or more people all contribute links to minute-by-minute breaking news. Sometimes the single most must-see publication on a given topic will have been created the day before.

23   Besides introducing valuable new sources of information to readers, these sites are also forcing their proprietors to act like journalists: choosing stories, judging the credibility of sources, writing headlines, taking pictures, developing prose styles, dealing with readers, building audience, weighing libel considerations, and occasionally conducting informed investigations on their own. Thousands of amateurs are learning how we do our work, becoming in the process more sophisticated readers and sharper critics. For lazy columnists and defensive gatekeepers, it can seem as if the hounds from a mediocre hell have been unleashed. But for curious professionals, it is a marvelous opportunity and entertaining spectacle; they discover what the audience finds important and encounter specialists who can rip apart the work of many a generalist. More than just A. J. Liebling-style press criticism, journalists finally have something approaching real peer review, in all its brutality. If they truly value the scientific method, they should

rejoice. Blogs can bring a collective intelligence to bear on a question.

And when the decentralized fact-checking army kicks into gear, 24 it can be an impressive thing to behold. On March 30, veteran British war correspondent Robert Fisk, who has been accused so often of anti-American bias and sloppiness by bloggers that his last name has become a verb (meaning, roughly, "to disprove loudly, point by point"), reported that a bomb hitting a crowded Baghdad market and killing dozens must have been fired by U.S. troops because of some Western numerals he found on a piece of twisted metal lying nearby. Australian blogger Tim Blair, a free-lance journalist, reprinted the partial numbers and asked his military-knowledgeable readers for insight. Within twenty-four hours, more than a dozen readers with specialized knowledge (retired Air Force, former Naval Air Systems Command employees, others) had written in describing the weapon (U.S. high-speed antiradiation missile), manufacturer (*Raytheon*), launch point (F-16), and dozens of other minute details not seen in press accounts days and weeks later. Their conclusion, much as it pained them to say so: Fisk was probably right.

In December 2001 a University of New Hampshire Economics and Women's Studies professor named Marc Herold pub- 25 lished a study, based mostly on press clippings, that estimated 3,767 civilians had died as a result of American military action in Afghanistan. Within a day, blogger Bruce Rolston, a Canadian military reservist, had already shot holes through Herold's methodology, noting that he conflated "casualties" with "fatalities," double-counted single events, and depended heavily on dubious news sources. Over the next two days, several other bloggers cut Herold's work to ribbons. Yet for the next month, Herold's study was presented not just as fact, but as an understatement, by the *Guardian,* as well as the *New Jersey Star-Ledger, The Hartford Courant,* and several other newspapers. When news organizations on the ground later conducted their surveys of Afghan civilian deaths, most set the number at closer to 1,000.

But the typical group fact-check is not necessarily a matter of 26 war. Bloggers were out in the lead in exposing the questionable research and behavior of gun-studying academics Michael Bellesiles and John Lott Jr. (the former resigned last year from *Emory University* after a blogger-propelled investigation found that he falsified data in his antigun book, *Arming America*; the latter, author of the pro-gun book, *More Guns, Less Crime,* was forced by bloggers to admit that he had no copies of his own controversial self-defense study he had repeatedly cited as proving his case, and that he had masqueraded in online gun-rights discussions as a vociferous John Lott supporter named "Mary Rosh"). The fact-checking bloggers have uncovered misleading use of quotations by opinion columnists, such as Maureen Dowd, and jumped all over the inaccurate or irresponsible comments of various 2004 presidential candidates. They have become part of the journalism conversation.

Breathing in Blogworld

27 Which is not to say that 90 percent of news-related blogs aren't crap. First of all, 90 percent of any new form of expression tends to be mediocre (think of band demos, or the cringe-inducing underground papers of years gone by), and judging a medium by its worst practitioners is not very sporting. Still, almost every criticism about blogs is valid—they often are filled with cheap shots, bad spelling, the worst kind of confirmation bias, and an extremely off-putting sense of self-worth (one that this article will do nothing to alleviate). But the "blogosphere," as many like to pompously call it, is too large and too varied to be defined as a single thing, and the action at the top 10 percent is among the most exciting new trends the profession has seen in a while. Are bloggers journalists? Will they soon replace newspapers?

28 The best answer to those two questions is: those are two really dumb questions; enough hot air has been expended in their name already.

29 A more productive, tangible line of inquiry is: Is journalism being produced by blogs, is it interesting, and how should journalists react to it? The answers, by my lights, are "yes," "yes," and "in many ways." After a slow start, news organizations are beginning to embrace the form. Tech journalists, such as the *San Jose Mercury News*'s Dan Gillmor, launched Weblogs long before "blogger" was a household word. Beat reporting is a natural fit for a blog—reporters can collect standing links to sites of interest, dribble out stories and anecdotes that don't necessarily belong in the paper, and attract a specific like-minded readership. One of the best such sites going is the recently created California Insider blog by the *Sacramento Bee*'s excellent political columnist, Daniel Weintraub, who has been covering the state's wacky recall news like a blanket. Blogs also make sense for opinion publications, such as the *National Review, The American Prospect,* and my employer, *Reason,* all of which have lively sites.

30 For those with time to notice, blogs are also a great cheap farm system for talent. You've got tens of thousands of potential columnists writing for free, fueled by passion, operating in a free market where the cream rises quickly.

31 Best of all, perhaps, the phenomenon is simply entertaining. When do you last recall reading some writer and thinking "damn, he sure looks like he's having fun"? It's what buttoned-down reporters thought of their long-haired brethren back in the 1960s. The 2003 version may not be so immediately identifiable on sight—and that may be the most promising development of all.

Rachel Smolkin

The Expanding Blogosphere

Rachel Smolkin, editor and writer for the American Journalism Review, explores the sometimes thin line in the "blogosphere" between activist and journalist, between the right to publish one's opinion and the responsibility to be accurate and true to the ideals of journalism. As you read this piece, consider how the issues raised here might, or should, influence the ways we interact with that which we read in blogs. What responsibilities does it place on readers? How does this set of ideas figure into the debate between Frank Partsch and Jeff Jarvis, also included in this section of *Conversations?*

W hen political bloggers bay in the blogosphere, do po- 1
litical reporters hear them?

The answer, I quickly learned, depends on four factors: how 2
you define "political blog"; which political bloggers you mean; which political reporters you mean; and—not to go all Bill Clinton on you—what the meaning of "hear" is.

Blog, for the uninitiated, is shorthand for "Web log," online 3
journals of thought and commentary. They feature a personal, distinctive voice, links to other sources and regular postings displayed in reverse chronological order with the newest entry first. Readers scroll down the screen to scan the blogs, which often include a place for reader input, archives of past entries and "blogrolls," lists of other blogs the author finds useful.

Political bloggers chew over the news of the day, frequently 4
skewering journalists' coverage or spotlighting what they feel are undercovered stories. Objectivity is generally verboten in the blogosphere, although ideology tends to be less rigid than the partisan debates that play out so repetitiously in newspapers and on television. And bloggers are a clubby bunch, referencing and linking to each other even when ideologies clash.

A few hours into my research, I felt a rising sense of panic— 5
there was SO MUCH OUT THERE.

There are the rock stars of political blogging—Glenn H. 6
Reynolds (www.instapundit.com), Andrew Sullivan (www. andrewsullivan.com), Joshua Micah Marshall (www. talkingpointsmemo.com) and Mickey Kaus (www.kausfiles. com)—moody maestros who stroke their keyboards more quietly but no less fervently than Coldplay's Chris Martin.

There are amateurs and pros and semi-pros and group blogs 7
and pure blogs and media blogs and blog-like-journals-that-

aren't-really-blogs-or-kinda-are-depending-on-your-point-of-view. There are more blogs out there than any one person could reasonably hope to read or even find. After new software made blogging easy and free in 1999, the phenomenon took off. The September 11 attacks and their aftermath spawned another wave of political blogs.

8   "The people are now talking," says Jeff Jarvis, the blogger behind Buzzmachine.com and president of Advance.net, which runs online services for Newhouse Newspapers. "The people are blogging. Millions of them are blogging."

9   Yes, in these hardened, cynical times, amid angst over media conglomerates and homogenization of news, political junkies are using cyberspace to opine and whine, to preach and beseech.

10   And the news media are gingerly following the people's lead. The line between pure political bloggers and "Big Journalism," as Reynolds calls it, is fading.

11   "Big Journalism," the target of so much contempt and derision in the blogosphere, is borrowing elements of blogs, experimenting with them and sometimes even co-opting the bloggers themselves.

12   Kaus, a former writer for *The New Republic* and *Newsweek*, moved his once independent Kausfiles to *Slate*, a Microsoft-owned online magazine, in May 2002. *The Washington Monthly*, a small but influential politics and policy magazine, hired blogger Kevin Drum in March. Reynolds blogs for MSNBC.com in addition to writing his own InstaPundit blog.

13   The conservative magazine *National Review* hosts a group blog called The Corner; the liberal magazine *The American Prospect* countered with Tapped. In September, the *Prospect* hired blogger Matthew Yglesias as a writing fellow; he now blogs for Tapped in addition to his own site.

14   Some journalists' blogs favor reported tidbits and analysis over swashbuckling commentary. Daniel Weintraub, a public affairs columnist at the *Sacramento Bee*, helped set the tone for coverage during his state's recall race with his California Insider blog. *The New Republic's* Ryan Lizza blogs about the presidential race on the magazine's Campaign Journal site. Even the *New York Times* has launched an edited campaign blog of sorts, Times on the Trail, which is breezier than the paper but more straitlaced than most blogs.

15   Political blogs add to the cacophony of 24/7 information sources available to journalists and the public. While cable news endlessly repeats political headlines, Weblogs chatter over inside information that mesmerizes the junkies.

16   "What Weblogs do, both professional and amateur, is they help spread detailed political information all day long," says Jonathan Dube, managing producer for MSNBC.com and publisher of CyberJournalist.net, an American Press Institute site tracking online journalism.

Dube believes amateur blogs have fostered public involvement   17
in politics and enhanced political dialogue. But he cautions, "It's
hard for people to weed through and know what is opinion,
what is fact. It may contribute to the spreading of misinformation and to misperceptions and to spin."

Bloggers and their defenders argue that their medium is ide-   18
ally suited to fixing errors because corrections can be posted
immediately rather than waiting until the next day's paper.
But the blogosphere has dished up its share of misinformation
and spin.

When Internet gossip columnist Matt Drudge in February   19
posted an unsubstantiated rumor of a John Kerry affair, it surfaced on Wonkette.com, The Corner and other blogs. The Drudge
Report itself often is considered a blog or at least blog-like.

While the mainstream news media overplayed Gov. Howard   20
Dean's scream, the blogosphere positively wallowed in it, setting
it to music and boogeying to its beat.

And bloggers' predictions about the primaries were just as   21
inaccurate, but less restrained, as those of newspaper and television pundits. Kaus held a "Kerry Withdrawal Contest" before the
primaries to "help" Kerry drop out of the race, saying he "faces
not just defeat but utter humiliation in the New Hampshire primary." That was, of course, before Kerry triumphed in New
Hampshire and quickly wrapped up the Democratic nomination.

Kaus notes that he suspended his contest after Saddam Hus-   22
sein was captured because he figured it gave candidates who
voted for war a "fresh opening." And, as Kaus once wrote, bloggers get to "go off half-cocked," trust their instincts and change
their minds later if they're wrong. He believes that this clash of
"insta-takes" from many sources on the Web gets to the truth
more quickly than the traditional, more contemplative method
of analysis long employed by political journalists such as the
Washington Post's David Broder.

If bloggers don't always get to the truth, they are at least bang-   23
ing out their beliefs with a pitch fevered enough to attract some
attention.

Walter Shapiro, a political columnist for *USA Today* and a   24
reader of blogs, says blogs collectively are "definitely having an
impact" on political journalism, "but we haven't figured out what
the impact is. About all these trends we get too gushy on the way
up, and too dismissive on the way down. And we're sort of in the
middle age on blogs, at least in Andy Warhol terms." As Warhol
showed, all "forms of communication get modified in the marketplace," Shapiro observes. Some of the blogs' "original functions have been absorbed by Web sites or people far removed
from the lonely law professor at the University of Tennessee."

That lonely Tennessee professor is Reynolds, who teaches con-   25
stitutional and Internet law. He was inspired by early bloggers

such as Kaus; Sullivan, a former editor of *The New Republic;* and Virginia Postrel, a *New York Times* economics columnist and former editor of *Reason* magazine.

26   In August 2001, Reynolds started InstaPundit, now among the most heavily visited political blogs. "Bloggers have very little power," says Reynolds. "What they have is influence. They have an ability to get ideas noticed that would otherwise be ignored and to shame people"—namely journalists—"into doing their jobs better."

27   Reynolds, who also started a paid blog for MSNBC.com in January 2003, notes "the blogosphere is pretty hard on big journalism, and I think rightly so. But most of the problems of big journalism is institutional . . . My experience with big-name journalists in general is that most of them are very supportive and encouraging."

28   Reynolds repeated an assertion that I heard often from bloggers and blogging enthusiasts: "There's not much doubt that most political journalists read a lot of the blogs."

29   Mark Halperin, ABC News political director and coauthor of The Note, reads political blogs and says many of his colleagues do as well. In April, on the morning of Bush's third prime-time news conference, The Note counseled readers: "Watch the blogs for insta-reaction."

30   But Halperin doesn't like hearing the popular online political trove he helps write called a blog, even though it shares some stylistic features. "A blog to me is opinion and observations from one brain," Halperin says. "We are producing news and analysis from a group of people across ABC News . . . We're not about opinions generating from one brain."

31   Some political reporters say they don't pay much attention to bloggers. "I must confess I don't track a whole lot of them," says *Washington Post* national political reporter Jim VandeHei, although readers do occasionally e-mail him about blogs trashing his work. "I would challenge someone to point to me where they've really had that much influence on the coverage." Noting the proliferation of sources for news commentary and roundup, VandeHei says Web surfing could easily consume all of a reporter's time, and "at some point, you really actually have to pick up the phone and do some reporting."

32   Ron Brownstein, a *Los Angeles Times* national political correspondent and CNN political analyst, reads campaign blogs, but that's about it. "There's just so much information out there," he says. "I feel like we're talking to ourselves with most of that stuff."

33   *New York Times* national political reporter Adam Nagourney says he's constantly surfing the Web, but he's doing Google searches or reading the online sites of newspapers or magazines. He does keep on eye on *The New Republic's* campaign blog and

sometimes looks at Talking Points Memo or InstaPundit, but not
regularly. "Otherwise I would spend all my day reading,"
Nagourney says, "and some of the stuff on the Web is so out
there that it doesn't really help to read it."

Nagourney's colleague Jodi Wilgoren, the *Times'* Chicago   34
bureau chief who also is covering the presidential campaign,
was the subject of The Wilgoren Watch, a blog dedicated to
"deconstructing" her coverage of Howard Dean.

"I'm not a journalist and never pretended to be," the unnamed   35
blogger wrote on January 11. "I'm just a guy (veterinarian by
trade) living in Northern Virginia who supports Gov. Howard
Dean in his run for the White House and happens to know a
little about HTML . . . I'm a lifelong Democrat who—like many
of us—was caught off guard by the degree to which Al Gore was
mistreated by the media in 2000. I just want to do my little part
to mount a little 'pre-emption' in case the same treatment is
applied to Gov. Dean this time around."

Dean's supporters, the self-proclaimed "Dean Defense Forces,"   36
launched what they dubbed an "Adopt-a-Journalist" effort, and
blogs also targeted Associated Press reporter Nedra Pickler, who
covered Dean. But media accounts have tended to focus on the
Wilgoren Watch. "I think mine got more attention because of
the alliteration. I know that sounds ridiculous," says Wilgoren,
who signed up to receive e-mail notification of new postings. "If
people were writing about my work and talking about my work,
I wanted to know what they were saying."

Wilgoren's fiancé and father were angered by what were some-   37
times very personal attacks against her. But she suggested they
suppress their urges to defend her and warned of "Lemon-
Lyman" syndrome—a reference to an episode of NBC's "The
West Wing" in which Deputy Chief of Staff Josh Lyman writes
to correct a Web site and becomes the target of a cyber frenzy.
"Beware of writing back," Wilgoren counseled. "No good can
come of it."

The reader feedback she received through Wilgoren Watch as   38
well as other blogs and e-mails "typically did not reflect much
knowledge about or understanding of mainstream journalism,"
Wilgoren says, and often came from passionate Dean supporters. "I got many, many letters accusing me of being a tool of the
Republican administration or trying to destroy Howard Dean."

She tracked Dean's Blog For America, has glanced at the   39
Kerry blog, "although it seems not to have much bite to it," and
has seen the liberal blog Daily Kos (www. dailykos. com). But
asked about InstaPandit, that blogging giant, Wilgoren replies,
"I've never been on InstaPundit. I don't even know what that is."

One newspaper fan of InstaPundit is *USA Today* columnist   40
Shapiro. "Any time John Ashcroft is in the news, I'm checking
Glenn Reynolds three times a day," says Shapiro, who enjoys the

right-leaning blogger's "libertarian skepticism of the conduct of the war on terror." And Shapiro reads the blog of Kaus, a longtime friend, "religiously."

41   Howard Fineman, *Newsweek's* chief political correspondent and an analyst for NBC, also looks at Kausfiles—Kaus is a friend and former *Newsweek* colleague—as well as at Sullivan's and Marshall's blogs.

42   Fineman says blogs give him a "feel for the conversation going on in the country about politics" and he reads them for the "same reason I try not to sit on my tush inside the Beltway, and get outside the Beltway as much as possible. Cyberspace is a place you need to go."

43   Karen Tumulty, *Time* magazine's national political correspondent, last October asked Dean's chief blogger, Mathew Gross, to recommend some blogs. She bookmarked some of them, including InstaPundit, Talking Points Memo and Daily Kos.

44   Tumulty's "absolute, total guilty pleasure is Wonkette," a biting politics and D.C. social scene blog authored by Ana Marie Cox. (The New York Times on April 18 described the blog by Cox, a self-proclaimed "failed journalist," as "gossipy, raunchy, potty-mouthed," a review Cox proudly posted on her site.)

45   Blogs are a "good indicator of what's in the political bloodstream at any given moment," says Tumulty, who adds that a turning point in blogs' impact came when National Journal's influential political newsletter Hotline began citing them. Tumulty likens reading blogs to "sitting around with a bunch of political reporters and having a beer—without the buzz."

46   Ryan Lizza, a reporter for *The New Republic* covering the presidential campaign, says he reads blogs "pretty religiously. I have a list of 10 or 15 blogs that I check in with at least once a day." Lizza thinks "one really smart blog that deserves to get more attention" is The Decembrist (markschmitt.typepad.com), which "tends to be more thoughtful, more of an essay style." But he cautions that "you don't want to get too wrapped up in what some parts of the blogosphere are obsessing about, because it can sometimes be this self-contained world."

47   In addition to writing for *The New Republic*, Lizza started a blog just before the primaries as an outlet for tidbits and other material that might not hold for a week until the print edition (www.tnr.com/blog/campaignjournal). "It's a little different," he says. "It's not a blog in the sense that it's a list of things that Ryan Lizza has read out there on the Internet. I'm trying to keep it more reportorial and not just a list of random thoughts."

48   Lizza has used his blog to break news. On April 2 he happened to be on the phone with Jim Margolis, Kerry's admaker, when Margolis said he was leaving the Kerry campaign and read Lizza a prepared statement. "It was a very inside story, but kind of cool because you could break it and put it on the blog," says Lizza,

who posted the news at 12:22 p.m. that day, beating the Associated Press with the scooplet by 11 minutes.

At the New York Times, Wilgoren learned about Margolis' 49 departure when a colleague e-mailed her Lizza's post. "My guess is that everybody who wrote about this heard about it" from there, Wilgoren says. "It seemed that everybody I called about Margolis had read Ryan's thing. So he broke news on the blog."

But in the annals of bloggers' impact on political journalism, 50 one story stands above the rest. It sired breathless newspaper articles about the burgeoning influence of bloggers and even inspired a Harvard University case study.

On December 5, 2002, then-Senate Majority Leader Trent Lott, 51 a Mississippi Republican, remarked at a birthday party for retiring Republican Sen. Strom Thurmond of South Carolina that the nation "wouldn't have had all these problems over all these years" had Thurmond triumphed in his 1948 segregationist bid for the presidency.

Initially, the media largely ignored Lott's shocking faux pas. 52 But ABC News aired a brief story at 4:30 a.m. on December 6 and described the incident on The Note, which other Internet sites then referenced, according to a study by Esther Scott, a case writer for Harvard's John F. Kennedy School of Government.

The blogosphere seized on Lott's comments, howling with 53 outrage and sleuthing for similar outrageous statements from Lott's past. "Oh, what could have been!!!" opined a sarcastic Josh Marshall on December 6, 2002. "Just another example of the hubris now reigning among Capitol Hill Republicans."

Bloggers on the right also were enraged. "Trent Lott Must Go," 54 declared a December 9, 2002, posting by Andrew Sullivan that called on the Republican Party to "get rid" of Lott as majority leader or "come out formally as a party that regrets desegregation and civil rights for African-Americans."

During the Lott post-mortem, the media paid homage to blog- 55 gers for refusing to let the story fade. "The papers did not make note of his comments until days after he had made them," observed a December 23, 2002, Time magazine cover story by Dan Goodgame and Tumulty. "But the stillness was broken by the bum of Internet 'bloggers' who were posting their outrage and compiling rap sheets of Lott's earlier comments."

New York Post columnist John Podhoretz wrote on December 56 13, 2002, that, "There's nothing more exciting than watching a new medium mature before your eyes . . . The drumbeat that turned this story into a major calamity for Lott, and led directly to President Bush's welcome disavowal of Lott's views yesterday was entirely driven by the Internet blogosphere."

Scott's study was somewhat more circumspect, concluding it 57 was difficult to determine how "much of the story made its way from the blogs—as opposed to other Internet sources such as

The Note—into the mainstream." But she found "anecdotal evidence" that some reporters and columnists picked up the story from a blog.

58   "The mainstream media had sort of a blind spot on that story, and it was really left to a number of blogs to keep the story going" says Marshall, a former Washington editor for *The American Prospect* whose thoughtful site won praise from several journalists interviewed for this article. But he cautions that it's easy to exaggerate bloggers' impact and describes them as "part of an ecosystem of news sources. They have a niche."

59   Media companies are experimenting with their own place in this expanding ecosystem. Leonard M. Apcar, editor in chief of NYTimes.com, doesn't describe his online roundup of campaign news, Times on the Trail, as a blog. But he says he was influenced by blogs and tried to borrow some elements to create "our own special space" about the campaign, which debuted in January (www.nytimes.com/onthetrail).

60   "If you define blogs as unedited opinion and sometimes just passing on rumors, that's not what Times on the Trail is," Apcar says. "We are edited: we're not opinion as much as we are analysis, and we don't report rumors . . . Blog purists would say this is not a blog. Call it a blog. Call it a flog. I don't care. We call it Times on the Trail."

61   When the *Sacramento Bee's* Daniel Weintraub started his California Insider blog in April 2003, the serendipitous (for him) recall contest soon offered a rare opportunity to showcase his new medium. (See *Free Press*, December/January.) His blog has provided an additional venue for communicating with sources. People Weintraub knows through his reporting read his blog and send him unsolicited ideas and responses. "You can't put out 100 telephone calls a day, but you can put something on the Web that people can read and either take the time to e-mail or call," he says.

62   But a few weeks before the recall election, some of Weintraub's writings about candidate Cruz Bustamante stirred criticism among Latino politicians, and some of his newsroom colleagues objected to the double standard for editing.

63   Editorial Page Editor David Holwerk decided that an editor would clear blog entries as with print columns to preserve the newspaper's obligations to credibility and accuracy. The blogosphere greeted his decision with outrage.

64   Weintraub says he may subconsciously eschew more trivial items to avoid wasting his editors' time on something completely lighthearted or fluffy. "It's probably not as light and spontaneous," he says. "It's a little more formal . . . But it's not like I'm holding back on commentary or anything significant." He also has noticed some friction between blogging and some of the

"historical norms" of print journalism: Print journalists don't particularly like to acknowledge competitors' work, but bloggers do so regularly.

One amateur political blogger stumbled over stricter rules in   65
another professional arena, that of politics. Markos Moulitsas Zuniga, 32, author of the Daily Kos, majored in journalism at Northern Illinois University, edited the student newspaper and freelanced for the *Chicago Tribune*. He graduated from law school and headed to Silicon Valley to make millions in the dot-com world, a venture that "didn't go well at all." Moulitsas, who was raised in El Salvador and served in the U.S. Army, started the Daily Kos in May 2002—drawing from his Army nickname, which rhymes with "rose."

He and his business partner, Jerome Armstrong, worked as   66
paid consultants to Dean's campaign: Moulitsas now consults for "a couple Democratic congressional campaigns and interest groups," though he declines to specify which ones.

His reluctance is perhaps understandable given an April con-   67
troversy that Moulitsas touched off with a callous observation about four American contractors killed in Iraq. "I feel nothing over the death of mercenaries," he wrote. "Screw them."

Moulitsas later clarified his remarks but stopped short of an   68
apology, and a cyberspace furor ensued. "Kos has been rather a weasel about first making the comments, then hiding them, then issuing a bogus pseudo-apology, and now—as if there were more to this than dumb statements on a blog that led to some angry commentary and e-mail—he's playing the victim," Reynolds declared on InstaPundit.

The Kerry campaign dropped its link to Daily Kos, and some   69
candidates pulled their advertisements from his blog. *The Washington Post* mentioned the brouhaha in an April 18 story that described how some political candidates are turning to blogs as a new, cheap venue for ads.

Moulitsas asserts, "I can write about whatever I want without   70
somebody telling me I can't talk about an issue. At the end of the day, I don't need advertisers."

He proudly proclaims himself an activist, not a journalist. "My   71
God, if I was a journalist, I'd be breaking half the canon of jour-nalistic ethics," Moulitsas says wryly. "I am one walking conflict of interest. I am the epitome of conflict of interest, but at least I don't pretend otherwise, like Cokie Roberts taking money from trade groups and talking before them." (ABC News' Roberts was criticized in the mid-1990s for accepting large fees for giving speeches to trade associations—see "Talk Is Expensive," May 1994, and "Take the Money and Talk," June 1995.)

Kevin Drum, a self-described "centrist liberal" and one of   72
the more contemplative bloggers, spent two decades as a

software-marketing executive before launching his blog in August 2002. In mid-March, he agreed to blog for The Washington Monthly (www.washingtonmonthly.com).

73   His unedited blog is a comfortable fit with the magazine's advocacy. But Drum notes that bloggers such as Reynolds and the anonymous Atrios (www.atrios.blogspot.com) are not nearly so sober, and that style "is part of what makes blogs a lot of fun." Drum worries "if you try to put the rules of mainstream journalism onto blogs, you end up sucking the life out of them."

74   While professional journalism has standards for sourcing and reporting, with blogs, the whole point "is that the standards are lower," Drum says. "They're able to toss stuff out that a reporter on a daily newspaper couldn't. They express opinions loudly and with fervor. It's not clear to me how those two things can intersect."

75   Drum, who holds a journalism degree from California State University, Long Beach, admits to "some doubt about whether blogging and professional journalism can go together . . . If it turns out at the end of the year that the five most popular blogs are associated with professional journalism, it would change the nature of blogging."

76   USA Today's Walter Shapiro also wonders whether blogs will change because of their success. "We don't know where this is going," Shapiro says. "But what we do know is there are not enough eyes and enough hours to support the entire blog world" at its current level.

77   "I have real affection for the underlying notion here of the original blogs, which were people sitting at their computers, reading the morning news and commenting on it," he adds. "And that lonely person element there, the one voice, is something that, however this all evolves, I hope will not be lost."

David Weinberger

Blogs and the Values of Journalism

David Weinberger, editor of *The Journal of Hyperlinked Organizations,* and a philosopher by training, has published in *The New York Times,* the *Harvard Business Review, Salon, Wired,* and *Smithsonian.* Weinberger has also served as a fellow at the Berkman Center for Internet and Society at Harvard Law School and was named Senior Internet Advisor to Howard Dean's 2004 presidential campaign. He is the author of *Everything Is Miscellaneous: The Power of the New Digital Disorder.* In this essay, first published in 2005 in *KM Magazine,* Weinberger explores the challenges to journalism posed by blogs and other Internet publications, questioning whether the aura of objectivity that has long been at the center of journalism is becoming a thing of the past because it "tries to remove the reporter's point of view." As you read, you might consider whether knowing the author's stance and point of view is useful to readers, or whether it has—as Caryl Rivers suggests—made for more contentious conversations.

For me, the defining moment at the "Blogging, Journalism and Credibility" conference held recently at Harvard (harvard.edu) came in an exchange between Jimmy Wales, creator of Wikipedia (wikipedia.org), and Jill Abramson, managing editor of *The New York Times* (nytimes.com). Abramson was responding to the idea that blogs could displace traditional newsgathering organizations. "Do you know how much it takes to run our Baghdad operation?" she asked. "One million dollars." 1

Wales responded that the Encyclopedia Britannica is a $350 million operation but Wikipedia is "kicking its butt." 2

Several of the media people there reacted with hostility. But the way I took Wales comment, he was saying something the established media ought to heed: Don't be so sure. Recent experience shows that having a large investment and being the established leader isn't absolute protection. So, be careful: Somewhere there might be a Wikipedia waiting to dethrone you. 3

Many of the representatives of the mass media in the room couldn't hear what Wales was saying for the usual, and very human, reasons: Not only do people want to ignore vague, dire warnings, but our own assumptions usually look like eternal verities. For a couple of centuries, newspapers have assumed that their value consists in fielding an organization that covers the world. Journalists are highly trained, dedicated professionals. It's easy for amateurs, like webloggers, to underestimate what it takes to get journalists everywhere they need to be and to underestimate just how demanding a craft journalism is. 4

And that's true. It is easy to underestimate both those facts. But it's also easy to overestimate how fiercely our culture will hold on to existing values. If you want to create a newspaper that reads like *The New York Times* (for example) and has the same standards of quality and accountability as *The Times,* you will have to spend billions of dollars. But, it's possible that we'd be willing to exchange some of those values for others. Maybe we'd trade the objectivity of *The Times'* faceless reporters—oh, sure, a few have become celebrities, but *The Times* works against that—for livelier, more personal writing. Maybe we'd be willing to trade the polished stories in which reporters pull together 5 quotes and ideas for greater access to the voices of those they are interviewing. Maybe, and maybe not. The point is that newspapers like *The Times* rightfully pride themselves on maintaining certain values, and so long as those are the values the populace cherishes, *The Times* will rule. But if those values change, anything could happen.

6   I believe two values in particular are in transition: voice and transparency.

7   The Net is getting us used to hearing people speaking in a natural tone of voice, each unique. Reportage, on the other hand, is written in the voiceless voice of objectivity that strips out the reporter's unique point of view and way of talking. That, I think, is beginning to sound more and more artificial to many of us. Newspapers already accommodate voice-y writing: op-eds, reviews and features. There will, I believe, be pressure on newspapers to write more reportage as features. This not only personalizes the article, it gives us readers inadvertent metadata that enables us to account for the inevitable biases and points of view of the author.

8   The second value that's changing is transparency, i.e., letting us see through an article to its sources and to the author writing it. Already a few journalists are posting the complete interviews from which they drew a story. And it would be helpful to know more about an author so we can get a sense of who she is and how she thinks. Transparency accomplishes some of the same goals as the attempt to be objective: Objectivity tries to remove the reporter's point of view, while transparency tries to make that point of view obvious so we can compensate for it as we read the story.

9   Most of the journalists that I've met chose their profession because they have a commitment to making democracy better. They are idealists in one of the most intensely pragmatic jobs ever. They're sure not doing it for the money or the great hours. That sort of dedication can only be underestimated. It can't be replaced. So, while I genuinely don't know what the media landscape will look like in 10 years, I am confident that journalists—and their values—will remain at the core of how we learn about our world.

Frank Partsch

Unbounded Misrepresentation

Frank Partsch served as the editorial page director of the *Omaha World-Herald,* and is a former member of the National Conference of Editorial Writers. In this brief piece,

Partsch defines the traditional understanding of the editorial genre and argues for its continuing importance in an age of blogging, which he compares to graffiti. Consider how Partsch's profession and his organizational ties inform this defense of the editorial genre, and how Jeff Jarvis's response that follows likewise defends his own turf as a blogger.

n the world as it once existed, an editorial had particular   1
marks by which it might be known.

It was institutional. Thus, it represented the views or com-   2
ments of not just an institution but also its owner or investors—
people who were willing each day to exercise leadership in the
community even at the risk of putting their investment on the
line. This characteristic of an institutional voice constituted a
tie to the community, its prosperity, and its quality of life.

It was considered. The institution, from the top down, had a   3
point of view. Editors and editorial writers consulted with publishers. An effort was made to achieve consistency over time, thus
presenting the community one voice, among all other voices, that
could be relied on as a touchstone.

It rose or fell on its record of accuracy and sound judgment.   4

Of course it was presented without signature. An institutional   5
opinion with one person's byline is an oxymoron.

And it is true that editors often did no fresh reporting. Some   6
editors follow the philosophy that the editorial should be a logic-
driven outgrowth from known facts. Others, of course, are frustrated by the lack of detail they get from the news side and thus
break news on their own. Both approaches have their merits.

Critics of editorial pages who have never gone inside an edito-   7
rial page office, perhaps including Jarvis, toss off our function as
"telling people how to think." I have never heard an editorial
writer claim to be doing that. We try to bring facts and arguments
to the fore, based on our institutional platform and the fact that
our sole occupation is (or should be) thinking and writing. It is a
misstatement, as others in this thread have noted, that we exist
to trumpet our own opinion and stifle or disrespect all others.

I have deep personal concerns about what seems to be inatten-   8
tion, among some editorial pages, to sound thinking and clear
writing. If we are losing readers, it's not because of an insufficient
amount of white space or display type but rather because of an
insufficient percentage of intelligent, stylishly stated text in our
institutional opinions. Such inadequacies as pointing out the
obvious, vacillating, and understating (or over-stating) the point
of view have never attracted respect, and they aren't about to start.

But this is a matter entirely separate from the utterances of the   9
blogging-is-the-new-journalism people. In a nutshell, editorial

writers speak for institutions; a blogger speaks only for herself. Her online opinion is indistinguishable from a shout in the crowd, and the posts proclaiming agreement no different from other shouts in the crowd.

10 Certainly shouts in the crowd can have some effect, and there's a danger that they may crowd editorial writing from the stage unless the practitioners of the craft elevate editorial page writing and thinking (as well as accommodating the public's changing needs in an era of technological change).

11 But a blog entry is no more an editorial than is graffiti. Few editorial pages would stoop to the caricaturing of a target and then attacking the caricature. But that's what happened here. Jarvis's attempts to force a comparison, so that the one might replace the other, are rooted in unbounded misrepresentation.

Jeff Jarvis

Response to Frank Partsch

Jeff Jarvis is a journalist and, more recently, a blogger whose *Buzz Machine* has become a popular site for the "buzz" about politics and media. Jarvis is an associate professor and director of the interactive journalism program at the City University of New York's Graduate School of Journalism and consults for media companies. In this piece, he continues the debate with Frank Partsch (see the previous piece) about the nature and value of the "editorial" in the current media world. How would you describe Jarvis's style? Is there something about that style which is more appropriate to the blog genre? Note the way that Jarvis moderates the discussion of this blog by commenting on the words of other bloggers.

1 Not surprisingly, when I wrote about the value of editorialists today and cried, 'Off with the headlines,' a few of them objected.

2 In the Spokesman-Review, Frank Partsch, a retired editorialist from Omaha, took issue with my dismissal of the institutional voice. (His piece is behind a pay wall—thus out of the conversation—but that link to a print page should work; he also did not mention the name of this blog let alone link to it, cutting his readers off from the conversation here, but so be it.) He wrote:

> A blogged statement by one Jeff Jarvis has attracted attention among members of the National Conference of Editorial

Writers in recent days. Jarvis argues that newspaper editorial-
izing should be abandoned in an age of plentiful opinion.

Actually, a more careful reading—or perhaps a more careful   3
writing on my part—would show that I did not necessarily call
for the death of all editorialists, but did call for an updating
of the role of the editorialists in their communities. In any case,
it's fair to say that I think many editorialists, especially the
would-be voices of institutions, are not needed today. Partsch
continues:

> The premise reflects the deterioration of vocabulary. "Editorial"
> is not any old opinion, whether stated in a letter to the editor or
> shouted by a street evangelist. An editorial, in its purest sense, is
> an institutional opinion, representing the views of the owner or
> investors—people willing each day to stand behind the leader-
> ship of the editorial page even at the risk of attracting the ire of
> the community and putting their investment at risk.

This characteristic of an institutional voice constitutes part of   4
the ties that bind a newspaper to its community, whether that
community is a city, a state or a nation.

But it is the institutional voice itself that I say is a non   5
sequitor, especially for old-style newspapers that tried so hard
to insist that the rest of the institution could operate without
opinion. But the real point is the Cluetrain's point:

1. Conversations among human beings sound human.
   They are conducted in a human voice.
2. Whether delivering information, opinions, perspectives,
   dissenting arguments or humorous asides, the human
   voice is typically open, natural, uncontrived.
3. People recognize each other as such from the sound of
   this voice.

I say it is disrespectful and cowardly to speak to me behind   6
the cloak of the institution and anonymity. (And, yes, I say the
same thing to anonymous posters and bloggers.)   7
Partsch again:

> An editorial, by definition, is considered, weighed, crafted,
> edited, discussed. Its tone and content signal that the institu-
> tion has a point of view, a philosophy about its relationship
> with its readers and their community.
>
> Editors and publishers, and the editorial boards that act in
> their name, make an effort to achieve consistency over time.
> The best editorial pages are rooted in a coherent set of

values, thus offering the community a voice, among all other voices, that can be relied on as a touchstone.

Jarvis faults editorials for being unsigned. The criticism would not be unexpected from one who considers an editorial merely another person's outburst of opinion. Of course editorials are unsigned. An institutional opinion with a byline is an oxymoron.

8   There is absolutely nothing that says this cannot be accomplished by a person writing under his or her name. Indeed, how much better it is to have an opinion that is "weighed, crafted, edited, discussed" in public. And then consistency can be balanced with openness.

9   Partsch wonders whether I have hanged around editorial offices—I emailed him to let him know that in more than a decade on newspapers, I had (and he charmingly apologized and said he then went to "Uncle Google" to ask about me). In his Spokesman-Review piece, he says that contrary to my argument, editorial writers do not believe they are telling people what to think. He goes on to be critical of some editorials:

> I have deep personal concerns about what seems to be inattention, among some editorial pages, to sound thinking and clear writing. If we are losing readers, it's not because of an insufficient amount of white space or display type but rather because of an insufficient percentage of intelligent, stylishly-stated text in our institutional opinions.

10   And then, sadly, we get to a war between editorialists and bloggers. I believe the opportunity for editorialists is to use this new form to bring in new voices and viewpoints and to collaborate on issues facing the community. Partsch writes:

> But this is a matter entirely separate from the utterances of the folks who want us to believe that blogging is the new journalism. In a nutshell, editorial writers speak for institutions; a blogger speaks only for herself. Her online opinion is indistinguishable, in substance, from a shout in the crowd, and the posts proclaiming agreement no different from other shouts in the crowd.
>
> Certainly shouts in the crowd can affect the course of events, and there's a danger that they may crowd editorial-writing from the stage—unless the practitioners of the craft elevate editorial-page writing and thinking. We also need to pay attention to the evolving expectations of the public in an era of technological change.

But as a potential replacement, blogging is an imperfect candidate. A blog entry is no more an editorial than is graffiti. Few editorial pages would stoop to the caricaturing of a target and then attacking the caricature. But that's what happened here. Jarvis' attempts to force a comparison, so that the one might replace the other, are rooted in unbounded misrepresentation.

The irony, of course, is that in his piece, Partsch did "stoop to   11
the caricaturing of a target and then attacking the caricature," his target being bloggers.

But in a most cordial email exchange, Partsch goes on to con-   12
tinue his criticism of too many editorials, badly done, and says that some are so bad they might as well be abandoned to try something new. So there we almost agree. But I'm not so much criticizing editorial pages as they exist as I am proposing that the opened conversation gives them new opportunities not possible before, opportunities that should be explored.

And the point is that once the conversation is enabled—not   13
through one-time blog posts and op-ed columns but through the back-and-forth technology now allows—we get to find shared ground. Partsch says he and I probably fundamentally agree about much of this. And once we have a conversation, that proves to be the case. So that is what I'm arguing to editorialists: Find the ways to have the conversation.

There was more discussion from the editorialists' listserv (too   14
bad it's not on an open forum or blog, where we could join in the discussion). I'll pass by the silly, snarky—dare I say it? blogesque—one-liners ("Jarvis never heard of a letter to the editor or Op/Ed Page, I guess") for some good and substantive posts there. Mike Vogel of the Buffalo News says:

> With all due respect to Mr. Jarvis, he's just wrong. If I may be forgiven a little Aristotle—and yes, this debate has roots at least that old, so don't worry unduly about job security just yet—the force of argumentation depends on three things: the character of the arguer, the character of the audience, and the strength of the argument itself. Mr. Jarvis's stand is based mostly on that last factor. He raises the banner of egalitarianism, and down with the aristocracy because the wider new world lets anyone combine intellect with key-stroke research to come up with an equally valid opinion.

Well, we do more than key-stroke research, but let's just con-   15
cede that one. The other two, though, do count. The character of the arguer, for example. Someone previously noted that the institutional voice rises or falls on accuracy—an argument for

credibility, carefully created, nurtured and protected over time, that lends weight and authority to the editorial that also has a strong intrinsic argument. That's a combination of institutional strength and individual talent that the blogosphere cannot yet widely claim. Is there a difference between the voice of John685@blogoworld.net (my apologies if there is one) and the voice of the New York Times? You bet—it's the New York Times. Even those on Jarvis's blog thread who dis the Wall Street Journal edboard instinctively acknowledge that collective force, although disparaging its credibility. Star bloggers may be establishing track records and building or attempting to build credibility, but the threads belong largely to what a previous writer terms "shouts in the crowd." Do they have opinions worth hearing? Absolutely, but how do you fully evaluate them?

16   The institutional see the world in institutional terms, it seems. If they can speak for an organization, then they see others as parts of an organization: We are part of a blogosphere. No, we're not. We are individuals just as editorial writers are individuals and we either have talent and intelligence and credibility and openness and generosity or we do not. That is what this argument is about: Does the institution grant credibility—or, in Vogel's word, character? That is the assumption of these institutional voices but I say they need to hear that the opposite may be the case: Some do not trust their institutions and some do not trust those who hide their identity. In our world, transparency is a virtue that lends more character than institutional anonymity. Vogel continues:

> The strength of newspaper editorial pages lies less in what we say on given subject on any given day than it does in how we shape the community agenda over time. The strength of the blogosphere, at least so far, has been in its reactive analysis of things said and claimed, and not so much in its proactive agenda-setting. In part that's because we have more well-defined communities/audiences, and in part because love us or hate us readers just know there are few community institutions that have more invested in their community and its progress than the local news media.

17   No, I'd say that bloggers are quite good at setting agendas. Perhaps the bloggers reading this, if they've gotten this far, would like to give some examples.

18   Geitner Simmons of the *Omaha World Herald* adds thoughtful perspective of both ends of this discussion:

> The attitudes that Jarvis give voice to are deeply embedded in the blog world, and they are not going away. Newspaper editorialists don't need to abandon the traditional editorial

voice, but in an increasingly wired world, editorialists need to understand these cultural shifts. Newspapers will, and obviously are, responding in various ways. And newspapers should do so, in accordance with the particular conditions of their communities and cultures.

At the same time, even in the midst of cultural change, Frank [Partsch] offers a vital admonition for newspapers to retain an appreciation for the fundamentals of strong argumentation, clear prose (which rests on clear thinking) and a firm institutional voice.

They didn't all disagree with me. Most did, not all. Matt Neistein, op-ed editor of The Post-Crescent in Appleton, Wis., said: 19

> I think the easy dismissal of what Jarvis is saying is Exhibit A in his defense. In particular, this line should resonate with us: "Embrace new voices and viewpoints. Listen before lecturing."
>
> I agree that we have long invited other viewpoints to our pages via letters, opeds, etc. But we would be wise to apply the aforementioned advice to ourselves.
>
> The most important single sentence in that blog is this: "But today, we do not trust institutions."
>
> Nearly every response I've seen on the listserv uses, at its core, the defense that newspapers are the institutional voice. But Jarvis is right. People don't believe in institutions anymore, newspapers or otherwise. Every six months or so, I hear about another poll where journalists rank just ahead of lawyers and just behind used-car salesmen on the trustworthiness scale.
>
> Skepticism reigns. The corporatization of newspapers doesn't help anymore, either. Publishers are transferred around, the company touts its ownership, and readers don't identify with their papers anymore, as they're not locally owned or operated and the face of the paper has only lived there for a couple of years.
>
> Call it cynicism or apathy in our readers, or just plain ignorance, if you're feeling particularly chipper. But you take any one of us off the editorial page with its gaudy masthead that says "Community Newspaper, est. 185-whatever," and we're just bloggers. Bloggers with journalism training and experience, but bloggers nonetheless. And since that masthead is no longer held with the esteem it once was—through our fault or others'—using it as the trump card in this discussion may only reinforce Jarvis's point that we're out of touch and elitist.
>
> Matt, the beer's on us.

Greg Gutfield

Mad About You

Greg Gutfield is a consciously polemical writer who has
served as editor of *Stuff Magazine*, *Men's Health*, and *Maxim*.
He now maintains a blog called *The Daily Gut* and writes a
monthly column for the *American Spectator*, which published
this piece in 2007. As you read his opinions about the
YouTube phenomenon, you might consider how well his
satiric style advances his opinions and the genre of satire
more generally. For satire to be successful, what
characteristics and effects must it have? Does it work best
with specific types of audiences? Where can it go wrong?

1   I am extremely excited. More excited than usual, because I've
just had three colas and a chocolate bar. It was a Milky Way,
which in England, is actually a Three Musketeers. Despite
being duped into this charade, I still eat it, for it is my dinner
and I am riveted to my TV, watching the capture of one suspect
in the Ipswich (semi-attractive) hooker murders. A perverse attention seeker, Tom Stephens, is a man who likes to paint eyeballs on his eyelids as well as wear floppy hats—two methods
of identification used by fellow nutters when attending confer-
ences on how to choke people with mung beans. Stephens appears weirder than most Brits, for he annoys but rarely sleeps
with hookers—making him as useful as dry ice at a wet bar.
Still, it's early days yet, and Stephens might not be guilty. In
fact, as I write this, another man has been arrested—a sinister
trucker named Steve. But Tom should still be proud.

2   After all, he was named *Time*'s Person of the Year.

3   Tom, or "the bishop" as we like to call him at the gym, is a regular user of MySpace, the web equivalent of a high school yearbook for self-absorbed puddle jumpers. He went there a lot,
posting hundreds of pictures of himself along with creepy platitudes about Gandhi—probably to impress Gwyneth Paltrow or
her lookalike, a lump of paste.

4   Since *Time* magazine recently named "You," as person of the
year—meaning those who enjoy and create content for the web—
it's really proactive web users like Tom who won this award.
Along with, I might add, a few million other cowards, crotch-
fondlers, and stalkers. And considering that past winners of the
award were Hitler, Ted Turner, and the "generation under 25," a
skittish loner who kills hookers seems to make perfect sense.

I love *Time* magazine, for it is the only thing I read in the der-   5
matologist office when there are no dog-eared copies of *Tramp
Duty*. I love how its editors littered the award announcement with
edgy takes on YouTube, MySpace, and "mash-ups," mimicking
middle-aged parents desperately attempting to impress their
teenage son's friends with cool lingo. And failing, badly. Perhaps
they knew that no one reads *Time* anymore, and if they gave an
award to a zillion people who don't know they exist—they might
see a bump in their circulation. I doubt they saw a bump, or even
a rash or a zit—because most people who read it pulled the article off the Internet in between bouts of furious self-abuse. At any
rate, the boneheaded award went to a bunch of boneheaded people who have never read the boneheaded magazine—which
smacks of boneheaded toadyism and boneheaded gimmickry—a
combination that makes me wonder if the boneheaded editors
lack the wit and intelligence of a bricklayer's nailbag.

So I present my first annual BRICKLAYER'S NAILBAG   6
AWARD to *Time* for awarding its stupid, senseless award to everyone who hides behind a laptop. Meaning, our nation of online
commenting cowards—paper tigers who spend their time dehumanizing each other, or rather, people they disagree with, but are
too scared to actually say it to their faces. These tackle-bags spend
their days defecating all over America, its government and anyone who supports it, without ever adding a single constructive
point among their anonymous rants. I would quote them—but
why? They are everywhere, and nowhere at once—creating cruel
stereotypes rather than arguments—to attack their opposition.
I want to hit them with bricks. And I would if I could only find
them.

Not bricks, mind you, but those who hide behind screen   7
names and hurl insults in darkness. I doubt I am the only person who notices this—and I imagine our enemies in terror love
it. They know we've cultivated a group of people who would
rather denigrate our country than defend it—simply to impress
their friends and, for a brief moment, appear cool. Recently, the
second in command of al Qaeda released a web announcement
promising an imminent attack. Even he understands that he's
got a receptive audience—they would rather "send" than defend.

Time has defined "YOU" as a global community united by the   8
Internet—but we're really just numb nuts united by a thirst for
anything that might divert attention from stuff we should be
thinking about. Like semi-attractive hookers at risk. This unity
is a lie: You may be chatting globally, but you're alienating yourself locally.

The web does not connect people—it ramps up a mob men-   9
tality masquerading as community—a sham considering no one
really does anything for anyone anymore. Unless, you count

circulating jpegs of one's privates—but I don't, especially after a few months of sending them out. I believe if the "You" from *Time* disappeared off the face of the earth, God would be pleased.

10   But maybe I hate "you" so much, because I am one of "You." It's now six P.M. on a Wednesday, for example, and I am still in my underwear. Granted, I work at home, and my wife is visiting her folks, but still—this just isn't right. Not for me, and certainly not for you. And not for the neighbors who can see me through the front window. They don't even stare, which I find pretty insulting.

11   I haven't been outside today. I, like many other shut-ins, have allowed the web—which is nothing more than a glorified phone that transmits information—to reduce my life experiences to sitting in front of a screen staring at videos of cats vomiting and teenagers falling off skateboards. I can't remember the last time I had a conversation with my wife without saying, "Hold on, I'm in the middle of something." That "something" is almost always a video of a cat vomiting or a teenager falling off a skateboard.

12   And my alienation doesn't stop there. I hate that I can spend hours on the web devouring countless blogs about media types who mean nothing to me, but can barely handle a five-minute conversation with my 82-year-old mom. I know why: my mom is nuts. But it's also likely if my mom isn't keeping up with my appetite for novelty, so I can't be bothered. I've known my mom for 42 years. But I've only heard of Lindsey Lohan for two. My mom will understand—she plays computer bridge in her bedroom. It keeps her busy.

13   But this will all change once I become famous, which will happen . . . it is only a matter of time. And when I do become famous, I will have "You" to thank. After all, in the *Time* article, they write about how great YouTube and MySpace are at rescuing people "drowning in obscurity."

14   Thank God for that. I mean, how on earth could you survive if you weren't famous? How would you get to work or feed your family? Sadly, there aren't any outreach programs for the non-famous, but there should be and this ambivalence strikes me as bigotry.

15   What we need now is a movement to save the obscure. It will come soon, I think: a recent "study," part of something called National Kids Day, found that the top three things a child wants is to be "famous," "good looking," and "rich." These kids admire Madonna more than God. Fifteen hundred children were polled to get to this answer—after which, sadly, not one of them was thrown off a cliff.

Moisés Naím

The YouTube Effect

Moisés Naím is editor and publisher of *Foreign Policy*, a
magazine that features articles about global politics and
economics. He has also authored or edited eight books and
published numerous essays and opinion columns in leading
newspapers. Naím holds a Ph.D. and a master's degree from
the Massachusetts Institute of Technology. In this essay,
published in *Foreign Policy* in 2007, Naím explores what he
calls the "mixed blessings" of YouTube and its reporting by
"citizen journalists." As you read, you might consider Naím's
predictions for the role of video in citizen journalism, and
whether these predictions have been validated in more recent
selections.

A video shows a single line of people slowly trudging up a   1
snow-covered footpath. A shot is heard; the first person in
line falls. A voice-over says, "They are shooting them like
dogs." Another shot, and another body drops to the ground.
A uniformed Chinese soldier fires his rifle again. Then, a group
of soldiers examines the fallen bodies.

These images were captured high in the Himalayas by a mem-   2
ber of a mountaineering expedition who claims to have stumbled
upon the killing. The video first aired on Romanian television, but
it only gained worldwide attention when it was posted on
YouTube, the popular video-sharing Web site. Human rights
groups explained that the slain were a group of Tibetan refugees
that included monks, women, and children. According to the Chinese government, the soldiers had fired in self-defense after they
were attacked by 70 refugees. The posted video seems to render
that explanation absurd. The U.S. ambassador to China quickly
lodged a complaint protesting China's treatment of the refugees.

Welcome to the YouTube effect. It is the phenomenon whereby   3
video clips, often produced by individuals acting on their own, are
rapidly disseminated throughout the world thanks to video-
sharing Web sites such as YouTube, Google Video, and others.
Every month, YouTube receives 20 million visitors, who watch
100 million video clips a day. There are 65,000 new videos posted
every day. Most of the videos are frivolous, produced by and for
teenagers. But some are serious. YouTube includes videos posted
by terrorists, human rights groups, and U.S. soldiers in Iraq.
Some are clips of incidents that have political consequences or
document important trends, such as global warming, illegal

immigration, and corruption. Some videos reveal truths. Others spread disinformation, propaganda, and outright lies. All are part of the YouTube effect.

4   Fifteen years ago, the world marveled at the fabled "CNN effect." The expectation was that the unblinking eyes of TV cameras, beyond the reach of censors, would bring greater accountability and transparency to governments and the international system. These expectations were, in some sense, fulfilled. Since the early 1990s, electoral frauds that might have remained hidden were exposed, democratic uprisings energized, famines contained, and wars started or stopped, thanks to the CNN effect. But the YouTube effect will be even more intense. Although the BBC, CNN, and other international news operations employ thousands of professional journalists, they will never be as omnipresent as millions of people carrying a cell phone that can record video. Thanks to their ubiquity, the world was able to witness a shooting on a 19,000-foot mountain pass.

5   This phenomenon is amplified by a double echo chamber: One is produced when content first posted on the Web is re-aired by main-stream TV networks. The second occurs when television moments, even the most fleeting, gain a permanent presence thanks to bloggers or activists who redistribute them through Web sites like YouTube. Activists everywhere are recognizing the power of citizen-produced and Web-distributed videos as the ultimate testimony. The human rights group Witness arms individuals in conflict zones with video cameras so they can record and expose human rights abuses. Electoral watchdogs are taping elections. Even Islamic terrorists have adapted to this trend. Al Qaeda created a special media production unit called Al Sahab ("The Cloud"), which routinely posts its videos online, with the realistic expectation that they will be picked up by major media outlets and other Web sites.

6   The YouTube effect has brought other mixed blessings. It is now harder to know what to believe. How do we know that what we see in a video clip posted by a "citizen journalist" is not a montage? How do we know, for example, that the YouTube video of terrorized American soldiers crying and praying for their lives while under fire was filmed in Iraq and not staged somewhere else to manipulate public opinion? The more than 86,000 people who viewed it in the first 10 days of its posting will never know.

7   Governments are already feeling the heat of the YouTube effect. The U.S. military recently ordered its soldiers to stop posting videos unless they have been vetted. The Iranian government restricts connection speeds to limit its people's access to video streaming. These measures have not stopped the proliferation of Web videos shot by U.S. soldiers in Iraq, or savvy Iranians from viewing the images they want to see. And though

Beijing has been effective in censoring the content its citizens can view, it has yet to figure out a way to prevent a growing number of videos of peasant rebellions from being posted online. In the long run, all such efforts will fail.

When it comes to having faith in what we see online, the good 8 news is that the YouTube effect is already creating a strong demand for reliable guides—individuals, institutions, and technologies that we can trust to help us sort facts from lies. That is important, because the hope of countering the downsides of the YouTube effect will never come from government intervention. Markets and democracy do a much better job of filtering the bad from the good in the confusing tsunami of Web videos coming our way. The millions of bloggers who are constantly watching, fact-checking, and exposing mistakes are a powerful example of "the wisdom of crowds" at work. Sure, markets and democracies often fail or disappoint. But the openness these political and economic forces promote are now being assisted by a technology that is as omnipresent as we are.

getting into the conversation ••• 3

Information and Misinformation in New Media Journalism

1. The articles in this section of *Conversations* raise some serious questions about the role of traditional journalism—the mass media that have been a central element of our democracy (though in different forms) over the course of our history. One key question that emerges is whether journalists can continue to uphold their ideals as protectors of "the truth" in an age of the Internet. As you read the pieces in this section, keep track of all of the reasons why traditional journalism seems to have lost its central place, as well as the arguments over why it may be important that at least part of that place be preserved. Based upon that information, try to formulate your own best hypothesis as to the future of journalism: Will it survive? In what form? What must it do to remain relevant? Who is best equipped to carry on this democracy's traditions of journalism and the free press?

2. In your writing course, you may have learned about the three "rhetorical appeals," *ethos* (appeals to credibility and character, *pathos* (appeals to emotion), and *logos* (appeals to evidence and reasoning). In her essay, Caryl Rivers suggests that "more and more Americans are moving to 'hot,' emotion-laden methods of getting news, and away from cool, more objective forms of information." That is, Rivers seems to be suggesting that pathos-based arguments, due to new media journalism, are overcoming ethos- and logos-based arguments. Do you tend to agree? Do the other authors in this chapter also see this as being the case? You might also consider whether the ideal of "objective reporting" has ever really been true or possible, or whether agendas and emotions have always been part of the equation. One way to investigate this further might be to choose a topic that interests you and to analyze the arguments you find about that topic on the Internet, paying special attention to the relative value of each of the rhetorical appeals.

3. One of the arguments that is made by Frank Partsch about the dangers of blogging is that it has replaced the more accurate, sound, and institutionally based editorial genre. Partsch notes that "in a nutshell, editorial writers speak for institutions; a blogger speaks only for herself." This point of view is contested by Jeff Jarvis. In order to find your own position on this topic, you might first consider the stasis points in this debate between Partsch and Jarvis (perhaps also considering the thoughts of other writers in this chapter), and then to analyze the differences you find in these two genres by comparing and contrasting a number of editorials published on a given topic by newspapers and the arguments on that same topic made by bloggers. Consider the level of objectivity, the quality of information, and the types of reasoning

applied by each group. Does your analysis seem to support Partsch's argument or lend validity to Jarvis's defense of bloggers?

4. The underlying question of most of the pieces in this section, in the end, is whether the democratization of journalism—giving voice to any citizens who wish to have that voice through new technology— has had a positive effect upon our culture. Although any simple answer to that question will likely be shortsighted, evaluating the effects of the technologies remains important. After reading a number of the pieces in the chapter, write a literature review that brings together the various voices on this topic. Begin by defining what you take to be the most important elements of journalism and the role of journalism in our culture. Then, using those elements as the criteria for judgment, and drawing upon the information supplied in articles in this chapter, try to reach some conclusions about whether new media technologies have served, or undermined, the ideals of journalism and democracy.

conversations in context ••• 2

What Good Is Wikipedia?

I. The Context

Wikipedia has become for many students and teachers the forbidden site, synonymous with unreliable or lazy research. It has, at the same time, become the first stop for many who research on the Internet, a nearly ubiquitous hit when we search for anything on the open Web. Few will admit relying upon what it provides, while many do in fact consult the more than 13 million articles in 271 languages (according to a recent *Time* magazine story) it provides on a regular basis. For others, it is a grand knowledge experiment, an attempt to collect and share—through the power and reach of the Internet—knowledge from individuals the world over. Hence, to truly understand the nature and effect of this online force in the production and dissemination of knowledge, we need to go beyond labeling it good or bad. Instead, we might ask what it is, and what it might be good (or not so good) for. To do so, we'll need some context.

We might begin with some definitions. The word *encyclopedia* literally means "general education" or "circular education," suggesting an ideal of the liberal arts education that relies upon knowledge about broad and diverse areas of inquiry. A wiki is an online tool that allows for editing by a large group of users. Taken together, then, the name Wikipedia connotes a collection of general knowledge that undergoes regular editing by its users. That editing process is both the strength and weakness of Wikipedia: It is an open dialogue about its over three million topics, but it is not limited to the "experts" that are invited to write the entries for more conventional—but more static—encyclopedias. That is, while it has the advantage of keeping up with the times through the speed of the Internet, it has what some see as a key disadvantage: Its entries are not formally refereed by panels of experts as are academic journal articles. Of course, that is not to say that other experts do not weigh in through the available editing process. But it equalizes access (though there are some checks on that equality), giving no special place to those deemed experts.

We might also ask about its purposes. Because Wikipedia has become for many users a source of fast, digested information, we sometimes do not think enough about the ways it was (and continues to be) constructed and its larger intentions. Indeed, if you Google the "history of Wikipedia," the very first hit is likely to be the Wikipedia entry on itself, where you will find the site contextualized (complete with hypertext links) within other grand knowledge experiments such as the Library of Alexandria and the 18th century encyclopedists:

> The concept of gathering all of the world's knowledge in a single place goes back to the ancient Library of Alexandria and Pergamon, but the modern concept of a general purpose, widely distributed, printed encyclopedia dates from shortly before Denis Diderot and the 18th century

encyclopedists. The idea of using automated machinery beyond the printing press to build a more useful encyclopedia can be traced to librarian Charles Ammi Cutter's article "The Buffalo Public Library in 1983" (*Library Journal,* 1883, p. 211–217), Paul Otlet's book *Traité de documentation* (1934; Otlet also founded the Mundaneum institution, 1910), H. G. Wells' book of essays *World Brain* (1938) and *Vannevar Bush's* future vision of the microfilm based Memex in *As We May Think* (1945). Another milestone was Ted Nelson's Project Xanadu in 1973.

While previous encyclopedias, notably the Encyclopedia Britannica, were book-based, Microsoft's Encarta, published in 1993, was available on CD-ROM and hyperlinked.

A more comprehensive context for this site, however, requires us to not only place it within the larger history of knowledge collection, but also to understand how it is a unique moment in that history. Marshall Poe's article, "The Hive," which follows, provides some of that deeper background.

Considering Contexts: Marshall Poe, "The Hive"

In this essay, first published in the Atlantic *in 2006, Marshall Poe (a historian and professor at the University of Iowa, who is currently completing a book about Wikipedia entitled* Everyone Knows Everything*) explores the origins of Wikipedia through the thoughts of those who were instrumental in its creation. From the start, Poe looks at this project with the wonder of a true researcher: "Wikipedia has the potential to be the greatest effort in collaborative knowledge the world has ever known, and it may well be the greatest effort in voluntary collaboration of any kind." From this perspective, Poe constructs a narrative with real characters and a real plot, to tell the story of this "effort in collaborative knowledge." As you read, try to see Wikipedia from the perspective of those characters; but also be sure to keep your critical eye open as well, and be ready to situate the perspectives from this article in the conversation about Wikipedia that follows.*

The Hive

By Marshall Poe

Several months ago, I discovered that I was being "considered for deletion." Or rather, the entry on me in the Internet behemoth that is Wikipedia was.

For those of you who are (as uncharitable Wikipedians sometimes say) "clueless newbies," Wikipedia is an online encyclopedia. But it is like no encyclopedia Diderot could have imagined. Instead of relying on experts to write articles according to their expertise, Wikipedia lets anyone write about anything. You, I, and any wired-up fool can add entries, change entries, even propose that entries be deleted. For reasons

I'd rather not share outside of therapy, I created a one-line biographical entry on "Marshall Poe." It didn't take long for my tiny article to come to the attention of Wikipedia's self-appointed guardians. Within a week, a very active—and by most accounts responsible—Scottish Wikipedian named "Alai" decided that . . . well, that I wasn't worth knowing about. Why? "No real evidence of notability," Alai cruelly but accurately wrote, "beyond the proverbial average college professor."

Wikipedia has the potential to be the greatest effort in collaborative knowledge gathering the world has ever known, and it may well be the greatest effort in voluntary collaboration of any kind. The English-language version alone has more than a million entries. It is consistently ranked among the most visited websites in the world. A quarter century ago it was inconceivable that a legion of unpaid, unorganized amateurs scattered about the globe could create anything of value, let alone what may one day be the most comprehensive repository of knowledge in human history. Back then we knew that people do not work for free; or if they do work for free, they do a poor job; and if they work for free in large numbers, the result is a muddle. Jimmy Wales and Larry Sanger knew all this when they began an online encyclopedia in 1999. Now, just seven years later, everyone knows different.

The Moderator

Jimmy Wales does not fit the profile of an Internet revolutionary. He was born in 1966 and raised in modest circumstances in Huntsville, Alabama. Wales majored in finance at Auburn, and after completing his degree enrolled in a graduate program at the University of Alabama. It was there that he developed a passion for the Internet. His entry point was typical for the nerdy set of his generation: fantasy games.

In 1974, Gary Gygax and Dave Arneson, two gamers who had obviously read *The Lord of the Rings*, invented the tabletop role-playing game Dungeons & Dragons. The game spread largely through networks of teenage boys, and by 1979, the year the classic *Dungeon Master's Guide* was published, it seemed that every youth who couldn't get a date was rolling the storied twenty-sided die in a shag-carpeted den. Meanwhile, a more electronically inclined crowd at the University of Illinois at Urbana-Champaign was experimenting with moving fantasy play from the basement to a computer network. The fruit of their labors was the unfortunately named MUD (Multi-User Dungeon). Allowing masses of players to create virtual fantasy worlds, MUDs garnered a large audience in the 1980s and 1990s under names like Zork, Myst, and Scepter of Goth. (MUDs came to be known as "Multi-Undergraduate Destroyers" for their tendency to divert college students from their studies.)

Wales began to play MUDs at Alabama in the late 1980s. It was in this context that he first encountered the power of networked computers to facilitate voluntary cooperation on a large scale. He did not, however, set up house in these fantasy worlds, nor did he show any evidence of wanting to begin a career in high tech. He completed a degree in finance at Auburn, received a master's in finance at the University of Alabama, and then pursued a Ph.D. in finance at Indiana University. He was interested, it would seem, in finance. In 1994, he quit his doctoral program and moved to Chicago to take a job as an options trader. There he made (as he has repeatedly said) "enough."

Wales is of a thoughtful cast of mind. He was a frequent contributor to the philosophical "discussion lists" (the first popular online discussion forums) that emerged in the late '80s as e-mail spread through the humanities. His particular passion was objectivism, the philosophical system developed by Ayn Rand. In 1989, he initiated the Ayn Rand Philosophy Discussion List and served as moderator— the person who invites and edits e-mails from subscribers. Though discussion lists were not new among the technorati in the 1980s, they were unfamiliar territory for most academics. In the oak-paneled seminar room, everyone had always been careful to behave properly—the chairman sat at the head of the table, and everyone spoke in turn and stuck to the topic. E-mail lists were something altogether different. Unrestrained by convention and cloaked by anonymity, participants could behave very badly without fear of real consequences. The term for such poor comportment—*flaming*— became one of the first bits of net jargon to enter common usage.

Wales had a careful moderation style:

First, I will frown—very much—on any flaming of any kind whatsoever . . . Second, I impose no restrictions on membership based on my own idea of what objectivism really is . . . Third, I hope that the list will be more "academic" than some of the others and tend toward discussions of technical details of epistemology . . . Fourth, I have chosen a "middle-ground" method of moderation, a sort of behind-the-scenes prodding.

Wales was an advocate of what is generically termed "openness" online. An "open" online community is one with few restrictions on membership or posting—everyone is welcome, and anyone can say anything as long as it's generally on point and doesn't include gratuitous ad hominem attacks. Openness fit not only Wales's idea of objectivism, with its emphasis on reason and rejection of force, but also his mild personality. He doesn't like to fight. He would rather suffer fools in silence, waiting for them to talk themselves out, than confront them. This patience would serve Wales well in the years to come.

Top-Down and Bottom-Up

In the mid-1990s, the great dream of Internet entrepreneurs was to create *the* entry point on the Web. "Portals," as they were called, would provide everything: e-mail, news, entertainment, and, most important, the tools to help users find what they wanted on the Web. As Google later showed, if you build the best "finding aid," you'll be a dominant player. In 1996, the smart money was on "Web directories," man-made guides to the Internet. Both Netscape and Yahoo relied on Web directories as their primary finding aids, and their IPOs in the mid-1990s suggested a bright future. In 1996, Wales and two partners founded a Web directory called Bomis.

Initially, the idea was to build a universal directory, like Yahoo's. The question was how to build it. At the time, there were two dominant models: top-down and bottom-up. The former is best exemplified by Yahoo, which began as *Jerry's Guide to the World Wide Web*. Jerry—in this case Jerry Yang, Yahoo's cofounder—set up a system of categories and began to classify Web sites accordingly. Web surfers flocked to the site because no one could find anything on the Web in the early 1990s. So Yang and his partner, David Filo, spent a mountain of venture capital to hire a team of surfers to classify the Web. Yahoo ("Yet Another Hierarchical Officious Oracle") was born.

Other would-be classifiers approached the problem of Web chaos more democratically. Beginning from the sound premise that it's good to share, a seventeen-year-old Oregonian named Sage Weil created the first "Web ring" at about the time Yang and Filo were assembling their army of paid Web librarians. A Web ring is nothing more than a set of topically related Web sites that have been linked together for ease of surfing. Rings are easy to find, easy to join, and easy to create; by 1997, they numbered 10,000.

Wales focused on the bottom-up strategy using Web rings, and it worked. Bomis users built hundreds of rings—on cars, computers, sports, and especially "babes" (e.g., the Anna Kournikova Web ring), effectively creating an index of the "laddie" Web. Instead of helping all users find all content, Bomis found itself positioned as the *Playboy* of the Internet, helping guys find guy stuff. Wales's experience with Web rings reinforced the lesson he had learned with MUDs: given the right technology, large groups of self-interested individuals will unite to create something they could not produce by themselves, be it a sword-and-sorcery world or an index of Web sites on Pamela Anderson. He saw the power of what we now call "peer-to-peer," or "distributed," content production.

Wales was not alone: Rich Skrenta and Bob Truel, two programmers at Sun Microsystems, saw it too. In June 1998, along with three partners, they launched GnuHoo, an all-volunteer alternative to the Yahoo Directory. (GNU, a recursive acronym for "GNUs Not Unix," is a free operating system created by the über-hacker Richard Stallman.) The project was an immediate success, and it quickly drew the attention of Netscape, which was eager to find a directory capable of competing with Yahoo's index. In November 1998, Netscape acquired GnuHoo (then called NewHoo), promising to both develop it and release it under an "open content" license, which meant anyone could use it. At the date of Netscape's acquisition, the directory had indexed some 100,000 URLs; a year later, it included about a million.

Wales clearly had the open-content movement in mind when, in the fall of 1999, he began thinking about a "volunteer-built" online encyclopedia. The idea—explored most prominently in Stallman's 1999 essay "The Free Universal Encyclopedia and Learning Resource"—had been around for some time. Wales says he had no direct knowledge of Stallman's essay when he embarked on his encyclopedia project, but two bits of evidence suggest that he was thinking of Stallman's GNU free documentation license. First, the name Wales adopted for his encyclopedia—Nupedia.org—strongly suggested a Stallman-esque venture. Second, he took the trouble of leasing a related domain name, GNUpedia.org. By January 2000, his encyclopedia project had acquired funding from Bomis and hired its first employee: Larry Sanger.

The Philosopher

Sanger was born in 1968 in Bellevue, Washington, a suburb of Seattle. When he was seven, his father, a marine biologist, moved the family to Anchorage, Alaska, where Sanger spent his youth. He excelled in high school, and in 1986 he enrolled at Reed College. Reed is the sort of school you attend if you are intelligent, are not interested in investment banking, and wonder a lot about truth. There Sanger found a question that fired his imagination: What is knowledge? He embarked on that most unremunerative of careers, epistemology, and entered a doctoral program in philosophy at Ohio State.

Sanger fits the profile of almost every Internet early adopter: he'd been a good student, played Dungeons & Dragons, and tinkered with PCs as a youth—going so far as to code a text-based adventure game in BASIC, the first popular programming language. He was drawn into the world of philosophy discussion lists and, in the early 1990s, was an active participant in Wales's objectivism forum. Sanger also hosted a mailing list as part of his own online philosophy project (eventually named the Association for Systematic Philosophy). The mission and mien of Sanger's list stood in stark contrast to Wales's Rand forum. Sanger was far more programmatic. As he wrote in his opening manifesto, dated March 22, 1994:

> The history of philosophy is full of disagreement and confusion. One reaction by philosophers to this state of things is to doubt whether the truth about philosophy can ever be known, or whether there is any such thing as the truth about philosophy. But there is another reaction: One may set out to think more carefully and methodically than one's intellectual forebears.

Wales's Rand forum was generally serious, but it was also a place for philosophically inclined laypeople to shoot the breeze: Wales permitted discussion of "objectivism in the movies" or "objectivism in Rush lyrics." Sanger's list was more disciplined, but he soon began to feel it, too, was of limited philosophical worth. He resigned after little more than a year. "I think that my time could really be better spent in the real world," Sanger wrote in his resignation letter, "as opposed to cyberspace, and in thinking to myself, rather than out loud to a bunch of other people." Sanger was seriously considering abandoning his academic career.

As the decade and the century came to a close, another opportunity arose, one that would let Sanger make a living away from academia, using the acumen he had developed on the Internet. In 1998, Sanger created a digest of news reports relating to the "Y2K problem." *Sanger's Review of Y2K News Reports* became a staple of IT managers across the globe. It also set him to thinking about how he might make a living in the new millennium. In January 2000, he sent Wales a business proposal for what was in essence a cultural news blog. Sanger's timing was excellent.

The Cathedral

Wales was looking for someone with good academic credentials to organize Nupedia, and Sanger fit the bill. Wales pitched the project to Sanger in terms of Eric S. Raymond's essay (and later book) "The Cathedral and the Bazaar." Raymond sketched two models of software development. Under the "cathedral model," source code was guarded by a core group of developers; under the "bazaar model," it was released on the Internet for anyone to tinker with. Raymond argued that the latter model was better, and he coined a now-famous hacker aphorism to capture its superiority: "Given enough eyeballs, all bugs are shallow." His point was simply that the speed with which a complex project is perfected is directly proportional to the number of informed people working on it. Wales was enthusiastic about Raymond's thesis. His experience with MUDs and Web rings had demonstrated to him the power of the bazaar. Sanger, the philosopher, was charier about the wisdom-of-crowds scheme but drawn to the idea of creating an open online encyclopedia that would break all the molds. Sanger signed on and moved to San Diego.

According to Sanger, Wales was very "hands-off." He gave Sanger only the loosest sketch of an open encyclopedia. "Open" meant two things: First, anyone, in principle, could contribute. Second, all of the content would be made freely available. Sanger proceeded to create, in effect, an online academic journal. There was simply no question in his mind that Nupedia would be guided by a board of experts, that submissions would be largely written by experts, and that articles would be published only after extensive peer review. Sanger set about recruiting academics to work on Nupedia. In early March 2000, he and Wales deemed the project ready to go public, and the Nupedia Web site was launched with the following words:

> Suppose scholars the world over were to learn of a serious online encyclopedia effort in which the results were not proprietary to the encyclopedists, but were freely distributable under an open content license in virtually any desired medium. How quickly would the encyclopedia grow?

The answer, as Wales and Sanger found out, was "not very." Over the first several months little was actually accomplished in terms of article assignment, writing, and publication. First, there was the competition. Wales and Sanger had the bad luck to launch Nupedia around the same time as *Encyclopedia Britannica* was made available for free on the Internet. Then there was the real problem: production. Sanger and the Nupedia board had worked out a multistage editorial system that could have been borrowed from any scholarly journal. In a sense, it worked: assignments were made, articles were submitted and evaluated, and copyediting was done. But, to both Wales and Sanger, it was all much too slow. They had built a cathedral.

The Bazaar

In the mid-1980s, a programmer named Ward Cunningham began trying to create a "pattern language" for software design. A pattern language is in essence a common vocabulary used in solving engineering problems—think of it as best practices for designers. Cunningham believed that software development should have a pattern language, and he proposed to find a way for software developers to create it.

Apple's Hypercard offered inspiration. Hypercard was a very flexible database application. It allowed users to create records ("cards"), add data fields to them, and link them in sets. Cunningham created a Hypercard "stack" of software patterns and shared it with colleagues. His stack was well liked but difficult to share, since it existed only on Cunningham's computer. In the 1990s, Cunningham found himself looking for a problem-solving technique that would allow software developers to fine-tune and accumulate their knowledge collaboratively. A variation on Hypercard seemed like an obvious option.

Cunningham coded and, in the spring of 1995, launched the first "wiki," calling it the "WikiWikiWeb." (*Wiki* is Hawaiian for "quick," which Cunningham chose to indicate the ease with which a user could edit the pages.) A wiki is a Web site that allows multiple users to create, edit, and hyperlink pages. As users work, a wiki can keep track of all changes; users can compare versions as they edit and, if necessary, revert to earlier states. Nothing is lost, and everything is transparent.

The wiki quickly gained a devoted following within the software community. And there it remained until January 2001, when Sanger

conversations in context ...2

had dinner with an old friend named Ben Kovitz. Kovitz was a fan of "extreme programming." Standard software engineering is very methodical—first you plan, then you plan and plan and plan, then you code. The premise is that you must correctly anticipate what the program will need to do in order to avoid drastic changes late in the coding process. In contrast, extreme programmers advocate going live with the earliest possible version of new software and letting many people work simultaneously to rapidly refine it.

Over tacos that night, Sanger explained his concerns about Nupedia's lack of progress, the root cause of which was its serial editorial system. As Nupedia was then structured, no stage of the editorial process could proceed before the previous stage was completed. Kovitz brought up the wiki and sketched out "wiki magic," the mysterious process by which communities with common interests work to improve wiki pages by incremental contributions. If it worked for the rambunctious hacker culture of programming, Kovitz said, it could work for any online collaborative project. The wiki could break the Nupedia bottleneck by permitting volunteers to work simultaneously all over the project. With Kovitz in tow, Sanger rushed back to his apartment and called Wales to share the idea. Over the next few days he wrote a formal proposal for Wales and started a page on Cunningham's wiki called "WikiPedia."

Wales and Sanger created the first Nupedia wiki on January 10, 2001. The initial purpose was to get the public to add entries that would then be "fed into the Nupedia process" of authorization. Most of Nupedia's expert volunteers, however, wanted nothing to do with this, so Sanger decided to launch a separate site called "Wikipedia." Neither Sanger nor Wales looked on Wikipedia as anything more than a lark. This is evident in Sanger's flip announcement of Wikipedia to the Nupedia discussion list. "Humor me," he wrote. "Go there and add a little article. It will take all of five or ten minutes." And, to Sanger's surprise, go they did. Within a few days, Wikipedia outstripped Nupedia in terms of quantity, if not quality, and a small community developed. In late January, Sanger created a Wikipedia discussion list (Wikipedia-L) to facilitate discussion of the project. At the end of January, Wikipedia had 17 "real" articles (entries with more than 200 characters). By the end of February, it had 150; March, 572; April, 835; May, 1,300; June, 1,700; July, 2,400; August, 3,700. At the end of the year, the site boasted approximately 15,000 articles and about 350 "Wikipedians."

Setting the Rules

Wikipedia's growth caught Wales and Sanger off guard. It forced them to make quick decisions about what Wikipedia would be, how to foster cooperation, and how to manage it. In the beginning it was by no means clear what an "open" encyclopedia should include. People posted all manner of things: dictionary definitions, autobiographies, position papers, historical documents, and original research. In response, Sanger created a "What Wikipedia Is Not" page. There he and the community defined Wikipedia by exclusion—not a dictionary, not a scientific journal, not a source collection, and so on. For everything else, they reasoned that if an article could conceivably have gone in *Britannica,* it was "encyclopedic" and permitted; if not, it was "not encyclopedic" and deleted.

Sanger and Wales knew that online collaborative ventures can easily slide into a morass of unproductive invective. They had already worked out a solution for Nupedia, called the "lack of bias" policy. On Wikipedia it became NPOV, or the "neutral point of view," and it brilliantly encouraged the work of the community. Under NPOV, authors were enjoined to present the conventionally acknowledged "facts" in an unbiased way, and, where arguments occurred, to accord space to both sides. The concept of neutrality, though philosophically unsatisfying, had a kind of everybody-lay-down-your-arms ring to it. Debates about what to include in the article were encouraged on the "discussion" page that attends every Wikipedia article.

The most important initial question, however, concerned governance. When Wikipedia was created, wikis were synonymous with creative anarchy. Both Wales and Sanger thought that the software might be useful, but that it was no way to build a trusted encyclopedia. Some sort of authority was assumed to be essential. Wales's part in it was clear: He owned Wikipedia. Sanger's role was murkier.

Citing the communal nature of the project, Sanger refused the title of "editor in chief," a position he held at Nupedia, opting instead to be "chief organizer." He governed the day-to-day operations of the project in close consultation with the "community," the roughly two dozen committed Wikipedians (most of them Nupedia converts) who were really designing the software and adding content to the site. Though the division of powers between Sanger and the community remained to be worked out, an important precedent had been set: Wikipedia would have an owner, but no leader.

The Cunctator

By October 2001, the number of Wikipedians was growing by about fifty a month. There were a lot of new voices, among them a user known as "The Cunctator" (Latin for "procrastinator" or "delayer"). "Cunc," as he was called, advocated a combination of anarchy (no hierarchy within the project) and radical openness (few or no limitations on contributions). Sanger was not favorably disposed to either of these positions, though he had not had much of a chance to air his opposition. Cunc offered such an opportunity by launching a prolonged "edit war" with Sanger in mid-October of that year. In an edit war, two or more parties cyclically cancel each other's work on an article with no attempt to find the NPOV. It's the wiki equivalent of "No, *your* mother wears combat boots."

With Cunc clearly in mind, Sanger curtly defended his role before the community on November 1, 2001:

> I need to be granted fairly broad authority by the community—by you, dear reader—if I am going to do my job effectively. Until fairly recently, I was granted such authority by Wikipedians. I was indeed not infrequently called to justify decisions I made, but not constantly and nearly always respectfully and helpfully. This place in the community did not make me an all-powerful editor who must be obeyed on pain of ousting; but it did make me a leader. That's what I want, again. This is my job.

Seen from the trenches, this was a striking statement. Sanger had so far said he was primus inter pares; now he seemed to be saying that he was just primus. Upon reading this post, one Wikipedian wrote: "Am I the only person who detects a change in [Sanger's] view of his own position? Am I the only person who fears this is a change for the worse?"

On November 4, the Sanger-Cunc contretemps exploded. Simon Kissane, a respected Wikipedian, accused Sanger of capriciously deleting pages, including some of Cunc's work. Sanger denied the allegation but implied that the excised material was no great loss. He then launched a defense of his position in words that bled resentment:

> I do reserve the right to permanently delete things—particularly when they have little merit and when they are posted by people whose main motive is evidently to undermine my authority and therefore, as far as I'm concerned, damage the project. Now suppose that, in my experience, if I make an attempt to justify this or other sorts of decisions, the people in question will simply co-opt huge amounts of my time and will never simply say, "Larry, you win; we realize that this decision is up to you, and we'll have to respect it." Then, in order to preserve my time and sanity, I have to act like an autocrat. In a way, I am being trained to act like an autocrat. It's rather clever in a way—if you think college-level stunts are clever. Frankly, it's hurting the project, guys—so stop it, already. Just write articles—please!

The blowup disturbed Wales to no end. As a list moderator, he had tried hard to keep his discussants out of flame wars. He weighed in with an unusually forceful posting that warned against a "culture of conflict." Wikipedia, he implied, was about building an encyclopedia, not about debating how to build or govern an encyclopedia. Echoing Sanger, he argued that the primary duty of community members was to contribute—by writing code, adding content, and editing. Enough talk, he seemed to be saying: we know what to do, now let's get to work. Yet he also seemed to take a quiet stand against Sanger's positions on openness and on his own authority:

> Just speaking off the top of my head, I think that total deletions seldom make sense. They should be reserved primarily for pages that

are just completely mistaken (typos, unlikely misspellings), or for pages that are nothing more than insults.

Wales also made a strong case that anyone deleting pages should record his or her identity, explain his or her reasons, and archive the entire affair.

Within several weeks, Sanger and Cunc were at each other's throats again. Sanger had proposed creating a "Wikipedia Militia" that would deal with issues arising from sudden massive influxes of new visitors. It was hardly a bad idea: such surges did occur (they're commonly called "slash-dottings"). But Cunc saw in Sanger's reasonable proposition a very slippery slope toward "central authority." "You start deputizing groups of people to do necessary and difficult tasks," he wrote, "fast-forward two/three years, and you have pernicious cabals."

Given the structure of Wikipedia there was little Sanger could do to defend himself. The principles of the project denied him real punitive authority: he couldn't ban "trolls"—users like Cunc who baited others for sport—and deleting posts was evidence of tyranny in the eyes of Sanger's detractors. A defensive strategy wouldn't work either, as the skilled moderator's tactic for fighting bad behavior—ignoring it—was blunted by the wiki. On e-mail lists, unanswered inflammatory posts quickly vanish under layers of new discussion; on a wiki, they remain visible to all, often near the tops of pages. Sanger was trapped by his own creation.

The "God-King"

Wales saw that Sanger was having trouble managing the project. Indeed, he seems to have sensed that Wikipedia really needed no manager. In mid-December 2001, citing financial shortfalls, he told Sanger that Bomis would be cutting its staff and that he should look for a new job. To that point, Wales and his partners had supported both Nupedia and Wikipedia. But with Bomis suffering in the Internet bust, there was financial pressure. Early on, Wales had said that advertising was a possibility, but the community was now set against any commercialization. In January 2002, Sanger loaded up his possessions and returned to Ohio.

Cunc responded to Sanger's departure with apparent appreciation:

> I know that we've hardly been on the best of terms, but I want you to know that I'll always consider you one of the most important Wikipedians, and I hope that you'll always think of yourself as a Wikipedian, even if you don't have much time to contribute. Herding cats ain't easy; you did a good job, all things considered.

Characteristically, Sanger took this as nothing more than provocation: "Oh, how nice and gracious this was. Oh, thank you SO much Cunctator. I'm sure glad I won't have to deal with you anymore, Cunctator. You're a friggin' piece of work." The next post on the list is from Wales, who showed a business-as-usual sangfroid:

conversations in context ...2

"With the resignation of Larry, there is a much less pressing need for funds."

Sanger made two great contributions to Wikipedia: he built it, and he left it. After forging a revolutionary mode of knowledge building, he came to realize—albeit dimly at first—that it was not to his liking. He found that he was not heading a disciplined crew of qualified writers and editors collaborating on authoritative statements (the Nupedia ideal), but trying to control an ill-disciplined crowd of volunteers fighting over ever-shifting articles. From Sanger's point of view, both the behavior of the participants and the quality of the scholarship were wanting. Even after seeing Wikipedia's explosive growth, Sanger continued to argue that Wikipedia should engage experts and that Nupedia should be saved.

Wales, though, was a businessman. He wanted to build a free encyclopedia, and Wikipedia offered a very rapid and economically efficient means to that end. The articles flooded in, many were good, and they cost him almost nothing. Why interfere? Moreover, Wales was not really the meddling kind. Early on, Wikipedians took to calling him the "God-King." The appellation is purely ironic. Over the past four years, Wales has repeatedly demonstrated an astounding reluctance to use his power, even when the community has begged him to. He wouldn't exile trolls or erase offensive material, much less settle on rules for how things should or should not be done. In 2003, Wales diminished his own authority by transferring Wikipedia and all of its assets to the nonprofit Wikimedia Foundation, whose sole purpose is to set general policy for Wikipedia and its allied projects. (He is one of five members of the foundation's board.)

Wales's benign rule has allowed Wikipedia to do what it does best: grow. The numbers are staggering. The English-language Wikipedia alone has well more than a million articles and expands by about 1,700 a day. (*Britannica*'s online version, by comparison, has about 100,000 articles.) As of mid-February 2006, more than 65,000 Wikipedians—registered users who have made at least ten edits since joining—had contributed to the English-language Wikipedia. The number of registered contributors is increasing by more than 6,000 a month; the number of unregistered contributors is presumably much larger. Then there are the 200-odd non-English-language Wikipedias. Nine of them already have more than 100,000 entries each, and nearly all of the major-language versions are growing on pace with the English version.

What is Wikipedia?

The Internet did not create the desire to collect human knowledge. For most of history, however, standardizing and gathering knowledge was hard to do very effectively. The main problem was rampant equivocation. Can we all agree on what an apple is exactly, or the shades of the color green? Not easily. The wiki offered a way for people to actually decide in common. On Wikipedia, an apple is what the contributors say it is *right now*. You can try to change the definition by throwing in your own two cents, but the community—the voices actually negotiating and renegotiating the definition—decides in the end. Wikipedia grew out of a natural impluse (communication) facilitated by a new technology (the wiki).

The power of the community to decide, of course, asks us to reexamine what we mean when we say that something is "true." We tend to think of truth as something that resides in the world. The fact that two plus two equals four is written in the stars—we merely discovered it. But Wikipedia suggests a different theory of truth. Just think about the way we learn what words mean. Generally speaking, we do so by listening to other people (our parents, first). Since we want to communicate with them (after all, they feed us), we use the words in the same way they do. Wikipedia says judgments of truth and falsehood work the same way. The community decides that two plus two equals four the same way it decides what an apple is: by consensus. Yes, that means that if the community changes its mind and decides that two plus two equals five, then two plus two does equal five. The community isn't likely to do such an absurd or useless thing, but it has the ability.

Early detractors commonly made two criticisms of Wikipedia. First, unless experts were writing and vetting the material, the articles were inevitably going to be inaccurate. Second, since anyone could edit, vandals would have their way with even the best articles, making them suspect. No encyclopedia produced in this way could be trusted. Last year, however, a study in the journal *Nature* compared *Britannica* and Wikipedia science articles and suggested that the former are usually only marginally more accurate than the latter. *Britannica* demonstrated that *Nature*'s analysis was seriously flawed ("Fatally Flawed" was the fair title of the response), and no one has produced a more authoritative study of Wikipedia's accuracy. Yet it is a widely accepted view that Wikipedia is comparable to *Britannica*. Vandalism also has proved much less of an issue than originally feared. A study by IBM suggests that although vandalism does occur (particularly on high-profile entries like "George W. Bush"), watchful members of the huge Wikipedia community usually swoop down to stop the malfeasance shortly after it begins.

There are, of course, exceptions, as in the case of the journalist John Seigenthaler, whose Wikipedia biography long contained a libel about his supposed complicity in the assassinations of John F. and Robert Kennedy. But even this example shows that the system is, if not perfect, at least responsive. When Seigenthaler became aware of the error, he contacted Wikipedia. The community (led in this instance by Wales) purged the entry of erroneous material, expanded it, and began to monitor it closely. Even though the Seigenthaler entry is often attacked by vandals, and is occasionally locked to block them, the page is more reliable precisely because it is now under "enough eyeballs." The same could be said about many controversial entries on Wikipedia: the quality of articles generally increases with the number of eyeballs. Given enough eyeballs, all errors are shallow.

Common Knowledge

In June 2001, only six months after Wikipedia was founded, a Polish Wikipedian named Krzysztof Jasiutowicz made an arresting and remarkably forward-looking observation. The Internet, he mused, was nothing but a "global Wikipedia without the end-user editing facility." The contents of the Internet—its pages—are created by a loose community of users, namely those on the Web. The contents of Wikipedia—its entries—are also created by a loose community of users, namely Wikipedians. On the Internet, contributors own their own pages, and only they can edit them. They can also create new pages as they see fit. On Wikipedia, contributors own *all* of the pages collectively, and each can edit nearly every page. Page creation is ultimately subject to community approval. The private-property regime that governs the Internet allows it to grow freely, but it makes organization and improvement very difficult. In contrast, Wikipedia's communal regime permits growth *plus* organization and improvement. The result of this difference is there for all to see: much of the Internet is a chaotic mess and therefore useless, whereas Wikipedia is well ordered and hence very useful.

Having seen all of this in prospect, Jasiutowicz asked a logical question: "Can someone please tell me what's the end point/goal of Wikipedia?" Wales responded, only half jokingly, "The goal of Wikipedia is fun for the contributors." He had a point. Editing Wikipedia *is* fun, and even rewarding. The site is huge, so somewhere on it there is probably something you know quite a bit about. Imagine that you happen upon your pet subject, or perhaps even look it up to see how it's being treated. And what do you find? Well, this date is wrong, that characterization is poor, and a word is mispelled. You click the "edit" tab and make the corrections, and you've just contributed to the progress of human knowledge. All in under five minutes, and at no cost.

Yet Wikipedia has a value that goes far beyond the enjoyment of its contributors. For all intents and purposes, the project is laying claim to a vast region of the Internet, a territory we might call "common knowledge." It is the place where all nominal information about objects of widely shared experience will be negotiated, stored, and renegotiated. When you want to find out *what something is,* you will go to Wikipedia, for that is where common knowledge will, by convention, be archived and updated and made freely available. And while you are there, you may just add or change a little something, and thereby feel the pride of authorship shared by the tens of thousands of Wikipedians.

conversations in context ...2

Keeper

One of the objects of common knowledge in Wikipedia, I'm relieved to report, is "Marshall Poe." Recall that the Scottish Wikipedian Alai said that I had no "notability" and therefore couldn't really be considered encyclopedic. On the same day that Alai suggested my entry be deleted, a rather vigorous discussion took place on the "discussion" page that attended the Marshall Poe entry. A Wikipedian who goes by "Dlyons493" discovered that I had indeed written an obscure dissertation on an obscure topic at a not-so-obscure university. He gave the article a "Weak Keep." Someone with the handle "Splash" searched Amazon and verified that I had indeed written books on Russian history, so my claim to be a historian was true. He gave me a "Keep." And finally, my champion and hero, a Wikipedian called "Tupsharru," dismissed my detractors with this:

> Keep. Obvious notability. Several books published with prestigious academic publishers. One of his books has even been translated into Swedish. I don't know why I have to repeat this again and again in these deletion discussions on academics, but don't just use Amazon when the Library of Congress catalogue is no farther than a couple of mouse clicks away.

Bear in mind that I knew none of these people, and they had, as far as I know, no interest other than truth in doing all of this work. Yet they didn't stop with verifying my claims and approving my article. They also searched the Web for material they could use to expand my one-line biography. After they were done, the Marshall Poe entry was two paragraphs long and included a good bibliography. Now that's wiki magic.

II. The Conversation

While Poe's article brings out the larger philosophical and technological purposes of this grand knowledge experiment, there is a larger conversation about Wikipedia that explores its effects, rather than its history and purposes. To engage in this conversation, one might explore the perspectives on the uses of this growing and changing collection of ideas, and consider how this site has been, and continues to be, used. The images and words that follow can give you some starting points for further exploration, if you choose to enter this conversation. As you read and view the array of perspectives here, read with a critical eye, and keep track of the more focused conversations that explore the world of Wikipedia. Consider also your own experiences with this site, thinking about your own use of this online tool and its treatment by teachers, parents, and fellow students, to help you explore questions about what good Wikipedia is, is not, or could be.

conversations in context ...2

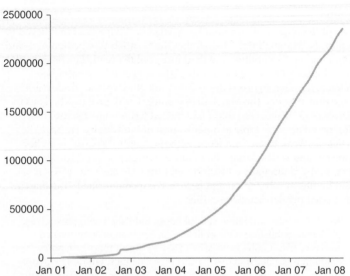

This graph appears on the Wikipedia entry for "History of Wikipedia"; what implicit argument does this graphic representation of the history of the site make?

The co-founder, Jimmy Wales, describes Wikipedia as "an effort to create and distribute a multilingual free encyclopedia of the highest quality to every single person on the planet in his or her own language. . . . Wikipedia exists to bring knowledge to everyone who seeks it."

Clearly, Wikipedia and its plethora of contributors are sincere and well-meaning; however, characterizing all contributed information as factual is unrealistic and, in many cases, patently false. Perhaps it would be more apt for Mr. Wales to describe Wikipedia as a great encyclopedia of an accumulation of biased opinions. For that, it is most definitely of the highest quality.

SOURCE: Jim Green http://www.associatedcontent.com/article/878207/why_ wikipedia_is_not_a_reliable_source.html

In order to test the reliability of Wikipedia, the well-respected journal, Nature, compared its reliability to that of Encyclopedia Brittanica. The results of that study were reported as follows by CNet News (http://news. cnet.com/2100-1038_3-5997332.html).

In the end, the journal found just eight serious errors, such as general misunderstandings of vital concepts, in the articles. Of those, four came from each site. They did, however, discover a series of factual errors, omissions, or misleading statements. All told, Wikipedia had 162 such problems, while Britannica had 123.

That averages out to 2.92 mistakes per article for Britannica and 3.86 for Wikipedia.

UBC professor grades students on Wikipedia status

VANCOUVER, Canada (AFP)— Wikipedia, the upstart Internet encyclopedia that most universities forbid students to use, has suddenly become a teaching tool for professors. Recently, university teachers have swapped student term papers for assignments to write entries for the free online encyclopedia.

Wikipedia is an "open-source" web site, which means that entries can be started or edited by anyone in the world with an Internet connection. Writing for Wikipedia "seems like a much larger stage, more of a challenge," than a term paper, said professor Jon Beasley-Murray, who teaches Latin American literature at the University of British Columbia in this western Canadian city.

SOURCE: by mtippett | May 12, 2008 at 05:32 pm. http://www.nowpublic. com/culture/ubc-professor-grades-students-wikipedia-status

Wikipedia breeds "unwitting trust" says IT professor
Students banned from citing Wikipedia in coursework.

Faced with the prospect of having brain surgery who would you rather it be performed by—a surgeon trained at medical school or someone who has read Wikipedia?

That's the view of Deakin University associate professor of information systems Sharman Lichtenstein, who believes the popular free encyclopedia that anyone can edit is fostering a climate of blind trust among people seeking information.

SOURCE: Rodney Gedda (Techworld Australia) 14 April, 2008 14:54 http://www.computerworld.com.au/ article/212258/wikipedia_breeds_ unwitting_trust_says_it_professor/

While plenty of professors have complained about the lack of accuracy or completeness of entries, and some have discouraged or tried to bar students from using it, the history department at Middlebury College is trying to take a stronger, collective stand. It voted this month to bar students from citing the Web site as a source in papers or other academic work. All faculty members will be telling students about the policy and explaining why material on Wikipedia—while convenient—may not be trustworthy. "As educators, we are in the business of reducing the dissemination of misinformation," said Don Wyatt, chair of the department. "Even though Wikipedia may have some value, particularly from the value of leading students to citable sources, it is not itself an appropriate source for citation," he said.

SOURCE: "A Stand Against Wikipedia," Inside Higher Ed, http://www.insidehighered.com/ news/2007/01/26/wiki

conversations in context ...2

"An encyclopedia? I don't know. Let's look
up what it is on Wikipedia."

How might this image comment as much about our educational system as about
Wikipedia? How might you use this image to make an argument about either topic?

*SOURCE: 400 x 355 - 70k - jpg - www.cartoonstock.com/lowres/rde02021.jpg. Image may
be subject to copyright. Below is the image at: www.cartoonstock.com/directory/e/
encyclopedia.asp*

Wikipedia, an online encyclopedia compiled by a distributed
network of volunteers, has often come under attack by academics as being shoddy and full of inaccuracies. Even
Wikipedia's founder, Jimmy Wales, says he wants to get the
message out to college students that they shouldn't use it for
class projects or serious research.

Speaking at a conference at the University of Pennsylvania
on Friday called "The Hyperlinked Society," Mr. Wales said
that he gets about 10 e-mail messages a week from students
who complain that Wikipedia has gotten them into academic
hot water. "They say, 'Please help me. I got an F on my paper
because I cited Wikipedia'" and the information turned out to
be wrong, he says. But he said he has no sympathy for their
plight, noting that he thinks to himself: "For God sake, you're
in college; don't cite the encyclopedia."

SOURCE: **Wikipedia Founder Discourages Academic Use of
His Creation** *By Jeff Young: http://chronicle.com/blogPost/
Wikipedia-Founder-Discourages/2305*

Last year a colleague in the English department described a conversation in which a friend revealed a dirty little secret: "I use Wikipedia all the time for my research—but I certainly wouldn't cite it." This got me wondering: How many humanities and social sciences researchers are discussing, using, and citing Wikipedia? To find out, I searched Project Muse and JSTOR, leading electronic journal collections for the humanities and social sciences, for the term "wikipedia," which picked up both references to Wikipedia and citations of the wikipedia URL. I retrieved 167 results from between 2002 and 2008, all but 8 of which came from Project Muse. (JSTOR covers more journals and a wider range of disciplines but does not provide access to issues published in the last 3-5 years.) In contrast, Project Muse lists 149 results in a search for "Encyclopedia Britannica" between 2002 and 2008, and JSTOR lists 3. I found that citations of Wikipedia have been increasing steadily: from 1 in 2002 (not surprisingly, by Yochai Benkler) to 17 in 2005 to 56 in 2007. So far Wikipedia has been cited 52 times in 2008, and it's only August.

Along with the increasing number of citations, another indicator that Wikipedia may be gaining respectability is its citation by well-known scholars. Indeed, several scholars both cite Wikipedia and are themselves subjects of Wikipedia entries, including Gayatri Spivak, Yochai Benkler, Hal Varian, Henry Jenkins, Jerome McGann, Lawrence Buell, and Donna Haraway.

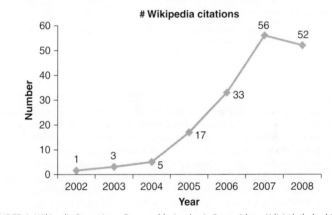

SOURCE: *Is Wikipedia Becoming a Respectable Academic Source?* http://digitalscholarship. wordpress.com/2008/09/01/is-wikipedia-becoming-a-respectable-academic-source

"HEY! LOOK WHAT I CAN DO!!"

This image makes a comment not only about Wikipedia, but also about the recording of history. Try to put into words that comment. Is the image or your written version more effective?

SOURCE: Wikipedia: Information hub or ruthless killer? (Christian Science Monitor)500 x 350 - 42k - jpg - blogs.nyu. edu/.../wikipedia_iraq.jpg.Image may be subject to copyright. http://blogs.nyu .edu/blogs/asr313/businessofmedia/2009/03/wikipedia_information_hub_or_r.html

When Bernardo Huberman looks at the chaos of millions of people online, he is often amazed at the order that emerges. And few destinations on the internet encompass this duality quite like the online encyclopedia Wikipedia, where almost five million volunteer editors have contributed over 50 million edits to close to 1.7 million articles with almost no supervision. "It's this strange, haphazard system, but it forms a kind of collective intelligence," said Huberman, the director of the Information Dynamics Lab at Hewlett Packard Laboratories and author of *The Laws of the Web: Patterns in Ecology of Information.* "People don't get paid and don't even get credit for the work they are doing," Huberman said to CBC News Online. "But somehow it has managed to thrive because of the value people place on knowledge."

SOURCE: The Wikipedia experiment Paul Jay, CBC NewsTechnology. CBC NEWS IN DEPTH: http://www.cbc.ca/news/background/tech/wikipedia.html

ACCOUNTING

Roy Delgado

" Don't worry, I checked the figures with wikopedia. "

What groups are the target of this cartoon? Does it comment on Wikipedia, or on the users?

SOURCE: 400 x 355 - 70k - jpg - www.cartoonstock.com/lowres/rde0202l.jpg Image may be subject to copyright. Below is the image at: www.cartoonstock.com/directory/e/ encyclopedia.asp

conversations in context ...2

This screen shot from the "history" tab of Wikipedia highlights edits to a Wikipedia entry on literacy. What does this show about the way this site works? Investigate this yourself; find an entry on a topic that interests you, and click the "history" tab to view the edits since the entry was created.

III. Entering the Conversation

Now that you have some background on both the history of and current opinions on Wikipedia, you can consider the ways to focus your own thoughts on this large topic. If you have been using the conversation model of reading and writing, you have kept track of the key points of debate or stasis points; you have made note of the arguments being made about the value and pitfalls of Wikipedia; and you have learned about who some of the key players in this debate are (such as founder Jimmy Wales or "the philosopher" of the project, Larry Sanger), as well as the views of other stakeholders in this dialogue.

Knowing some of the bases of the various arguments that have been made about Wikipedia from this collection of voices—those who see it as a noble experiment and those see it as a dangerous leveling of knowledge that makes reliable and unreliable information seem equal—you are now ready to take on a specific area of inquiry and to present your own informed views on some facet of this topic. Each of the writers whose views you have read formed their opinion in this way as well, based on their own contexts and their own place in the conversation. Professors and teachers, technologists, parents, students, historians, philosophers, cartoonists, and many more all weigh in on this topic. Depending upon your own interests and context, you might take on a particular facet of the topic through specific questions. Here are some possible lines of inquiry, which represent only a fraction of the possibilities:

- Whether Wikipedia has become what its founders imagined, something altogether different, or somewhere in the middle
- Whether the reaction to Wikipedia by educators is justified
- Whether, while reliability is an issue, Wikipedia is useful for some things—and what those things are
- Whether contributors to Wikipedia have a certain profile—are they experts, activists, gamers? What motivates them?
- Whether Wikipedia is an accurate measure of, if not reliable facts, at least public opinion?
- Whether there are other competing sites with similar functions, and whether they have solved some of the problems of Wikipedia
- How wikis have been used by other groups or organizations to share information
- How policies and practices about the use of Wikipedia vary across educational institutions
- How Wikipedia fits into larger conversations about technology and the sharing of information (Here, you could draw upon many of the other pieces in this part of *Conversations*.)
- Whether there are generational splits about the use of Wikipedia, or how students themselves have strong opinions about its use
- Whether specific features of Wikipedia (like its bibliographies) are useful and reliable

The list, of course, could go on; indeed, you would find many other conversations on this topic should you do more research. In any case, as you weigh in on this topic, be sure to draw upon what you have learned by seeing this conversation within the larger contexts and to consider what other information you need to write in more informed ways on this topic. The following are a few ways for you to get started on extending the conversation about Wikipedia through your own reading and research. You can use them as jumping-off points. Feel free to take them in whatever directions your interests and your research take you, or to develop related topics on your own.

1. One key question about Wikipedia is whether allowing editing by users corrupts its reliability. Studies have been done on this, and so you might begin by examining what has been found about reliability so far—both the absolute reliability and its reliability in comparison to other types of sources that researchers use. But you might also add to this conversation by doing some primary research. Begin by imagining how you might set up a focused study of this. First, you would need methods. For example, you might start by deciding to check Wikipedia articles on one or two specific topics that interest you. Then, you

could do what is sometimes called "fact-checking." Select some of the claims made in each article, and do some research to see whether those claims have a reasonable level of support from other experts. You can also use the history tab of the Wikipedia entry to see (1) how frequently it has been edited and by whom and (2) whether the edits are reliable and tend to keep the entry up to date, or whether it seems to be more about the agenda of each editor. Then, you can write an essay that shows—using those specific examples—the degree to which this article is reliable and what this one example might tell us about the reliability of Wikipedia more generally.

2. Like any source of information, and especially that which is available on the open Web, one might consider whether Wikipedia is sometimes used as a site of advocacy for a particular point of view, and so whether the information posted there is meant to persuade others of that point of view. Pick a particularly contentious topic—gun control, reproductive rights, global warming, evolution—and test whether the edits to the page seem to be about factual accuracy and objectivity, or whether they are more about individual users attempting to forward his or her own agenda. You can use methods similar to those noted in #1 above to do fact checking and to study the history of the entry. But in this case, your goal would be to build an argument about how the site's articles on controversial topics are treated by users, and whether there are particular kinds of topics that do not lend themselves to wiki technology in terms of reliability. By doing this, you might also learn a great deal about the use of emotional appeals, bias, and the relationship between disinterested research and advocacy. Consider also whether advocating for a particular agenda in this way is itself fair game or unethical.

3. Wikipedia is of interest not only because of its content, but also because of the technology that allows it to exist. If your interests are there, you might learn more about wiki technology (the "Marshall Poe" piece included here might be a good start), and bring an engineer or software developer's eye to this, considering the current and potential uses of this technology. Do some research on the development of this software, the ways that it works, and how the programs have developed since their invention. You might also trace the various uses of wikis in different kinds of settings. For example, some companies now use wikis as a form of brainstorming, as do some classrooms. You can also learn more about how wikis are used in closed rather than open environments: wikis open only to members of professional or academic organizations, wikis for activist groups, wikis for collaborative writing projects, and so on. Or, you could compare wiki technology to other related collaborative technologies like Google docs. After you have done this research, you might write an essay for a number of purposes: to show how it has developed and is being used, its potential for other uses (especially in your field of study), and so forth.

CHAPTER 4

Is Technology Making Us Stupid?

Nicholas Carr

Is Google Making Us Stupid?

Nicholas Carr, who writes on the effects of technology upon our culture and economy, has published in many periodicals, including *The Atlantic Monthly* (where this piece was first published in 2008), *The New York Times Magazine, Wired, The Financial Times, Die Zeit, The Futurist,* and *Advertising Age.* He is also the author of the 2008 *Wall Street Journal* bestseller *The Big Switch: Rewiring the World, from Edison to Google.* This essay was the catalyst for a great deal of debate about not only the effects of Google specifically, but also about the ways that technology more generally affects our cognitive processes and our relationship with information. As you read, you might consider not only the title question, but also your own practices of interacting with information, and whether technological applications like Google are changing what it means to think and to be human. Does technology advance our abilities, or does it, as Carr suggests, flatten our own intelligence into "artificial intelligence"?

"Dave, stop Stop, will you? Stop, Dave. Will you stop, 1 Dave?" So the supercomputer HAL pleads with the implacable astronaut Dave Bowman in a famous and weirdly poignant scene toward the end of Stanley Kubrick's *2001: A Space Odyssey.* Bowman, having nearly been sent to a deep-space death by the malfunctioning machine, is calmly, coldly disconnecting the memory circuits that control its artificial brain. "Dave, my mind is going," HAL says, forlornly. "I can feel it. I can feel it."

2   I can feel it, too. Over the past few years I've had an uncomfortable sense that someone, or something, has been tinkering with my brain, remapping the neural circuitry, reprogramming the memory. My mind isn't going—so far as I can tell—but it's changing. I'm not thinking the way I used to think. I can feel it most strongly when I'm reading. Immersing myself in a book or a lengthy article used to be easy. My mind would get caught up in the narrative or the turns of the argument, and I'd spend hours strolling through long stretches of prose. That's rarely the case anymore. Now my concentration often starts to drift after two or three pages. I get fidgety, lose the thread, begin looking for something else to do. I feel as if I'm always dragging my wayward brain back to the text. The deep reading that used to come naturally has become a struggle.

3   I think I know what's going on. For more than a decade now, I've been spending a lot of time online, searching and surfing and sometimes adding to the great databases of the Internet. The Web has been a godsend to me as a writer. Research that once required days in the stacks or periodical rooms of libraries can now be done in minutes. A few Google searches, some quick clicks on hyperlinks, and I've got the telltale fact or pithy quote I was after. Even when I'm not working, I'm as likely as not to be foraging in the Web's info-thickets, reading and writing e-mails, scanning headlines and blog posts, watching videos and listening to podcasts, or just tripping from link to link to link. (Unlike footnotes, to which they're sometimes likened, hyperlinks don't merely point to related works; they propel you toward them.)

4   For me, as for others, the Net is becoming a universal medium, the conduit for most of the information that flows through my eyes and ears and into my mind. The advantages of having immediate access to such an incredibly rich store of information are many, and they've been widely described and duly applauded. "The perfect recall of silicon memory," *Wired's* Clive Thompson has written, "can be an enormous boon to thinking." But that boon comes at a price. As the media theorist Marshall McLuhan pointed out in the 1960s, media are not just passive channels of information. They supply the stuff of thought, but they also shape the process of thought. And what the Net seems to be doing is chipping away my capacity for concentration and contemplation. My mind now expects to take in information the way the Net distributes it: in a swiftly moving stream of particles. Once I was a scuba diver in the sea of words. Now I zip along the surface like a guy on a Jet Ski.

5   I'm not the only one. When I mention my troubles with reading to friends and acquaintances—literary types, most of them—many say they're having similar experiences. The more they use the Web, the more they have to fight to stay focused on long pieces of writing. Some of the bloggers I follow have also begun

mentioning the phenomenon. Scott Karp, who writes a blog about online media, recently confessed that he has stopped reading books altogether. "I was a lit major in college, and used to be [a] voracious book reader," he wrote. "What happened?" He speculates on the answer: "What if I do all my reading on the web not so much because the way I read has changed, i.e. I'm just seeking convenience, but because the way I THINK has changed?"

Bruce Friedman, who blogs regularly about the use of comput-   6
ers in medicine, also has described how the Internet has altered his mental habits. "I now have almost totally lost the ability to read and absorb a longish article on the Web or in print," he wrote earlier this year. A pathologist who has long been on the faculty of the University of Michigan Medical School, Friedman elaborated on his comment in a telephone conversation with me. His thinking, he said, has taken on a "staccato" quality, reflecting the way he quickly scants short passages of text from many sources online. "I can't read *War and Peace* anymore," he admitted. "I've lost the ability to do that. Even a blog post of more than three or four paragraphs is too much to absorb. I skim it."

Anecdotes alone don't prove much. And we still await the long-   7
term neurological and psychological experiments that will provide a definitive picture of how Internet use affects cognition. But a recently published study of online research habits, conducted by scholars from University College London, suggests that we may well be in the midst of a sea change in the way we read and think. As part of the five-year research program, the scholars examined computer logs documenting the behavior of visitors to two popular research sites, one operated by the British Library and one by a U.K. educational consortium, that provide access to journal articles, e-books, and other sources of written information. They found that people using the sites exhibited "a form of skimming activity," hopping from one source to another and rarely returning to any source they'd already visited. They typically read no more than one or two pages of an article or book before they would "bounce" out to another site. Sometimes they'd save a long article, but there's no evidence that they ever went back and actually read it. The authors of the study report:

> It is clear that users are not reading online in the traditional sense; indeed there are signs that new forms of "reading" are emerging as users "power browse" horizontally through titles, contents pages and abstracts going for quick wins. It almost seems that they go online to avoid reading in the traditional sense.

Thanks to the ubiquity of text on the Internet, not to mention   8
the popularity of text-messaging on cell phones, we may well be

reading more today than we did in the 1970s or 1980s, when television was our medium of choice. But its a different kind of reading, and behind it lies a different kind of thinking—perhaps even a new sense of the self. "We are not only *what* we read," says Maryanne Wolf, a developmental psychologist at Tufts University and the author of *Proust and the Squid: The Story and Science of the Reading Brain.* "We are *how* we read." Wolf worries that the style of reading promoted by the Net, a style that puts "efficiency" and "immediacy" above all else, may be weakening our capacity for the kind of deep reading that emerged when an earlier technology, the printing press, made long and complex works of prose commonplace. When we read online, she says, we tend to become "mere decoders of information." Our ability to interpret text, to make the rich mental connections that form when we read deeply and without distraction, remains largely disengaged.

9   Reading, explains Wolf, is not an instinctive skill for human beings. It's not etched into our genes the way speech is. We have to teach our minds how to translate the symbolic characters we see into the language we understand. And the media of other technologies we use in learning and practicing the craft of reading play an important part in shaping the neural circuits inside our brains. Experiments demonstrate that readers of ideograms, such as the Chinese, develop a mental circuitry for reading that is very different from the circuitry found in those of us whose written language employs an alphabet. The variations extend across many regions of the brain, including those that govern such essential cognitive functions as memory and the interpretation of visual and auditory stimuli. We can expect as well that the circuits woven by our use of the Net will be different from those woven by our reading of books and other printed works.

10   Sometime in 1882, Friedrich Nietzsche bought a typewriter—a Malling-Hansen Writing Ball, to be precise. His vision was failing, and keeping his eyes focused on a page had become exhausting and painful, often bringing on crushing headaches. He had been forced to curtail his writing, and he feared that he would soon have to give it up. The typewriter rescued him, at least for a time. Once he had mastered touch-typing, he was able to write with his eyes closed, using only the tips of his fingers. Words could once again flow from his mind to the page.

11   But the machine had a subtler effect on his work. One of Nietzsche's friends, a composer, noticed a change in the style of his writing. His already terse prose had become even tighter, more telegraphic. "Perhaps you will through this instrument even take to a new idiom," the friend wrote in a letter, noting that, in his own work, his "'thoughts' in music and language often depend on the quality of pen and paper."

12   "You are right," Nietzsche replied, "our writing equipment takes part in the forming of our thoughts." Under the sway of

the machine, writes the German media scholar Friedrich A. Kittler, Nietzsche's prose "changed from arguments to aphorisms, from thoughts to puns, from rhetoric to telegram style."

The human brain is almost infinitely malleable. People used   13
to think that our mental meshwork, the dense connections formed among the 100 billion or so neurons inside our skulls, was largely fixed by the time we reached adulthood. But brain researchers have discovered that that's not the case. James Olds, a professor of neuroscience who directs the Krasnow Institute for Advanced Study at George Mason University, says that even the adult mind "is very plastic." Nerve cells routinely break old connections and form new ones. "The brain," according to Olds, "has the ability to reprogram itself on the fly, altering the way it functions."

As we use what the sociologist Daniel Bell has called our   14
"intellectual technologies"—the tools that extend our mental rather than our physical capacities—we inevitably begin to take on the qualities of those technologies. The mechanical clock, which came into common use in the 14th century, provides a compelling example. In *Technics and Civilization,* the historian and cultural critic Lewis Mumford described how the clock "disassociated time from human events and helped create the belief in an independent world of mathematically measurable sequences." The "abstract framework of divided time" became "the point of reference for both action and thought."

The clock's methodical ticking helped bring into being the sci-   15
entific mind and the scientific man. But it also took something away. As the late MIT computer scientist Joseph Weizenbaum observed in his 1976 book, *Computer Power and Human Reason: From Judgment to Calculation,* the conception of the world that emerged from the widespread use of timekeeping instruments "remains an impoverished version of the older one, for it rests on a rejection of those direct experiences that formed the basis for, and indeed constituted, the old reality." In deciding when to eat, to work, to sleep, to rise, we stopped listening to our senses and started obeying the clock.

The process of adapting to new intellectual technologies is   16
reflected in the changing metaphors we use to explain ourselves to ourselves. When the mechanical clock arrived, people began thinking of their brains as operating "like clockwork." Today, in the age of software, we have come to think of them as operating "like computers." But the changes, neuroscience tells us, go much deeper than metaphor. Thanks to our brain's plasticity, the adaptation occurs also at a biological level.

The Internet promises to have particularly far-reaching effects   17
on cognition. In a paper published in 1936, the British mathematician Alan Turing proved that a digital computer, which at the time existed only as a theoretical machine, could be programmed

to perform the function of any other information-processing device. And that's what we're seeing today. The Internet, an immeasurably powerful computing system, is subsuming most of our other intellectual technologies. It's becoming our map and our clock, our printing press and our typewriter, our calculator and our telephone, and our radio and TV.

18   When the Net absorbs a medium, that medium is re-created in the Net's image. It injects the medium's content with hyperlinks, blinking ads, and other digital gewgaws, and it surrounds the content with the content of all the other media it has absorbed. A new e-mail message, for instance, may announce its arrival as we're glancing over the latest headlines at a newspaper's site. The result is to scatter our attention and diffuse our concentration.

19   The Net's influence doesn't end at the edges of a computer screen, either. As people's minds become attuned to the crazy quilt of Internet media, traditional media have to adapt to the audience's new expectations. Television programs add text crawls and pop-up ads, and magazines and newspapers shorten their articles, introduce capsule summaries, and crowd their pages with easy-to-browse info-snippets. When, in March of this year, *The New York Times* decided to devote the second and third pages of every edition to article abstracts, its design director, Tom Bodkin, explained that the "shortcuts" would give harried readers a quick "taste" of the day's news, sparing them the "less efficient" method of actually turning the pages and reading the articles. Old media have little choice but to play by the new-media rules.

20   Never has a communications system played so many roles in our lives—or exerted such broad influence over our thoughts— as the Internet does today. Yet, for all that's been written about the Net, there's been little consideration of how, exactly, it's reprogramming us. The Net's intellectual ethic remains obscure.

21   About the same time that Nietzsche started using his type-writer, an earnest young man named Frederick Winslow Taylor carried a stopwatch into the Midvale Steel plant in Philadelphia and began a historic series of experiments aimed at improving the efficiency of the plant's machinists. With the approval of Midvale's owners, he recruited a group of factory hands, set them to work on various metalworking machines, and recorded and timed their every movement as well as the operations of the machines. By breaking down every job into a sequence of small, discrete steps and then testing different ways of performing each one, Taylor created a set of precise instructions—an "algorithm," we might say today—for how each worker should work. Midvale's employees grumbled about the strict new regime, claiming that it turned them into little more than automatons, but the factory's productivity soared.

22   More than a hundred years after the invention of the steam engine, the Industrial Revolution had at last found its philosophy

and its philosopher. Taylor's tight industrial choreography—his "system," as he liked to call it—was embraced by manufacturers throughout the country and, in time, around the world. Seeking maximum speed, maximum efficiency, and maximum output, factory owners used time-and-motion studies to organize their work and configure the jobs of their workers. The goal, as Taylor defined it in his celebrated 1911 treatise, *The Principles of Scientific Management,* was to identify and adopt, for every job, the "one best method" of work and thereby to effect "the gradual substitution of science for rule of thumb throughout the mechanic arts." Once his system was applied to all acts of manual labor, Taylor assured his followers, it would bring about a restructuring not only of industry but of society, creating a utopia of perfect efficiency. "In the past the man has been first," he declared; "in the future the system must be first."

Taylor's system is still very much with us; it remains the ethic 23 of industrial manufacturing. And now, thanks to the growing power that computer engineers and software coders wield over our intellectual lives, Taylor's ethic is beginning to govern the realm of the mind as well. The Internet is a machine designed for the efficient and automated collection, transmission, and manipulation of information, and its legions of programmers are intent on finding the "one best method"—the perfect algorithm—to carry out every mental movement of what we've come to describe as "knowledge work."

Google's headquarters, in Mountain View, California—the 24 Googleplex—is the Internet's high church, and the religion practiced inside its walls is Taylorism. Google, says its chief executive, Eric Schmidt, is "a company that's founded around the science of measurement," and it is striving to "systematize everything" it does. Drawing on the terabytes of behavioral data it collects through its search engine and other sites, it carries out thousands of experiments a day, according to the *Harvard Business Review,* and it uses the results to refine the algorithms that increasingly control how people find information and extract meaning from it. What Taylor did for the work of the hand, Google is doing for the work of the mind.

The company has declared that its mission is "to organize the 25 world's information and make it universally accessible and useful." It seeks to develop "the perfect search engine," which it defines as something that "understands exactly what you mean and gives you back exactly what you want." In Google's view, information is a kind of commodity, a utilitarian resource that can be mined and processed with industrial efficiency. The more pieces of information we can "access" and the faster we can extract their gist, the more productive we become as thinkers.

Where does it end? Sergey Brin and Larry Page, the gifted 26 young men who founded Google while pursuing doctoral degrees in computer science at Stanford, speak frequently of their desire to turn their search engine into an artificial intelligence, a HAL-like machine that might be connected directly to our brains. "The ultimate search engine is something as smart as people—or smarter," Page said in a speech a few years back. "For us, working on search is a way to work on artificial intelligence." In a 2004 interview with *Newsweek*, Brin said, "Certainly if you had all the world's information directly attached to your brain, or an artificial brain that was smarter than your brain, you'd he better off." Last year, Page told a convention of scientists that Google is "really trying to build artificial intelligence and to do it on a large scale."

27   Such an ambition is a natural one, even an admirable one, for a pair of math whizzes with vast quantities of cash at their disposal and a small army of computer scientists in their employ. A fundamentally scientific enterprise, Google is motivated by a desire to use technology, in Eric Schmidt's words, "to solve problems that have never been solved before," and artificial intelligence is the hardest problem out there. Why wouldn't Brin and Page want to be the ones to crack it?

28   Still, their easy assumption that we'd all "be better off" if our brains were supplemented, or even replaced, by an artificial intelligence is unsettling. It suggests a belief that intelligence is the output of a mechanical process, a series of discrete steps that can be isolated, measured, and optimized. In Google's world, the world we enter when we go online, there's little place for the fuzziness of contemplation. Ambiguity is not an opening for insight but a bug to be fixed. The human brain is just an outdated computer that needs a faster processor and a bigger hard drive.

29   The idea that our minds should operate as high-speed data-processing machines is not only built into the workings of the Internet, it is the network's reigning business model as well. The faster we surf across the Web—the more links we click and pages we view—the more opportunities Google and other companies gain to collect information about us and to feed us advertisements. Most of the proprietors of the commercial Internet have a financial stake in collecting the crumbs of data we leave behind as we flit from link to link—the more crumbs, the better. The last thing these companies want is to encourage leisurely reading or slow, concentrated thought. It's in their economic interest to drive us to distraction.

30   Maybe I'm just a worrywart. Just as there's a tendency to glorify technological progress, there's a countertendency to expect the worst of every new tool or machine. In Plato's *Phaedrus*, Socrates bemoaned the development of writing. He feared that, as people came to rely on the written word as a substitute for the knowledge they used to carry inside their heads, they would,

in the words of one of the dialogue's characters, "cease to exercise their memory and become forgetful." And because they would be able to "receive a quantity of information without proper instruction," they would "be thought very knowledgeable when they are for the most part quite ignorant." They would be "filled with the conceit of wisdom instead of real wisdom." Socrates wasn't wrong—the new technology did often have the affects he feared—but he was shortsighted. He couldn't foresee the many ways that writing and reading would serve to spread information, spur fresh ideas, and expand human knowledge (if not wisdom).

The arrival of Gutenberg's printing press, in the 15th century, 31 set off another round of teeth gnashing. The Italian humanist Hieronimo Squarciafico worried that the easy availability of books would lead to intellectual laziness, making men "less studious" and weakening their minds. Others argued that cheaply printed books and broadsheets would undermine religious authority, demean the work of scholars and scribes, and spread sedition and debauchery. As New York University professor Clay Shirky notes, "Most of the arguments made against the printing press were correct, even prescient." But, again, the doomsayers were unable to imagine the myriad blessings that the printed word would deliver.

So, yes, you should be skeptical of my skepticism. Perhaps those 32 who dismiss critics of the Internet as Luddites or nostalgists will he proved correct, and from our hyperactive, data-stoked minds will spring a golden age of intellectual discovery and universal wisdom. Then again, the Net isn't the alphabet, and although it may replace the printing press, it produces something altogether different. The kind of deep reading that a sequence of printed pages promotes is valuable not just for the knowledge we acquire from the author's words but for the intellectual vibrations those words set off within our own minds. In the quiet spaces opened up by the sustained, undistracted reading of a book, or by any other act of contemplation, for that matter, we make our own associations, draw our own inferences and analogies, foster our own ideas. Deep reading, as Maryanne Wolf argues, is indistinguishable from deep thinking.

If we lose those quiet spaces, or fill them up with "content," we 33 will sacrifice something important not only in our selves but in our culture. In a recent essay, the playwright Richard Foreman eloquently described what's at stake:

> I come from a tradition of Western culture, in which the ideal (my ideal) was the complex, dense and "cathedral-like" structure of the highly educated and articulate personality— a man or woman who carried inside themselves a personally constructed and unique version of the entire heritage of the

West. [But now] I see within us all (myself included) the replacement of complex inner density with a new kind of self—evolving under the pressure of information overload and the technology of the "instantly available."

34   As we are drained of our "inner repertory of dense cultural inheritance," Foreman concluded, we risk turning into "'pancake people'—spread wide and thin as we connect with that vast network of information accessed by the mere touch of a button."

35   I'm haunted by that scene in *2001*. What makes it so poignant, and so weird, is the computer's emotional response to the disassembly of its mind: its despair as one circuit after another goes dark, its childlike pleading with the astronaut—"I can feel it. I can feel it. I'm afraid"—and its final reversion to what can only be called a state of innocence. HAL's outpouring of feeling contrasts with the emotionlessness that characterizes the human figures in the film, who go about their business with an almost robotic efficiency. Their thoughts and actions feel scripted, as if they're following the steps of an algorithm. In the world of *2001*, people have become so machinelike that the most human character turns out to be a machine. That's the essence of Kubrick's dark prophecy: as we come to rely on computers to mediate our understanding of the world, it is our own intelligence that flattens into artificial intelligence.

Pew Research Center

Does Google Make Us Stupid?

The Pew Research Center for the People & the Press is "an independent, non-partisan public opinion research organization that studies attitudes toward politics, the press, and public policy issues." As a public opinion research group, it uses polling data to gauge public opinion on a variety of topics that impact our culture and its relationship with various media. This report, issued by Janna Quitney Anderson and Lee Rainie, summarizes a 2010 poll of Internet experts who were asked their opinions on Nicholas Carr's "Is Google Making Us Stupid?" As you read, note the way that these authors use not only quantitative information, but also responses to open-ended questions to demonstrate the range of thoughts about this topic. Think also about the ways that the authors have chosen to organize those responses into specific categories, illustrating well the kind of synthesis that writers create to bring some order to a wide range of opinions—a skill that is necessary as you develop a review of the literature (as discussed in the Introduction to *Conversations*).

Respondents to the fourth "Future of the Internet" survey, conducted by the Pew Internet & American Life Project and Elon University's Imagining the Internet Center, were asked to consider the future of the internet-connected world between now and 2020 and the likely innovation that will occur. The survey required them to assess 10 different "tension pairs"—each pair offering two different 2020 scenarios with the same overall theme and opposite outcomes—and to select the one most likely choice of two statements. Although a wide range of opinion from experts, organizations, and interested institutions was sought, this survey, fielded from Dec. 2, 2009 to Jan. 11, 2010, should not be taken as a representative canvassing of internet experts. By design, the survey was an "opt in," self-selecting effort.

Among the issues addressed in the survey was the provocative question raised by eminent tech scholar Nicholas Carr in a cover story for the Atlantic Monthly magazine in the summer of 2008[1]: "Is Google Making us Stupid?" Carr argued that the ease of online searching and distractions of browsing through the web were possibly limiting his capacity to concentrate. "I'm not thinking the way I used to," he wrote, in part because he is becoming a skimming, browsing reader, rather than a deep and engaged reader. "The kind of deep reading that a sequence of printed pages promotes is valuable not just for the knowledge we acquire from the author's words but for the intellectual vibrations those words set off within our own minds. In the quiet spaces opened up by the sustained, undistracted reading of a book, or by any other act of contemplation, for that matter, we make our own associations, draw our own inferences and analogies, foster our own ideas. . . . If we lose those quiet spaces, or fill them up with 'content,' we will sacrifice something important not only in our selves but in our culture."

Jamais Cascio, an affiliate at the Institute for the Future and senior fellow at the Institute for Ethics and Emerging Technologies, challenged Carr in a subsequent article in the *Atlantic Monthly*. Cascio made the case that the array of problems facing humanity—the end of the fossil-fuel era, the fragility of the global food web, growing population density, and the spread of pandemics, among others—will force us to get smarter if we are to survive. "Most people don't realize that this process is already under way," he wrote. "In fact, it's happening all around us, across the full spectrum of how we understand intelligence. It's visible in the hive mind of the Internet, in the powerful tools for simulation and visualization that are jump-starting new scientific disciplines, and in the development of drugs that some people (myself included) have discovered let them study harder, focus better, and stay awake longer with full clarity." He argued that while the proliferation of technology and media can challenge humans' capacity to concentrate there were signs that we are developing "fluid intelligence-the ability to find meaning in confusion and solve new problems, independent of acquired knowledge." He also expressed hope that techies will develop tools to help people find and assess information smartly.

4   With that as backdrop, respondents were asked to indicate which of two statements best reflected their view on Google's effect on intelligence. The chart shows the distribution of responses to the paired statements. The first column covers the answers of 371 longtime experts who have regularly participated in these surveys. The second column covers the answers of all the respondents, including the 524 who were recruited by other experts or by their association with the Pew Internet Project. As shown, 76% of the experts agreed with the statement, "By 2020, people's use of the internet has enhanced human intelligence; as people are allowed unprecedented access to more information they become smarter and make better choices. Nicholas Carr was wrong: Google does not make us stupid."

Current experts N=371	Current total N=371	
■ 81%	■ 76%	By 2020, people's use of the internet has enhanced human intelligence; as people are allowed unprecedented access to more information, they become smarter and make better choices. Nicholas Carr was wrong: Google does not make us stupid (http://www.theatlantic.com/doc/200807/google).
— 16%	— 21%	By 2020, people's use of the internet has not enhanced human intelligence and it could even be lowering the IQs of most people who use it a lot. Nicholas Carr was right: Google makes us stupid.
- - · 4%	- - · 2%	Did not respond

5   Respondents were also asked to "share your view of the Internet's influence on the future of human intelligence in 2020—what is likely to stay the same and what will be different in the way human intellect evolves?" What follows is a selection of the hundreds of written elaborations and some of the recurring themes in those answers:

Nicholas Carr and Google staffers have their say:

- "I feel compelled to agree with myself. But I would add that the Net's effect on our intellectual lives will not be measured simply by average IQ scores. What the Net does is shift the emphasis of our intelligence, away from what might be called a meditative or contemplative intelligence and more toward what might be called a utilitarian intelligence. The price of zipping among lots of bits of information is a loss of depth in our thinking."—*Nicholas Carr*
- "My conclusion is that when the only information on a topic is a handful of essays or books, the best strategy is to read these works with total concentration. But when you have access to thousands of articles, blogs, videos, and people with expertise on the topic, a good strategy is to skim first to get an overview. Skimming and concentrating can and should coexist. I would also like to say that Carr has it mostly backwards when he says that Google is built on the principles of Taylorism [the institution of time-management and worker-activity standards in industrial settings]. Taylorism shifts responsibility from worker to management, institutes a standard method for each job, and selects workers with skills unique for a specific job. Google does the opposite, shifting responsibility from management to the worker, encouraging creativity in each job, and encouraging workers to shift among many different roles in their career. . . Carr is of course right that Google thrives on understanding data. But making sense of data (both for Google internally and for its users) is not like building the same artifact over and over on an assembly line; rather it requires creativity, a mix of broad and deep knowledge, and a host of connections to other people. That is what Google is trying to facilitate."—*Peter Norvig, Google Research Director*
- "Google will make us more informed. The smartest person in the world could well be behind a plow in China or India. Providing universal access to information will allow such people to realize their full potential, providing benefits to the entire world."—*Hal Varian, Google, chief economist*

The resources of the internet and search engines will shift cognitive capacities. We won't have to remember as much, but we'll have to think harder and have better critical thinking and analytical skills. Less time devoted to memorization gives people more time to master those new skills.

- "Google allows us to be more creative in approaching problems and more integrative in our thinking. We spend less time trying to recall and more time generating solutions."—*Paul Jones, ibiblio, University of North Carolina—Chapel Hill*

- "Google will make us stupid and intelligent at the same time. In the future, we will live in a transparent 3D mobile media cloud that surrounds us everywhere. In this cloud, we will use intelligent machines, to whom we delegate both simple and complex tasks. Therefore, we will lose the skills we needed in the old days (e.g., reading paper maps while driving a car). But we will gain the skill to make better choices (e.g., knowing to choose the mortgage that is best for you instead of best for the bank). All in all, I think the gains outweigh the losses."—*Marcel Bullinga, Dutch Futurist at futurecheck.com*

- "I think that certain tasks will be 'offloaded' to Google or other Internet services rather than performed in the mind, especially remembering minor details. But really, that is a role that paper has taken over many centuries: did Gutenberg make us stupid? On the other hand, the Internet is likely to be front-and-centre in any developments related to improvements in neuroscience and human cognition research."—*Dean Bubley, wireless industry consultant*

- "What the internet (here subsumed tongue-in-cheek under "Google") does is to support SOME parts of human intelligence, such as analysis, by REPLACING other parts such as memory. Thus, people will be more intelligent about, say, the logistics of moving around a geography because "Google" will remember the facts and relationships of various locations on their behalf. People will be better able to compare the revolutions of 1848 and 1789 because "Google" will remind them of all the details as needed. This is the continuation ad infinitum of the process launched by abacuses and calculators: we have become more "stupid" by losing our arithmetic skills but more intelligent at evaluating numbers."—*Andreas Kluth, writer, Economist magazine*

- "It's a mistake to treat intelligence as an undifferentiated whole. No doubt we will become worse at doing some things ('more stupid') requiring rote memory of information that is now available through Google. But with this capacity freed, we may (and probably will) be capable of more advanced integration and evaluation of information ('more intelligent')."—*Stephen Downes, National Research Council, Canada*

- "The new learning system, more informal perhaps than formal, will eventually win since we must use technology to cause everyone to learn more, more economically and faster if everyone is to be economically productive and prosperous. Maintaining the status quo will only continue the existing win/lose society that we have with those who can learn in present school structure doing ok, while more and more students drop out, learn less, and fail to find a productive niche in the future."—*Ed Lyell, former member of the Colorado State Board of Education and Telecommunication Advisory Commission*

- "The question is flawed: Google will make intelligence different. As Carr himself suggests, Plato argued that reading and writing would make us stupid, and from the perspective of a preliterate, he was correct. Holding in your head information that is easily discoverable on Google will no longer be a mark of intelligence, but a side-show act. Being able to quickly and effectively discover information and solve problems, rather than do it "in your head," will be the metric we use."—*Alex Halavais, Vice President, Association of Internet Researchers*

- "What Google does do is simply to enable us to shift certain tasks to the network—we no longer need to rote-learn certain seldomly-used facts (the periodic table, the post code of Ballarat) if they're only a search away, for example. That's problematic, of course—we put an awful amount of trust in places such as Wikipedia where such information is stored, and in search engines like Google through which we retrieve it—but it doesn't make us stupid, any more than having access to a library (or in fact, access to writing) makes us stupid. That said, I don't know that the reverse is true, either: Google and the Net also don't automatically make us smarter. By 2020, we will have even more access to even more information, using even more sophisticated search and retrieval tools—but how smartly we can make use of this potential depends on whether our media literacies and capacities have caught up, too."—*Axel Bruns, Associate Professor, Queensland University of Technology*

- "My ability to do mental arithmetic is worse than my grandfather's because I grew up in an era with pervasive personal calculators. . . . I am not stupid compared to my grandfather, but I believe the development of my brain has been changed by the availability of technology. The same will happen (or is happening) as a result of the Googleization of knowledge. People are becoming used to bite sized chunks of information that are compiled and sorted by an algorithm. This must be having an impact on our brains, but it is too simplistic to say that we are becoming stupid as a result of Google."—*Robert Acklund, Australian National University*

- "We become adept at using useful tools, and hence perfect new skills. Other skills may diminish. I agree with Carr that we may on the average become less patient, less willing to read through a long, linear text, but we may also become more adept at dealing with multiple factors. ... Note that I said 'less patient,' which is not the same as 'lower IQ.' I suspect that emotional and personality changes will probably more marked than 'intelligence' changes."—*Larry Press, California State University, Dominguz Hills*

Technology isn't the problem here. It is people's inherent character traits. The internet and search engines just enable people to be more of what they already are. If they are motivated to learn and shrewd, they will use new tools to explore in exciting new ways. If they are lazy or incapable of concentrating, they will find new ways to be distracted and goof off.

- "The question is all about people's choices. If we value introspection as a road to insight, if we believe that long experience with issues contributes to good judgment on those issues, if we (in short) want knowledge that search engines don't give us, we'll maintain our depth of thinking and Google will only enhance it. There is a trend, of course, toward instant analysis and knee-jerk responses to events that degrades a lot of writing and discussion. We can't blame search engines for that . . . What search engines do is provide more information, which we can use either to become dilettantes (Carr's worry) or to bolster our knowledge around the edges and do fact-checking while we rely mostly on information we've gained in more robust ways for our core analyses. Google frees the time we used to spend pulling together the last 10% of facts we need to complete our research. I read Carr's article when *The Atlantic* first published it, but I used a web search to pull it back up and review it before writing this response. Google is my friend."—*Andy Oram, editor and blogger, O'Reilly Media*
- "Google isn't making us stupid—but it is making many of us intellectually lazy. This has already become a big problem in university classrooms. For my undergrad majors in Communication Studies, Google may take over the hard work involved in finding good source material for written assignments. Unless pushed in the right direction, students will opt for the top 10 or 15 hits as their research strategy. And it's the students most in need of research training who are the least likely to avail themselves of more sophisticated tools like Google Scholar. Like other major technologies, Google's search functionality won't push the human intellect in one predetermined direction. It will reinforce certain dispositions in the end-user: stronger intellects will use Google as a creative tool, while others will let Google do the thinking for them."—*David Ellis, York University, Toronto*

- "For people who are readers and who are willing to explore new sources and new arguments, we can only be made better by the kinds of searches we will be able to do. Of course, the kind of Googled future that I am concerned about is the one in which my every desire is anticipated, and my every fear avoided by my guardian Google. Even then, I might not be stupid, just not terribly interesting."— *Oscar Gandy, emeritus professor, University of Pennsylvania*

- "I don't think having access to information can ever make anyone stupider. I don't think an adult's IQ can be influenced much either way by reading anything and I would guess that smart people will use the Internet for smart things and stupid people will use it for stupid things in the same way that smart people read literature and stupid people read crap fiction. On the whole, having easy access to more information will make society as a group smarter though."—*Sandra Kelly, market researcher, 3M Corporation*

- "The story of humankind is that of work substitution and human enhancement. The Neolithic revolution brought the substitution of some human physical work by animal work. The Industrial revolution brought more substitution of human physical work by machine work. The Digital revolution is implying a significant substitution of human brain work by computers and ICTs in general. Whenever a substitution has taken place, men have been able to focus on more qualitative tasks, entering a virtuous cycle: the more qualitative the tasks, the more his intelligence develops; and the more intelligent he gets, more qualitative tasks he can perform . . . As obesity might be the side-effect of physical work substitution by machines, mental laziness can become the watermark of mental work substitution by computers, thus having a negative effect instead of a positive one."—*Ismael Peña-Lopez, lecturer at the Open University of Catalonia, School of Law and Political Science*

- "Well, of course, it depends on what one means by 'stupid'— I imagine that Google, and its as yet unimaginable new features and capabilities will both improve and decrease some of our human capabilities. Certainly it's much easier to find out stuff, including historical, accurate, and true stuff, as well as entertaining, ironic, and creative stuff. It's also making some folks lazier, less concerned about investing in the time and energy to arrive at conclusions, etc."—*Ron Rice, University of California, Santa Barbara*

- "Nick [Carr] says, 'Once I was a scuba diver in the sea of words. Now I zip along the surface like a guy on a Jet Ski.' Besides finding that a little hard to believe (I know Nick to be a deep diver, still), there is nothing about Google, or the Net, to keep anyone from diving—and to depths that were not reachable before the Net came along."—*Doc Searls, co-author of "The Cluetrain Manifesto"*

It's not Google's fault if users create stupid queries.

- "To be more precise, unthinking use of the Internet, and in particular untutored use of Google, has the ability to make us stupid, but that is not a foregone conclusion. More and more of us experience attention deficit, like Bruce Friedman in the Nicholas Carr article, but that alone does not stop us making good choices provided that the 'factoids' of information are sound that we use to make out decisions. The potential for stupidity comes where we rely on Google (or Yahoo, or Bing, or any engine) to provide relevant information in response to poorly constructed queries, frequently one-word queries, and then base decisions or conclusions on those returned items."—*Peter Griffiths, former Head of Information at the Home Office within the Office of the Chief Information Officer, United Kingdom*
- "The problem isn't Google; it's what Google helps us find. For some, Google will let them find useless content that does not challenge their minds. But for others, Google will lead them to expect answers to questions, to explore the world, to see and think for themselves."—*Esther Dyson, longtime internet expert and investor*
- "People are already using Google as an adjunct to their own memory. For example, I have a hunch about something, need facts to support, and Google comes through for me. Sometimes, I see I'm wrong, and I appreciate finding that out before I open my mouth."—*Craig Newmark, founder Craig's List*
- "Google is a data access tool. Not all of that data is useful or correct. I suspect the amount of misleading data is increasing faster than the amount of correct data. There should also be a distinction made between data and information. Data is meaningless in the absence of an organizing context. That means that different people looking at the same data are likely to come to different conclusions. There is a big difference with what a world class artist can do with a paint brush as opposed to a monkey. In other words, the value of Google will depend on what the user brings to the game. The value of data is highly dependent on the quality of the question being asked."—*Robert Lunn, consultant, FocalPoint Analytics*

The big struggle is over what kind of information Google and other search engines kick back to users. In the age of social media where users can be their own content creators it might get harder and harder to separate high-quality material from junk.

- "Access to more information isn't enough—the information needs to be correct, timely, and presented in a manner that enables the reader to learn from it. The current network is full of inaccurate, misleading, and biased information that often crowds out the valid information. People have not learned that 'popular' or 'available' information is not necessarily valid."—*Gene Spafford, Purdue University CERIAS, Association for Computing Machinery U.S. Public Policy Council*
- "If we take 'Google' to mean the complex social, economic and cultural phenomenon that is a massively interactive search and retrieval information system used by people and yet also using them to generate its data, I think Google will, at the very least, not make us smarter and probably will make us more stupid in the sense of being reliant on crude, generalised approximations of truth and information finding. Where the questions are easy, Google will therefore help; where the questions are complex, we will flounder."—*Matt Allen, former President of the Association of Internet Researchers and Associate Professor of Internet Studies at Curtin University in Australia*
- "The challenge is in separating that wheat from the chaff, as it always has been with any other source of mass information, which has been the case all the way back to ancient institutions like libraries. Those users (of Google, cable TV, or libraries) who can do so efficiently will beat the odds, becoming 'smarter' and making better choices. However, the unfortunately majority will continue to remain, as Carr says, stupid."—*Christopher Saunders, managing editor, internetnews.com*
- "The problem with Google that is lurking just under the clean design home page is the "tragedy of the commons": the link quality seems to go down every year. The link quality may actually not be going down but the signal to noise is getting worse as commercial schemes lead to more and more junk links."—*Glen Edens, former Senior Vice President and Director at Sun Microsystems Laboratories, Chief Scientist Hewlett Packard*

Literary intelligence is very much under threat.

- "If one defines—or partially defines—IQ as literary intelligence, the ability to sit with a piece of textual material and analyze it for complex meaning and retain derived knowledge, then we are indeed in trouble. Literary culture is in trouble . . . We are spending less time reading books, but the amount of pure information that we produce as a civilization continues to expand exponentially. That these trends are linked, that the rise of the latter is causing the decline of the former, is not impossible . . . One could draw reassurance from today's vibrant Web culture if the general surfing public, which is becoming more at home in this new medium, displayed a growing propensity for literate, critical thought. But take a careful look at the many blogs, post comments, Facebook pages, and online conversations that characterize today's Web 2.0 environment . . . This type of content generation, this method of 'writing,' is not only sub-literate, it may actually undermine the literary impulse . . . Hours spent texting and e-mailing, according to this view, do not translate into improved writing or reading skills."—*Patrick Tucker, Senior Editor, The Futurist magazine*

New literacies will be required to function in this world. In fact, the internet might change the very notion of what it means to be smart. Retrieval of good information will be prized. Maybe a race of "extreme Googlers" will come into being.

- "The critical uncertainty here is whether people will learn and be taught the essential literacies necessary for thriving in the current infosphere: attention, participation, collaboration, crap detection, and network awareness are the ones I'm concentrating on. I have no reason to believe that people will be any less credulous, gullible, lazy, or prejudiced in ten years, and am not optimistic about the rate of change in our education systems, but it is clear to me that people are not going to be smarter without learning the ropes."—*Howard Rheingold, author of several prominent books on technology, teacher at Stanford University and University of California-Berkeley*
- "Google makes us simultaneously smarter and stupider. Got a question? With instant access to practically every piece of information ever known to humankind, we take for granted we're only a quick Web search away from the answer. Of course, that doesn't mean we understand it. In the coming years we will have to continue to teach people to think critically so they can better understand the wealth of information available to them."—*Jeska Dzwigalski, Linden Lab*
- "We might imagine that in ten years, our definition of intelligence will look very different. By then, we might agree on 'smart' as something like a 'networked' or 'distributed' intelligence where knowledge is our ability to piece together various and disparate bits of information

into coherent and novel forms."—*Christine Greenhow, educational researcher, University of Minnesota and Yale Information and Society Project*

- "Human intellect will shift from the ability to retain knowledge towards the skills to discover the information i.e. a race of extreme Googlers (or whatever discovery tools come next). The world of information technology will be dominated by the algorithm designers and their librarian cohorts. Of course, the information they're searching has to be right in the first place. And who decides that?"—*Sam Michel, founder Chinwag, community for digital media practitioners in the United Kingdom*

One new "literacy" that might help is the capacity to build and use social networks to help people solve problems.

- "There's no doubt that the internet is an extension of human intelligence, both individual and collective. But the extent to which it's able to augment intelligence depends on how much people are able to make it conform to their needs. Being able to look up who starred in the 2nd season of the Tracey Ullman show on Wikipedia is the lowest form of intelligence augmentation; being able to build social networks and interactive software that helps you answer specific questions or enrich your intellectual life is much more powerful. This will matter even more as the internet becomes more pervasive. Already my iPhone functions as the external, silicon lobe of my brain. For it to help me become even smarter, it will need to be even more effective and flexible than it already is. What worries me is that device manufacturers and internet developers are more concerned with lock-in than they are with making people smarter. That means it will be a constant struggle for individuals to reclaim their intelligence from the networks they increasingly depend upon."—*Dylan Tweney, Senior Editor, Wired magazine*

Nothing can be bad that delivers more information to people, more efficiently. It might be that some people lose their way in this world, but overall, societies will be substantially smarter.

- "The Internet has facilitated orders of magnitude improvements in access to information. People now answer questions in a few moments that a couple of decades back they would not have bothered to ask, since getting the answer would have been impossibly difficult."—*John Pike, Director, globalsecurity.org*
- "Google is simply one step, albeit a major one, in the continuing continuum of how technology changes our

generation and use of data, information, and knowledge that has been evolving for decades. As the data and information goes digital and new information is created, which is at an ever increasing rate, the resultant ability to evaluate, distill, coordinate, collaborate, problem solve only increases along a similar line. Where it may appear a 'dumbing down' has occurred on one hand, it is offset (I believe in multiples) by how we learn in new ways to learn, generate new knowledge, problem solve, and innovate."—*Mario Morino, Chairman, Venture Philanthropy Partners*

Google itself and other search technologies will get better over time and that will help solve problems created by too-much-information and too-much-distraction.

- "I'm optimistic that Google will get smarter by 2020 or will be replaced by a utility that is far better than Google. That tool will allow queries to trigger chains of high-quality information—much closer to knowledge than flood. Humans who are able to access these chains in high-speed, immersive ways will have more patters available to them that will aid decision-making. All of this optimism will only work out if the battle for the soul of the Internet is won by the right people—the people who believe that open, fast, networks are good for all of us."—*Susan Crawford, former member of President Obama's National Economic Council, now on the law faculty at the University of Michigan*
- "If I am using Google to find an answer, it is very likely the answer I find will be on a message board in which other humans are collaboratively debating answers to questions. I will have to choose between the answer I like the best. Or it will force me to do more research to find more information. Google never breeds passivity or stupidity in me: It catalyzes me to explore further. And along the way I bump into more humans, more ideas and more answers."—*Joshua Fouts, Senior Fellow for Digital Media & Public Policy at the Center for the Study of the Presidency*

The more we use the internet and search, the more dependent on it we will become.

- "As the Internet gets more sophisticated it will enable a greater sense of empowerment among users. We will not be more stupid, but we will probably be more dependent upon it."—*Bernie Hogan, Oxford Internet Institute*

Even in little ways, including in dinner table chitchat, Google can make people smarter.

- "[Family dinner conversations] have changed markedly because we can now look things up at will. That's just one small piece of evidence I see that having Google at hand is great for civilization."—*Jerry Michalski, president, Sociate*

'We know more than ever, and this makes us crazy.'

- "The answer is really: both. Google has already made us smarter, able to make faster choices from more information. Children, to say nothing of adults, scientists, and professionals in virtually every field, can seek and discover knowledge in ways and with scope and scale that was unfathomable before Google. Google has undoubtedly expanded our access to knowledge that can be experienced on a screen, or even processed through algorithms, or mapped. Yet Google has also made us careless too, or stupid when, for instance, Google driving directions don't get us to the right place. It has confused and overwhelmed us with choices, and with sources that are not easily differentiated or verified. Perhaps it's even alienated us from the physical world itself—from knowledge and intelligence that comes from seeing, touching, hearing, breathing and tasting life. From looking into someone's eyes and having them look back into ours. Perhaps it's made us impatient, or shortened our attention spans, or diminished our ability to understand long thoughts. It's enlightened anxiety. We know more than ever, and this makes us crazy."— *Andrew Nachison, co-founder, We Media*

A final thought: Maybe Google won't make us more stupid, but it should make us more modest.

- "There is and will be lots more to think about, and a lot more are thinking. No, not more stupid. Maybe more humble."—*Sheizaf Rafaeli, Center for the Study of the Information Society, University of Haifa*

Notes

1. Nicholes Carr's article "Is Google Making Us Stupid?" was published in the summer of 2008, not the summer of 2009 as this report originally stated.

Trent Batson

Response to Nicholas Carr's "Is Google Making Us Stupid?"

Trent Batson has served as a professor of English, as Director of Academic Computing at two universities, and as a communications strategist at MIT. He is Director of the Association for Authentic, Experiential, and Evidence-Based Learning. His research areas include e-portfolios, teaching digital writing, and other areas that bring together technological literacy and learning. In this essay, first published in 2009 in *Campus Technology*, Batson takes issue with Carr's contention that technologies like Google are harmful, suggesting instead that they are creating a wider conversation, "like listening to a bunch of people talking." As you read, then, you might consider the stasis points between Carr and Batson and, more specifically, whether technology has indeed provided a useful and effective form of public dialogue.

1   Criticism of the Web most often questions whether we are becoming more superficial and scattered in our thinking. In the July–August 2008 *Atlantic* magazine, Nicholas Carr published "Is Google Making Us Stupid?" Like other critics, he sees change as loss and not as gain. But, his own criticism is superficial and misses the humanizing impact of Web 2.0.

2   Nicholas Carr is an important voice today in pointing to the nervousness that many people have about technology. He recently published *The Big Switch; Rewiring the World, from Edison to Google*, which is in its seventh printing. His blog is well worth reading regularly: *http://www.roughtype.com/*. His views are carefully constructed and researched. He is a skilled writer and is widely read.

3   And, academics often express the same concerns Carr does in his *Atlantic* article. Our concerns are about the qualitative differences in how net-gen students think and write and learn. Nicholas Carr is giving voice to these concerns. This article is about one skill that he believes is being eroded, that of reading:

> "I'm not thinking the way I used to think. I can feel it most strongly when I'm reading. Immersing myself in a book or a lengthy article used to be easy. My mind would get caught up in the narrative or the turns of the argument, and I'd spend

hours strolling through long stretches of prose. That's rarely the case anymore. Now my concentration often starts to drift after two or three pages. I get fidgety, lose the thread, begin looking for something else to do. I feel as if I'm always dragging my wayward brain back to the text. The deep reading that used to come naturally has become a struggle."

He says this change is because of all the time he spends online.   4
As a writer, he finds the Web a valuable tool, but he thinks it's having a bad effect on his concentration. He says "Once I was a scuba diver in the sea of words. Now I zip along the surface like a guy on a Jet Ski." He refers to a 5-year study in the UK, which found that people visiting their sites "exhibited 'a form of skimming activity,' hopping from one source to another and rarely returning to any source they'd already visited."

Carr admits that we, as a culture, read a lot more because of   5
the Web, but laments that "our ability to interpret text, to make the rich mental connections that form when we read deeply and without distraction, remains largely disengaged." And he highlights a quote from an essay by the playwright Richard Foreman:

> "I come from a tradition of Western culture, in which the ideal (my ideal) was the complex, dense, and 'cathedral-like' structure of the highly educated and articulate personality— a man or woman who carried inside themselves a personally constructed and unique version of the entire heritage of the West. [But now] I see within us all (myself included) there placement of complex inner density with a new kind of self—evolving under the pressure of information overload and the technology of the 'instantly available.'"

As an advocate for technology in higher education over the past   6
20 years, I've heard similar warnings for years. Indeed, some people reading this article may believe that Carr has hit the nail on the head. There is no question that our habits are changing: The Web has captured our attention and is now the default starting point for almost all work. The Web is different in almost all aspects from a book. Printed books have contained the essential truths of humanity for half a millennium. The Web is where we look for knowledge that usually exists not in final, authoritative, single-author text blocks but in the aggregate of wisdom from many sites.

Carr sees only one side of the change we are going through, the   7
loss of book habits. But, for us over our thousands of years of learning, the book is the anomaly, not the Web. The book led us to think that one person could write a permanent compilation of truth. Books lived on over the years, separated from their authors,

a single voice, implying that knowledge is a thing or a commodity, creating the legal fiction that one person "owned" the ideas in a book as though the author had grown up in isolation from all other humans and all the ideas had sprung, fully-formed, from his or her brain.

8   Books are heavy and expensive and take a long time to produce. Knowledge based in books, therefore, is slow to develop, hard to respond to, and is scarce. People responded to books with reviews, with articles, and with new books. Human gregariousness was therefore slowed to a snail's pace as conversation around a book was carried out in the lengthy print process. Books built our culture, don't get me wrong, and have provided wonderful wealth, but ultimately they also undervalued and ignored the natural ways that humans learn: through oral interaction and in a group.

9   It is easy to criticize a new technology; it is much harder to understand how the new technology can help create new abilities in humans. And even much harder to understand how technology can actually recapture and re-enable human abilities.

10   What Carr describes and is most worried about, how we "skim" and "bounce" around in our reading, is actually a kind of new orality: We are reading as we speak when we are in a group. We "listen" to one statement, then another and another in quick succession: Our reading on the Web is like listening to a bunch of people talking. It's hybrid orality. We find ourselves once again the naturally gregarious humans we always were. We find ourselves creating knowledge continually and rapidly as our social contacts on the Web expand. We have rediscovered new ways to enjoy learning in a social setting.

11   No, Google is not making us stupid. What Google and the Web are doing is helping us reclaim our human legacy of learning through a rapid exchange of ideas in a social setting. Google is, indeed, making us smarter as we rediscover new ways to learn.

Conversations 2.0: Is Google Making Us Stupid?

12
In the current environment, many public conversations take place in a virtual, online space. And while calling these conversations "virtual conversations" might make them seem less real or less important, that is not the case. In fact, online conversations have become one of the central locations for public debate on key issues, including the issues that are included in this book. To enrich your understanding of public conversations, you can make use of the array of online discussion boards, listservs, blogs, Facebook pages, and Twitter sites that are available via the web. The Conversations 2.0 *pages in this book suggest some possible*

ways to do so, and point out some particularly useful and credible online conversations; you of course can use your own online forums and communities to add to these suggestions—or even to start your own.

Nicholas Carr's essay, which asked an extremely provocative   13
question ("Is google making us stupid") strikes at the heart of the
cyber-world. It thus predictably caused a great deal of buzz in
online communities. If you were to (ironically) google the title,
you would find a great many responses to that question which
range from complete agreement to excoriating attacks upon
Carr's contentions. You might also try just searching the terms
"is making us stupid," and you would find a whole host of technologies and new discoveries that some suggest are leading to a
dumbed-down society. Try it out, and as you browse some of the
results, analyze the various arguments you find there, judging
them by credibility, quality of evidence, and motivations of the
writers. You can also consider your own use of online resources.
One specific site that would be worth investigating is maintained   14
by a group called "The Reality Club." Just search "reality club and
Google" and you'll find it. This group of responses to Nicholas
Carr's essay was published by The Edge Foundation, an organization whose mission is "to promote inquiry into and discussion of
intellectual, philosophical, artistic, and literary issues, as well as
to work for the intellectual and social achievement of society." Contributors include: W. Daniel Hillis, an American inventor and
entrepreneur who founded Thinking Machines Corporation; Kevin
Kelly, co-founder and former Senior Editor of *Wired* magazine;
Larry Sanger, co-founder of Wikpedia; George Dyson, a scientific
historian and author of *Project Orion: The Atomic Spaceship
1957–1965* and *Darwin Among the Machines: The Evolution of
Global Intelligence*; Jaron Lanier, an artist and computer scientist
with expertise in—and a frequent speaker and author on—virtual
reality issues; and Douglas Rushkoff, who teaches Media Studies
at The New School and who is the author of ten best selling books,
including *Cyberia, Media Virus, Playing the Future,* and *Get Back in
the Box: Innovation from the Inside Out.* Unlike some sites, then,
this one is comprised of a group of high-level experts on technology's effects, and so are particularly qualified to comment upon
Carr's controversial essay. As you read, consider the points of contention among them, searching for specific topics that might
inform your own further reading and research.

Katherine Allen

Is Technology Making Us Dumb?

At the time this essay was written, Katherine Allen was a senior at University Laboratory High School in Urbana, Illinois. *The Online Gargoyle,* where this piece first appeared in 2009, is a publication of that school. In her essay, she brings the perspective of her own generation to this discussion of technology's effects, examining the various technologies that inform that generation's world, and how they affect the "reading and thinking styles" of young people. As you read and reflect on this piece, you might consider whether you believe that students educated in today's environment do in fact have fundamental differences in learning styles and methods from those of previous generations—and if so, what the effects of those differences are.

1   You've all heard tales of travelers who got stuck on unnavigable back roads or who ended up hundreds of miles off course after blindly following the directions on their global positioning systems. Their unquestioning reliance on technology negated the need to look at actual "ye olde mappes," or heed roadside warnings.

2   I yearned for a map at times during my college road trip this past summer. (Unfortunately the maps were stuck in the trunk in a very un-get-at-able spot.) At any given moment I, with the assistance of Maggie (our somewhat-trusty Magellan GPS), could pinpoint my exact coordinates on earth. Sadly, unless I paid attention, I was not always entirely certain which state I was in.

3   GPS navigation, like any other technology, is quite reliable, so it is easy for us to let our guard down—to let it do all the thinking for us. Sometimes we may lose something in the process. Who still plans a route or bothers to memorize a phone number?

In elementary school I knew my friends' phone numbers, 4
addresses, and even birthdays off by heart. Apart from a few
emergency numbers I no longer make an effort—and why
should I? It is right there on my phone. Memorizing this type of
information is not really terribly important. The simple fact of
memorization, however, is, and any Uni student can tell you that
there is plenty of that going on in our daily lives.

Luddites have decried new "tools" since the first workers were 5
displaced by less labor-intensive technologies. Their tendency to
expect the worst of every new technology should not alarm us.
Yet it is foolish to dismiss their concerns.

Claims like "Google is making us stupid" deserve attention. 6
Supposedly the Internet has changed the way we read—as
Nicholas Carr laments, "Once I was a scuba diver in the sea of
words. Now I zip along the surface like a guy on a Jet Ski."

Apparently old classics like *War and Peace* have become chal- 7
lenging reading because the Internet has dumbed us down.
Reading with concentration and contemplation is no longer possible. The Internet seems to have weaned us from that.

Technology and its concurrent ills are more a symptom of the 8
world we live in than a cause of the "decline." Sure, we rapidly
navigate through pages and "randomly" follow links from topic
to topic (down the rabbit hole to subjects we would never have
dreamt of reading about).

This style may indeed decrease our capacity for concentration 9
and contemplation, but given the vast amount of information
available to us, we have to make choices about what we will
skim and what we will read in depth.

It's inevitable that our reading and thinking styles will not be 10
the same as those of readers who lived in an isolated, slow, and
less complicated world. Having grown up with the Internet we
(my generation) are capable of a "skimming Internet" style of
reading as well as "deep *War and Peace*" style of reading. How
many readers from the previous generation can say they read
700-page novels nonstop in their preteens? Being comfortable
with both big fat books and the Internet, we actually end up
reading more than previous generations.

Technology is a benefit to curious people since they have 11
tremendous resources at their disposal. People who are too lazy
to think will always end up doing something odd or lazy, and
technology should not be blamed for it.

Chris DeWolfe

The MySpace Generation

Chris DeWolfe is one of the creators of MySpace (along with Tom Anderson), and currently serves as its CEO. (MySpace was recently sold to News Corporation for $580 million dollars.) He holds a degree from the University of Southern California. In this essay, which was published as the cover story of Forbes, a respected business magazine, DeWolfe touts what he feels are the strengths of the MySpace generation, which gets its news not from newspapers or television, but which rather "shapes its world through networks of friends." Compare this perspective on MySpace to the essay by Alex Williams that follows, considering how much of a political influence social networking sites are likely to have on our political future.

1   Last year two guys in Los Angeles came up with an elegantly simple idea. Why not hit a grocery store, load up on tortillas, rice and beans, go home to make burritos and distribute them to the homeless? It's cheap, it's easy and, while it may not precisely comply with health code regulations, it's an immediate way to feed hungry people.

2   As they started their work, what would come to be known as the Burrito Project acquired a few more friends in L.A. who liked the idea, were up for chipping in a few bucks now and then and were excited to cycle around town helping the homeless.

3   The Burrito Project guys created a MySpace page (www.myspace.com/burritoproject) to share their work with others. Without spending a dime on advertising, their MySpace community grew to 4,800, and word spread to other cities. In short order burrito projects were launched in nearby San Bernardino, Calif., and across the country in Charlotte, N.C.

4   In November, MySpace launched the Impact Awards (www.myspace.com/impactawards), a program honoring individuals and organizations having a positive effect on the world through the site. In just days we received tens of thousands of nominations for deserving groups, including dozens of nominations for the Burrito Project. The MySpace community voted in overwhelming numbers, and the Burrito Project was a landslide winner, taking home a $10,000 check and a hefty package of promotion on our site.

As a consequence the Burrito Project has gone global. There   5
are now projects not only in Phoenix, Detroit and Denver, but
also in Mexico City and Damascus, Syria, where MySpace users
created a Falafel Project (www.myspace.com/falafelproject).

At MySpace we've expanded rapidly overseas, launching in   6
more than a country a month since June of last year, but
we don't have a site in Syria and we're not yet translated into
Arabic. Still, Syrians learned about the project through MySpace
and were moved enough to act. All of which just blows me away.

People have come to expect stories about musicians or filmmak-   7
ers who get the big breaks because they were discovered on
MySpace. But the mainstream media have so far missed the boat
on the extent to which MySpace serves as a platform for doing
good.

The generation that has flocked to MySpace is thought by   8
many to be so self-involved that it has no idea what's happening
in the rest of the world. Understandable judgment, perhaps, but
it couldn't be further from the truth. They care about community, and they're actively engaged in civic causes. Young people
balance their interests in the latest fashions and the hottest dubs
with intrigue about going carbon-neutral and concern for entire
villages being wiped out in Darfur.

We created a site and a community that offer a truly level play-   9
ing field. It's free, it's easy and it has an equal chance to work for
everyone. We offer a democracy of ideas and tools to communicate them.

As we create avenues for the consumption of culture, we are   10
enabling people-powered politics in new ways. If Thomas Paine
were around today, he wouldn't be pamphleteering, he'd be vlog-
ging (video blogging).

In January we ran a contest called MyState of the Union, ask-   11
ing users to submit a minute of video giving their own views on
what's going on in our country. A panel of judges that included
former Senate Majority Leader Bill Frist and onetime White
House Chief of Staff John Podesta selected the best submissions.
The day before President Bush's address our community chose
a 32-year-old from Boise, Idaho as the winner. His message
spread through MySpace, and his appearances on broadcast and
cable news outlets allowed him to reach a broad swath of the
American public (www.myspace.com/mystateoftheunion).

The recent launch of a recut version of Apple's famous 1984   12
advertisement illustrates how user-generated video puts political power back in the hands of everyday people. The defining ad
of this upcoming political cycle may not be produced by a group
of Beltway campaign hands or even this election's version of the
Swift Boat Veterans—it will come from a young person with a
$100 digital camera and Final Cut software.

13   The MySpace generation is not reinventing political communication on its own; modern day politicians are doing their part, as well. The leading candidates for President have MySpace pages; some are offering users customized banners, wallpapers and news feeds, creating, so to speak, digital yard signs for their campaigns. But unlike cardboard posters, these signs can be interactive, shared virally and spread rapidly through an intricately connected virtual neighborhood.

14   The MySpace generation doesn't really read newspapers or watch a lot of television. This group shapes its views of the world through networks of friends. In past elections it was almost impossible for young voters to touch candidates, to interact with them directly, to get a feel for who they are. Now citizens of the Web have the chance to discover the issues by getting to know candidates just as they interact with their buddies, as well as with comedians and bands. That's why John McCain was smart to post his March Madness picks, and John Edwards did well to offer a candid behind-the-scenes video that didn't have an overproduced feel.

15   We offer a far more immediate and intuitive means of two-way communication than has ever existed. It has the potential to redemocratize politics—not just in America but around the world. This is social networking at its very best. And we're only at the very beginning. This revolution will not be televised—it will be Webcast. It's already happening.

Edward Tufte

PowerPoint Is Evil

Edward Tufte is among the foremost experts in the ways that we communicate quantitative and technological information. He teaches statistics, graphic design, and political economics at Yale University, and is the author of the highly influential books, *The Visual Display of Quantitative Information, Visual Explanations, Political Control of the Economy*, and *Data Analysis for Politics and Policy*. In this brief essay published in *Wired* in 2009, Tufte draws upon his extensive studies of the ways that information is communicated and his longer work, *The Cognitive Style of PowerPoint*, to suggest the ways that he believes PowerPoint "disrupts, dominates, and trivializes content." As you read, consider your experience with

PowerPoint presentations—both as a user and as an audience—in order to respond to Tufte's argument. More specifically, you might consider the ways that using PowerPoint either helps you organize your argument and effectively present information, or how it constrains your abilities to do so.

Power Corrupts.
PowerPoint Corrupts Absolutely.

I magine a widely used and expensive prescription drug that 1 promised to make us beautiful but didn't. Instead the drug had frequent, serious side effects: It induced stupidity, turned everyone into bores, wasted time, and degraded the quality and credibility of communication. These side effects would rightly lead to a worldwide product recall.

Yet slideware—computer programs for presentations—is 2 everywhere: in corporate America, in government bureaucracies, even in our schools. Several hundred million copies of Microsoft PowerPoint are churning out trillions of slides each year. Slideware may help speakers outline their talks, but convenience for the speaker can be punishing to both content and audience. The standard PowerPoint presentation elevates format over content, betraying an attitude of commercialism that turns everything into a sales pitch.

Of course, data-driven meetings are nothing new. Years before 3 today's slideware, presentations at companies such as IBM and in the military used bullet lists shown by overhead projectors. But the format has become ubiquitous under PowerPoint, which was created in 1984 and later acquired by Microsoft. Power-Point's pushy style seeks to set up a speaker's dominance over the audience. The speaker, after all, is making power points with bullets to followers. Could any metaphor be worse? Voicemail menu systems? Billboards? Television? Stalin?

Particularly disturbing is the adoption of the PowerPoint cog- 4 nitive style in our schools. Rather than learning to write a report using sentences, children are being taught how to formulate client pitches and infomercials. Elementary school PowerPoint exercises (as seen in teacher guides and in student work posted on the Internet) typically consist of 10 to 20 words and a piece of clip art on each slide in a presentation of three to six slides—a total of perhaps 80 words (15 seconds of silent reading) for a week of work. Students would be better off if the schools simply closed down on those days and everyone went to the Exploratorium or wrote an illustrated essay explaining something.

In a business setting, a PowerPoint slide typically shows 40 5 words, which is about eight seconds' worth of silent reading material. With so little information per slide, many, many slides are needed. Audiences consequently endure a relentless sequentiality, one damn slide after another. When information is stacked in time, it is difficult to understand context and evaluate relationships. Visual reasoning usually works more effectively when relevant information is shown side by side. Often, the more intense the detail, the greater the clarity and understanding. This is especially so for statistical data, where the fundamental analytical act is to make comparisons.

6   Consider an important and intriguing table of survival rates for those with cancer relative to those without cancer for the same time period. Some 196 numbers and 57 words describe survival rates and their standard errors for 24 cancers.

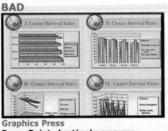

GOOD

Graphics Press
A traditional table: rich, informative, clear.

BAD

Graphics Press
PowerPoint chartjunk: smarmy, chaotic, incoherent.

7   Applying the PowerPoint templates to this nice, straightforward table yields an analytical disaster. The data explodes into six separate chaotic slides, consuming 2.9 times the area of the table. Everything is wrong with these smarmy, incoherent graphs: the encoded legends, the meaningless color, the logo-type branding. They are uncomparative, indifferent to content and evidence, and so data-starved as to be almost pointless. Chartjunk is a clear sign of statistical stupidity. Poking a finger into the eye of thought, these data graphics would turn into a nasty travesty if used for a

serious purpose, such as helping cancer patients assess their survival chances. To sell a product that messes up data with such systematic intensity, Microsoft abandons any pretense of statistical integrity and reasoning.

Presentations largely stand or fall on the quality, relevance, 8 and integrity of the content. If your numbers are boring, then you've got the wrong numbers. If your words or images are not on point, making them dance in color won't make them relevant. Audience boredom is usually a content failure, not a decoration failure.

At a minimum, a presentation format should do no harm. Yet 9 the PowerPoint style routinely disrupts, dominates, and trivializes content. Thus, PowerPoint presentations too often resemble a school play—very loud, very slow, and very simple.

The practical conclusions are clear. PowerPoint is a competent 10 slide manager and projector. But rather than supplementing a presentation, it has become a substitute for it. Such misuse ignores the most important rule of speaking: Respect your audience.

getting into the conversation •••4

Is Technology Making Us Stupid?

1. One of the key stasis points of the articles in this section surrounds whether new technologies are dumbing down our culture by minimizing the work done by our own minds. This is not a new argument; in fact, Socrates once questioned whether writing, as a new technology, would undermine our memories by making it less important for us to remember information. In order to find your own position on this topic, first listen in to the various arguments made about the effects of various technologies upon the use of our own brains. Create a list of what you take to be the main arguments made by each, categorizing and organizing them in a way that will allow you to compare the quality of each argument. Then, write a review of the key arguments against technology that are being made, developing discussion points that might then be used if you decide to do further primary or secondary research on this topic. Consider whether such arguments are valid or whether they are overreactions.

2. Although the question about whether Google—and other technologies— "makes us stupid" is common to many of the pieces in this section, many different methods are used to enter into that debate. For example, the Pew Research Center uses survey information to collect public opinion on the topic, drawing upon methods common in the social sciences. The expert views you can access through the Conversations 2.0 section draw upon the background of each of these technology experts. Katharine Allen draws from her experience as a student and "digital native"—one who grew up on technology—while Chris DeWolfe defends his generation and the MySpace technology that he helped to create. And Edward Tufte builds upon his great expertise in visual rhetoric to show the shortcomings of PowerPoint. In order to demonstrate the ways in which each writer's opinions are built upon the discipline (field of study) of that author, write an analysis of the ways that the answer to the question about whether technology is making us stupid depends upon the disciplinary perspective and experience from which the argument is made.

3. While part of the question about how technology affects our minds involves the ways that we collect information, another thread of the conversation in this chapter involves how presentation technologies likewise can enhance, or limit, the way that we frame and deliver that information to our audiences. In particular, Edward Tufte argues that PowerPoint tends to limit the richness of information by placing it within a pre-set and linear template. You can find many other such arguments if you search for "PowerPoint and effects." Drawing upon the ways these arguments are made, create your own argument about another technology: Does YouTube make for diverse or pre-digested forms of arguments? Does blog technology set up rules for the presentation of information and/or arguments that limit, or expand, the way

those arguments are made? Does Twitter's limitations predispose us to dumbed-down arguments, or do the uses of this technology make it versatile and diverse? Pick whatever technology for the presentation of arguments that you feel is particularly important, and discuss the ways that it has affected the mental processes of both the author and the audience.

4. Although new literacies tend to develop naturally, based both upon need and available technologies, some argue that educational methods have not kept pace with those new technologies by preparing students to use them effectively and thoughtfully. A report by the National Commission on Writing, entitled *Writing, Technology, and Teens* (which is readily available through the Web—just search the title and you'll find it easily), draws similar conclusions. It also begins with this statement: "Teens write a lot but do not think of their emails, instant, and text messaging as writing." Drawing upon your own experiences, some further research on the writing habits of current students, and perhaps some primary research (surveys, focus groups, and so forth), write an essay that explores the effects of new technology upon the amount and types of writing done—and whether the ways writing is taught is in fact addressing these new literacies. You could do this on a local level, asking whether national statistics about writing apply to those in your community. Or you could investigate how what we mean by "writing" has changed, whether young people do consider things like texting or Twitter a kind of writing. In the end, you could investigate the effects of these technologies on school writing, asking whether education is keeping pace with these changes, and perhaps proposing some ways that it might do so more effectively. However you frame the question, exploring the relationship between writing, technology, and educational methods can provide some excellent topics for investigation.

extending the conversation ···2

Opportunities for Reading, Writing, and Research

Although the readings in *Conversations* are organized into specific topic areas, they can also be used to start your research into other related areas of interest. The following writing opportunities can help you extend the conversations across the various subjects discussed in the book—and beyond the book into research areas you might explore on your own. These examples demonstrate how you might develop the readings from this book into larger projects; you can come up with many more on your own. As you do so, think especially about how your major field of study or other interests you have can inform your research.

1. One common element in writing about technology is many authors' attempts to act as "futurists," predicting which innovations will have a particularly important effect—and what that effect is likely to be. You can see that element represented in Matt Welch's "Blogworld and Its Gravity," Rachel Smolkin's "The Expanding Blogosphere," and several other pieces in Chapter 3. Following this method of many "futurists," choose a technology that you think is likely to be the next big thing, and do some research on how that technology works, how it is being received, and what populations seem to be most intrigued by its use. Then, after gathering that information on this up-and-coming technology, develop your own argument about its potential to affect some facet of our culture in significant ways. To do so, you might include examples about how it is being used now, visuals that illustrate its potential, testimony by individuals who have developed or used it, and so forth. You might also assess the possible negative or deleterious effects of this technology, as several of the pieces in this section do. One key to building a convincing argument will be to be as specific as possible in showing the potential of this technology and tying that potential to the needs that it will serve.

2. Historical perspectives can be particularly important in fully under-standing the present. But those historical perspectives must be accu-rate in order to provide a useful lens on our own times. Many of the arguments in Chapter 3 are based on traditions of journalism that some of the authors believe are being lost in a new media world. In order to put these critiques into the proper historical perspective, do some research on the history of American journalism, locating authori-tative sources of information that can help you gain insight into the role of the "fourth branch of government" in founding and maintaining our democracy. How did the founders view journalism? What free-doms and restrictions were put into place in order to assure a free—but responsible—press? What landmark court cases have weighed in on issues related to journalism? Who have been some of the key play-ers in founding, developing, and protecting the role of the press? What

kinds of standards are taught to professional journalists, and how have those standards developed or changed over the years? (For this question, you might interview faculty members in your Communications department, if your college has one.) Questions like these can help you become more informed on the history of journalism, and thus see what is at stake in a time of new media or "citizen" journalism. Then, once you have educated yourself (and your readers) on this topic, go on to demonstrate the ways in which new methods of journalism extend, support, and/or violate the role of journalism in our culture. Because this is a very large question, it would be useful for you to focus upon one particular effect and its implications.

3. While several of the pieces in Chapter 4 of *Conversations* speculate on the ways that technology is making us "stupid," few provide any real depth on the actual changes to cognition—brain processes—that these technologies have brought about, or are likely to bring about. But many natural scientists, and particularly neuroscientists, have done studies of the actual physiology of brain activity that is brought about by various technologies. In order to enrich this conversation and to bring it into the realm of scientific disciplines, do some research on this topic. You might, for example, examine whether technology use changes specific brain functions. Does it enhance or impair our memory? Does it create new brain activities that might, in fact, make us more adaptable to our environments, or does it create a dependence that makes us less capable to function on our own? Does it stimulate active thought processes, or does it tend to suppress them? Questions like these will help you discover not only their findings and conclusions, but also can help you learn more about the ways that scientists conduct such research—how they assure reliability and objectivity, how they ethically use human or animal subjects for such tests, and so forth. The questions can also help you consider the likely direction of future research on these topics—perhaps research topics you may want to take on in your further college studies.

Conversations About Identity: Gender, Race, and Ethnicity

Introduction

We form our identity in a great many ways. Scientists who completed the human genome project might suggest that we are products of our DNA, our identities determined in many ways before we are born. Some suggest that identity is formed as we live in the world, responding to the influences of our parents, taking on roles depending upon the circumstances of our lives, and changing all along. Some see the question as a matter of chemistry and physiology, others as a matter for sociology or philosophy or religion. Some suggest that our identities are now less stable because of technological advances, extreme makeovers, and plastic surgery—that is, we can control and change our identities in ways never before possible.

But coming to grips with our own identity—or at least trying to do so—is also a fundamental human need. We feel compelled to see not only what we are as individuals, but also how we fit in as part of larger social groups. In our attempt to do so, specific physical and cultural features are among the most visible signs to others—and to ourselves—about who we are. Our gender and our race and/or ethnicity are among the most prominent of these signs. We are identified as man, as woman, or as "white man" or "Asian woman" more readily than even by our name. And with each designation come predispositions that affect not only others' views of us, but also, in many cases, our own view of ourselves. This chapter examines the ways that those categories, for better or worse, define us.

The essays in Chapter 5 explore identity through the lens of gender. More specifically, this chapter looks at changing conceptions of the role of gender, beginning from a time when women were openly considered to be "the weaker sex" (a contention that even in the 19th century, women like Sojourner Truth denied) and moving through feminism's battles to attain equal rights and equal respect for women. That struggle was held on many fronts, from language issues, which framed women as inferior, limited, or circumscribed into particular roles, to societal pressures that placed upon women expectations of proper "ladylike" behaviors. But times have indeed changed, and, more recently, a new conversation on gender has emerged, a conversation that has begun to question whether men are now placed at a disadvantage and whether there is "a war against boys." Fueled by new societal trends—the dominance of women in education and their growing numbers in college (approaching 60%), the suspicion of men's behaviors by feminists, and so forth—some writers are now suggesting that it is men who are in decline. Not all agree, of course; many would suggest that such arguments are merely backlash against feminism, an attempt to resolidify the dominance of men. But this debate is certainly an important one, and, by reading the varied perspectives of authors in this section, you can start to learn the terms of this conversation and consider your own entry point into it.

One of the places where women, traditionally, and men, more recently, struggle with identity issues surrounds what Naomi Wolf dubbed "the beauty myth." Wolf's 1991 book on this topic crystallized one portion of the gender conversation, examining the ways, to quote her subtitle, "How images of beauty are used against women." Although discussions about the ways that standards of beauty—often unobtainable standards—have long been an issue for women's identity, this book was released within a new context, that of the modern feminist movement. This part's *Conversations in Context*, then, explores in both words and images (as this is a very visual debate) the ways in which physical expectations dictate identity issues for women and the ways in which they can undermine one's identity formation when those ideals cannot be attained. Further, as with gender issues more generally, there is growing evidence that ideals of beauty are also affecting men's self-image; as such, this section also explores the growing importance that men seem to be placing upon their own physicality. Finally, this section also acknowledges that ideals of beauty are also connected to race and ethnicity, asking whether our culture's definitions of beauty are tied to skin color and other physical features.

Chapter 6 delves into a related conversation and a conversation that is crucial for a society that is, at its very base, multicultural. As with the previous chapter, the readings here allow you to trace the development of this conversation across time. Beginning with the struggles of African-Americans during the Civil Rights struggles of the 1960s and 1970s, the essays in this chapter explore how personal identity is affected by racial and ethnic identity. In some cases, the authors argue for ways to overcome oppressive standards that stunt the mental horizon of individuals; in others, the authors simply tell the story of how their own self-image is affected by the outside world. You will find here the voices of activists and leaders and the stories of teenagers who are just starting to find their own place and their own identity amidst the larger world. You will also read, both explicitly and implicitly, a discussion about whether attention to categories of race and ethnicity help us find an identity, or whether we have moved beyond the need for those categories that serve only to divide us.

Taken as a group, what these authors share is a concern with the relationship between the individual and the culture, between the struggle to find ourselves and the struggle to find our place among others. Whether the issue is race, ethnicity, or gender, whether one feels liberated and celebratory by one's group identity or constricted by it, there is little doubt that this is a crucial conversation and one that can help you come to grips with your own identity formation. So as you read, consider not only the ways in which these authors have articulated their own sense of self, but also use it as a way of developing—and writing about—your own identity.

CHAPTER 5

Gender Identities

Sojourner Truth

Ain't I a Woman?

Sojourner Truth's story is fascinating and moving. Born into slavery in Ulster County, New York, around 1797 and given the name Isabella, she was sold three times before she turned twelve. Perhaps sexually abused by one of her owners, she fled to freedom in 1827, a year before slavery was outlawed in New York. In New York City she worked as a domestic and fell in with an evangelical preacher who encouraged her efforts to convert prostitutes. Though illiterate, she managed to negate the sale of her son Peter to the South when her former "owner" tried to accomplish the sale. In 1843, inspired by mystical visions, she took the name Sojourner Truth and set off alone and undeterred by her illiteracy to preach and sing about religion and the abolition of slavery. By 1850, huge crowds were coming to witness the oratory of the ex-slave with the resounding voice and message. During the Civil War she was presented to President Lincoln at the White House. After the war she spoke out for women's suffrage, but she never gave up her spiritual and racial themes—or her humor and exuberance. She continued to lecture until near her death in Battle Creek, Michigan, in 1883.

Sojourner Truth accepted neither the physical inferiority of women nor the idea that they should be placed on pedestals; nor did she subordinate women's rights to the pursuit of racial equality. At a women's rights convention in May 1851, Sojourner Truth rose extemporaneously to rebut speakers who had impugned the rights and capabilities of women. What you will read below is what, according to an eyewitness who recorded the scene in his diary, she said. As you read, consider what this foundational document suggests about the early stages of American Feminism and the female identity.

279

1   Well, children, where there is so much racket there must be something out of kilter. I think that 'twixt the negroes of the South and the women at the North, all talking about rights, the white men will be in a fix pretty soon. But what's all this here talking about?

2   That man over there says that women need to be helped into carriages, and lifted over ditches, and to have the best place everywhere. Nobody ever helps me into carriages, or over mud-puddles, or gives me any best place! And ain't I a woman? Look at me! Look at my arm! I have ploughed and planted, and gathered into barns, and no man could head me! And ain't I a woman? I could work as much and eat as much as a man—when I could get it—and bear the lash as well! And ain't I a woman? I have borne thirteen children, and seen them most all sold off to slavery, and when I cried out with my mother's grief, none but Jesus heard me! And ain't I a woman?

3   Then they talk about this thing in the head; what's this they call it? [Intellect, someone whispers.] That's it, honey. What's that got to do with women's rights or negro's rights? If my cup won't hold but a pint, and yours holds a quart, wouldn't you be mean not to let me have my little half-measure full?

4   Then that little man in black there, he says women can't have as much rights as men, 'cause Christ wasn't a woman! Where did your Christ come from? Where did your Christ come from? From God and a woman! Man had nothing to do with Him.

5   If the first woman God ever made was strong enough to turn the world upside down all alone, these women together ought to be able to turn it back, and get it right side up again! And now they is asking to do it, the men better let them.

6   Obliged to you for hearing on me, and now old Sojourner ain't got nothing more to say.

Sherryl Kleinman

Why Sexist Language Matters

Though our attention to sexist language is sometimes considered no more than "political correctness" or a method of controlling free speech, Sherryl Kleinman, a sociologist, essayist, and poet, argues here that sexist language does matter. Kleinman has taught at UNC–Chapel Hill since 1980, offering courses in social psychology, race, class and gender, and social and economic justice. Her books include *Equals before God: Seminarians as Humanistic Professionals* (1984), *Emotions and Fieldwork* (with Martha Copp, 1993), and *Opposing Ambitions: Gender and Identity in an Alternative Organization* (1996). As you read, consider how her background as a sociologist influences her methods of argument and the evidence she presents. To what alternative views does her title and the essay itself, first published in *Qualitative Sociology* in 2002, seem to be responding?

For eleven years I've been teaching a sociology course at the University of North Carolina on gender inequality. I cover such topics as the wage gap, the "second shift" (the disproportionate amount of housework and child care that heterosexual women do at home), the equation of women's worth with physical attractiveness, the sexualizing of women in the media, lack of reproductive rights for women (especially poor women), sexual harassment, and men's violence against women. But the issue that both female and male students have the most trouble understanding—or, as I see it, share a strong unwillingness to understand—is sexist language.

I'm not referring to such words as "bitch," "whore," and "slut." What I focus on instead are words that most people consider just fine: male (so-called) generics. Some of these words refer to persons occupying a position: postman, chairman, freshman, congressman, fireman. Other words refer to the entire universe of human beings: "mankind" or "he." Then we've got manpower, man-made lakes, and "Oh, man, where did I leave my keys?" There's "manning" the tables in a country where we learn that "all men are created equal."

The most insidious, from my observations, is the popular expression "you guys." People like to tell me it's a regional term. But I've heard it in Chapel Hill, New York, Chicago, San Francisco, and Montreal. I've seen it in print in national magazines, newsletters, and books. I've heard it on television and in films. And even if it were regional, that doesn't make it right. I bet we can all think of a lot of practices in our home regions we'd like to get rid of.

Try making up a female-based generic, such as "freshwoman," and using it with a group of male students, or calling your male boss "chairwoman." Then again, don't. There could be serious consequences for referring to a man as a woman—a term that still means "lesser" in our society. If not, why do men get so upset at the idea of being called women?

5   What's the big deal? Why does all this "man-ning" and "guys-ing" deserve a place on my list of items of gender inequality?

6   The answer is because male-based generics are another indicator—and, more importantly, a *reinforcer*—of a system in which "man" in the abstract and men in the flesh are privileged over women. Some say that language merely reflects reality and so we should ignore our words and work on changing the unequal gender arrangements that are reflected in our language. Well, yes, in part.

7   It's no accident that "man" is the anchor in our language and "woman" is not. And of course we should make social change all over the place. But the words we use can also reinforce current realities when they are sexist (or racist or heterosexist). Words are the tools of thought. We can use words to maintain the status quo or to think in new ways—which in turn creates the possibility of a new *reality*. It makes a difference if I think of myself as a "girl" or a "woman"; it makes a difference if we talk about "Negroes" or "African Americans." Do we want a truly inclusive language or one that just pretends?

8   For a moment, imagine a world—as the philosopher Douglas R. Hofstadter did in his 1986 satire on sexist language—where people used generics based on race rather than gender. In that world, people would use "freshwhite," "chairwhite," and, yes, "you whiteys." People of color would hear "all whites are created equal"—and be expected to feel included. In an addendum to his article, Hofstadter says that he wrote "A Person Paper on Purity in Language" to shock readers: Only by substituting "white" for "man" does it become easy to see the pervasiveness of male-based generics and to recognize that using "man" for all human beings is wrong. Yet, women are expected to feel flattered by "fresh-man," "chairman," and "you guys."

9   And why do so many women cling to "freshman," "chairman," and "you guys?"

10   I think it's because women want to be included in the term that refers to the higher-status group: men. But while being labeled "one of the guys" might make women *feel* included, it's only a guise of inclusion, not the reality. If women were really included we wouldn't have to disappear into the word "guys."

11   At the same time that women in my classes throw around "you guys"—even here in the southern United States, where "y'all" is an alternative—they call themselves "girls." I'm not sure if this has gotten worse over the years or I've just noticed it more. When I was an undergraduate in the early to mid 1970s, we wanted to be women. Who would take us seriously at college or at work if we were "girls"? To many of my students today, "woman" is old enough to be "over the hill." A "girl" is youthful and thus more

attractive to men than a "woman." Since they like the term so much, I suggest that we rename Women's Studies "Girls' Studies." And since the Women's Center on campus provides services for them, why not call it "The Girls' Center." They laugh. "Girls" sounds ridiculous, they say. The students begin to see that "girl"—as a label for twenty-one-year-olds—is infantilizing, not flattering.

"Girl" and "you guys" aren't the only linguistic problems on   12 campus. A few years ago Bob, a student in my class, said that his fraternity is now open to women as well as men and that a controversy had erupted over whether to continue to use the term "brother" to refer to all fraternity members, or to use "sister" for female members. Almost all the women in his fraternity, he said, voted to be called brother rather than sister. As with "you guys," the women wanted to take on the word that has more value. Yet the practice of using "brother" reinforces the idea that a real member of the group is a brother (i.e., a man). I asked what would happen if he had suggested that all fraternity members be called sisters rather than brothers, or that they rename the fraternity a sorority. Everyone laughed at the absurdity of this suggestion. Exactly. Yet it is not absurd, but acceptable, to call women by the term "guys" or "brothers."

Since the "fraternity" Bob referred to is no longer exclusively   13 male, and since gender is no longer a criterion for membership, I asked him how he thought others might react if he suggested they substitute "association" or "society" for "fraternity." Perhaps they could call both men and women "members," or, if students preferred a more informal term, "friends"?

"Yes, that makes sense." Bob told us. "But, I just don't think   14 they'll go for it." He paused. "I'm not sure why."

We talked as a class about why this simple solution might meet   15 with resistance. We concluded that many men would resist losing these linguistic signifiers of male superiority, and many women would resist losing the valued maleness implied by "brother" and "fraternity." "Member" would feel like a drop in status for both women and men!

The students, like most people who use male "generics," don't   16 have bad intentions. But as sociologists, we know that it's important to look at the *consequences*. All those "man" words—said many times a day by millions of people every day—cumulatively reinforce the message that men are the standard and that women should be subsumed by the male category.

I worry about what people with the best of intentions are   17 teaching our children. A colleague's five-year-old daughter recently left her classroom crying after a teacher said, "What do you guys think?" She thought the teacher didn't care about what *she* thought. When the teacher told her that of course she was included, her tears stopped. But what was the lesson? She learned that her opinion as a girl mattered only when she's a guy. She learned that men are the norm.

18   A friend's six-year-old son refused to believe that the female firefighter who came to his school to talk to the class—dressed in uniform—actually fought fires. The firefighter repeatedly referred to herself as a "fireman." Despite the protests of the teacher and the firefighter, the boy would not be convinced. "A fire*man* can't be a woman," he said. His mother, who is fastidious in her use of nonsexist language, had a tough time doing damage control.

19   So, is it any surprise that the worst insult a boy can hurl at another boy is "girl"?

20   We know from history that making a group invisible makes it easier for the powerful to do what they want with members of that group. Perhaps that's why linguists use the strong language of "symbolic annihilation" to refer to the disappearance of women into male-based terms. And we know, from too many past and current studies, that far too many men are doing "what they want" with women. Most of us can see a link between calling women "sluts" and "whores" and men's sexual violence against women. We need to recognize that making women linguistically a subset of man/men through terms like "mankind" and "guys" also makes women into objects. If we, as women, aren't worthy of such true generics as "first-year," "chair," or "you all," then how can we expect to be paid a "man's wage," be respected as people rather than objects (sexual or otherwise) on the job and at home, be treated as equals rather than servers or caretakers of others, be considered responsible enough to make our own decisions about reproduction, and define who and what we want as sexual beings? If we aren't even deserving of our place in humanity in language, why should we expect to be treated as decent human beings otherwise?

21   Some people tell me that making English nonsexist is a slippery slope. As one colleague said to me, "Soon we'll have to say 'waitperson,' which sounds awful. We won't be able to 'man' the table at Orientation. And we'll become 'fellowpersons' at the Institute!" I told him that "server" works well. We can "staff" the table. And why not use "scholars" instead of "fellows"? We've got a big language to roam in. Let's have fun figuring out how to speak and write without making "man" the center. If sliding down that slope takes us to a place where we speak nonsexist English, I'm ready for the ride.

22   And this doesn't mean that every word with "m-e-n" in it is a problem. Menstruation and mending are fine. Making amends is good, too. There's only a problem when "men," as part of a word, is meant to refer to everyone (freshmen, chairmen, and so on).

23   Now and then someone says that I should work on more important issues—like men's violence against women—rather

than on "trivial" issues like language. Well, I work on lots of issues. But that's not the point. Working against sexist language *is* working against men's violence against women. It's one step. If we cringe at "freshwhite" and "you whiteys" and would protest such terms with loud voices, then why don't we work as hard at changing "freshman" and "you guys"? Don't women deserve it? That women primarily exist in language as "girls" (children), "sluts" (sex objects) and "guys" (a subset of men) makes it less of a surprise that we still have a long list of gendered inequalities to fix.

We've got to work on *every* item on the list. Language is one 24
we can work on right now, if we're willing. It's easier to start saying "you all," "y'all" or "you folks" instead of "you guys" than to change the wage gap tomorrow.

And what might help us make changes in our language? About 25
a year ago I was complaining, as usual, about the "you guys" problem. "What we need is a card that explains why we don't want to be called guys!" Smita Varia, a veteran of my gender course, said. "Let's write one."

And so we did. Smita enlisted T. Christian Helms, another for- 26
mer student, to design a graphic for the card. You can access the layout of this business-sized card from our website: www.youall.freeservers.com. Make lots of copies. Give the cards to friends and ask them to think about sexist language. Leave one with a big tip after you've been "you guysed" during a meal. The card explains the problem and offers alternatives.

"Hey, You Guys!"

Imagine someone walking up to a group of guys and saying, "Hey, girls, how're ya doing?" We doubt they'd be amused! So isn't it weird that women are supposed to accept—even like— being called "one of the guys"? We're also supposed to like "freshman," "chairman" and "mankind."

Get over it, some people say. Those words are generic. They apply to everyone. But then how come so-called generics are always male?

What if generics ended in "white"? Freshwhite, chairwhite, and "hey, you whiteys!" Would people of color like being called "one of the whites"? We don't think so.

The terms "guys" makes women invisible by lumping them in with men. Let's quit doing that. When you're talking to a group of customers, gender doesn't really matter, so why not replace "you guys" with "you all," "folks," or "y'all." Or simply say "what can I get you?" That would take care of us all.

Thanks for your help.

27   And institutional change is also possible. Some universities have adopted "first-year student" (instead of "freshman") because some students and faculty got angry about the male-based generics embedded in university documents. The American Psychological Association has a policy of using only inclusive language in their publications. Wherever you work or play, get together with other progressive people and suggest that your organization use "chair" instead of "chairman," "Ms." instead of "Mrs." or "Miss," "humankind" instead of "mankind," and "she or he" instead of "he." In my experience, members of some activist groups think sexist language is less important than other issues. But if we're going to work on social change, shouldn't we start by practicing nonsexist English among ourselves? Let's begin creating *now* the kind of society we want to live in later.

28   Nonsexist English is a resource we have at the tip of our tongues. Let's start using it.

Reference

1. Hofstadter, D. R. (1986). A person paper on purity in language. In D. R. Hofstadter, Metamagical themas: A questing for the essence of mind and pattern (pp. 159–167). New York: Bantam.

Scott Russell Sanders

The Men We Carry In Our Minds

Scott Russell Sanders (born 1945 in Memphis) grew up in rural Ohio and Tennessee. Active in the environmental movement through organizations such as the Nature Conservancy, the Audubon Society, and the Wilderness Society, he has the ability to cross between the so-called two cultures (science and the humanities) in his fiction, science fiction, and essays. A member of the faculty at Indiana University and the author of many books, he recently told the editors of *Contemporary Authors* that "a writer should be a servant of language, community, and nature." As you read this piece, first published in 1984, consider how this author offers a male perspective on the feminist movement through his

personal reflections. In what ways does his narrative style
build an argument about the male identity?

"T his must be a hard time for women," I say to my friend 1
Anneke. "They have so many paths to choose from, and
so many voices calling them."

"I think it's a lot harder for men," she replies. 2

"How do you figure that?" 3

"The women I know feel excited, innocent, like crusaders in a 4
just cause. The men I know are eaten up with guilt."

"Women feel such pressure to be everything, do everything," 5
I say. "Career, kids, art, politics. Have their babies and get back
to the office a week later. It's as if they're trying to overcome a
million years' worth of evolution in one lifetime."

"But we help one another. And we have this deep-down sense 6
that we're in the *right*—we've been held back, passed over,
used—while men feel they're in the wrong. Men are the ones
who've been discredited, who have to search their souls."

I search my soul. I discover guilty feelings aplenty—toward 7
the poor, the Vietnamese, Native Americans, the whales, an endless list of debts. But toward women I feel something more confused, a snarl of shame, envy, wary, tenderness, and amazement.
This muddle troubles me. To hide my unease I say, "You're right,
it's tough being a man these days."

"Don't laugh," Anneke frowns at me. "I wouldn't be a man for 8
anything. It's much easier being the victim. All the victim has to
do is break free. The persecutor has to live with his past."

How deep is that past? I find myself wondering. How much 9
of an inheritance do I have to throw off?

When I was a boy growing up on the back roads of Tennessee 10
and Ohio, the men I knew labored with their bodies. They were
marginal farmers, just scraping by, or welders, steelworkers, carpenters; they swept floors, dug ditches, mined coal, or drove
trucks, their forearms ropy with muscle; they trained horses,
stoked furnaces, made tires, stood on assembly lines wrestling
parts onto cars and refrigerators. They got up before light,
worked all day long whatever the weather, and when they came
home at night they looked as though somebody had been whip-
ping them. In the evenings and on weekends they worked on
their own places, tilling gardens that were lumpy with clay, fixing broken-down cars, hammering on houses that were always
too drafty, too leaky, too small.

The bodies of the men I knew were twisted and maimed in 11
ways visible and invisible. The nails of their hands were black
and split, the hands tattooed with scars. Some had lost fingers.
Heavy lifting had given many of them finicky backs and guts

weak from hernias. Racing against conveyor belts had given them ulcers. Their ankles and knees ached from years of standing on concrete. Anyone who had worked for long around machines was hard of hearing. They squinted, and the skin of their faces was creased like the leather of old work gloves. There were times, studying them, when I dreaded growing up. Most of them coughed, from dust or cigarettes, and most of them drank cheap wine or whiskey, so their eyes looked bloodshot and bruised. The fathers of my friends always seemed older than the mothers. Men wore out sooner. Only women lived into old age.

12   As a boy I also knew another sort of men, who did not sweat and break down like mules. They were soldiers, and so far as I could tell they scarcely worked at all. But when the shooting started, many of them would die. This was what soldiers were *for*, just as a hammer was for driving nails.

13   Warriors and toilers; those seemed, in my boyhood vision, to be the chief destinies for men. They weren't the only destinies, as I learned from having a few male teachers, from reading books, and from watching television. But the men on television—the politicians, the astronauts, the generals, the savvy lawyers, the philosophical doctors, the bosses who gave orders to both soldiers and laborers—seemed as remote and unreal to me as the figures in Renaissance tapestries. I could no more imagine growing up to become one of these cool, potent creatures than I could imagine becoming a prince.

14   A nearer and more hopeful example was that of my father, who had escaped from a red-dirt farm to a tire factory, and from the assembly line to the front office. Eventually he dressed in a white shirt and tie. He carried himself as if he had been born to work with his mind. But his body, remembering the earlier years of slogging work, began to give out on him in his fifties, and it quit on him entirely before he turned 65.

15   A scholarship enabled me not only to attend college, a rare enough feat in my circle, but even to study in a university meant for the children of the rich. Here I met for the first time young men who had assumed from birth that they would lead lives of comfort and power. And for the first time I met women who told me that men were guilty of having kept all the joys and privileges of the earth for themselves. I was baffled. What privileges? What joys? I thought about the maimed, dismal lives of most of the men back home. What had they stolen from their wives and daughters? The right to go five days a week, 12 months a year, for 30 or 40 years to a steel mill or a coal mine? The right to drop bombs and die in war? The right to feel every leak in the roof, every gap in the fence, every cough in the engine as a wound they must mend? The right to feel, when the layoff comes or the plant shuts down, not only afraid but ashamed?

I was slow to understand the deep grievances of women. This   16
was because, as a boy, I had envied them. Before college, the only
people I had ever known who were interested in art or music or
literature, the only ones who read books, the only ones who ever
seemed to enjoy a sense of ease and grace were the mothers and
daughters. Like the menfolk, they fretted about money, they
scrimped and made do. But, when the pay stopped coming in,
they were not the ones who had failed. Nor did they have to go
to war, and that seemed to me a blessed fact. By comparison with
the narrow, ironclad days of fathers, there was an expansiveness,
I thought, in the days of mothers. They went to see neighbors, to
shop in town, to run errands at school, at the library, at church.
No doubt, had I looked harder at their lives, I would have envied
them less. It was not my fate to become a woman, so it was easier for me to see the graces. I didn't see, then, what a prison a
house could be, since houses seemed to me brighter, handsomer
places than any factory. I did not realize—because such things
were never spoken of—how often women suffered from men's
bullying. Even then I could see how exhausting it was for a mother to cater all day to the needs of young children. But if I had been
asked, as a boy, to choose between tending a baby and tending a
machine, I think I would have chosen the baby. (Having now
tended both, I know I would choose the baby.)

So I was baffled when the women at college accused me and   17
my sex of having cornered the world's pleasures. I think something like my bafflement has been felt by other boys (and by girls
as well) who grew up in dirt-poor farm country, in mining country, in black ghettos, in Hispanic barrios, in the shadows of factories, in Third World nations—any place where the fate of men
is just as grim and bleak as the fate of women.

When the women I met at college thought about the joys and   18
privileges of men, they did not carry in their minds the sort of
men I had known in my childhood. They thought of their
fathers, who were bankers, physicians, architects, stockbrokers,
the big wheels of the big cities. They were never laid off, never
short of cash at month's end, never lined up for welfare. These
fathers made decisions that mattered. They ran the world.

The daughters of such men wanted to share in this power,   19
this glory. So did I. They yearned for a say over their future, for
jobs worthy of their abilities, for the right to live at peace, unmo-
lested, whole. Yes, I thought, yes yes. The difference between
me and these daughters was that they saw me, because of my
sex, as destined from birth to become like their fathers, and
therefore as an enemy to their desires. But I knew better. I wasn't
an enemy, in fact or in feeling. I was an ally. If I had known,
then, how to tell them so, would they have believed me? Would
they now?

Michael Norman

From Carol Gilligan's Chair

Michael Norman is an author, journalist, and professor of narrative journalism in the Literary Reportage Program at New York University. The author of *These Good Men: Friendships Forged From War*, Norman has also served as a correspondent for the *New York Times*, where this piece was first published in 1997. In this article, Norman interviews Carol Gilligan, a developmental psychologist whose work on women's minds and experiences has made her one of the key voices in gender studies and, more specifically, in the women's movement in the United States. This interview focuses upon the experiences of men and women, and can set the context for the response to Gilligan's important work by Christina Hoff Sommers that follows. As you read, consider the ways in which gender studies—often seen as the study of women— is situated here as also including the relationship between the sexes.

1   What began as an idea jotted down at her kitchen table has grown into a central tenet of feminist thought: Women differ from men; they are more concerned with the nexus of relationships that holds society together. Their psychological and moral development must be considered in their own light, not against criteria used to measure the behavior of men. That common-sense idea first came to Carol Gilligan, a developmental psychologist, in the early seventies, when she noticed that researchers were drawing conclusions about girls from studies of boys. In 1975 she published a paper that grew into a landmark book, *In a Different Voice*. In September, at 60, Gilligan was named the first holder of a chair in gender studies at Harvard's School of Education—a rare commitment for such work and one that carries with it a research endowment of half a million dollars.

2   Q: Can we talk about your new work—your research on boys?

3   A: I don't see it as new work. It's really an extension of the work I have been doing with women and girls.

4   I noticed that there was an asymmetry between boys and girls. Girls are more at risk psychologically in adolescence, whereas boys are more at risk—more stuttering, more bed-wetting, more

learning problems—in early childhood, when cultural norms pressure them to separate from their mothers. I was observing a boy just yesterday. His face was very still. It didn't register a lot of emotion. He was around 6, when boys want to become "one of the boys." They feel they have to separate from women. And they are not allowed to feel that separation as a real loss.

Q: What accounts for the asymmetry? 5

A: I think boys are at risk in early childhood because their 6 initiation comes earlier. Girls are ignored until the edge of adolescence. This made me and a colleague, Normi Noel, ask, "Is anybody listening to boys?" And we ask this knowing that they have less language skill.

Q: Sounds as if you're trying to discover in boys the 7 reasons men feel compelled to adopt certain cultural models of what it means to be a man—models that many men feel are enslaving.

A: That's exactly it. 8

Q: Earlier you said you were making a new move in your life. 9

A: A really scary move—I've been writing fiction. I've written 10 a cycle of short stories and about 150 pages of a novel.

Q: Why fiction? 11

A: I wanted to get out of my academic voice and into the sub- 12 ject's voice. Which is what a fiction writer does.

Q: When you assume your academic voice, what are some of 13 the research projects you're directing?

A: One is being conducted by Judy Chu, a doctoral student, 14 among preschool and adolescent boys in the Boston area. It's called "Listening to Boys' Voices." We are trying to discover a research relationship that will free boys' voices, to create conditions that allow boys to say what they know. Another student, Ilina Singh, is trying to get a historical perspective on the use of Ritalin and the diagnosis of attention-deficit-hyperactivity disorder in boys. She is interested in what it means to medicalize all this—the relationship between the biological and the psychological. The fact that the neurological symptoms are real doesn't mean that it wouldn't be interesting to hear their voices.

15   Q: What else are you looking at?

16   A: Well, a doctoral student named Barney Brawer and I started "The Harvard Project on Women, Psychology, Boys' Development and the Culture of Manhood."

17   Q: Which looks at?

18   A: Actually, which asks a lot of other questions: are boys in early childhood experiencing a crisis of relationship? What kind of support could prevent trouble? What are men's responses to being in relationships with 3- and 4-year-old boys? What are women's responses? Does all of this open for women the question of our relationships to men? How do we keep alive parts of our sons that we think are valuable for them but that are also at risk when their masculinity is questioned? Does adolescence bring up feelings that were pushed down in early childhood? Is it, as psychoanalysts suggest, a kind of second chance for boys?

19   What we are discovering is how vulnerable boys are. How, under the surface, behind that psychic shield, is a tender creature who's hiding his humanity. I often say about my own three boys, who are now grown, that I feel that the world muffles the very best qualities in them, meaning their sensitivity.

20   Q: You would argue that men's biology is not so powerful that we can't change the culture of men?

21   A: Right. We have to build a culture that doesn't reward that separation from the person who raised them. We might be close to a time similar to the Reformation, where the fundamental structure of authority is about to change. I think now the issues turn on love and work and on gender. To shift our understanding of what it means to be a man and to be a woman is to think about how we work and how we love. And what's more basic than that?

22   Q: Everything you've said suggests that unless men change in fundamental ways, we're not going to have a sea change in the culture.

23   A: That seems right to me.

Christina Hoff Sommers

Do Boys Need to Be Saved?

Christina Hoff Sommers, a former philosophy professor, is best known for her criticisms of the late 20th century feminist movement. She is the author of *Who Stole Feminism? How Women Have Betrayed Women* (1995) and *The War against Boys: How Misguided Feminism is Harming our Young Men* (2001), from which this excerpt is taken. In this piece, Sommers critiques the work of Carol Gilligan, a leader in the feminist movement who has also written on the ways that the male ethos is harmed by the values imposed upon them. As you read, you might consider how each author frames not only the place of women, but also how the male identity is affected by one's relationship with women and with a culture that places specific expectations upon men. To do so, you might look back to the comments made by Gilligan in her interview with Michael Norman in the preceding piece.

C arol Gilligan's theory about boys' development includes   1
three hypothetical claims: (1) that boys are being deformed and made sick by traumatic, forced separation
from their mothers; (2) that seemingly healthy boys are cut
off from their own feelings and are relationally damaged; and
(3) that the well-being of society may depend on freeing
boys from "cultures that value or valorize heroism, honor, war,
competition—the culture of the warrior, the economy of capitalism." Let us consider each proposition in turn.

According to Gilligan, boys are at special risk in early child-   2
hood: they suffer "more stuttering, more bed-wetting, more learning problems . . . when cultural norms pressure them to separate
from their mother."[1] (Sometimes she adds allergies, depression,
attention deficit disorder, and attempted suicide to the list.)[2] She
does not cite any pediatric research that supports her theories
about the origin of these various early-childhood disorders. Is
there a single study, for example, that shows that young males
who remain intimately bonded with their mothers are less likely
to develop allergies or wet their beds?

More boys than girls suffer from speech and learning disorders,   3
but many girls are similarly afflicted. Are these girls disconnected
from their mothers? The more plausible explanations for boys'
greater vulnerability to language disabilities are neurological.[3]

4   Gilligan's speculative assertion that the "pressure of cultural norms" causing boys to separate from their mothers generates a host of early disorders is never tested empirically. She offers no indication of how it *could* be tested. Gilligan herself does not seem to feel that her assertions need to be confirmed empirically. She is confident that boys must be protected from what the culture is doing to them, a culture that initiates them into a manhood that "valorizes" war and the economy of capitalism, a culture that desensitizes boys and, by submerging their humanity, is the root cause of "out-of-control and out-of-touch behavior" and the ultimate source of war and male violence.

5   But are boys aggressive and violent because they are psychically separated from their mothers? Thirty years of research suggest that it is the absence of the male parent that is more often the problem. The boys who are most at risk for juvenile delinquency and violence are boys who are *literally* separated from their fathers. The U.S. Bureau of the Census reports that in 1960, 5.1 million children lived with only their mother; by 1996, the number was more than 16 million.[4] As the phenomenon of fatherlessness has increased, so has violence. As far back as 1965, Senator Daniel Patrick Moynihan called attention to the social dangers of raising boys without benefit of paternal presence. "A community that allows a large number of young men to grow up in broken families, dominated by women, never acquiring any stable relationship to male authority, never acquiring any rational expectations about the future—that community asks for and gets chaos."[5]

6   *In Fatherless America*, the sociologist David Blankenhorn notes that "Despite the difficulty of proving causation in social sciences, the wealth of evidence increasingly supports the conclusion that fatherlessness is a primary generator of violence among young men."[6] William Galston, a former domestic policy adviser to the Clinton administration (now at the University of Maryland), and Elaine Kamarck, a lecturer at Harvard's J. F. Kennedy School of Government, concur. Commenting on the relationship between crime and one-parent families, they say, "The relationship is so strong that controlling for family configuration erases the relationship between race and crime and between low income and crime. This conclusion shows up time and again in the literature."[7]

7   It showed up, for example, in 1998, when Cynthia Harper of the University of Pennsylvania and Sara McLanahan of Princeton University studied the incarceration rates of six thousand males aged fourteen to twenty-two between 1979 and 1993.[8] Boys who lived in homes without fathers were twice as likely to have spent time in jail. These results held even after the researchers controlled for race, income, and parents' education. (Having a stepfather did not decrease the likelihood of incarceration.)

Fathers appear to be central in helping sons develop a con-   8
science and a sense of responsible manhood. Fathers teach boys
that being manly need not mean being predatory or aggressive.
By contrast, when the father is absent, male children tend to get
their ideas of what it means to be a man from their peers. Fathers
play an indispensable civilizing role in the social ecosystem;
therefore, fewer fathers, more male violence.

According to Blankenhorn, effective fathers need not be   9
paragons of emotional sensitivity. In fact, they may possess qualities that would distress the gender experts at the Harvard Graduate School of Education. The typically masculine dad who plays
roughly with his kids, who teaches his sons to be stoical and
competitive, who is often glued to the television set watching
football or crime dramas—is in fact unlikely to produce a violent
son. As Blankenhorn explains, "There are exceptions, of course.
But here is the rule. Boys raised by traditionally masculine
fathers generally do not commit crimes. Fatherless boys commit
crimes."[9]

Given Gilligan's general animus toward the "patriarchal social   10
order," it is not surprising that her research appears to attach no
importance to fathers. All the same, the more we learn about the
reasons for juvenile violence, the clearer it becomes that the progressive weakening of the family—in particular, the absence of
fathers from the home—plays a major role.

Restoring fathers to the home is nowhere on Gilligan's list of   11
priorities. Instead, Gilligan and her Harvard associates concentrate on changing things like boys' play preferences. In an interview for *Education Week* Gilligan talks of a moment when each
little boy stands at a cross-road: "You see this picture of a little
boy with a stuffed bunny in one hand and a Lego gun in the
other. You could almost freeze-frame that moment in development."[10] The interviewer reports Gilligan's comment on this crucial development period in boys' lives: "If becoming a boy means
becoming tough, Gilligan says, then boys may feel at an early age
that they have to hide the part of themselves that is more caring
or stereotypically feminine."

Recall the suggestion of Gilligan's colleague, Elizabeth Debold,   12
that it is superheroes and macho toys that "cause [boys] to be
angry and act aggressive." The patriarchal pressures on boys to
hide their feminine side create the problem. This is something the
Harvard team hopes a new "Reformation" will radically change.

Describing the purpose of the Harvard Project on Women's Psy-   13
chology, Boys' Development and the Culture of Manhood, Carol
Gilligan and her codirector, Barney Brawer, state the following
"working theory":

- "that the relational crisis which men typically experience
  in early childhood occurs for women in adolescence"

- "that this relational crisis in boys and girls involves disconnection from women which is essential to the perpetuation of patriarchal societies"[11]

14   A project that posits a "crisis" engulfing both boys and girls, caused by a patriarchal order that perpetuates itself by forcing children to "disconnect" from women, is not about to take a serious look at the problem of absent fathers. In his contribution to the statement describing the purpose of the Harvard Project, Brawer seeks to address this point by "adding two additional questions to Gilligan's analysis":

> First: How do we include in our view of boyhood and manhood not only the problems of the traditional model but also potential strengths?
> Second: What is the particular conundrum of boys living *without* fathers *within a culture of patriarchy?*

15   To the first of Brawer's questions, the answer is, How indeed? Having identified the "traditional model" of manhood as the cause of boys' crisis, how can we now turn around to acknowledge that the traditional manly virtues (courage, honor, self-discipline, competitiveness) play a vital role in the healthy socialization of boys? The second question oddly hints that the problems being caused by fatherlessness are some-how due to the culture of patriarchy—the default villain of the piece. We can see why Brawer finds fatherlessness a conundrum. The puzzle is why, in a Gilliganesque world where the ills suffered by boys are caused by a male culture that forcibly separates boys from their mothers, the absence of fathers wouldn't be a blessing. In the real world, of course, widespread fatherlessness is not a conundrum but a personal and social tragedy.

16   In 1998, Brawer moved the Harvard Project to Tufts University and renamed it the Boys' Project. As he now describes it, it is a "collaborative community" of teachers, counselors, researchers, and parents who will develop new "experiments in connection."[12] Reconstructing boys is the ultimate aim. How to do so is still undetermined.[13] Back at Harvard, Gilligan, Judy Chu, and their colleagues are moving forward with their own well-funded studies on how to rescue boys from the harmful culture of boyhood. According to *The New York Times,* Gilligan's chair carries with it a half-million-dollar research endowment.[14]

Boys Out of Touch with their Feelings

17   Oblivious to all the factual evidence that points to paternal separation as a significant cause of aberrant behavior in boys, Gilligan bravely calls for a fundamental change in the rearing of boys that

would keep them in a more sensitive relationship with their feminine side: we need to free young men from a destructive culture of manhood that "impedes their capacity to feel their own and other people's hurt, to know their own and other people's sadness."[15] Since, as she has diagnosed it, the purported disorder is universal, the cure must be radical. We must change the very nature of childhood: we must find ways to keep boys bonded to their mothers. We must undercut the system of socialization that is so "essential to the perpetuation of patriarchal societies."

Gilligan's views are attractive to many who believe that boys   18
could well profit by being more sensitive and empathetic. But before anyone enlists in Gilligan's project of getting boys in touch with their inner nurturer, he or she would do well to note that Gilligan's central thesis—that boys are being imprisoned by their conventional masculinity—is not a scientific hypothesis. It is an extravagant piece of speculative psychology of the kind that sometimes finds acceptance in schools of education but is not creditable in most professional departments of psychology.

On a less academic plane, we may simply fault Gilligan's pro-   19
posed reformation for straining common sense. It is obvious that a boy needs his father (or a father figure) to help him become a young man and that the ideal of belonging to the culture of manhood is terribly important to every boy. To impugn his desire to become "one of the boys" is to deny that a boy's biology determines much of what he prefers and is attracted to. Unfortunately, when education theorists deny boys' nature, they are in a position to cause them much misery.

Gilligan talks about radically reforming "the fundamental struc-   20
ture of authority" by making changes that will free boys from the masculine stereotypes that bind them. But in what sense are American boys unfree? Was the young Mark Twain or the young Teddy Roosevelt enslaved by conventional modes of boyhood? Is the average Little Leaguer or Cub Scout defective in the ways suggested by Gilligan? In practice, getting boys to be more like girls means getting them to stop segregating themselves into all-male groups. That's the darker, coercive side of the project to "free" boys from their masculine straitjackets.

It is certainly true that a small subset of male children fit Gilli-   21
gan's description of being desensitized and cut off from feelings of tenderness and care. However, these boys do not represent the sex as a whole. Gilligan speaks of boys in general as "hiding their humanity" and showing a capacity to "hurt without feeling hurt." This, she maintains, is a general condition brought about because the vast majority of boys are forced into separation from their nurturers. But the idea that boys are abnormally insensitive flies in the face of everyday experience. Boys are competitive and often aggressive. But anyone in close contact with them—parents,

grandparents, teachers, coaches, friends—gets daily proof of most boys' humanity, loyalty, and compassion.

22   Gilligan appears to be making the same mistake with boys that she made with girls. She observes a few children and interprets their problems as indicative of a deep and general malaise caused by the way our society imposes sex-role stereotypes on them. By adolescence, she concludes, the pressure to meet these stereotypes has impaired, distressed, and deformed both sexes. In fact, with the important exception of boys whose fathers are absent and who get their concept of maleness from peer groups, most boys are not violent. Most are not unfeeling or antisocial. They are just boys—and being a boy is not in itself a defect.

23   Does Gilligan really understand boys? She finds boys lacking in empathy, but does *she* empathize with *them*? Is she free of the tiresome misandry that infects so many gender theorists who never stop blaming the "male culture" for all social and psychological ills? Nothing we have seen or heard offers the slightest reassurance that Gilligan and her colleagues are wise enough or objective enough to be trusted to lead the field in devising new ways of socializing boys.

24   We have yet to see a single reasonable argument for radically reforming the identities of boys and girls. There is no reason to believe that such reform is achievable, but even if it were, the attempt to obtrude on boys and girls at this level of their natures is morally wrong. The new pedagogies designed to "educate boys more like girls" (in Gloria Steinem's phrase) are not harmless. Their approach to boys is unacceptably meddlesome, even subtly abusive.

A Good Word for the Capitalist Patriarchy and Martial Virtues

25   Gilligan's work on boys irresponsibly downplays biological factors and ignores problems caused by family breakdown. Instead, it is heavy on cultural ideology and speculative psychology and light on common sense. In particular, it displays little sympathy for the males she is seeking to help.

26   Consider her criticism of how American boys are initiated into a patriarchal social order that valorizes heroism, honor, war, and competition. In Gilligan's world, the military man is one of the potent and deplorable stereotypes that "the culture of manhood" holds up to boys as a male ideal. But her criticism of military culture is flawed in a number of ways. First, the military ethos that Gilligan castigates as insensitive and uncaring is probably less influential in the lives of boys today than at most periods in our history. At the same time, it needs to be pointed out, the American military and its culture are nothing to be ashamed of. Indeed, if you want to cite an American institution

that inculcates high levels of human concern, cooperation, and sacrifice, you could aptly choose the military.

Anyone who has firsthand knowledge of American military personnel knows that most are highly competent, self-disciplined, honorable, and moral young men and women ready to risk their lives for their country. Gilligan and her followers are confused about military ethics. Yes, the military "valorizes" honor, competition, and winning. Offering no reasons for impugning these values, which in fact are necessary for an effective life, she contents herself with insinuating that they are dehumanizing by contrast with the values she admires: cooperation, caring, self-sacrifice. She seems unaware that the values she holds dear are also essential to the military ethos. To suggest that the military ethic promotes callousness and heedlessness is a travesty of the facts. To accuse the military of being uncaring is to ignore the selflessness and camaraderie that make the martial ethos so attractive to those who intensely desire to live lives of high purpose and service.   27

The historian Stephen Ambrose, who has spent half his career listening to the stories of soldiers, tells of a course on the Second World War he gave at the University of Wisconsin in 1996 to an overflow class of 350. Most students were unfamiliar with the salient events of that war. According to Ambrose, "They were dumbstruck by descriptions of what it was like to be on the front lines. They were even more amazed by the responsibilities carried by junior officers . . . who were as young as they . . . they wondered how anyone could have done it."[16]   28

Ambrose tried to explain to them what had brought so many men and women to such feats of courage, such levels of excellence. He told them it hadn't been anything abstract. It had involved two things: "unit cohesion"—a concern for the safety and well-being of their soldier comrades that equaled and sometimes exceeded their concern for their own well-being—and an understanding of the moral dimensions of the fight: "At the core, the American citizen soldiers knew the difference between right and wrong, and they didn't want to live in a world in which wrong prevailed. So they fought, and won, and we all of us, living and yet to be born, must be forever profoundly grateful."[17]   29

What Ambrose understands and Gilligan does not is that an overarching ethic of duty encompasses the ethic of care. The so-called manly virtues of honor, duty, and self-sacrifice *are* caring virtues, and it is wrong to deride them as lesser virtues. Gilligan's depreciation of the military is academically fashionable. Ambrose says that after he finished college in the late 1950s, he too shared the antimilitary, antibusiness snobbery that prevails in many universities today. He writes: 30

> By the time I was a graduate student, I was full of scorn for [ex-GIs] . . . But in fact these were the men who built modern

America. They had learned to work together in the armed services in World War II. They had seen enough destruction: they wanted to construct. They built the Interstate Highway system, the St. Lawrence Seaway, the suburbs . . . They had seen enough killing; they wanted to save lives. They licked polio and made other revolutionary advances in medicine. They had learned in the army the virtues of a solid organization and teamwork, and the value of individual initiative, inventiveness, and responsibility.[18]

31   Carol Gilligan's many disciples, who teach in schools of education, work in the U.S. Department of Education, and shape policy in the nation's lower schools, show little awareness of the noble and constructive side of the military ethos. They seem not to appreciate or even understand the manly virtues. The thought seems never to have crossed their minds that the military virtues—stoicism, honor, cooperation, sacrifice, striving for excellence—are the virtues that sustain our civilization.

Gilligan's Direction

32   Finally, what are we to make of Carol Gilligan's contribution and influence? Her earlier work on the different moral voices of males and females had merit; her demand that psychologists and philosophers take into account the possibility that women and men have different styles of moral reasoning was altogether appropriate. As it turns out, the differences are less important than Gilligan predicted. All the same, her suggestive ideas on sex and moral psychology stimulated an important discussion. For that she deserved recognition.

33   Her later work on adolescent girls and their "silenced" voices shows us a different Gilligan. Her ideas were successful in the sense that they inspired activists in organizations such as the AAUW and the Ms. Foundation to go on red alert in an effort to save the nation's "drowning and disappearing" daughters. But all their activism was based on a false premise: that girls were subdued, neglected, and diminished. In fact, the opposite was true: girls were moving ahead of boys in most of the ways that count. Gilligan's powerful myth of the incredible shrinking girl did far more harm than good. It patronized girls, portraying them as victims of the culture. It diverted attention from the academic deficits of boys. It also gave urgency and credibility to a specious self-esteem movement that wasted everybody's time.

34   Gilligan's latest work on boys is even more reckless and removed from reality. The myth of the emotionally repressed boy has great destructive potential. If taken seriously, it could lead to even more distracting and insipid school programs designed to

get boys in touch with their feelings. More ominously, it could lead to increasingly aggressive efforts to feminize boys—for their own sakes and the supposed good of society.

Gilligan's work on girls led to an outpouring of writing about   36 the shattered Ophelias in our midst. We are now facing a second spate of Gilligan-inspired books and articles, this time sounding the tocsin about the plight of our nation's isolated, repressed, and silenced young males. Boys, we hear, are being traumatized by a culture of manhood that surrounds them with harmful "myths of boyhood."[19] Boys, like girls, need to be rescued from the male culture. In this call for deliverance, Gilligan has been joined by some prominent male disciples. I shall now consider their research, their claims, and their overwrought recommendations for restoring psychic health to a nation of stricken young Hamlets.

Notes:

1. Norman, "From Carol Gilligan's Chair," p. 50.
2. Gilligan, "The Centrality of Relationship in Human Development," p. 238; Franklin, "The Toll of Gender Roles," p. 9.
3. See Chapter 3 for a discussion of how biological differences between males and females may account for differences in reading abilities.
4. http://www.census.gov/population/socdemo.
5. Daniel Patrick Moynihan, *The Negro Family: The Case for National Action* (Washington, D.C.: U.S. Department of Labor, 1965). Quoted in National Fatherhood Initiative, *Father Facts* (Gaithersburg, Md.: National Fatherhood Initiative, 1998), p. 57.
6. David Blankenhorn, *Fatherless America: Confronting Our Most Urgent Social Problem* (New York: Basic Books, 1995), p. 31.
7. Elaine Ciulla Kamarck and William Galston, *Putting Children First: A Progressive Family Policy for the 1990s* (Washington, D.C.: Progressive Policy Institute, 1990), p. 14.
8. Cynthia Harper and Sara McLanahan, "Father Absence and Youth Incarceration," presented at annual meeting of the American Sociological Association, San Francisco, August 1998.
9. Blankenhorn, *Fatherless America.*
10. Debra Viadero, "Their Own Voice," *Education Week,* May 13, 1998, p. 38.
11. Information sheet from Harvard Graduate School of Education, "Women's Psychology, Boys' Development and the Culture of Manhood," September 1995.
12. Information sheet from the Program for Educational Change Agents, Tufts University, Medford, Massachusetts, 1998–99.
13. Viadero, "Their Own Voice," p. 37.
14. Norman, "From Carol Gilligan's Chair," p. 50.
15. Gilligan, "The Centrality of Relationship in Human Development," p. 251.
16. Stephen Ambrose, *Citizen Soldiers* (New York: Simon & Schuster, 1997), p. 473.
17. Ibid.
18. Ibid., pp. 471–72.
19. The most popular book calling for the rescue of boys from the constraints of a harmful masculinity is William Pollack, *Real Boys: Rescuing Our Sons from the Myths of Boyhood* (New York: Random House, 1998).

Michael Kimmel

A War Against Boys?

A sociologist and professor at the State University of New York at Stony Brook, Michael S. Kimmel writes frequently on the topic of masculinity. His publications include *Changing Men: New Directions in Research on Men and Masculinity* (1987) and *Men Confront Pornography* (1990). His *Against the Tide: Pro-Feminist Men in the United States, 1776–1990* (1992) traces the role of men in advancing feminism. More recently, he has published *Manhood in America: A Cultural History* (1996) and *The Gendered Society* (2003). Unlike other writers on masculinity, Kimmel considers himself a feminist; he is National Spokesperson for the National Organization for Men Against Sexism. In what ways does Kimmel's feminism in this 2006 article from Dissent underlie his examination of the so-called "War Against Boys"? How does this piece respond to Christina Hot Sommers' contention of a "war against boys"?

1   Doug Anglin isn't likely to flash across the radar screen at an Ivy League admissions office. A seventeen-year-old senior at Milton High School, a suburb outside Boston, Anglin has a B-minus average and plays soccer and baseball. But he's done something that millions of other teenagers haven't: he's sued his school district for sex discrimination.

2   Anglin's lawsuit, brought with the aid of his father, a Boston lawyer, claims that schools routinely discriminate against males. "From the elementary level, they establish a philosophy that if you sit down, follow orders, and listen to what they say, you'll do well and get good grades," he told a journalist. "Men naturally rebel against this." He may have a point: overworked teachers might well look more kindly on classroom docility and decorum. But his proposed remedies—such as raising boys' grades retroactively—are laughable.

3   And though it's tempting to parse the statements of a mediocre high school senior—what's so "natural" about rebelling against blindly following orders, a military tactician might ask—Anglin's apparent admissions angle is but the latest skirmish of a much bigger battle in the culture wars. The current salvos concern boys. The "trouble with boys" has become a staple on talk-radio, the cover story in *Newsweek,* and the subject of dozens of columns in newspapers and magazines. And when the First Lady offers a

helping hand to boys, you know something political is in the works. "Rescuing" boys actually translates into bashing feminism. There is no doubt that boys are not faring well in school. From 4 elementary schools to high schools they have lower grades, lower class rank, and fewer honors than girls. They're 50 percent more likely to repeat a grade in elementary school, one-third more likely to drop out of high school, and about six times more likely to be diagnosed with attention deficit and hyperactivity disorder (ADHD).

College statistics are similar—if the boys get there at all. Women 5 now constitute the majority of students on college campuses, having passed men in 1982, so that in eight years women will earn 58 percent of bachelor's degrees in U.S. colleges. One expert, Tom Mortensen, warns that if current trends continue, "the graduation line in 2068 will be all females." Mortensen may be a competent higher education policy analyst but he's a lousy statistician. His dire prediction is analogous to predicting forty years ago that, if the enrollment of black students at Ol' Miss was one in 1964, and, say, two hundred in 1968 and one thousand in 1976, then "if present trends continue" there would be no white students on campus by 1982. Doomsayers lament that women now outnumber men in the social and behavioral sciences by about three to one, and that they've invaded such traditionally male bastions as engineering (where they now make up 20 percent) and biology and business (virtually par).

These three issues—declining numbers, declining achievement, 6 and increasingly problematic behavior—form the empirical basis of the current debate. But its political origins are significantly older and ominously more familiar. Peeking underneath the empirical façade helps explain much of the current lineup.

Why Now?

If boys are doing worse, whose fault is it? To many of the current 7 critics, it's women's fault, either as feminists, as mothers, or as both. Feminists, we read, have been so successful that the earlier "chilly classroom climate" has now become overheated to the detriment of boys. Feminist-inspired programs have enabled a whole generation of girls to enter the sciences, medicine, law, and the professions; to continue their education; to imagine careers outside the home. But in so doing, these same feminists have pathologized boyhood. Elementary schools are, we read, "anti-boy"—emphasizing reading and restricting the movements of young boys. They "feminize" boys, forcing active, healthy, and naturally exuberant boys to conform to a regime of obedience, "pathologizing what is simply normal for boys," as one psychologist puts it. Schools are an "inhospitable" environment for boys, writes Christina Hoff Sommers, where their natural propensities for rough-and-tumble play, competition, aggression, and rambunctious violence are cast as social problems in the making. Michael Gurian argues in *The Wonder of Boys*, that, with testosterone surging through their little limbs, we demand that they sit still, raise their hands, and take naps. We're giving them the message, he says, that "boyhood is defective." By the time they get to college, they've been steeped in anti-male propaganda. "Why would any self-respecting boy want to attend one of America's increasingly feminized universities?" asks George Gilder in *National Review*. The American university is now a "fluffy pink playpen of feminist studies and agitprop 'herstory,' taught amid a green goo of eco-motherism . . . "

8   Such claims sound tinnily familiar. At the turn of the last century, cultural critics were concerned that the rise of white-collar businesses meant increasing indolence for men, whose sons were being feminized by mothers and female teachers. Then, as now, the solutions were to find arenas in which boys could simply be boys, and where men could be men as well. So fraternal lodges offered men a homo-social sanctuary, and dude ranches and sports provided a place where these sedentary men could experience what Theodore Roosevelt called the strenuous life. Boys could troop off with the Boy Scouts, designed as a fin-de-siècle "boys' liberation movement." Modern society was turning hardy, robust boys, as Boy Scouts' founder Ernest Thompson Seton put it, into "a lot of flat chested cigarette smokers with shaky nerves and doubtful vitality." Today, women teachers are once again to blame for boys' feminization. "It's the teacher's job to create a classroom environment that accommodates both male and female energy, not just mainly female energy," explains Gurian.

9   What's wrong with this picture? Well, for one thing, it creates a false opposition between girls and boys, assuming that educational reforms undertaken to enable girls to perform better hinder boys' educational development. But these reforms—new classroom arrangements, teacher training, increased attentiveness to individual learning styles—actually enable larger numbers of boys to get a better education. Though the current boy advocates claim that schools used to be more "boy friendly" before all these "feminist" reforms, they obviously didn't go to school in those halcyon days, the 1950s, say, when the classroom was far more regimented, corporal punishment common, and teachers far more authoritarian: they even gave grades for "deportment." Rambunctious boys were simply not tolerated; they dropped out.

10   Gender stereotyping hurts both boys and girls. If there is a zero-sum game, it's not because of some putative feminization of the classroom. The net effect of the No Child Left Behind Act has been zero-sum competition, as school districts scramble to

stretch inadequate funding, leaving them little choice but to cut noncurricular programs so as to ensure that curricular mandates are followed. This disadvantages "rambunctious" boys, because many of these programs are after-school athletics, gym, and recess. And cutting "unnecessary" school counselors and other remedial programs also disadvantages boys, who compose the majority of children in behavioral and remedial educational programs. The problem of inadequate school funding lies not at feminists' door, but in the halls of Congress. This is further compounded by changes in the insurance industry, which often pressure therapists to put children on medication for ADHD rather than pay for expensive therapy.

Another problem is that the frequently cited numbers are mis-   11
leading. More *people*—that is, males and females—are going to college than ever before. In 1960, 54 percent of boys and 38 percent of girls went directly to college; today the numbers are 64 percent of boys and 70 percent of girls. It is true that the *rate of increase* among girls is higher than the rate of increase among boys, but the numbers are increasing for both.

The gender imbalance does not apply to the nation's most elite   12
colleges and universities, where percentages for men and women are, and have remained, similar. Of the top colleges and universities in the nation, only Stanford sports a fifty-fifty gender balance. Harvard and Amherst enroll 56 percent men, Princeton and Chicago 54 percent men, Duke and Berkeley 52 percent, and Yale 51 percent. In science and engineering, the gender imbalance still tilts decidedly toward men: Cal Tech is 65 percent male and 35 percent female; MIT is 62 percent male, 38 percent female.

And the imbalance is not uniform across class and race. It   13
remains the case that far more working-class women—of all races—go to college than do working-class men. Part of this is a seemingly rational individual decision: a college-educated woman still earns about the same as a high-school educated man, $35,000 to $31,000. By race, the disparities are more starkly drawn. Among middle-class, white, high school graduates going to college this year, half are male and half are female. But only 37 percent of black college students and 45 percent of Hispanic students are male. The numerical imbalance turns out to be more a problem of race and class than gender. It is what Cynthia Fuchs Epstein calls a "deceptive distinction"—a difference that appears to be about gender, but is actually about something else.

Why don't the critics acknowledge these race and class differ-   14
ences? To many who now propose to "rescue" boys, such differences are incidental because, in their eyes, all boys are the same aggressive, competitive, rambunctious little devils. They operate from a facile, and inaccurate, essentialist dichotomy between males and females. Boys must be allowed to be boys—so that they grow up to be men.

15   This facile biologism leads the critics to propose some distasteful remedies to allow these testosterone-juiced boys to express themselves. Gurian, for example, celebrates all masculine rites of passage, "like military boot camp, fraternity hazings, graduation day, and bar mitzvah" as "essential parts of every boy's life." He also suggests reviving corporal punishment, both at home and at school—but only when administered privately with cool indifference and never in the heat of adult anger. He calls it "spanking responsibly," though I suspect school boards and child welfare agencies might have another term for it.

16   But what boys need turns out to be pretty much what girls need. In their best-selling *Raising Cain*, Michael Thompson and Dan Kindlon describe *boys'* needs: to be loved, get sex, and not be hurt. Parents are counseled to allow boys their emotions: accept a high level of activity; speak their language; and treat them with respect. They are to teach the many ways a boy can be a man, use discipline to guide and build, and model manhood as emotionally attached. Aside from the obvious tautologies, what they advocate is exactly what feminists have been advocating for girls for some time.

Boys' Lives and Fatherlessness

17   However, those feminist women, many of whom are also involved mothers, are seen not as boys' natural allies in claiming a better education but as their enemies. Fears of "momism"—that peculiar cultural malady that periodically rears its head—have returned. Remember those World War II best sellers, like Philip Wylie's *Generation of Vipers*, David Levy's *Maternal Overprotection*, and Edward Strecker's *Their Mothers' Sons* that laid men's problems at the foot of overdominant mothers, who drained their boys of ambition and hardy manliness and led them straight to the summit of Brokeback Mountain?

18   Well, they're back. Now the problem with mothers is that they read *The Feminine Mystique* and ran out to pursue careers, which caused a mass exodus of fathers from the lives of their sons. Feminist women not only promoted girls at the expense of boys, but they kicked dad out of the house and left boys wallowing in an anomic genderless soup.

19   The cause of the boy crisis, we hear, is fatherlessness. Boys lack adequate role models because their fathers are either at work all the time or are divorced with limited custody and visitation privileges. Discussions of boys' problems almost invariably circle back to fathers or, rather the lack of them. But fatherlessness is not Dad's fault. It's Mom's. The debate about boys instantly morphs into a discussion of unwed mothers, single-parent families, babies having babies, and punitive and vindictive ex-wives (and their equally punitive and vindictive lawyers) who prevent men from

being more present in their lives of their children. Women left the home in search of work and fulfillment, abandoning their natural role of taming men and rearing children. Feminism declares war against nature. The battle for boys is only the latest front.

This antifeminist political argument is best, and most simply,   20 made by Harvey Mansfield, author of the recent *Manliness*, in a November 3, 1997, op-ed essay in the *Wall Street Journal*. "The protective element of manliness is endangered when women have equal access to jobs outside the home," he writes. "Women who do not consider themselves feminist often seem unaware of what they are doing to manliness when they work to support themselves. They think only that people should be hired and promoted on merit, regardless of sex." When Lionel Tiger argues that "the principal victims of moving toward a merit-based society have been male," one feels a certain resigned sadness. Imagine that: it's feminists who actually believe in meritocracy.

Fathers *would* be present in their sons lives (in this debate,   21 fathers don't seem to have daughters)—if only women would let them. "Fortunately," writes pro-fatherhood activist Steve Biddulph, "fathers are fighting their way back into family life." Fighting against whom exactly? Feminist women have been pleading with men to come home and share housework and child care— let alone to help raise their sons—for what, 150 years?

As role models, fathers could provide a model of decisiveness,   22 discipline, and emotional control—which would be useful for their naturally aggressive, testosterone-juiced sons at school. But how do these same biologically driven, rambunctious boys magically grow up to be strong, silent, decisive, and controlled fathers?

It's easy—if women do what *they* are biologically programmed   23 to do: stay home and raise boys (but not for too long) and constrain the natural predatory, aggressive, and lustful impulses of their men. In leaving the home and going to work, women abandoned their naturally prescribed role of sexual constraint. Presto: a debate about fatherhood and boyhood becomes a debate about feminism.

The boy crisis would be magically solved if fathers were not   24 exiled from family life. The spate of works about fatherhood that appeared several years ago is now being recycled in the debate about boys. Fathers, by virtue of being men, bring something irreplaceable to the family, something "inherently masculine" notes Wade Horn, assistant secretary in the U.S. Department of Health and Human Services, Administration for Children and Families. (It is Horn who is promoting the backward idea that marriage-based programs will alleviate poverty when all available evidence suggests the opposite relationship, that alleviating poverty would actually lead to an increase in marriages.) That "inherently masculine" influence is a triumph of form over content. David Blankenhorn's catalog of specious correlations, *Fatherless America*, that saw fathers' absence as the source of virtually every social problem in America, doesn't call for a new fatherhood, based on emotional receptivity and responsiveness, compassion and patience, care and nurture. Instead he rails against such a father in this sarcastic passage:

> He is nurturing. He expresses his emotions. He is a healer, a companion, a colleague. He is a deeply involved parent. He changes diapers, gets up at 2:00 a.m. to feed the baby, goes beyond "helping out" . . . to share equally in the work, joys, and responsibilities of domestic life.

25   How utterly "selfish" of him. This "reflects the puerile desire for human omnipotentiality in the form of genderless parenthood, a direct repudiation of fatherhood as a gendered social role for men." What he means is that the real father is neither nurturing nor expressive; he is neither a partner nor a friend to his wife, and he sleeps through most of the young baby's infantile helplessness, oblivious to the needs of his wife and child. This guy is a father simply because he has a Y chromosome. Men are fathers, but they are not required to do any real parenting. The father "protects his family, provides for its material needs, devotes himself to the education of his children, and represents his family's interests in the larger world"—all valuable behaviors, to be sure. But he need not ever set foot in his child's room.

26   The notion that men should be exempt from mundane housework and child care, which should be left to their wives, is deeply insulting to women. Feminism taught us that. But it's also deeply insulting to men, because it assumes that the nurturing of life itself cannot be our province; given how clumsy and aggressive we are, it had better be done at a distance.

Masculinity: The Missing Piece

27   What, then, is missing from the debate about boys? In a word, the boys themselves—or rather, what the boys feel, think, and believe—especially what they believe will make them men. None of the antifeminist pundits who seek to rescue boys from the emasculating clutches of feminism ever talks about what masculinity means to boys. The beliefs, attitudes, and traits that form the foundation of gender identity and ideology are nowhere to be found—except as some mythic endocrine derivative. "Males" are the topic, not "masculinity." Countless surveys suggest that young boys today subscribe to a traditional definition of masculinity, stressing the suppression of emotion, stoic resolve, aggression, power, success, and other stereotypic features. Indeed, the point of such successful books as William Pollack's *Real Boys* and Thompson and Kindlon's *Raising Cain* is to expand

the emotional and psychological repertoire of boys, enabling them to express a wider emotional and creative range.

How does a focus on the ideology of masculinity explain what 28 is happening to boys in school? Consider the parallel for girls. Carol Gilligan's work on adolescent girls describes how these assertive, confident, and proud young girls "lose their voices" when they hit adolescence. At that same moment, Pollack notes, boys become *more* confident, even beyond their abilities. You might even say that boys *find* their voices, but it is the inauthentic voice of bravado, posturing, foolish risk-taking, and gratuitous violence. He calls it "the boy code." The boy code teaches them that they are supposed to be in power, and so they begin to act as if they are. They "ruffle in a manly pose," as William Butler Yeats once put it, "for all their timid heart."

In adolescence, both boys and girls get their first real dose of 29 gender inequality: girls suppress ambition, boys inflate it. Recent research on the gender gap in school achievement bears this out. Girls are more likely to undervalue their abilities, especially in the more traditionally "masculine" educational arenas such as math and science. Only the most able and most secure girls take courses in those fields. Thus, their numbers tend to be few, and their mean test scores high. Boys, however, possessed of this false voice of bravado (and facing strong family pressure) are likely to *overvalue* their abilities, to remain in programs though they are less capable of succeeding.

This difference, and not some putative discrimination against 30 boys, is the reason that girls' mean test scores in math and science are now, on average, approaching that of boys. Too many boys remain in difficult math and science courses longer than they should; they pull the boys' mean scores down. By contrast, the smaller number of girls, whose abilities and self-esteem are sufficient to enable them to "trespass" into a male domain, skew female data upward.

A parallel process is at work in the humanities and social sci- 31 ences. Girls' mean test scores in English and foreign languages, for example, outpace those of boys. But this is not the result of "reverse discrimination"; it is because the boys bump up against the norms of masculinity. Boys regard English as a "feminine" subject. Pioneering research by Wayne Martino in Australia and Britain found that boys avoid English because of what it might say about their (inauthentic) masculine pose. "Reading is lame, sitting down and looking at words is pathetic," commented one boy. "Most guys who like English are faggots." The traditional liberal arts curriculum, as it was before feminism, is seen as feminizing. As Catharine Stimpson recently put it, "Real men don't speak French."

Boys tend to hate English and foreign languages for the same 32 reasons that girls love them. In English, they observe, there are no hard-and-fast rules, one expresses one's opinion about the topic and everyone's opinion is equally valued. "The answer can be a variety of things, you're never really wrong," observed one boy. "It's not like maths and science where there is one set answer to everything." Another boy noted:

> I find English hard. It's because there are no set rules for reading texts . . . English isn't like maths where you have rules on how to do things and where there are right and wrong answers. In English you have to write down how you feel and that's what I don't like.

33   Compare this to the comments of girls in the same study:

> I feel motivated to study English because . . . you have freedom in English—unlike subjects such as maths and science—and your view isn't necessarily wrong. There is no definite right or wrong answer, and you have the freedom to say what you feel is right without it being rejected as a wrong answer.

34   It is not the school experience that "feminizes" boys, but rather the ideology of traditional masculinity that keeps boys from wanting to succeed. "The work you do here is girls work," one boy commented to a researcher. "It's not real work."

35   "Real work" involves a confrontation—not with feminist women, whose sensible educational reforms have opened countless doors to women while closing off none to men—but with an anachronistic definition of masculinity that stresses many of its vices (anti-intellectualism, entitlement, arrogance, and aggression) but few of its virtues. When the self-appointed rescuers demand that we accept boys' "hardwiring," could they possibly have such a monochromatic and relentlessly negative view of male biology? Maybe they do. But simply shrugging our collective shoulders in resignation and saying "boys will be boys" sets the bar much too low. Boys can do better than that. They can be men.

36   Perhaps the real "male bashers" are those who promise to rescue boys from the clutches of feminists. Are males not also "hardwired" toward compassion, nurturing, and love? If not, would we allow males to be parents? It is never a biological question of whether we are "hardwired" for some behavior; it is, rather, a political question of which "hardwiring" we choose to respect and which we choose to challenge.

37   The antifeminist pundits have an unyielding view of men as irredeemably awful. We men, they tell us, are savage, lustful, violent, sexually omnivorous, rapacious, predatory animals, who will rape, murder, pillage, and leave towels on the bathroom floor—unless women fulfill their biological duty and constrain

us. "Every society must be wary of the unattached male, for he is universally the cause of numerous ills," writes David Popenoe. Young males, says Charles Murray, are "essentially barbarians for whom marriage . . . is an indispensable civilizing force."

By contrast, feminists believe that men are better than that, 38 that boys can be raised to be competent and compassionate, ambitious and attentive, and that men are fully capable of love, care, and nurturance. It's feminists who are really "pro-boy" and "pro-father"—who want young boys and their fathers to expand the definition of masculinity and to become fully human.

Marshall Poe

The Other Gender Gap

Marshall Poe was born in 1961 has served as a lecturer at both Harvard and Columbia Universities. He has written on topics as varied as Russian and American history and the state of American education. In the piece below, originally published in *The Atlantic Monthly in 2004,* Poe explores what he calls the "educational stagnation" of boys, who are outnumbered by women in colleges nationally. This piece (which was subtitled "Maybe Boys Just Weren't Meant for the Classroom") might help you to consider how gender plays a role in issues of education. You might also compare Poe's contention that boys are being left behind in schooling because educational systems don't account for boys' natural tendencies toward kinesthetic activities, to the argument made on a similar topic by Michael Kimmel in "A War Against Boys" as well as the arguments on gender issues made throughout this section of this book.

The women's movement has taught us many things, one of 1 the more surprising being that boys are not performing in school as well as they might.

Three decades ago reformers attention was focused on the 2 "higher-education gap"—the fact that not as many girls went on to college, graduate school, and professional school as boys. Advocates of equality between the sexes fought hard to create gender-specific education programs, fair admissions policies, and professional societies for women. There efforts were rewarded:

from 1970 to 2000 the number of women attending college rose by 136 percent, graduate school by 168 percent, and professional school by 853 percent.

3   Yet soon the higher-education gap opened again—but this time girls were on the other side of it. In the late 1970s more girls than boys began to enroll in college, and the disparity has since increased. Today woman make up approximately 56 percent of all undergraduates, outnumbering men by about 1.7 million. In addition, about 300,000 more women than men enter graduate school each year. (The gap does not particularly affect professional school; almost as many women as men attend.) In short, equal opportunity brought an unequal result.

4   The advance of girls relative to boys might well have been predicted from patterns in K–12 schooling, where girls have long been outperforming boys on several measures. In both primary and secondary school girls tend to receive higher marks than boys. Since the inception, in 1969, of the National Assessment of Educational Progress (a standardized exam given to nine-, thirteen-, and seventeen-year-olds), girls at all grade levels have scored much higher, on average, than boys in language skills, and about the same in math. (True college-bound boys have long outperformed girls overall on the SAT, but it is likely that boys average scores are statistically elevated by the fact that roughly 10 percent fewer of them take the exam—and those who opt out tend to be lower achievers.) It is hardly surprising then, that once various cultural barriers were removed, girls began entering college at a greater rate.

5   The continuing advance among girls has thrown a spotlight on the stagnation of boys. During the past decade the percentage of boys who complete high school (about 70), enter college (about 40), and go on to graduate school (about eight) has risen only slightly or not at all. And this despite the fact that the economic payoff of higher education has never been greater. Whereas girls continue to demonstrate that society has not yet reached any "natural" limit on college-attendance rates, boys have somehow gotten stuck. If boys and girls have roughly equal abilities, then why aren't they doing equally well?

6   From kindergarten on, the education system rewards self-control, obedience, and concentration—qualities that, any teacher can tell you, are much more common among girls than boys, particularly at young ages. Boys fidget, fool around, fight, and worse. Thirty years ago teachers may have accommodated and managed this behavior in part by devoting more attention to boys than to girls. But as girls have come to attract equal attention, as an inability to sit still has been medicalized, and as the options for curbing student misbehavior have been ever more curtailed, boys may have suffered. Boys make up three quarters of all children categorized as learning disabled today, and they

are put in special education at a much higher rate (special education is often misused as a place to stick "problem kids," and children seldom switch from there to the college track). Shorter recess times, less physical education, and more time spent on more rote learning (in order to meet testing standards) may have exacerbated the problems that boys tend to experience in the classroom. It is no wonder then, that many boys disengage academically. Boys, are also subject to a range of extrinsic factors that hinder their academic performance and pull them out of school at greater rates than girls. First among these is the labor market. Young men, with or without high school diplomas, earn more than young women, so they are more likely to see work as an *alternative* to school. Employment gives many men immediate monetary gratification along with relief from the drudgery of the classroom.

But boys' educational stagnation has long-term economic 7 implications. Not even half the boys in the country are taking advantage of the opportunity to go to college, which has become almost a prerequisite for a middle-class lifestyle. And languishing academic attainment among a large portion of our population spells trouble for the prospects of continued economic growth. Unless more boys begin attending college, the nation may face a shortage of highly skilled workers in the coming decades.

The trouble with boys is not confined to the United States; boys 8 are being outperformed by girls throughout the developed world. The United Kingdom and Australia are currently testing programs aimed at making education more boy-friendly. Single-sex schools, single-sex classes, and gender-specific curricula are all being tried. Here the United States lags; there are several local initiatives aimed at boys, but nothing on the national level—perhaps owing to a residual anxiety over the idea of helping boys in a society where men for so long enjoyed special advantages.

getting into the conversation ...5

Gender Identities

1. The articles in this chapter of *Conversations* all address the ways that our identity is influenced by our gender. But gender itself is a complex concept. Does it refer to specific biological or sex characteristics, or do the more important identity issues come from "socially constructed" norms—that is, from societal expectations for particular genders? As you read the pieces in this section, keep track of the ways that each author addresses questions of biology and questions about the norms that are imposed upon each gender, and build an argument that demonstrates how identity issues related to gender are either naturally occurring or socially constructed. To do so, you might also do some further research on the construction of gender roles.

2. For the last 40 years or so, modern feminists have been working toward civil and economic rights for women. As a consequence, most gender studies have focused upon the changing role and place of women. But there is a growing trend toward studies of the male gender. Many of the pieces in this section explore the ways in which feminism has affected the male identity (and there are numerous other such studies written over the past few years). Compare and contrast the views on the effect of feminism on male identity contained in these pieces, and try to formulate a position on whether men are somehow being put at a disadvantage in the current environment, or whether perhaps these pieces represent a backlash against attempts to find equality for women.

3. One of the key points of debate here is whether feminism has gone too far in its quest for equality for women. Implicit in that question is whether times have changed enough to suggest that we have entered a post-gendered society (just as some have suggested that we have entered a post-racial society). As you read these pieces, which span over 150 years of the feminist thought, consider both the contexts that led to the feminist movement and whether the conditions of women that are described in these pieces have been fully overcome enough to suggest that feminism is no longer necessary. What social conditions that now exist suggest that some of these problems still persist? What conditions suggest that the feminist movement still has work to do? In order to make this argument reliably, you will need to seek out further information about the current condition of women in areas such as leadership, pay scales, access to education, and so forth.

4. One of the identity issues explored here surrounds feminism itself and whether men can also be considered feminists. Scott Russell Sanders, for example, sees himself as stereotyped by the feminists that he encountered in his education, and Michael Kimmel describes himself as a feminist. On the other hand, Christina Hoff Sommers writes in

defense of men. Do you believe, from what you have read here and from your own experiences, that men can be part of the feminist movement, or that women can play a serious role in fighting against the supposed "war against boys"? Writing from your own gender perspective, argue for or against this proposition, suggesting whether our personal gender identity can include the kind of empathy necessary to see the world through the lens of the opposite sex, or whether such empathy is not fully possible.

conversations in context ••• 3

The Beauty Myth and Personal Identity

I. The Context

> The beauty myth tells a story: The quality called "beauty" objectively and universally exists. Women must want to embody it and men must want to possess women who embody it.
>
> Naomi Wolf, The Beauty Myth

> Beauty exists, and it's unevenly distributed. . . . Asking women to say they're beautiful is like asking intellectuals to say they're geniuses. Most know that they simply don't qualify.
>
> Virginia Postrel, "The Truth about Beauty"

Beauty is in the eye of the beholder. Beauty is only skin deep. Phrases like those have long existed in our mental landscape, helping us to consider various definitions of beauty which go beyond superficial definitions of beauty that only consider a single, universal, and for many, unobtainable ideal of beauty.

As the above quotation from Naomi Wolf's landmark *The Beauty Myth* suggests, this preeminence of beauty as an ideal has been of special significance to women's self-image. But is this really a myth, or a reality? The problem may be, Virginia Postrel suggests, that beauty is not wholly in the eye of the beholder—it "exists, and it's unevenly distributed," she argues in the essay included below. And as recent studies have begun to show, ideals of physical beauty have also become more central in the self-image of men and of various ethnic and racial groups, evidenced by the growth of magazines devoted to attaining a perfect male body and of the male cosmetic industry.

Of course, the praise of—and struggle to attain—physical beauty is no new thing. Even William Shakespeare critiqued the idealization of women's appearance in his well-known Sonnet 130:

> My mistress' eyes are nothing like the sun;
> Coral is far more red than her lips' red;
> If snow be white, why then her breasts are dun;
> If hairs be wires, black wires grow on her head.
> I have seen roses damask'd, red and white,
> But no such roses see I in her cheeks;
> And in some perfumes is there more delight
> Than in the breath that from my mistress reeks.
> I love to hear her speak, yet well I know
> That music hath a far more pleasing sound;
> I grant I never saw a goddess go;
> My mistress, when she walks, treads on the ground:
>   And yet, by heaven, I think my love as rare
>   As any she belied with false compare.

This "false compare" or idealization of beauty to which women have been subjected is at the heart of the more recent conversations about the beauty myth that were brought into the public eye by Naomi Wolf's work. *The Beauty Myth,* published in 1991, became an international bestseller, speaking to the reception and effect of this work as part of the larger feminist movement. This more recent context, rooted in feminist thought, suggests that "though there has been, of course, been a beauty myth in some form for as long as there has been patriarchy, the beauty myth in its modern form is a fairly recent invention," an invention that Wolf sees as an attempt at social control of women. She argues that "the beauty myth is always actually prescribing *behavior* and not appearance"—behavior that puts women into competition with one another for the title of most beautiful.

As you read Virginia Postrel's "The Truth about Beauty, "you will find that the conversation on this topic is more complex than simply a statement that "we pay too much attention to physical beauty." Your job as a careful reader of these pieces, and the words and images that follow them in this section, is to go beyond the simpler versions of this notion, and to consider the contexts surrounding the various incarnations of this concept as it evolved. But if you choose to look deeper into this topic, you will find that there are many perspectives and contexts that can help you focus upon a particular part of this issue—and to bring your own voice into the conversation.

Considering Contexts: Virginia Postrel, "The Truth About Beauty"

Virginia Postrel, a graduate of Princeton University with a degree in English literature, writes regularly for the Atlantic Monthly, Forbes, *and other noted publications. She also served as the editor of* Reason *magazine and as a reporter for the* Wall Street Journal. *This essay explores underlying implications of Dove Soap's campaign to show "real women," not perfect models. In what ways does Dove's campaign respond to the images of beauty that Naomi Wolf's* The Beauty Myth *decries? Why does Postrel seem to take issue with this campaign? Would Wolf agree with Postrel?*

Virginia Postrel

The Truth About Beauty

Cosmetics makers have always sold "hope in a jar"—creams and potions that promise youth, beauty, sex appeal, and even love for the women who use them. Over the last few years, the marketers at Dove have added some new-and-improved enticements. They're now promising self-esteem and cultural transformation. Dove's "Campaign for Real Beauty," declares a press release, is "a global effort that is intended to serve as a starting point for societal change and act as a catalyst for widening the definition and discussion of beauty." Along with its thigh-firming creams, self-tanners, and hair conditioners, Dove is peddling the crowd-pleasing notions that beauty is a media creation, that recognizing plural forms of beauty is the same as declaring every woman beautiful, and that self-esteem means ignoring imperfections.

Dove won widespread acclaim in June 2005 when it rolled out its thigh-firming cream with billboards of attractive but variously sized "real women" frolicking in their underwear. It advertised its hair-care products by showing hundreds of women in identical platinum-blonde wigs—described as "the kind of hair found in magazines"—tossing off those artificial manes and celebrating their real (perfectly styled, colored, and conditioned) hair. It ran print ads that featured atypical models, including a plump brunette and a ninety-five-year-old, and invited readers to choose between pejorative and complimentary adjectives: "Wrinkled or wonderful?" "Oversized or outstanding?" The public and press got the point, and Dove got attention. Oprah covered the story, and so did the *Today* show. Dove's campaign, wrote *Advertising Age*, "undermines the basic proposition of decades of beauty-care advertising by telling women—and young girls—they're beautiful just the way they are."

Last fall, Dove extended its image building with a successful bit of viral marketing: a seventy-five-second online video called *Evolution*. Created by Ogilvy & Mather, the video is a close-up of a seemingly ordinary woman, shot in harsh lighting that calls attention to her uneven skin tone, slightly lopsided eyes, and dull, flat hair. In twenty seconds of time-lapse video, makeup artists and hair stylists turn her into a wide-eyed, big-haired beauty with sculpted cheeks and perfect skin. It's *Extreme Makeover* without the surgical gore.

But that's only the beginning. Next comes the digital transformation, as a designer points-and-clicks on the model's photo, giving her a longer, slimmer neck, a slightly narrower upper face, fuller lips, bigger eyes, and more space between her eyebrows and eyes. The perfected image rises to fill a billboard advertising a fictitious line of makeup. Fade to black, with the message "No wonder our perception of beauty is distorted." The video has attracted more than 3 million YouTube views. It also appears on Dove's campaignforrealbeauty.com Web site, where it concludes, "Every girl deserves to feel beautiful just the way she is."

Every girl certainly wants to, which explains the popularity of Dove's campaign. There's only one problem: Beauty exists, and it's unevenly distributed. Our eyes and brains pretty consistently like some human forms better than others. Shown photos of strangers, even babies look longer at the faces adults rank the best-looking. Whether you prefer Nicole Kidman to Angelina Jolie, Jennifer Lopez to Halle Berry, or Queen Latifah to Kate Moss may be a matter of taste, but rare is the beholder who would declare Holly Hunter or Whoopi Goldberg—neither of whom is homely—more beautiful than any of these women.

For similar reasons, we still thrill to the centuries-old bust of Nefertiti, the Venus de Milo, and the exquisite faces painted by Leonardo and Botticelli. Greta Garbo's acting style seems stilted today, but her face transcends time. We know beauty when we see it, and our reactions are remarkably consistent. Beauty is not just a social construct, and not every girl is beautiful just the way she is.

Take Dove's *Evolution* video. The digital transformation is fascinating because it magically makes a beautiful woman more striking. Her face's new geometry triggers an immediate, visceral response—and the video's storytelling impact is dependent on that predictable reaction. The video makes its point about artifice only because most people find the manipulated face more beautiful than the natural one.

In *Survival of the Prettiest: The Science of Beauty*, Nancy Etcoff, a psychologist at Harvard Medical School, reported on experiments that let people rate faces and digitally "breed" ever-more-attractive composite generations. The results for female faces look a lot like the finished product in the Dove video: "thinner jaws, larger eyes relative to the size of their faces, and shorter distances between their mouths and chins" in one case, and "fuller lips, a less robust jaw, a smaller nose and smaller chin than the population average" in another. These features, wrote Etcoff, "exaggerate the ways that adult female faces differ from adult male faces. They also exaggerate the youthfulness of the face." More than youth, the full lips and small jaws of beautiful women reflect relatively high levels of female hormones and low levels of male hormones—indicating greater fertility—according to psychologist Victor Johnston, who did some of these experiments.

More generally, evolutionary psychologists suggest that the features we see as beautiful—including indicators of good health like smooth skin and symmetry—have been rewarded through countless generations of competition for mates. The same evolutionary pressures, this research suggests, have biologically programmed human minds to perceive these features as beautiful. "Some scientists believe that our beauty detectors are really detectors for the combination of youth and femininity," wrote Etcoff. Whether the beauty we detect arises from nature or artifice doesn't change that visceral reflex.

Perhaps surprisingly, Etcoff herself advised Dove on several rounds of survey research and helped the company create workshops for girls. Dove touts her involvement (and her doctorate and Harvard affiliation) in its publicity materials. She sees the campaign as a useful corrective. Media images, Etcoff notes in an e-mail, are often so rarefied that "they change our ideas about what people look like and what normal looks like . . . Our brains did not evolve with media, and many people see more media images of women than actual women. The contrast effect makes even the most beautiful non-model look less attractive; it produces a new 'normal.'"

Dove began its campaign by recognizing the diverse manifestations of universally beautiful patterns. The "real women" pictured in the thigh-cream billboards may not have looked like supermodels, but they were all young, with symmetrical faces, feminine features, great skin, white teeth, and hourglass shapes. Even the most zaftig had relatively flat stomachs and clearly defined waists. These pretty women were not a random sample of the population. Dove diversified the portrait of beauty without abandoning the concept altogether.

But the campaign didn't stop there. Dove is defining itself as the brand that loves regular women—and regular women, by definition, are not extraordinarily beautiful. The company can't afford a precise definition of *real beauty* that might exclude half the population—not a good strategy for selling mass-market consumer products. So the campaign leaves *real beauty* ambiguous, enabling the viewers to fill in the concept with their own desires. Some take *real beauty* to mean "nature unretouched" and interpret the *Evolution* video as suggesting that uncannily beautiful faces are not merely rare but nonexistent. Others emphasize the importance of character and personality: Real beauty comes from the inside, not physical appearance. And *Advertising Age*'s interpretation is common: that Dove is reminding women that "they're beautiful just the way they are."

Another Dove ad, focusing on girls' insecurities about their looks, concludes, "Every girl deserves to feel good about herself and see how beautiful she really is." Here, Dove is encouraging the myth that phys- ical beauty is a false concept, and, at the same time, falsely equating beauty with goodness and self-worth. If you don't see perfection in the mirror, it suggests, you've been duped by the media and suffer from low self-esteem.

But adult women have a more realistic view. "Only two percent of women describe themselves as beautiful" trumpets the headline of Dove's press release. Contrary to what the company wants readers to believe, however, that statistic doesn't necessarily represent a crisis of confidence; it may simply reflect the power of the word *beautiful*. Dove's surveys don't ask women if they think they're unattractive or ugly, so it's hard to differentiate between knowing you have flaws, be- lieving you're acceptably but unimpressively plain, and feeling worth- lessly hideous. In another Dove survey, 88 percent of the American women polled said they're at least somewhat satisfied with their face, while 76 percent said they're at least somewhat satisfied with their body. But dissatisfaction is not the same as unhappiness or insecurity.

Like the rest of the genetic lottery, beauty is unfair. Everyone falls short of perfection, but some are luckier than others. Real confidence requires self-knowledge, which includes recognizing one's shortcom- ings as well as one's strengths. At a recent conference on biological ma- nipulations, I heard a philosopher declare during lunch that she'd never have plastic surgery or even dye her hair. But, she confessed, she'd pay just about anything for fifteen more IQ points. This woman is not inse- cure about her intelligence, which is far above average; she'd just like to be smarter. Asking women to say they're beautiful is like asking intel- lectuals to say they're geniuses. Most know they simply don't qualify.

II. The Conversation

Postrel's essay (and its connection to Wolf's *The Beauty Myth*) has several key stasis points. While Wolf saw beauty as a myth, for example, Postrel complicates that equation, asserting that "Dove is encouraging the myth that physical beauty is a false concept, and, at the same time, falsely equating beauty with goodness and self-worth." This and other points of debate are not limited, however, to these two authors. To hear the wider conversation, and to enter into it once you have listened in for a while, consider the various voices in the excerpts below. Also, since this is clearly a visual issue, you should also consider the impact of the depictions of beauty that are presented here and many more that you might examine on your own in magazines, websites, television commercials, and so forth.

As you read and reflect, try to go beyond superficial understandings of what is "good" or "bad" about these depictions of beauty, and look to more developed discussions of the topic. There are many academic and professional fields that have brought their thoughts to this conversation, from business, advertising and mass media to philosophy, gender studies, psychology, history, and medical fields (since the search for ideals of beauty can have a great impact upon an individual's health). So, if you choose to further research, you might do so in an interdisciplinary way, examining the perspective on this issue that comes from the fields in which you are most interested.

conversations in context ...3

Ready-to-Wear, Shoes, Leather Goods, Watches, Jewelry.
Sold exclusively at Louis Vuitton stores, www.vuitton.com, 866-VUITTON

LOUIS VUITTON

What is the message about female beauty that this image portrays? How much of that image is based upon the person, and how much upon the product? What does it suggest about the relationship between the two? Are there any messages about ethnicity also carried by this image?

Whilst I agree that in essence, there is a grain of truth in her accusations that big businesses use pressure in the media to sell more goods, I naturally disagree with her views that cosmetic surgery is wrapped up in The Beauty Myth too. I believe that Wolf is potentially seeing a conspiracy where there is none. What I think Wolf has missed is that science has progressed incredibly since the 1960's; treatments that are safe and painless have arrived at a reasonable price for the average consumer. I can't help but feel that Wolf has been rather judgmental of those seeking to improve themselves subtly.

Paul Lanham, Cosmetic Surgery and the Beauty Myth. http://ezinearticles.com/?Cosmetic-Surgery-and-the-Beauty-Myth&id=3470315

What promises does this advertisement seem to make about the relationship between physical beauty and success? How do the words and the images work together to form that message?

In 1997, American men spent:

- $4 billion on exercise equipment and health club memberships
- $3 billion on grooming aids and fragrances
- $800 million on hair transplants

In 1996, American men spent:

- $500 million on male cosmetic surgery procedures
- $300 million on procedures such as pectoral implants, chin surgery, and penis enlargement
- $200 million on procedures such as liposuction and rhinoplasty (nose jobs)

It does appear that men are growing increasingly concerned with the appearance of their body, and are willing to fork over millions of dollars to enhance their physical image.

Milwaukee School of Engineering, *Newsletter for Mental Health*

What message about male beauty is sent by these images? In what ways does it set up an ideal of beauty for men? How does this ideal borrow from traditional images of female beauty? What facets of this image are specific to male beauty? What expectations does it set for what it means to be an attractive man?

"I looked at a Barbie doll when I was six and said, 'This is what I want to look like.'"

—*Cindy Jackson, 54. Holder of the Guinness Book of World Records for having more cosmetic procedures than anyone else in the world.*

What message does this image suggest about the role of the Barbie doll in creating the ideal of female beauty?

☐ fat?
☐ fit?

Does true beauty only squeeze into size 6?

campaignforrealbeauty.co.uk Dove

conversations in context ...3

Recently, a small number of consumer researchers voiced concern regarding the question of how and to what degree advertising involving thin/attractive endorsers is linked with chronic dieting, body dissatisfaction, and eating disorders in American females (Peterson 1987; Richins 1991; Solomon 1992). Richins (1991) found that while exposure to ads with highly attractive models can indeed increase women's dissatisfaction with their facial and overall attractiveness, such exposure does not appear to increase dissatisfaction with body shape in particular. Richins observed that college women who participated in her study were far less satisfied with their physique than with their face or overall attractiveness. (Richins 1991, 81).

SOURCE: Cynthia Hanson. *The beauty myth and female consumers: the controversial role of advertising. Journal of Consumer Affairs. Wednesday, June 22, 1994. http://www. allbusiness.com/marketing-advertising/advertising/462627-1.html*

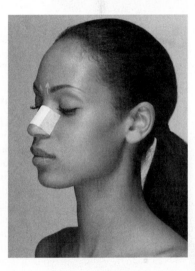

You see, for far too long, African women have allowed the West to dictate to us what a beautiful woman should look like. If we are to believe the women we see taking part in beauty pageants, advertising campaigns and music videos, or if we look at the type of models on catwalks or magazine covers, famous actresses, singers, sportswomen and television personalities, then a beautiful woman is clearly defined as one with long straight hair. Often her complexion is light and she is so thin one can only wonder if she is anorexic.

Akua Djanie,

SOURCE: *The Black Woman and the Beauty Myth. http://www.thefreelibrary. com/The+black+woman+and+the+bea uty+myth.-a0210161437*

□ gray?
□ gorgeous?
Why aren't women
glad to be gray?

Like it or not, we live in a society where all things are driven by consensus. Which is why our insistence that beauty comes in all ages, as well as shapes and sizes, is crucial to changing the plethora of images that blind us to our beauty. Only then will we stop buying into the myth of beautiful woman as young woman. Or thin woman. Or light-skinned woman. Only then will real transformation come.

SOURCE: *Laura Randolph Lancaster, The Beauty Myth—Brief Article. Ebony, September, 2000. http://findarticles. com/p/articles/mi_m1077/is_11_55/ ai_65014605/?tag+content;col1*

How do the two quotations on this page complicate the idea of what we mean by beauty as we also consider race and ethnicity? Does the myth of one race or gender influence that in others?

III. Entering the Conversation

The words and images included here—and many more that you might find on your own—demonstrate the ways in which Naomi Wolf's work began a conversation that continues through the present times—a conversation that is reflected in the essay by Virginia Postrel. That conversation has expanded to include many stakeholders and many parties interested in the beauty myth, creating dialogues about the role of media, body image's effect upon eating disorders, the growth of cosmetics and cosmetic surgery, changes in the concept of male beauty, images of beauty among people of color, and so forth. This concept has also given rise to campaigns such as that led by Dove Soap to combat the problems associated with those negative body image by valuing all types of beauty.

Knowing some of the bases of the various arguments that have been made about the beauty myth, you are now ready to take on a specific area of inquiry and to present your own informed views on some facet of this topic. Each of the writers whose views you have read formed their opinion in this way as well—based on their own contexts and their own place in the conversation. This topic has been approached from many perspectives—from the standpoint of feminism, sociology, ethnic and race studies, psychology, business, media studies and, in many cases, a combination of those perspectives. Depending upon your own interests and context, you might take on a particular facet of the topic through specific questions. Here are some possible lines of inquiry, which represent only a fraction of the possibilities:

- Whether the beauty myth has fueled self-image problems, or self-image problems fuel the beauty myth;

conversations in context ...3

- Whether products (such as Barbie or cosmetics) have created unachievable ideals or whether they are simply responding to people's own desire to be attractive
- Whether what we take to be beautiful is defined by the mass media or, as some biologists have suggested, definitions of, and attraction to, beauty is a natural instinct
- Whether men are now also subject to the beauty myth and its negative consequences
- Whether the quest to attain beauty might have positive consequences (such as increased attention to exercise or proper eating)
- Whether racial or ethnic groups have their own definitions of beauty, or if those definitions are controlled by dominant groups
- Whether businesses and media outlets have an ethical responsibility to avoid sustaining unobtainable ideals of beauty, or consumers have an obligation to be savvy enough to keep those ideals in context
- Whether the feminist movement, in the last two decades, has succeeded in overcoming some of the problems posed by Wolf

The list, of course, could go on; indeed, you would find many other conversations on this topic should you do more research. In any case, as you weigh in on this topic, be sure to draw upon what you have learned by seeing this conversation within the larger contexts here and to consider what other information you need to write in more informed ways on this topic. Below are a few ways for you to get started on extending the conversation about beauty through your own reading and research. You can use them as jumping off points. Feel free to take them in whatever directions your interests and your research take you, or to develop related topics on your own.

1. Since the beauty myth is so directly tied to our visual culture, you might develop a research project that analyzes the ways in which the many images of beauty that bombard us daily affects self-image, consumer behavior, the way we dress, how we interact with others, how we feel about our ethnicity or race, and so forth. To do so, you might do both secondary and primary research. Secondary research—reading the results of studies and analyses by others—is a good place to start. After narrowing your topic to one particular set of effects of the beauty myth, do a literature review of the books, articles, and other reliable sources that you might find on this topic; in doing so, you might focus your search within a particular field or discipline. As you read these secondary sources, pay special attention to the methodologies of the studies—how the writers set up ways to test their theories and how they gathered results: Did they use surveys? Focus groups? Interviews? Did they show specific images to people and test their reactions, or did they attempt to find which images by which they seem most affected in their daily lives? Then, test out those results by doing some primary research of your own, replicating the methods used with your own population. For example, if a study was done of high school students, you might test it on college students; if the population tested in a study

was women, you might consider studying men. If the study was done with one set of images, you might try it with others. In doing so, you will not only gain experience doing primary research, but you can extend the research of others beyond the scope offered in those studies.

2. Both Naomi Wolf (whose book you can likely find in your library)and Virginia Postrel drew upon the analytical skills learned through their degrees in English literature to show the ways that images and ideals of beauty can affect women; there are of course other disciplinary approaches that could also be used to test those analyses, and to contribute other perspectives to the conversation. For example, a psychologist might study the behaviors of individuals who are exposed to differing home or societal circumstances; a neuroscientist might attempt to explain the cognitive processes that lead one to react to images of beauty; an anthropologist or sociologist might study differences in perspectives on beauty differ across cultures, and historians might study differences across time. You might, then, try to bring these various perspectives together, creating an interdisciplinary study which highlights the ways in which the beauty myth has been studied by a range of disciplines. In order to organize such a paper, you might begin by introducing the topic, and then include a section on the contributions of each discipline to the study of this topic. As an alternative, you could focus upon the contributions of one discipline that especially interests you.

3. While both Wolf and Postrel focus their analyses of the beauty myth upon its effect upon women, as some of the excerpts included here suggest, others have asked similar questions as they apply to ethnicity or race. One specific area of study has to do with variations and gradations of skin color within races (light-skinned African-Americans versus darker skinned individuals; Latinos and their concept of being "brown"; Arab-Americans and Asian-Americans as non-white). In order to better understand the ways that definitions of beauty are affected by skin color, you will also need to consider both how those definitions are formed within and outside of those communities. For example, are supposed preferences for lighter skin as prevalent among African-Americans as they are by the wider population? You might also study the origin of these preferences—have they been imposed upon groups, or have members of the group developed such preferences on their own? There is a great deal of research on the topic of skin color that you might draw upon to correlate images of beauty with questions about skin color. Or, as an alternative, you might also consider the effect of other external physical features associated with race and ethnicity, studying the origins and effects of their relationship to definitions of beauty.

CHAPTER 6

Racial and Ethnic Identities

Conversations 2.0: Racial and Ethnic Identities in the Civil Rights Movement and the Legacy of Martin Luther King

In the current environment, many public conversations take place in a virtual, online space. And while calling these conversations "virtual conversations" might make them seem less real or less important, that is not the case. In fact, online conversations have become one of the central locations for public debate on key issues, including the issues that are included in this book. To enrich your understanding of public conversations, you can make use of the array of online discussion boards, listservs, blogs, Facebook pages, and Twitter sites that are available via the web. The Conversations 2.0 *pages in this book suggest some possible ways to do so, and point out some particularly useful and credible online conversations; you of course can use your own online forums and communities to add to these suggestions—or even to start your own.*

While the concept of racial or ethnic identity is clearly a current topic—especially as it relates to issues of citizenship, immigration, and community—it has a long history as well. And while we think of the world wide web as a technology devoted to the most current information, it also acts as a storehouse or archive of past documents. Many historically significant documents that used to require extensive travel or special privileges to view are now at our fingertips as we sit at a computer terminal. Thus, to do some background research on the history of inter-racial and inter-ethnic relationships, you might access some of these primary documents: the records of court cases surrounding the Jim Crow laws or Brown v. the Board of Education; the civil rights bills of the 1960s and 1990s passed by Congress; or the U. S. Constitution and its various amendments. You can also gain access to many of the key speeches and writings of the civil rights movements surrounding specific ethnicities and races.

Some of the most significant, and most rhetorically effective, of those pieces were authored by Martin Luther King. You can find text and audio versions of many of these works by searching the web using King's name and terms like "speeches," "texts," "writings," etc. One particularly useful work for studying the ways that rhetoric can persuade and change things around us is Kings' "Letter from a Birmingham Jail" (and the "Public Statement by 8 Alabama Clergymen" that prompted King's letter). This 1963 letter, later published in his collection called *Why We Can't Wait*, lays out clearly the reasons why those of his race needed to act in order to find justice. In doing so, he draws upon a number of key strategies, including: refutation (of the clergymen who urged him to call of his protests); appeals to his own *ethos* (character) as a minister, and as a black man and father; appeals to *pathos* (emotions) through narratives of injustice and incivility; and appeals to *logos* (reasoning) through his argument that granting equal rights would create a stronger union. If you search the web, you will also find online a series of analyses, responses, tributes, and blogs/discussion boards that demonstrate that this document is clearly still very much part of the conversation about race in America.

bell hooks

Overcoming White Supremacy: A Comment

bell hooks (born Gloria Jean Watkins) is a respected author of works on gender, race, and class, and an activist on issues related to all three of those social issues. She has served as Distinguished Professor of English at City College in New York and as Distinguished Professor in Residence at Berea College in Kentucky. Deeply influenced by the work of Sojourner Truth (whose "Ain't I a Woman" is included in Chapter 5), hooks has published over 30 books and numerous articles in both scholarly and public venues. In this essay, first published in 1989 as a chapter in her *Talking Back: Thinking Feminist, Thinking Black,* hooks explores the persistence of white supremacy even amidst the advances made by black women. She also explores the ways that fellow blacks are somewhat complicit in this ongoing hierarchy, and the ways that racial identities are (at least to a degree) chosen by individuals.

To help make this case, she cites Toni Morrison, who said during an interview: "Now people choose their identities. Now people choose to be Black." (You might consider the ways in which President Barack Obama consciously chose his black identity over his white identity, for example.) Consider also the ways in which hooks brings together the identity issues related to gender and feminism with those related to race.

B lack people in the United States share with black people   1
in South Africa and with people of color globally both
the pain of white-supremacist oppression and exploitation and the pain that comes from resistance and struggle. The
first pain wounds us, the second pain helps heal our wounds. It
often troubles me that black people in the United States have
not risen *en masse* to declare solidarity with our black sisters
and brothers in South Africa. Perhaps one day soon—say
Martin Luther King's birthday—we will enter the streets at a
certain hour, wherever we are, to stand for a moment, naming
and affirming the primacy of black liberation.

As I write, I try to remember when the word racism ceased to   2
be the term which best expressed for me exploitation of black
people and other people of color in this society and when I
began to understand that the most useful term was white
supremacy. It was certainly a necessary term when confronted
with the liberal attitudes of white women active in feminist
movement who were unlike their racist ancestors—white
women in the early woman's rights movement who did not wish
to be caught dead in fellowship with black women. In fact, these
women often requested and longed for the presence of black
women. Yet when present, what we saw was that they wished to
exercise control over our bodies and thoughts as their racist
ancestors had—that this need to exercise power over us
expressed how much they had internalized the values and attitudes of white supremacy.

It may have been this contact or contact with fellow white   3
English professors who want very much to have "a" black person in "their" department as long as that person thinks and acts
like them, shares their values and beliefs, is in no way different,
that first compelled me to use the term white supremacy to identify the ideology that most determines how white people in this
society (irrespective of their political leanings to the right or left)
perceive and relate to black people and other people of color. It
is the very small but highly visible liberal movement away from
the perpetuation of overtly racist discrimination, exploitation,
and oppression of black people which often masks how all-
pervasive white supremacy is in this society, both as ideology

and as behavior. When liberal whites fail to understand how they can and/or do embody white-supremacist values and beliefs even though they may not embrace racism as prejudice or domination (especially domination that involves coercive control), they cannot recognize the ways their actions support and affirm the very structure of racist domination and oppression that they profess to wish to see eradicated.

4   Likewise, "white supremacy" is a much more useful term for understanding the complicity of people of color in upholding and maintaining racial hierarchies that do not involve force (i.e., slavery, apartheid) than the term "internalized racism"—a term most often used to suggest that black people have absorbed negative feelings and attitudes about blackness held by white people. The term "white supremacy" enables us to recognize not only that black people are socialized to embody the values and attitudes of white supremacy, but that we can exercise "white-supremacist control" over other black people. This is important, for unlike the term "uncle tom," which carried with it the recognition of complicity and internalized racism, a new terminology must accurately name the way we as black people directly exercise power over one another when we perpetuate white-supremacist beliefs. Speaking about changing perspectives on black identity, writer Toni Morrison said in a recent interview: "Now people choose their identities. Now people choose to be Black." At this historical moment, when a few black people no longer experience the racial apartheid and brutal racism that still determine the lot of many black people, it is easier for that few to ally themselves politically with the dominant racist white group.

5   Assimilation is the strategy that has provided social legitimation for this shift in allegiance. It is a strategy deeply rooted in the ideology of white supremacy and its advocates urge black people to negate blackness, to imitate racist white people so as to better absorb their values, their way of life. Ironically, many changes in social policy and social attitudes that were once seen as ways to end racial domination have served to reinforce and perpetuate white supremacy. This is especially true of social policy that has encouraged and promoted racial integration. Given the continued force of racism, racial integration translated into assimilation ultimately serves to reinforce and maintain white supremacy. Without an ongoing active movement to end white supremacy, without ongoing black liberation struggle, no social environment can exist in the United States that truly supports integration. When black people enter social contexts that remain unchanged, unaltered, in no way stripped of the framework of white supremacy, we are pressured to assimilate. We are rewarded for assimilation. Black people working or socializing in predominately white settings whose very structures are informed

by the principles of white supremacy who dare to affirm blackness, love of black culture and identity, do so at great risk. We
must continually challenge, protest, resist while working to leave
no gaps in our defense that will allow us to be crushed. This is
especially true in work settings where we risk being fired or not
receiving deserved promotions. Resisting the pressure to assimilate is a part of our struggle to end white supremacy.

When I talk with audiences around the United States about   6
feminist issues of race and gender, my use of the term "white
supremacy" always sparks a reaction, usually of a critical or hostile nature. Individual white people and even some non-whites
insist that this is not a white-supremacist society, that racism is
not nearly the problem it used to be (it is downright frightening
to hear people argue vehemently that the problem of racism has
been solved), that there has been change. While it is true that
the nature of racist oppression and exploitation has changed as
slavery has ended and the apartheid structure of Jim Crow has
legally changed, white supremacy continues to shape perspectives on reality and to inform the social status of black people
and all people of color. Nowhere is this more evident than in university settings. And often it is the liberal folks in those settings
who are unwilling to acknowledge this truth.

Recently in a conversation with a white male lawyer at his   7
home where I was a guest, he informed me that someone had
commented to him that children are learning very little history
these days in school, that the attempt to be all-inclusive, to talk
about Native Americans, blacks, women, etc. has led to a frag-
mented focus on particular representative individuals with no
larger historical framework. I responded to this comment by
suggesting that it has been easier for white people to practice
this inclusion rather than change the larger framework; that it
is easier to change the focus from Christopher Columbus, the
important white man who "discovered" America, to Sitting Bull
or Harriet Tubman, than it is to cease telling a distorted version
of U.S. history which upholds white supremacy. Really teaching
history in a new way would require abandoning the old myths
informed by white supremacy like the notion that Columbus discovered America. It would mean talking about imperialism, col-
onization, about the Africans who came here before Columbus
(see Ivan Van Sertima's *They Came Before Columbus*). It would
mean talking about genocide, about the white colonizers'
exploitation and betrayal of Native American Indians; about
ways the legal and governmental structures of this society from
the Constitution on supported and upheld slavery, apartheid (see
Derrick Bell's *And We Are Not Saved*). This history can be taught
only when the perspectives of teachers are no longer shaped by
white supremacy. Our conversation is one of many examples
that reveal the way black people and white people can socialize

in a friendly manner, be racially integrated, while deeply ingrained notions of white supremacy remain intact. Incidents like this make it necessary for concerned folks, for righteous white people, to begin to fully explore the way white supremacy determines how they see the world, even as their actions are not informed by the type of racial prejudice that promotes overt discrimination and separation.

8   Significantly, assimilation was a term that began to be more commonly used after the revolts against white supremacy in the late 1960s and early 1970s. The intense, passionate rebellion against racism and white supremacy of this period was crucial because it created a context for politicization, for education for critical consciousness, one in which black people could begin to confront the extent of our complicity, our internalization of white supremacy and begin the process of self-recovery and collective renewal. Describing this effort in his work, *The Search for a Common Ground*, black theologian Howard Thurman commented:

> "Black is Beautiful" became not merely a phrase—it was a stance, a total attitude, a metaphysics. In very positive and exciting terms it began undermining the idea that had developed over so many years into a central aspect of white mythology: that black is ugly, black is evil, black is demonic. In so doing it fundamentally attacked the front line of the defense of the myth of white supremacy and superiority.

9   Clearly, assimilation as a social policy upholding white supremacy was strategically an important counter-defense, one that would serve to deflect the call for radical transformation of black consciousness. Suddenly the terms for success (that is getting a job, acquiring the means to provide materially for oneself and one's family) were redefined. It was not enough for black people to enter institutions of higher education and acquire the necessary skills to effectively compete for jobs previously occupied solely by whites; the demand was that blacks become "honorary whites," that black people assimilate to succeed.

10   The force that gave the social policy of assimilation power to influence and change the direction of black liberation struggle was economic. Economic distress created a climate wherein militancy—overt resistance to white supremacy and racism (which included the presentation of self in a manner that suggests black pride)—was no longer deemed a viable survival strategy. Natural hair styles, African dress, etc. were discarded as signs of militancy that might keep one from getting ahead. A similar regressive, reactionary move was taking place among young white radicals, many of whom had been fiercely engaged

in left politics, who suddenly began to seek reincorporation into the liberal and conservative mainstream. Again the force behind their re-entry into the system was economic. On a very basic level, changes in the cost of housing (as in the great apartment one had in 1965 for $100 a month cost $400 by 1975) had a frightening impact on college-educated young people of all ethnicities who thought they were committed to transforming society, but who were unable to face living without choice, without the means to escape, who feared living in poverty. Coupled with economic forces exerting pressure, many radicals despaired of the possibility that this white-supremacist, capitalist patriarchy could really be changed.

Tragically, many radical whites who had been allies in the   11
black liberation struggle began to question whether the struggle to end racism was really that significant, or to suggest that the struggle was over, as they moved into their new liberal positions. Radical white youth who had worked in civil rights struggles, protested the war in Vietnam, and even denounced U.S. imperialism could not reconstruct their ties to prevailing systems of domination without creating a new layer of false consciousness—the assertion that racism was no longer pervasive, that race was no longer an important issue. Similarly, critiques of capitalism, especially those that urged individuals to try and live differently within the framework of capitalism, were also relegated to the back burner as people "discovered" that it was important to have class privilege so that one could better help the exploited.

It is no wonder that black radicals met these betrayals with   12
despair and hopelessness. What had all the contemporary struggle to resist racism really achieved? What did it mean to have this period of radical questioning of white supremacy, of black is beautiful, only to witness a few years later the successful mass production by white corporations of hair care products to straighten black hair? What did it mean to witness the assault on black culture by capitalist forces which stress the production on all fronts of an image, a cultural product that can "cross over"— that is, that can speak more directly to the concerns, to the popular imagination of white consumers, while still attracting the dollars of black consumers. And what does it mean in 1987 when television viewers watch a morning talk show on black beauty, where black women suggest that these trends are only related to personal preferences and have no relation to racism; when viewers witness a privileged white male, Phil Donahue, shaking his head and trying to persuade the audience to acknowledge the reality of racism and its impact on black people? Or what does it mean when many black people say that what they like most about the Bill Cosby show is that there is little emphasis on blackness, that they are "just people"? And again to hear

reported on national news that little black children prefer playing with white dolls rather than black dolls? All these popular narratives remind us that "we are not yet saved," that white supremacy prevails, that the racist oppression and exploitation which daily assaults the bodies and spirits of black people in South Africa, assaults black people here.

13   Years ago when I was a high school student experiencing racial desegregation, there was a current of resistance and militancy that was so fierce. It swept over and through our bodies as we—black students—stood, pressed against the red brick walls, watching the national guard with their guns, waiting for those moments when we would enter, when we would break through racism, waiting for the moments of change—of victory. And now even within myself I find that spirit of militancy growing faint; all too often it is assaulted by feelings of despair and powerlessness. I find that I must work to nourish it, to keep it strong. Feelings of despair and powerlessness are intensified by all the images of black self-hate that indicate that those militant 1960s did not have sustained radical impact—that the politicization and transformation of black consciousness did not become an ongoing revolutionary practice in black life. This causes such frustration and despair because it means that we must return to this basic agenda, that we must renew efforts at politicization, that we must go over old ground. Perhaps what is more disheartening is the fear that the seeds, though planted again, will never survive, will never grow strong. Right now it is anger and rage (see Audre Lorde's "The Uses of Anger" in *Sister Outsider*) at the continued racial genocide that rekindles within me that spirit of militancy.

14   Like so many radical black folks who work in university settings, I often feel very isolated. Often we work in environments predominately peopled by white folks (some of whom are well-meaning and concerned) who are not committed to working to end white supremacy, or who are unsure about what that commitment means. Certainly feminist movement has been one of the places where there has been renewed interest in challenging and resisting racism. There too it has been easier for white women to confront racism as overt exploitation and domination, or as personal prejudice, than to confront the encompassing and profound reality of white supremacy.

15   In talking about race and gender recently, the question most often asked by white women has to do with white women's response to black women or women of color insisting that they are not willing to teach them about their racism—to show the way. They want to know: What should a white person do who is attempting to resist racism? It is problematic to assert that black people and other people of color who are sincerely committed to struggling against white supremacy should be unwilling to

help or teach white people. Challenging black folks in the 19th century, Frederick Douglass made the crucial point that "power accedes nothing without demand." For the racially oppressed to demand of white people, of black people, of all people that we eradicate white supremacy, that those who benefit materially by exercising white-supremacist power, either actively or passively, willingly give up that privilege in response to that demand, and then to refuse to show the way is to undermine our own cause. We must show the way. There must exist a paradigm, a practical model for social change that includes an understanding of ways to transform consciousness that are linked to efforts to transform structures.

Fundamentally, it is our collective responsibility as radical   16 black people and people of color, and as white people to construct models for social change. To abdicate that responsibility, to suggest that change is just something an individual can do on his or her own or in isolation with other racist white people is utterly misleading. If as a black person I say to a white person who shows a willingness to commit herself or himself to the struggle to end white supremacy that I refuse to affirm, or help in that endeavor is a gesture that undermines my commitment to that struggle. Many black people have essentially responded in this way because we do not want to do the work for white people, and most importantly we cannot do the work, yet this often seems to be what is asked of us. Rejecting the work does not mean that we cannot and do not show the way by our actions, by the information we share. Those white people who want to continue the dominate/subordinate relationship so endemic to racist exploitation by insisting that we "serve" them—that we do the work of challenging and changing their consciousness—are acting in bad faith. In his work, *Pedagogy in Progress: The Letters to Guinea-Bissau,* Paulo Freire reminds us:

> Authentic help means that all who are involved help each other mutually, growing together in the common effort to understand the reality which they seek to transform.

It is our collective responsibility as people of color and as white   17 people who are committed to ending white supremacy to help one another. It is our collective responsibility to educate for critical consciousness. If I commit myself politically to black liberation struggle, to the struggle to end white supremacy, I am not making a commitment to working only for and with black people, I must engage in struggle with all willing comrades to strengthen our awareness and our resistance. (See *The Autobiography of Malcolm X* and *The Last Year of Malcolm X—The Evolution of a Revolutionary* by George Breitman.) Malcolm X is an important role model for those of us who wish to transform our consciousness for he was engaged in on going critical self-reflection, in changing both his words and his deeds. In thinking about black response to white people, about what they can do to end racism, I am reminded of that memorable example when Malcolm X expressed regret about an incident with a white female college student who asked him what she could do and he told her: "nothing." He later saw that there was much that she could have done. For each of us, it is work to educate ourselves to understand the nature of white supremacy with a critical consciousness. Black people are not born into this world with innate understanding of racism and white supremacy. (See John Hodge, ed., *Cultural Bases of Racism and Group Oppression*.)

18   In recent years, particularly among women active in feminist movement, much effort to confront racism has focussed on individual prejudice. While it is important that individuals work to transform their consciousness, striving to be anti-racist, it is important for us to remember that the struggle to end white supremacy is a struggle to change a system, a structure. Hodge emphasizes in his book "the problem of racism is not prejudice but domination." For our efforts to end white supremacy to be truly effective, individual struggle to change consciousness must be fundamentally linked to collective effort to transform those structures that reinforce and perpetuate white supremacy.

Amitai Etzioni

Leaving Race Behind

Amitai Etzioni, who holds a doctorate in sociology from the University of California at Berkeley, is the author of 24 books. He is perhaps most famous for his formation of the Communitarian movement, which builds itself on its vision of moral, social, and political foundations of society. Communitarians emphasize the role and good of the whole community, and so differ from Libertarians in shifting emphasis away from the individual. In this piece, first published in 2006 in *The American Scholar*, Etzioni asks whether focusing upon racial categories, even in the attempt to advance our culture's fairness, might cause as many problems as it solves. It also can help you to think about whether racial categories are a natural identity category, or one imposed from the outside. How might Martin Luther King or bell hooks respond to Etzioni? Or have times changed enough since the publication of their works so as to justify Etzionzi's suggestion?

Some years ago the United States government asked me 1 what my race was. I was reluctant to respond because my 50 years of practicing sociology—and some powerful personal experiences—have underscored for me what we all know to one degree or another, that racial divisions bedevil America, just as they do many other societies across the world. Not wanting to encourage these divisions, I refused to check off one of the specific racial options on the U.S. Census form and instead marked a box labeled "Other." I later found out that the federal government did not accept such an attempt to de-emphasize race, by me or by some 6.75 million other Americans who tried it. Instead the government assigned me to a racial category, one it chose for me. Learning this made me conjure up what I admit is a far-fetched association. I was in this place once before. When I was a Jewish child in Nazi Germany in the early 1930s, many Jews who saw themselves as good Germans wanted to "pass" as Aryans. But the Nazi regime would have none of it. Never mind, they told these Jews, *we determine* who is Jewish and who is not. A similar practice prevailed in the Old South, where if you had one drop of African blood you were a Negro, disregarding all other facts and considerations, including how you saw yourself.

You might suppose that in the years since my little Census-form 2 protest the growing enlightenment about race in our society would have been accompanied by a loosening of racial categories by our government. But in recent years the United States government has acted in a deliberate way to make it even more difficult for individuals to move beyond racial boxes and for American society as a whole to move beyond race.

Why the government perpetuates racialization and what 3 might be done to diminish the role of race in our lives are topics that have become especially timely as Hispanics begin to take a more important role demographically, having displaced African-Americans as the largest American minority. How Hispanics view themselves and how they are viewed by others are among the most important factors affecting whether or not we can end race as a major social divide in America.

Treating people differently according to their race is as un- 4 American as a hereditary aristocracy, and as American as slavery. The American ethos was formed by people who left the social stratification of the Old World to live in a freer, more fluid society. They sought to be defined by what they accomplished, not by what they were born with. As Arthur M. Schlesinger Jr. puts it in his book *The Disuniting of America*, one of the great virtues of America is that it defines individuals by where they are going rather than by where they have been. Achievement matters, not origin. The national ideal says that all Americans should be able to compete as equals, whatever their background.

5   American society has been divided along racial lines since its earliest days. Racial characterizations have trumped the achievement ideal; people born into a non-white race, whatever their accomplishments, have been unable to change their racial status. Worse, race has often been their most defining characteristic, affecting most, if not all, aspects of their being.

6   As a result, we have been caught, at least since the onset of the civil rights movement, in an ambivalence. On the one hand, we continue to dream of the day when all Americans will be treated equally, whatever their race; we rail against—and sometimes punish—those who discriminate according to race in hiring, housing, and social life. At the same time, we have ensconced in law many claims based on race: requirements that a given proportion of public subsidies, loans, job training, educational assistance, and admission slots at choice colleges be set aside for people of color. Many Americans, including African-Americans, are uneasy about what some people consider reverse discrimination. Courts have limited its scope; politicians have made hay by opposing it; and some of its beneficiaries feel that their successes are hollow because they are unsure whether their gains reflect hard-won achievements or special favors. There must be a better way to deal with past and current injustice. And the rapid changes in American demographics call for a reexamination of the place of race in America.

Enter the Hispanic

7   We have grown accustomed to thinking about America in black and white, and might well have continued to do so for decades to come except that Hispanics complicate this simplistic scheme: they do not fit into the old racial categories. Some Hispanics appear to many Americans to be black (for example, quite a few Cuban-Americans), others as white (especially immigrants from Argentina and Chile), and the appearance of still others is hard for many people to pigeonhole. Anyone seeing the lineup of baseball players honored as Major League Baseball's "Latino Legends Team" would find that the players vary from those who are as fair-skinned as Roger Clemens to those who are as dark-skinned as Jackie Robinson. More important by far, survey after survey shows that most Hispanics object to being

classified as either black or white. A national survey conducted in 2002 indicated that 76 percent of Hispanics say the standard racial categories used by the U.S. Census do not address their preferences. The last thing most of those surveyed desire is to be treated as yet another race—as "brown" Americans.

Hispanics would have forced the question of how we define one   8
another even if they were just another group of immigrants among the many that have made America what it is. But Hispanics are not just one more group of immigrants. Not only have Hispanic numbers surpassed those of black Americans, who until 2003 made up America's largest minority group, Hispanics have been reliably projected to grow much faster than African-Americans or any other American group. Thus, according to the Census, in 1990 blacks constituted 12 percent of the population and Hispanics 9 percent. By 2000, Hispanics caught up with blacks, amounting to 12.5 percent of the population compared to 12.3 percent for blacks. By 2050, Hispanics are projected to be 24.3 percent of the American population, compared to 14.7 percent for blacks. In many cities, from Miami to Los Angeles, in which African-Americans have been the largest minority group, Hispanics' numbers are increasingly felt. While once Hispanics were concentrated in the areas bordering Mexico, their numbers are now growing in places like Denver, St. Paul, and even New England.

Immigration fuels the growth of Hispanics relative to the   9
growth of African-Americans because Latin American immigration, legal and illegal, continues at an explosive pace, while immigration from Africa is minuscule. Hispanics also have more children than African-Americans. During the most recent year for which data is available, 2003–2004, one of every two people added to America's population was Hispanic. And while black Americans have long been politically mobilized and active, Hispanics are just beginning to make their weight felt in American politics.

The rapid growth in the number, visibility, and power of His-   10
panics will largely determine the future of race in America, a point highlighted by Clara E. Rodriguez in her book *Changing Race: Latinos, the Census, and the History of Ethnicity in the U.S.* If Hispanics are to be viewed as brown or black (and some on the left aspire to color them), and above all if Hispanics develop the sense of disenfranchisement and alienation that many African-Americans have acquired (often for very good reasons), then America's immutable racial categories will only deepen.

If, on the other hand, most Hispanics continue to see them-   11
selves as members of one or more ethnic groups, then race in America might be pushed to the margins. Racial categories have historically set us apart; ethnic categories are part of the mosaic that makes up America. It has been much easier for an individual to assimilate from an ethnic perspective than from a racial

one. Race is considered a biological attribute, a part of your being that cannot be dropped or modified. Ethnic origin, in contrast, is where you came from. All Americans have one hyphen or another attached to their ethnic status: we're Polish-, or German-, or Anglo-, or Italian-Americans. Adding Cuban-Americans or Mexican-Americans to this collage would create more comfortable categories of a comparable sort.

The Race Trap

12   Many people take it for granted that genes determine race, just as genes determine gender. And we also tend to believe that racial categories are easy to discern (though we all know of exceptions).

13   One way to show how contrived racial divisions actually are is to recall that practically all of the DNA in all human beings is the same. Our differences are truly skin deep. Moreover, the notion that most of us are of one race or another has little basis in science. The Human Genome Project informs us not only that 99.9 percent of genetic material is shared by all humans, but also that variation in the remaining 0.1 percent is greater *within* racial groups than across them. That is, not only are 99.9 percent of the genes of a black person the same as those of a white person, but the genes of a particular black person may be more similar to the genes of a white person than they are to another black person.

14   This point was driven home to college students in a sociology class at Penn State in April 2005. Following their professor's suggestion, the students took DNA tests that had surprising results. A student who identified himself as "a proud black man" found that only 52 percent of his ancestry traced back to Africa, while the other 48 percent was European. Another student who said she takes flak from black friends for having a white boyfriend found that her ancestry was 58 percent European and only 42 percent African. These two students are not alone: an estimated one-third of the African-American population has European ancestry.

15   Which people make up a distinct race and which are considered dark-skinned constantly changes as social prejudices change. Jewish-, Slavic-, Irish-, and Polish-Americans were considered distinct races in the mid-19th and early 20th centuries—and dark races at that, as chronicled in great detail in Matthew Frye Jacobson's book *Whiteness of a Different Color: European Immigrants and the Alchemy of Race* and in a well-documented book by Noel Ignatiev, *How the Irish Became White*. Ignatiev found that in the 1850s, Irish people were considered non-white in America and were frequently referred to as "niggers turned inside out." (Blacks were sometimes called "smoked Irish.")

The capriciousness of racial classifications is further high- 16
lighted by the way the U.S. Census, the most authoritative and
widely used source of social classifications, divides Americans
into races. When I ask my students how many races they think
there are in America, they typically count four: white, black,
Asian, and Native American. The Census says there are 15 racial
categories: white, African-American, American Indian/Alaska
Native, Asian Indian, Chinese, Filipino, Japanese, Korean, Vietnamese, "other Asian," Native Hawaiian, Guamanian/ Chamorro,
Samoan, and "other Pacific Islander," and as of 2000 one more
for those who feel they are of some other race. (Hispanic is not
on this list because the Census treats Hispanic as an ethnicity
and asks about it on a separate question, but immediately following that question, the Census asks, "So what is your race,
anyhow?")

The arbitrary nature of these classifications is demonstrated by 17
the Census Bureau itself, which can change the race of millions
of Americans by the stroke of a pen. The Census changed the race
of Indian- and Pakistani-Americans from white in 1970 to Asian
in 1980. In 1930 the Census made Mexicans into a different race
but then withdrew this category. Similarly, Hindu made a brief
appearance as a race in the 1930 and 1940 Censuses but was
subsequently withdrawn.

Anthropologists have found that some tribes do not see colors 18
the way many of us do; for instance, they do not "see" a difference between brown and yellow. Members of these tribes are not
colorblind, but some differences found in nature (in the color
spectrum) simply don't register with them, just as young American children are unaware of racial differences until someone
introduces them to these distinctions. We draw a line between
white and black, but people's skin colors have many shades.
It is our social prejudices that lead us to make sharp racial
categories.

I am not one of those postmodernists who, influenced by Niet- 19
zsche and Foucault, claim that there are no epistemological
truths, that all facts are a matter of social construction. I disagree with Nietzsche's description of truth as "a mobile army of
metaphors, metonyms, and anthropomorphisms—in short a
sum of human relations, which have been enhanced, trans-
posed, and embellished poetically and rhetorically and which
after long use seem firm, canonical, and obligatory to a people."
However, there is no doubt that social construction plays a significant role in the way we "see" racial differences, although our
views may in turn be affected by other factors that are less
subject to construction, for example, historical differences.

Most important is the significance we attribute to race and 20
the interpretations we impose on it. When we are told only that
a person is, say, Asian-American, we often jump to a whole list

of conclusions regarding that person's looks, intelligence, work ethic, character; we make the same sort of jumps for Native Americans, blacks, and other races. Many things follow from these knee-jerk characterizations: whether we will fear or like this person, whether we will wish to have him or her as a neighbor or as a spouse for one of our children—all on the basis of race. In short, we load on to race a great deal of social importance that is not a reflection of the "objective" biological differences that exist. To paraphrase the UNESCO Constitution, racial divisions are made in the minds of men and women, and that is where they will have to be ended.

Defining the Hispanic

21   If racial categories have long been settled, the social characterization of the Hispanic is up for grabs. We still don't know whether Hispanics will be defined as a brown race and align themselves with those in the United States who are or who see themselves as marginalized or victimized—or if they will be viewed as a conglomerate of ethnic groups, of Mexican-Americans, Cuban-Americans, Dominican-Americans, and so forth, who will fit snuggly into the social mosaic.

22   The term *Hispanic* was first used in the Census in 1980. Before that, Mexican-Americans and Cuban-Americans were classified as white (except when a Census interviewer identified an individual as the member of a different racial group). Until 1980, Hispanics were part of the great American panorama of ethnic groups. Then the Census combined these groups into a distinct category unlike any other. It was as if the federal government were to one day lump together Spanish-, Italian-, and Greek-Americans into a group called "Southern European" and begin issuing statistics on how their income, educational achievements, number of offspring, and so on compare to those of Northern Europeans.

23   And as we've seen, those who define themselves as Hispanic are asked to declare a race. In the 1980 Census, the options included, aside from the usual menu of races, that ambiguous category "Other." There were 6.75 million Americans, including me, who chose this option in 1980. Most revealing: 40 percent of Hispanics chose this option. (Note that they—and I—chose this category despite the nature of the word *Other*, which suggests the idea of "not being one of us." Had the category been accorded a less loaded label, say "wish not to be identified with any one group," it seems likely that many millions more would have chosen this box.)

24   To have millions of Americans choose to identify themselves as "Other" created a political backlash because Census statistics

are used both to allocate public funds to benefit minority groups and to assess their political strength. Some African-American groups, especially, feared that if African-Americans chose "Other" instead of marking the "African-American" box, they would lose public allotments and political heft.

But never underestimate our government. The Census Bureau has used a statistical procedure to assign racial categories to those millions of us who sought to butt out of this divisive classification scheme. Federal regulations outlined by the Office of Management and Budget, a White House agency, ruled that the Census must "impute" a specific race to those who do not choose one. For several key public policy purposes, a good deal of social and economic data must be aggregated into five racial groups: white, black, Asian, American Indian or Alaska Native, and native Hawaiian or other Pacific Islander. How does the government pick a race for a person who checked the "Other" box? They turn to the answers for other Census questions: for example, income, neighborhood, education level, or last name. The resulting profiles of the U.S. population (referred to as the "age-race modified profile") are then used by government agencies in allotting public funds and for other official and public purposes.

But the Census isn't alone in oversimplifying the data. Increasingly, other entities, including the media, have treated Hispanics as a race rather than an ethnic group. This occurs implicitly when those who generate social data—such as government agencies or social scientists—break down the data into four categories: white, black, Asian, and Hispanic, which is comparable to listing apples, oranges, bananas, and yams. In their profile of jail inmates, the Bureau of Justice Statistics lists inmates' origins as "white, black, *Hispanic,* American Indian/Alaska Native, Asian/Pacific Islander, and more than one race." *The New York Times* ran a front-page story last September in which it compared the first names used by whites, blacks, Asians, and Hispanics. Replace the word *Hispanics* with the name of another ethnic group, say Jews, and the unwitting racial implication of this classification will stand out.

Still other studies include Hispanics when they explicitly refer to racial groups. For example, a 2001 paper by Sean Reardon and John T. Yun examines what they call "racial balkanization among suburban schools," where there is increased segregation among black, Hispanic, and Asian students. A 2005 *Seattle Times* story uses racial terminology when it reports "Latinos have the fewest numbers among racial groups in master's-of-business programs nationwide, with about 5,000 enrolling annually." Similarly, *The San Diego Union Tribune* states: "A brawl between Latino and black students resulted in a lockdown of the school and revealed tensions between the two largest racial groups on campus."

28   A handful of others go a step further and refer to Hispanics as a brown race. For example, following the recent Los Angeles mayoral election, *The Houston Chronicle* informed us that "Villaraigosa's broad-based support has analysts wondering whether it is evidence of an emerging black-brown coalition." And, National Public Radio reported: "There is no black and brown alliance at a South Central Los Angeles high school."

29   One way or another, all of these references push us in the wrong direction—toward racializing Hispanics and deepening social divisions. America would be best served if we moved in the opposite direction.

A New Taxonomy

30   Thus far, workers at the U.S. Census Bureau, following the White House's instructions, seem determined to prevent any de-emphasis of race. They are testing iterations of the wording for the relevant questions in the 2010 Census—but all of these possibilities continue to require people to identify themselves by race. Moreover, Census bureaucrats will continue to impute race to those who refuse to do so themselves, ignoring the ever-growing number of people, especially Hispanics, who do not fit into this scheme.

31   Imagine if instead the federal government classified people by their country (or countries) of origin. For some governmental purposes, it might suffice to use large categories, such as Africa (which would exclude other so-called black groups, such as Haitians and West Indians that are now included in references to "black" Americans), Asia, Europe, Central America, and South America (the last two categories would not, of course, include Spain). For other purposes, a more detailed breakdown might work better—using regions such as the Middle East and Southeast Asia, for example—and if still more detail was desired, specific countries could be used, as we do for identifying ethnic groups (Irish, Polish, Cuban, Mexican, Japanese, Ethiopian, and so on). Kenneth Prewitt, a former director of the U.S. Census Bureau, has suggested the use of ethnic categories. As we have seen, ethnic origins carry some implications for who we are, but these implications decline in importance over time. Above all, they do not define us in some immutable way, as racial categories do. A category called something like "wish not to be identified with any particular group" should be included for those who do not want to be characterized even by ethnicity or for others who view themselves as having a varied and combined heritage.

32   The classification of Americans who are second-generation, and beyond, highlights the importance of the no-particular-group

category. Although a fourth-generation Italian-American might still wish to be identified as Italian, he might not, particularly if he has grandparents or parents who are, say, Greek, Korean, and Native American. Forcing such a person to classify himself as a member of one ethnic group conceals the significance of the most important American development in social matters: out-marriage. Out-marriage rates for all groups other than African-Americans are so high that most of us will soon be tied to Americans of a large variety of backgrounds by the closest possible social tie, the familial one. Approximately 30 percent of third-generation Hispanics and 40 percent of third-generation Asians marry people of a different racial or ethnic origin. Altogether, the proportion of marriages among people of different racial or ethnic origins has increased by 72 percent since 1970. The trend suggests more of this in the future. Even if your spouse is of the same background, chances are high that the spouse of a sibling or cousin will represent a different part of the American collage. At holidays and other family events, from birthdays to funerals, we will increasingly be in close connection with "Others." Before too long most Americans will be "Tiger Woods" Americans, whose parental heritage is black, Native American, Chinese, Caucasian, and Thai. Now is the time for our social categories to reflect this trend—and its capacity for building a sense of one community—rather than conceal it.

Where Do We Go from Here?

Changing the way we divide up society will not magically resolve our differences or abolish racial prejudices. Nor does a movement toward a colorblind nation mean that we should stop working for a more just America. A combination of three major approaches that deal with economic and legal change could allow us to greatly downgrade the importance of race as a social criterion and still advance social justice. These approaches include reparations, class-based social programs, and fighting discrimination on an individual basis.   33

To make amends for the grave injustice that has been done to African-Americans by slavery and racial prejudice, as well as to bring to a close claims based on *past* injustices—and the sense of victimhood and entitlement that often accompanies these claims—major reparations are called for. One possible plan might allot a trillion dollars in education, training, and housing vouchers to African-Americans over a period of 20 years. (The same sort of plan might be devised for Native Americans.)   34

Such reparations cannot make full compensation for the sins of slavery, of course. But nothing can. Even so, if Jews could accept restitution from Germany and move on (Germany and   35

Israel now have normal international relations, and the Jewish community in Germany is rapidly growing), could not a similar reconciliation between black and white Americans follow reparations? A precedent in our own history is the payment of reparations to Japanese-Americans because of their internment in World War II. In 1988, the U.S. government issued a formal apology in the Civil Liberties Act and awarded $20,000 to each living person who had been interned. About 80,000 claims were awarded, totaling $1.6 billion.

36   Part of the deal should be that once reparations are made for the sins against African-Americans in the past, black people could no longer claim special entitlements or privileges on the basis of their race. Reparations thus would end affirmative action and minority set-asides as we have known them.

37   At the same time, Americans who are disadvantaged for any reason not of their own doing—the handicapped; those who grew up in parts of the country, such as Appalachia, in which the economy has long been lagging; those whose jobs were sent overseas who are too old to be retrained—would be given extra aid in applying for college admissions and scholarships, housing allowances, small-business loans, and other social benefits. The basis for such aid would be socioeconomic status, not race. The child of a black billionaire would no longer be entitled to special consideration in college admissions, for instance, but the child of a poor white worker who lost his job to outsourcing and could not find new employment would be.

38   Social scientists differ in their estimates of the extent to which differences in opportunity and upward mobility between blacks and whites are due to racial prejudice and the extent to which they are due to economic class differences. But most scholars who have studied the matter agree that economic factors are stronger than racial ones, possibly accounting for as much as 80 percent of the differences we observe. A vivid example: In recent years, Wake County in North Carolina made sure that its public school classes were composed of students of different economic backgrounds, disregarding racial and ethnic differences. The results of this economic integration overshadowed previous attempts to improve achievement via racial integration. While a decade ago, only 40 percent of blacks in grades three through eight scored at grade level, in the spring of 2005, 80 percent did so.

39   Class differences affect not only educational achievement, health, and job selection, but also how people are regarded or stereotyped. Fifty years ago, a study conducted at Howard University showed that although adjectives used to describe whites and blacks were quite different, that variance was greatly reduced when class was held constant. People described upper-class whites and upper-class blacks in a remarkably similar fashion, as

intelligent and ambitious. People also described lower-class whites and lower-class blacks in a similar way, as dirty and ignorant. The author concluded that "stereotypes vary more as a function of class than of race."

If race-based discrimination were a thing of the past, and   40 black Americans were no longer subjected to it, then my argument that reparations can lead to closure would be easier to sustain. Strong evidence shows, however, that discrimination remains very much with us. A 1990 Urban Institute study found that when two people of different races applied for the same job, one in eight times the white was offered the job and an equally qualified African-American was not. Another Urban Institute study, released in 1999, found that racial minorities received less time and information from loan officers and were quoted higher interest rates than whites in most of the cities where tests were conducted.

The victims of current racial discrimination should be fully   41 entitled to remedies in court and through such federal agencies as the Equal Employment Opportunity Commission. These cases should be dealt with on an individual basis or in a class-action suit where evidence exists to support one. Those who sense discrimination should be required to prove it. It shouldn't be assumed that because a given workplace has more people of race *x* than race *y*, discrimination must exist.

A Vision of the Future

In the end, it comes down to what Americans envision for our   42 future together: either an open society, in which everyone is equally respected (an elusive goal but perhaps closer at hand than we realize), or an even more racialized nation, in which "people of color" are arrayed in perpetual conflict with white people. The first possibility is a vision of America as a community in which people work out their differences and make up for past injustices in a peaceful and fair manner; the other is one in which charges of prejudice and discrimination are mixed with real injustices, and in which a frustrated sense of victimhood and entitlement on the one hand is met with guilt and rejection on the other.

A good part of what is at stake is all too real: the distribution   43 of assets, income, and power, which reparations, class-based reforms, and the courts should be able to sort out. But don't overlook the importance of symbols, attitudes, and feelings, which can't be changed legislatively. One place to start is with a debate over the official ways in which we classify ourselves and the ways we gather social data, because these classifications and data are used as a mirror in which we see ourselves reflected.

44   Let us begin with a fairly modest request of the powers that
be: Give us a chance. Don't make me define my children and
myself in racial terms; don't "impute" a race to me or to any of
the millions of Americans who feel as I do. Allow us to describe
ourselves simply as Americans. I bet my 50 years as a sociologist that we will all be better for it.

Richard Rodriguez

The Third Man

Born in 1944 to Mexican immigrants, Richard Rodriguez
earned a bachelor's degree at Stanford University and a
master's degree from Columbia University. His work exploring
race and ethnicity has been highly acclaimed, including the
awarding of the Commonwealth Gold Medal for his 1982
memoir about assimilation into American culture, *Hunger of
Memory: The Education of Richard Rodriguez*. The piece that
follows is excerpted from his 2002 book, *Brown: The Last
Discovery of America*. In this essay, Rodriguez searches for
an identity in the space "between black and white." In that
space, he sees himself as a type of "third man" who has
resisted the identity of a "minority." As you read, you might
consider how, despite similarities among the experiences of
non-whites, each racial or ethnic group has its own set of
identity issues—a perspective that is also important in the two
pieces about the Asian-American experience that follow.
What specific issues about being "brown" does Rodriguez
explore here? Why are those issues particularly poignant for
his ethnicity and as an individual?

1   A Chinese or an Eskimo or a countertenor could play this
role as well. Anyone in America who does not describe
himself as black or white can take the role. But the reason I am here, on this dais, in a hotel ballroom, is numerical.

2   Our subject today is the perennial American subject: Race
Relations. You understand, by this time, I am not a race. I do
not have a race. To my left, standing at the microphone, is an
African-American academic who refers to himself as "black." To
my right sits a journalist who calls himself "white." My role is
the man in the middle, the third man; neither.

Situated thus, between black and white—occupying the passing   3
lane in American demographics—the Hispanic should logically be
gray or at least a blur.

Americans dislike gray. Gray areas, gray skies, gray flannel   4
suits, mice, hair, cities, seas. Moscow. Hera's eyes.

But I am not gray, I am brown as you can see, or rather you   5
can't see, but my name on this book is brown. Rodriguez is a
brown name—or gray—halfway between Greenwich and Tim
buktu. I am brown all right—darkish reddish, terra-cotta-ish,
dirt-like, burnt Sienna in the manner of the middle Bellini.

At the microphone, the African-American professor refers (in   6
one breath) to "blacks-and-Latinos," his synonym for the disadvantaged in America—the dropout, the lost, the under arrest.
The professor's rhetorical generosity leaves me abashed.

In truth, African Americans are in fierce competition with   7
Hispanics in this country. We compete for the meanest jobs or
for the security of civil service positions or for political office or
for white noise. If I were an African American I would not be so
generous toward Hispanics, especially if I had to read every
morning of their ascending totals. The *Wall Street Journal*,
March 8, 2001: NUMBER OF HISPANICS BALLOONED IN 1990S; GROUP
IS ABOUT TO BECOME BIGGEST MINORITY. I would resent the
incurious gabble of Spanish invading African-American neighborhoods; Hispanics demanding from the federal government
the largest slice of black metaphor; and this—my brown intru-
sion into the tragic dialectic of America, the black and white
conversation.

Not so long ago, Hispanics, particularly Mexicans and Cubans,   8
resisted the label of "minority." In a black-and-white America,
Hispanics tended toward white, or at least tended to keep their
distance from black. I remember my young Mexican mother saying to her children, in Spanish, "We are not minorities," in the
same voice she would use decades later to refuse the term "senior citizen." One day in the 1980s, my mother became a senior
citizen because it got her on the bus for a nickel. One day, in the
1960s, the success of the Negro Civil Rights movement encouraged Hispanics (along with other groups of Americans) to insist
on the coveted black analogy, and thus claim the spoils of
affirmative action.

Today you will see us listed on surveys and charts, between   9
Black and White, as though Hispanics are necessarily distinct
from either Black or White; as though Hispanics are comparable to either Black or White.

Out of mischief or stupidity, federal demographers have taken to   10
predicting that Hispanics are destined to replace African Americans as "American's largest minority." The Census Bureau manages
both to trivialize the significance of Hispanics to our national life,
and to insult African Americans by describing Hispanics as

supplanters. To date, the nation's Hispanic political leadership has remained silent about the Census Bureau's grammar.

11   The notion of African Americans as a minority is one born of a distinct and terrible history of exclusion—the sin of slavery, later decades of segregation, and every conceivable humiliation visited upon a people, lasting through generations. To say, today, that Hispanics are becoming America's largest minority is to mock history, to pervert language, to dilute the noun "minority" until it means little more than a population segment.

12   This is exactly what Hispanics have become—a population segment, an ad-agency target audience, a market share. Not coincidentally, it was an advertising agency that got the point of Hispanic totals as early as the 1980s. It was then that Coors Beer erected billboards throughout the Southwest that flattered "The Decade of the Hispanic."

13   By telling you these things, I do not betray "my people." I think of the nation entire—all Americans—as my people. Though I call myself Hispanic, I see myself within the history of African Americans and Irish Catholics and American Jews and the Chinese of California.

14   When citizens feel themselves excluded, it is appropriate that they lobby, petition, attract the interest of government and employers. But when Americans organize into subgroups, it should be with an eye to merging with the whole, not remaining separate. What was the point of the Negro Civil Rights movement of the early twentieth century, if not integration?

15   The trouble with today's ethnic and racial and sexual identifications is that they become evasions of citizenship. Groups beget subgroups: Last week in Atlanta there was a meeting of Colombian Americans, their first convention. In parody of Hispanics nationally, Colombian Americans declared themselves to be "America's fastest-growing minority."

16   At Yale University, I was recently trailed by a white graduate student—truly Hispanic—who kept boasting that she was the "first Latina to win" and the "first Latina named." The moment we sat down to talk, this white Hispanic referred to herself as "a person of color" and I realized she had no idea.

17   Alone among the five (White, Black, Asian, et cetera) options placed at one's disposal on affirmative action applications. Hispanic is the only category that has no reference to blood. One can be an Asian-Hispanic or an Indian-Hispanic, et cetera. Indeed, I know Hispanics who are of a complexion most Americans would call black but who elect to name themselves Hispanic. I know Hispanics who are blithe as daffodils.

18   Here is what I will say when it is my turn to get up and speak: *Hispanicity is culture. Not blood. Not race. Culture, or the illusion of culture—ghost-ridden. A belief that the dead have a hold on the living.*

What I will not say, when I get up to speak, is that from child- 19
hood I have resisted the notion of culture in Spanish. There was
not another noun in my childish Spanish vocabulary that made
me more uneasy than the word *"cultura"* (which was always
used against me, but as indistinguishable from me—something
I had betrayed). I did not shrink from culture's cousin-noun,
"costumbre"—custom, habit—which was visible, tangible,
comestible, conditional.

In Spanish, culture is indissoluble; culture is everything that 20
connects me to the past and with a sense of myself as beyond
myself. When I was a boy and refused to speak Spanish (because
I spoke English), then could not speak Spanish from awkward-
ness, then guilt, Mexican relatives criticized my parents for
letting me "lose it"—my culture, they said. (So it was possible to
lose, after all? If culture is so fated, how could I have lost it?)
Many years later, complete strangers—Hispanic readers and
academics, even non-Hispanic readers and academics—picked
up the taunting refrain. As if culture were a suitcase left too long
unclaimed. I had lost my culture. The penalty for my sin was a
life of inauthenticity. Then they commenced hurling coconuts—
all those unchivalric taunts that are the stock of racial and
sexual and patriotic bullies.

The audience is bound to misunderstand what I will tell them. 21
There is nothing fateful about the notion of culture in American
English. (The English word means exactly the opposite of the
Spanish word.) The word "culture" in America comes equipped
with add-on component jacks. The word "culture" in America
pivots on a belief in the individual's freedom to choose, to
become a person different from her past. Culture in American
English separates children from grandparents, the living from
the dead, this moment from what I believed only yesterday. "Culture gaps" and "culture shocks," "cultural pride" and "counter-
culture" are American specialties, presupposing obsolescence.

Insofar as I remain culturally influenced by Latin America, I 22
must notice the fallacy that supports the American "I": American individualism is a communally derived value, not truly an
expression of individuality. The teenager persists in rebelling
against her parents, against tradition or custom, because she is
shielded (blindfolded, entranced, drugged) by American culture
from the knowledge that she inherited her rebellion from dead
ancestors and living parents.

But insofar as I am culturally American, my gringo eye sees 23
only diversity among the millions of people who call themselves
Hispanic. The songwriter from Buenos Aires, the Bolivian from
a high mountain village, the Mayan Indian who refuses Spanish, the Mayan Indian who exaggerates Spanish, the Salvadoran
evangelical Protestant, the Cuban anticommunist, the Cuban
communist, the green criminal, the Catholic nun, the red poet,

the city dweller, the inhabitant of the desert, the swimmer from the tropics, the agnostic scientist with a German surname—Hispanics all! In no sense can so many different lives be said to inhabit a singular culture. Save one sense: Hispanics in the United States are united in the belief (a Latin American belief) that culture is a more uniform source of identity than blood.

24   The African-American professor has concluded his speech. He catches my eye as he sits. We smile conspiratorially. He assumes we plot the same course. Then the white journalist rises to speak. The journalist says, "Racism has not gone away, it haunts our streets, it haunts our courtrooms, it haunts our boardrooms, it haunts our classrooms . . . "

When Americans speak about "race" they remind me of Latin Americans speaking of "culture."

Culture in Latin American Spanish is fated.

Culture in American English yields to idiosyncracy.

Race in American English is fated.

Race in Latin American Spanish yields to idiosyncracy.

25   I hardly mean to imply racism does not exist in Latin America. Latin America predictably favors light over dark. Certainly in Mexico, the Latin American country I know best, white ascends. Certainly, the whitest dinner party I ever attended was a Mexico City dinner party where a Mexican squire of exquisite manner, mustache, and flán-like jowl, expressed himself surprised, so surprised, to learn that I am a writer. One thought he would never get over it. *Un escritor . . . ¿Un escritor . . . ?* Turning the word on a lathe of tooth and tongue, until: "You know, in Mexico, I think we do not have writers who look like you," he said. He meant dark skin, thick lips, Indian nose, bugger your mother.

26   No one in the United States has ever matched the confidence of that gentleman's insult. I believe it would not occur to the deepest-dyed racist in the United States to question whether I am a writer. The racist might say I look like a monkey, but he would not say I don't look like a writer.

27   The dream of Mexico is an apotheosis of bleach. Nevertheless, Mexico has for centuries compiled a ravishing lexicon of brown because in Mexico race is capricious as history is capricious. From the colonial era, the verbal glamour of Mexico has been to entertain a spectrum of brown—of impurity—as rich and as wet as a Hollander palette: *mestizo, castizo, alvina, chino, negro torno atras, morisco, canbujo, albarrasado, tente en el aire, canpa mulato, coyote, vorsino, lobo . . .*

28   By contrast, white and black discussions of race in America are Victorian; leave out the obvious part. In light of postmodern

America's obsession with sex, it is remarkable how reluctant we are to sexualize American history. In an American conversation, where there is no admission of brown, the full meaning of the phrase "New World" lies always out of sight.

In eighteenth-century Mexico there was a popular genre of paintings on the subject of *las castas*—descriptive not of social caste, but of racial admixture. The paintings were illustrations of racial equations: If mama is *negra* and papa is *indio*, then baby is . . . An auxiliary convention of these paintings is that they catalog and display fruits and fauna of the New World—dogs, lizards, parrots, as well as costume, fabric. Both words and paintings describe domestic bliss or comic discord. In one panel, *la negra* is about to brain her Spanish spouse with an indigenous frying pan—à la Maggie and Jiggs—and the entire adventure and preoccupation of the New World is seen as genetic. But comically so. This, despite Latin America's fame for a tragic disposition. This, despite the fame of the United States for optimism. 29

In American English, mulatto traces the distance from a contaminant. In eighteenth-century Latin America, mulatto was only one pinion on a carnival wheel. In the United States of the eighteenth century, the condition of being a mulatto was an offense when it was thought to issue from black male desire. When mulatto was the issue of white male desire, mulatto was unspoken, invisible, impossible. 30

Brown made Americans mindful of tunnels within their bodies, about which they did not speak; about their ties to nature, about which they did not speak; about their ties to one another, about which they did not speak. 31

This undermining brown motif, this erotic tunnel, was the private history and making of America. Brown was the light of day. Brown, the plain evidence. Fugue and funk. Brown, the color of consort; brown, the color of illicit passion—not blue—brown, the shade of love and drawn shades and of love children, so-called, with straight hair and gothic noses: secret cousins; brown, the stench of rape and of shame, sin, slippage, birth. 32

After several brown centuries, I sit on a dais, in a hotel ballroom, brown. I do not hesitate to say into a microphone what everyone knows, what no one says. *Most American blacks are not black*. The erotic history of America kept pace with segregation. From the inception of America, interracial desire proceeded apace with segregated history. (The biological impulse of creatures is stronger than any cultural impulse, apparently.) Desire and sympathy, as well as cruelty and revulsion, undermined and propelled America's New World experiment from the beginning. In spite of dire social prohibitions, white slave owners placed their ancestors in the bodies of their slaves. 33

34   We know from the gossip outside books that generations before Thomas Jefferson and Sally Hemmings, black female and white male pairings existed, some lasting from youth till death did them part. But the issue of such white-black eroticism was not recognized as being brown, or both. Mulattos, quadroons, octoroons, tracing distance from the contaminant, were ultimately an irrelevance under the dictum of the American racial theory called the "one-drop" theory.

35   In the American musical *Showboat*, a backwater sheriff boards the *Cotton Blossom*, or whatever that showboat was called, to declaim, in cadences of Racine (and to make himself plain to the second balcony), *One drop o'nigger blood 'sall it takes . . .*

36   To make a nigger. Here was an anthropology, a biology, indeed an alchemy, that allowed plantation owners to protect their investment, to preserve the assumption of racial superiority, to accommodate, as well, their sexual curiosity and to redouble their chattel.

37   A child of black-and-white eroticism remained "black" in the light of day, no matter how light her skin, straight his hair, gothic her nose; she was black as midnight, black as tar, black as the ace of spades, black as your hat. Under the one-drop theorem, it was possible for a white mother to give birth to a black child in America, but no black mother ever gave birth to a white child. A New World paradox.

38   One of the first lessons in America, the color-book lesson, instructs that color should stay within the lines. The river should not flood its banks. The tree should not smear the sky.

39   It is interesting to note the two American fictions of the nineteenth century that continue to romance us were about interracial relationships, exclusively male. I mean *The Adventures of Huckleberry Finn* and *Moby-Dick*—both dreams of escape from convention and family. At a time when America was preoccupied with land and settlement, with cultivating the land, Twain and Melville wrote of water, of suspension, of being carried outward. The river cares nothing for its bank, the ocean cares nothing for the shore, each consorts with the sky. In the first, a white boy and a runaway slave abandon town and the constriction of the shore for the freedom of the river. In the latter, a crew of men from every corner of the world board a ship in search of a ghostly whale. In both stories there are only undomesticated men or boys. And the male pairings are odd, interracial, even homoerotic; violations of the town's conventions.

40   After the Civil War, in American places where water seduced or penetrated the landscape, the promiscuity of the horizon encouraged African Americans who lived near those places to speak the truth about themselves. In New Orleans and Charleston. African Americans often described themselves as "Creoles" or

"mulattos"—washes, watercolors—some Latin influence, perhaps. But the landlocked places kept to the shackle of blood-as-fate; color within the lines.

The notion that a brown is black—a paucity of choice—   41
created segregated drinking fountains and schoolrooms and colored platoons in the Second World War. But that same notion—the one-drop notion—also undermined segregation in America by forging a solidarity among African Americans over and above any extenuations such as occupation or age or income or complexion.

My friend Darrell. Darrell says he is black. Darrell says he is   42
black because *that is what the white cop sees when he looks at me.*

If it is fair for me to notice that the white Latina at Yale is   43
not objectively a person of color, is it fair to notice you are not exactly black? Darrell?

You know what I'm talking about . . .   44

Of course I understand what you're talking about. Race is the   45
sine qua non among American transactions. Without race, we wouldn't have music, movies, prisons, politics, history, libraries, colleges, private conversations, motives. Dorothy Dandridge. Bill Clinton. Race is America's theme—not freedom, not democracy (as we say in company). What are you? we say. Well, we don't say anymore, but we mean. And you say black.

What do you say?   46

I don't.   47

Yes you do. You say, queer Indian Catholic—some sidestep bull-   48
shit like that.

I don't say brown. Anyway, how should I know what race I am,   49
my ancestors go back a long way. I grant you, were it not for America's preoccupation with distinguishing feathers. I would have to learn a trade other than brown. To be a warbler is not the same as being a brown warbler.

Speaking of warblers. I saw a blackbird the other day—Avian-   50
American—he was sitting in the sun. Little patch of lawn. In this particular sun—or was it just the Fabergé of the moment?—the blackbird appeared green, green as ink, and with gold tracery upon the nib of his folded wing; the green of the grayest recesses of the swooniest forest of Fragonard.

Blackbirds are green,   51
Violets blue . . . So?   52

So, I believe I do not truly understand you. Darrell, your resort   53
to imprecision to color yourself from another's regard. Maybe because I have never been taken, mistaken, though I do get stopped often enough by cops for jogging in my whiteout neighborhood. Do you believe you uphold the one-drop theory by your insistence on black, because that is the way the white cop sees you?

Too easy, Rodriguez.   54

55   *It doesn't matter if my complexion is lemon or redbone or licorice, I'm black—the word that drips down indelible as India ink through the language because black is incapable of qualification. You can have black and blue. You can have black and white. You can have* The Red and the Black. *But you can't have reddish black or light black or blackish, as you have reddish brown. Black is historically dense because it is linguistically dense; it overwhelms any more complicated shading. You can say I'm self-consciously black. You want to say that instead of black? That's my race. Self-Conscious. I dream about an unself-conscious gesture or moment or thought. Or step. An unself-conscious boulevard. Or fellowship. I won't find it. Not in Harlem. Not in Paris. Not in Oakland on Easter Sunday morning. There's always a split-second delay between you and me—a linguistic felt-tip line. I am the line in the color book! Is my fly open? Am I scaring somebody? Is your tone ironic or condescending? Is there a third choice? No, I don't believe there is a third choice. I can detect the slightest tremor of misgiving faster than Jane Austen. Sensibility, she called her faculty, and that's what black folk are masters of—sensibility. My eyes are two-way mirrors. My deliberation is reflexive. Because my hue cannot reflect? What do they think of me? And speaking of mirrors: Mirror, mirror on the wall, does this outfit look too spooky? Too out there? Rap stars and kids can get away with an outlaw look, as you call it, but a black man better stick with Lands' End. When I say I'm black-because-that's-what-the-white-cop-sees, I mean I'm a man of sensibility. Buck is the thinnest skin there is, babe. Absorbs everything.*

56   *Uphold the one-drop theory? Come on! I don't make this stuff up, you know. And if you'll kindly advise the San Francisco Police Department their way of thinking is recherché, I'll be much obliged and I'll call myself something else.*

57   What of white, then? White flesh is reductive. Caucasian is a term of no scientific currency. White is an impulse to remain innocent of history.

58   For many generations, the American paint box was predicated upon an unsullied white, an irreducible, an unblushing, a bloodless white—let us say, cadmium—let us say, rather, the white of the powder on George Washington's head; let us say, rather, the white of the driven snow, for the first white Americans imagined themselves innocent. And white is universally accepted, among white people, as the color of innocence.

59   It is impossible to depict or portray white in time—even the white of philosophy, even the white of an hour—without a complex palette. (Though Japanese painting portrays white—the cloud obscuring a mountaintop or the mist in a valley—as an absence of paint.) Fra Angelico's *Transfiguration* might serve us here. Christ's transfigured robes are described in Scripture as whiter than any bleach could make them. In order to paint

(rather than to absent) a supernaturally irradiated garment, a garment outside time, Fra Angelico must call upon time—drape and shadow—and, in so doing, must call upon pigment, literally mortal clay, yellow and red and gray and brown and black. Later, we see, Christ used dirt and spit as a healing paste; a mixture to restore sight.

Brown marks the passage of time.   60

After a speech or a panel discussion like the one I here   61
rehearse, someone from the audience will approach me, "someone who is white," she says. She feels she has no culture. She envies me. She envies what I have been at pains to escape—the Mexican sense of culture.

The price of entering white America is an acid bath, a bleach-   62
ing bath—a transfiguration—that burns away memory. I mean the freedom to become; I mean the freedom to imagine oneself free.

The point of Noel Ignatiev's *How the Irish Became White* (by   63
distancing themselves from black) may be extended to any number of other European immigrants to America. *How the Germans became white. How Sicilian Catholics became white. How Russian Jews became white.*

Extended even to non-Europeans: *How my mother and father*   64
became white. My Mexican parents were described as White on their citizenship papers by an unimaginative federal agent. (An honorary degree.)

Who can blame the Irish steward or the Sicilian hatmaker for   65
wanting to be white? White in America was the freedom to disappear from a crowded tenement and to reappear in a Long Island suburb, in an all-electric kitchen, with a set of matching plates.

I grew up wanting to be white. That is, to the extent of want-   66
ing to be colorless and to feel complete freedom of movement. The other night at a neighborhood restaurant the waiter, after mentioning he had read my books, said about himself, "I'm white, I'm nothing." But that was what I wanted, you see, growing up in America—the freedom of being nothing, the confidence of it, the arrogance. And I achieved it.

Growing up an honorary white—which meant only that I was   67
not black—I never wanted to be black, like the white kids wanted to be black (Elvis Presley wanting to be black), such was their white freedom! White, which began as an idea of no color; which defined itself against black and was therefore always bordered with black; white in America ended up as freedom from color—an idea of no boundary. Call me Ishmael.

Whereas whites regarded their Americanization as a freedom   68
from culture, black was fated because black was blood. Blood was essence; black was essence. *Yo, blood!* If you are black, to this day, if you are young, black, you can end up with siblings,

classmates, who will challenge you for speaking "white," thinking "white," even though every white kid assumes the right to sing black and talk black and move black. So "black," once a restriction imposed by whites in defiance of obvious history, black now is a culture (in the fated sense) imposed by blacks.

69   Within their restriction, using restriction subversively, using whatever was not valued by the ugly stepsisters (using poverty, bruise, prayer), African Americans created the most vibrant culture of America, now the defining culture of America. White Americans would end up feeling themselves bloodless. White Americans would end up hungering for black culture, which they understood curiously as freedom of expression, glamour of transcendence.

70   To make black culture, so the American myth goes, one needs to connect to misery; one needs to be bad or battered to sing the blues. How many millions of African Americans today need to rot in jail cells to maintain the culture of partition, to keep black culture outlaw, to keep outlaw black culture at the center of white yearning?

71   What I want for African Americans is white freedom. The same as I wanted for myself.

72   The last white freedom in America will be the freedom of the African American to admit brown. Miscegenation. To speak freely of ancestors, of Indian and Scots and German and plantation owner. To speak the truth of themselves. That is the great advantage I can see for blacks in the rise of the so-called Hispanic.

73   What Latin America might give the United States is a playful notion of race. Already the definitive blond in America is Tina Turner.

74   What the United States might give Latin America is a more playful notion of culture. Culture as freedom. Culture as invitation. Culture as lure. Already, the definitive blond in Latin America is Ricky Martin. Ricky Martin is so blond he can afford to be brunette.

75   Only further confusion can save us. My favorite San Francisco couple is a Chinese-American man and an African-American woman who both have blond hair and wear Hawaiian shirts and ride around town in a vintage red Pontiac convertible with white leather upholstery. The use of vegetable hair dyes is a great boon to American youth, wouldn't you say? Such wonderfully false colors allow young Americans to be and not to be. Blue or chartreuse or Lucille Ball. And at the same time to proclaim themselves to be just kidding. And contact lenses. My niece has dyed her hair red and thinks she might like to try blue eyes for a change. Nothing permanent. It all washes out. Tomorrow and tomorrow and tomorrow.

76   Ding-dong. It's the UPS man. The Filipino guy in shorts, his hair just beginning to magenta at the temples. Home, as I said, is a

Victorian in San Francisco with Indians stomping around on the roof. And I am left (on such a nice day, too) sitting inside, deconstructing the American English word for myself—Hispanic [*sic*]—by which I celebrate my own deliverance from *cultura*; the deliverance of the United States of America from race.

Rosie Molinary

The Latina Mystique

Rosie Molinary is the author of *Hijas Americanas: Beauty, Body Image, and Growing Up Latina* and *Beautiful You: A Daily Guide to Radical Self-Acceptance.* She has also been a high school teacher, coach, and college administrator. She holds an MFA in Creative Writing, and has contributed to a number of publications including *Teen Vogue, Latina, Women's Health,* and *Philanthropy Journal.* As you read this piece, note the ways that various identity issues discussed in this part of *Conversations* merge as she brings together the expectations of her gender with that of her culture. You might also consider the various factors that influence your own identity, how they come together, and what conflicts they may cause in your own self-image.

Latina. It's an identity that's often burdened by other peo- 1 ple's expectations. The women who shared their stories for this book seemed to be relieved to have the opportunity to voice their experiences about dealing with these expectations.

We mine words to label our experiences, and yet sometimes 2 those words become too much, morphing into ideas that convey something larger than what we mean. "Being Latina" doesn't mean for me what it might mean to another woman, just as my experience of being raised in America surely differs from others', even my own sister's. Over and over again, I was struck by the various ways in which we articulate our experiences as Latinas—many of which are based on the words that are put upon us, the identities that others give us in an attempt to define for us who we are. In my conversations with Latinas from around the country, I found how loaded the concept of "being Latina" is for so many of us; how such concepts sometimes set us up for disappointment, failure, and dissatisfaction; and how they are often based on things that we don't even understand.

3   The notion of the "Latina mystique" is one of the most prevailing stereotypes in American culture, and yet there are several other stereotypes about Latinas. Confronting how we're perceived can be an awakening. By acknowledging these images as stereotypes, we are more able to see why they're invalid, and how important it is to live our lives as examples of the multidimensional Latina experience.

4   When I was in my mid-twenties, the Latina in me was frustrated. She stayed up late into the night and contemplated marriage and feminism. My friends were starting to marry and have kids, and my Latin mother was dropping hints about marrying the man I described as her "Great White Hope." Meanwhile, the gringa in me tried to ignore what she perceived as unfair expectations. Mamacita had been praying for a husband for me for far too long. She lit candles and recited rosaries for her *hijita soltera.*

5   "Don't ask for an *esposo* in my name," I would implore over the phone line, agitated.

6   "*¿Y si no, qué?*" she replied, implying that she would always do what she damn well pleased.

7   "Pray for starving children. That's the type of prayer you call on God for." My head hurt from having this conversation with my mother yet again. I was twenty-four and absorbed in a teaching career that I loved. I wasn't ready to get married and have children. I already had two hundred kids whom I worked with every day. I just wanted to give my everything to the kids who showed up in my classroom or on the soccer field without having to worry about a husband. I felt like I had a lifetime ahead of me—and plenty of time to get married if I chose. But I was also just fine with the idea of not getting married.

8   My mom had gotten married in her mid-twenties, unusually late in her day, especially for Puerto Rico. I always thought her experience would make her more laid back about her children's children. Yes, this was an assurance, even insurance, that I would become the Latina I had never fully been in her eyes. I'd always been too independent, too willful, too American. I tried to ignore her disappointment in my casual appearance, my autonomy, my dismissal of the importance of men, marriage, and children.

9   The idea that there was just one way to be a Latina—and a stereotypical way at that—rendered me silent, frozen on the borderlands between my Latina and my gringa. The pressure of the Latina mystique chilled me. I was coming into my own at a time when Latinas were figuring more prominently in hip-hop videos and mainstream media. *Selena* had just come out, and the Fly

Girls on *In Living Color* were giving Latinas like Jennifer Lopez real airtime. And there I was, a twentysomething who favored long skirts and baggy sweaters. I didn't look the part of those Latinas, and I certainly couldn't compete with the more commonplace images I saw all around me in the South: the pretty blond cheerleaders, the fair-skinned, highlight-streaked athletes.

As I got older and traveled, I experienced a different sort of frustration. I began to encounter boys and men in my hometown and around the country who found me sexy and seductive, as well as "free game"—not because I was those things, but because I was ethnic, a girl from the Island, a Latina who would surely be able to titillate them in whole new ways. Suddenly, my Latina had to deal with the pressure to be the curvy J.Lo type, while my gringa was dealing with Barbie-doll pressure. And for who I was—a girl with a casual, girl-next-door vibe—I couldn't muster up a good impersonation of *either* of those two extreme stereotypes.

But soon I got to the point where I truly grasped the idea that nobody, not even J.Lo, is so incredibly one-dimensional. The expectations being placed on me and other Latinas were part and parcel of the stereotypes we have to live with and move beyond—not realities. I didn't perceive myself as sexy and exotic. After all, I was struggling with two identities. I wasn't wholly identified with the idea of being so different that men would pay me attention simply for my look. And yet clearly, I'd felt different enough all my life that I yearned for connection, for that elusive friend who came from where I did. So there I was: I couldn't be a white girl, and I couldn't totally embrace being just a Puerto Rican. Why? Because life can't be boiled down that simply. The Latina mystique, the Barbie mystique, mystique *period,* is based in mystery, not reality.

For years, I never really knew how to perceive myself, because I was waiting for the answers to come from someone else. I was waiting for someone to tell me how much of a Latina I was, or how much of a gringa. I let other people's judgment of me determine whether I was pretty or plain, alluring or unappealing, exciting or mundane.

I wanted something to resonate in me, to know that something was right because I *felt* it; but I was grasping, because I was still also, somehow, waiting for the confirmation to come from the outside. Ultimately, I realized that the only way I could make peace with myself and find a consistent view that reflected the woman I was becoming was to search for the confirmation I was seeking on the inside. I needed to inform others about how to interpret me, rather than the other way around. That was something that required coming to terms with my Latina and my gringa, and then owning both parts of who I was. The most important issue was not how other people defined what they

saw when they looked at me, but how I defined what I felt, and
how I melded my parts.

Emma Violand-Sánchez and Julia Hainer-Violand

The Power of Positive Identity

This essay, first published in 2006 in *Educational Leadership*, a
trade journal for teachers and school administrators, addresses
the issue of ethnic identity largely—but not exclusively—
through the issue of bilingualism. It examines the importance
of language in the formation of identity for Latino students,
both in terms of the importance of retaining their mother
tongue and in terms of other words like "illegals" and "aliens"
that affect students' self-perception. Both authors bring a
background in education to this issue. Emma Violand-Sánchez
is the supervisor of English for Speakers of Other Languages
and High-Intensity Language Training programs in the
Arlington Public Schools, Arlington, Virginia. She also teaches
as an adjunct professor at Georgetown University. Julia
Hainer-Violand serves as a third-grade teacher at Oyster
Elementary School in Washington, D.C. You might consider
how the issue of identity formation for students speaks to other
educational issues discussed in Part One of *Conversations*.

1   Acknowledging the strengths that Latinos bring to school
and community is crucial for their academic and social
success.

2   As the largest minority group in the United States, Latinos
account for 14 percent of the U.S. population. By 2050, they will
account for 25 percent. Despite the hefty increase, many children of immigrants consider themselves members of a minority
group in a way that negatively affects their behavior, school performance, and social integration (Tienda & Mitchell, 2006). As
educators, we should develop a better understanding of the culture and issues that affect the well-being of Latino English language learners because these issues will ultimately affect the
future of the United States.

Addressing the needs of Latino students means acknowledg-   3
ing and capitalizing on the cultural and linguistic strengths that
they bring to the classroom. Schools should

- Foster a positive ethnic identity by viewing bilingualism
  and biculturalism as an asset and immigration as a
  source of pride.
- Empower Latino students through leadership roles within the school and community.
- Encourage student voice by having students speak and
  write from experience.

Adding or Subtracting?

Latinos are a varied ethnic group representing 20 countries,   4
including Mexico, Puerto Rico, Cuba, El Salvador, Guatemala,
and the United States. Despite class, race, and national differences, Latinos have found ways to coalesce on the basis of a
shared language and a common identity (Tienda & Mitchell,
2006). Recent studies have found that a strong, positive ethnic
identity is associated with high self-esteem, a commitment to
doing well in school, a sense of purpose in life, confidence in
one's own efficacy, and high academic achievement (Benard,
2004).

Developing identity is one of the socio-cultural tasks of ado-   5
lescence. During adolescence, many immigrant youths are
learning to become members of a non-dominant group. They
need to strike a balance between the native culture found in
their homes and communities and the dominant U.S. culture
that exists in most schools. This culture often assumes that students will quickly assimilate by learning English and forgetting
about their home countries. Students may experience this
process of assimilation as a subtraction of their first culture and
language, leaving them vulnerable and alienated from both
cultures (Valenzuela, 1999). But a more hopeful outcome is possible: These students may integrate the two cultures, thereby
fostering a new, additive bicultural identity that takes from
various sources.

David Hernandez, a bilingual community liaison in Virginia's   6
Arlington Public School District, created the concept of "Remix-
tino," the process through which students blend language with
family and cultural values to create their own sense of a U.S.-
Latino identity. These students move fluidly within the Latino
community; at the same time, they are fully aware of their
multilayered identity. As Hernandez puts it, "The students see
the Remix-tino process as a production, as their ultimate composition" (personal communication, June 2006).

7   Unfortunately, immigrant students face many challenges daily that exacerbate their problems adapting to the culture, such as financial problems, discrimination on the basis of their immigration status, linguistic differences, and family separations. Moreover, Latino students can easily experience U.S. culture as an onslaught of materialism, television, pop culture, and technology. For example, because they do not have an iPod or a computer with Internet access at home, they might see themselves as poor and as disconnected from the school community.

8   Immigrant students need increased guidance as well as family and community support to succeed in this society. School leaders can facilitate this transition and tap into Latino students' strengths by providing a number of services, including instructional programs that build on language and Latin American culture, English language courses for parents, student access to computers, Latino role models and mentors, bilingual counseling, and clubs and family involvement activities in Spanish.

9   It would also be helpful for educators to participate in staff development through which they learn Spanish and familiarize themselves with Latino culture and related issues. Partnering with community-based organizations is also an excellent strategy. The Arlington Public School District has partnered with a nonprofit organization, Escuela Bolivia, Inc. On Saturdays, students and adults from various countries learn Spanish, Quechua, and English, and they participate in cultural and family leadership activities (Osterling, Violand-Sánchez, & von Vacano, 1999).

Identity as Bilingual

10   More than 100 empirical studies show a positive association between additive bilingualism and students' linguistic, cognitive, or academic growth (Cummins, 2000). Developing literacy in two or more languages not only results in linguistic and academic benefits for individual students but also prepares students to work in both national and international contexts. Advances in technology, communication, and transportation have created a global environment that depends on interaction among nations and businesses in every corner of the world. Nevertheless, many critics continue to argue that English language learners should focus solely on learning English, leaving their home language behind.

11   We have taken a different tack in Arlington Public Schools, where 44 percent of our student body speaks a home language other than English and 33 percent of students are Latino, with Bolivians representing the largest group. We have implemented

several programs that provide a supportive environment for all students' academic and socio-cultural development:

- Dual-language immersion programs, in which native English-speaking students and Spanish-speaking students take science and mathematics in Spanish.
- First-language support programs, in which Spanish-speaking students with parental permission receive content instruction in Spanish for approximately 6–10 hours each week. While they are learning English, Spanish students take social studies and science in Spanish.
- Spanish for fluent speakers programs at the middle and high school levels. In high school, advanced placement classes in Spanish offer students the opportunity to continue developing their language skills and cultural knowledge while gaining access to college courses.

Arlington also promotes various supportive practices. Both monolingual and bilingual teachers often tap into the background knowledge of students by allowing them to express their knowledge or thoughts in their native language, either in a small group setting or through free writing. This approach gives students the chance to be "equal" in the classroom to their native English-speaking peers and helps prepare them to learn new information. In fact, using their native language while they learn English facilitates English acquisition and can reduce students' anxiety about learning. Quite often, students use native language when new information is unclear or when they explain an important concept or abstract idea to another student who is struggling with it. Using native language becomes a foundation for acquiring new information—regardless of whether that information is presented in English or in the native language.   12

The school system also provides books, dictionaries, and other resources in students' native languages in the library and classrooms. Teachers can prepare units that incorporate languages other than English in meaningful ways, by using bilingual storytellers, for example, or implementing a school pen pal program in which students communicate with one another in their first language through e-mail (Collier, 1995). Students can also use the Internet to do research in Spanish.   13

Many Latinos are driven to succeed when they adhere to the enabling values of love of and loyalty to family, community participation, respect for education, and a strong work ethic. To encourage the academic success of English language learners, educators should recognize and nurture the close relationship among these values and each students home language and social identity.   14

Identity as an Immigrant

15   The image of tongue-tied students who occupy a marginal position within U.S. schools and society leads to the misrepresentation of immigrants, not only in mainstream media but also in the nation's psyche. Latino students complain that it's hard to fight the negativism about being immigrants, especially when people underestimate their potential.

16   Some of this negativism insidiously works its way into the language that we use. For example, Latino students have expressed their frustration and anger that some teachers and classmates refer to immigrants as "illegals" or "aliens." The words that teachers use matter, because they set the tone for language in the classroom. To improve relationships and create a classroom atmosphere that welcomes diversity, teachers should avoid such terminology, going beyond even the neutral language of "undocumented" to promote the positive notion of "immigrants as essential workers" (Lakoff, in Rodriguez, 2006).

17   Moreover, we often forget that many immigrants have a legal presence in the United States—students on temporary visas, for example, or with "protected" status. Under the current quota system, many families have been waiting for years to get their permanent residency. Meanwhile, students suffer. For example, one Latino student, who was valedictorian of her high school class and whose family had a legal presence in the United States, was recently offered admission to a prestigious university. However, her "temporary" immigration status prevented her from receiving any state or federal aid.

Students Learn to Lead

18   To flourish, immigrant students need to feel that they belong. Schools should provide English language learners with opportunities to participate in activities that promote a sense of community by sponsoring clubs that foster leadership skills and pride and that honor the heritage of students who speak different languages. Creating leadership opportunities for Latino students is a natural outgrowth of any approach that capitalizes on student strengths.

19   Arlington schools boast many clubs—such as the Arabic Club, the Vietnamese Club, and Latinos and Latinas en Acción—that cater to a diverse student body. For example, the members of the ESOL Club of Arlington's Washington-Lee High School hail from such countries as Equatorial Guinea, Bolivia, Mongolia, Ethiopia, and El Salvador. The club provides students with a place to bond outside the classroom after school and during various club outings. When students participate and take leadership positions in a club in which they experience a sense of

belonging, they often will participate and become leaders in other organizations beyond their language and cultural groups.

At Conferences . . .

For the past 12 years, Arlington has held an annual Latino Youth   20
Leadership Conference, which involves nearly 400 Latino secondary students in the Arlington Public Schools. Coordinated by Congreso Estudiantil Latino (CELA), the conference fosters leadership among Latino students by showcasing positive Latino role models, such as Walter Tejada, the first Latino elected to the Arlington County Board. The conference also offers presentations on career and college topics. Deeply involved in coordinating the event, students develop conference themes—for example, Honoring Our Identity, What It Means to Be Latino, and Our Road to Success. They select topics for workshops and manage the event down to the details of what food to serve.

The conference brings students together from the various high   21
schools and middle schools in Arlington, fostering connections among students who often become future leaders and organizers of Latino clubs at the university level. One former student conference leader organized an Equal Access Education group at his high school and participated in a lawsuit filed in 2003 by the Mexican Legal Education Fund against several Virginia colleges for their admission policies dealing with undocumented students. Now at Virginia Tech, he serves as a liaison, welcoming prospective Latino students from his former high school.

In Classrooms . . .

Students helping students is a wonderful way to build commu-   22
nity among students with diverse linguistic and cultural backgrounds. One English as a second language (ESL) peer tutor explained that he volunteers because he wants to give back to the group that helped him when he first arrived in the United States from Bolivia.

The Latino Student Association staffs the peer tutoring group   23
at Washington-Lee High School. ESL students drop in whenever they need help completing schoolwork, but they also form friendships and learn from one another as they converse. For example, one student, on discovering that one of his Spanish-speaking peers had managed to change his placement to a more advanced math class, learned to advocate for himself and do the same.

Tutoring has proven highly successful, not only to the tutees   24
but also to the tutors. When students have mastered enough English to tutor with confidence, they reinforce both their

language and leadership skills as they take on a meaningful role in school. Peer tutoring creates a model community among English language learners that can extend to activities outside school as well.

And on the Streets!

25   As the U.S. Congress debated future immigration policy in spring 2006, Arlington Latino students stepped up and displayed leadership in organizing peaceful student protests. Directly affected by the possible criminalization of undocumented immigrants, students recognized the immediate need to rouse themselves out of silent complacency and speak out for their families and their future. Students came alive with the energy of organizing the Latino population for a student march and rally.

Student organizers worked with county representatives, police officers, and the school administration to plan an after-school rally and discussions that would highlight the contributions of the immigrant community in Arlington. The student organizers experienced a sense of pride, autonomy, and empowerment; shy students bloomed as they worked with community leaders.

Coming to Voice

26   Once English language learners have a taste of leadership, they will no longer fall back into silence. The student leaders who naturally emerged in the process of creating and managing a successful rally exercised their freedom of expression through constientizaçao, a deepened awareness arising out of a state of oppression (Freire, 2000). Once a person awakens to conscintização, he or she recognizes the systematic inequity in this world and the need to actively dismantle its mechanisms to prevent its continuation.

27   Latino students also need to find their voices in the classroom. By tapping into the personal experience of immigrants, teachers can help English language learners become comfortable speaking and writing from their own perspectives. In Arlington, one author gave "zine" workshops (magazine self-publishing) to ESL classes. One 6th grade class chose to write on the topic of family. A student wrote about how courageous his mother was to come to the United States when she didn't speak English and about how tenacious she'd become about learning the language. Another wrote about how thankful she was that her mother always took time to sit with her and talk. Students enthusiastically shared in English their interpretations of what family

meant to them. Student blogs are another popular medium in which students can engage one another on a variety of topics.

Latinos are frequently interested in writing about who they 28 are, about their identities as Latinos. The issue is complex. When many Latinos arrive in the United States, they tend to think of themselves as "Bolivian" or "San Salvadoran," for example, but bureaucracy reduces them to a single box to check on a form—"Hispanic." As they try to untangle who they really are, both ethnically and individually, Latino students often have much to say.

Teachers might sponsor a student-run newsletter that pub- 29 lishes student-selected topics. Latino students value a community space in which they can discuss their identities as Latinos, as well as any number of issues of interest: music, sports, relationships, culture, current events, immigration, and education opportunities. Students develop their voice and critical thinking skills while gaining self-confidence in managing a publication, from the early brainstorming days to final distribution. Through a monthly publication like this, students can help shape the community's perception of its immigrant members.

Honoring Experience

Experience is the best teacher. By focusing on their own experi- 30 ence, students can "claim a knowledge base from which they can speak" (Scrapp, in hooks, 1994, p. 148). By honoring the complexity of language and culture as well as the tenacious spirit that Latino students bring to the classroom, schools can teach to Latino students' strengths. This will not only enrich our lessons, but also our schools, our communities, and our world.

As they try to untangle who they really are, both ethnically 31 and individually, Latino students often have much to say.

Latino students can easily experience U.S. culture as an 32 onslaught of materialism, television, pop culture, and technology.

Creating leadership opportunities for Latino students is a nat- 33 ural outgrowth of any approach that capitalizes on student strengths.

References

Benard, B. (2004). *Resiliency: What we have learned.* San Francisco: West Ed.

Collier, V. (1995). *Promoting academic success for ESL students.* NJ: Teachers of Other Languages.

Cummins, J. (2000). *Beyond adversarial discourse: Searching for a common ground in the education of bilingual students.* In C. Ovando & P. McLaren (Eds.), *Multiculturalism and bilingual education.* Boston: McGraw Hill.

Freire, P. (2000). *Pedagogy of the oppressed.* New York: Continuum.
hooks, b. (1994). *Teaching to transgress: Education as the practice of freedom.* New York: Routledge Press.
Osterling, J. P., Violand-Sánchez, E., & von Vacano, M. (1999, October). Latino families learning together. *Educational Leadership,* 57(2), 64–68.
Rodriguez, C. (2006, April 4). "Illegal" as a noun breaks law of reason. *Denver Post.*
Tienda, M., & Mitchell, F. (Eds.). (2006). *Hispanics and the future of America.* Washington, DC: National Academies Press.
Valenzuela, A. (1999). *Subtractive schooling.* New York: SUNY Press.

Helen Zia

From Nothing, a Consciousness

A second-generation Chinese-American, Helen Zia is an author, civil rights activist, and journalist who served as Executive Editor of *Ms.* magazine. She is the coauthor of *My Country Versus Me* (2002), an account of the false arrest of a Los Alamos scientist accused of being a spy for China and of *Asian American Dreams: The Emergence of an American People* (2001), from which the follow essay is excerpted. In this piece, Zia explores identity issues related to her name, her education, and to queries about where she is "from"—an experience she suggests is shared by many Asian-Americans. As you read, consider what specific identity issues surround being "Asian-American," some of which might be shared by other racial or ethnic groups, and some of which are specific to this group. Think also about the ways in which Zia's discussions about her name might reveal the ways the status of members of particular groups changes, depending upon current events and U. S. relations with their countries (or even continents) of origin.

1
2   "Little China doll, what's your name?"
       This question always made me feel awkward. I knew there was something unwholesome in being seen as a doll, and a fragile china one at that. But, taught to respect my elders at all times, I would answer dutifully, mumbling my name.

3   "Zia," they would cluck and nod. "It means 'aunt' in Italian, you know?"

The Zia family in 1957: Dad and Mom with (left to right) Henry, Hugo, Hoyt, and the author

To me, growing up in New Jersey, along the New York– 4 Philadelphia axis, it seemed almost everyone was a little Italian, or at least had an Italian aunt.

One day in the early 1980s, the routine changed unexpectedly. 5 I was introduced to a colleague, a newspaper editor. Making small talk, he said, "Your name is very interesting . . . " I noted his Euro-Anglo heritage and braced myself for yet another Italian lesson.

"Zia, hmm," he said. "Are you Pakistani?" 6

I nearly choked. For many people, Pakistan is not familiar 7 geography. In those days it was inconceivable that a stranger might connect this South Asian, Pakistani name with my East Asian, Chinese face.

Through the unscientific process of converting Asian names 8 into an alphabetic form, my romanized Chinese last name became identical to a common romanized Pakistani name. In fact, it was homonymous with a much despised ruler of Pakistan. Newspaper headlines about him read: "President Zia Hated by Masses" and "Pakistanis Cry, Zia Must Go." I'd clip out the headlines and send them to my siblings in jest. When President Zia's plane mysteriously crashed, I grew wary. After years of being mistaken for Japanese and nearly every other East Asian ethnicity, I added Pakistani to my list.

I soon discovered this would be the first of many such inci- 9 dents. Zia Maria began to give way to Mohammad Zia ul-Haq. A new awareness of Asian Americans was emerging.

The abrupt change in my name ritual signaled my personal 10 awakening to a modern-day American revolution in progress. In 1965, an immigration policy that had given racial preferences to Europeans for nearly two hundred years officially came to an end. Millions of new immigrants to America were no longer the standard vanilla but Hispanic, African, Caribbean, and—most dramatically for me—Asian. Though I was intellectually aware of the explosive growth in my community, I hadn't yet adjusted my own sense of self, or the way I imagined other Americans viewed me.

11   Up until then, I was someone living in the shadows of American society, struggling to find some way into a portrait that was firmly etched in white and, occasionally, black. And there were plenty of reminders that I wasn't relevant. Like the voices of my 1960s high school friends Rose and Julie. Rose was black, and Julie was white. One day we stood in the school yard, talking about the civil rights movement swirling around us, about cities engulfed in flames and the dreams for justice and equality that burned in each of us.

12   As I offered my thoughts, Rose abruptly turned to me and said, "Helen, you've got to decide if you're black or white." Stunned, I was unable to say that I was neither, that I had an identity of my own. I didn't know the words "Asian American." It was a concept yet to be articulated.

13   Somewhere between my school yard conversation and the confrontation with my Pakistani namesake, Asian Americans began to break through the shadows. By then we had already named ourselves "Asian American" and we were having raging debates and fantastic visions of an America *we* fit into. But few outside of Asian America cared about our shadow dreams.

14   Gradually we began to be visible, although not necessarily seen the way we wished. Then we had to discover what it meant to be in the light.

15   When I was growing up in the 1950s and 1960s, there were barely a half-million Asian Americans in the nation. Of those, only 150,000 were Chinese Americans—not enough to populate a small midwestern city. We made up less than 0.1 percent of the population. Most of us lived on the islands of Hawaii or in a few scattered Chinatown ghettoes.

16   My parents met in New York City's Chinatown in 1950. They were among the new wave of Northern Chinese who fled China as a result of the Japanese occupation, the devastation of World War II, and the rise of the Chinese Communist Party. My father, Yee Chen Zia, was a poet and scholar from the canaled, garden city of Suzhou, known as the Venice of China. Like many Chinese of his generation, he had been a patriotic warrior against Japan, later becoming a newspaper editor and a member of the Chinese diplomatic corps in the United States. After the war, he decided to settle in New York, taking on various odd jobs— cabdriver, Fuller Brush salesperson, Good Humor ice cream truck driver.

17   My mother, Beilin Woo, was raised not far from Suzhou, in the metropolis of Shanghai. She fled its postwar chaos as a

tubercular teenager aboard the *General Gordon*, the last American ship to leave Shanghai before the Communist government took power. Her first task upon arrival at the port of San Francisco was to find a husband who could not only ensure her continued stay in the United States but also help her repay her sister for the cost of the passage to America.

Finding marriageable suitors was not a problem for women   18
from Asia. For more than half a century before World War II, several racially discriminatory laws prohibited Asian men from becoming U.S. citizens or marrying outside their race. The United States also barred women from China, India, and the Philippines from immigrating. The combined impact of these prohibitions created generations of lonely Asian bachelor societies in America. But World War II forced the United States to change such policies, so obviously offensive to its allies in Asia as well as to the thousands of Asian and Asian American GIs fighting for America. The shameful citizenship laws were eventually repealed and women like my mother gained entry into the country.

Among the many Chinese American men who courted my   19
mother at her boardinghouse near San Francisco's Chinatown was a bank clerk who had come all the way from New York City in search of a wife. His jovial disposition and stable job appealed to her, even though he said he was forty years old. They were married in Reno, Nevada, on October 31, 1949. My twenty-year-old mother was on her way to New York as Mrs. John Yee.

Communicating with her new husband, however, was not   20
easy. Like the vast majority of Chinese in America at that time, he was from Canton Province, a thousand miles away from Shanghai. The language, customs, and even facial features of the regions' peoples were different. Their local Chinese dialects of Shanghainese and Cantonese were unintelligible to each other. Cantonese people were considered more easygoing, lighthearted in spirit and darker in complexion, while Northern Chinese were taller and thought to be arrogant and hot-tempered. To get around in Chinatown, my mother had to learn some Cantonese. In the meantime she and her husband communicated in a mixture of pidgin English and pidgin Cantonese.

They settled into a dank tenement on Henry Street, where   21
many new arrivals made their first home in New York. It stands today, with the shared bathroom down the hall and the bathtub in the kitchen, still home to new generations of Chinese immigrants. A year later, my older brother was born. They named him Henry, after the street. Had he been a girl, they planned to name him Catherine, after the nearby cross street. During the day, Henry's father worked a few blocks away in Chatham Square, at the Bank of China, while my mother found new friends. New York's Chinatown had only 15,000 residents in 1950, compared

to more than 100,000 in 1990; a tiny but growing number came from Shanghai and its neighboring cities of Hangzhou, Ningbo, Suzhou, and Nanjing. Bound by their similar dialects and regional cuisine, which were so unlike those of the larger Cantonese community surrounding them, the Shanghainese speakers congregated at the curio shop of a Mrs. Fung, on the corner of Doyers and Pell. That's where my mother met my father.

22   When Henry was still an infant, his father suffered a massive stroke and died. From his death certificate my mother learned that her husband was ten years older than he had disclosed. The young widow was eligible for marriage again in the Chinatown society, with my father in pursuit. Months later they wed and moved to Newark, New Jersey, where my father was trying, unsuccessfully, to run a small furniture store. I soon came on the scene, another member of the post–World War II Asian American baby boom.

23   On a clear day the Manhattan skyline is visible from Newark, but the insular familiarity of Chinatown was worlds away. Outside of Chinatown it was rare to encounter another person of Chinese or other Asian descent. In Newark and the various New Jersey communities where we later moved, the only way to meet Asians was to stop complete strangers on the street, while shopping, or at the bus stop—anywhere that we happened to see the occasional person who looked like us. At an A&P supermarket checkout counter, my mother met her friend Sue, who came to the United States as a war bride, having married a GI during the postwar occupation of Japan. The animosity between China and Japan that brought both women to New Jersey was never an issue. Each was so thrilled to find someone like herself.

24   Auntie Sue and her son Kim, who was of mixed race, white and Japanese, were regular visitors to our home. Though our mothers bonded readily, it was harder for their Asian American kids to connect simply because we looked alike. Mom and Auntie Sue had the shared experience of leaving their war-ravaged Asian homes for a new culture, but Kim and I shared little except for our Asian features; we stuck out like yellow streaks on a white-and-black canvas. Outside of Chinatown, looking Asian meant looking foreign, alien, un-American. The pressure on us was to fit in with the "American" kids we looked so unlike, to conform and assimilate. Why would we want to be around other Asian kids who reminded us of our poor fit? At the tender age of six, I already felt different from the "real" Americans. I didn't feel comfortable with Kim and sensed his ambivalence to me. But the joke was on us, because no matter how hard we might try to blend in with the scenery, our faces gave us away.

25   Still, I was proud to be Chinese. Mom and Dad filled us with stories about their childhoods in China. Dad was born in 1912, one year after the founding of the Chinese Republic, and was

imbued with a deep love for his native country. He was the second son of a widow who was spurned by her in-laws. His mother
sold her own clothes to pay for his schooling. She beat my father
every day so that he would study harder—this he told us proudly
whenever we slacked off. Dad modeled his life after the ideal of
the Confucian scholar-official: by studying assiduously he won
academic honors and scholarships and achieved recognition as
a poet and writer. China's system of open examinations was the
foundation of the civil service—a Chinese creation, Dad point-
edly reminded us as he turned the TV off. Studying hard, he
said, was a time-honored route to advancement for even the
poorest Chinese.

Mom grew up in Shanghai under the Japanese occupation. 26
From the time she was a small child she lived with a fear and
dislike of Japanese soldiers. Because of the war, her education
was disrupted and she never went beyond the fourth grade—a
source of regret that made her value education for her children.
Mom's childhood memories were of wartime hardships and days
spent picking out grains of rice from the dirt that had been
mixed in as a way to tip the scales. Her stories taught me to be
proud of the strength and endurance of the Chinese people.

Dad told us about our heritage. When other children made 27
fun of us, or if news reports demeaned China, he reminded us
that our ancestors wore luxurious silks and invented gunpow-
der while Europeans still huddled naked in caves. Of course, I
knew that Europeans had discovered clothing, too, but the
image was a reassuring one for a kid who didn't fit. My father
wanted us to speak flawless English to spare us from ridicule
and the language discrimination he faced. He forbade my mother
to speak to us in Chinese, which was hard, since Mom spoke little English then. We grew up monolingual, learning only simple
Chinese expressions—*che ve le*, "Come and eat"—and various
Shanghainese epithets, like the popular phrase for a naughty
child—*fei si le*, or "devilish to death." Dad also expected us
to excel in school, since, he said, our Asian cranial capacities
were larger than those of any other race. Pulling out the
Encyclopaedia Britannica to prove his point, he'd make us study
the entry, then test us to make sure we got the message. He told
us about the Bering Strait and the land bridge from Asia to
America, saying that we had a right to be in this country because
we were cousins to the Native Americans.

These tidbits were critical to my self-esteem. In New Jersey, 28
it zwas so unusual to see a person of Asian descent that
people would stop what they were doing to gawk rudely at my
family wherever we went. When we walked into a store or a
diner, we were like the freak show at Barnum & Bailey's circus,
where Chinese were displayed as exotic creatures in the late
1800s, along with the two-headed dog. A sense of our own

heritage and worth gave us the courage and cockiness to challenge their rudeness and stare down the gawkers.

29   What Mom and Dad couldn't tell us was what it meant to be Chinese in America. They didn't know—they were just learning about America themselves. We found little help in the world around us. Asians were referred to most often as Orientals, Mongols, Asiatics, heathens, the yellow hordes, and an assortment of even less endearing terms. Whatever the terminology, the message was clear: we were definitely not Americans.

30   There is a drill that nearly all Asians in America have experienced more times than they can count. Total strangers will interrupt with the absurdly existential question "What are you?" Or the equally common inquiry "Where are you from?" The queries are generally well intentioned, made in the same detached manner that you might use to inquire about a pooch's breed.

31   My standard reply to "What are you?" is "American," and to "Where are you from?" "New Jersey." These, in my experience, cause great displeasure. Eyebrows arch as the questioner tries again. "No, where are you really from?" I patiently explain that, really, I am from New Jersey. Inevitably this will lead to something like "Well then, what country are your people from?" Sooner or later I relent and tell them that my "people" are from China. But when I turn the tables and ask, "And what country are your people from?" the reply is invariably an indignant "I'm from America, of course."

32   The sad truth was that I didn't know much about my own history. I knew that Chinese had built the railroads, and then were persecuted. That was about it. I didn't know that in the 1700s a group of Filipinos settled in Louisiana, or that in 1825 the first Chinese was born in New York City. I didn't know that Asian laborers were brought to the Americas as a replacement for African slaves—by slave traders whose ships had been rerouted from Africa to Asia. I didn't even know that Japanese Americans had been imprisoned only a decade before my birth. Had I known more about my Asian American history I might have felt less foreign. Instead, I grew up thinking that perhaps China, a place I had never seen, was my true home, since so many people didn't think I belonged here.

33   I did figure out, however, that relations between America and any Asian nation had a direct impact on me. Whenever a movie about Japan and World War II played at the local theater, my brothers and I became the enemy. It didn't matter that we weren't Japanese—we looked Japanese. What's worse, by now my family had moved to a new housing development, one of the mass-produced Levittowns close to Fort Dix, the huge army base. Most of our neighbors had some connection to the military.

34   At the Saturday matinee, my brothers and I would sit with all the other kids in town watching the sinister Zero pilots prepare

to ambush their unsuspecting prey, only to be thwarted by the all-American heroes—who were, of course, always white. These movies would have their defining moment, that crescendo of emotion when the entire theater would rise up, screaming, "Kill them, kill them, kill them!"—them being the Japanese. When the movie was over and the lights came on, I wanted to be invisible so that my neighbors wouldn't direct their patriotic fervor toward me.

As China became the evil Communist menace behind the   35 Bamboo Curtain, and the United States was forced to deal with its stalemate in the Korean War, the Asian countries seemed interchangeable. Back when Japan was the enemy, China was the good ally—after all, that's how my mom and dad got to come to America. But now, quixotically, Japan was good and China was evil.

Chinese in America were suspected to be the fifth column of   36 Chinese Communists, as J. Edgar Hoover frequently said before Congress and throughout the McCarthy era witch-hunts. In the 1950s, while Japanese American families attempted to return to normalcy after their release from American concentration camps during the war, the FBI switched its surveillance eye onto hundreds of Chinese Americans. My father was one.

Our mail routinely arrived opened and damaged, and our   37 phone reception was erratic. I thought everyone's mail service and phone lines were bad. Polite FBI agents interviewed our neighbors, asking if my father was up to anything suspicious. What attracted the attention of the FBI was Dad's tendency to write letters to newspapers and politicians when he disagreed with their views on China or anything else. Nothing ever came of the FBI investigations of my father, nor was a ring of Chinese American spies ever found—but I later learned that the probes succeeded in intimidating the Chinese American communities of the 1950s, creating a distrust of and inhibiting their participation in politics.

The FBI queries hardly bolstered our acceptance in our   38 working-class housing tract. Neighbor kids would nose around and ask, "So what *does* your father do?" It didn't help that my father had instructed us to say, "He's self-employed." This only added to our sense of foreignness.

Like so many Asian immigrants unable to break into the   39 mainstream American labor market, my father had to rely on his own resourcefulness and his family's labor. In the back room of our house we made "baby novelties" with little trinkets and baby toys and pink or blue vases that my father then sold to flower shops. Every day, in addition to doing our schoolwork, we helped out in the family business.

Our home was our workplace, the means to our livelihood,   40 and therefore the center of everything. This conveniently matched the Confucian notion of family, whereby the father, as patriarch, is the master of the universe. In our household it was understood that no one should ever disobey, contradict, or argue with the patriarch, who, in the Confucian hierarchy, is a stand-in for God. My mother, and of course the children, were expected to obey God absolutely.

41   This system occasionally broke down when my mother and father quarreled, usually about my father's rigid expectations of us. But in the end, God always seemed to win. Growing up female, I could see the Confucian order of the Three Obediences in action: the daughter obeys the father, the wife obeys the husband, and, eventually, the widow obeys the son. The Confucian tradition was obviously stacked against me, as a girl.

42   I found similar lessons in the world beyond our walls. Mom's best friend from the Chinatown Shanghainese clique had followed us to New Jersey, attracted by the low home costs and the fact that we already lived there. Auntie Ching and her husband opened a Chinese restaurant at a major intersection of the highway. In those days, there were few places outside Chinatown to get real Chinese food. After they had spent their own money to upgrade the kitchen and remodel the restaurant, business was booming. But Auntie Ching had no lease for the restaurant— and the German American owner, sensing an opportunity for himself, evicted the Chings and set up his own shop.

43   Our tiny Chinese American community was horrified that the Chings would be treated so unjustly. My cantankerous dad urged them to fight it out in court. But they chose not to, believing that it would be better not to make waves. Chinese cannot win, they said, so why make trouble for ourselves? Such defeatism disturbed my father, who would often say in disgust, "In America, a 'Chinaman's chance' means no chance." He felt that the Chinese way of dealing with obstacles—to either accept or go around them, but not to confront them directly—would never get us very far in the United States.

44   As a child, I didn't see Chinese or other Asian Americans speaking up to challenge such indignities. When my parents were denied the right to rent or buy a home in various Philadelphia neighborhoods, they had to walk away despite my father's outrage. We could only internalize our shame when my mother and her troop of small children were thrown out of supermarkets because we were wrongly accused of opening packages and stealing. Or when Henry was singled out of a group of noisy third graders for talking and he alone was expelled from the lunchroom for the rest of the year. Or when my younger brother Hoyt and the few other Asian boys in school were rounded up because another kid said he thought he saw an "Oriental" boy go into his locker.

Other times the discomfort was less tangible. Why did my   45
fifth-grade teacher, a Korean War veteran, become so agitated
when topics of China and Asian culture came up? Was there a
reason for his apparent dislike of me and my brothers, who also
had him as a teacher? After my Girl Scout troop leader asked all
the girls to state their religions, what caused her to scowl in disgust at me when I answered Buddhist? My family didn't practice an organized religion, so I didn't know what else to say.

Absorbing the uncertainty of my status in American society, I   46
assumed the role that I observed for myself—one of silence and
invisibility. I enjoyed school and, following my father's example,
studied hard and performed well academically, but I consciously
avoided bringing attention to myself and rarely spoke up, even
on matters related to me.

For example, there was Mrs. George. From second grade until   47
I graduated from John F. Kennedy High School, Mrs. George
was my physical education teacher. She was the aunt of Olympic
track star Carl Lewis and was always kind to me. But for those
ten years, Mrs. George called me Zi, as though it rhymed with
"eye." One day, when I was in twelfth grade, she yelled over at
me, "Zi, come over here." A classmate standing nearby said,
"Mrs. George, Helen's name isn't Zi, it's Zia." Mrs. George looked
at me and let out a huge laugh. "Zi," she said, then corrected herself. "I mean, Zia, how come you never told me how to say your
name after all these years?"

I didn't know how to answer. It had never occurred to me to   48
correct my teacher. In the Confucian order of the world, teachers were right up there with parents in commanding respect and
obedience. I simply had no voice to raise to my teacher.

getting into the conversation ···6

Racial and Ethnic Identities

1. Most of the pieces in this chapter of *Conversations,* because they deal
   with identity issues, incorporate a particularly narrative and personal
   style. That is, these pieces tend to tell stories, and to do so in ways that
   incorporate personal experience, individual reflections, and emotion-
   based arguments. In order to better understand the ways that authors
   frame issues of a personal nature, try to articulate some of the stylistic
   features of this form of writing. Look for common elements of each
   piece's style, demonstrating the ways that writers help readers share
   their personal experiences through their use of anecdotes, descriptive
   language, dialogue, and so forth. Then write an essay that demonstrates how this form of argument functions and its effect upon readers. As you do so, you might consider how this style is affected by audience: Is each piece meant for others who share a particular identity,
   or is it primarily meant to address outsiders, in order to help them understand the identity issues raised?

2. Clearly, issues related to racial and ethnic identity can be very sensitive topics, both for the writer and for the reader. As such, the tone of
   the author is crucial in expressing the nature of the conversation that
   is created between a writer and his or her audience. Analyze the tonal
   choices of the authors, comparing the intent and effectiveness of the
   tone of several of the pieces. For example, you might consider how
   Martin Luther King, Jr. attempts to establish a conciliatory tone, but, at
   times, is quite direct about the outrages that were endured by blacks.
   How does that tone compare to that of bell hooks as she addresses the
   concept of white supremacy and its causes? How does the experience
   of ethnicity captured in the pieces by Zia or Rodriguez differ in tone
   from those of authors writing about race? What tone does Amitai
   Etzioni use in order to argue for the abandonment of racial categories
   in his support for a communitarian agenda? Try to reach some conclusions about how the tone chosen is related to the rhetorical situation—
   the topic, purpose, and audience—of each piece.

3. While the term *minority* was once used to describe many of the races
   and ethnicities described here, the term *underrepresented* is now
   more frequently used. This term is meant to suggest that some groups,
   even when they are large, still lack access to power structures or leadership positions. (After all, women outnumber men, but still—many
   would argue—lack the power of men in our culture and are certainly
   not proportionally represented in government and other high-level positions.) Consider the implications of this change in terminology, and
   focusing upon one of the groups represented in these readings, discuss
   the ways in which personal identity is related to the positions that are
   held—or not held—by members of this group. How has the election
   of the first black president affected the identity of that group? How

might the appointment of a Latina to the Supreme Court change the identity of other Latinos and Latinas? What is the effect of having an Asian-American as the Secretary of Energy? Write an essay that explores the ways in which the personal identity issues explored by writers in this section might be changed as members of that group attain positions of power and authority.

4. While America has long thought of itself as a "nation of immigrants," conversations about illegal immigration and threats of terrorism have changed the way many Americans view immigration. This is particularly true for Latinos because the large number of illegal immigrants from Mexico is much in the public eye. Consider how attitudes toward immigration might affect the identity of Latinos as a group, and how ethnic or racial identity might differ for other non-white groups— including perhaps, Arab-Americans. Does the conversation about illegal immigration create particular challenges for those groups? How do attitudes toward immigration—and stereotypes about particular ethnicities or races—affect other groups? Do language issues (the terms used to describe particular groups) also come into consideration in terms of personal identity—and how people of different races and ethnicities are treated within our current culture? In what ways do the issues raised by Violand-Sanchez and Hainer-Violand link language with identity? Choose one focal point that helps develop the identity of a particular group, and use those identity issues to weigh in on current conversations about our immigration policies.

extending the conversation •••3

Opportunities for Reading, Writing, and Research

Although the readings in Conversations are organized into specific topic areas, they can also be used to start your research into other related areas of interest. The writing opportunities suggested in the following can help you extend the conversations across the various subjects discussed in the book—and beyond the book into research areas you might explore on your own. These examples demonstrate how you might develop the readings from this book into larger projects; you can come up with many more on your own. As you do so, think especially about how your major field of study or other interests you have can inform your research.

1. Although gender and race are clearly separate categories or lenses through which people see their own identity, it is also clear that our identities are multifaceted. That is, we might examine, as does bell hooks, whether the experience of being black is influenced by the experience of being a woman, and vice versa. Or we might note the ways in which the experience of being Latina—or any ethnicity—is different for a woman than it is for a man, as Rosie Molinary seems to suggest. Likewise, we might ask whether the experience of being male in the 21st century differs for people of various ethnicities. In order to explore this question, you might do some research on the ways in which identity is affected by the multiple categories within which we might identify ourselves. You can begin by examining your own identity and the many ways you might describe yourself. Then, after doing some research on the various stereotypes surrounding your own backgrounds and some research about your own heritage, develop a personal essay that examines the intersections of the various facets of your own identity.

2. Although identity is clearly a very personal issue, it is also the topic of much of the work of philosophers, psychologists, and other social scientists. That is, identity is not only the topic of personal essays, but also of academic and scholarly research. Using your own major or possible major as a starting point, research the ways in which that field or discipline considers questions of identity. For example, you might look at how literary critics have studied identity as it appears in stories or poetry. Or you might study the identity theories of a particular psychological theory. Or you might consider how anthropologists study identity issues with a particular current or past culture. Then, using those theories as background, apply them to one or a number of essays in this section of *Conversations*. What might a psychologist make of Helen Zia's ruminations about her childhood? What would a sociologist or political scientist say about the attempts at amalgamation discussed by bell hooks? What would a language specialist say about the effect of words upon our identity? Develop a research paper that

extends the personal writings of one of these authors into a more academic, scholarly realm.

3. Although much of our identity is socially constructed—that is, the product of our individual and collective experiences of social norms—there is also much discussion about whether there are biological bases for the categories within which we find ourselves, and how finely we are able to define or parse out those categories. The recent work done through the Human Genome Project, for example, has called into question whether the category of race even exists in genetic terms. Some biologists question whether the division of people into two and only two genders is accurate, suggesting that gender (and even sex) is a continuum with gradations rather than sharp divisions. In order to provide further context for the discussions of race and gender in this part of *Conversations,* research current scientific findings about gender and race, developing an essay that details the ways in which one particular area of scientific inquiry attempts to address whether societal racial and gender categories are in keeping with the actual physical make-up of human beings.

Conversations About Love Relationships and Marriage

Introduction

Among the many things that make us human, motivate our daily lives, and bring us fulfillment, our love relationships are clearly among the most central. But how we define love and the nature of the relationships we seek vary widely from individual to individual and from culture to culture. Those cultural values and norms are negotiated in groups, groups that come together with shared (and disputed) religious and moral norms, with shared interests in gender roles and equality, with shared beliefs about the relative importance of the individual versus the couple or the collective, and with shared beliefs about family, ethnic, or regional norms. So, although love relationships are perhaps the most individual of concepts, we converse a great deal about them, both for personal and public reasons. This part of *Conversations* will help you listen in on some of those dialogues and find a place amidst them.

The nature of love relationships and marriage puts them at the intersection of tradition and change. On one hand, the norms associated with how one interacts with one's partner and how partnered people interact with the larger culture are deeply traditional. There are many expectations of what it means to be a supportive partner, what constitutes healthy and fulfilling sexual practices, and how committed love and family is celebrated through marriage and the ceremony surrounding it. Through these cultural values, we learn about the expectations about how we are to relate to our loved ones. Those traditions and values are deeply engrained within our culture and passed down from generation to generation. On the other hand, each new generation and each shift in the larger culture brings with it many discussions: whether "mixed marriages" (a term that has been used to refer to both race and religion) are supported, whether sexual relations are to be reserved for committed relationships, whether marriage is only between one man and one women, and even whether being in a long-term relationship is the ideal, just to name a few. The readings in these two chapters of *Conversations* form a dialogue between the forces of tradition and those of change.

The readings in Chapter 7 examine the ways that twenty-first-century love relationships are changing in a number of ways. In this chapter, you will find writers who are expressing their thoughts—thoughts that are sometimes informed by social research, sometimes by personal experience, and often by a bit of both—about the world of human love. This conversation goes from fundamental questions (Do we really need to be in a committed relationship to find fulfillment?) to specific practices. (How has technology changed the dating scene? Is monogamy the only, or the best, form of sexual partnering? Is "hooking up"—casual sex without commitment—a fulfilling and morally acceptable practice?) Depending upon your own cultural values, you may find the contentions and arguments made here enlightening, troubling, and/or no big deal. You may find the descriptions of current cultural values accurate or misguided. You might see these changes as tectonic shifts, or simply a reasonable evolution of values. As you read, then, it is important that you ask good questions, keep track of points of agreement and disagreement, and develop ways for you to enter this dialogue with your own further writing and research. Because so much of this chapter deals with issues that represent generational change, the readings will open up many possibilities for you to do primary research to test out the ideas that are floated here.

One of the driving forces behind changes in love relationships is the growing presence of technology as a mediating element in those relationships. This section's *Conversations in Context* examines the ways that love relationships have been influenced by—and lived within—our online lives and identities. Those technologies include some that are used in the service of actual, physical relationships—dating sites and the like. But they also include a growing tendency for those love relationships to be actually carried out online, with virtual contact largely or completely substituting for physical contact. Although this may seem to some as a poor substitute for "the real thing," many who are engaged in these practices find them quite fulfilling. As you read the words and images that comprise this section, you will be challenged to consider not only the value of such relationships, but also to consider how they have grown from a context that is so current that it changes daily.

The pieces in Chapter 8 take on questions related more directly to the institution of marriage. It first provides you with a few pieces that provide findings from social science research, past and present, about the nature of marriage as a social institution, and its potential to continue as a relatively stable practice. Although we all know a great deal about marriage from our own experiences, these pieces can help you form a more analytical perspective about this institution and its place in American culture. Then, the remainder of the readings allow you to listen in to more personal reflections on the experience of marriage from individuals who are facing its dissolution and who are (or are not) struggling to hold it together. This conversation can help you move from an analytical perspective on marriage back to the fundamentally private and personal facets of this topic.

All in all, this part of *Conversations* allows you to hear varied and impassioned discussions surrounding a set of values that are among the most revered in our culture, but which are undergoing a period of radical changes. For some, change means abandoning those values; for others, it means widening access to them; and still for others, it is the values themselves that need to change. Without a doubt, it is a conversation that will also ask you to examine your own values.

CHAPTER 7

Hooking Up: Relationships in the 21st Century

Jillian Straus

Lone Stars: Being Single

Born in 1973, Jillian Straus received a B.A. and an M.A. at the Medill School of Journalism at Northwestern University and is a fellow of the Woodhull Institute for Ethical Leadership, training young women in communications. She has worked as a television producer for ABC News and producing programs for *The Oprah Winfrey Show*. In the latter position, she interviewed hundreds of men and women about their love relationships. This work led to the publication in 2006 of *Unhooked Generation: The Truth About Why We're Still Single*. In this piece, published in 2006 in *Psychology Today*, a magazine meant for nonexperts, Straus explores another challenge faced by marriage in the twenty-first century—the conscious choice of many to remain single. As you read, you might consider your own views about marriage, and those of your generation, to assess whether the ideas here seem to match your own perspectives on love relationships. You might also consider whether men and women seem to share these views.

For 23 years—her whole career—Bella DePaulo built a stellar 1 reputation as the go-to expert on the subject of deception, the lying and the detecting we do in our everyday social life. She published dozens of papers, wrote scores of chapters and found a tenured professional home at the University of Virginia. At the same time, she was building a wide web of friendships, a vibrant intellectual life, traveling extensively and generally enjoying life as a single, unattached human being.

Research psychologist that she is, she also began collecting data on attitudes about singles in America.

2   Two years ago, she went out West on sabbatical. She liked it so much she chose to stay. Moreover, she was ready to put aside her work on deception for a while. "I decided to take a chance on writing a book about singles and not look for a full-time job," she reports. She signed on as a visiting professor at the University of California at Santa Barbara and teaches an occasional course.

3   Sacrificing her status, following her passion and taking a huge personal and professional leap into the unknown—"I never could have considered that if I were part of a couple," says DePaulo. "Even now I'm not sure it will pay off. But in a marriage, I would have felt that I was not pulling my weight."

4   DePaulo's own path exemplifies a seismic shift in the place of singles in American culture—in the lives they lead, in the way others see them and, more profoundly, in the way they see themselves. Not only are singles the fastest-growing population group in the country, most of us will spend more of our adult lives single than married. That hard demographic fact is rapidly turning singlehood into a satisfying destination rather than an anxiety-ridden way station, a sign of independence rather than a mark of shame, an opportunity to develop a variety of relationships rather than a demand to stuff all one's emotional eggs into one basket.

5   "Singlehood is no longer a state to be overcome as soon as possible," says social historian Stephanie Coontz. "It has its own rewards. Marriage is not the gateway to adulthood anymore. For most people it's the dessert—desirable, but no longer the main course." People may still be eager to meet a long-term partner, but they are a lot less desperate, she adds. Increasingly, individuals are finding singlehood preferable to being in an unsatisfactory relationship. In fact, the possibility of singlehood as a viable life path throws into high relief a finding that is slowly emerging from mountains of social science data—that neither the coupled nor uncoupled life is an automatic ticket to bliss; much depends on the achievement of meaningful life goals and quality of the relationships you create.

6   While polls show that men are warming to the idea of marriage, women are increasingly in a financial, emotional and professional position to weigh carefully all the trappings that come with the institution. Because they are more conscious of the tradeoffs—women still do more of the housework and childcare—they are increasingly unwilling, Coontz finds, "to put up with something that violates their sense of fairness."

7   Married-couple households have dominated America's demographic landscape since the country's founding. In the 1950s, according to the U.S. Census Bureau, they comprised 80 percent of all households. But married couples make up only 50.7 percent

of households today. Any moment now, 86 million single adults will define the new majority, some by design and some by default. While many are actively looking for Ms. or Mr. Right, most 8 are also busy leading full lives, including having children. Today, unmarried Americans make up 42 percent of the workforce, 40 percent of home buyers, 35 percent of voters. There is even an official holiday dubbed "National Singles Week."

Holy "Matrimania"

DePaulo believes the growing number of singles is the hidden force 9 behind what she calls "matrimania," the glorification of marriage and, especially, the cultural obsession with weddings. "Americans feel insecure about the place of marriage," she observes. "It no longer appears to be the only path to happiness."

Even as singlehood is becoming the de facto norm, people who 10 choose to go through life solo are deliberately kept in a state of confusion about their own motives by a culture that clings to the marriage standard. Typically, says DePaulo, singles are told that they are selfish for pursuing their own life goals. If you're single and you have a great job to which you devote energy, you're typically told your job won't love you back. Of course, singles are always suspect as tragic losers in the game of love. But most of all they are told through commercials, images and endless articles that they will never be *truly* happy and deeply fulfilled unless they are married.

"The battlefield is now psychological," says DePaulo. Single 11 women today have work opportunities, economic independence and reproductive freedom. "The things that can be legislated are all done," she notes. "The last great way to keep women in their place is to remind them that they are incomplete. Even if you think you're happy, the messages go, you don't know *real* happiness." There's a hunger out there for a new view of singles.

Still, we've come a long way since the 19th century, when 12 unmarried women were labeled spinsters or old maids and relegated to an inferior status. In the 1970s, a single Mary Tyler Moore bounced into America's heart with her professional ambition, dream of independence—and an endearing faux-family of coworkers and neighbors. Today television singles like Carrie Bradshaw lead such full, active lives that, like their real-life counterparts, they are sometimes ambivalent about marriage. As a 26-year-old account executive puts it, "I don't need a man in my life. I don't need or want a relationship because I am lacking anything. I want it only to add or enrich."

The notion that singles are uniformly lonely and miserable is a 13 myth, one that is dying hard—nowhere harder than in the psyche of singles themselves. There are countless singles living lives of "secret contentment," DePaulo insists. "They like their lives—they have friends, they travel and yet what they see and hear all around them is that you don't have a happy life unless you are matched up. I think it is hard for single people to fully recognize or say to other people 'I am happy. I like my life.' It is not even a part of our cultural imagination that you could embrace being single and want to be single."

14   The reality today is that being single is manageable and brings freedom, says Ellen McGrath, a clinical psychologist who is president of Bridge Coaching Institute in New York. "It could be the better choice." By staying single, you may be more likely to develop into your best self, says DePaulo, whose book, *Singled Out: How Singles Are Stereotyped, Stigmatized, and Ignored and Still Live Happily Ever After* (St. Martin's) is scheduled for publication in November. "I feel very emotionally empowered by pursuing what is meaningful to me, even if it is risky. When you are single, you have more opportunities to do what seems right to you without looking to another person for approval."

15   Many singles may be so satisfied on their own that they claim they have no desire to look for a mate. In a recent survey by the Pew Research Center, 55 percent of 3,000 singles reported that they are not in a committed relationship and have no active interest in seeking a romantic partner. It is hard to know if these singles will someday want a special someone in their lives, or if they are hesitant to admit they want a partner or if indeed they are satisfied with being forever unpartnered; but being single today is no longer necessarily a default position, as most were socialized to believe.

16   In her extensive counseling of single men and women, McGrath finds that a necessary first step for them to embrace their status is to reconfigure their own mindset. "Tradition tells us you have to be part of a pair. There was a time when that might have been necessary for survival, but it is no longer the case. Singles must actively update their mental files to see that being unmarried is just as valuable a choice as being in a couple."

17   Today, women especially have all they need to lead an independent life. There's no shame in having sex out of marriage. They can have sex without kids and kids without sex. They can be financially self-sufficient and purchase homes. Not very long ago, the "American dream" was all wound up in the marital ball. Banks, for example, happily accepted deposits from women but drew the line at lending them money for mortgages.

18   Yet sociologist E. Kay Trimberger has found that having a real home is critical for the single psyche. "Owning your own home is a strong cultural value," says Trimberger, professor emeritus at Sonoma (California) State University, who followed 27 single women over a 10-year period. Home ownership makes singles feel independent and secure, she reports in her 2005 book *The New Single Woman*.

As one real estate agent puts it, "Single women are delaying   19
marriage but not real estate." After married couples, they now
make up the largest segment of home buyers—21 percent in
2005, up from 18 percent the year before. By contrast, single men
make up 9 percent of home buyers, according to a recent survey
by the National Association of Realtors. Forgoing marriage
doesn't mean abandoning nesting: The concept of home profoundly matters to women, less as a place to do laundry, more as
a sacred space for personal happiness. Just as important, it is a
safe way to plan for the future.

So many women are buying homes without waiting for   20
Mr. Right that the building industry is adding design features
specifically to appeal to them (secure courtyards, more street
lights, extra closet space), offering maintenance services to make
upkeep easy and—reversing decades of financial discrimination—
teaming with mortgage lenders to help women qualify for loans.
Signing a check for hundreds of thousands of dollars can be emotionally daunting. But there's an immediate return on investment:
an immeasurable boost in sense of self-worth.

Builders find it takes a lot less to satisfy single men: A flat-screen   21
TV will often do it. "Men still see marriage as a way they settle
down," observes Coontz. Women settle down on their own. In fact,
they are often willing to go all the way and independently invest
in parenthood if no suitable marriage partner appears.

The psychological benefits of having a home are not limited to   22
purchasers, says Trimberger. "Whether you rent or own, decorat-
ing and making a home helps you feel psychologically rooted." It's
making a place that is not temporary. What's more, creating a
home helps singles build relationships. Reina, a 37-year-old single
woman, explains, "Once I invested time and money in my home,
I saw my family and friends more often because I was excited to
host dinner parties."

Work and Worth

Satisfying work is another component of a psychologically fulfill-   23
ing life, and it's especially important for singles, Trimberger finds.
"If you love what you're doing, it gives you a sense of self-worth
and autonomy. It makes you feel good about yourself that you are
engaged in something important." Work has countless other benefits. A sense of identity is chief among them, particularly for singles. "In our society, we value work, self-creation and autonomy,"
says the Sonoma sociologist. "Satisfying work provides a sense
that you have achieved something worthwhile."

Work also tends to supply important social networks, people   24
of similar educational background and, often enough, values
and interests. A single woman in her late thirties found herself
much happier when she went back to work after time off: "I had

a sense of purpose and a place to be. It gave me a reason to get out of bed in the morning and people to do things with in the evening."

25   Although work may be just as rewarding for women as for men, women still can't always reap all the benefits, DePaulo says. Single men who are highly dedicated to their careers and spend lots of time at work are generally viewed very positively in the culture. But single women are sometimes seen as "compensating" for not having a spouse. "Women can be blamed for being too hard-driving to be good in relationships," she notes.

26   Men and women alike suggest that the main reason they are fulfilled as singles today is that they have lots of company. "Most of my friends are single. I have plenty of people to go out with, travel with and spend time with," says 29-year-old Tom. Sasha Cagan, author of *Quirkyalone: A Manifesto for Uncompromising Romantics,* agrees. "There is an elevated importance of friendship for my generation. It has a vastly larger place in our lives because there isn't a wholesale rush to get married. You maintain a level of intimacy with many significant others. It makes singledom a lot more viable and satisfying."

27   The soulmate culture insists that one person can satisfy all your emotional needs, says DePaulo. "But that's like putting all of your money in one stock and hoping it's not Enron." Marriage today forces many people to put their friendships on the back burner. Singles, on the other hand, are free to develop deeper relationships with their friends without fear that they are betraying closeness. The flip side is that singles have to be more proactive about building their social lives; it takes an effort.

28   "Single people are more likely to have a good relationship investment strategy. They tend to have a diversified portfolio of relationships—friends, siblings, colleagues—and to value a number of them," says DePaulo. "They have not invested their entire emotional capital in one person." Having a broad social network is physiologically as well as emotionally protective, although society perceives singles as psychologically vulnerable precisely because they lack the built-in support system of a spouse.

Building a Better Self

29   A broad array of friendships also appears to be a developmental plus. "Having a number of relationships allows you to develop different parts of yourself and a more complex, autonomous self," Trimberger finds. Among women, Coontz points out, this development is more a return to 19th-century patterns, before "heterosexual pressures made close same-sex friendships seem suspect and even deviant." Beyond friendships, a broad social network

contributes a sense of community. Many singles without children feel the need to create connections to the next generation. "You feel valued as a single person when a younger person respects the life you have created," says Trimberger.

Where are singles more likely to build their social networks?   30
In 2006, the happy news is that it can happen almost anywhere. Some observers find that cities are easiest for unmarrieds to live in and form "urban tribes." Trimberger contends the suburbs are actually an ideal place to settle into life—single *or* married.   31

Comprehensive sex studies show that married couples have more and better sex than singles, but the unattached may actually have more exciting sex lives. Psychologist McGrath finds that single men and women are often more sexually adventurous. "They get more variety and learning from others. Because they are not emotionally invested, they can cut their losses faster and leave when sex is not desirable." In interviews with single men and women, I found that singles almost unanimously viewed their sex lives as more exciting than those of their married friends. "I don't think my married friends even have sex anymore," sighed Nick, a 30-year-old legal recruiter. DePaulo concurs. "It's erroneous to assume that just because someone has a permanent partner, his or her sexual needs are *automatically* being met. If you are single, you have to go out and find someone. But if you are in a serious relationship, you can still have issues with sex."   32

More and more, that someone singles find is likely to be a friend. "They're not even looking for another person to be their every-thing," says DePaulo. Coontz agrees, citing broad new socializa-tion patterns emerging in the culture, particularly a greater degree of nonromantic friendship across genders in which people are physically affectionate, though not necessarily sexual. It's most vis-ible among the young. "There has been lots of negative talk about casual sex for teenagers, who are emotionally immature," says Coontz. "But some casual sex is actually between friends—'friends with benefits,' in the parlance of the young—and that's probably healthy, especially among older individuals. Male-female relations don't have to be based on the excitement of insecurity."   33

While it has disadvantages among the young, an increasingly casual attitude about sex enables older singles to disentangle their sexual needs from other needs, Coontz observes. "You don't have to talk yourself into falling in love to have sex." That frees people to more thoughtfully explore other passions and drives. "People accept a wide range of passions in life—from food to gardening to the need to feel competent—and they don't all reduce to sex."

That may explain why middle-aged singles are especially likely   34
to enjoy their solo status. What's more, there are more of them—28.6 percent of adults age 45 to 59 in 2003, versus 18.8 percent in

1980—and they are often financially and emotionally independent. "A really interesting renaissance happens for people in their 50s," Trimberger explains. "There is more social support for settling into a single life." There are internal changes as well, DePaulo points out. "There is a perspective that comes with age. You may know the reality of coupling. You probably know other people who are living their lives rather than waiting for someone to transform theirs."

35   So the next time your mother points to a table of five beautiful women dining out without dates and wonders why they're single, smile and tell her the truth: "Mom, they are having the time of their lives." And you can add that the tables have been turned. It's marriage, not singlehood, that's now the transitional state.

Live Your Life to the Fullest, Now

- Don't postpone home buying or other major endeavors. See your life as something to totally engage in rather than as marking time.
- Travel now. It's liberating to immerse yourself in the experiences you want to have.
- Pay attention to basic needs for meaningfulness and competence. Companionship is important, but it's not the only requisite of complete and satisfied adults.
- Pursue your passions, whatever they may be.

Stay Connected

- Maintain contact with married friends. The soulmate ethic is no truer for them than for you—no one partner can satisfy all needs for companionship.
- Establish ongoing contact with the next generation through meaningful activities.
- Cultivate a broad array of friendships. Companionship comes in many forms. You don't have to pour all your energy into one person.
- Use the Internet to find partners for activities you enjoy.
- Remember that you're not the only single person enjoying life—there are many others who may think they're the only ones comfortable with their solo status.

Jessica Bennett

Only You. And You. And You.

Jessica Bennett is a senior writer at *Newsweek,* where she writes
on topics related to social trends, women's issues, and sexuality.
She has also served as a reporter for the *Boston Globe.* In this
piece, first published in *Newsweek* in 2009, she discusses
polyamory—relationships among multiple, consenting partners.
Although this trend clearly violates what many consider to be
the norm—the monogamous relationship—Bennett notes that
some researchers have estimated the number of "polyamorous
families" in the United States at more than half a million. As
you read, you might not only consider your own moral and
ethical views on this lifestyle, but also the ways in which this
phenomenon might affect larger societal norms. Think also
about whether these groups constitute "families," and how the
concept of a family has changed over recent years.

Terisa Greenan and her boyfriend, Matt, are enjoying a rare   1
day of Seattle sun, sharing a beet carpaccio on the patio of
a local restaurant. Matt holds Terisa's hand, as his 6-year-
old son squeezes in between the couple to give Terisa a kiss. His
mother, Vera, looks over and smiles; she's there with her
boyfriend, Larry. Suddenly it starts to rain, and the group must
move inside. In the process, they rearrange themselves: Matt's
hand touches Vera's leg. Terisa gives Larry a kiss. The child,
seemingly unconcerned, puts his arms around his mother and
digs into his meal.

Terisa and Matt and Vera and Larry—along with Scott, who's   2
also at this dinner—are not swingers, per se; they aren't pursuing casual sex. Nor are they polygamists of the sort portrayed
on HBO's *Big Love*; they aren't religious, and they don't have
multiple wives. But they do believe in "ethical nonmonogamy,"
or engaging in loving, intimate relationships with more than one
person—based upon the knowledge and consent of everyone
involved. They are polyamorous, to use the term of art applied
to multiple-partner families like theirs, and they wouldn't want
to live any other way.

Terisa, 41, is at the center of this particular polyamorous clus-   3
ter. A filmmaker and actress, she is well-spoken, slender and
attractive, with dark, shoulder-length hair, porcelain skin—and a
powerful need for attention. Twelve years ago, she started dating
Scott, a writer and classical-album merchant. A couple years later,

Scott introduced her to Larry, a software developer at Microsoft, and the two quickly fell in love, with Scott's assent. The three have been living together for a decade now, but continue to date others casually on the side. Recently, Terisa decided to add Matt, a London transplant to Seattle, to the mix. Matt's wife, Vera, was OK with that; soon, she was dating Terisa's husband Larry. If Scott starts feeling neglected, he can call the woman he's been dating casually on the side. Everyone in this group is heterosexual, and they insist they never sleep with more than one person at a time.

4   It's enough to make any monogamist's head spin. But the traditionalists had better get used to it.

5   Researchers are just beginning to study the phenomenon, but the few who do estimate that openly polyamorous families in the United States number more than half a million, with thriving contingents in nearly every major city. Over the past year, books like *Open*, by journalist Jenny Block; *Opening Up*, by sex columnist Tristan Taormino; and an updated version of *The Ethical Slut*— widely considered the modern "poly" Bible—have helped publicize the concept. Today there are poly blogs and podcasts, local get-togethers, and an online polyamory magazine called *Loving More* with 15,000 regular readers. Celebrities like actress Tilda Swinton and Carla Bruni, the first lady of France, have voiced support for nonmonogamy, while Greenan herself has become somewhat of an unofficial spokesperson, as the creator of a comic Web series about the practice—called "Family"—that's loosely based on her life. "There have always been some loud-mouthed ironclads talking about the labors of monogamy and multiple-partner relationships," says Ken Haslam, a retired anesthesiologist who curates a polyamory library at the Indiana University-based Kinsey Institute for Research in Sex, Gender and Reproduction. "But finally, with the Internet, the thing has really come about."

6   With polyamorists' higher profile has come some growing pains. The majority of them don't seem particularly interested in pressing a political agenda; the joke in the community is that the complexities of their relationships leave little time for activism. But they are beginning to show up on the radar screen of the religious right, some of whose leaders have publicly condemned polyamory as one of a host of deviant behaviors sure to become normalized if gay marriage wins federal sanction. "This group is really rising up from the underground, emboldened by the success of the gay-marriage movement," says Glenn Stanton, the director of family studies for Focus on the Family, an evangelical Christian group. "And while there's part of me that says, 'Oh, my goodness, I don't think I could see them make grounds,' there's another part of me that says, 'Well, just watch them.'"

7   Conservatives are not alone in watching warily. Gay-marriage advocates have become leery of public association with the poly cause—lest it give their enemies ammunition. As Andrew Sullivan, the *Atlantic* columnist, wrote recently, "I believe that

someone's sexual orientation is a deeper issue than the number of people they want to express that orientation with." In other words, polyamory is a choice; homosexuality is not. It's these dynamics that have made polyamory, as longtime poly advocate Anita Wagner puts it, "the political football in the culture war as it relates to same-sex marriage."

Polys themselves are not visibly crusading for their civil rights.   8 But there is one policy issue rousing concern: legal precedents concerning their ability to parent. Custody battles among poly parents are not uncommon; the most public of them was a 1999 case in which a 22-year-old Tennessee woman lost rights to parent her daughter after outing herself on an MTV documentary. Anecdotally, research shows that children can do well in poly families—as long as they're in a stable home with loving parents, says Elisabeth Sheff, a sociologist at Georgia State University, who is conducting the first large-scale study of children of poly parents, which has been ongoing for a decade. But because academia is only beginning to study the phenomenon—Sheff's study is too recent to have drawn conclusions about the children's well-being over time—there is little data to support that notion in court. Today, the nonprofit Polyamory Society posts a warning to parents on its Web site: *If your PolyFamily has children, please do not put your children and family at risk by coming out to the public or by being interviewed [by] the press!*

The notion of multiple-partner relationships is as old as the   9 human race itself. But polyamorists trace the foundation of their movement to the utopian Oneida commune of upstate New York, founded in 1848 by Yale theologian John Humphrey Noyes. Noyes believed in a kind of communalism he hoped would fix relations between men and women; both genders had equal voice in community governance, and every man was considered to be married to every woman. But it wasn't until the late-1960s and 1970s "free love" movement that polyamory truly came into vogue; when books like *Open Marriage* topped best-seller lists and groups like the North American Swingers Club began experimenting with the concept. The term "polyamory," coined in the 1990s, popped up in both the Merriam-Webster and Oxford English dictionaries in 2006.

Polyamory might sound like heaven to some: a variety of part-   10 ners, adding spice and a respite from the familiarity and boredom that's doomed many a traditional couple. But humans are hard-wired to be jealous, and though it may be possible to overcome it, polyamorous couples are "fighting Mother Nature" when they try, says biological anthropologist Helen Fisher, a professor at Rutgers University who has long studied the chemistry of love. Polys say they aren't so much denying their biological instincts as insisting they can work around them—through open communication, patience, and honesty. Polys call this process "compersion"—or learning to find personal fulfillment in the emotional and sexual satisfaction of your partner, even if you're not the one doing the satisfying. "It's about making sure that *everybody's* needs are met, including your own," says Terisa. "And that's not always easy, but it's part of the fun."

11   It's complicated, to say the least: tending to the needs of multiple partners, figuring out what to tell the kids, making sure that nobody's feelings are hurt. "I like to call it poly*agony*," jokes Haslam, the Kinsey researcher, who is himself polyamorous. "It works for some perfectly, and for others it's a f—king disaster."

12   Some polyamorists are married with multiple love interests, while others practice informal group marriage. Some have group sex—and many are bisexual—while those like Greenan have a series of heterosexual, one-on-one relationships. Still others don't identify as poly but live a recognizably poly lifestyle. Terisa describes her particular cluster as a "triad," for the number of people involved, and a "vee" for its organization, with Terisa at the center (the point of the V) and her two primary partners, Scott and Larry (who are not intimate with each other) as the tips of each arm. Other poly vocabulary exists, too: "spice" is the plural of "spouse"; "polygeometry" is how a polyamorous group describes their connections; "polyfidelitous" refers to folks who don't date outside their menage; and a "quad" is a four-member poly group.

13   It's easy to dismiss polyamory as a kind of frat-house fantasy gone wild. But in truth, the community has a decidedly feminist bent: women have been central to its creation, and "gender equality" is a publicly recognized tenet of the practice. Terisa herself is proof of that proposition, as the center of her cluster. She, Scott, and Larry have all been polyamorous since meeting in the Bay Area in the '90s, where they were all involved with the same theater community.

14   Terisa and Scott started dating first. Both were getting out of long-term monogamous relationships—Terisa had been married for six years—and knew they wanted something different. They fell in love, and though they were committed, they began dating around. Two years in, Scott introduced her to Larry, a pit violinist and mutual acquaintance. When Larry was offered the Microsoft job in Seattle, he asked Terisa and Scott to go with him. "We were like, 'Wow, are we really going to do this?'" Terisa remembers. "And we sort of just said, 'Well let's jump in!'"

15   It wasn't long before they realized there was a thriving community of Seattleites living the same way. There were local outings, monthly poly potlucks, and a Sea-Poly e-mail list that served to keep everyone informed. Larry even found a poly club for Microsoft employees—listed openly on the company's internal Website. (Microsoft declined to comment on the message board, or whether it still exists.) The trio has been together ever since, and they share a lakeside home in Seattle's Mt. Baker neighborhood, where they have a vegetable garden and three dogs. They often go

on walks along the lake, hand in hand in hand. "I think if we were all given a choice, everyone would choose some form of open relationship," Scott explains, sitting in the family's hillside gazebo overlooking Lake Washington. "And I just like variety," Terisa chimes in, laughing. "I get bored!"

The trio have had emotional moments. Scott had a hard time 16 the first time he heard Larry called Terisa "sweetie" nine years ago. Larry was nervous when Terisa began semiseriously dating somebody outside the group. There are times when Scott has had to put up with hearing his girlfriend have sex with someone else in the home they share. And there have been moments when each of them have felt neglected in their own way. But they agreed early on that they weren't going to be sexually monogamous, and they are open about their affairs. "So it's not as if anybody is betraying anybody else's trust," says Larry.

There are, of course, some things that are personal. "Terisa 17 doesn't tell me a lot of the private stuff between her and Matt, and I respect that," says Scott. When there are twinges of jealousy, they talk them out—by getting to the root of what's causing the feeling. "It's one of those things that sounds really basic, but I think a lot of people in conventional relationships don't take the time to actually tell their partner when they're feeling dissatisfied in some way," says Terisa. "And sometimes it's as simple as saying, 'Hey, Larry,' or 'Hey, Scott, I really want to have dinner alone with you tonight—I'm feeling neglected.' We really don't let anything go unsaid." As Haslam puts it: "It's all very straight forward if everybody is just honest about what's going on in their brains—and between their legs."

Larry and Terisa married last year—with Scott's permission— 18 in part for tax purposes. Larry owns the house they all live in, and Scott pays rent. Household expenses require a complicated spreadsheet. Terisa, Larry, and Scott all have their own bedrooms, but sleeping arrangements must be discussed. Larry snores, so Terisa spends most nights with Scott—which means she must be mindful of making up for lost time with Larry. Terisa and Larry only recently began dating Matt and Vera, after meeting on Facebook, and now every Friday, the couple bring their son over to the house and the three of them stay all weekend. Matt will usually sleep with Terisa, and Vera with Larry, or they'll switch it up, depending on how everyone feels.

The child, meanwhile, has his own room. And he's clearly the 19 most delicate part of the equation. Matt and Vera have asked *Newsweek* not to use their last names—or the name of their child— for fear, even in liberal Seattle, they might draw unwanted attention. Though Terisa doesn't have children—and doesn't want them—she adores Matt and Vera's son, who calls her Auntie. Recently, the child asked his father who he loved more: Mommy or Terisa. "I said, 'Of course I love momma more,' because that's the answer he needed to hear," Matt says. He and Vera say they are honest with him, in an age-appropriate way. "We don't do anything any regular parents of a 6-year-old wouldn't do," he says. For the moment, it seems to be working. The child is happy, and there are two extra people to help him with his homework, or to pick him up or drop him off at school. They expect the questions to increase with age, but in the long run, "what's healthy for children is stability," says Fischer, the anthropologist.

20   It's a new paradigm, certainly—and it does break some rules. "Polyamory scares people—it shakes up their world view," says Allena Gabosch, the director of the Seattle-based Center for Sex Positive Culture. But perhaps the practice is more natural than we think: a response to the challenges of monogamous relationships, whose shortcomings—in a culture where divorce has become a commonplace—are clear. Everyone in a relationship wrestles at some point with an eternal question: *can one person really satisfy every need?* Polyamorists think the answer is obvious—and that it's only a matter of time before the monogamous world sees there's more than one way to live and love. "The people I feel sorry for are the ones who don't ever realize they have any other choices beyond the traditional options society presents," says Scott. "To look at an option like polyamory and say 'That's not for me' is fine. To look at it and not realize you can choose it is just sad."

Sandra Barron

R We D8Ting?

Sandra Barron is a freelance journalist who lives in Brooklyn, New York. This piece was published in 2005 in the Modern Love section of the *New York Times,* a column that addresses issues related to current relationship trends. Told as a personal narrative, it addresses the ways in which new technologies have changed the idea of "dating." As you read, however, you might consider whether there are even wider implications for issues of privacy, safety, and the ways that technology has changed the ways that we relate to one another more generally—a topic that is at the heart of the *Conversations in Context* section of this part of the book as well. You might also consider how your own relationships have been affected by new communication methods such as text messaging and social networking.

T HE orange message light on my cellphone started blink- 1
ing as I was getting ready for bed. Barely an hour had
passed since our quick kiss goodnight at the subway, and
I was surprised to see the screen light up with the initials I'd
just entered into my phone. It wasn't voice mail; it was a text
message, and it made me smile.

U miss me? ;-) 2

I'd met him a week before at my usual Wednesday night hang- 3
out. He was alone but gregarious, and he seemed to be pals with
the female bartender—a tacit vote of confidence. He chatted with
my friends and me and then left with a wave from the door, and
when my friend Kate and I ordered our next drinks, the bartender
said this round was on the guy we'd been talking to.

Surprised, we debated his motivations. I insisted that perfectly 4
normal people sometimes buy strangers drinks just to be nice.
Kate thought he was way too aggressive.

When I saw him at the bar the next Wednesday, I thanked him 5
for the drink. He asked if he could take me to dinner sometime; I
said I'd think about it. He walked me to the subway and we
exchanged numbers, but I thought it would be days before I heard
from him, if ever, making this late-night text message all the more
unexpected.

I like text messages. They fill an ever-narrowing gap in modern 6
communication tools, combining the immediacy of a phone call
with the convenience of an answering machine message and the
premeditation of e-mail. And if they happen to be from a crush
and pop up late at night, they have the giddy re-readability of a
note left on a pillow.

So did I miss him? Certainly not yet. But I was flying from 7
New York to West Virginia in the morning for work; maybe I'd
miss him while I was away? I could already hear my friends citing his enthusiasm as evidence he was coming on too strong,
but I'd had enough of aloof. I found his boldness refreshing.

Before I turned out the light and snapped the phone into its 8
charger, I allowed myself one more grin at his message and a gri-
mace at his middle-school style ("U"? A winking smiley face?).
Then I deleted it.

He called the next afternoon while I was grounded in Pittsburgh 9
between flights. He kept me company while I ambled down moving walkways and wandered through a loop of food courts. We
talked about work for the first time; he said he worked intense
hours as a freelancer so he could take months off at a time to
travel, and he showed he had been paying attention by asking me
about things we had discussed at the bar. He asked if we could
have dinner when I got back to town, and I said sure.

A few hours later, as the prop plane taxied toward the gate in 10
West Virginia, I turned on my phone and an animated lighthouse
beacon indicated that it was searching for a signal. For three days,

the light swept the dark cartoon sea in vain. Every time I saw "no signal" on the screen I felt unmoored and isolated. But as soon as the signal bars sprang to life on my trip home on Monday, that orange light flashed on and, sure enough, it was him.

9   Miss me now?

10   I'd missed having cellphone service, and my mind had indeed wandered at times to our airport conversation. But that degree of nuance was too much for the 12-button keypad, so I wrote, Hi! Sure. Talk when I get back.

11   This set off a volley of texts. Where did I live? What day is good? What about tonight? Tomorrow? We decided on dinner that Thursday and I finally signed off, thumb sore and eyes tired.

12   At the office on Tuesday, as the light blinked on again (Din in SoHo then drinks in the E Vil, and maybe a kiss), I wondered, Just who is this guy?

13   Google failed me. One time, armed with only a guy's first name and the fact that he sold sneakers, I had found his full details and photos online. But all I had here was a cellphone number and initials, and Friendster, MySpace and Technorati—the entire digital detective squad of the modem dater—were stumped.

14   I would actually have to learn about him the old-fashioned way, in person. Which is partly why, on a slushy, windy Wednesday afternoon, I liked his next message:

15   Dinner Raoul's 2morrow, I just made reservations 4 7:30.

16   I couldn't remember the last time I'd gone out with someone who'd made reservations.

17   Sounds good! I replied.

18   A message came back as I was leaving the office: Its better than good—u r with me! Maybe I'll stop by the bar 2nite.

19   So he remembered I usually went on Wednesdays.

20   On the way over, feet soaked and fingers numb, I knew that I didn't want him to brave the sleet just to see me, especially since it would be awkward trying to get to know him better while hanging out with people he had never met. And after all, we had reservations for the next night.

21   Don't come out in this weather! I wrote. Can't really hang out anyway, see you tomorrow.

22   His reply was impossibly swift for its length: I live 45 seconds from there and I would be doing my own thing. I am not leachy. Very independent boy I am. I may or may not, depends where the wind takes me.

23   Was it just me, or had things just taken a hairpin turn for the hostile? My message was meant to be friendly. Had it come out that way? Or was I reading him wrong? I needed to find a way to respond that was light, in case I was only imagining he was angry, but not flippant, in case he actually was.

24   I swallowed my distaste for cutesy abbreviations and tried: LOL! As you like, then. :-) I cringed slightly as I hit send; this suddenly seemed like a dangerously clumsy way of communicating.

Minutes later: Would u like me 2 stay away?   24

Oh, dear. At this point, yes. Wires were crossing that would   25
probably be best untangled in person, the next day.

Entering the bar, I waved to my friends in their booth and,   26
before joining them, whipped off a quick response, attempting
to be polite and clear: Yeah, I guess that'd be better; you'd dis-
tract me if you were here.

A minute later, after I'd settled in with my friends, the orange   27
light looked like a warning: 2 late, im here.

I looked up. Sure enough, there he was, talking to two girls at   28
the bar. He drifted closer and hovered nearby but didn't make
eye contact. By the time he came over and sat down, a full hour
had passed.

He'd clearly had a few drinks, and our conversation went down-   29
hill as fast as it had on our phone screens. He said that I'd tried
to "control" him by saying he shouldn't come to the bar and added
that he hadn't come to see me but to see other people. After going
on in this vein for a while, he suddenly softened and asked me to
"promise one thing": a kiss before the night was over.

I stammered that I couldn't make any promises. He shook his   30
head and stormed off, sloshing the beers on the table and sending a pool cue clattering to the floor.

Before I could process what had happened, he looked over   31
from his perch on a nearby barstool and smiled, winked and
waved over his shoulder as if we'd never met. My friends, wide-
eyed, asked what was going on. I wasn't sure, but I did know one
thing: reservations or not, tomorrow's date was off.

Not so that evil blinking light. Only half an hour later, with   32
both of us still in the bar, no, was it possible? Another message?

What was that all about? he'd written. R we still on 4 2morrow?   33

I deleted the message and put my phone away, hoping to erase   34
the whole encounter. Soon he seemed to have left, and as long
as my phone stayed in the dark recesses of my purse, I believed
that he was powerless to bother me.

But suddenly there he was again, standing a few feet from our   35
booth, smiling and crooking his finger at me.

I shook my head.   36

"I need to talk to you," he said.   37

I told him we had nothing to talk about.   38

Turns out I wasn't the only person who found him menacing;   39
within minutes the bartender took the stocky wine glass out of
his hand and told him to leave.

I hoped he would be so embarrassed that he wouldn't dream   40
of contacting me again. But the next morning the blinking
orange light seemed louder than my bleating alarm clock. Three
new messages. Mailbox full.

From 6:30 a.m.: I am done boozing for a while!! ;-)   41

From 6:38 a.m.: What did I do 2 upset u? Do u not want to   42
have dinner?

43   At 6:45, as if he had waited long enough for a reply: Anyway, 2 bad, I would have liked 2 have gotten 2 know u.

44   I liked the finality of that one.

But had he really given up, or was there simply no more room in the inbox? I deleted those three and got on the subway. I emerged to find: Pls forgive me and join me 4 dinner. ;-(

45   We are not going out, I wrote.

46   What did I do?

47   I'm at work and we're not discussing this.

48   Whatever, he wrote. U don't have 2 b ignorant. Peace.

49   I turned off the phone, dumbfounded. How had this happened? How had we managed to speed through all the stages of an actual relationship almost solely via text message? I'd gone from butterflies to doubt to anger at his name on the screen, before we even knew each other.

50   That was it, I decided: no more text-message flirtations for me. From now on I'd stick to more old-fashioned ways of getting to know a guy. Like e-mail.

Tom Wolfe

Hooking Up: What Life Was Like At the Turn of the Second Millennium*

Tom Wolfe is one of America's most prolific and popular living authors. Wolfe holds a Ph.D. in American Studies from Yale University and has served as a reporter for the *New York Herald-Tribune*. His bestselling books chronicle many key moments in American history and culture, including his examinations of the turbulent 1960s in *The Pump House Gang* and *The Electric Kool-Aid Acid Test,* and his book about the racial struggles in the United States in the 1970s, *Radical Chic & Mau-Mauing the Flak Catchers*. He is also the author of *The Right Stuff,* a type of ethnography of the test pilots who became America's first astronauts. In the piece excerpted here

*With a tip of the hat to Robert Lacey and Danny Danziger and their delightful book *The Year 1000: What Life Was Like at the Turn of the First Millennium: An Englishman's World* (London: Little, Brown and Company, 1999).

from his 2000 book *Hooking Up,* Wolfe explores the trends
that characterize love relationships of young people in the
new millennium. As you read, you might consider how
Wolfe's experiences in studying the "free love" culture of the
1960s and 70s might have informed this piece, and what his
tone tells you about the author's attitudes about new trends in
love relationships. You can also compare his thoughts on the
"hooking up" culture with those of the authors who follow in
this chapter.

B y the year 2000, the term "working class" had fallen into
   disuse in the United States, and "proletariat" was so obsolete it was known only to a few bitter old Marxist academics with wire hair sprouting out of their ears. The average
electrician, air-conditioning mechanic, or burglar-alarm repairman lived a life that would have made the Sun King blink. He
spent his vacations in Puerto Vallarta, Barbados, or St. Kitts.
Before dinner he would be out on the terrace of some resort hotel
with his third wife, wearing his Ricky Martin cane-cutter shirt
open down to the sternum, the better to allow his gold chains to
twinkle in his chest hairs. The two of them would have just
ordered a round of Quibel sparkling water, from the state of West
Virginia, because by 2000 the once-favored European sparkling
waters Perrier and San Pellegrino seemed so tacky.

European labels no longer held even the slightest snob appeal
except among people known as "intellectuals," whom we will
visit in a moment. Our typical mechanic or tradesman took it
for granted that things European were second-rate. Aside from
three German luxury automobiles—the Mercedes-Benz, the
BMW, and the Audi—he regarded European-manufactured
goods as mediocre to shoddy. On his trips abroad, our electrician, like any American businessman, would go to superhuman
lengths to avoid being treated in European hospitals, which
struck him as little better than those in the Third World. He considered European hygiene so primitive that to receive an injec-
tion in a European clinic voluntarily was sheer madness.

Indirectly, subconsciously, his views perhaps had to do with
the fact that his own country, the United States, was now the
mightiest power on earth, as omnipotent as Macedon under
Alexander the Great, Rome under Julius Caesar, Mongolia
under Genghis Khan, Turkey under Mohammed II, or Britain
under Queen Victoria. His country was so powerful, it had
begun to invade or rain missiles upon small nations in Europe,
Africa, Asia, and the Caribbean for no other reason than that
their leaders were lording it over their subjects at home.

Our air-conditioning mechanic had probably never heard of
Saint-Simon, but he was fulfilling Saint-Simon's and the other

nineteenth-century utopian socialists' dreams of a day when the ordinary workingman would have the political and personal freedom, the free time and the wherewithal to express himself in any way he saw fit and to unleash his full potential. Not only that, any ethnic or racial group—*any,* even recent refugees from a Latin country—could take over the government of any American city, if they had the votes and a modicum of organization. Americans could boast of a freedom as well as a power unparalleled in the history of the world.

5   Our typical burglar-alarm repairman didn't display one erg of chauvinistic swagger, however. He had been numbed by the aforementioned "intellectuals," who had spent the preceding eighty years being indignant over what a "puritanical," "repressive," "bigoted," "capitalistic," and "fascist" nation America was beneath its democratic façade. It made his head hurt. Besides, he was too busy coping with what was known as the "sexual revolution." If anything, "sexual revolution" was rather a prim term for the lurid carnival actually taking place in the mightiest country on earth in the year 2000. Every magazine stand was a riot of bare flesh, rouged areolae, moistened crevices, and stiffened giblets: boys with girls, girls with girls, boys with boys, bare-breasted female bodybuilders, so-called boys with breasts, riding backseat behind steroid-gorged bodybuilding bikers, naked except for *cache-sexes* and Panzer helmets, on huge chromed Honda or Harley-Davidson motor-cycles.

6   But the magazines were nothing compared with what was offered on an invention of the 1990s, the Internet. By 2000, an estimated 50 percent of all hits, or "log-ons," were at Web sites purveying what was known as "adult material." The word "pornography" had disappeared down the memory hole along with "proletariat." Instances of marriages breaking up because of Web-sex addiction were rising in number. The husband, some fifty-two-year-old MRI technician or systems analyst, would sit in front of the computer for twenty-four or more hours at a stretch. Nothing that the wife could offer him in the way of sexual delights or food could compare with the one-handing he was doing day and night as he sat before the PC and logged on to such images as a girl with bare breasts and a black leather corset standing with one foot on the small of a naked boy's back, brandishing a whip.

7   In 1999, the year before, this particular sexual kink—sadomasochism—had achieved not merely respectability but high chic, and the word "perversion" had become as obsolete as "pornography" and "proletariat." Fashion pages presented the black leather and rubber paraphernalia as style's cutting edge. An actress named Rene Russo blithely recounted in the Living section of one of America's biggest newspapers how she had consulted a former dominatrix named Eva Norvind, who maintained a dungeon replete with whips and chains and assorted baffling leather masks, chokers, and cuffs, in order to prepare for a part

as an aggressive, self-obsessed agent provocateur in *The Thomas Crown Affair,* Miss Russo's latest movie.

"Sexy" was beginning to replace "chic" as the adjective indi- 8 cating what was smart and up-to-the-minute. In the year 2000, it was standard practice for the successful chief executive officer of a corporation to shuck his wife of two to three decades' standing for the simple reason that her subcutaneous packing was deteriorating, her shoulders and upper back were thickening like a shot-putter's—in short, she was no longer sexy. Once he set up the old wife in a needlepoint shop where she could sell yarn to her friends, he was free to take on a new wife, a "trophy wife," preferably a woman in her twenties, and preferably blond, as in an expression from that time, a "lemon tart." What was the downside? Was the new couple considered radioactive socially? Did people talk *sotto voce,* behind the hand, when the tainted pair came by? Not for a moment. All that happened was that everybody got on the cell phone or the Internet and rang up or E-mailed one another to find out the spelling of the new wife's first name, because it was always some name like Serena and nobody was sure how to spell it. Once that was written down in the little red Scully & Scully address book that was so popular among people of means, the lemon tart and her big CEO catch were invited to all the parties, as though nothing had happened.

Meanwhile, sexual stimuli bombarded the young so incessantly 9 and intensely they were inflamed with a randy itch long before reaching puberty. At puberty the dams, if any were left, burst. In the nineteenth century, entire shelves used to be filled with novels whose stories turned on the need for women, such as Anna Karenina or Madame Bovary, to remain chaste or to maintain a façade of chastity. In the year 2000, a Tolstoy or a Flaubert wouldn't have stood a chance in the United States. From age thirteen, American girls were under pressure to maintain a façade of sexual experience and sophistication. Among girls, "virgin" was a term of contempt. The old term "dating"—referring to a practice in which a boy asked a girl out for the evening and took her to the movies or dinner—was now deader than "proletariat" or "pornography" or "perversion." In junior high school, high school, and college, girls headed out in packs in the evening, and boys headed out in packs, hoping to meet each other fortuitously. If they met and some girl liked the looks of some boy, she would give him the nod, or he would give her the nod, and the two of them would retire to a halfway-private room and "hook up."

"Hooking up" was a term known in the year 2000 to almost 10 every American child over the age of nine, but to only a relatively small percentage of their parents, who, even if they heard it, thought it was being used in the old sense of "meeting" someone. Among the children, hooking up was always a sexual experience, but the nature and extent of what they did could vary widely. Back

at the brilliant example the United States had set for the world as the third millennium began. And yet there was a cloud on the millennial horizon.

22   America had shown the world the way in every area save one. In matters intellectual and artistic, she remained an obedient colony of Europe. American architecture had never recovered from the deadening influence of the German Bauhaus movement of the twenties. American painting and sculpture had never recovered from the deadening influence of various theory-driven French movements, beginning with Cubism early in the twentieth century. In music, the early-twentieth-century innovations of George Gershwin, Aaron Copland, Duke Ellington, and Ferde Grofé had been swept away by the abstract, mathematical formulas of the Austrian composer Arnold Schoenberg. Schoenberg's influence had faded in the 1990s, but the damage had been done. The American theater had never recovered from the Absurdism of Samuel Beckett, Bertolt Brecht, and Luigi Pirandello.

23   But, above all, there was the curious case of American philosophy—which no longer existed. It was as if Emerson, Charles Peirce, William James, and John Dewey had never lived. The reigning doctrine was deconstruction, whose hierophants were two Frenchmen, Michel Foucault and Jacques Derrida. They began with a hyperdilation of a pronouncement of Nietzsche's to the effect that there can be no absolute truth, merely many "truths," which are the tools of various groups, classes, or forces. From this, the deconstructionists proceeded to the doctrine that language is the most insidious tool of all. The philosopher's duty was to deconstruct the language, expose its hidden agendas, and help save the victims of the American "Establishment": women, the poor, nonwhites, homosexuals, and hardwood trees.

24   Oddly, when deconstructionists required appendectomies or bypass surgery or even a root-canal job, they never deconstructed medical or dental "truth," but went along with whatever their board-certified, profit-oriented surgeons proclaimed was the last word.

25   Confused and bored, our electrician, our air-conditioning mechanic, and our burglar-alarm repairman sat down in the evening and watched his favorite TV show (*The Simpsons*), played his favorite computer game (*Tony Hawk's Pro Skater*) with the children, logged on to the Internet, stayed up until 2 a.m. planning a trip to this fabulous-sounding resort just outside Bangkok, then "crashed" (went to bed exhausted), and fell asleep faster than it takes to tell it, secure in the knowledge that the sun would once more shine blessedly upon him in the morning. It was the year 2000.

Matt Sigl

You Aught to Remember Blog Post

You Aught to Remember is a blog designed to count and describe "the 100 trends, fashions, memes, personalities, and ideas that shaped the first decade of the 21st century." Contributions to this blog form a type of virtual time capsule that speak to future generations about what life was like during this time period. In this post, signed as "Matt Sigl," the author explores the term "hooking up" and the implications of this way of describing casual sexual relationships, the "sexual politics" of the 21st century. As you read, consider how close study of the terms we use to describe phenomena can be used to better understand the nature of the phenomenon itself. As you develop topics for your own writing, you might also consider how key terms and their definitions can help you invent ways to write about those topics.

I n the aughts, one expression has surged in popularity, espe- 1
cially among the young. One expression embodied, in itself, a shift in the culture's sexual mores. This shift, I hope to prove, could not have occurred without the expression, the language facilitating the needed symbolic restructuring that social pressures demanded. Eventually, so common was the expression's use that it itself began to alter behavioral patterns, as opposed to merely accommodating them.

I am, of course, talking about "hooking-up," the aughts' catch- 2
all term for any casual sexual interaction. By deconstructing the subtle ways in which the word functions, we can analyze both how behavior dictates language and, reciprocally, how language dictates behavior. A dialectic analysis allows us to trace the evolution of the expression and its widespread integration in society.

Employing the dialectic concepts of thesis, anti-thesis and synthesis we can trace how "hooking-up" became such a dominant phrase in our collective vocabulary. In a traditional dialectic, within each thesis is a contradiction which leads to the antithesis—which then brings about synthesis.

What was the thesis here? As the 21st century approached, a 3
generation was coming of age that had never lived through the sexual revolution of the sixties or the gender politics of the seventies. Women were equals to men prima facie; they no longer

had greater pressure to get married than men and were actively discouraged from having children at too young an age. Concurrently, sexual interactions outside of marriage were by now the norm, safe-sex education and the pill rendering the activity consequence-free for those responsible enough to take precautions. The result was a society where casual sex, of one sort or another, was becoming more and more prominent.

4   And here we arrive at the contradiction. Even though social pressures were creating a need for loose and easily-disposable romantic detachments, the lexicon of terms to describe this variety of sexual behavior was wanting. Options of expression were limited and inadequate. There was a severity to saying that you "had sex." The disclosure was too invasive, too clear, too forward. It was even worse to "make love" when obviously you were doing no such thing. Expressions with a more casual feel were tainted by a misogynistic cant: *"Get laid," "scored," "hit a home run," "got some," "nailed her"* (which is almost impossible to imagine or make sense of with the opposite pronoun, continuing a tradition of male-centric slang descriptions of sex), are but a few examples. They all share a view of sex as conquest, a vantage point almost always masculine in perspective. Suddenly these terms began to sound as antiquated as "free love." There simply was no word to express the new sexual politics of the 21st century.

5   What kind of language would be required to accommodate these new social pressures? It would have to be gender neutral, for one; women as much as men were engaging in this casual sexual behavior, and it sometimes involved two women or two men. It would have to deflate the importance of sex, making the activity as mundane and routine as walking the dog or getting a latte. It would need to maintain a certain level of discretion, allowing people to discuss the topic without admitting much in the way of specifics. And finally, it should allude to easy detachment. "Hooking-up" was the perfect candidate.

6   Already an expression in common—though different—usage before the aughts, to "hook-up" with someone meant little more than to meet them in person. It was inevitable in retrospect that the word would get re-appropriated to imply, now almost exclusively, some sort of sexual interaction. This re-appropriation *was* the anti-thesis to the contradiction created by a vocabulary and social climate that were deeply mismatched. "Hooking-up" could mean anything from a stolen smooch at a party to full-blown intercourse. In either case, one was not inclined to press the point further and inquire just what a person meant when they said they had "hooked-up" with someone. "Hooking-up" was a catch-all; a phrase allowing people to both confess their intimate behavior to others and simultaneously reveal almost nothing. The verb "to hook" was the perfect symbolic image for interpersonal connection in the aughts. Hooking implies easy unhooking. Other verbs

in the vicinity carry with them a deeper sense of permanence: to link, to join, to latch, to meld. Hooking, with its intimations of tenous permanence, was the ideal metaphor for sex in the aughts.

As the phrase caught on we reached the synthesis point in the   7 dialectic. From first accommodating new social realities, the phrase began to proactively create them. "Hooking-up," as an expression more than an activity, normalized casual sex to such a degree that inhibitions against such behavior were slackened to the point of non-existence. "Hooking-up" became an expectation, a fully integrated aspect of modern life for the young. Language, not merely expressing our ideas, actively sets the coordinates of our social reality, creating culture, not just defining it. There needs to be a stabilization between external behaviors and internal representations of such behaviors, these representations being embodied by words and expressions. The relationship is a two way street. The important thing is that they not get too mis-aligned; such tensions, as seen in the early aughts, can lead to dra-matic change, both within a individual and society as a whole.

Does "Hooking-up" have a half-life in our collective conscious-   8 ness, or is the notion here to stay? I suspect the former. The syn-thesis of the dialectic that brought us to this point may itself be a new thesis with its own internal contradictions. The cagey ambiguity at the center of the expression—its failure to express much at all—implies a certain retrograde prudishness that we still hold with us. There is something dishonest about "hooking-up," something delusional. "Hooking-up" takes away the sex from sex, neutralizing its awesome power. We still feel anxiety about the broken down gender roles and sexual negotiations that the modern world foists upon us, unable as we are to inte-grate a truly coherent sexual ethos into a world where procre-ation can be accomplished in a lab and men and women share social equality (in theory if not practice). "Hooking-up" may not, in the final analysis, resolve this neurotic predicament. It's a temporary solution to a long-term problem: the human animal.

Laura Sessions Stepp

The Unrelationship

Laura Sessions Stepp, a Pulitzer Prize winning journalist, writes for the *Washington Post*. She is also the author of *Our Last Best Shot: Guiding Our Children Through Early Adolescence (2001)* and *Unhooked: How Young Women*

Pursue Sex, Delay Love, and Lose at Both (2007), from which this excerpt was taken. The book follows three groups of young women in high school and college, gathering information about their sexual attitudes and practices. As you read this account of the how the "relationship" has become the "unrelationship," you might consider how Stepp distinguishes "hooking up" from previous forms of casual sex. You also may pay attention to the ways that Stepp incorporates the words of her subjects within the text in order to make her explanations of the phenomenon more compelling, real, and effective—a technique that you might use if you conduct primary research that includes interviews.

1   U nless you've lived in a cave for the last couple of years, you've heard about hooking up, the most common way young people, male and female, straight and gay, relate intimately to each other, beginning as early as ages twelve and thirteen, and continuing into early adulthood. But what is it exactly?

2   It isn't exactly anything.

3   Hooking up can consist entirely of one kiss, or it can involve fondling, oral sex, anal sex, intercourse or any combination of those things. It can happen only once with a partner, several times during a week or over many months. Partners may know each other well, only slightly or not at all, even after they have hooked up regularly. A hookup often happens in a bedroom, although other places will do: dance floors, bars, bathrooms, auditoriums or any deserted room on campus. It is frequently unplanned, though it need not be. It can mean the start of something, the end of something or the whole something.

4   Feelings are discouraged, and both partners share an understanding that either of them can walk away at any time. Their behavior bewilders older generations, for they appear unhooked not only from guys but from our social expectations. Even those of us who didn't expect to find a marriage partner in college went there believing that our undergraduate years would deliver not only a great education but our first major, serious relationship, free of parental oversight. We looked forward to that. Young people today don't seem to feel that way.

5   So how is hooking up different from what we used to call "casual sex"? Casual sex always meant intercourse—and it was the exception in college even during the '60s, '70s and early '80s, when most of these kids' parents were dating. Social historians now say that the "free love" phrase tossed around in the early part of that period characterized only a small proportion of young Americans. More girls didn't engage in casual sex than did, and if

they did, they had to sneak around to do it lest they become known as promiscuous. With some exceptions, intercourse took place within a relationship that, at least on the young woman's part, implied some degree of commitment, and it followed several earlier stages of affection.

I was reminded of just how different things are today when, early in my research for this book, I was having dinner in San Francisco with a friend and her twenty-one-year-old stepdaughter, who had just graduated from a small state school. My friend was saying that in high school in the early 1970s, she "slept with" her boyfriend, "but only after going through the whole spectrum of behaviors, each of which signaled a new level of intimacy. We started with holding hands." 6

Her stepdaughter choked on the sip of water she had just taken. "You held hands?" she managed to say between coughs. "Oh my God, are you kidding me?" 7

None of this is meant to say that girls don't want to love and be loved, as Jamie did. But for reasons ranging from career plans to distrust of men, their prevailing philosophy is that love should wait, the result being that when, by what seems like accident or error, attachment occurs, they are torn up inside. Hooking up leaves them wholly unprepared for both the steadfastness and the flexibility a loving relationship requires. 8

To illustrate what hooking up can look like, let's return briefly to the dating that preceded it. A friend of mine, a Duke alumna in her early fifties, described a possible scene in a women's dorm at Duke early on a Tuesday evening in the fall of 1970: 9

The telephone rings at the switchboard, and a student operator, probably on a work-study grant, puts one finger on the page of the textbook she has been reading and with her other hand picks up the phone. 10

She listens for a couple of seconds and then switches on the microphone in front of her. "Susie Jenkins, telephone! Susie Jenkins, telephone!" Her no-nonsense voice sails through the dorm's public-address system, letting everyone in the dorm know that Susie may have a suitor. 11

Susie sprints down the hall to the phone at the end of the corridor. While other girls pop out of their rooms to make faces at her, she listens carefully and begins to smile. Frank, the frat boy in her European studies class, is calling to see if she'll go out with him on Saturday night. He asks if he can pick her up at her dorm at seven o'clock for dinner at The Ivy Room and later take her to the Sigma Chi party. She hesitates just long enough to let him squirm, and then accepts his invitation. 12

That Saturday, shortly before seven, she's in her room listening to the Carpenters sing "Close to You" on the radio when she hears the same receptionist's voice announcing, "Susie Jenkins, caller! Susie Jenkins, caller!" Susie asks her roommate to look over her 13 outfit—a pink-and-gray plaid skirt and soft pink angora sweater—before heading out to meet Frank in the lobby. She signs his name in the registry at the desk and reminds him of the eleven p.m. curfew.

14   As excited as Susie is, she's also slightly nervous. She has never gone out with Frank before and has no idea how the two of them will get along. She sends up a silent prayer of thanks for the curfew system, grateful for the built-in excuse it provides if she isn't having a good time or Frank is having too good a time.

15   If she and Frank hit it off, they will know exactly what to expect as they progress from one date to the next, perhaps getting a little more sexual each time, maybe going steady. They may find a way eventually to sleep together when Susie's roommate is gone for the weekend, but such opportunities will be rare. Even in the next decade, as curfews were lifted and dorms went coed, the majority of Susies and Franks would have agreed that the goal of serious dating—and sex—was finding someone you wanted to be with permanently, or at least learning what it took to play for keeps.

16   Now fast-forward to fall of 2004 and a country-style saloon called Shooters a couple of miles from Duke in a gritty part of downtown Durham. The last stop before bed on a student's drunken weekend binge, it features dancing cages, a mechanical bull and dark, recessed corners. On this night, the disk jockey is spinning the hip-hop song "Back That Azz Up," and on the scuffed wooden dance floor, girls and guys are following the order, grinding their front- and backsides with one or two partners, known or unknown.

17   A sophomore we'll call Lindsay arrives with a bunch of girlfriends, flashes a fake ID to the bouncer outside and within a few minutes is sipping Smirnoff and tonic. She loves to dance and, once her drink is finished, is on the dance floor in her tight jeans and off-the-shoulder knit top, moving her torso and long, tanned arms seductively with the beat. Sometimes she dances with a female partner, sometimes alone.

18   Somewhere around one a.m., she spots a guy in khakis and a popped-collar Oxford shirt, which he wears, of course, with the sleeves pushed up to reveal his tan, muscular forearms. She knows his name is Adam, and not much else, but she likes what she sees and makes eye contact with him. He joins her on the dance floor for a short while and gradually they work their way over to a dark corner where they kiss and grope. He suggests that they get in her car and drive to her dorm, and she readily agrees. When they arrive at her room, she asks her roommate, Tasha, to find someplace else to sleep—a practice called "sexiling"—and Tasha agrees because at some point, she'll want to ask the same thing of Lindsay.

19   Lindsay and Adam have sex. Adam, like many guys, keeps a couple of condoms in his wallet for times like this. Eventually,

he leaves. She has no idea whether she'll go out with him again or whether she even wants to.

That afternoon, a girlfriend asks her what she did the previ-   20
ous night: "Did you hook up or *hook up?*"

That's the beauty of the term "hooking up" for girls: It's so vague   21
that they can do whatever they want and not feel bad or even awkward when dishing with a girlfriend. Despite wanting to appear
cool, they may still feel like used goods after a night in the sack.
As one college professor explained, "Saying 'I hooked up last night
with this guy whose name I don't remember' is a lot easier than
saying 'I gave this guy whose name I don't remember a blow job
last night.'"

You've got to give them credit; they've come up with a vocabu-   22
lary that gives them maximum freedom. The distance between
what one says and what one means has never been greater. They
don't have boyfriends and girlfriends; they have "friends with benefits" or, to confuse classmates even more, just "friends." They
don't go on dates but may say they're dating someone. They also
may be "talking to" someone but not "having a conversation"
unless it's serious. If they declare themselves a couple and then
argue over something, they may "go on a break" and hook up with
other partners while they decide whether to resume the relationship. If they leave high school for different colleges, they may
declare themselves neither finished nor faithful but in an "open
relationship," meaning both of them can be "sort of seeing" someone else on the side.

When they actually describe intimate encounters, they do so   23
in terms of performance—and how well they perform—rather
than how they feel about what they're doing or why they chose
to do it. A girl will say she "teabagged" a guy, meaning she took
his testicles into her mouth. A guy will say he "had a roast beef
sandwich" if he went down on a girl.

Like past generations, these young people enjoy making up   24
words to describe the aspects of their sexual culture that only they
are meant to understand, such as "shack pack" (toothbrushes,
toothpaste and other supplies given to pledges by sororities),
"horority" (sorority), and the "roll and scream" when, according
to one female Dukie, "you roll over the next morning so horrified
at what you find next to you that you scream."

It's hard not to laugh at their colorful language, and equally   25
hard not to be a bit disturbed by the attitude that intimacy is
disposable. Teachers remark on this frequently. "There's always
been a lot of sex in college," says Harvard University psychologist Mark O'Connell. "It's the quality of sex that's changed. It's
increasingly disconnected."

Robin Sawyer, a public-health professor who teaches a popu-   26
lar human sexuality course at the University of Maryland, surveyed three hundred students, asking what hooking up means.

"My favorite response," he recalls, "was 'random oral sex.' I said, 'What the hell does that mean? You walk into the student union and say I'll pick every third boy or girl I see?' I've been teaching for over twenty years and seen a lot of pushing the envelope. This hanging out and hooking up has been a trip for me."

27   "Come on," some students say to such comments. "We use condoms." (And indeed they do, more frequently than past generations.) "Can't we just enjoy sex without grown-ups getting on our case? Sex without love may be meaningless, but on the list of meaningless things that are fun, it's pretty high up there." Two students in the sexuality class I taught at George Washington University, a guy and a girl, made this point one evening. Tony, a junior from New York, had earlier described himself as a "man-whore." Sacha was also a junior.

28   Eleven of us were sitting around a conference table in a small library. Tony began:

29   "There's a girl who calls me when we're both single, just because she likes to have sex with me. Nothing else. I could never have a conversation with her if I wanted to. It was just purely . . . the time is right to be havin' some sex. And . . . the next day I'll see her on the street and it's, 'Hey, what's goin' on?' And that's it."

30   He continued, "I was the one who actually stopped the whole situation. Because I was baffled. It was mind-boggling. I'd try to talk to her, I'd be like, 'Hey . . . wanna talk about something?' She never did."

31   Sacha picked up the discussion.

32   "I hooked up with a guy on and off for a year, and I don't think we ever had a conversation. Like, really, it was just, like, 'See you later.' And it was fun. I mean we both had a good time."

33   Several "Yeahs" and "Mm-hmms" were heard around the table.

34   Hooking up first surfaced as a sexual concept in porn magazines in the early 1990s. Within a few years, the term had made its way onto college campuses across the United States, starting with the pricey private schools. "Everyone here seems intent on hooking up as fast as possible," a freshman at Columbia University told National Public Radio in 1996. A year later, in 1997, a Brown University student told *The New York Times*, "In a normal relationship, you meet, get drunk, hook up." A major research project on gender issues at Duke, led by undergraduates and supervised by faculty during the 2002–2003 school year, reported that "students rarely go on formal dates but instead attend parties in large groups, followed by 'hook-ups'—unplanned sexual encounters fueled by alcohol."

35   Social trends such as hooking up may start with privileged kids, but they're rarely confined to one class. In 2000, Elizabeth Paul, a professor at the College of New Jersey (formerly a teacher's college known as Trenton State), surveyed 555 undergrads and found that almost four out of five students had

hooked up; half said they started their evenings planning to have some form of sex, with no particular person in mind. A study a couple of years later at James Madison University in Virginia, with 15,000 students, reported similar proportions, one at the University of Wisconsin, whose undergraduates number about 28,000, only slightly less. In my own reporting in the Washington, D.C.–Baltimore corridor, I've talked about hooking up with students on campuses as diverse as the University of the District of Columbia, a predominantly black commuter school, and Towson University, a residential state college just north of Baltimore.

Certainly, traditional dating can be found on campuses as well, 36 particularly those with active religious affiliations or located in the South. As Jessica, a student from Atlanta in my GW class, told me, "My girlfriends at Auburn, Savannah College of Art and Design and Georgia Southern seem to always go on dates and then date boys for longer periods of time." But at many other colleges and universities, dating is like an elderly aunt who sits alone and forgotten at the dining table rather than a lively guest next to whom everyone wants to sit.

Accounts in the late 1990s of hooking up in college were fol- 37 lowed by reports, first in *The Washington Post* and later in other national publications, that it had surfaced in high schools and even some middle schools, with girls as young as twelve and thirteen saying they had given blow jobs to boys. This shouldn't have surprised anyone: Sexual trends among older youths, once established, tend to be imitated by younger kids. At the time, little data existed to expand on these accounts because squeamish federal bureaucrats, who dole out most of the dollars for research on sexuality, had told surveyors *not* to ask about oral sex, anal sex, heavy petting or sex with a homosexual partner—in short, most of the sexual behaviors included in the catch-all phrase "hooking up."

Scientists in the 1990s did, however, start noticing a first-ever 38 decline in dating among high school students of all racial, ethnic and income groups. Researchers at Bowling Green State University in Ohio picked up something else as well among Toledo-area students: Of the fifty-five percent of eleventh-graders who reported having intercourse, one-third said it was with someone who was only a friend, not a boyfriend or girlfriend. Presumably, the proportion would have been higher if the survey had included sexual activities other than intercourse.

In mid-2005, a study funded by the Centers for Disease Control 39 and Prevention (CDC) gave credence to these unofficial reports of early sexual behavior. Figures showed that while the percentage of high school students having intercourse was declining slightly, those who did have sex were starting at a younger age. This was particularly true for girls—and tipped me off to the fact that in public conversations, we were missing a significant point: Hooking up—or more precisely, unhooking—might have been just a footnote in social history, the curious behavior of a promiscuous few, had it not fit so neatly into the new lives young women were creating.

Kathleen Bogle

Hooking Up and Dating: A Comparison

Kathleen Bogle is an assistant professor of sociology and criminal justice at La Salle University in Philadelphia. Bogle's recent research interests have centered on dating practices, leading to her 2008 book, *Hooking Up: Sex, Dating, and Relationships on Campus,* from which this excerpt was taken. As a sociologist, Bogle collects and analzyes primary research in ordet to draw conclusions about human behavior. As you read, pay attention to the ways that she uses her analytical skills to move from the evidence to the conclusions she draws. You might also compare her more academic method of writing with that of other authors in this section; in particular, you might compare the way Bogle uses her interview information with the ways it is used by Laura Sessions Stepp in the previous piece. Does Bogle seem to take a position about these practices, in the ways that Sessions does?

1   n *The Way We Never Were: American Families and the Nostalgia Trap*, historian Stephanie Coontz challenges those who lament the loss of "traditional family values" by debunking myths about families of the past.[1] Coontz contends that the images of ideal family life that many people conjure up resemble a hodgepodge of old television shows' depictions of a bygone era (i.e., *The Waltons* [1930s], *Leave It to Beaver* [1950s], etc.), which often misrepresent the realities that families faced during those time periods. Thus, sentimental views of the past are often presented using revisionist history. Likewise, many critics of the hooking-up phenomenon have compared it to the rose-tinted version of dating, emphasizing the deterioration of courtship customs since the glory days of the dating era.[2] This raises the question: How significant is the shift from dating to hooking up? In *Dating, Mating and*

Marriage, sociologist Martin Whyte states that "the topic of continuity and change in premarital relations is a 'blank spot' in the study of social change in America."[3] With this in mind, let's consider the similarities and differences between the traditional dating script and the contemporary hookup script in college.

Sex

The most notable difference in the shift from the dating script   2
to the hookup script is how sexual behavior fits into the equation. But it would be a mistake to assume that men and women in the dating era were any less interested in sexual interaction than those in today's hookup culture. In some cases, a man asking a woman on a date was a thinly veiled attempt to see how much she would "put out" sexually.[4] Therefore, one of the primary objectives of a date was the same as that of a hookup (i.e., that something sexual would happen). Although men and women in both the hooking-up and dating eras had sexual objectives, the timing has changed. With traditional dating, sexual interaction occurred after the two parties had gone on a date or series of dates. With hooking up, the sexual interaction comes first; going on a date comes later, or not at all for those who never make it to the point of "going out" or at least "hanging out." Marie, a senior at State University, discussed what typically happens after an initial hookup. "Most [girls] who hook up initially get a lot of bullshit, like a lot of guys will be like: 'Yeah, I'll call you,' but they don't. You know, so it might take them a while to see you out and then hook up with you more before they really, you know, want to like call and hang out."

Some college women I interviewed said they would prefer to   3
"get to know someone" before engaging in sexually intimate acts. The hookup script does not preclude getting to know someone prior to the first hookup; however, it does not require it, either. The dating script did require it.

The content of what can fall under the rubric of a "sexual   4
encounter" has also changed with the shift to the hookup script. Most college students during the dating era restricted their sexual experimentation on dates to so-called "necking" and "petting."[5] Oral sex was not a part of the sexual script for the majority of people during the dating era.[6] The sexual possibilities are much greater for the contemporary hookup script. According to the college students I spoke with, hooking up can mean "just kissing," "fooling around" (i.e., petting), "oral sex," or "sex-sex" (i.e., sexual intercourse).[7] Although "going all the way" was not unheard of during the dating era, it was not the norm. There is evidence that many women had sexual intercourse prior to

marriage, but most did so only with the man they would eventually marry.[8] In the hookup era, intercourse is not limited to exclusive, marriage-bound relationships. The hookup script includes the potential for a wide array of sexual behavior, including intercourse, even in the most casual encounters.[9] This represents a significant departure from what the dating script allowed.

The Rules

In the dating era the rules were clear: young people, especially women, were not supposed to have sexual intercourse prior to marriage.[10] Religious leaders played a primary role in communicating this standard to the American public. Since the sexual revolution, Americans largely rebuffed religious reasons for delaying sexual intimacy, and attitudes toward premarital sex became more lax.[11] For example, most approve of sexual intercourse prior to marriage, but only in the context of an ongoing, exclusive relationship.[12] Most of the college men and women I interviewed indicated that neither their religious affiliation nor their religious beliefs had a major effect on their participation in the hookup culture. Adrienne, a senior at Faith University, considered herself a practicing Catholic. She also indicated that her religious beliefs affected her day-to-day behavior; however, these beliefs did not prevent her from hooking up or engaging in premarital sex with her boyfriend.

> *KB*: Do you think that [Faith University] is any different because it's a Catholic school with regard to male-female stuff?
>
> *Adrienne*: Not really. I don't think so . . . well, obviously they don't like hand out condoms. And I don't think you'd be able, like I don't even know if you had a problem with your birth control or anything, I don't even know if you could like say anything to the health people. I think that might make people a little more like apprehensive to go [to the campus health center]. I mean you might have [some people who] come here that want to wait until marriage [to have sex] and stuff like that. . . . Once a year you might see a poster or something [that says] like: "Wait until marriage" or something. But it's not like anything else [is different than any other school]. Like [I said before] there's not condoms in the bathroom or anything like that. But I think the girls and the guys, they pretty much hook up, they just hook up the same [whether they are at a Catholic college or not]. Because I

5

think you can still be like religious, like I said before, I'm religious, but I still engage in like premarital sex. But I don't think that's wrong necessarily. So I think that's where a lot of people are right now.

The change in the script for sexual behavior on the college 6 campus is part of a larger trend toward increased premarital sexual experience throughout our culture.[13] In one of the most comprehensive studies on sexual behavior of men and women in the United States, Laumann et al. found that the median age at first sexual intercourse decreased throughout the twentieth century, particularly for white women. In the latest birth cohort, the median age at first intercourse was approximately 17 for white men and women.[14] This change, coupled with the increased age at first marriage, has led those who came of age in more recent years to accumulate more sexual partners than those in the pre-sexual-revolution dating era.[15] Changing times and circumstances have led to a change in society's standards regarding premarital sex. In the dating era, "waiting for marriage" meant delaying intercourse for a relatively short period of time. In the hookup era, men and women spend more time being single adults, so delaying intercourse for marriage has become an increasingly difficult standard to achieve. Therefore, in the hookup era, society does not strictly dictate that men and women wait for marriage, and any religious regulations to that effect are not staunchly followed.[16]

Although the contemporary ideal may be for intercourse to 7 occur only in committed relationships, on the college campus many students were willing to have sex under other circumstances when the ideal was not available or, in the case of some college men, when the ideal was not desired. The increased sexual possibilities with the hookup script may seem to create more options for college students. In other words, while those in the dating era were not supposed to engage in sexual intercourse on dates, those in the hookup era can choose to have sexual intercourse or choose to abstain (until they are in an exclusive relationship or married). However, increased choice has also brought about a sense of normlessness.

The fact that there are no clear standards has led to confusion 8 for students trying to decide when sex is appropriate. Many students believe that having sex is simply a matter of personal choice. The problem is that students' "personal" choices are affected by what they perceive "everybody else" is doing sexually. Unfortunately, students' perceptions are often distorted. For example, if students perceive other students as being highly sexually active under a wide array of circumstances via the hookup scene, they may not want to be left behind. This helps explain how virginity, at least for women, went from a "treasure to be safeguarded" (in the dating era) to a "problem to be solved" (in the post-sexual-revolution hooking-up era).[17] In fact, some college students spoke of virginity as something to "get rid of" to avoid being "known as a virgin."[18]

> *KB*: Do you know any people that are virgins?
>
> *Larry*: Very few. Very few.
>
> *KB*: How is that viewed? Is it males or females that you know that are virgins?
>
> *Larry*: I'd say I know both and it's very shady. People that are virgins I've found, I find out that they are virgins because they won't come out and tell you. They kind of seem a little shameful of it. They haven't "done it" yet, if you want to put it that way.
>
> *KB*: Guys are embarrassed about it or girls are embarrassed about it too?
>
> *Larry*: Both.
>
> *KB*: Okay. Is that something people would get teased about?
>
> *Larry*: Sure. Sometimes [people will say] like: "You haven't done it yet, what are you waiting for?" I've seen that before. [Senior, Faith University]
>
> *Rebecca*: I know a lot of people who just want to get the sex thing, well one person, who just wanted to get the sex thing over with. She didn't need it really to mean a lot, she just needed it to be over, so she could have her virginity gone, you know [laughing]. [But losing your virginity is] supposed to be a special moment kind of thing. [Sophomore, State University]

9   The lack of a clear standard in the hookup era has also led to some problematic behavior. For those students who believe "anything goes," college social life can take the form of excessive drinking and exploitive sexual encounters. In 2006, the media spotlight turned to Duke University when rape allegations were made against three members of their lacrosse team. Although this scandal held the attention of the public for a variety of reasons, it underscored the problem many college campuses face with regard to the extremes of the hookup culture. Regardless of the outcome of the criminal investigation, it was clear that members of this team were engaging in heavy alcohol consumption and creating a sex-charged atmosphere by hiring two exotic dancers.

It is this type of behavior that has concerned many scholars who have studied binge drinking, fraternity life, and rape.[19]

Students define normal sexual behavior relative to their peers.   10 Those who get caught up with certain groups on campus, who define their college experience as the characters did in the movie *Animal House,* might have trouble distinguishing the behavior of their friends from that of a typical college student. With no firm guidelines decreeing when, where, and with whom sex is appropriate, some students can engage in lewd behavior and think it's permissible because there are no rules saying otherwise.

What's Love got to do with it?

Along with the rule forbidding premarital sex, the conventions   11 of the dating script pertaining to the emotional side of relationships also wavered in the shift to hooking up. In the dating era, the script offered an opportunity for men and women to learn about their dating partners. While there may have been plenty of cross-sex interaction generally, going on a date represented a distinct time where the pair could get to know each other. While the dating script dictated that men and women spend "quality time" together, hooking up does not. Although the hookup script does not preclude two people from getting to know each other (aside from sexually), it does not require it, either. Liz, a freshman at Faith University, began hooking up with someone she met in the first weeks of school. Although hooking up continued for months and eventually led to sexual intercourse, it never became a romantic relationship. When Liz's partner began to show less interest in frequent hookup encounters and the sexual aspect of the relationship fizzled, she found that there was not much of a foundation for a relationship. Even building a close friendship was a struggle.

> *KB*: If you could paint an ideal scenario of how you would meet and get together with someone, how would it be?
>
> *Liz*: Well, I guess . . . seeing them at a party or something and having a nice conversation, realizing that we have something in common or that we seem to hit it off. And then, um, like maybe he would get my number and then we'd talk or I would see him on campus or something. And then we would hang out the next weekend and see where it went from there. I don't like jumping into things because that always ends up bad, I feel like.
>
> *KB*: Why do you think it does?
>
> *Liz*: Because you don't give it a chance to become friends with someone or you don't really know someone [if you hook

up with him right away]. I think that's what happened to me in the beginning [of this year] because we just jumped into it so fast and . . . we're just starting now to like become like real friends . . . Of course we were friends before, but it was more on like a physical level and now that it's backed off [and we don't hook up as often anymore] it's kind of like upsetting. Like I feel bad for myself, you know, that I let that happen. Like, I don't want to be like that. I don't want to just like meet someone and jump right into something because it doesn't give it enough like . . . like um . . .

KB: The time to develop the friendship aspect?

Liz: Yeah, yeah, things just like, yeah. I don't know, and when things fizzled with that person it was like: "What are you left with?"

12   Men and women in the hookup scene seem to have to work harder to build a relationship of any kind. Thus, to the extent that relationship formation is a goal, dating offered a better script for doing this. This point was emphasized by many recent graduates. After college, the men and women I interviewed became increasingly focused on finding a boyfriend/girlfriend, and in order to do so, most virtually abandoned hooking up in favor of traditional dating.

13   Getting to know someone, via the dating script, was also a way for men and women to ascertain whether or not they had romantic feelings toward their dating partner. Presumably, if feelings got stronger as the couple continued dating, sexual intimacy would also increase. Thus, in the dating era, there was some expectation that the degree of sexual intimacy would match the degree of emotional intimacy. In other words, two people would become increasingly sexually intimate as they grew "closer."[20] In fact, during the dating era there was a level of sexual intimacy deemed appropriate for each stage of the dating process.[21] Ideally, young men and women would initially limit their sexual interaction to kissing.[22] Within an ongoing dating relationship, necking and petting were hallmarks of the dating experience.[23] Sexual intercourse was supposed to be reserved for marriage, but often took place with dating couples once marriage was imminent.[24] These rules were not always followed, but there was a standard sense of appropriate behavior for each stage of the dating script, and love or a strong romantic attachment was a part of the equation.

14   Sexual intimacy in the hookup era is no longer as symbolic of relationship status as it was in the dating era. There is still a sequential pattern for relationships: hooking up, seeing each other, and going out, but it is not altogether clear what the corresponding sexual behavior is for each stage. Sexual intercourse

is expected in many of the "going out" relationships; however, it is less clear what one should do sexually in the other contexts.[25] The students I spoke with were vague in response to questions about when certain degrees of sexual intimacy were appropriate. Some suggested one should wait (at least for sexual intercourse) until "it feels right" or "until you can trust someone." Interestingly, none of the men and women mentioned love as a prerequisite for sex.

It is safe to say that in the hookup era the degree of sexual inti-   15
macy is often unrelated to the level of commitment to the relationship. In fact, many of the college students, particularly women, indicated that they were more likely to "go farther" sexually with someone during a hookup if they did not like the person that much or believed there was no relationship potential. This is not to say that romantic feelings are absent among hookup partners, but that the hookup script does not dictate an emotional attachment.

Walking the Line

Men's greater control has led to the sexual exploitation of   16
women in both the dating and hooking-up eras. According to Waller's study of the dating era, exploitation occurred when one party was more interested in a continuing relationship than the other and thereby she or he was willing to give in to the other's demands. Among dating partners during this time, women might exploit men by "gold digging," while men could exploit women for sexual favors or "thrills."[26] Therefore, in a case where a woman had stronger feelings toward a man and was trying to secure him, she might offer more sexual favors. In the hookup era, sexual exploitation continues to be an issue for women. Since hooking up does not involve men spending money on women, college men have no fear of gold digging.[27] Women, on the other hand, must be cautious about being used. Many of the college men I spoke with were aware that women were desirous of more committed relationships, yet men were often able to keep a woman as just a hookup partner.

Exploitation was an issue not just for women in some version   17
of a relationship, but for those seeking relationships, too. Throughout the dating era, women who had a reputation for "putting out" might be asked on dates by a variety of men, each having the purpose of seeing how much he could get sexually.[28] Certain women might be sought after for dates because they were defined as being sexually available merely due to their social class or occupation.[29] For example, student nurses were stereotyped as a "good time" by college men. Thus, college men sought dates with student nurses in order to "get a little" sexually.[30] Some college men in the hookup era who are interested

in accumulating various hookup partners do so by going after certain women, as men did in the dating era. For example, several college students mentioned that freshman males have a great deal of difficulty getting into campus parties unless they know one of the hosts personally, while freshman women are granted free admission. This practice increases the likelihood of upperclassmen being able to hook up with freshman women who are a target because they are naive about the unwritten rules of the hookup scene.

18   Like women of the dating era, college women in the hookup culture must walk a fine line between being exploited and being excluded. Those who choose to take part in the script not only risk being used for sex, but also risk their reputations. There are a host of norms to which contemporary college women must adhere in order to avoid being labeled a "slut." College women can be negatively labeled if they hook up too often or with too many different partners. Indeed, women must be careful not even to appear to be conducting themselves in an overtly provocative manner or they will be perceived as "easy." Kyle, a senior at State University, summarized it this way: "One night can screw up a girl's reputation."

19   Another pitfall for women is going "too far" sexually during a hookup. Many of the students I spoke with took for granted that it is a woman's responsibility to decide "how far" a sexual encounter will go. Lee, a freshman at Faith University, explained this attitude: "Because I think guys will always try to make [sexual] advances and it's up to the girl to go along with that or not. And I think girls are scared to say no and to say that they are not into doing that because they don't want to look stupid . . . But I think ultimately it is up to the girl."

20   In the hookup culture, college women's reputations can be affected not only by their own behavior, but even by whom they associate with on campus. For example, certain sororities on the campuses I studied were given nicknames having a sexual connotation. Similarly, an article in *Rolling Stone* magazine about Duke University quotes an anonymous blog entry entitled "How-to Guide to Banging a Sorority Girl," which ranks the women of the "Core Four" sororities on campus in terms of their attractiveness. The blogger contends: "I would include a ranking for sluttiness, but in general all four are equally slutty." The blogger goes on to say it may be difficult to have sex with women in one of the "hottest" sororities, "unless you are part of the lucky group of dudes that pass these bitches around."[31] Although this blogger's point of view may be more extreme than that of most students on campus, it demonstrates how college women exist in a fishbowl, for others to watch and judge.

21   In the dating era, women's sexual behavior was also scrutinized.[32] Women were permitted to allow some necking and pet-

ting, but were absolutely supposed to maintain their virginity. Advice books were filled with suggestions for women on how to conduct themselves in sexual matters.[33] These books suggested that women were responsible for playing the "gatekeeper" role during sexual interaction on dates.[34] The 1958 advice book *The Art of Dating* warned young women about what men really think about girls who go "all the way." It suggested that if a girl allows a guy to go all the way, afterwards he is haunted by the question: "If she went all the way with me, how can I be sure there have not been others?" It continues by saying that men do not want to get "stuck with a tramp" for a long-term relationship.[35]

Although the dating script and the hookup script differ with   22 regard to specific sexual norms, women's sexual conduct continues to be scrutinized in a way that men's behavior is not. Thus, the sexual double standard, which prevailed during the dating era, is still very much a part of the hookup scene. This scrutiny makes navigating sex and relationships in the hookup era difficult for women. Women want "romantic" interaction with men, but there are many pitfalls for them in doing so. The catch is that a woman needs to hook up in order to find someone with whom to have a potential relationship, yet her very participation in hooking up can mean that she is not taken seriously as a potential girlfriend, is exploited for sex, and/or is labeled a slut. Women of the dating era faced the same dilemma. For example, student nurses found themselves in a difficult situation because of the stereotype that they were promiscuous.

> If she is not cooperative and does not meet the college boys' expectations of sexual permissiveness, she is likely to be dropped immediately and have no further dates. If she is cooperative, she easily builds a reputation and becomes fair game for her current dating partner and later his friends and fraternity brothers. The authors suspect that more girls than not choose to solve the dilemma by being more permissive than they normally would, just in order to keep dating.[36]

Despite this dilemma, women actively participate in hooking   23 up, as they did in dating. Why? Because the prevailing script in any era is seen as the only way, or at least the most likely way, to get together with men and feel a part of the social scene of their peers.

Conclusion

In the final analysis, much has changed since the dating era.   24 Some of the changes can be seen as an improvement, and others can be viewed as negative. One of the most interesting things to examine about the shift from dating to hooking up is its impact on women. Since the emergence of hooking up can be traced back to the sexual revolution period, it begs the question: Have the goals of the women's liberation movement been met? If the objective of women's rights activists was for women to be able to have sexual experiences without having to barter exclusive sexual access in exchange for a wedding ring, there is evidence that it has been realized. Women's sexual behavior has changed more than men's since the 1960s, and on several key indicators women are reaching "parity" with men. For example, historically men had their first experience of sexual intercourse earlier than women; today, it is roughly equal.[37] Historically, men also had a higher number of sexual partners than women; however, in more recent decades gender differences are less pronounced.[38] These changes were precisely what many architects of the women's liberation movement had in mind.

25   However, even as similarities between men and women increased, the double standard remains. On the campuses I studied, contemporary college women may be permitted to engage in a wider variety of sexual behaviors under a wider array of circumstances than their dating-era counterparts, but there are no clear rules guiding what they should do and under what conditions. The ostensible lack of rules in the hookup script may seem to be liberating, and perhaps it can be, but it is also problematic because there are many unwritten rules that women must learn as they go along. These unwritten rules continue to limit the options available to women who are interested in pursuing sexual relationships.

26   Despite the double standard, women do have more sexual freedom today than they did in the dating era. But, it was not only women who gained sexual freedom since the sexual revolution; men did also. Since "respectable" women were not supposed to have premarital sex in the dating era, men who wanted to engage in sexual intercourse (while society looked the other way) had to do so with women of ill repute.[39] In the hooking-up era, men have many more women to choose from for potential sexual encounters. For better or worse, men also do not have to put forth the amount of effort (e.g., phone calls, flowers, expensive dates, etc.) that their grandfathers did for sexual interaction to take place. Men today also do not have to propose marriage or walk down the aisle in order to have regular access to sexual intercourse. Indeed, men can have sex without entering into a relationship at all. Thus, hooking up is a system whereby men can engage in sexual encounters without the pretext of a relationship and where no guarantee of an ongoing or future bond with the woman is required. In a sense, it can be

argued that men are the ones who really benefited from the sexual revolution. Robert, a sophomore at Faith University, opined:

> *Robert*: It almost seems like [the hookup scene] is a guy's paradise. No real commitment, no real feelings involved, this is like a guy's paradise. This age [era] that we are in I guess.
>
> *KB*: So you think guys are pretty happy with the [hookup] system?
>
> *Robert*: Yeah! I mean this is what guys have been wanting for many, many years. And women have always resisted, but now they are going along with it. It just seems like that is the trend.

Clearly, women's rights activists who called for sexual equality with men did not intend to promote a form of interaction that would be considered a "guy's paradise."   27

Despite the increase in sexual freedom since the dating era, the hookup culture is not as out of control as some observers (and college students) believe. Hooking up is dominant on campus, but it represents a wide range in terms of level of participation and sexual behavior. There are many students who do not take part in hooking up at all and others who, for various reasons (e.g., they are in a relationship), have only hooked up a few times.[40] For those students who have engaged in hooking up, many encounters involved nothing more than kissing. Although a hookup can involve casual sex between two parties who just met that evening, a hookup could also mean two people kissing after having a crush on each other for a year. Likewise, a hookup encounter may happen only once or evolve into repeatedly hooking up or even become a relationship. The point is that hooking up can mean different things, and it is too often assumed, by scholars and commentators alike, that it refers to only the most promiscuous scenarios.   28

This is not to say that extreme behavior is not happening in the hookup culture. For some students, college life can become an endless spring break. These are the same students who consume a disproportionate amount of alcohol on campus and hook up with different partners on a weekly basis. This behavior raises a variety of health concerns, particularly with regard to the level of binge drinking and the potential for STD transmission or rape. It is students caught up in the extremes of the hookup culture who, to the exclusion of their more moderate classmates, have captured the attention of critics. Although this behavior needs attention, it can also distort the reality of life on campus for the student body as a whole.   29

Acknowledging the variation in the hookup culture is important not only for students generally, but also for understanding differences between genders. Although I chose to highlight the   30 differences between men and women throughout the preceding chapters, there is, no doubt, as much variation within gender as there is across it. Just as not all students fit the mold of the most raucous partiers, not *all* men want sex and not *all* women want relationships. I spoke with some men who preferred being in a relationship over hookup encounters with new partners. I also spoke to some women who enjoyed the freedom and experimentation of the hookup scene (at least during freshman year). Therefore, it would be unfair to oversimplify the behavior of the sexes. However, I found that women's interest in hookup encounters evolving into some semblance of a relationship and men's interest in "playing the field" was a theme that fundamentally affects the dynamic between men and women in the hookup culture.

31   Given that there is a wide range of possibilities available to men and women coming of age in the hookup era, it would seem that there is an almost endless array of choices an individual can make. For example, if a student wants to go to parties and hook up every weekend, he or she can choose to do so. Likewise, if a student wants to be part of the hookup scene, but as a more moderate participant, he or she can do that too. However, in many ways, the hookup system creates an illusion of choice. Although students have many options about how they conduct themselves within the hookup culture, they cannot change the fact that hooking up is the dominant script on campus. An individual student may decide to abstain from hooking up altogether, but they are more or less on their own to figure out an alternative. In other words, no other script exists side-by-side with hooking up that students can opt to use instead. Emily, a sophomore at Faith University, put it this way: "If [hooking up] is not what you're looking for, then I guess it is hard to escape it."

32   Students who would prefer to go out on traditional dates every weekend cannot change the fact that they did not enter college during a time when that was the "in" thing to do. Thus, students can use their own moral compass to make personal decisions on how to use the hookup script, but their decisions are constrained by their environment and the time period. The modern college campus is conducive to hooking up, and no individual can change that.

33   It is my hope that readers have gained a better understanding of the hooking-up phenomenon. I believe that the stories of college students and young alumni presented here provide a look into the world of campus life and single life after college as many young people experience it today. The information in this book can be useful for those on the outside looking in at campus life, particularly college administrators and parents seeking to guide students through their college careers. I hope that they,

and other commentators, will come away with an appreciation for the systemic issues that impact individual experiences.

I also hope that my work will be useful to researchers who   34 study social problems on the college campus, such as binge drinking, STD transmission, and sexual assault. Understanding the relationship between hooking up and these issues is crucial because, I believe, these campus problems grow out of a larger context of how students socialize and form sexual and romantic relationships. Without understanding this context, it would be difficult to find any effective solutions.

For recent graduates who are trying to make sense of a new   35 singles scene, this book can provide insight into where they have been, where they are going, and why things change (almost overnight) after they leave the campus environment. Although hooking up ceases to play the dominant role in social life that it did in college, it has lasting effects for alumni. After college, individuals must learn to adapt to a new script (i.e., formal dating), yet prepare to switch back to the hookup script when circumstances make it possible to do so. I hope alumni readers will find the views of other twenty-something singles insightful.

Most importantly, I believe that college students who are   36 learning to navigate the hookup system will find the information in this book helpful. Many students I interviewed spoke of having to find out how hooking up works as they made their way through college. By sharing their experiences of college life, they have given current students a point of reference on the hookup culture. Although students may not identify with all of the individuals in the preceding chapters, I think that the stories of some men and women will resonate with each reader. Understanding others' perspectives on hooking up will allow students to see how their intimate lives fit into the bigger picture. I hope my work will give students the opportunity to reflect on what they are doing, why they are doing it, and will ultimately help them to make informed, and possibly better, decisions about their lives.

Notes

1. Coontz 1992.
2 For example, see Glenn and Marquardt (2001).
3. Although Whyte (1990), in his quantitative study of women in Detroit, examined changes and continuities in dating throughout most of the twentieth century, he did not consider the contemporary hookup scene on the college campus.
4. Skipper and Nass 1966.
5. Bailey 1988.
6. Gagnon and Simon 1987.
7. This finding confirms what previous researchers have found (see Glenn and Marquardt 2001; Paul, McManus, and Hayes 2000; Williams 1998).
8. Whyte 1990. See also Kinsey 1953.

9. In fact, Paul, McManus, and Hayes (2000) found that 30.4 percent of the college students in their study had engaged in at least one hookup that culminated in sexual intercourse. This finding is particularly interesting when one considers that the definition of hooking up employed by Paul, McManus, and Hayes referred to encounters with a stranger or brief acquaintance (or what interviewees in my sample referred to as "random" hookups).
10. Rubin 1990.
11. Carpenter 2005.
12. Reiss 1997; Harding and Jencks 2003.
13. Laumann et al. 1994.
14. Those born between 1933 and 1942 had their first experience of intercourse at approximately 18, while the age for those born 20 to 30 years later decreased by six months (Laumann et al. 1994).
15. Laumann et al. 1994.
16. See Hollander (1997) for a discussion of how different religious affiliations (i.e., Catholics and "mainstream" Protestants versus conservative or fundamentalist Christians) affect attitudes on premarital sex.
17. Rubin 1990, 46.
18. See Carpenter (2005) for more on how many people view virginity as a stigma.
19. See Martin and Hummer 1989; Boswell and Spade 1996; Sanday 1992.
20. Bailey 1988; Whyte 1990. See also Thornton (1990).
21. See King and Christensen (1983) for a discussion of the stages in dating relationships.
22. Women were advised to avoid kissing on the first date (Duvall 1958).
23. Bailey 1988.
24. Goffman 1977.
25. Despite the fact that sexual intercourse is expected in exclusive relationships, some research indicates that a sizable percentage of college couples are not having intercourse. Specifically, Glenn and Marquardt (2001) found that 24 percent of the college women they surveyed had a boyfriend but had never had sexual intercourse.
26. Waller 1937.
27. Although none of the college men in my sample were afraid that women might exploit them financially, many feared women "clinging onto them" by trying to form an unwanted serious relationship.
28. Rubin 1990.
29. Rubin 1990; Skipper and Nass 1966.
30. Skipper and Nass 1966, 417.
31. Reitman 2006.
32. Rubin 1990.
33. See Duvall 1958.
34. See Holland and Eisenhart (1990) for a discussion of gender roles, sexual intimacy, and the cultural model of romance.
35. Duvall 1958, 205.
36. Skipper and Nass 1966, 417.
37. Laumann et al. 1994.
38. Laumann et al. 1994.
39. Rubin 1990.
40. Paul et al. (2000) found in their quantitative study of a large university in the northeastern United States that approximately 22 percent of undergraduate students had never engaged in a hookup.

getting into the conversation ... 7

Hooking Up: Relationships in the 21st Century

1. Although many assume that finding one's soul mate is fundamental to a happy and fulfilling life, that assumption itself is worth examining. Jillian Straus' "Lone Star" chronicles the stories of individuals who have consciously chosen to remain single and who have found happiness through networks of friends instead of through a reliance upon a single other individual. To consider the issues that are raised in this chapter— about more fleeting and purely physical love relationships or those that involve more than two individuals—you might begin by examining the assumption that human beings have a natural tendency to pair off. To do so, you can use the readings in this section—and the many views on love relationships not only of the authors, but also of those who were interviewed in these pieces—to reach some conclusions about whether this central cultural assumption is valid and useful, or whether perhaps casting it aside might open up new paths to happiness.

2. Although love relationships clearly involve both genders, the perspective upon them varies in significant ways across genders. The readings here provide a great many perspectives on both love and sexuality from individuals of both genders. You might look back through the readings in this section and notes that you have taken as you read them and then create a synthesis of these readings organized by the similarities and differences in perspectives on love and sex according to gender. First, review the techniques for synthesis in the Introduction to *Conversations*. Then, organize your notes in a way that allows you to find the stasis points that seem to exist between men and women on a concept like hooking up, dating, or monogamy. From those notes, you can then construct an essay that allows you to hypothesize about points of agreement and disagreement across genders. If you want to test those hypotheses, you could also go on to do more primary and/ or secondary research.

3. One question raised about the "hookup culture" is whether the phenomenon is one that represents a fleeting and youthful practice, or a real change in the ways that human beings are viewing the goals and purposes of relationships. Do some interviews with people of your generation, and try to gauge whether current sexual practices have displaced, or simply delayed, traditional attitudes toward monogamy and marriage.

4. Sandra Barron addresses the ways that technology has influenced current love relationships. But the discussions of how current technologies have changed the ways we relate to one another are not limited to the ideas in those pieces; technology is an implicit part of hook-up culture as well. Try to bring together these two threads of the readings in this chapter to examine the ways that hooking up and virtual communication are related phenomenon. To enrich this discussion, you might also refer to the materials in the *Conversations in Context* section which follows.

conversations in context ...4

Loving Online

I. The Context

As Chapter 2 of *Conversations* makes clear, new technologies have changed the ways that we gather information, get the news, communicate, and perhaps even the ways that we learn. But technology has also affected the ways that we relate to one another as human beings—even in intimate love relationships. Not only are many actual love relationships *found* online through dating services, Facebook, and other cyber-talk, but some love relationships are actually *carried out* exclusively online. There has even been talk about the ways in which some partners cheat online, finding emotional fulfillment outside of their actual, physical relationships with others in cyberspace. As complicated as love relationships can be in any case, this added dimension has added further complexity. And people are talking and writing about it.

Those conversations take many forms. There are online forums that provide outlets for narratives of cyber relationships, essays describing those relationships, and even a growing number of serious sociological and psychological studies of these phenomena that have been published by experts. These various venues have allowed us to listen in on the formation and progress of relationships in an almost voyeuristic way. Like a diary left open for the world, some of these very personal moments have become very public ones. One only needs to peruse Facebook or love blogs to realize that what was once seen as the province of the most private conversations has now been opened up for the wider world. That phenomenon, too, has become the subject of study for those interested in human behavior and its motivations, which have asked both behavioral and ethical questions about where the lines between privacy and self-disclosure lie. And there has been a great deal of talk about how the revelation of the private has affected people's work lives, now that some potential employers regularly check online to find out information about those that have applied for work. For this reason, too, this is a topic worth your consideration.

One of the key questions that the concept of the cyber-relationship raises is how we are to define (or re-define) what a "good" love relationship is. For some, it might seem patently absurd that one might consider words transferred across electronic media a significant emotional tie, something that we might raise to the level of love. But for others, this form of communication is considered rich, fulfilling, even intimate. Some find that the level of self that is revealed in such relationships goes beyond anything that they could achieve in face-to-face communication, while others find that kind of communication thin at best, and cowardly at worst. And what of physicality? Can cyber-flirting be considered a satisfying, even a healthy, form of sexual activity between consenting adults?

Clearly, we are only beginning to understand the implications of this new form of human love, love that is transmitted via machines. And because it is new, there is clearly much to be explored, making it an area rife with research potential. As you read the excerpt from Nicola Döring's, *Studying Online-Love and Cyber-Romance,* consider the ways in which this piece provides methods for studying this phenomenon that you might use in your own writing. Then, as you peruse the varied thoughts, opinions, reflections, and images that follow Döring's piece, consider how these artifacts (and others you find on your own) can lead to a research project you could take on, and how some further research (both primary and secondary) might help you write about this topic.

Considering Contexts: Nicola Döring, "Studying Online-Love and Cyber-Romance"

Nicola Döring is an Assistant Professor of Communication Studies at the Ilmenau Technological University in Germany. She studies the effects of technology upon personal, gender, and love relationships. In the excerpt from her Studying Online-Love and Cyber-Romance *that follows, Döring lays out some of the key definitions and methodologies that researchers should take into account as they study the phenomena of online relationships. As you read, consider how these methods of study might help you to develop your own study of some facet of cyber-love, using the excerpts and visuals that follow as jumping off points for that research.*

Studying Online-Love and Cyber-Romance

Nicola Döring

The fact that people fall in love on the net, and truly experience deep feelings during the course of their cyber-romance, has been demonstrated too often to still be denied. Nevertheless, it is often doubted that *genuine* love relationships exist on the net. How can it be possible to lead a close, intimate relationship if participants are only there for each other primarily via their computer-mediated messages? The first section of this contribution argues that cyber-romance should no longer be treated as an exotic fringe phenomenon, and, instead, should be regarded as a serious sociopsychological research topic. The second section discusses the most important data collection methods used to study cyber-romance.

Why Study Cyber-Romance?

Studying cyber-romance is significant for three reasons: first, cyber-romantic relationships can be reconstructed theoretically in the form of normal social relationships. Besides, they are quite common among people active on the net (20.1.2). Finally, in the context of social relationships research, cyber-romantic relationships provoke a number of interesting new research questions.

20.1.1 Definition of Cyber-Romance

In order to clarify whether, or under which circumstances, a cyber-romance counts as a genuine romantic relationship or merely represents a pseudo relationship, we must first clarify the term relationship.

A social relationship develops between two people if they repeatedly have contact with one another, be it in form of asynchronous communication (e.g. letters, notes) or synchronous interaction (e.g., telephone calls, personal conversations, joint activities). In contrast to a social contact as an individual event, social relationships *continue* over a period of several occasions, so that each individual contact is affected both by the preceding contacts and by expectations of future contacts. During the course of the development of the relationship, participants get to know each other and have to negotiate a common relationship definition, for instance by mutually spelling out their expectations and by continually renewing their commitment to the relationship. Since the relationship continues in the periods between individual contacts, apart from open communication and interactive behavior patterns, emotional, motivational and cognitive processes within each partner (e.g., a feeling of longing, preparing for the next meeting, remembering common experiences) also play an important role in the quality and continuity of the relationship. This sociopsychological interpretation of personal relationships (see Hinde, 1997) places no restrictions on the type of media used for the individual contacts, and thereby allows one, theoretically, to speak of genuine social relationships when the participants predominantly or exclusively contact each other in a computer-mediated environment.

Such relationships based on contacts mediated primarily via computers, where the first contact normally takes place on the net, are today called *on-line relationships* or *cyber-relationships*. This distinguishes them from "conventional" relationships, where the first contact and the important following contacts take place face-to-face. In net discourse, these conventional relationships are now called *off-line relationships, real life relationships, 3D-relationships,* or *in-person relationships.*

Social relationships can roughly be divided into *formal* (e.g., salesman - customer) and *personal* (e.g., father - son) relationships, whereby personal relationships are further divided into *strong* (e.g., friendship) and *weak* (e.g., acquaintance) ties. *Romantic relationships* (to a large extent synonymous with love affairs or partnerships) are strong personal bonds which clearly differ from family and friendship relationships because of their potential to develop into family relationships and because of their open sexuality. Passion, intimacy and commitment are three of the core elements of romantic relationships (Steinberg, 1986). Theoretically, nothing can be held against the fact that a love relationship is primarily or exclusively based on net contacts, since in principle, passion (e.g., shared arousal when articulating sexual fantasies), intimacy (e.g., support in times of personal problems), and commitment (e.g., regular contact) can also be passed on via the asynchronous or synchronous exchange of digital text, tone, or image messages. Whether and how people on the net actually make use of these options and thereby actually lead genuine *romantic on-line relationships* (synonymous with *cyber love affairs, cyber-romance*) must, in contrast, be ascertained with the help of empirical analysis. If one of the participants in a cyber-romance also lives in a committed relationship outside of the net, then the cyber-romance is called a *cyber-affair*.

Pervasiveness of Cyber-Romance

How common are romantic on-line relationships? Although a majority of net contacts occur between people who already know each other offline (which affects the *density of the social network;* cf. Hamman, 1998), many people also find new contacts directly after accessing the net (which affects the *size of the social network,* cf. Wellman & Gulia, 1999). Most of the new online relationships are *weak ties:* information is exchanged with colleagues overseas or the last episode of a favorite TV series is discussed with other fans worldwide. Those people who develop *strong ties* on the net in the form of friendships or romantic relationships represent a minority of the online population, a minority which nevertheless might, in absolute numbers, include several million worldwide. In a representative telephone survey in 1995, 14% of (n=601) US citizens who had access to the net reported having become acquainted with people on the net whom they would refer to as "friends". Unfortunately, no differentiation was made between romantic and non-romantic relationships (Katz & Aspden, 1997). In surveys aimed at persons active in newsgroups, the portion of those who maintain close relationships on the net increases to 61% (53% friendships, 8% romantic relationships; Park & Floyd, 1996). If one considers MUD (Multi User Dungeons/ Domains) participants only, the portion of those with close net relationships shoots up to 91% (Schildmann, Wirausky & Zielke, 1995), or 93% (67% friendships, 26% romantic relationships; Park & Robert, 1997). Among people who use chat forums, cyber-romance seems to be especially prevalent, as most chat forums promote flirting and fooling around.

In summary: romantic net relationships neither represent an exotic fringe phenomenon nor an epidemic mass phenomenon. Instead, net relationships are an experience that belongs to the everyday life of a considerable portion of the net population, and one which is growing exponentially. Furthermore, an increasing number of people are also *indirectly* affected by cyber-romance and cyber-affairs, because friends, relatives, partners or clients fall in love online. According to the results of an ongoing public WWW questionnaire on cyber-romance that has been conducted since 1997 in the free WWW magazine *Self-Help & Psychology Magazine*, as of October 1999 the majority (70% of n=2,174) of respondents (64% women, 36% men) admitted having experienced at least one case of cyber-romance in their immediate social surroundings (Maheu, 1999). Psychologist Storm King, active in the areas of clinical and socio-psychological Internet research, provides the following anecdotal evidence that demonstrates the everyday nature of cyber-romantic affairs:

> This author has presented at several psychology conferences, talking about Internet interpersonal relationships. At each of four presentations, the audience, composed of psychologists and mental health workers, was asked to raise their hand if they knew of someone (friend, family or client) that had partaken in a cyber romance. Each time, of the approximately 50 people in the audience, about half the hands went up. (King, 1999)

The fact that most cyber-romantic relationships are also cyber-affairs is a result of the socio-statistic composition of the net population, in which singles are the minority. Of the 9,177 people active on the net (14% women, 86% men), who participated in Cooper, Scherer, Boies and Gordon's (1999) WWW survey, 80% had a steady partner and approximately 50% were married, which mirrors the situation outside of the net: even today's hi-tech nations are *not* "single societies".

Research Questions

Who is most likely to actually fall in love on the net? Which net forums are particularly suitable for making romantic acquaintances or for strengthening existing relationships? What personal and behavioral characteristics are indicative of interpersonal (and particularly of erotic) attraction, if we confront each other on the net only in the form of our text contributions written on machines? After becoming acquainted via a Chat, a MUD or a web site, how, when and why do people agree to switch over to private e-mail contact, telephone calls, exchange of pictures, or personal meetings? How, when and why do they consciously abstain from such a change in media, and thus maintain the "virtual" character of the relationship? How do people involved in a cyber-romantic relationship deal with the fact that one can control one's own self-presentation much better via computer-mediated text communication than in face-to-face situations? What effect does tactical self-presentation in online love (e.g., consciously withholding certain personal traits, or information) have on misgivings, or an increase in them, for the other partner? How widely spread is "love at first byte" really, or at what point in time in the media mediated acquaintance do participants claim to have fallen in love, or actually love each other? How do online lovers officially seal their status as a couple? What is their degree of commitment to their cyber-romance? If, during the course of the strengthening of a cyber-romance, various media changes took place before the face-to-face meeting, the romantic relationship is considered less of an online relationship and more of an offline relationship. Which definition criteria do participants apply to the relationship in order to illustrate the dichotomous online versus offline relationship construction in the continuum of the relative significance of net communication? How large is the share of multinational and long distance relationships amongst cyber-romantic relationships? How do online lovers deal with the (sometimes considerable) geographical distances, and cultural differences? Such research questions are initially aimed at establishing a detailed definition. Systematic studies may thereby help to qualify the occurrence frequency and/or subjective meaning of those characteristics of cyber-romance, which so often arouse interest in the public eye (e.g., cyber-weddings or online gender swapping).

Foremost, a descriptive examination of cyber-romance is necessary but studies which use the net context as a new test bed for well-known impression formation, self-presentation, attraction and social relationship theories are also required. Even if other people are initially invisible on the net, one nevertheless gets a general impression of what someone is like on the basis of their communication behavior. In interpersonal exchange outside of as well as within the net, cooperation, sincerity, spontaneity and empathy for others are valued traits. The fear those who are egocentric, socially incompetent, and incapable of forming relationships can comfortably "consume" social contacts without any risk merely by pushing a button on a keyboard should be analyzed in view of this background. After all, even on the net, compassion for other people is a prerequisite for getting to know somebody more closely. Concepts such as intimacy, self-disclosure, social skills or interpersonal proximity should be examined according to the role they play in a particular medium. "Genuine" interpersonal proximity, as is always maintained intuitively, requires face-to-face contact, even though the psychosocial dimensions of such categorical claims are not confirmed. The common fear that net relationships, which will play an increasingly important role for younger generations, cause deficits in social skills is also questionable: computer-mediated relationships also require, apart from technical expertise in operating the system, various social skills, such as explicitly articulating one's feelings in absence of non-verbal communication. If teenagers' first loves are increasingly online love relationships, will certain development psychology and socialization theory concepts have to be reformulated? If cyber-romance particularly stresses emotional intimacy, because the partners usually communicate with each other for days, weeks, or months on an exclusively verbal basis, and otherwise do not pursue common activities, should they then be characterized as "female" forms of communication? Or wouldn't they pose a reason, in view of the amount of male participation, to

conversations in context ...4

question the hypothesis of two distinctly gender specific communication styles? It is not the repeatedly alleged possibility of falling for a gender switch, or of presenting oneself on the net as a neuter that make cyber relationships so interesting from a gender theory point of view. Instead, it is the fact that we encounter and desire each other on the net explicitly as men or as women, while we realize unusual forms of self-presentation and of coming closer which may deviate from traditional gender roles and from conventional rituals of homosexual, heterosexual or bisexual paradigms.

Studies on cyber-romance not only contribute to basic scientific research into social relationships, they are also relevant from the perspective of applied science. Under certain circumstances, excessive devotion to cyber-romantic relationships can be an indicator, or catalyst, of psychosocial problems and disturbances. As a result, some people limit their radius of behavior drastically during the course of a cyber-romance, and then increase their net activities even if these already have serious negative consequences within their psychological, physical or social environment. If a person is on her computer for nights on end in order to chat with her online love, neglects all other areas of life and nevertheless tends to increase her time online, then this is often referred to as an "online addiction" (see Young, 1998). Such pathological labeling can, however, be problematic. Loss of control, development of tolerance, and withdrawal symptoms may be characteristic for addictions as well as for falling in love. Overly enthusiastic net activity seldom is caused by an obsession with technology in itself. Rather it is a symptom of a—more or less conflicted—search for interpersonal proximity. With regard to problematic patterns of net use, the focus of research needs to be centered on pathological relationship behavior, its determinants and moderators, instead of projecting the problem onto the medium itself. Since computer-mediated communication is a part of the everyday lifestyle of an increasing portion of the population, cyber-romance and cyber-affairs will increasingly become a topic in the context of psychological consultation and therapy (see Cooper et al., 1999; Greenfield & Cooper, 1999). An expert treatment of these new forms of relationships and their various psychosocial functions, (e.g., besides escapism, compensation or exploration) is therefore required and should be based on sound social scientific research instead of on storytelling and prejudices (see Döring, 1999).

How to Study Cyber-Romance?

If one wants to get a precise idea of the characteristics of romantic net relationships, different data collection *methods* are at our disposal. Observational studies (20.2.1), interviews and surveys (20.2.2), personal narratives (20.2.3) and practical suggestions (20.2.4) are four particularly important sources of data.

conversations in context ...4

Due to space restrictions, this chapter focuses on *data collection* and does not go into *data analysis*. In the case of *offline data* about online love, all the conventional analytical methods are applicable. In the case of *online data,* conventional data analysis methods can also be used for standardized online interviews or surveys whose data output can easily be processed by the common statistical packages. More difficult to analyze are natural online data such as chat conversations, newsgroup postings or web sites. As Rössler (this volume) points out, a content analysis of natural online data is a challenge for traditional methodology in many ways. "Online content analysis," he summarizes, "is a lot of work with little gains but yet an important and responsible task because content on the net cannot be reproduced or studied by communication scholars in the future." In fact, natural online data on cyber-romances are not only historically but also psychologically unique since the most important discourses on the phenomenon take place online. Even though we know that the analysis of natural online data is not an easy task, it should not stop us from collecting such data. On the contrary, even purely exploratory data collection and inspection are key prerequisites of any further development in online methodology as well as in our understanding of online social phenomena.

Observational Studies

Observation of computer-mediated communication and interaction processes is facilitated by the fact that the medium allows complete documentation of interpersonal events without any additional technology and without the target persons noticing the documentation process. For example, we can completely log public behavior in mailing lists, newsgroups, chat forums or MUDs (Multi User Dungeons) for hours, days and weeks, and on the basis of this observation data examine flirtation behavior, acquaintance processes, but also communication within couples. *Automatically compiled observation logs* can be analyzed qualitatively, and/or quantitatively. Since romantic online encounters are so prevalent and online (participatory) observation in Chats and MUDs is quite a well-known data collection method (see Utz, this volume) it's surprising that there have been as yet no online observational studies examining romantic net relationships systematically on the basis of automatic observation logs. As illustrated on the basis of two chat interaction log files, such observational studies could contribute to our understanding of cyber-romance.

The first log file documents a meeting between *Bekin* and *ABC* on the mainly German-language chat channel #germany (February 18th, 1999; only the messages of the two focus persons will be listed). Bekin and ABC both address their respective names, home towns and leisure interests during the first ten minutes of the online dialogue. The interspersed smileys underscore the friendly atmosphere, while the rapid reactions show mutual interest. Just as in face-to-face situations, small talk normally takes place at the beginning of a potential net relationship:

<Bekin> are u here ABC

<abc> yes

<Bekin> ok

<Bekin> whats ur name

<abc> Sandra

<Bekin> my name is bekin

<abc> Nice to meet you bekin:)

<Bekin> and i am Turkish

<abc>:)

<Bekin> do u speak german

<abc> so, when did you came into germany?

<abc> No, I can understand, but can't speak

<Bekin> i born here

<abc> I have learned german language in primary school

<Bekin>: -)

<abc> but as I am working in english language, I have forgot lots of words

<Bekin> and i learned English in Primary scool

<abc>:)

<abc> I am trying to learn German language again

<Bekin> Wow thats great

<abc> thanks

<Bekin> do u speak Tuerkish? -)

<abc> No, just Bosnian . . . but we have some similar words

<Bekin> what a words?

<abc> I don't know precisely but lots of Bosnian words are Turkish origin

<Bekin> yes

<Bekin> are u visit Germany?

<abc> Long time ago

<Bekin> when?

<abc> I was in Koeln

<Bekin> Koeln is a Wunderfull City

<abc> 1987

<abc> yes, it is

<Bekin> but the city where i leave is better

<abc> where do you live?

<Bekin> Mannheim

<Bekin> u know

<abc> yes I know, but I never been there

<abc> what are you doing except working

The second log file documents romantic communication on the #38plus-de (February 19th, 1999) chat channel. Morrison and Janina, who are officially a couple, refer to each other with their nicknames (Morri, Jani, sweetie). To a third person (BlueMan), Janina stresses the monogamous nature of her relationship with Morrison. She kisses Morrison virtually and publicly. Morrison plays a love song for Janina on the channel. What becomes clear is the way the partners use verbal and nonverbal means of expression via computer-mediated communication, in order to create a friendly, attentive first contact (Bekin and ABC) or an euphoric, amorous rendezvous (Janina and Morrison):

* * * Joins: Morrison (user5@ 146.usk.de)

<Morrison> morning fans:))

<janina> morri!!!!

<Morrison> jani,:)))))))))))))))))))))))

<Morrison> how are we feeling today?

* janina is sad, because she has to go soon

<BlueMan> janina: you have to leave so soon???

<janina> morri, my sweetie, were you also here yesterday?????

<Morrison> jani, not me

<janina> blueman, well I'll stay for a bit

<BlueMan> janina: *smile*

<janina> blueman, also *smile* (however don't cuddle me again, otherwise morri will get mad)

<BlueMan> janina: I don't care *grin*

* Morrison plays i can't stop loving you.mp^3 3304kb

<janina> morri, No. 10 is simply the most beautiful song *kiss*

<Morrison> jani, I can't play it often enough

<janina> morri, here's a rose @-;-;—-;— for you

Field observations, which include longer participation in selected net forums, as well as field interviews with their participants, permit the reconstruction of romantic net relationships from the first encounter to the happy ending, the split-up or the change of the relationship. Active participation in the respective net forum and private contacts to members of the forum during field research provide insight into the participants' biographies. From his one year of field observation in various Compuserve chat forums (SIGs: Special Interest Groups), Sannicolas

(1997) offers the following information on the "success ratio" of romantic chat relationships: In the year that this researcher has spent visiting SIG's I have seen approximately 50 relationships form on-line. In many of those instances, one party has moved a great distance to be with the other person, without giving much time to spend time together face to face getting to know one another. All of the knowledge about the other person has come from their interaction over the "puter." Thus, it is not surprising that out of these approximately 50 relationships, only a very small number (3) have worked out to last more than 6 months. (Sannicolas, 1997) As a participating observer, Debatin (1997) frequented an anonymous CompuServe chat room between December 1995 and July 1997, and thereby gained insight into the resident virtual group's structure as well as into the relationships between the individual group members. The author presents observation logs of individual channel discussions and interprets these against the background of his own experiences on the channel. As a result, he managed to solve an alleged forum participant's leukemia death as a dramatized retreat from a complicated online love affair:

> E. was suffering, as she had told many regulars in confidence, from leukemia. After her disappearance from the forum it was said that she had died. Her death was received mournfully in the forum, and Showan, her cyber-lover, disappeared from the forum for several months. Later, we found out that E. had only feigned her illness and death in order to free herself from an emotionally complicated affair with Showan. Approx. 15 years her younger, single Showan wanted to begin a "new life" with E., who was tied up in an unhappy marriage. This was out of the question for her. Some months later, E. got back in contact with Showan, and even occasionally returned to the forum. (Debatin, 1997)

Automatic observation logs document participants' behavior in public forums. Beyond that, by means of participatory field observation we can gain information on the happening behind the scenes and on the partakers' subjective experiences. Outsiders cannot register how private net communication comes about in detail, but even more so by the participants themselves. Many mail clients not only store sent messages, but also receive e-mails, meaning that a glance in his or her private mailbox is all a net user needs to be able give precise information on the communication with his or her cyber-love:

> It has been 2 months now that we've been together and so far I have received a total of 140 e-mail messages and he has approx. 160 from me. (Story 20 in the *Archive of Cyber Love Stories:* http://www.love life.com/LS/)

People who are active on the net usually archive large parts of their e-mail correspondence, and in particular their electronic love letters. Occasionally, they will also record their private online discussions, which is unproblematic for many chat and MUD programs to execute (without the opposite side's knowledge). In this manner, we can cull objective behavior data on intimate social events, which normally remain undocumented and can at most be recalled from memory if the participants do not associate with one another via media. Logs of private (and more or less openly sexual) net contacts in the context of cyber-romance are occasionally incorporated into personal narratives (see section 20.2.3). They can also be used as data for empirical social research, provided the participants agree to supply the appropriate documents.

Automatic registration of computer-mediated communication processes generally presents a particularly economically and ecologically viable form of data acquisition. It is, however, afflicted by ethical problems. One of the core problems is the fact that nowadays privacy is the subject of extremely controversial debate in most net contexts. The argument postulated by participants and outsiders states that any open group communication on the net is public domain, in principle, and thereby qua implicit agreement open for documentation by anybody interested, just as the case may be with, for instance, television talk shows or panel discussions on political meetings. The opposite viewpoint states that net forums are not addressed at a dispersed, broad audience, and instead fulfill an internal exchange aimed at only those people who are currently enlisted. Incognito logging of group interactions in the net would thus be equivalent to the secret recording of a table conversation in a restaurant or a multi-person chat at a party, and would represent an unethical infringement of privacy laws. Ethical problems in the context of online observational studies cannot be resolved by simply applying overall guidelines. Rather, we should make conscious decisions for each study based on our respective research aim as well as on the specific social norms of the observed forum. In light of these considerations, the names and computer addresses of all persons involved in the two log files presented in this section have, for purposes of data privacy, been changed.

Anonymity is still ensured, even the names of the forums and the times at which the interactions took place have been listed for purposes of documentation.

Interviews and Surveys

Interviews and surveys are particularly suitable for researching romantic online relationships, since they can equally address past events and future expectations, and can also include those contacts that remain hidden to observation.

In *interviews*, direct dialogue is established between the researcher and the respondent. Research interviews can be conducted face to face, over the telephone, or in a chat or MUD. Standardized interviews stick to a fixed catalog of questions and give the respondent a choice of answers from a set of pre-selected alternatives. In this way, a lot of people can be interviewed efficiently, and the responses can be easily compared (for a standardized telephone survey on personal net relationships see Katz & Aspden, 1997). In contrast, semi-open or open interviews adapt the questions to the course of the interview. Additionally, the respondents have the opportunity of expressing themselves in their own words. The variety and quantity of the data gained in this way with a relatively small numbers of informants permit detailed descriptions of individual cases, however, it hardly permits generalizations on how common or typical the described phenomena and constellations are. Face-to-face interviews, which focus on net relationships among other things, were either conducted as semi-open interviews, such as those carried out by Wetzstein, Dahm, Steinmetz, Lentes, Schampaul and Eckert (1995) or as open or clinical interviews, such as those by Turkle (1995). In both studies, the interviews are, unfortunately, only documented in the form of individual quotations. In his open interview study, Shaw (1997) gave his (n=12) student informants the option of giving information on their experiences with gay chat contacts either via e-mail, chat, or over the telephone. Albright and Conran (1995) interviewed n=33 chatters on their cyber-romantic relationships by asking the following questions:

Initial meeting and Attraction   Where and how did you meet the person or persons with whom you became intimately involved? What first attracted you? What got you interested? What fascinated you most? How did you know this person (or persons) was "right" for you?

Development of Relationship   What was the frequency, intensity, and content of your online communications? How did you augment and shape your messages for each other? Did you speak on the telephone, send photos, and plan a time to flesh meet? If you did some or all of these, how was it decided and what happened? How did your relationship transform, grow, or end over time? Did you develop an offline relationship? If so, how did that evolve, and what, if any online communication was still used?

Truth and Deception   How did you learn to trust the other or others? How quickly did you experience a meeting of the minds, a sense of intimacy? What, if any, nice surprises or disappointments did you experience? What, if any, fantasies or simulations did you do online?

In *surveys* there is no direct contact between researcher and respondent. The questions in the questionnaire are fixed and the answers are entered there. The questionnaire can be handed out personally on paper, or sent via the postal service, as a private e-mail, as a posting to a mailing list or newsgroup, or be made available as an online document on the WWW. The choice of distribution medium affects the composition of the sample.

Communications scientist, Traci Anderson, (1999a) is currently examining cyber-love on the basis of a WWW questionnaire. The questionnaire includes closed questions (e.g., multiple-choice question on the communication media used) and open questions (e.g., "How do you feel about online romantic relationships compared to in-person romantic relationships?" or "How do you feel about your current or most recent online romantic partner?"). Additionally, general attitudes towards romantic love are measured on a scale (example item: "I believe that to be truly in love is to be in love forever."). A second WWW questionnaire (Anderson, 1999b) is concerned with cyber-affairs. Apart from questions on quantity and quality of Internet use and on personal dispositions, it also asks about direct participation in or indirect suffering caused by cyber-affairs. For three years, the current WWW Self-Help & Psychology Magazine questionnaire (Maheu, 1999) has in particular been concerned with the sexual dimensions of cyber-romance (example item: "Can cyber-sex be as satisfying as physical sex?"), and also allows the respondents to enter a personal statement "pro" or "contra" cyber-romance. In her Online Romance Survey, psychologist Pamela McManus (1999) addresses, among other things, the announcement of cyber-relationships in the social network (e.g. to parents or friends), as well as the ensuing reactions from the direct social environment.

WWW Surveys employing self-selected samples (for instance, Anderson, 1999a, 1999b, Maheu, 1999, McManus, 1999), are more likely to be answered by people who are both particularly active on the Internet (and therefore more likely to find the questionnaire in the first place) and particularly interested in questions concerning romance and love on the net (and thus more motivated to answer the questionnaire). Surveys based on self-selected online samples therefore have a tendency to *overrate* the frequency, intensity and significance of online romance. In contrast to this, the studies of Parks and Floyd (1995), and Parks and Robert's (1997) using random online samples are protected against such distortions (for generalizability issues in internet-based survey research see Brenner, this volume). In the field of net relationships, research interviews and surveys are more common than observational studies. Since interviews and surveys are reactive methods, the volunteers must give explicit consent to the investigation, which eliminates a lot of ethical problems related to observational studies. As Sassenberg and Kreutz (this volume) point out, anonymity is a crucial issue in online surveys influencing both participation rate and honesty of answers. Whenever we guarantee the anonymity of an online survey to make our respondents feel safe, we should make an extra effort to ensure actual non-identifiability. In some cases (depending on the survey design) we should direct potential respondents to anonymous e-mailing or surfing services to prevent them from inadvertently handing over delicate information such as their personal e-mail or IP addresses in the course of responding to the survey. Since the results of a web survey are online themselves one has to make sure that the respective data file cannot be downloaded or inspected by any third party, which inadvertently was the case in one of the above-mentioned cyber-romance surveys.

Personal Narratives

Firsthand personal narratives can be found in some of the standard *sociopsychological literature* on cyber-romance. In the rarest cases they originate from the social scientists themselves, who would—according to prevailing social norms in academia—possibly endanger their professional integrity if they were to reveal self-aspects related to love and sexuality. Instead, guest contributions are used. In the anthology *Wired Women* the programmer Liv Ullman (1996) talks about e-mail love; in the online magazine *Cybersociology* an anonymous author Sue (1997), who is likewise foreign to the social sciences, reports of her cyber-liaisons. The anthropologist Cleo Odzer (1997) combines the descriptive and detailed reports of her own romantic and sexual net experiences with general reflections based on feminism and cultural criticism; as an independent writer, she is unconstrained by academic norms.

Without a doubt, the largest collection of personal narratives on online love affairs can be found on the net itself. Contrary to frequent claims in the context of net communication, an inspection of the narratives does not indicate fictitious self-portrayals being produced on a large scale, a process sometimes referred to as "masquerade". Besides, from a psychological point of view, it seems implausible that people should invest so much time and trouble in publishing fictitious accounts under a fictitious alias if they have the opportunity of expressing that which really moves them without having to fear a loss of face or discrimination in their direct social environment (e.g., family, colleagues).

What a psychology student from Switzerland experienced under her nickname *Priscilla* in the net, in particular her romantic net relationship with *MrNorth*, is illustrated in her online diary on a separate web site (Priscilla, 1999) purposely not linked to her personal homepage. Again and again, Priscilla invites her readers to send reactions to her often meta-reflexive diary entries, and also publishes some of the detailed comments, so that dialogues develop (e.g., on unfaithfulness). Between April 1998 and May 1999, Priscilla wrote entries in her online diary on a nearly daily basis. Then she said farewell to the Internet world that over the months had started to seem more and more shallow and futile to her. With her diploma thesis, the separation from her boyfriend and her retreat from MrNorth behind her, she was about to begin her first career.

14th December 1998

How words can grab hold of you. MrNorth was so far away from me, I did not know him in person—and nevertheless I thought of him so often. The little flag on my e-mail program, which possibly indicated a new message from him, was the center of my attention. And the evenings we arranged to chat were the highlights of my day. I do not know anymore what we always talked about. I only know that I sat there for hours, with

an empty stomach a lot of the time, because I had skipped dinner to be online, and I laughed. It was unbelievable. As absurd
as it seemed to me to sit in the office at night and laugh with not
a soul in the house. We played with words, invented dream
worlds, strange irrealities, we split ourselves up into several people and let four people speak with each other, we were horses,
elephants, bears, sailed across the sea in a Viking galleon—it was
an unbelievably fantastic playground which we filled together
with life, a world, as it had never existed before, neither for him,
nor for me. And in this fairytale world feelings also arose [. . .]

15th December 1998

When does infidelity begin? The longer this continued, the more
I was surprised at myself by the way MrNorth accompanied me
in my everyday life. I bought a jumper and asked myself whether
it would please him. I walked down the streets and watched for
men with short, blond hair—in the meantime he had revealed
that much about his looks. I lay in the arms of my boyfriend—
and thought of the man who I had never seen nor heard.

What is infidelity? I had a bad conscience. One evening I told
my boyfriend about my unbelievable experiences, wanted to let
him in on the secret, warn him, what do I know—but he did not
get what it really meant. Language is not his thing, and he probably had no idea of how very much this world was displaced to
his. So I remained alone and tried to get along in this new
ground [. . .]

Shorter autobiographic accounts, which are typically incorporated
into the personal homepage, are more common than complete online
diaries. Cyber-couples like to link their homepages with each other's,
or even offer a joint homepage. Online diaries or private homepages,
which contain empirical reports on cyber-romantic relationships, are
individually accessible over search engines, or bundled in the appropriate *webrings*. The most common webrings (http://www.webring.
org/) are *Love On-line* (62 homepages), *Love at first Byte* (82 homepages), *Internet Romance* (184 homepages), or *I Met My Mate on the
Net* (241 homepages), whereby most usually involve heterosexual
couples. Reports on gay or lesbian cyber-romantic relationships can
be found individually, for example in the *Queer Wedding Webring* (e.g.,
Kim & Kellie, 1999) or in the *Women Loving Women Webring* (e.g.,
Pedds & Birdie, 1999).

Finally, various free online archives are also accessible, which
publish personal narratives on online romances. Some archives allow
users to submit their own narratives into the archives via an online
form. In this way, 170 contributions have so far been submitted to the
Archive of Cyber Love Stories, which is administered by a chat forum,
Hawaii Chat Universe (HCU: http://www.lovelife.com/LS/). The lack
of editorial control of these archives is most apparent in the fact that
54 of the 170 contributions are either double postings, or off topic
(e.g., description of offline romances). The actual database therefore

consists of n=116 empirical reports of cyber-romantic relationships (valid: October 1999): 78% (n=89) of these contributions came from women, 22% (n=26) were contributed by men; in one case no gender could be allocated. All of the described relationships are heterosexual relationships. This indicates that the relatively small rate of male participation in the cyber-romance and cyber-sex discourse has nothing to do with lack of experience in the phenomenon and can instead be attributed to less willingness to bring the subject up for discussion. The contributors age spectrum ranges from 15 to 55 years, and the cyber-romances described are accordingly of different biographic values in each case. In 59% of the cases (n=68), a reference was found to the participants' hometowns. Geographical distance was small in only 9 cases (e.g. neighboring town, same city), whilst in all other cases distances of several hundred miles were registered, as well as different countries and even continents of origin. Nearly every fourth cyber-romance was a cyber-affair with at least one person married (n=15), or living in a committed relationship (n=12).

In other archives, new entries are made by the archives' administrators to whom the material has been submitted via e-mail. The central archives administration facilitates selecting and classifying the contributions. The administrator of the *Safer Dating* web site (http://www.saferdating.com/) offers archives with n=37 *True Stories* (valid: October 1999). One must assume that in the entire spectrum of experiences with cyber-romantic relationships, spectacular cases will be somewhat over-represented in the personal narratives, since unusually positive or negative experiences are the first thing that motivate people to produce and publish a contribution. From an ethical perspective, personal narratives published on the WWW can be interpreted as freely available for social scientific purposes (providing correct citation is used), since the potential audience on the WWW is far larger and more uncontrollable than the target group of a scientific publication. Therefore, the use of WWW contributions does not pose an infringement of privacy laws. The reference to the web source frequently does not contain any reference to the author's identity, since these archived contributions usually only indicate the author's nickname. If one were, to a larger extent, to use individuals' narratives, and if the authors concerned can be identified or at least contacted, then information on the research project would be appropriate. A critical issue for the authors of online contributions is not only an unwanted distribution of their accounts in front of a larger audience, but also an undesirable re-contextualization, including quoting out of context which would suggest an interpretation of their personal narratives that they might not agree with (Sharf, 1999, p. 248).

Practical Suggestions

If we wanted to know how to flirt successfully on the net, how to unmask unfaithful cyber-lovers, or get to grips with the unhappy ending of a cyber-romance, it would be futile to turn to the sociopsychological literature in search of assistance. In the meantime, the market for *counseling literature* has adopted this topic. Typically, the so-called experts are all people who have either had the required personal net experiences (e.g., Phlegar, 1996; Skrilloff & Gould, 1997; Theman, 1997) or have a psychological or psychotherapeutic background (e.g., Adamse & Motta, 1996; Booth & Jung, 1996; Gwinnell, 1998). Such counseling books are strongly shaded by their authors' personal opinions, and may give questionable advice ("Cyber-sex: most women—if they're honest about it—have faked one orgasm or two. Just fake one on the screen", "Check his fidelity: change your screen name and try seducing him in your new persona", Skrilloff & Gould, 1997, p. 70, p. 97). Some of the counseling literature can nevertheless provide researchers with interesting suggestions and case descriptions.

Besides the conventional book publications, counseling literature written by experts is also available on the net, in the form of *online magazines*, which may not primarily, but at least marginally address cyber romance. These include the *Self-Help & Psychology Magazine* (http://www.shpm.com/), the *Friends and Lovers—Relationship Magazine* (http://www.friends-lovers.com/), *Cybergrrl* (http://www.cybergrrl.com/) or the *Love, Romance & Relationships* web site (http:// www.lovingyou.com/).

However, even more frequently, lay persons meet to assist and support each other on the net in *discussion forums* and *online self-help groups*. This typically takes place on newsboards in the WWW, newsgroups in the Usenet, in mailing lists as well as in chat forums. Of relevance in cases of problems with cyber-romance and cyber-affairs are the web newsboard *Cyber Romance* (via http://members.lovingyou.com/boards/), the "Cyberdating" mailing list (via: http://www.onlinelist.com/), and the <alt.irc.romance> newsgroup. The following excerpts from a thread in the web newsboard *Cyber Romance* address typical problems and uncertainties from different perspectives:

1st contribution (5.10.1999)

Subject: Am I insane or is it possible?

Hi, Ok this is the story about a month ago I was chatting on ICQ and I was in the Romance room, I usually go to these rooms just for the fun of it. I was already seeing someone in real life so I wasn't really looking for anything new. Well I was scrolling the names and I came across the a name that I really thought was interesting. So I began a chat with this guy, we chatted for over five hours and neither of us had even realized it. We were so absorbed in our conversation that time no longer seemed to matter. During that first talk, we discovered so much about each other. It was like we could feel each other. I don't really know how to explain it. All I knew was that from the moment I talked with him I had this deep longing and caring for him. He felt the same for me. We've talked every day since this first meeting, as I said about a month, and we feel more and more for each other. I love him, I know I do, but what I'm asking is how can this be? I mean is it wrong to care so deeply for someone I have never even met in person and have only known a short time? We have exchanged pictures and I have to admit that having his picture and knowing what he looks like just cements my feelings more. He lives in Italy and I live in the States so that makes our relationship even more frustrating. The logical side of me is saying that I'm crazy and that it isn't right, but my heart is saying how can someone who makes me feel so good about myself and makes me happy be wrong. So can anyone give me some advice? Are things going too fast or what??

2nd contribution (5.10.1999)

Sometimes you just meet "the one". You don't know when or where. And it's not wrong to feel this way at all. HOWEVER, you are dating someone now. How do you really feel about him? How serious is your relationship with your bf? It's good to be friends but if you are thinking about more than friends then you have to decide who you want. Don't let distance stop you or your heart. My fiancé is 1300 miles from me and we just celebrated our 9th month together. Just don't start a new love relationship unless you are finished with the old.

4th contribution (5.10.1999)

Hey, I just wanted to tell you that I think it's really cool that you met someone you have so much in common with, and that i know how you feel. I have fallen in love with someone online, and I know how frustrating it is, because he lives in Germany and I live in the states. So, hang in there. It doesn't sound like you're going too fast, to me. But, it's always best to listen to your heart. That's the easiest way to tell if you are going too fast or not, and no matter what . . . never listen to anyone else's advice, comments, etc.

5th contribution (10.10.1999)

Believe me I know what you are feeling. The same thing happened to me too. I had been happily married for 21 yrs when I played around in a chat room and met a man that would forever change my life. We connected right away and are now engaged. I am leaving my husband and children in Dec. for a new life with him in Hawaii. He is also leaving his marriage and family also. It sounds worst than it really is. Anyway, like I did, You just gotta follow your heart and listen to No one.

7th contribution (13.10.1999)

First, I thought the reason that people posted in this forum was to get advice . . . now everyone is saying don't follow anyone's advice (sorry I don't get it). [. . .] I think we all know that there is no such thing as a "perfect" relationship and they all have their ups and downs. I've always said that if we worked half as hard at making our current relationships work as we do complaining about them and eyeing others life would be so much better. I think it's right that you have to do what is in your heart . . . but in this case I think she knows in her heart this is not a good situation and will only cause problems in the long run (the distance thing alone). Why cause problems for yourself if you don't have to? I've never understood that.

If quotations from a public net forum (i.e., web newsboards) are used here for illustration purposes, then only with indication of the date, but without mention of the authors' names. In this manner, the authors of the newsboard postings are only identifiable (if at all) to those who have the necessary competence and motivation to read the appropriate net forums themselves. In contrast to web newsboard contributions that seldom reveal the authors' e-mail addresses, in mailing lists and newsgroups every posting comes with an e-mail address. This means that explicit agreement for the use of quotations can be obtained, and the mode of citation can be coordinated (e.g., anonymous or with mention of the name). Beyond the ethical purpose of informed consent, contacting the respective authors of the online contributions analyzed may provide valuable additional background information (Sharf, 1999, p. 251). But getting in touch with posters is not always possible. If postings whose publication date is several years old are used for analyses, then one must assume that many of the indicated e-mail addresses are already outdated. If a larger amount of postings is analyzed, contacting all posters might be too costly. In addition, some posters of worthwhile online contributions will be slow or unreliable when it comes to responding to a researcher's request for citation permission. Furthermore, many researchers feel that data collection without explicit permission is ethical if a content analysis of the postings is conducted and the published results summarize individual statements. The lack of general ethical rules in online research should encourage us to discuss our respective ethical decisions and their implications in more detail.

Conclusion

For the investigation of cyber-romance, data can be collected via observational studies, interviews and surveys as well as via naturally occurring personal narratives and practical suggestions. The possibility of logging and documenting online communication automatically, unnoticed by the participants, and without the use of any additional technical equipment is a major advantage of online research. In addition, the fact that many lay persons publish their experiences with and attitudes towards cyber-romantic relationships makes net forums valuable data sources, whereby there is no cause to generally doubt the accounts' authenticity. In view of diverging concepts of privacy and copyright, harvesting net documents raises ethical problems, which have to be solved individually in each specific context.

Although research activities in the field of cyber-romance are on the rise and several characteristics of cyber-romances have meanwhile been well-replicated (e.g., accelerated self-disclosure), there is still call for systematic empirical data. The economy of online data collection may, on the one hand, be conducive for relatively unprepared ad-hoc studies, but can, on the other hand, save resources better invested in designing the study. Representative results can be obtained from observational studies, interviews and surveys for example by selecting net forums, observation times or respondent samples from defined populations according to random sample principles. In contrast, analyses based on personal narratives or discussion contributions cannot be regarded as representative since we still know too little about the motives that prompt certain net users to publicly tell the story of their online love or to publicly give advice on cyber-romance. It would be worthwhile to examine in which respect descriptions of cyber-romance published on the internet deviate from descriptions recollected in the framework of representative studies. So it must be assumed that personal narratives published on the net turn out to be more spectacular and eccentric. That cyber-romance is not a homogeneous phenomenon determined by media technology is easily proven through an explorative analysis of personal narratives, in which totally different experiences are represented (Archive of Cyber Love Stories: http://www.lovelife.com/LS/):

- "Love is hard. CyberLove is impossible. I have learned this." (Story 130)
- "A sad cyberlove story, but a true one. On one hand the skeptics were right, it didn't work out, but it did for 3 months, and those three months, were among the best of my life." (Story 119)
- "I have found my one true love and for anyone that thinks that it can't happen on-line, you are wrong! Love can be found online!" (Story 161)

If one takes into account that people clearly differ both in the way they build social relationships, and in how they deal with computer-mediated communication, then it is not surprising to which extent the experiences are heterogeneous. If further research activities manage to process this heterogeneity, then mono-causal explanation models, which either attribute the existence of cyber-romance to personal deficits ("Only the social inept, lonely computer freak searches for love on the net."), and/or are directly derived from media characteristics ("In the computer-based virtual reality illusionary love flourishes and people get addicted to those mock feelings."), should lose some of their persuasive power. Contrasting virtuality with reality, the mind against the flesh, or the online relationship against the offline relationship is doubtful and at the same time necessary. Doubtful because dichotomous schematizing as a willful neglect of ambiguity and interdependence generally has the disadvantage of oversimplification. Contrasting is necessary, however, because the participants themselves frequently interpret their experiences in terms of dichotomous concepts, and then tend to contrast for example the "virtual life" with the "real life". The hypothesis of two distinct experiential realms prove then to be illusory when instructive irritations crop up:

> Of course I then asked myself what MrNorth looks like. That means: first I simply had an imaginary picture of him. Approx. 1,85 meters [6' 1"] tall, brown hair, brown eyes. How on earth did I deduce that? Lautrec says it isn't cool to ask a new chat acquaintance about their looks. And nevertheless most do it. MrNorth and I were cool. We did not ask each other for a long time. But nevertheless it did once strike me that that he might have a moustache and wire-framed spectacles. After that I had to ask nevertheless. He asked whether I knew Cyrano de Bergerac—that was him. He neither wears a moustache, nor spectacles, but is 1,65 meters [5' 5"] tall. How that frightened me. It disappointed me—I had wished him to be taller. The idea of chatting with such a small man dampened my joy in our talks. And then frightened me again. His looks meant that much to me? Me, who always stressed the importance of values? Now that was definitely uncool. And it was all different again. It turned out to be a joke—my virtual interlocutor had wanted to put me to the test. In reality he is some centimeters taller than I am. Although the "joke" had annoyed me a little—it had had its effect. I began to have second thoughts about my expectations. And discovered in me some completely narrow-minded ideal conceptions which I thought I had long overcome. That on the one hand—and on the other hand I became conscious of what is really important to me in a man's looks. Some other ideas, hitherto unquestioned, also changed. (Priscilla, 1999, December 9th, 1998)

An online love affair does not necessarily lend itself to better self-realization, though. Instead, dispositions independent of media technology might be decisive here (e.g., cognitive and motivational requirements for self-reflection).

About fifteen years ago, computer-mediated contacts were accused of being impersonal, unemotional, and solely determined by facts and logic due to their "technological nature." Today the exact opposite is claimed. Communication technology is blamed for inventing a dreamland, encouraging people to quickly and openly express romantic feelings and sexual attraction instead of sticking to a matter-of-fact information exchange. Caution and reserve when dealing with net acquaintances are frequently advised these days in order to resist the temptations of online love and cyber-romance. For further research into online relationships, it seems particularly sensible not to interpret anonymity and intimacy, physical distance and sensual presence, the ability to control and unpredictability as pairs of opposites, but instead to explore them as interrelated complements that affect the quality of both our online and offline romances.

References

Adamse, M. & Motta, S. (1996). Online Friendship, Chat-Room Romance and Cybersex. Your Guide to Affairs of the Net. Deerfield Beach, FL: Health Communications Inc.

Albright, J. & Conran, T. (1995). Online Love: Sex, Gender and Relationships in Cyberspace. [Online]. Retrieved 15.10.1999. Available: http://www-scf.usc.edu/~albright/onlineluv.txt

Anderson, T. (1999a). The Experience of Online Romance. [Online]. Retrieved 15.10.1999. Available: http://members.aol.com/andersontl/surveys/romancesurvey.htm

Anderson, T. (1999b). Perceptions of Online Relationships and Affairs. [Online]. Retrieved 15.10.1999. Available: http://members.aol.com/andersontl/surveys/CMRTsurvey.htm

Booth, R. & Jung, M. (1996). Romancing the Net. A "Tell-All" Guide to Love Online. Rocklin, CA: Prima Publishing.

Cooper, A.; Scherer, C.; Boies, S.; & Gordon, B. (1999). Sexuality on the Internet: From Sexual Exploration to Pathological Expression. Professional Psychology: Research and Practice, 30 (2), 154–164. Also [Online]. Available: http://www.apa.org/journals/pro/pro302154.html

Debatin, B. (1997). Analyse einer öffentlichen Gruppenkonversation im Chat-Room. Referenzformen, kommunikationspraktische Regularitäten und soziale Strukturen in einem kontextarmen Medium (Vortrag gehalten auf der Jahrestagung der Fachgruppe Computervermittelte Kommunikation der DGPuK in München 1997). [Online]. Available: http://www.uni-leipzig.de/~debatin/German/Chat.htm

Döring, N. (2000). Romantische Beziehungen im Netz. [Romantic Online Relationships] In C. Thimm (Hrsg.), Soziales im Netz. Sprache, Beziehungen und Kommunikationskulturen im Netz [The Social on the Net. Language, Social Relationships, and Communication Cultures on the Net] (S. 39-70). Opladen: Westdeutscher Verlag.

Döring, N. (1999). Sozialpsychologie des Internet [Social Psychology of the Internet]. Göttingen: Hogrefe.

Greenfield, D. & Cooper, A. (o.J.). Crossing the Line—On Line. Self-Help and Psychology Magazine, Rubrik "Cyber-Affairs". [Online]. Available: http://www.shpm.com/articles/sex/sexcross.html

Gwinnell, E. (1998). Online Seductions. Falling in Love with Strangers on the Internet. New York, NY: Kodansha International.

Hamman, R. (1998). The Online/Offline Dichotomy: Debunking Some Myths about AOL Users and the Affects of Their Being Online Upon Offline Friendships and Offline Community (MPhil Dissertation, University of Liverpool, Department of Communication Studies). [Online]. Available: http://www.cybersoc.com/mphil.html

Hinde, R.A. (1997). Relationships: A Dialectical Perspective. Hove, East Sussex: Psychology Press.

Katz, J. & Aspden, P. (1997). A nation of strangers? Friendship patterns and community involvement of Internet users. Communications of the ACM, 40 (12), 81–86. Also [Online]. Available: http://www.iaginteractive.com/emfa/friendship.htm

Kim & Kellie (1999). Kim and Kellie's Commitment Ceremony. [Online]. Available: http://www.geocities.com/WestHollywood/Village/6400/cc.html

King, S.A. (1999). Internet Gambling and Pornography: Illustrative Examples of the Psychological Consequences of Communication Anarchy. CyberPsychology and Behavior, 2 (3), 175–184.

Maheu, M.M. (1999). Cyber-affairs Survey Results. Self-Help & Psychology Magazine, Rubrik "Cyber-affairs". [Online]. Available: http://www.shpm.com/articles/cyber_romance/

McManus, P. (1999). Online Romantic Relationship Survey. [Online]. Available: http://www.shsu.edu/~ccp_pwm/

Odzer, C. (1997). Virtual Spaces. Sex and the Cyber Citizen. New York, NY: Berkley Books.

Parks, M. & Floyd, K. (1996). Making Friends in Cyberspace. Journal of Computer-Mediated Communication, 1 (4), March 1996 [Online]. Available: http://www.ascusc.org/jcmc/vol1/issue4/parks.html

Parks, M. & Roberts, L. (1997). "Making MOOsic": The development of personal relationships on-line and a comparison to their off-line counterparts (Paper presented at the Annual Conference of the Western Speech Communication Association. Monterey, California.). [Online]. Available: http://psych.curtin.edu.au/people/robertsl/moosic.htm

Pedds & Birdie (1999). Peddler & Nitebird's Beachouse. [Online]. Available: http://members.xoom.com/Beachouse/

Phlegar, P. (1996). Love Online: A Practical Guide to Digital Dating. Cambridge, MA: Addison Wesley Longman.

Priscilla (1999). Priscillas Tagebuch. [Online]. Available: http://www.priscilla.ch/ or Mirror-Site Available: http://paeps.psi.uni-heidelberg.de/doering/priscilla/

Sannicolas, N. (1997). Erving Goffman, Dramaturgy, and On-Line Relationships. Cybersociology Magazine, 1. [Online]. Available: http://members.aol.com/Cybersoc/islnikki.html

Schildmann, I., Wirausky, H. & Zielke, A. (1995). Spiel- und Sozialverhalten im MorgenGrauen (Hausarbeit für das Seminar "Technik und Gesellschaft" an der Universität Bielefeld). [Online]. Available: http://www.mud.de/Forschung/verhalten.html

Sharf, B.F. (1999). Beyond Netiquette: The Ethics of Doing Naturalistic Discourse Research on the Internet. In Steve Jones (Ed.), Doing Internet Research. Critical Issues and Methods for Examining the Net (pp. 243-256). Thousand Oaks, CA: Sage.

Shaw, D. (1997). Gay Men and Computer Communication: A Discourse of Sex and Identity in Cyberspace. In Jones, Steven G. (Ed.), Virtual Culture. Identity and Communication in Cybersociety (pp. 133-145). London: Sage.

Skrilloff, L. & Gould, J. (1997). Men are from Cyberspace. The Single Woman's Guide to Flirting, Dating and Finding Love On-Line. New York, NY: St. Martin's Press.

Sternberg, R. (1986). A triangular theory of love. Psychological Review, 93, 119-135.

Sue (1997). New to Cyber Liaisons. Cybersociology Magazine 1. [Online]. Available: http://members.aol.com/Cybersoc/is1sue.html

Theman, D. (1997). Beyond Cybersex: Charming Her Online, Meeting Her Offline. San Francisco, CA: Liberty Publishing.

Turkle, S. (1995). Life on the Screen: Identity in the Age of the Internet. New York, NY: Simon and Schuster.

Ullman, E. (1996). Come in, CQ: The Body and the Wire. In L. Cherny & E. Weise (Eds.)

Wired Women. Gender and New Realities in Cyberspace (pp. 3-23). Seattle: Seal Press.

Wellman, B. & Gulia, M. (1999). Virtual communities as communities. Net surfers don't ride alone. In M. A. Smith & P. Kollock (Eds.), Communities in Cyberspace (pp. 167-194). London & New York: Routledge.

Wetzstein, T.; Dahm, H.; Steinmetz, L.; Lentes, A.; Schampaul, S. & Eckert, R. (1995). Datenreisende. Die Kultur der Computernetze. Opladen: Westdeutscher Verlag.

Young, K. (1998). Caught in the Net: How to Recognize the Signs of Internet Addiction And a Winning Strategy for Recovery. New York: Wiley.

conversations in context ...4

II. The Conversation

In research on cyber-relationships, true inquiry does not limit itself to deciding if online relationships are "good" or "bad," "normal" or "abnormal," "real" or "pretend." Other points of inquiry help us to ask larger, less simplified questions: How does one define an online relationship? What human needs does it serve? What features of a healthy relationship does it seem to have, and what does it lack? Which forms of communication does it develop, and which does it neglect? Are both genders equally served, or equally under-served, by such relationships? And what effect does it have upon younger folks, who are just learning about love relationships? As you can see, the array of potential conversations about this topic is rich, varied, and current.

What follows is just a sample of some of those conversations—and some artifacts of the phenomenon as well. That is, this conversation is comprised not only of people writing about the topic, but also some sample words and images from the actual relationships themselves and the virtual "places" where they meet. As you read, don't just look for conclusions, but also for further research questions that you might ask.

> "Women find cyberspace comforting because they are not being judged by their looks. But they also leave themselves very open to manipulation because there is a tendency, in chat rooms particularly, to give away a lot about yourself very quickly." *Jenny Madden, the founder of Women in Cyberspace*
>
> *Source: BBC NEWS World Edition, Aug 17, 2002 http://news.bbc.co.uk/2/hi/uknews/ 2199695.stm*

> Some of the research exploring online romantic relationships has focussed on the issue of online adultery or cybercheating, which may be defined as forming an intimate relationship with someone other than the primary partner through the internet. There have been increasing reports of internet infidelity (Gwinnell 2001) and suggestions that online adultery is becoming an increasingly attractive form of social and/or sexual behaviour (Cooper, McLoughlin & Campbell 2000). In addition, some have claimed that online adultery accounts for a growing number of divorces in the USA (Quitter 1997). Thus, it is perhaps not surprising that Schwartz and Southern (2000) reported that the majority of their respondents who were involved in online sex were married. Similarly, Wysocki (1998) found that half the respondents who said they were involved in online sexual relationships also reported that they were married, some with up to three children. Although both men and women were found to be involved in internet infidelity, the majority of these self-confessed online adulterers were male. *Elizabeth Hardie and Simone Buzwell*
>
> *Source: Australian Journal of Emerging Technologies and Society Vol. 4, No. 1, 2006, pp: 1-14. **Finding Love Online: The Nature and Frequency of Australian Adults' Internet Relationships** http://www.swinburne.edu.au/hosting/ijets/journal/V4N1/ pdf/v4n1-1-hardie.pdf*

conversations in context ...4

When theorists discuss relationships developed in cyberspace, they also often focus their writings on the absence of the body. Cybersex, for instance, has been a popular topic of discussion. In their discussions of cybersex, theorists often emphasize the idea that participants can engage in virtual sex without the *real presence* of bodies. In respect to Internet romantic relationships, one writer has commented that 'some Internet lovers come to the conclusion that they love each other before they even meet or without ever meeting' (Gwinnell, 1998, p. 89). The implication here is that bodies can only meet offline. To give a further example, McRae (1996) has defined cybersex or virtual sex as 'a generic term for erotic interaction between individuals whose bodies may never touch' (p. 243). Again this writer is focusing on the lack of bodies online. An alternative view of cyberspace is that it existed before the origins of the Internet, in the form of telephone calls. As such, theorists such as Stratton (1997) argue, cyberspace should essentially be understood 'simply as the space produced by human communication when it is mediated by technology in such a way that the body is absent' (p. 29). . . .

In contrast to this very restricted view, which is somewhat of a metaphysical interpretation, it is argued in this paper that the phenomenon of flirting behavior in cyberspace is such that it is in fact there construction of the body that is imperative to the success of many interpersonal interactions over the Internet. For example, Stone (1995) has discussed the importance of the body in telephone sex. She has pointed out that telephone sex is clearly a different kind of sex to physical or 'embodied' sex. Physical sex involves a range of senses, touch, sight, sound, smell and hearing. In contrast, telephone sex workers are required to translate the physical experience of sex into an audible form. In turn, the receiver at the other end of the line needs to reconstitute these images. As Stone (1995) describes, 'what's being sent back and forth over the wires isn't merely information, it's bodies, not physical objects, but the information necessary to reconstruct the meaning of body to almost any desired depth and complexity' (p. 244). In respect to cyberspace, while it cannot be denied that the physical body is not present in the textual exchanges in cyberspace, how the real physical body is reconstructed should be of interest to researchers. For although we do not have physical, tangible bodies in cyberspace, we do nevertheless have bodies.
Monica Therese Whitty

Source: Monica Therese Whitty, **Cyber-Flirting: Playing at Love on the Internet**
   http://tap.sagepub.com/cgi/reprint/13/3/339 Theory & Psychology
   DOI: 10.1177/0959354303013003003

conversations in context ...4

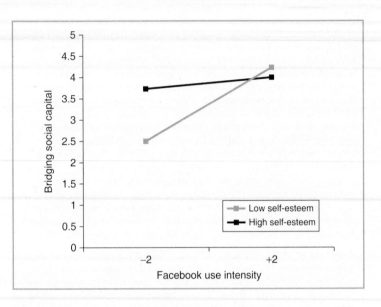

Online social network sites may play a role different from that described in early literature on virtual communities. Online interactions do not necessarily remove people from their offline world but may indeed be used to support relationships and keep people in contact, even when life changes move them away from each other. In addition to helping student populations, this use of technology could support a variety of populations, including professional researchers, neighborhood and community members, employees of companies, or others who benefit from maintained ties.

Source: The Benefits of Facebook "Friends:" Social Capital and College Students' Use of Online Social Network Sites Nicole B. Ellison, Charles Steinfield, Cliff Lampe Michigan State University http://jcmc. indiana.edu/vol12/issue4/ellison.html

From Voyeurs to Actors

Not too long ago there was a major change in Cyberspace, and it had to do with how people explore social relationships online. In the days of Web 1.0, we were voyeurs. We passively looked up words and images and watched. In the past, for a long time, the most popular way people used the Internet was to access pornography. Web 2.0 means the read-write Internet—where people aren't just passive observers of published content, but they contribute and interact. So recently that long-held statistic that the Internet was mostly for porn, was overturned. Now the most popular way people use the Internet is for social networking sites like *Facebook*. Porn use is down.

Source: Karen Dill, Ph.D. Love Is . . . Online. Psychology Today blog. Created Feb 14 2010 9:46am. http://www.psychologytoday.com/blog/how-fantasy-becomes-reality/201002/love-isonline.

"We're not looking for clones, but our models emphasize similarities in personality and in values. It's fairly common that differences can initially be appealing, but they're not so cute after two years. If you have someone who's Type A and real hard charging, put them with someone else like that. It's just much easier for people to relate if they don't have to negotiate all these differences." *Galen Buckwalter, psychologist, on his computer program for finding mates.*

Source: John Tierney, Hitting It Off, Thanks to Algorithms of Love. New York Times, January 29, 2008. http://www.nytimes.com/2008/01/29/science/29tier.html

Millions of lovelorn people turn to self-help books, searching for the magic words that might save a relationship. But their *own* writing may provide the key to everlasting love, according to researchers at The University of Texas at Austin.

In a study titled "How Do I Love Thee? Let Me Count the Words," Psychology Professor James W. Pennebaker and graduate student Richard B. Slatcher found writing about one's romantic relationship may help it last longer.

Source: Tracy Mueller, Language of Love: http://www.utexas.edu/features/2007/writing/index.html

conversations in context ...4

He Faded Out of the Relationship

by collegegirlNk
(louisiana)

More Important Articles

Financially secure
How to apologize
Trust issues
Looking for a husband?
Understanding men
Seduce him!
Laser hair removal
Cure acne now!
Tempted to cheat?
Building self-esteem
Does he like you?
Get your ex back
Best internet dating sites
Sexy things to say
How to be beautiful
Dealing with jealousy
Signs of lying
Find a husband
How to flirt
No contact rule

My ex and I dated near three years, mostly long distance. The first year was fine. He loved me to death, a nice gentleman, spoke to me nearly every day. Of course, half the time we spent arguing over pointless things but in the end we always got a good laugh out of it.

Then things started going downhill for him which changed him through and through. He started hanging with the wrong crowd and treating me badly, disrespecting me and such. Soon after he got out of the crowd, his grandmother died who he was close to then a few short months later his mom died from a wreck. He was so devestated and depressed. He couldn't sleep over nightmares and so he would call or text me and I would stay up with him talking no matter school night or not.

Eventually he started pulling further away from me and he just faded out of the relationship. He wouldn't tell me how he was feeling, he became snappy and moody. He even quit some of his favorite hobbies over the situation. I know everyone handles deaths differently and I gave him space did all I could to help him because I have been in similar situation before, but nothing seemed to help. Sometimes he even went to the point he wouldn't argue with me anymore. He would just tell me the famous words "Whatever, do what you like."

He was slowly crushing my heart and it nearly killed me being so far from him not being able

What do open sites like this suggest about individuals' desire to make their love relationships public? Is this a new phenomenon, or just a new medium for this desire?

Source: http://www.dating-relationship-advice-for-women.com/he-faded-out-of-the-relationship.html

---

Last month, three unrelated stories challenged the idea that internet relationships are just fantasy and therefore less important, less powerful and less real than offline relationships.

They aren't . . .

The common thread among these stories is that people get deeply involved in online relationships and make decisions about their real lives. Calling any of these online relationships "fantasy" dismisses the impact they have on the people involved and on those closest to them. We all know we do things in the heat of the moment that we might not if we stepped back and thought about it for a while. Online environments can extend that "heat of the moment" feeling over long periods of time; physical environments often don't. . . .

I have broadened my horizons since the first *Sex Drive* column more than four years ago. And I have yet to encounter anything that challenges my core belief: Relationships are real wherever they form.

Regina Lynn, *Sex Drive Column*

Source: Regina Lynn, Don't Dismiss Online Relationships as Fantasy. 09.07.07. www.wired.com/culture/lifestyle/commentary/sexdrive/2007/09/sexdrive_0907.

Story 1

So, what is Cyberlove?

Thanks to the late 20th century technology the Danish Maria and Martijn of Holland met on a chatline. For months they've talked and sent letters to each other with the help of their computers as they found themselves falling head over heels in love. It was then they've decided to meet in the real, not only the virtual, world. It was not easy to arrange as the young man and his lady were separated by 700 very real kilometers, but the date was a success and Maria and Martijn have been living together happily ever since. They've created a home page to let the world know how they've found happiness via the Internet and introduce couples who've met under similar circumstances.

MsGreenFields had hoped for a similar romance when she met her love on the internet. They've arranged to meet. The lonely young woman felt she'd finally found the man with whom she can live with in harmony and realize her dreams. Their personalities and interests were so similar and even their goals seemed to match well. She was not disappointed in his physical appearance either—the man was elegantly dressed, and the romantic champagne dinner, dance and the man's compliments and attention toward her during the evening all served to fuel her feelings of happy expectation. What could have been the happiest of nights turned into a nightmare when they got to her apartment. The man she just spent a wonderful evening with turned into Mr. Hyde and brutally raped her and disappeared. She didn't even have the opportunity to report the incident to the police. What could she have said about the man she knew only as StandByMe through electronic contact and who supposedly, just arrived from Las Vegas. More than likely, StandByMe continues to prowl cyberspace looking for new victims probably under a new nickname and, of course, unpunished.

These two stories are merely two samples of the many experiences you may find on different web sites that feature the topic cyberlove.

Story 53

I Seriously Doubt We Shall Ever Meet

Hello Andrea,

I just happened to come across your site and was fascinated by the varied stories portrayed in those pages. One of the things that struck me was the ephemeral nature of those relationships. They seemed like flowers that either bloomed or were blighted in mere heartbeats.

My story is somewhat different for, you see, I have been conducting a relationship by email and now ICQ with a woman 9,000 miles away since 1991. In that time we have never met, and I seriously doubt we ever shall.

It started in a newsgroup dedicated to an organisation we both belong to. She sent in a cheeky message and I replied in kind. Without any apparent effort we were soon emailing each other daily, sharing our stories, fears, and hopes in ways that I would dread to do with anybody else. In a way, I talked to her in deeper ways than I did my wife (yes, I am married and so is she). A spark developed between us that seemed almost miraculous. In 1994 she lost her job and with it her access to the internet. We tried to maintain the relationship through "snail-mail" but the time between letters did not suit the quickfire nature of our minds.

Source for all three is Cyberlove 101: http://www.cyberlove101.com/

III. Entering the Conversation

Loving online—whether it constitutes the *source* of a physical relationship, or the *whole* of that relationship—might seem just "virtual" rather than "real." But as the excerpts above suggest, there are clearly many who rely upon these electronic means of relating to others, and some who vehemently protest against the idea that such means are somehow a mere substitute for the real thing. And the wide variety of websites, wikis, blogs, and other means of electronic romance suggest that this phenomenon is more than just a passing fad or an oddity restricted to a small segment of our culture. As such, this is a topic well worth your further study and consideration. It is also a topic that is of serious interest to a wide range of fields and disciplines.

For psychologists, who have long studied the functioning of emotions, this twist has added an important new research area. But there are many other fields that are interested as well; entrepreneurs who see this as a source of profit, philosophers and ethicists that are intrigued by this new human activity and its implications, natural scientists who consider how these relationships fit into natural drives toward love and sex, scholars of gender studies who can study the ways that the sexes engage in these activities, and so forth, all have a stake in this discussion. And as one who has likely grown up in a time in which new technologies are constantly emerging, you have a large stake as well.

There are many ways in to this discussion, and many questions that might lead you into further research, including (but certainly not limited to) the following.

- whether exclusively online relationships really fit into the category we would call "love"—or whether an online relationship conducted by someone in a committed relationship in real life could be considered "cheating" or even "adultery";

- whether online relationships can satisfy the human need to connect to others;

- whether men have differing perspectives about online relationships than women;

- whether online relationships often also develop into physical relationships;

- whether the communication in online relationships is as rich, or even richer, than that in physical relationships;

- whether emerging technologies have also changed the nature of online love relationships;

- whether online love relationships are more prominent upon particular demographic groups;

- whether online love relationships have affected the development of young people's attitudes toward, or perspectives on, love;

- whether visual imagery plays a role in online love communication;

- whether the growth of this phenomenon has been driven by business ventures.

The list, of course, could go on; indeed, you would find many other conversations on this topic should you do more research—drawing upon some of the methods suggested by Döring's piece. In any case, as you weigh in on this topic, be sure to consider this topic within the larger contexts here, and to decide what other information you may need to write in more informed ways. Below are a few ways for you to get started on extending the conversation about the implications of online love relationships through your own reading and research. You can use them as jumping off points. Feel free to take them in whatever directions your interests and your research take you, or to develop related topics on your own.

1. While the idea of disclosing one's innermost feelings for another through something as public as the worldwide web might seem like a huge change on how we see the "personal," making one's emotions for another the subject of our writing is in some ways nothing new. Love poetry, intimate novels and memoires, and artworks devoted to the love we feel have been a form of human expression from the start of our species. So in what ways has the ways that we go public with our private emotions changed in the last quarter century due to

technological change? In order to study this question, or related questions, you might do a rhetorical analysis that compares other forms of expressive writing with the kinds of disclosure that we now see on blogs, websites, and other electronic communication. Has the role of the visual changed? Is the language used to express oneself different? Are the relationships formed via the internet different in kind from those that were formed in love letters, journal entries, and other more private forms of communication? In order to write on this topic, you might collect primary artifacts that are available in historical or family records (letters, photo albums, and so forth), and do a comparative analysis with those forms of expression that are now seen via the web. As you do so, go beyond just the media used and compare the language, tone, and forms of expression across time to reach some conclusions about what has changed, and what has remained constant, in the expression of human love relationships.

2. Dating sites have gone beyond a last resort for "lonely hearts" to a frequently used medium for finding love. If you listen to the advertisements for these sites, you will hear the stories of individuals who have found their soul mate via these services. But how successful are these sites in matching individuals with common beliefs, worldviews, and interests? To study this question, you might do a combination of primary and secondary research. Start with the secondary research, and seek out some of the many studies of the success of such sites, paying special attention to the methods used to measure that "success." Is success measured by the length of relationships formed there? By the rate of marriages? By whether individuals who "meet" there proceed to physical relationships? By case studies of individuals that met via electronic means? And how were these studies conducted? Did the researchers use interviews? Surveys? Ethnographies, where they spent time among couples that had met through a dating service? Drawing upon the methods you find most effective and most feasible for you as a researcher, you then might go on to conduct your own study of those who use these sites, collecting and analyzing data about the success of these services among a particular demographic group (college students, divorced individuals, senior citizens, and so on). As you analyze, you should also formulate a definition of what might be considered a successful relationship.

3. While many of the relationships that are formed (and in some cases carried out) online are between otherwise unattached individuals, recent studies have also begun to look at cyber cheating—that is, the development of love relationships by those who are married or in committed physical relationships. The question here, of course, is whether such online relationships (or even online flirting) constitute an act of betrayal or even an act of adultery. To study this question, you might proceed in a number of ways. You could analyze the discussions of such relationships that have been conducted by behavioral scientists or ethicists. You might consider how religious views play into

this. Or you might look at the available artifacts or narratives of the relationships that are readily available on the web. You could also use a survey or questionnaire to see how many individuals admit to such cyber-cheating or flirting, and gather their perspectives on its moral implications. In the end, you may be able to formulate—and write about—the informed opinions that emerge from this research about when lines are crossed, whether online love banter represents an actual betrayal, whether it rises to the level of adultery, and so forth.

conversations in context ...4

CHAPTER 8

The Ideal and Real of Marriage

Stephanie Coontz

The Evolution of Matrimony: The Changing Social Context of Marriage

Stephanie Coontz is Director of Research and Public Education for the Council on Contemporary Families. She is the author of *Marriage, A History: From Obedience to Intimacy, or How Love Conquered Marriage* (2005); *The Way We Never Were: American Families and the Nostalgia Trap* (1992 and 2000); *The Way We Really Are: Coming to Terms with America's Changing Families* (1997); and *The Social Origins of Private Life: A History of American Families, 1600–1900* (1988). As is evident by her associations and writings, Coontz has long concerned herself with the study of marriage. In this piece, she notes that marriage has changed more in the last 30 years than in the last 3,000. If that is true, you should be able to trace some serious differences between the conception of marriage as noted in this piece, published in 2005, and the ways it was seen by earlier writings about marriage. You might also look forward, considering whether the predictions made by Coontz in 2005 have already begun to come true.

1   As both a social institution and a personal experience, marriage has changed more in the past 30 years than the preceding 3,000 years. The changes in marriage have rolled across the West at different rates and have taken different

forms depending on each region's cultural and religious traditions, political institutions, and economic conditions. No area
has been exempt. Even people who are completely committed
to "traditional" family life and communities that have laws and
values to penalize departures from older norms have been
caught up in these marital changes.

Right in America's Bible belt exist some of the highest rates of   2
divorce and unwed motherhood in the country, and born again
Christians divorce just as often as atheists. In 2000, Belgium, the
only European state still without no-fault divorce, had higher
divorce rates than its more liberal neighbors. As of 2004, Chile
was the only country in the Western Hemisphere that still prohibited divorce entirely. Yet between 1990 and 2003, the number of marriages in Chile fell from 100,000 to 60,000 a year, and
nearly half of all children born in Chile in the early years of the
twenty-first century were born to unmarried couples.

The revolution in marriage is changing everything therapists   3
used to think they knew about how families work and how to
work with families. It is rendering obsolete many older sociological findings about who marries and why, who divorces, what
predicts a good marriage, and what the consequences of non-
marriage may be. It challenges our work practices, school sched-
ules, health benefits, and interpersonal ethics, and even our
most cherished emotional assumptions about marriage, divorce,
parenting, sexuality, and gender roles.

Many people believe that the essence of the marriage revolution   4
is the multiplication of diverse family arrangements. However, this
is not what's new about marriage and family life. Through most of
history, family diversity was the norm, and some of the variations
in marriage that were acceptable in the past make our own supposedly "anything goes" society look downright conservative.

The most commonly approved form of marriage across the   5
ages was polygamy, in which one man could marry several
women, but in a few parts of Asia and India, one woman might
be married to several men. Single parent families and stepfam-
ilies were much more widespread in the past than they are
today, although unlike today there were around an equal number of single-father and single-mother households. Usually, these
family forms were created by high death rates. In many traditional hunting and gathering societies, in parts of nineteenth-
century Japan, and in twentieth-century Malaysia, divorce rates
were higher than those in the United States today. Also, half of
all children born in nineteenth-century Austria, compared to
less than a third in contemporary America, were born out of
wedlock (Coontz, 2005; Therborn, 2004).

Contrary to the ethnocentric notion that there are universal   6
emotional reactions and child outcomes attached to particular

marital arrangements, some cultures have happily accepted arrangements that would lead to misery or even murder in today's context. In many cultures women welcomed the presence of co-wives because it gave them more freedom to come and go. "Without co-wives," they said, "a woman's work is never done." The Innuit of Alaska believed that divorce should be accomplished without jealousy and that remarriage created lasting ties between the ex-husband and the new one. A remarried woman's partner had the obligation to allow the former spouse, as well as any children of that union, to fish, hunt, and gather in the territory of the new spouse. In ancient Rome, men who had been successively married to and divorced from the same woman sometimes chipped in to jointly build her a monument after her death (Coontz, 2005).

7   Perhaps the most startling example of the cultural specificity of marital values is found in several small-scale societies in South America, where people believe that any man who has sex with a woman during her pregnancy contributes part of his biological substance to the child. The husband is recognized as the primary father, but all such supplementary fathers have a duty to share food with the woman and her child in the future. During the 1990s, researchers taking oral histories found that many women took lovers during their pregnancy for this very reason, and a child with a secondary father was twice as likely to survive to age 15 as a child whose mother had only slept with her husband during her pregnancy (Coontz, 2005).

8   Even with marital arrangements and family forms that look more familiar on the surface, interpersonal dynamics and family values often differ radically from our own. Today we stress the importance of open communication and the expression of intimate feelings or inner truths. By contrast, when seventeenth- and eighteenth-century American lovers said they wanted candor from each other, they did not mean the kind of soul-baring intimacy that most modern Americans expect, nor the idea that in a good relationship you talk frankly about your disappointments with your partner and get your grievances off your chest. Instead, candor referred to fairness, kindliness, and good temper. People wanted a mate who did not pry too deeply under the surface. The ideal mate, as U.S. President John Adams put it in his diary, was willing "to palliate faults and mistakes, to put the best construction upon words and action, and to forgive injuries" (Rothman, 1984, p. 43).

9   In the contemporary world, there are many regional, class, and ethnic variations in the kinds of marital interactions that are considered desirable and healthy. The public expression of tender emotions toward a lover or spouse is frowned upon in many peasant and working-class communities because this is seen as cutting across the other solidarities that are needed

when neighbors vitally depend upon each other. Husbands and wives often relate to each other in public through a ritualized language of gender hostility, hiding any fondness they may really feel for each other. They refer to each other as "the old man" or, in the Cockney rhyming slang for a wife, "the trouble and strife" (Medick & Sabean, 1984).

Modern Americans tend to interpret such patterns as a sign 10 of people's inability to reach their true or deepest inner feelings, but many Japanese citizens, according to Takeo Doi, feel that "those who are close to each other—that is to say, who are privileged to merge with each other—do not need words to express their feelings. One surely would not feel merged with another . . . if one had to verbalize a need to do so!" (Morsbach & Tyler, 1986, p. 290).

Anthropologists Lila Abu-Lughod and Catherine Lutz suggest 11 that inner truths and emotions are just as much culturally constructed as are the behaviors that we tend to label superficial social conventions. Some cultures see emotions as expressions of rules that govern social relationships. As such, an opposition between what you should feel and what you really feel may be inexplicable to them (Abu-Lughod & Lutz, 1990).

In contemporary America it is taken for granted that loyalty 12 to a spouse should trump other personal ties. However, through most of history marriage was not supposed to be the most powerful wellspring of sentiment and obligation. Ministers in seventeenth-century America and England warned women against using affectionate nicknames for their husbands because that would undermine the authority relations essential to a proper marriage. A common Chinese saying was "you have only one family, but you can always get another wife." A Kiowa Indian woman summed up a widespread sentiment in less patriarchal societies when she told a researcher, "a woman can always get another husband, but she has only one brother" (Coontz, 2005).

Novels and diaries from eighteenth- and nineteenth-century 13 Europe and America reveal that same-sex friendships and sibling ties were sometimes more intense than marital relationships, and no one saw anything deviant about this. Sociologist Vern Bengtson argues that today the extension of the life span, combined with the prevalence of non-marriage and divorce, has created a situation where multi-generational ties are surpassing nuclear family attachments and marriage as a source of well-being and social support for many individuals (Bengtson, 2001).

Not all family relations and marital values are equally valid. 14 Human beings have a cluster of biological and emotional needs, some of which are universal, but many of which depend on the particular culture, environment, and social group in which they live. Since the most universal fact about human nature is that we are social animals, it stands to reason that our psychological needs vary according to how our societies or subgroups within a society are organized. The outcome of family relations depends on the fit between the internal dynamics of a family and its social environment. The fit between marriage, gender roles, and socio-economic institutions is in the process of unprecedented change today. Thus, we should be cautious about positing universal rules in marital and family dynamics.

15   Despite all the variety of marital arrangements and family values in the past, there were two cross-cultural commonalities that characterized family life through most of history. The first was that, for thousands of years, marriage was not about a man and a woman falling in love and deciding to take their personal relationship to a higher level. Marriage was a way of acquiring influential in-laws, sealing business deals, raising capital, and expanding the family labor force. So one almost universal cross-cultural value was that young people should not be allowed to freely choose their own marriage partner, especially for such a self-indulgent reason as love.

16   It was only 200 years ago that it became respectable and even preferable for people to marry for love, and only 100 years ago that husbands and wives began to be encouraged to develop intense sexual ties and to put their relationship ahead of all other family and friendship ties. The result was that over the course of the twentieth century marriage gradually became more fulfilling, more loving, and more central to people's identity than in the past, but it also became more fragile. Heightened expectations about fairness and mutual consideration made a good marriage work better for both the husband and wife than ever before, but also led many people to find it less bearable to enter or stay in a marriage that did not live up to those expectations.

17   The second common theme in the overwhelming majority of marriages through the ages, and one that lasted even longer than the barriers to romantic and sexualized love between husband and wife, was that marriage was traditionally based on the legal, economic, and reproductive subordination of women. "Husband and wife are one, and that one is the husband" said the English common law, which was also adopted in America and regulated marriage relations until the early twentieth century. A man had the legal right to forcibly restrain, imprison, and "correct" his wife until the late nineteenth century. As late as the 1970s, many states and most Western European countries had Head and Master laws, which gave husbands the final say over family decisions such as whether the wife could take a job and where the couple would live. Until the 1980s, the idea of marital rape was considered a contradiction in terms

because courts held that when a wife said "I do" to marriage she had said "I will" to sex whenever her husband wanted it (Coontz, 2005).

Until the 1970s, also, women's economic dependence was so   18 pervasive that most women had to get married, even if it meant settling for someone very different than who they wanted. They could not afford to turn down a shotgun marriage if it was an option, were required to make most of the adjustments that made a marriage work, and could very seldom leave a marriage even if it wasn't working and didn't seem like it ever would. It was only in the last 30 years that sizable numbers of women in the industrial countries of the world became free to truly marry for love and equally able to refuse a shotgun marriage or leave a marriage with a man they found unsatisfactory.

Never before in history have so many young people had   19 the right to make their own decisions about sexuality, courtship, and marriage, and never before in history have so many women had the amount of legal, economic, and reproductive self-determination that they have gained—however incompletely—over the past few decades. These two changes—in young people's independence from the dictates of parents and in women's independence from the dictates of men—have revolutionized marriage in Western Europe and the United States and Canada. They are also eroding its traditional roles and forms all around the globe.

Marriage is certainly not dead. Indeed, most people hold the   20 marital relationship in higher esteem than they did when the institution used to be practically mandatory. Marriage as a relationship between two individuals is taken more seriously and comes with higher emotional expectations than ever before in history. However, marriage as an institution exerts less power over people's lives than it once did. Historian Nancy Cott suggests that a good way to understand the changes in marriage in much of the industrial world is to see them as analogous to the disestablishment of religion. When the state stopped supporting one official church, religion did not disappear, but new churches and sects proliferated. When people stayed in the old church or joined it for the first time they did so for different reasons than when it was the only route to economic and political respectability, so even the traditional church had to change the way it recruited members and had to adapt to the new reasons that people chose one church over another.

The same is true of marriage. Therapists can help people "do"   21 marriage better than they currently do, but couples will have to learn how to do it differently than in the past. Researchers and clinicians need to learn more about the new reasons that people marry in this new context, along with the changing factors that keep people in marriages—or drive them away from marriage—now that marriage is more optional and less hierarchical than in the past. Relying on old adages and coasting on old techniques is no longer an option.

References

Abu-Lughod, L., & Lutz, C. (1990). Introduction. In C. Lutz & L. Abu-Lughod, (Eds.), *Language and the Politics of Emotion*. Cambridge, England: Cambridge University Press.

Bengtson, V. (2001). Beyond the nuclear family: The increasing importance of multigenerational bonds. *Journal of Marriage and Family*, 63(1) 1–16.

Coontz, S. (2005). *Marriage, a history: From obedience to intimacy, or how love conquered marriage*. New York: Viking Press.

Morsbach, H., & Tyler, W.J. (1986). A Japanese Emotion: Amae. In R. Harre (Ed.), *The social construction of emotion*. Oxford, England: Basil Blackwell.

Medick, H. & Sabean, D. (1984). *Interest and emotion: Essays on the study of family and kinship*. Cambridge, England: Cambridge University Press.

Pfister, J. (1997). On conceptualizing the cultural history of emotional and psychological life in America. In J. Pfister & N. Schnog (Eds.), *Inventing the Psychological: Toward a cultural history of emotional life in America*. New Haven, CT: Yale University Press.

Rothman, E. (1984). *Hands and hearts: A history of courtship in America*. New York: Basic Books.

Therborn, G. (2004). *Between sex and power: Families in the world, 1900-2000*. London: Routledge Press.

Jennifer Marshall

Marriage: What Social Science Says and Doesn't Say

Jennifer Marshall is the director of domestic policy studies at The Heritage Foundation, a conservative think tank that describes its mission as the formulation and promotion of "conservative public policies based on principles of free enterprise, limited government, individual freedom, traditional American values, and a strong national defense." As you read Marshall's piece, which was published in the "Research" section of Heritage's website, you might consider how it serves that organization's mission—and how it uses "research" and "social science" to bolster its argument.

S ocial science data indicate that the intact family—defined 1 as a man and a woman who marry, conceive, and raise their children together—best ensures the current and future welfare of children and society when compared with other common forms of households. As alternative family forms have become more prevalent since the 1960s, social science research and government surveys have indicated an accompanying rise in a number of serious social problems.

Government's interest in marriage has been based primarily 2 on its interest in the welfare of the next generation. Among the many types of social relationships, marriage has always had a special place in all legal traditions, our own included, because it is the essential foundation of the intact family, and no other family form has been able to provide a commensurate level of social security.

In all other common family and household forms, the risk of 3 negative individual outcomes and family disintegration is much greater, increasing the risk of dependence on state services. A free society requires a critical mass of individuals in stable households who are not dependent on the state. The most stable and secure household, the available research shows, is the intact family. Therefore, the state has an interest in protecting the intact family and we should be cautious about facilitating other forms of household, the effects of which are either deleterious or unknown.

Compared with counterparts in other common household 4 arrangements, adolescents in intact families have better health, are less likely to be depressed, are less likely to repeat a grade in school, and have fewer developmental problems, data show. By contrast, national surveys reveal that, as a group, children in other family forms studied are more likely to experience poverty, abuse, behavioral and emotional problems, lower academic achievement, and drug use. These surveys illustrate

- Adolescents in intact families, as a group, are the least likely to feel depressed compared to those with divorced, step-, cohabiting, or single parents; (National Longitudinal Survey of Adolescent Health)
- The national average grade-point scores of children in intact families is 2.98, compared to 2.79 for children of cohabiting parents and 2.71 for children living in step-families; (National Longitudinal Survey of Adolescent Health)
- The rate of youth incarceration is significantly greater for children raised in single-mother and stepfamily homes than for those raised in intact families, even after controlling for parental income and education; (National Longitudinal Survey of Youth)

- Children in non-intact families are three times as likely to have children outside of marriage; (National Longitudinal Survey of Youth) and
- Rates of engaging in problem behaviors such as lying, stealing, drunkenness, and violence are sharply higher for children of divorce compared to children in intact families. (National Longitudinal Survey of Adolescent Health)

5   During the 1990s, a serious public policy debate resulted when emerging social science data showed the consequences of several decades of experimentation with family forms. Out of this increased awareness grew a movement for policy and cultural changes to reinforce and restore marriage in America. Policy decisions—such as welfare reform—were grounded in these data. We have seen some of the fruit of those efforts in declining rates of teen sex and childbearing.

6   By contrast, the current debate over same-sex marriage is not anchored in sound research, and data on the consequences of children being brought up by same-sex couples remains scarce. Same-sex couples with children constitute a new form of household that has not been carefully studied. Nor has the objective of this policy discussion been clearly defined as the interest of children or the future of the nation's families.

7   Same-sex marriage advocates propose that we institutionalize a social experiment in its early stages by elevating it in law to the status of the oldest of institutions: marriage. That experiment is the same-sex coupling and parenting recently taking place around us. To be sure, Americans have become more accepting of other types of sexual experimentation—sex outside of marriage, cohabitation, single parenting—but do not equate them with or see them as a substitute for marriage. None of these experiments has been regarded in law as the equivalent of the intact family. Yet this is precisely the proposal before us on the question of same-sex marriage: that we institutionalize in law an experiment about which we have very little knowledge.

8   The data on the homosexual household is extremely limited. We know relatively little about the long-term effects of homosexual relationships on partners and even less about the children that will be raised in such households. Such an absence of data should give us pause before reconfiguring the basic institution of society. Thus we should study the results of the current experiment in homosexual households with children rather than forcing communities at large to accept, by law, same-sex marriage and parenting.

9   We should also further explore what it is about marriage that sets the intact family apart in the current research. Many would contend that the unique natures and contributions of a male and

a female constitute the critical characteristic of marriage, and that the distinctive sexual nature and identity of each parent, along with their number (two rather than one) and relationship status (marriage rather than cohabitation), gives the intact family the exceptional quality it exhibits. This needs to be examined carefully, to determine how having two parents of opposite sexes contributes to the upbringing of a child.

In the meantime, with the policy debate forced by same-sex   10
marriage advocates beyond the conclusions of existent social science research, we must look to the best evidence currently available about family forms and their social impacts. What we know about alternative family forms is a good indicator of what we might expect from this variant.

Modern policymaking should be informed by the realities of   11
available empirical evidence. In time, the data will be forthcoming on this newest form of experimentation, same-sex partnering and parenting, and its effects on homosexual men and women and on those who live with them. In the meantime America's marriage and family law should stay the course based on what we *do* know.

Sandra Tsing Loh

Let's Call the Whole Thing Off

Sandra Tsing Loh is an author and performer, whose solo show "Mother on Fire" garnered a good deal of critical acclaim. Her books include *A Year in Van Nuys, Aliens in America, Depth Takes a Holiday: Essays From Lesser Los Angeles,* and her novel, *If You Lived Here, You'd Be Home By Now.* She is also a commentator on National Public Radio. This piece, first published in the *Atlantic Monthly* in 2009, chronicles her decision to divorce her husband, with whom she had had a relationship for 20 years. In this exploration of the work involved in maintaining her marriage and her relationship with her children, she also examines the institution of marriage more generally, concluding with her "final piece of advice: avoid marriage." As you read this essay, consider which parts of this essay are personal narrative and which are social commentary, as well as whether the perspective she provides is unique to her gendered—and feminist—perspective.

1   Sadly, and to my horror, I am divorcing. This was a 20-year partnership. My husband is a good man, though he did travel 20 weeks a year for work. I am a 47-year-old woman whose commitment to monogamy, at the very end, came unglued. This turn of events was a surprise. I don't generally even enjoy men; I had an entirely manageable life and planned to go to my grave taking with me, as I do most nights to my bed, a glass of merlot and a good book. Cataclysmically changed, I disclosed everything. We cried, we rent our hair, we bewailed the fate of our children. And yet at the end of the day—literally during a five o'clock counseling appointment, as the golden late-afternoon sunlight spilled over the wall of Balinese masks—when given the final choice by our longtime family therapist, who stands in as our shaman, mother, or priest, I realized . . . no. Heart-shattering as this moment was—a gravestone sunk down on two decades of history—I would not be able to replace the romantic memory of my fellow transgressor with the more suitable image of my husband, which is what it would take in modern-therapy terms to knit our family's domestic construct back together. In women's-magazine parlance, I did not have the strength to "work on" falling in love again in my marriage. And as Laura Kipnis railed in *Against Love*, and as everyone knows, *Good relationships take work*.

2   Which is not to say I'm against work. Indeed, what also came out that afternoon were the many tasks I—like so many other working/co-parenting/married mothers—have been doing for so many years and tearfully declared I would continue doing. I can pick up our girls from school every day; I can feed them dinner and kiss their noses and tell them stories; I can take them to their doctor and dentist appointments; I can earn my half—sometimes more—of the money; I can pay the bills; I can refinance the house at the best possible interest rate; I can drive my husband to the airport; in his absence, I can sort his mail; I can be home to let the plumber in on Thursday between nine and three, and I can wait for the cable guy; I can make dinner conversation with any family member; I can ask friendly questions about anybody's day; I can administer hugs as needed to children, adults, dogs, cats; I can empty the litter box; I can stir wet food into dry.

3   Which is to say I can work at a career and child care and joint homeownership and even platonic male-female friendship. However, in this cluttered forest of my 40s, what I cannot authentically reconjure is the ancient dream of brides, even with the Oprah fluffery of weekly "date nights," when gauzy candlelight obscures the messy house, child talk is nixed and silky lingerie donned, so the two of you can look into each other's eyes and feel that "spark" again. Do you see? Given my

staggering working mother's to-do list, I cannot take on yet another arduous home- and self-improvement project, that of rekindling our romance. Sobered by this failure as a mother—which is to say, my failure as a wife—I've since begun a journey of reading, thinking, and listening to what's going on in other 21st-century American families. And along the way, I've begun to wonder, what with all the abject and swallowed misery: Why do we still insist on marriage? Sure, it made sense to agrarian families before 1900, when to farm the land, one needed two spouses, grandparents, and a raft of children. But now that we have white-collar work and washing machines, and our life expectancy has shot from 47 to 77, isn't the idea of lifelong marriage obsolete?

I sense you picking up the first stone to hurl, even if you your-   4 self may be twice or even three times divorced. Such a contradiction turns out to be uniquely American. Just because marriage didn't work for us doesn't mean we don't believe in the institution. Just because our own marital track records are mixed doesn't mean our hearts don't lift at the sight of our daughters' Tiffany-blue wedding invitations. After all, we can easily arrange to sit far from our exes, across the flower-bedecked aisle, so as not to roil the festive day. Just because we know that nearly half of U.S. marriages end in divorce—including perhaps even those of our own parents (my dearest childhood wish was not just that my parents would divorce, but also that my raging father would burst into flames)—doesn't mean we aren't confident ours is the one that will beat the odds. At least that is the attitudinal yin/yang described by Andrew J. Cherlin in his scrupulously argued *Marriage-Go-Round*: compared with our western European counterparts, Americans are far more credulous about marriage. In World Values Surveys taken at the turn of the millennium, fewer Americans agreed with the statement "Marriage is an outdated institution" than citizens of any other Western country surveyed (compare the U.S.'s tiny 10 percent with France's 36 percent). We are also more religious—more Americans (60 percent) say they attend religious services once a month than do the Vatican-centric Italians (54 percent) or, no surprise, the laissez-faire French (12 percent). At the same time, Americans endure the highest divorce rate in the Western world. In short, although we say we love religion *and* marriage, Cherlin notes, "religious Americans are more likely to divorce than secular Swedes."

Cherlin believes the reason for this paradox is that Americans   5 hold two values at once: a culture of marriage and a culture of individualism. Or is it an American spirit of optimism wedded, if you will, to a Tocquevillian spirit of restlessness that inspires three out of four Americans to say they believe marriage is for life, while only one in four agreed with the notion that even if a marriage is unhappy, one should stay put for the sake of the children. If America is a "divorce culture," it may be partly because we are a "marriage culture," since we both divorce *and* marry (a projected 90 percent of us) at some of the highest rates anywhere on the globe. Hence, Cherlin's cautionary advice consists of two words—"Slow down"—his chief worry about our frenetic marriage-go-round being its negative impact on our children. In fact, while having two biological parents at home is, the statistics tell us, best for children, a single-parent household is almost as good. The harm comes, Cherlin argues, from parents continually coupling with new partners, so that the children are forced to bond, or compete for attention, with ever-new actors. These are the youngsters who are likely to suffer, according to a measurable matrix of factors such as truancy, disobedience in school, and teen pregnancy. Instead of preaching marriage, Cherlin says, we should preach domestic stability for children. Is marriage the best way to ensure this? Apparently not, at least not the way we do it in America.

6   Rachel is one of the women I regularly dine with, now that I have a divorced person's oddly relaxed—oddly civilized, even horribly French?—joint-custody schedule. It has been almost 10 years since I dined with adults on a weekly basis. My domestic evenings have typically revolved around five o'clock mac and cheese under bright lighting and then a slow melt into dishes and *SpongeBob* . . . because yet another of my marital failings was that I was never able to commit to a nanny. Even though my husband and I both drew full-time incomes, I, as a writer, worked at home and hence was ambivalent, because if I had daily in-house help, what was my role as a mother? Would I be emotionally displaced? Also, I secretly worried that using domestic help was exploitative—recall Barbara Ehrenreich's dictum that she'd never let another woman scrub her toilets. Yea, these are the various postfeminist hurdles that stretched before me at 2:00 a.m. as I lay awake in our bed, contorted not just by cats but by two children kicking me from both sides—Exhibit A of lazy, undisciplined attachment parenting.

7   Imagine driving with me now to Rachel's house for our new 40-something social hobby—the Girls' Night dinner. Leap not from my car, even though I realize—given my confessed extramarital affair, avowed childhood desire to see my father explode into flames, and carpet of tattered Happy Meal wrappers—I may not strike you as the most reliable explicator of modern marriage. Still, we forge on, and what I'd like to do now is recant for a moment and not be quite so hard on marriage, which I think is a very good fit for *some* people. It certainly has been for Judith

S. Wallerstein (married more than 48 years, as the jacket flap indicates), co-author with Sandra Blakeslee of the 1995 book *The Good Marriage: How and Why Love Lasts*. Through close observation of 50 happily married couples, the authors identified four templates for lasting nuptial success. The Romantic Marriage thrives on the spark of love that never dies. (Think of those affectionate 80-somethings in convalescent homes, still holding hands.) The Rescue Marriage features partners who fit each other like lost puzzle pieces, healing each other from mutual childhood traumas. (And then there are those shrieky co-dependent pairs: think of fiercely attached couples whose commitment is cemented by a commitment to unwholesome habits. Said a friend of his 70-something WASP parents, who sally off to their frequent cruises with huge Lavoris bottles filled with gin: "What they share is an enthusiasm for drinking.") The Traditional Marriage succeeds because the man works while the woman runs the home, a clear and valuable division of labor.

Today, the most common type of marriage is the Companionate Marriage, in which husband and wife each have a career, and they co-parent and co-housekeep according to gender-free norms they negotiate. Three decades ago, in their 1972 runaway best seller, *Open Marriage,* Nena and George O'Neill suggested that such a modern arrangement might even include sexual freedom. But as we all know, the Sexually Open Marriage fizzled with the lava lamp, because it is just downright icky for most people. How, then, has marriage evolved? In what sorts of partnerships do we find ourselves in the 21st century? Enter with me, finally, the home of my friend Rachel. (To appease the diligent *Atlantic* fact checkers, I must now pause to announce that I've carefully disguised some of the individuals whose lives we're about to dissect.) Picture a stunning two-story Craftsman—exposed wood, Batchelder tile fireplace, caramel-warm beams, Tiffany lamps on Mission tables—nestled in the historic enclave in Pasadena dubbed Bungalow Heaven. Rachel, 49, an environmental lawyer, is married to Ian, 48, a documentary-film editor. They have two sons, 9 and 11, whom Ian—in every way the model dad—has whisked off this evening to junior soccer camp (or drum lessons or similar; the boys' impressive whirl of activities is hard to keep track of). Rachel is cooking dinner for three of us: Ellen (a writer, married with children), Renata (violinist, single, lithe, and prowling at 45), and me. Rachel is, more accurately, reheating dinner; the dish is something wonderfully subtle yet complex, like a saffron-infused porcini risotto, that Ian made over the weekend and froze for us, in Tupperware neatly labeled with a Sharpie, because this is the sort of thoughtful thing he does. Ian subscribes to *Cook's Illustrated* online and a bevy of other technically advanced gourmet publications—he's always perfecting some polenta or bouillabaisse. If someone

8

requests a cheeseburger, he will fire back with an über-cheese-burger, a fluffy creation of marbled Angus beef, Stilton, and homemade ketchup. Picture him in bike shorts (he's a cyclist), hovering over a mandala of pots that are always simmering, quietly simmering. To Ian's culinary adventurousness, Rachel attributes the boys' sophisticated taste buds—they eagerly eat everything: curry, paella, seaweed, soba noodles. My own girls are strictly mac-and-cheese-centric (but I've been told in therapy not to keep beating myself up over the small things).

9   Since her own home fires seemed to roar so warmly, I was hesitant to hit Rachel with news of my breakup, and it is true that her first reaction was a degree of disbelief and horror even more pronounced than everyone else's in our village of longtime marrieds. "But what about the children?" she wailed. I explained that since their parents had been in parallel motion since they were born, the girls appeared—on the surface at least—to be unfazed. On top of my musician husband's roadwork, some years I'd logged 200 shows as a theater performer, carrying my babies in buckets to hotel rooms. In addition, when my girls' cousins—at ages 6, 5, and 2—suddenly lost their mother, through illness, we had done an emergency move-in with my brother for two years (while my husband remained on the road), so my girls were more used to sitting down to dinner with an extended family tribe than with one father and one mother. Now elementary age, my children seem relatively content as long as they remain in their own house, their own beds, and their own school, with Mom and Dad coming and going as usual (and when Dad's in the house, I pick them up from school every day so they always see me). Their most ardent daily fixations continue to be amassing more Pokémon cards and getting a dog named Noodles to add to their menagerie of five fish and two cats, Midnite and Cuteface.

10   But it is now our second Girls' Night dinner since my horrifying announcement, and Rachel has eschewed Ian's customary wine-club Bordeaux and is mixing some alarmingly strong martinis.

11   Leaning forward heavily across the bar, she swirls her glass and huskily drops the bomb: "I have to tell you—since we talked, I too have started thinking divorce." "No!" we girls exclaim. With a stab of nausea, I suddenly feel as though now that I've touched my pool of friends with my black pen, a cloud of ink is enveloping them.

12   "You can't!" Renata cries. "Ian—he's the perfect father! The perfect husband! Look at this . . . kitchen!"

13   It's true: the kitchen is a prime example of Ian's contribution to their union. He based the design of the remodel on an old farmhouse kitchen they saw during their trip to Tuscany, and of course—carpentry being another of his hobbies—he did all the details himself, including building the shelves. One of the room's

marvels is how ingeniously and snugly all the specialty kitchen-ware is housed—the hanging copper pots, the garlic press, the mandolin, the lemon zester, the French press coffeemaker . . .

"Ian won't have sex with me," Rachel says flatly. "He has not   14
touched my body in two years. He says it's because I've gained weight." Again, we stoutly protest, but she goes on. "And he thinks I'm a bad mother—he says I'm sloppy and inattentive."

The list of violations unfurls. Last week, Rachel mistakenly   15
gave the wrong medication to the dog, a mistake Ian would never make. She also forgot to deglaze the saucepan and missed the window to book the family's Seattle flights on Expedia, whose chiming bargains Ian meticulously tracks.

Rachel sees herself as a failed mother, and is depressed and   16
chronically overworked at her $120,000-a-year job (which she must cling to for the benefits because Ian freelances). At night, horny and sleepless, she paces the exquisite kitchen, gobbling mini Dove bars. The main breadwinner, Rachel is really the Tra-ditional Dad, but instead of being handed her pipe and slippers at six, she appears to be marooned in a sexless remodeling proj-ect with a passive-aggressive Competitive Wife.

Rachel had even asked Ian point-blank: "Do you want a   17
divorce?" And Ian said absolutely not—they must show disci-pline and work at the marriage (again with the *work*!), since any domestic upset could negatively affect the boys, who were now facing a particularly fraught time at their new school, where they have an extraordinarily challenging roster of extracurricu-lar activities and a quarterly testing schedule.

"You know, it's funny," says Ellen, after a moment of gloom.   18
(Passing note: Ellen has been married for 18 years, and she also, famously, never has sex. There were the hot 20s with Ron and the making-the-babies 30s, and in the 40s there is . . . nothing. Ellen had originally picked Ron because she was tired of all the bad boys, and Ron was settle-down husband material. What she didn't know was that after the age of 38, thanks to Mr. Very Settled-Down, she was never going to have regular sex with a man again.)

"When marriage was invented," Ellen continues, "it was con-   19
sidered to be a kind of trade union for a woman, her protection against the sexually wandering male. But what's happened to the sexually wandering male?"

In our parents' era, the guy hit 45, got the toupee, drove the   20
red Porsche, and left his family for the young, hot secretary. We are unable to imagine any of the husbands driving anything with fewer than five seat belts.

"Ron only goes as far as the den," Ellen says. "He has his Inter-   21
net porn bookmarked on the computer."

"Ian has his *Cook's Illustrated*," Rachel adds. "And his—his   22
men's online fennel club."

23   Of the four of us, Renata has the fastest-thrumming engine, as evidenced by her rabid in-the-moment sex-tryst texting ("omg he flyz in 2nite on red i @ 2 am!!!"). One imagines a string of men toppled behind her in ditches like crashed race cars. "My problem is, I'm a dopamine freak!" She waggles her hands in the air. "Dopamine!"

24   "Helen Fisher!" Ellen exclaims, pointing at her.

25   Fisher, a women's cult figure and an anthropologist, has long argued that falling in love—and falling out of love—is part of our evolutionary biology and that humans are programmed not for lifelong monogamy, but for serial monogamy. (In stretches of four years, to be exact, approximately the time it takes to get one kid safely through infancy.)

26   *Why Him? Why Her?* explains the hormonal forces that trigger humans to be romantically attracted to some people and not to others (a phenomenon also documented in the animal world). Fisher posits that each of us gets dosed in the womb with different levels of hormones that impel us toward one of four basic personality types:

> **The Explorer**—the libidinous, creative adventurer who acts "on the spur of the moment." Operative neurochemical: dopamine.
>
> **The Builder**—the much calmer person who has "traditional values." The Builder also "would rather have loyal friends than interesting friends," enjoys routines, and places a high priority on taking care of his or her possessions. Operative neurotransmitter: serotonin.
>
> **The Director**—the "analytical and logical" thinker who enjoys a good argument. The Director wants to discover all the features of his or her new camera or computer. Operative hormone: testosterone.
>
> **The Negotiator**—the touchy-feely communicator who imagines "both wonderful and horrible things happening" to him- or herself. Operative hormone: estrogen, then oxytocin.

27   Fisher reviewed personality data from 39,913 members of Chemistry.com. Explorers made up 26 percent of the sample, Builders 28.6 percent, Directors 16.3 percent, Negotiators 29.1 percent. While Explorers tend to be attracted to Explorers, and Builders tend to be attracted to Builders, Directors are attracted to Negotiators, and vice versa.

28   Exclaims Ellen, slapping the book: "This is why my marriage has been dead for 15 years. I'm an Explorer married to a Builder!" (Ron literally is a builder—like Ian, he crafts wonderful shelves and also, of course, cooks.) But what can Ellen do?

Explorer-Explorer tends to be one of the most unstable combinations, whereas Fisher suspects "most of the world's fifty-year marriages are made by Builders who marry other Builders."
While a Rutgers study suggests that only 38 percent of mar-   29
ried people in America describe themselves as happy, we stay married for many good reasons. Take, for instance, the otherwise unaffordability of homeownership.
Some of us stay married because we're in competition with   30
our divorcing 1960s and 1970s parents, who made such a hash of it. What looks appealing to us now, in an increasingly frenetic, digital world, is the 1950s marriage. Writes Karen Karbo, in *Generation Ex*, reminiscing about her mother's evening routine of serving old-fashioneds to her dad by the pool:

> At the turn of the millennium, our marriages and remarriages bear almost no resemblance to these single-paycheck, cocktail-hour unions. Once considered sexist and monotonous, these staid marriages are emblems of an easier time. What seemed too dull and constricting a mere fifteen years ago now looks luxurious, like those huge gas-guzzling cars with all that chrome and the tuck-and-roll seats.

Some of us stay married because along with fancy schools,   31
tae kwon do lessons, and home-cooked organic food, the two-parent marriage is another impressive—and rare—attainment to bestow on our fragile, gifted children.
Some of us stay married because . . . what else is there? A   32
lonely apartment and a hot plate?
That said, it's clear that females are dissatisfied—more and   33
more, divorce seems to be initiated by women. If marriage is the Old World and what lies beyond is the New World, it's the apparently stable men (comfortable alone in their postfeminist den with their *Cook's Illustrated* and their porn) who are Old Worlders, and the Girls' Night Out, questionnaire-completing women who are the questing New Worlders. They most embody what Tocqueville described as America's "restless temper," or *l'inquiétude du caractère*. (Interestingly, according to *Enlighten Next* magazine, some northern European women are reportedly eschewing their progressive northern European male counterparts and dating Muslims, who are more like "real men.")
To work, to parent, to housekeep, to be the ones who sched-   34
ule "date night," only to be reprimanded in the home by male kitchen bitches, and then, in the bedroom, to be ignored—it's a bum deal. And then our women's magazines exhort *us* to rekindle the romance. You rarely see men's magazines exhorting men to rekindle the romance.

35   So, herewith, some modest proposals. Clearly, research shows that what's best for children is domestic stability and not having to bond with, and to be left by, ever new stepparent figures. Less important is whether or not their overworked parents are logging "date night" (or feeling the magic). So why don't we accept marriage as a splitting-the-mortgage arrangement? As Fisher suggests, rekindling the romance is, for many of us, biologically unnatural, particularly after the kids come. (Says another friend of mine, about his wife of 23 years: "My heart doesn't lift when she walks in the room. It sinks, slightly.") If high-revving women are sexually frustrated, let them have some sort of French arrangement where they have two men, the post-feminist model dad building shelves, cooking bouillabaise, and ignoring them in the home, and the occasional fun-loving boyfriend the kids never see. Alternately, if both spouses find life already rather exhausting, never mind chasing around for sex. Long-married husbands and wives should pleasantly agree to be friends, to set the bedroom aglow at night by the mute opening of separate laptops and just be done with it. More than anything, aside from providing insulation from the world at large, that kind of arrangement could be the perfect way to be left alone.

36   As far as the children are concerned, how about the tribal approach (a natural, according to both primate and human evolution)? Let children between the ages of 1 and 5 be raised in a household of mothers and their female kin. Let the men/husbands/boyfriends come in once or twice a week to build shelves, prepare that bouillabaisse, or provide sex.

37   Or best of all, after the breast-feeding and toddler years are through, let those nurturing superdads be the custodial parents! Let the Type A moms obsessively work, write checks, and forget to feed the dog. Let the dads then, if they wish, kick out those sloppy working mothers and run effective households, hiring the appropriate staff, if need be. To a certain extent, men today may have more clarity about what it takes to raise children in the modern age. They don't, for instance, have today's working mother's ambivalence and emotional stickiness.

38   In any case, here's my final piece of advice: avoid marriage—or you too may suffer the emotional pain, the humiliation, and the logistical difficulty, not to mention the expense, of breaking up a long-term union at midlife for something as demonstrably fleeting as love.

Amy Benfer

When Date Night Is Not Enough

Amy Benfer is a freelance writer and former editor of *Salon's* "Mothers Who Think" department. She also contributes regularly to *San Francisco Magazine* and *The New York Times Book Review*. In this piece, first published in 2009 in Salon.com, Benfer reacts to Sandra Tsing Loh's "Let's Call the Whole Thing Off." She uses her essay not only to explore the reasons for marriage and divorce, but also to explore the genre of the personal essay, which she lauds for showing readers not the ideal, but "the real." After reading Benfer's essay, you might return to Loh's piece as well, considering how the genre of the personal essay works, and how its fierce honesty appeals to readers. You might also try writing a personal essay of your own, testing out your ability to be detailed, open, and direct as you reflect upon one of your own experiences.

I had just settled down with a glass of wine last Saturday night and was rifling through that day's mail when I spied the new copy of the *Atlantic*. As I have done each month for the past few years, the first thing I did was turn to see if this was a good month, a *Sandra Tsing Loh month*. Hooray! It was. Watching back DVDs of "The Wire" would have to wait. But as I scanned the column, I started to panic. The headline: "Let's call the whole thing off." The subhead: "The author is ending her marriage. Isn't it time you did the same?" My reaction was immediate and personal: Wait, I thought, does that mean Sandra is leaving *Mike*? Immediately thereafter, like someone who had just found out that LiLo and Sam had broken up, I started frantically e-mailing friends at midnight to ask if they, too, had heard the news.

My horror did not come from personal fear for the state of my own domestic bliss (though I live with my partner of the last five years, we are not married). Nor did it come from some sort of intimate relationship with the concerned parties: Sandra Tsing Loh, much to my regret, is a writer I don't know. But in that moment, I felt for the first time that I really understood something new about what the first-person essay—so in vogue for the past decade and a half—has meant to us as readers.

3   As I pointed out in Broadsheet last week, these essays—about the politics and day-to-day life of sex, dating, marriage and children or lack thereof—are more often than not written by women; moreover, as a study I quoted last week found, they are the most common form of nonfiction writing by women published in the most prestigious magazines. Plenty of these, of course, have been published by Salon (Anne Lamott's essays, often credited for kicking off the newfound popularity of the form, were published on Salon back when the Life section was known as "Mothers Who Think"). And in some ways they've become, to borrow the title of Lamott's first book, "Operating Instructions," a way to spy on the hideous mistakes, hard-won insights, and daily flimflam of a quirky, hopefully interesting person other than ourselves.

4   At one time, those of us who read got this vicarious pleasure mostly from reading novels (previously considered a better place to vent the flaws of others and oneself without having to be branded an asshole). But even though I have spent a good portion of the past 10 years working, among other things, as a book critic, in recent years, I've had to admit that the best television— "Mad Men," "The Sopranos," "The Wire," "Lost" and the rest of the usual suspects—are as good and often better at developing a character over time. (This comes from a woman who didn't even own a television for about 15 years.) The reasons for this seem clear: The narrative is episodic, and, unlike most novels— the vast majority of which, with the exception of series, are read in a matter of days or a week—we are invited to follow these characters in one-hour increments over the course of years, in their own lives and our own.

5   This, I realized this past weekend, is the same way I've been reading Sandra Tsing Loh. I can be wildly ambivalent about the personal essay as a form. It's all about the person: If the narrator seems narcissistic, self-absorbed and concerned with trivialities, well, so does the work. But I've never been ambivalent about Loh: I flat-out fucking love her. This is a woman who, when writing on women and work, can admit that for most Americans their jobs come down to "makin' kahpies," who can make fun of the bohemian pretensions of Harvard grad millionaires who insist on wearing grimy Red Sox caps, and admit that her fondness for her own flinty Ramones T-shirt betrays her own Bobo pretensions. She can admit that she spent a year trying to get her kid into the fanciest schools in L.A. but ultimately chose to stick it out in the public schools where she and the Latino and Armenian mothers banded together to get a VH-1 grant for a new music program. She'll tell us about going to a party at a gazillionaire friend's house, and follow it with a zinger about being mistaken for her blond daughter's third-world nanny.

And throughout the past 15 or so years, she has written fondly   6
about her compatriot in the struggle to carve out a career, then
a family as a member of what she dubs the urban "middle-class
poor"—her lovable, child-raising, tomato-growing, lowly paid
musician husband, Mike, whom she described in last year's
memoir, "Mother on Fire" as having "the soul of Mr. Darcy with
the income of Mr. Collins." Back in the '90s they discovered Ikea
and Trader Joe's and sat at home gorging on knock-off Brie on
their flimsy sofa, until their tummies were noticeably distended
and their sofa kicked to the curb. He was her partner in raising
their two little girls, and when Loh freaked out about having to
send the eldest to the seemingly crappy elementary school down
the street, he responded that he'd love for their daughter to
be bilingual (the school was mostly Latino). But there were
also signs: Loh wrote in "Mother on Fire" about telling her
pierced, Kahlo-loving undergraduates that after 40, "the wheels
fall off," and drew what she called a "portrait of a narrative in a
post-feminist age," as a circle with a line through it that read:
"NO MORE MR. DARCY!" While it seemed like her usual self-
deprecating way to cut through idealized, romantic bullshit, perhaps, in retrospect, it was a sign that she, too, was interested in
a little romantic illusion?

In some ways, yes. Loh admits that she is "A 47-year-old   7
woman whose commitment to monogamy, at the very end, came
unglued." Coincidentally, today I also published on Salon an
interview with Kate Christensen, whose most recent novel,
"Trouble," is about a therapist almost exactly the same age as
Loh who ends her 15-year marriage to rediscover sex and passion. But Loh, though she cops to that one-time old-fashioned
sin of adultery, sounds jaded on the long-term prospects of
romance altogether. She points out that the reason America may
have "a divorce culture" might be because we *marry* too damn
often—"we both divorce *and* marry (a projected 90 percent of
us) at some of the highest rates on the globe." Most of all, she
delivers a scathing indictment of the difficulty of kindling
romance in that peculiarly modern invention, the "Companionate Marriage, in which husband and wife each have a career, and
they co-parent and co-housekeep according to gender free
norms they negotiate." Acknowledging that, as we are all told,
"good relationships take work" Loh admits in therapy that that
is the one thing she is having the hardest time doing:

> Which is not to say I am against work. Indeed, what came
> out of that afternoon were the many tasks I—like so many
> working/co-parenting/married mothers—have been doing for
> so many years and tearfully declared I would continue doing.
> I can pick up our girls from school every day; I can make
> them dinner and kiss their noses and tell them stories; . . .

I can earn my half—sometimes more—of the money; . . . I can refinance the house at the best possible interest rate; I can drive my husband to the airport; in his absence, I can sort his mail . . . Which is to say I can work at a career and child care and joint home ownership and even platonic male-female friendship. However, in the cluttered forest of my 40s, what I can't authentically reconjure is the ancient dream of brides, even with the Oprah fluffery of weekly "date nights" . . . Do you see? Given my staggering working mother's to-do list, I cannot take on another arduous home- and self-improvement project, that of rekindling our romance.

8   Loh's essay on the demise of her marriage provides the darker counterpoint to the idealized, soft-focused, "date-night" loving Obamas. Last week, Amanda Fortini applied some of Susan Sontag's ideas in "Illness as Metaphor" to show how our current fascination with self-help can lead us to demonize those who seem to refuse to help themselves: "If you can help yourself, then it's your fault if you don't. If there are ways to resuscitate a marriage, however corny or contrived they may seem, you have only yourself to blame if you don't try them." No doubt some will blame Loh for not trying hard enough. But she's never been one to show us the ideal; just what's real. Good luck, Sandra and Mike, and please, let us know how it all shakes out.

Amanda Fortini

Why Your Marriage Sucks

Amanda Fortini is an essayist for the *New Yorker*, *Slate*, *Elle*, and *New York*, among other publications. In this piece, first published in Salon.com, Fortini reviews and comments on two other works about marriage—Sandra Tsing Loh's "Let's Call the Whole Thing Off" (included earlier in this chapter) and Christina Nehring's "A Vindication of Love." In doing so, Fortini is able to weave her own thoughts into this dialogue on the state of marriage as well. As you read, note the methods that Fortini uses to bring together the ideas of these other authors with her own, using techniques like those discussed in the Introduction to *Conversations*. Note in particular the ways that she is able to use ideas and quotations from the other pieces to build toward her concluding paragraph.

Why would anyone submit to the doomed delusion that 1
is marriage? The unmarried among us have surely
begun to ask this question. (No doubt the married
have, too, though in the past tense.) For several years now, disdain for heterosexual unions has been on the rise—or at least
the disdainful have been more vocal—and it's become increasingly difficult to believe that a lasting marriage is possible. If it
is possible, the "hard work" it requires will wring the partnership of all passion and wonderment and joy. From the narratives of wifely grievance routinely published in women's
magazines to the spectacular public bust-ups of numerous
celebrity marriages in which we have placed our bruised faith,
it's easy to glean that we currently inhabit a vast and bleak
landscape of marital discontent.

There are numbers to corroborate this: In a much-discussed 2
recent survey of 35,000 American women, published in the July
issue of *Woman's Day*, 72 percent of married women said they
had considered leaving their husbands. Seventy-nine percent said
they'd like sex more often, and 52 percent said they have no sex
life to speak of. Contemporary marriage, all signs would indicate,
is a long, tedious slog toward sex-starved paunchiness via an endless, embittering negotiation of banalities: who will shuttle the
kids, walk the dog, prepare the meals, wash the laundry.

Last week, as though timed to the release of the survey find- 3
ings, two female writers offered their respective takes on the
subject. In a heavily parsed essay in the July/August issue of the
Atlantic Monthly titled "Let's Call the Whole Thing Off," writer
Sandra Tsing Loh explores the dissolution of her 20-year marriage, pinpointing as the superficial cause her extramarital affair
and subsequent inability "to take on yet another home- and self-
improvement project, that of rekindling [her] romance." From
her personal predicament she diagnoses a broader epidemic of
dissatisfaction—emotional, social, familial and, most of all,
sexual—among women. "To work, to parent, to housekeep, to
be the ones who schedule 'date night' . . . and then, in the bedroom, to be ignored—it's a bum deal," she writes. Literary critic and essayist Cristina Nehring, who also happens to write for
the *Atlantic*, takes a more impersonal approach in her contrarian polemic, "A Vindication of Love"; she writes of the bankrupt
state of romantic love in our society: "We inhabit a world in
which every aspect of romance from meeting to mating has been
streamlined, safety-checked and emptied of spiritual consequence . . . Romance in our day is a poor and shrunken thing."

Do our problems with marriage arise from our impoverished 4
ideas about romance? Though Loh cites lack of love, a fairly
standard excuse, as a reason for her divorce—"I did not have
the strength to 'work on' falling in love again in our marriage,"
she says, in the therapeutic parlance of our day—Nehring is

convinced that love as we currently define it, or at least as we practice it, is too safe, too sterile, acculturated and tamed. We are apparently unwilling to acknowledge love in all its unresolved messiness, unable to recognize that transgression, obsession, power inequities and strife might enflame our passions rather than diminish them, saving us from blandness and boredom. "It is the trivialization of love that is the tragedy of our time," Nehring writes, with signature melodrama. "It is the methodical demystification, recreationalization, automatization, commercialization, medicalization, and domestication of Eros that is making today's world a much flatter place." Her solution is a kind of perceptual readjustment. "Romantic love needs to be reinvented for our time. For those of us as bored by the cult of safe love as we are by the man-hating clichés of old-style feminism, it needs to be formulated afresh." A change in ideology, perhaps, will bring about a change in attitude.

5   But I don't believe that our notions of romantic love are at fault, nor are they all that different from the ideal Nehring propounds. For many of us, our models of deep romantic feeling have been formed through books and films and television. Romance novels comprise 32 percent of adult mass-market paperback sales; Harlequin, the predominant publisher of bodice-ripping tales, sold 130 million books in 2007, notes a recent article on the genre. These portraits rarely involve what Loh calls "companionate marriage," with partners divvying up the childcare and chores. Fictional love tends to be obsessive, transgressive, regressive, operatic, unequal, full of conflict or a disaster of the grandest proportions—in other words, characterized by many of the elements on which Nehring places such a premium.

6   As with most Americans, my own ideas about love were formed not only by books—*Jane Eyre* and *Pride and Prejudice, Emma* and *Wuthering Heights,* yes, as well as the incestuous *Flowers in the Attic* series, *The Thorn Birds,* and the Andrew Greeley books with their fornicating priests—but also by soap operas and romantic comedies: the tempestuous on-again-off-again affair of Bo and Hope on *Days of Our Lives,* the jaunty repartee of *When Harry Met Sally.* "Almost everything in modern society militates against our falling in love hard or long. It militates against love as risk, love as sacrifice, love as heroism," writes Nehring. This is not entirely true. Even if the self-help establishment promotes romance as an "organized adult activity with safety rails on the left and right, rubber ceilings, no-skid floors, and a clear, clean destination: marriage"—and I'm not sure it does—tension exists between the domesticated romance of relationship manuals and the many depictions of outlaw love in the culture around us.

7   As a result, most people long to experience love, especially love of the wildest, most complicated sort. And I would venture

to guess that many have—romance born of mischief, with a co-worker, perhaps, or a professor or student; obsessive love characterized by vigilant waiting for calls and e-mails, or a humiliating inability to stop calling even after the relationship is broken. Most of us have not consciously or categorically banished passionate love from our lives, we just can't seem to make it fit. Indeed, if being in love is such a stimulating and gratifying state—and it is, of course—why would we do without it unless, in some sense, we had to? One of the reasons that we have resigned ourselves to a certain dearth of passion may be that we can't seem to afford it economically or temporally. Here is Cathi Hanauer, editor of the bestselling anthology *The Bitch in the House*, describing her typical day: "nursing a baby at the computer while trying to make a deadline; sprinting home from my daughter's nursery school, both kids in tow, to return phone calls; handing the children off to Dan [her husband], the instant he walked in at night so I could rush off to a coffee shop to get my work done." And here is Loh, on her inability to cram romance into her life: "Which is to say I can work at a career and child care and joint homeownership and even platonic male-female friendship. However, in this cluttered forest of my 40s, what I cannot authentically reconjure is the ancient dream of brides, even with the Oprah fluffery of weekly 'date nights,' when gauzy candlelight obscures the messy house, child talk is nixed, and sexy lingerie is donned."

When the bureaucratic nightmare that is everyday life has 8 become so intrusive, when both parents work out of the home, the circumstances that allow for intimacy and passion are imperiled. (Sandra Tsing Loh tells us that her musician-husband traveled 20 weeks a year.) When are we to form deep connections? How and where is this hot sex supposed to happen? You can't stay up all night when you have to wake up and go to work the next day; no one is going to grant you a leave of absence for passion. (In an interview with the Telegraph, Arianna Huffington once discussed sleep deprivation as a negative byproduct of love affairs. "So I've gotten to be a good breaker-upper," said Huffington.) We have, you might say, been forced to adapt to a world that is hostile to romance, our lives full of ever-clamoring responsibilities: bills to pay, BlackBerrys to monitor, e-mails to answer. Talk to almost any therapist, and he or she will tell you that the primary reason people don't have sex is that they're too tired, or have built up a little mountain of resentments over the difficulty of running a household together. If you want an intense, consuming passion, you're probably not going to be as productive, to put it in mundane terms. This is in part why we are so fascinated with marriages that appear, from the outside at least, highly functional and romantic: How do the Obamas make time for "date night" when Barack has a country to run?

How, while raising their brood, do the Jolie-Pitts manage philanthropic work and careers?

9   What's particularly frustrating about Nehring's sophomoric and overlong book (like most book-length polemics, a magazine article would have sufficed) is the vagueness at its core: She ignores reality, writing as though social life takes place entirely in a vacuum, as though culture occurs on some astral plane. In the course of many pages of rather pedestrian literary analysis—on Chaucer's "The Wife of Bath's Tale," Tristan and Iseult, and Emily Dickinson's "Master" letters, among others—she hardly comments on how we currently live. Nor does she offer any prescriptions as to what sort of configurations or lifestyle choices might be more conducive to the sort of love she values. (By examining the literature of the past, she attempts "to identify alternative modes and arresting new visions of romantic behavior for the twenty-first century.") But there's something dishonest about advocating for a kind of instantaneous sentimental or intellectual reorientation, when a withdrawal from the systems and obligations of contemporary life is what would be required: to stop worrying, say, whether your husband had bought the right brand of detergent or that e-mail messages are idling unopened in your in box. On a larger level, this may mean nothing less than a sacrifice of ambitions or possessions; it may mean simplifying, downsizing or moving. Reading a few books and applying nostrums about transgression and difference hardly seems sufficient.

10   In the end, I'm not sure the message of *A Vindication of Love* is all that different from any other exhortation to transgression we have seen over the years—books like *The Sensuous Woman* or articles in *Cosmopolitan*. If anything has dulled our love nerves, it might be decades of detailed instructions on how to spice up our sex life and marriage. The other night, while loitering in the kitchen of some friends in their 20s, I noticed, pinned to their refrigerator, a page ripped from *Cosmo*, the title something along the lines of "101 Sex Tips to Try Before You Die," that contained pointers so explicit (let's just say the word "perineum" was in there), it made me blush. I write this article from a hotel room in New York City, where nearly a dozen porn movies are on offer, and, among the potato chips and dry-roasted nuts in the mini-bar, there sits a "pleasure kit" with "silk bondage ties." If romantic love is uncommon or endangered, it's not for lack of trying. It may, in fact, be from trying too hard, from attempting to control a willful, quixotic, emotional impulse. Nehring's argument also left me somewhat bewildered: The female literary figures she praises as models of romantic derring-do acted in repressive, often very religious societies; these days, really, when nothing is taboo, what are we to transgress against?

It's interesting that even as heterosexual women are sounding   11
the death knell for their nuptials, homosexual men and women
are fighting for the right to marry traditionally. It may be that
you can't properly loathe an institution of which you are not yet
a member. And gay marriage, for many in this country, remains
intriguingly unfamiliar. Come to think of it, if the current vent-
ing among the unhappily married accomplishes anything, it
may send the rebellious and romantic-minded to the altar with
a defiant sneer. After all, the more marriage is maligned, the
more dangerous and transgressive it will appear.

Elizabeth Weil

Married (Happily) with Issues

Elizabeth Weil writes for the *New York Times Magazine* and
has also published her work in *Mother Jones, Outside,* and
Vogue. She is the author of *Crib Notes: A Random Reference
for the Modern Parent, Love Notes: A Random Reference for
the Modern Romantic,* and *They All Laughed at Christopher
Columbus.* In this piece, published in 2009 in the *New York
Times Magazine,* Weil chronicles her attempts to improve her
marriage, first examining what "a better marriage would look
like." Unlike Sandra Tsing Loh, who in "Let's Call the Whole
Thing Off" concludes that she "did not have the strength to
'work on' falling in love again in my marriage," Weil cogently
and honestly describes the process of doing that work. As you
read, you might compare these two perspectives and consider
what each author seems to suggest about the necessary
elements of a successful marriage, and whether those
elements are attainable and worth the effort they require. You
might also consider how the underlying belief systems of
each author inform the conclusions that are drawn.

I

I have a pretty good marriage. It could be better. There are   1
things about my husband that drive me crazy. Last spring
he cut apart a frozen pig's head with his compound miter
saw in our basement. He needed the head to fit into a pot so
that he could make pork stock. I'm no saint of a spouse, either.

I hate French kissing, compulsively disagree and fake sleep when Dan vomits in the middle of the night. Dan also once threatened to punch my brother at a family reunion at a lodge in Maine. But in general we do O.K.

2   The idea of trying to improve our union came to me one night in bed. I've never really believed that you just marry one day at the altar or before a justice of the peace. I believe that you become married—truly married—slowly, over time, through all the road-rage incidents and precolonoscopy enemas, all the small and large moments that you never expected to happen and certainly didn't plan to endure. But then you do: you endure. And as I lay there, I started wondering why I wasn't applying myself to the project of being a spouse. My marriage was good, utterly central to my existence, yet in no other important aspect of my life was I so laissez-faire. Like most of my peers, I applied myself to school, friendship, work, health and, ad nauseam, raising my children. But in this critical area, marriage, we had all turned away. I wanted to understand why. I wanted not to accept this. Dan, too, had worked tirelessly—some might say obsessively—at skill acquisition. Over the nine years of our marriage, he taught himself to be a master carpenter and a master chef. He was now reading Soviet-era weight-training manuals in order to transform his 41-year-old body into that of a Marine. Yet he shared the seemingly widespread aversion to the very idea of marriage improvement. Why such passivity? What did we all fear?

3   That night, the image that came to mind, which I shared with Dan, was that I had been viewing our marriage like the waves on the ocean, a fact of life, determined by the sandbars below, shaped by fate and the universe, not by me. And this, suddenly, seemed ridiculous. I am not a fatalistic person. In my 20s I even believed that people made their own luck. Part of the luck I believed I made arrived in the form of Dan himself, a charming, handsome surfer and writer I met three days after I moved to San Francisco. Eleven years later we had two kids, two jobs, a house, a tenant, a huge extended family—what Nikos Kazantzakis described in "Zorba the Greek" as "the full catastrophe." We were going to be careless about how our union worked out?

4   So I decided to apply myself to my marriage, to work at improving ours now, while it felt strong. Our children, two girls who are now 4 and 7, were no longer desperately needy; our careers had stabilized; we had survived gutting our own house. Viewed darkly, you could say that I feared stasis; more positively, that I had energy for Dan once again. From the myriad psychology books that quickly stacked up on my desk, I learned that my concept was sound, if a bit unusual. The average couple is unhappy six years before first attending therapy, at which point, according to "The Science of Clinical Psychology," the marital

therapist's job is "less like an emergency-room physician who is called upon to set a fracture that happened a few hours ago and more like a general practitioner who is asked to treat a patient who broke his or her leg several months ago and then continued to hobble around on it; we have to attend not only to the broken bone but also to the swelling and bruising, the sore hip and foot and the infection that ensued."

Still, Dan was not 100 percent enthusiastic, at least at first. He 5 feared—not mistakenly, it turns out—that marriage is not great terrain for overachievers. He met my ocean analogy with the veiled threat of California ranch-hand wisdom: if you're going to poke around the bushes, you'd best be prepared to scare out some snakes.

II

A quick bit of background: Dan and I married on July 1, 2000, 6 in Olema, Calif. I wore a white dress. Dan was 32; I was 30. We vowed to have and to hold, to love and to cherish in sickness and in health, etc. We were optimistic, cocky and vague about the concept of marriage. We never discussed, or considered discussing, why we were getting married or what a good marriage would mean. It all seemed obvious. I loved Dan; I loved how I felt with him. Ergo I wanted to be his wife.

During the first nine years of our marriage—that is, until we 7 tried to improve it—Dan and I thought little about our expectations and even less about our parents' marriages, both of which have lasted more than 40 years. Our families had set very different examples of how a marriage could be good. Dan was raised in Berkeley, Calif., by VW-bus-driving lefties who were so utterly committed to their own romance that Dan sometimes felt left out. Each meal and each sunset was the most exquisite. When girls refused to talk to Dan in high school, his mother told him they were just too intimidated by his incredible good looks. My parents' marriage, meanwhile, resembled nothing so much as a small business. They raised their three children in Wellesley, Mass., where civic life was so tidy that kids held bake sales at the town dump. All conjugal affection took place out of sight. "You're a good Do Bee" was considered high praise.

After our wedding, with some money from a boom-time book 8 advance, we bought a run-down house in San Francisco. We assumed that our big problems would be money (or lack thereof; we're both freelance writers) and religion (I'm Jewish; Dan's Christian). Neither turned out to be true. We built—or more accurately fell—into a 21st-century companionate marriage. But Dan and I were not just economic partners, lovers, (soon enough) co-parents and best friends. We were also each other's co-workers, editors and primary readers. Both working from home, our lives resembled a D-list version of Joan Didion's and John Gregory Dunne's, whose days, according to Didion, "were filled with the sound of each other's voices"—except with what I can only assume is a much more egregious lack of boundaries. We lost steam 95 percent of the way through our D.I.Y. home remodeling and, as a result, have no master-bathroom door.

III

9   But how to start? What would a better marriage look like? More happiness? Intimacy? Stability? Laughter? Fewer fights? A smoother partnership? More intriguing conversation? More excellent sex? Our goal and how to reach it were strangely unclear. We all know what marriage is: a legal commitment between two people. But a good marriage? For guidance I turned to the standard assessments. The Locke-Wallace Marital Adjustment Test instructs spouses, among other things, to rank themselves along the "always agree" to "always disagree" continuum on matters ranging from recreation to in-laws. This struck me as scattershot and beside the point. For all the endless talk about marriage—who should have the right to be in one, whether the declining numbers of married-parent households are hurting America's children—we don't know much about what makes a marriage satisfying or how to keep one that way. John Gottman, in his Love Lab in Seattle, claims that he can analyze a conversation between spouses and predict with 94 percent accuracy whether that couple will divorce over the course of six years. But many academics say that Gottman's powers of prophecy are overblown, that he can't truly predict if a couple will split. Those not selling books, workshops or counseling admit to knowing surprisingly little. Harry Reis, a professor of psychology at the University of Rochester, likens our current understanding of "relationship science" to the Buddhist parable of the blind men and the elephant. One blind man "feels the tusk, inferring that elephants are hard and sharp-edged, like a blade. Another touches the soft, flexible ear, concluding that elephants are supple, resembling felt. A third imagines massive strength from grasping the pillar-like structure of the leg. The perspective of each person touching the elephant is valid, as far as it goes . . . " But no one understands the whole beast.

10   Dan and I decided to dive in, trusting that the terms of our better marriage and the yardstick by which to measure those terms would emerge along the way. It seemed safest to start in private, so we began our putative improving with Harville Hendrix's Oprah-sanctioned self-help best seller, *Getting the Love You Want*. I let Dan pick the first exercise. It seemed only

sporting. I assumed he would choose "positive flooding," which includes making a list of all the qualities you wish your partner would praise you for but never does and then sitting in a chair as your spouse walks circles around you, reading that list in an increasingly loud and emphatic voice. (I was terrible at giving Dan compliments, even though he craved them; I sided with the psychoanalyst Adam Phillips, who writes that in marriage "the long applause becomes baffling.") But instead Dan chose "reromanticizing." In hindsight, no surprise—Dan's parents were dreamy and passionate.

Step 1: Complete this sentence in as many ways as possible: 11
"I feel loved and cared about when you . . ."

Dan quickly jotted down "submit to kissing, clean the kitchen,   12
tell me I look studly."

"Let's try for 10," I said.   13

"Ten!" Dan said, teasing but serious, one of our most common   14
modes of conversation. "You can think of 10?"

In "Intimate Terrorism: The Crisis of Love in an Age of Disil-   15
lusion," the psychologist Michael Vincent Miller describes marriage as mocking our "fondest dreams," because the institution
is not the wellspring of love we imagine it to be. Instead it's an
environment of scarcity, it's "a barbaric competition over whose
needs get met"; it's "two people trying to make a go of it on emotional and psychological supplies that are only sufficient for one."
And true enough, with "Getting the Love You Want" splayed on
our bed, I began seeing Dan as my adversary, the person against
whom I was negotiating the terms of our lives. I remembered
well, but not fondly, this feeling from early in our marriage, when
nearly everything was still up for grabs: Where would we live?
How much money was enough? What algorithm would determine who would watch the baby and who would go to the gym?
Recently those questions had settled, and our marriage felt better for it. But now the competitive mind-set came roaring back,
as I reasoned, unconsciously anyway, that any changes we made
would either be toward Dan's vision of marriage and away from
mine or the other way around. Admitting too much satisfaction
seemed tantamount to ceding the upper hand. So I held my
ground. I, too, failed to think of 10 things Dan did that made me
feel loved. "O.K.," I said, "let's quit after 8."

Step 2: Recall the romantic stage of your relationship. Com-   16
plete this sentence: "I used to feel loved and cared about when
you . . ."

Dan made one of those circles with a line through it on his   17
paper, symbolizing, he ribbed, "the null set." Then he grabbed
my list. "'Looked giddy to come through the door and see me,'"
Dan read. "Are you kidding me? You don't even see me when you
come through the door. It's like you're blind and deaf to everyone but the kids."

18   I thought I had avoided becoming one of those mothers who transferred all of her romantic energy from her husband to her children. Apparently I failed. But Dan, in my view, hadn't mastered the spouse-parent balance, either, only his problem was the opposite: at times he ignored the kids. While reromanticizing, I asked him, testily, "Do you really think a 6-2, 200-pound man who works at home with his wife needs to compete with his small children for their mother's attention before those children leave for school?" Great. Now we were having a fight. Dan retreated to the bathroom to check his progress on his six-pack. My doubts set in. This was the fear, right? You set out to improve your marriage; it implodes. What if my good marriage was not floating atop a sea of goodness, adrift but fairly stable when pushed? What if my good marriage was teetering on a precipice and any change would mean a toppling, a crashing down?

19   Much of the commentary on modern marriage is frankly terrifying. Miller describes "the marital ghetto"—the marital ghetto?—as "the human equivalent of a balanced aquarium, where the fish and the plants manage to live indefinitely off each other's waste products." Perhaps we'd been striving in raising children and not in marriage because child-rearing is a dictatorship and marriage is a democracy. The children do not get to vote on the direction of the relationship, on which sleep-training or discipline philosophy they like best. But with a spouse, particularly a contemporary American spouse, equality is foundational, assumed. A friend had recently told me that he thought I was the boss in my marriage. Did I really want to negotiate my marriage anew and risk losing that power? From the bathroom, Dan asked, "Do you really think this project is a good idea?"

20   I realized that my favorite books about marriage—Calvin Trillin's *About Alice* and Joan Didion's *Year of Magical Thinking*—included one spouse who was dead.

21   Still, one Saturday last spring, we drove across the Golden Gate Bridge to Mill Valley to attend a marriage-education class. In academic circles, marriage education is known as a "prevention" program, an implicit admission that by the time most couples get to the subsequent program—therapy—it's too late. The classes, sadly, have all the intellectual glamour of driver's ed. But they're based on the optimistic idea that you can learn to be better at marriage. As Bernard G. Guerney Jr., a clinical psychologist, family therapist and the godfather of the marriage-education movement, wrote in his 1977 book "Relationship Enhancement," unless an unhappily married spouse "is suffering a biochemical deficiency or imbalance, he is no more sick than someone who wants to play tennis and does not know how, and the professional is no more providing 'therapy' or 'curing' his or her client than a tennis coach is 'curing' his clients."

We enrolled in a 16-hour, two-Saturday course called "Mastering the Mysteries of Love." The classes teach students how to have "skilled conversations" or rather, I should say, how to stop having the let's-see-who-rhetorically-wins skirmishes that were standard in our house. A skilled conversation is an exercise in forced empathy. One person starts by describing his or her feelings. The other person then validates those feelings, repeating them back nearly verbatim. 22

Midmorning, with the gongs of the supposedly soothing spa music crashing in the background, Dan and I retreated to a couch with a template for having a skilled conversation about a "small disagreement." Among our most longstanding fights was how much energy and money should go into Dan's cooking. Shortly after our first child, Hannah, was born, Dan and I started having the same conversation every night: do you want to cook dinner or look after the kid? He always picked cook, I always picked kid, and now, seven years later, Dan was an excellent, compulsive and profligate chef. We spent far more money on food than we did on our mortgage. Sure, we ate well. Very well. Our refrigerator held, depending on the season: homemade gravlax, Strauss organic milk, salt-packed anchovies, little gem lettuces, preserved Meyer lemons, imported Parmesan, mozzarella and goat cheese, baby leeks, green garlic, Blue Bottle coffee ($18 a pound), supergroovy pastured eggs. On a ho-hum weeknight Dan might make me pan-roasted salmon with truffled polenta in a Madeira shallot reduction. But this was only a partial joy. Dan's cooking enabled him to hide out in plain sight; he was home but busy—What? I'm cooking dinner!—for hours every evening. During this time I was left to attend to our increasingly hungry, tired and frantic children and to worry about money. That was our division of labor: Dan cooked, I tended finances. Because of the cooking, in part, we saved little for retirement and nothing for our children's college educations. 23

I garnered no sympathy from our friends. Still, Dan's cooking and the chaos it created drove me mad, a position I expressed by leaving whole pigeons untouched on my plate. Dan, meanwhile, entrenched and retaliated, slipping crispy fried pigs' ears into my salads and making preposterously indulgent weekday breakfasts, the girls upending flour bowls and competing for Dad's attention as he made them crepes with grapes and Champagne sauce at 6:45 a.m. I knew Dan's cooking and his obsessions in general were mechanisms to bind his anxiety, attempts to bring order to an unruly mind. Without an outlet, Dan tended toward depression, and his depression vented as anger. In his early 20s, he learned the trick of focusing and applying himself, at nearly all times, so his energy would not, as he put it, "turn bad." I respected this, even appreciated it, in theory. But I struggled with 24 the specifics. Dan cooked, because he needed to cook, blitzing through one cookbook after another, putting little check marks next to every recipe. He was not cooking for me, not for the girls. Yet now in our marriage class, following the skilled-conversation template, the emotional distance between us on this issue seemed to collapse. I said, then Dan mirrored back to me, "The chaos is really upsetting, and you'd like to find a way to maintain more peace and calm in our home." Then Dan said, and I mirrored to him: "Food is a truly important part of family. For you it's health and pleasure bound together, and it lets you express and pursue the life you want to live three times a day."

25   That afternoon, as we talked in this stilted, earnest style—covering such esteemed topics as backrubs and stray socks, the utter banalities of married life—I felt a trapdoor crack open in our marriage. According to a widely accepted model, intimacy begins when one person expresses revealing feelings, builds when the listener responds with support and empathy and is achieved when the discloser hears these things and feels understood, validated and cared for. This is not news. It's not even advice. Offering a married couple this model is like informing an obese person that he should eat less and move more. But in the days and nights that followed that course, our intimacy grew. We had never considered our verbal jousting to be protecting uncomfortable feelings. Clearly it was. Back home, that first irony-free evening, I found myself telling Dan a raft of antiheroic stories about my childhood, stories I'd never told him, I realized, because I felt insecure. They were tales about suburban bat mitzvahs and the pedal pushers I wore to them, anecdotes from a conventional East Coast world our marriage eschewed. Without the ironclad guarantee of empathy, I had felt that they might go over poorly, especially alongside Dan's epics of a glorious youth spent playing Frisbee in Berkeley's Tilden Park.

26   For the next few weeks, even our sex was more intimate, more open and trusting. Then I found myself recoiling. As if I were obeying Newton's third law of motion, I had an innate equal and opposite reaction to our newfound intimacy, to living our lives, as the saccharine marriage-improvement phrase goes, as we instead of as me. I loved the idea of digging out of my emotional bunker and going over to Dan's to live with him. And I liked being there, for a while. But Dan has a bigger, flashier personality than I do. I feared, in our intimacy, I might be subsumed. As many women had, I read in fascinated horror, a few years back, about a Buddhist couple who took vows never to be parted by more than 15 feet. They inhaled and exhaled in unison while doing yoga, walked each other to writing desks when inspiration struck in the middle of the night. "It is very intimate," the male partner explained. That vision of intimacy as a chain-link leash filled me with dread. Yes, I loved the emotional security of

knowing that if I said, "I'm upset," Dan would repeat back, "You're upset." But while such command empathy was comforting to a point, it felt unsustainable, even cloying.

Some days, following intimate nights, I'd walk up to our   27
kitchen from our bedroom below and want to pretend it didn't happen. Dan would caress the small of my back. I'd squirm away. I knew older couples who slept in separate bedrooms, an arrangement that unsettled me as a newlywed but now struck me as a sound approach to running the chute between intimacy and autonomy over the course of 50 years. Yet Dan and I weren't going to stop sharing a room—for one thing, we lacked the space. So while working to improve our marriage, I found myself pushing my husband away. I had started our project assuming the more closeness, the better. But that wasn't turning out to be true, at least for me.

A few weeks later we drove through San Francisco to the tony   28
Laurel Village neighborhood from our house in Bernal Heights for some psychoanalytic couple's therapy. En route we discussed not shaking the bushes of our union too hard. Dan had just flown home from London where he was working on a story about Fergus Henderson, a chef who defines half a pig's head as "a perfect romantic supper for two." Henderson has Parkinson's but told Dan he stopped reading about the disease, because in his experience "the more I know, the more symptoms I have." Following suit, we thought it best to stick to dissecting the good parts of our marriage and how to improve them, as marriage can bring out people's worst. Even those who are tolerant, wise and giving are often short and rude to their mates. I had always winced at the opening of Chekov's "Lady With the Dog." The narrator describes the protagonist's wife as "a tall, erect woman with dark eyebrows, staid and dignified." Then he gives us her husband's view: "he secretly considered her unintelligent, narrow, inelegant, was afraid of her and did not like to be at home." How much did we really want to share?

A word here about psychoanalytic reasoning: I've never been   29
a big fan. I've long favored the fake-it-till-you-make-it approach to life. Why turn over the rocks of your history just to see what's underneath? In marriage therapy, this fear makes particular sense, because the therapy carries not only the threat of learning things about yourself that you might prefer not to know but also the hazard of saying things to your spouse that are better left unsaid, as well as hearing things from your spouse that you might prefer not to hear. Some in the field are outwardly critical of most marriage therapy; among them is William J. Doherty, a psychologist and the director of the Marriage and Family Therapy Program at the University of Minnesota, who writes, "If you talk to a therapist in the United States about problems in your marriage, I believe that you stand a good risk of

harming your marriage." The science behind marital counseling is also less precise than you might imagine. In clinical trials, among the most effective protocols is Integrative Behavioral Couple Therapy, an unabashed mash-up of two schools of thought. Couples work on "change-oriented strategies," trying to find ways to remedy each other's complaints. They also do "acceptance work," trying to learn to love the relationships as is.

30   Holly Gordon, our reed-thin psychoanalyst, did not think much of our plan. "To get the most out of your time here we need to talk about some dissatisfaction or problem, something you're trying to improve," she instructed, closing a double set of soundproof doors. So we settled into airing some well-rehearsed gripes—the time Dan came to the hospital to visit me and four-pound, premature Hannah, and all he could talk about was the San Francisco building code. (He'd torn the front stairs off our house and kept rebuilding them and ripping them off again, fearing they were imperfect.) The time Dan proposed a trade: he would clean up more, he swore he would, if I would just French-kiss him spontaneously once a day; I gave up first. (I found the forced affection claustrophobic. I was also still stung, I later realized, by critical comments Dan had made about my kissing style before we were engaged.) These were many-times-told tales, and as such we both felt inured to their dark content. We used them to avoid committing what Doherty calls "therapist-induced marital suicide." We did not want therapy to set a pick for our divorce.

31   So instead of speaking our harshest truths, for six weeks running Dan and I pursued the lesser offense of making the other sound crazy. Holly cooperated, too, offering feedback that we used to confirm our sense that the other was neurotic. Some weeks Dan took it in the teeth; others, I did. At home, Dan and I had been following a de facto acceptance strategy. He even convinced me that the best response to his lecturing me, again, about conjugate-periodization strength training was for me to say, "Oh, you lovable, obsessive man, you!" and walk away. But Holly took a fix-it, or at least diagnose-it, approach. This is another major complaint about marital therapy: mental-health professionals find mental-health problems. All of a sudden you're married to a narcissistic personality disorder; who wants to stick around for that? One day Holly ended our session with this synopsis: "On the first count, you find Dan unavailable because he's not relating to you. He's just using you as a sounding board. But on the other hand he feels he can't reach you either. He wants you to accept his affection and praise, but those attentions make you feel smothered, and that makes him feel alone." I still believed our marriage was good. But I felt that Holly had reduced it to an unappealing, perhaps unfixable conundrum. Would her vote of little confidence hurt or help?

I did start watching my reactions when Dan told me that I   32
looked beautiful. Did he mean it? What did he want from me? I
would try to accept the compliment graciously, even offer one
in return. But the endless therapy required to become less neurotic generally seemed outside the scope of this project. I felt
confident we could build a better marriage, less so that our individual personalities would change. Marital therapy, to me,
seemed akin to chemo: helpful but toxic. Leaving Holly's office
one day, Dan, ever valiant, made a strong play to titrate how
much negative feedback we let in. "Do they spray shrink powder in these places," he asked, "to make them extra depressing?"

IV

Monogamy is one of the most basic concepts of modern mar-   33
riage. It is also its most confounding. In psychoanalytic thought,
the template for monogamy is forged in infancy, a baby with its
mother. Marriage is considered to be a mainline back to this
relationship, its direct heir. But there is a crucial problem: as
infants we are monogamous with our mothers, but our mothers are not monogamous with us. That first monogamy—that
template—is much less pure than we allow. "So when we think
about monogamy, we think about it as though we are still children and not adults as well," Adam Phillips notes. This was true
for us. On our wedding day, Dan and I performed that elaborate
charade: I walked down the aisle with my father. I left him to
join my husband. We all shed what we told ourselves were tears
of joy. Dan and I promised to forsake all others, and sexually we
had. But we had not shed all attachments, naturally, and as we
waded further into our project the question of allegiances
became more pressing. Was our monogamy from the child's or
the mother's perspective? Did my love for Dan—must my love
for Dan—always come first?

This all came pouring out last summer in the worst fight of   34
our marriage. At the time, we were at my parents' house, an
hour northeast of San Francisco. More than food, more than
child-rearing, we fought about weekends—in particular, how
many summer weekends to spend up there. I liked the place: out
of the fog, free grandparental day care; the kids could swim. Dan
loathed it, describing the locale as "that totally sterile golf community in which your mother feeds our kids popsicles for break-
fast and I'm forbidden to cook."

For the past few years I dismissed Dan's complaints by say-   35
ing, "Fine, don't go." I told myself this was justified, if not altru-
istic: I was taking our girls; Dan could do what he wanted with
his free time. But underneath lay a tangle of subtext. Dan wished
he spent even more time with his own parents, who were quite
private. I felt an outsize obligation toward mine, because they

moved to the Bay Area to be closer to us. We'd had some skilled conversations, which helped a bit, as I now knew those weekends with his in-laws made Dan feel alienated and left out of our family decision-making. Yet at root we fought because the issue rubbed a weak point in our marriage, in our monogamy: I didn't want to see my devotion to my parents as an infidelity to Dan. To him, it was.

36   That June weekend my folks weren't home, we'd gone up with friends, but Dan hated the place more than ever. Saturday morning I woke up early, went for a run and came back to find Dan on a small AstroTurf putting green with the girls, ranting about how he hated all the houses that looked the same, with tinted windows blocking the natural light; the golf course that obliterated the landscape and all the jerks that played golf on it. The next day was Father's Day. I took the girls to do errands with what I thought were the best of intentions, but I was so angered by Dan's relentless crabbiness that I failed to buy a gift. The final insult came Sunday afternoon as we packed to go home. I informed Dan that I told my mother that she could bring the girls back up the following weekend. Dan erupted in rage. "Those are my actual children. Why do you insist on treating me like I'm some potted plant? I, too, get to decide what happens in this family. Do I need to tell you to tell your mother, 'O.K., Mom, I'm not allowed to make any plans for our children without getting permission from my husband?' Do I need to be telling you, 'I'm sorry, little girl, I make the plans in this family, and I'll tell you what to tell your mother about where my children are going?'"

37   I stiffened and said, "Of course not."

38   "How far are you going to let this go?" Dan kept screaming. "Are you willing to get divorced so you can keep spending weekends with your mom?"

39   This was the first time in our marriage either of us had ever invoked divorce.

40   The following Thursday, as we entered Holly's office, I still felt certain she would side with me: Dan needed to get over his holier-than-thou Berkeley hang-ups. Sure, golf communities are snobbish, but family is much more important. Especially my family, right now—my parents had moved from Massachusetts to California to be near their grandchildren, for God's sake. And besides, I dealt more with the kids, and I let Dan run amok in the kitchen. So I got this.

41   Holly, who'd thrown out her back and was reclining in a lawn chair in front of the couch she used for psychoanalytic clients, did not think much of my reasoning. "It sounds like you've created these little enclaves of rationalizations: 'I give on all these other fronts, so I'm entitled not to give on this one.'"

42   She was right. I felt entitled.

"But that does pose a problem—for Dan. Because he feels he's 43
really not taken into account."

Dan brightened. "Just as you were talking there, I was having 44
all these fears come up again. I have a real fear of being an
appendage in that family, and that Liz's real family is her and her
mother, and I was just a sperm donor. That it would be really fine
if I disappeared. Nothing much would change."

"Really?" I asked. I knew some of the ways I betrayed Dan 45
with the girls. As they grew older we found ourselves forming
cross-generation allegiances. Hannah, our elder, and I would
wish Dan wasn't so chronically messy and emotionally florid.
Audrey, our younger, would promise to be Dan's perfect companion; she would do the things I wouldn't do: climb huge over-
hanging rock crags, eat whole fried smelt. But I understood less
well why there was a conflict with my parents. I often spent
21 hours a day with Dan. When my mother called, I frequently
didn't answer the phone.

I could not believe Dan thought my primary relationship was 46
with my mother. I needed to know if he felt that way generally
or just on these weekends. Dan declared the distinction moot:
any rupture in our monogamy weakened the whole. I wondered
if improving my marriage had to mean cutting myself off from
the world? I wanted to gain strength from my marriage—that
was increasingly clear. In many ways I did. Dan had faith in me,
and that helped me have faith in myself. But clearly I owed Dan
a debt of constancy and consideration. Our marriage needed to
be a place to gain strength for him too.

Near the end of our session, Holly asked what I thought would 47
happen if I let go of my rationalizations, if I accepted a fuller
monogamy. I said I would feel vulnerable, "like a beating heart
with no rib cage."

"So there's a feeling that if you take Dan into account, he's 48
going to take it all away, or you're going to have to give yourself
over to him?"

"Yes," I said. "I imagine I'm going to be squashed." 49

Holly sat up in her lawn chair. "We're going to have to stop for 50
the day."

V

Since the beginning of this project, Dan had been waiting for 51
one thing: sex therapy. And I have good and bad news on this
front: improving the sex in our marriage was much easier than
you might guess, and the process of doing so made us want to
throw up.

Here again we began with books. In "Can Love Last? The Fate 52
of Romance Over Time," Stephen A. Mitchell, a psychoanalyst,
presents a strong case for the idea that those thoughts you might

have about your spouse or your sex life being predictable or boring—that's just an "elaborate fantasy," a reflection of your need to see your partner as safe and knowable, so you don't have to freak out over the possibility that he could veer off in an unforeseen direction, away from you.

53   Inspired by Mitchell, I decided to try a thought exercise: to think, while we were making love, that Dan was not predictable in the least. Before this, Dan and I were having regular sex, in every sense: a couple of times a week, not terribly inventive. As in many areas of our lives, we'd found a stable point that well enough satisfied our desires, and we just stayed there. But now I imagined Dan as a free actor, capable of doing anything at any time and paradoxically, by telling myself I did not know what to expect, I wanted to move toward him, to uncover the mystery. For years, of course, I felt I knew Dan well, worried that lessening the little distance between us could lead to collapse. Now I was having the same sweaty feelings I had in my 20s, when I would let my psyche ooze into that of a new lover at the start of an affair.

54   This was great, right? A better marriage meant more passionate sex, this went without saying. But by now I noticed a pattern: improving my marriage in one area often caused problems in another. More intimacy meant less autonomy. More passion meant less stability. I spent a lot of time feeling bad about this, particularly the fact that better sex made me retreat. There's a school of thought that views sex as a metaphor for marriage. Its proponents write rational-minded books like Patricia Love and Jo Robinson's "Hot Monogamy," in which they argue, "When couples share their thoughts and emotions freely throughout the day, they create between them a high degree of trust and emotional connection, which gives them the freedom to explore their sexuality more fully." But there's this opposing school: sex—even sex in marriage—requires barriers and uncertainty, and we are fools to imagine otherwise. "Romantic love, at the start of this century, is cause for embarrassment," Cristina Nehring moans in "A Vindication of Love: Reclaiming Romance for the Twenty-First Century." She berates the conventional marital set-up: two spouses, one house, one bedroom. She's aghast at those who strive for equality. "It is precisely equality that destroys our libidos, equality that bores men and women alike." I can only imagine what scorn she'd feel for hypercompanionate idiots like us.

55   Still, I agreed with Nehring's argument that we need "to rediscover the right to impose distances, the right to remain strangers." Could my postcoital flitting away be a means to re-establish erotic distance? An appealing thought but not the whole truth. My relationship with Dan started on rocky footing. When we met, Dan was working through the aftershocks of a torrid affair with an emotionally sadistic, sexually self-aggrandizing woman. She said

mean things to him; he said mean things to me ("Why do you kiss like that?"). Not a perfect foundation for a marriage. Nor was the fact that Dan spent the early years of ours writing an erotic bildungsroman about this nightmare ex-girlfriend, the novel at one point ballooning to 500 pages and including references to everyone he'd ever slept with. Even after the book was published, I never quite shook the feeling that my role in Dan's life was to be the steady, vanilla lay. We never discussed this. We just had a strenuously normal sex, year after year after year.

Then one day at my desk I started reading "The Multi-Orgasmic   56
Couple: Sexual Secrets Every Couple Should Know." I sent Dan an e-mail message entitled "Nine Taoists Thrusts."

Page 123, from the seventh-century physician Li T'ung-hsuan   57
Tzu:

1. Strike left and right as a brave general breaking through the enemy ranks.
2. Rise and suddenly plunge like a wild horse bucking through a mountain stream.
3. Push and pull out like a flock of seagulls playing on the waves.
4. Use deep thrusts and shallow teasing strokes, like a sparrow plucking pieces of rice.
5. Make shallow and then deeper thrusts in steady succession.
6. Push in slowly as a snake entering its hole.
7. Charge quickly like a frightened mouse running into its hole.
8. Hover and then strike like an eagle catching an elusive hare.
9. Rise up and then plunge down low like a great sailboat in a wild wind.

This e-mail was partly in response to one Dan sent me a few   58
months earlier, just to see how much he could tweak my type-A sensibility. It was entitled "Strength Benchmarks for Women" and indicated that I should be able to do 10 pull-ups, 20 bar dips, front squat and bench press my body weight and dead lift one and a half times my body weight. Upon receiving the thrust e-mail, Dan ran up to my office in the attic from his in the basement and asked which thrust sounded best. This was a departure for us—after I felt rebuffed in some early attempts to make use of some kitschy erotic wedding presents, we settled into our safe, narrow little bowling alley of a sex life.

Now, high above noisy Franklin Street, in the office of our   59
therapist, Betsy Kassoff, our issues came pouring out. (We chose to see a psychologist who worked on sexuality, because we weren't contending with physical dysfunction.) Dan began with

an exhaustive history. "When I was 15 years old I was dating a girl . . . " I can't tell you how monumentally tired I was of hearing about Dan's ex-girlfriends. Could we please never discuss this again? "We had this completely psychological sadistic thing that was incredibly disturbing to me . . . Every few years I'd have a relationship that mirrored that one, and then I had the bull moose of these relationships. It was like sticking my finger in the electrical socket of my own unconscious."

60   Betsy, who had a touch as deft as Bill Clinton at a barbecue, just said, "Wow."

61   Dan and I had talked around the edges of this before—the trauma of the bull moose, our romance's unpleasant start. But by the time either of us had any clarity on the matter, we were desperate to pack it away. Strange, now, what relief we felt in opening that rank old hamper. Betsy could not have said more than 50 words before Dan paused, and I jumped in.

62   Remember that searing detail from the Eliot Spitzer scandal: that he had sex in his socks? Way worse stuff came out. Like how Dan and I hadn't been talking to each other while having sex. And not making eye contact either. "And what about the darker, more aggressive side of sexuality you talked about in your earlier relationships?" Betsy asked Dan. "Would you say it's been more difficult to bring those parts of yourself to this relationship?"

63   Betsy worked gently and efficiently, a nurse undressing a wound. I confessed my craving but also my worry that we could not be sexually aggressive without conjuring the bull moose. Dan swore—eagerly—that this was not the case. The layers of our erotic life kept pulling back. I allowed that I felt hemmed in by our excessively regular sex life and annoyed that, in the context of our marriage, Dan supposedly had an important sexual history while I had none. Dan then admitted his fantasies about my past lovers, his fear that they had accessed parts of me that were walled off from him. How, nine years into our marriage, could our sex life still be under the thumbs of exes we no longer talked to or even desired? The thought made me angry and nauseated.

64   Fifty minutes later, Dan and I stumbled down onto the street, wrung out and dazed. Then we went home and solved the problem, at least at first. I hate to sound all Ayelet Waldman here, trumpeting her steamy sex life with Michael Chabon, but we had excellent sex. We were terrified not to. Yet once we proved to ourselves that we weren't fools to be married—that we could have as charged an erotic life with each other as we had with others before—the backslide began. This time, the retreat was painful and abrupt. One day Dan found a box of old snapshots in the basement and brought it upstairs, thinking he'd show his old self to our daughters. The cache turned out to include

pictures I saved of ex-boyfriends, photos Dan proceeded to fling, to the girls' great amusement, across the room. "Remind me again why you invited so many ex-lovers to our 65 wedding?" Dan e-mailed me at 6 the following morning—neither of us could sleep. "Also, at the time, you had told me that you'd never slept with two of them. It only emerged later over time that you had. So what was going on there? Not completely ready to relinquish the past? Immaturity? Self-protection? Are you enjoying having a sexual history, too?"

In his novel "Before She Met Me," Julian Barnes explores the 66 rabid jealousy we feel for spouses' former lovers, as if we expect our partners to have lived in anticipation of meeting us. This jealousy, Barnes writes, comes "in rushes, in sudden, intimate bursts that winded you." It then lingers on "unwanted, resented." This was our experience. The inquisition continued for days. Why had I not told Dan I'd slept with _____? I lied 11 years earlier for the weakest of reasons: I lacked the presence of mind to tell Dan the truth, that I did not yet think he had a right to know all the details of my sex life before him. But now Dan was my husband, my full catastrophe. He allowed this reckless poking into all corners of our marriage. He even stopped seeing me as predictable and tame, and the old lie hurt. "This is the central trust issue in a marriage," Dan said the next day as he made me lunch. "Can I trust you when you tell me you haven't slept with somebody else?"

The following weekend: jealousy again (or was it an attempt 67 to fuel our eroticism with tension?). I said yes a bit too forcefully when Dan asked if I'd noticed a well-muscled young man at the pool. Dan was allowing for my sexual free agency, granting me my full humanity. We lived, raised children, worked and slept together. Now we needed to gouge out a gap to bridge, an erotic synapse to cross. It was exhausting. "That guy did the epitome of bad-values hypertrophy training"—vanity weight lifting, in Dan's estimation, just to get buff. "You're like a guy admitting he likes fake boobs. And he had chicken legs. Did you notice that, too?"

VI

What is a good marriage? How good is good enough? Ultimately 68 each philosophy of what makes a good marriage felt like a four-fingered glove. The passion apologists placed no stock in the pleasures of home. The communication gurus ignored life history. I came to view the project as a giant attempt to throw everything out of the messy closet that was our life and put it back in a way that resembled an ad for the Container Store. Not everything fit. It never would. We could tidy up any given area and more quickly and easily than we anticipated. But despite ongoing sessions with endless professionals, we couldn't keep the entirety of our marriage shipshape at once.

69   Still, night after night, I'd slide into bed next to Dan. He often slept in a white T-shirt and white boxer briefs, a white-cased pillow wrapped over his head to block out my reading light, his toppled stacks of cookbooks and workout manuals strewn on the floor. He looked like a baby, fresh and full of promise. In psychiatry, the term "good-enough mother" describes the parent who loves her child well enough for him to grow into an emotionally healthy adult. The goal is mental health, defined as the fortitude and flexibility to live one's own life—not happiness. This is a crucial distinction. Similarly the "good-enough marriage" is characterized by its capacity to allow spouses to keep growing, to afford them the strength and bravery required to face the world.

70   In the end, I settled on this vision of marriage, felt the logic of applying myself to it. Maybe the perversity we all feel in the idea of striving at marriage—the reason so few of us do it—stems from a misapprehension of the proper goal. In the early years, we take our marriages to be vehicles for wish fulfillment: we get the mate, maybe even a house, an end to loneliness, some kids. But to keep expecting our marriages to fulfill our desires—to bring us the unending happiness or passion or intimacy or stability we crave—and to measure our unions by their capacity to satisfy those longings, is naïve, even demeaning. Of course we strain against marriage; it's a bound canvas, a yoke. Over the months Dan and I applied ourselves to our marriage, we struggled, we bridled, we jockeyed for position. Dan grew enraged at me; I pulled away from him. I learned things about myself and my relationship with Dan I had worked hard not to know. But as I watched Dan sleep—his beef-heart recipe earmarked, his power lift planned—I felt more committed than ever. I also felt our project could begin in earnest: we could demand of ourselves, and each other, the courage and patience to grow.

Conversations 2.0: Debates About Non-Traditional Marriage

71   *In the current environment, many public conversations take place in a virtual, online space. And while calling these conversations "virtual conversations" might make them seem less real or less important, that is not the case. In fact, online conversations have become one of the central locations for public debate on key issues, including the issues that are included in this book. To enrich your understanding of public conversations, you can make use of the array of online discussion boards, listservs, blogs, Facebook pages,*

and Twitter sites that are available via the web. The Conversations 2.0 *pages in this book suggest some possible ways to do so, and point out some particularly useful and credible online conversations; you of course can use your own online forums and communities to add to these suggestions—or even to start your own.*

While most of the pieces in this chapter (and in the previous   72
one) address issues related to male/female relationships, love exists in forms that are often termed "non-traditional." Not only same-sex marriage, but open marriage, polygamy, and other variations have encroached upon what others suggest is the sacred union that should only exist between one man and one woman. Because of the passion on all sides of this conversation, the world wide web has become the site of a wealth of information on the variety of relationships which make claims to the term marriage. Just search terms like "gay marriage," "same-sex marriage," "non-traditional marriage," "varieties of marriage," or other related terms, and you will find people engaged in virtual conversations on the topic. Your job, of course, is to sort through this mass of data and decide, based upon your own areas of interest and research, which would provide the most useful documents.

In order to negotiate the wealth of conversations on the topic   73
of same-sex marriage, you might begin with an excellent e-bibliography maintained by Rutgers University (just search same-sex marriage and Rutgers to find it). This site can help you to gain some background on the topic, providing resources such as web sources, transcripts of symposia, effects upon children and parenting, the Defense of Marriage Act, international facets, and articles on all sides of the topics. As such, it is a very useful jumping off point for your research.

getting into the conversation ...8

The Ideal and Real of Marriage

1. Many media depictions about the state of marriage suggest that marriage is endangered. For example, Caitlin Flanagan's *Time* magazine cover story asks "Is There Hope for the American Marriage?" While this is presented as a question, it certainly leads readers toward the belief that the institution is in trouble. But a good reader will also look more closely; in this case, you might ask yourself if we are indeed in a time of decline for marriage, or if media depictions are overstating or sensationalizing the issue. Start out by doing a survey of recent media stories about marriage. Then do some research on the demographics of marriage in more scholarly research sources in order to test out the validity of the claims that are being made in those media sources, writing a comparative essay on the topic.

2. Feminism has had much to say about marriage as a social institution. As early as the 17th century, Mary Astell was asking in *Some Reflections on Marriage*, "If marriage be such a blessed state, how comes it, may you say, that there are so few happy marriages?" Astell and others of this period saw marriage as a detriment to women's educational, and even spiritual, progress. Many recent feminists have also seen marriage as an unequal state that keeps women in subservient roles. As you examine the views on marriage in this chapter of *Conversations*, ask yourself how many of the critiques that are made by these authors have their root in feminist ideas. Then, go on to write an essay that places recent discussions of marriage into the context of feminism, considering the degree to which changes in the value assigned to marriage is due to feminism, and whether those changes are a positive sign for our culture.

3. While the ideal of marriage imagines a blissful, pleasant, and easy relationship, the reality—as is noted by many of the authors in this section—is that maintaining a good marriage takes a great deal of work. But what kind of "work," specifically, is necessary for a marriage to succeed? Look back over the pieces in this chapter, and drawing upon the most relevant parts of those essays, write an essay that details the most important efforts that these authors suggest must be made toward a happy and fulfilling marriage. In order to further enrich this essay, you might go on to do some further research, seeking studies that predict the likelihood of a marriage's success based upon specific behaviors.

4. While writers like Jennifer Marshall and Stephanie Coontz base their arguments on sociological research, many of the pieces in this chapter use personal experience from their own lives and relationships as evidence. Study the forms of evidence and reasoning that are used in several essays in this section, and write an analysis of how the styles of

argument differ. Pay attention not only to the evidence that is offered, but also to the ways in which that evidence is used as a form of "proof" for each writer's main argument, using specific examples to illustrate each. You might also consider whether one form of proof is more compelling and/or more reliable than others.

extending the conversation ...4

Opportunities for Reading, Writing, and Research

Though the readings in *Conversations* are organized into specific topic areas, they can also be used to start your research into other related areas of interest. The following writing opportunities suggested can help you extend the conversations across the various subjects discussed in the book—and beyond the book into research areas you might explore on your own. These examples demonstrate how you might develop the readings from this book into larger projects; you can come up with many more on your own. As you do so, think especially about how your major field of study or other interests you have can inform your research.

1. While the reading you have done in this chapter provides you with a good deal of knowledge about changes in love relationships among current youth, you are living amidst another key source of information on that topic—your own college. In fact, both Laura Sessions Stepp and Kathleen Bogle collected information on this topic by interviewing and observing college students' behaviors. You might enter the conversation with similar methods, observing and collecting perspectives on this topic from classmates. First, look back over the essays to determine the methodologies that are used in these and other pieces in order to collect information from students. Then, develop your own methodology. How large a sample of students will you need? Will you do interviews, focus groups, or surveys? Might you do a case study, learning more about the lives of a few specific students? How will you assure the privacy of those individuals you study? (Each college has its own standards for doing ethical research; check with your Institutional Review Board to be sure that your research methods meet college standards.) After you have designed a methodology, carry out your research, taking careful field notes, or perhaps audio or video taping the conversations. After you have collected this informtion, you can compare your own primary evidence with that of the authors in this section (and others you might read) in order to draw some conclusions about the validity of those studies in the context of your own college.

2. While "hooking up" is a relatively new term, the idea of "free love" or "casual sex" is not. In fact, "free love" was one of the driving forces behind the last revolution in social norms during the 1960s and 1970s in America. In order to get some perspective on the hook-up phenomenon, you might do some further reading on that earlier period (or other periods of social revolution) and develop a comparison between our own times and that other period. There are a number of ways that you might gather information on the topic. You can do some historical research on a past period and its attitudes toward sexuality. You could also interview or survey individuals who lived during this time period. You could also study artifacts of that period, gathering and analyzing visuals, advertisements, films, and other remnants of the past to

demonstrate how that past revolution, and the present one, relate to one another. Doing so can also give you experience on the kinds of work done by historians and other social scientists.

3. The pieces in this chapter focus largely upon heterosexual relationships. However, love relationships are not exclusively heterosexual, and so you might consider whether the claims made about love relationships and/or marriage in this section apply equally well to same-sex relationships. Are the values in same-sex marriage, where that is legal, also deteriorating? What is the rate of same-sex divorce? Do same-sex relationships require the same kinds of work as those in heterosexual relationships? Has the hookup culture made changes in homosexual relationships as well? What is the state of virtual homosexual relationships, and do they differ for men and women? If marriage is declining, why do so many gay activists fight for the right to marry? These, and many other questions, might give you the opportunity to extend the conversation beyond its focus on heterosexuals into a comparative analysis with same-sex couples. Choose one specific area of analysis in order to keep your study focused.

Conversations About Sustainability

Introduction

For some, it is easy to think of the environmentalist movement as univocal and peaceful, a group of concerned individuals who are trying to save the world. For others, it is just as
easy to see sustainability advocates as extremists and reactionary doomsayers, constantly and irrationally predicting
disaster. But although there are always fringe elements in any
group, the truth is that those who are interested in issues of
environmental sustainability are a diverse group. This group
comprises scientists and artists, philosophers and social scientists, conservatives and liberals; but you cannot predict
with ease what stance they will take on this issue by their
associations. Conservatives and liberals have a long record
of interest in environmental conservation. Both scientists
and artists are contributing their work to sustainability efforts.
Many not associated with any particular discipline or field
find themselves engaged in this debate simply as concerned
citizens. Thus, the dialogue about what practices are most
likely to preserve a livable world are wide-ranging, and this
conversation is both internal (among other members of
the movement) and external (an attempt to involve the wider
citizenry).

As a reader and writer, there is much to learn from the
ways that arguments about sustainability are formed in this
section of *Conversations*. Because this is an issue that
involves such a diverse group of stakeholders, the motivations to write differ widely. Businesspeople are interested in
the issue from an economic perspective. Scientists and engineers are intrigued by the challenge of solving the problems
associated with sustainability. Ethicists ask questions about
the imperatives and obligations we have to each other
and the natural environment, whereas political scientists
examine the ways that public policies and public opinion
affect the progress of the movement. Each brings a different
set of topics and their own modes of persuasion. Some arguments are emotionally based, pulling at the heartstrings of
those who they wish to influence. Others develop ethos- or
character-based arguments, arguing for their own credibility on the issue, and many use a set of facts and diverse forms
of reasoning to build their case. So as you read, you will be
able to track not only the issues that are raised, but also the
methods that are used to forward those perspectives.

One of the newer focuses of the sustainability movement
focuses upon ways toward a sustainable and environmentally
friendly food production system. The selections in Chapter 9

will provide you with a wide range of conversations about the effects of food production and consumption and policy perspectives on how we might provide a stable and sustainable food supply to our people without doing long-term damage to the soil, to our water supply, or to the animals with which humans share the earth. You will hear from those who are concerned about the chemical content of many of our foods, from those who suggest that eating meat is a cause of environmental degradation, and from those who question farming practices and the intricate web of how our food is transported around the country and the globe. You will hear from those who find present practices deleterious and those who suggest that new movements such as the "local foods" initiative are risky. You will hear about the motives of those involved in this debate and the questioning of the motives of others. You will also learn about what one author calls the "twinkie-industrial" complex, an intricate web of food additives that have dubbed chemicals and chemically enhanced products "food" despite their lack of nutritional value. As you listen in to these dialogues, your job will be to assess the validity and impact of each.

This section's *Conversations in Context* features a discussion of one front in the attempt to provide sustainable energy to a country that is attempting to overcome what the Obama administration has dubbed our "oil addiction"—the movement toward re-centering the place of nuclear energy. Nuclear energy, of course, carries with it the stigma of past disasters (Chernobyl) and near-disasters (Three-Mile Island), events that are still tied to any discussion of nuclear energy, as is the association with nuclear weaponry. This conversation is thus conducted in the space between the reasoned science of the Secretary of Energy and the emotional responses of those who continue to have deep fears of this form of energy production and its by-products. The range of voices and images here show how both ends of that spectrum and the whole range in between have a place in this discussion, and they indicate the need to find stasis points if there is to be any real resolution.

Finally, Chapter 10 asks a slightly different set of questions: Who are the best guardians of our environment, and what methods are available to them in terms of both effectiveness and ethics as members of a sustainability movement? The players and stakeholders in this conversation include environmental activists who are willing to go to almost any lengths, and those who prefer more collaborative methods; business persons who have used their resources to develop more environmentally friendly practices; governmental representatives, who are involved in legislating toward more sustainable outcomes; engineers, who are setting about the task of solving our dual problems of supplying the goods and services necessary, and doing so in ways that do as little damage to the environment as possible; and private citizens who are examining their own practices and practices of others like them, which might contribute to more positive outcomes.

What emerges from the group of readings in this chapter, then, is a set of arguments as diverse as those making those arguments. Although this makes finding your place in the conversation somewhat challenging, it also enriches the conversation to which you are listening and to which you may become a party. The key is, as with each of the topics broached in this book, to find the areas of shared concern and debate and to use that common ground as a staging point for your own writing.

CHAPTER 9

Feeding the World: Toward Sustainable Foods

Eric Schlosser

Fast Food Nation

"Fast Food Nation," the title of this essay, is also the title of Eric Schlosser's best-selling first book. Schlosser, a correspondent for the *Atlantic Monthly*, received great acclaim for that work, and subsequently appeared on *60 Minutes, CNN, CBS Evening News, NBC Nightly News, FOX News, The O'Reilly Factor,* and *Extra!* and has been interviewed on NPR and for *Entertainment Weekly, USA Today,* and the *New York Times.* This essay was published in April 2004, in the *Ecologist,* a widely read environmental magazine that is published on four continents and read by over 200,000 people in 150 countries. It considers itself an activist journal as well, describing itself as a "key player in major environmental campaigns against GM [genetically modified] crops, rainforest destruction, climate change and the impact of globalization." You might consider why an environmental journal such as this decided to publish Schlosser's piece on fast food. Also, consider how his work may have played a role in starting the many discussions of food that are represented in the pieces that follow.

In February a report by George W. Bush's Council of Economic Advisers (CEA) suggested that fast food workers might in the future be classified as manufacturing workers. A CEA report asked: "When a fast-food restaurant sells a hamburger, for example, is it providing a 'service,' or is it combining inputs to 'manufacture' a product?"   1

2   Reclassifying fast-food restaurants as 'factories' would have a number of benefits for the Bush administration. It would, in a single stroke, add about 3.5 million manufacturing jobs to the U.S. economy, at a time when such jobs are rapidly being exported overseas. From a statistical point of view, it would make the U.S. seem like an industrial powerhouse once again, instead of an ageing superpower threatened by low-cost competitors. And it would allow the fast-food industry, a strong backer of the Republican Party, to enjoy the tax breaks provided to U.S. manufacturers.

3   The CEA's chairman N. Gregory Mankiw was derided and ridiculed in the press for making the proposal, and his plan is likely to go nowhere. Yet there was an underlying logic to it. Fast food is indeed factory food, perhaps the most heavily processed food on the planet, and the low-paid workers who defrost, reheat and reconstitute it have jobs as boring, highly regimented and strictly supervised as the workers in a 19th century textile mill would have had. Moreover, the founding fathers of the industry probably wouldn't have minded the manufacturing label at all. Bringing the philosophy of the assembly line to the commercial restaurant kitchen was the simple innovation responsible for Ronald McDonald's global conquest.

4   The fast-food industry began in 1948. Richard and Maurice McDonald were growing tired of running their successful drive-in restaurant in San Bernadino, California. They were tired of constantly hiring new carhops, the teenaged girls who took food to customers waiting in parked automobiles. They were tired of replacing the dishes and glasses broken by their adolescent customers. But most of all, they were tired of paying the high wages demanded by skilled short-order cooks.

5   So the McDonalds decided to shut down their drive-in and replace it with a revolutionary new form of restaurant. The McDonald brothers started by firing all their car-hops and short-order cooks. They simplified the menu, hired unskilled workers and made each worker perform the same task again and again. One person only made french fries. Another only made shakes. Another only flipped burgers. By getting rid of skilled workers, by serving food and drinks in paper cups and plates, by demanding that customers wait in line for their own meals, the new 'Speedee Service System' allowed the brothers to serve fast, cheap food.

6   The new restaurant was an instant success. It fitted perfectly with the new culture emerging in post-war southern California—a car culture that worshipped speed, convenience and the latest technology. Ray Kroc, the milk shake machine salesman who bought out the McDonald brothers in the early 1960s and later exported their Speedee system around the world, embraced a blind faith in science: a Disneyesque vision of society

transformed through chemistry and families living happily in plastic homes and travelling in sleek, nuclear-powered cars.

Kroc also believed fervently in the ethic of mass production. 7 A philosophy of uniformity, conformity and total control that had long dictated the manufacture of steel wire was now applied not only to food, but to the people who prepared the food. "We have found out . . . that we cannot trust some people who are non-conformists," Kroc declared. "We will make conformists out of them in a hurry . . . The organisation cannot trust the individual; the individual must trust the organisation."

For the first two decades of its existence, the McDonald's oper- 8 ating system had little impact on the way people lived and ate. In 1968 there were only 1,000 McDonald's restaurants, all of them in the U.S. The chain bought fresh ground beef and potatoes from hundreds of local suppliers. But the desire for rapid growth and the desire for everything to taste exactly the same at thousands of different locations transformed not only the McDonald's supply system, but also the agricultural economy of the entire U.S.

McDonald's switched entirely to frozen hamburger patties and 9 frozen fries, relying on a handful of large companies to manufacture them. Other fast food chains spread nationwide at the same time, helping to drive local restaurants, small suppliers, independent ranchers and farmers out of business. And by the 1970s McDonald's began to expand overseas, taking with it a mentality perfectly expressed years later in one of the company's slogans—One taste worldwide.

Half a century after Richard and Maurice McDonald decided 10 to fire their carhops, the world's food supply is dominated by an agro-industrial complex in which the fast-food chains occupy the highest rung. Monsanto developed genetically-modified potatoes to supply McDonald's with perfectly uniform French fries—and then halted production of the "New Leaf GM Potato" when McDonald's decided, for publicity reasons, not to buy it. When the fast-food industry wants something, the major food processors rush to supply it.

Although many of the foods we eat look the same as the ones 11 we ate a generation ago, they have been fundamentally changed. They have become industrial commodities, with various components (flavour, colour, fats) manufactured and assembled at different facilities. If you bought a hamburger in the U.S. 30 years ago, it would most probably have contained meat from one steer or cow, which would have been processed at a local butcher shop or small meat-packing plant. Today a typical fast-food hamburger patty contains meat from more than 1,000 different cattle, raised in as many as five different countries. It looks like an old-fashioned hamburger, but is a fundamentally different thing.

12   Here is a partial list of what fast food and the fast-food mentality have recently brought us: the homogenisation of culture, both regionally and worldwide; the malling and sprawling of the landscape; the feeling that everywhere looks and feels the same; a low-wage, alienated service-sector workforce; a low-wage, terribly exploited meat-packing workforce; a widening gap between rich and poor; concentration of economic power; the control of local and national government by agribusiness; an eagerness to aim sophisticated mass marketing at children; a view of farm animals as industrial commodities; unspeakable cruelty toward those animals; the spread of factory farms; extraordinary air and water pollution; the rise of foodborne illnesses; antibiotic resistance; BSE; soaring obesity rates that have caused soaring rates of asthma, heart disease and early-onset diabetes; reduced life expectancy; a cloying, fake, manipulative, disposable, plastic worldview, the sole aim of which is to make a buck.

13   None of this was inevitable. The triumph of the fast-food system was aided at almost every step by government subsidies, lack of proper regulation, misleading advertisements, and a widespread ignorance of how fast, cheap food is actually produced. This system is not sustainable. In less than three decades it has already done extraordinary harm. When the fast-food industry is made to bear the costs it is now imposing on the rest of society, it will collapse. The alternative to fast food now seems obvious: slow food.

14   By "slow food" I do not mean precious, gourmet food, sold by celebrity chefs and prepared according to recipes in glossy cookbooks. I mean food that is authentic, that has been grown and prepared using methods that are local, organic and sustainable. Most slow foods are peasant foods. Somehow mankind existed for thousands of years without Chicken McNuggets. And I'd argue that our future survival depends on living without them.

15   What's the difference between fast food and slow food?

16   Here are the ingredients you need to make a strawberry milk shake the old-fashioned, slow-food way: milk, cream, sugar, ice, vanilla beans and strawberries.

17   And here are the ingredients you need to make a fast-food strawberry milk shake: milk-fat, non-fat milk, sugar, sweet whey, high-fructose corn syrup, corn syrup, guar gum, mono- and diglycerides, cellulose gum, sodium phosphate, carrageenan, citric acid, sodium benzoate, red colouring #40 and artificial strawberry flavour (amyl acetate, amyl butyrate, amyl valerate, anethol, anisyl formate, benzyl acetate, benzyl isobutyrate, butyric acid, cinnamyl isobutyrate, cinnamyl valerate, cognac essential oil, diacetyl, dipropyl kentone, ethyl acetate, ethyl amylketone, ethyl butyrate, ethyl cinnamate, ethyl heptanoate, ethyl heptylate, ethyl lactate, ethyl methylphenyl-glycidate,

ethyl nitrate, ethyl propionate, ethyl valerate, heliotropin, hydroxyphenyl-2-bulanone, xionone, isobutyl anthranilale, isobutyl anthranilate, isobutyl butyrate, lemon essential oil, maltol, 4-methylacetophenone, methyl anthranilate, methyl benzoate, methyl cinnamate, methyl heptine carbonate, methyl naphthyl ketone, methyl salicylate, mint essential oil, neroli essential oil, nerolin, neryl isobutyrate, orris butter, phenethyl alcohol, rose, rum ether, yundecalactone, vannilin and solvent).

Steve Ettinger

Consider the Twinkie

Steve Ettinger is a prolific author and editor who has authored, co-authored, or edited over 40 books. Six of his books have focused upon food, including his 2007 book, *Twinkie, Deconstructed,* from which this excerpt is taken. Ettinger has also appeared regularly on *The Today Show, CBS This Morning, ABC Nightline, Good Morning America,* and many other popular shows. *Twinkie, Deconstructed* uses this iconic junk food as a way of discussing the ways that our definitions of "food" have come to include the many chemical ingredients that are used in the food industry and to let his readers know "what you're eating." As you read this piece, consider the ways that the author is able to make larger points about the food industry by examining this single product. What do you take to be the crux of Ettinger's argument here? In what ways does it relate to Eric Schlosser's argument in "Fast Food Nation"? You might also imagine what other food products, in your own writing, you might examine in order to cast light upon the issue of food and its relation to issues of sustainability and health.

Finding that Twinkies ingredients may come from as far   1 away as Chinese and Middle Eastern oilfields and involve products from facilities as wide-ranging as steel mills and deep mines may be surprising, especially for such a familiar, small, sweet, everyday item. "All this just for a little cake?" is the obvious question. The answer is yes—because the implications extend far beyond the Twinkie.

The Twinkie-Industrial Complex

2   When you consider the Twinkie as a product—which it truly is, in every sense of the term—it's not that hard to fathom its link to the world economy. Twinkies' ingredients are the products of a rural-industrial complex, made from a web of chemicals and raw materials produced by or dependent on nearly every basic industry we know. Where do they come from, my kids wanted to know. They come from an international nexus: the Twinkie Nexus.

3   Twinkies are obviously connected to food industries such as corn, soybeans, wheat, eggs, and milk, but, in fact, Twinkies ingredients are also manufactured with fourteen of the top twenty chemicals made in the United States, not even including salt (which goes into chlorine) or petroleum. The unlikely food subingredients sulfuric acid, ethylene, lime, and phosphoric acid top the list. The Twinkie Nexus is huge and complex.

4   That industrial aspect of our food—and Twinkies are but one among tens of thousands of processed foods—would be less troubling if it were easier to still see where it all comes from. There is often no terroir to an ingredient, no one place that it is actually *from*. And between commoditization and competition, most industrial food ingredient suppliers are not easily identified. Most of the vitamins are made in China, essentially placing their manufacture beyond normal scrutiny, and most of the enormous and politically powerful agricultural commodity or global chemical conglomerates simply will not make themselves available. The whole scene is quite opaque. These companies' embrace of science is simply limited by their obedience to the marketplace and governmental policies. One only need recall the recent discovery that partially hydrogenated oils, which were supposed to be better for us than butter, are actually worse, because of trans fats, or that they unrelentingly promote the unnatural use of corn to feed cattle, or that they fully embrace genetic engineering. But we love the results and express this feeling unequivocally with our purchasing power, enthusiastically demanding more protein sources, a wider range of food choices, lower prices, presumably safer and less spoiled food. These are plainly political angles on biology—there are choices to be made—so it is up to us to keep on top of things in the food world.

5   The fact is that chemicals, especially those in foods, are part of nature. Perhaps a pertinent question is, "When does a chemical become a food?" ("It becomes a food when you decide it is a food," is the tantalizingly vague answer offered by a food scientist with whom I spoke. And what about when you use a food ingredient as a chemical—like the use of cellulose gum in oil well-drilling?) It appears to be a matter of perspective. Take flour, for example. Even this most basic, common ingredient seems

a product of global technology and commerce when you account for the enriching and bleaching that goes into producing it for Twinkies' use. Parse those words—enriched, bleached—and you learn that flour is mixed with some of the most heavily processed chemicals in the world: vitamins and bleach. It takes a global industrial effort to make enriched flour, to build strong bodies— and to make little snack cakes.

From the Cradle of Civilization to Every Supermarket Shelf

Twinkies' role in history is best understood in the inverse: history's   6
role in shaping the ingredient list. If all of civilization started with the farming of barley (to make beer), then all of the innovations since have led directly from flour and baking to the Twinkie and its emblematic quest for perfection in food.

Probably two of the most fascinating aspects of Twinkies ingre-   7
dients are that the scientific discoveries in the name of shelf life, taste, texture, and reduced cost are directly rooted in the Industrial Revolution, and that the key inventions of ingredients or processes are tied into historic moments. Especially in the United States after the Civil War, mass supply started to feed mass demand that existed thanks to the arrival of mass communication and transportation systems. The developments are all connected.

Over the years, wars and politics, as key events in history,   8
played key roles in inspiring the development of things like the modern, mechanized flour mill, baking soda, baking powder, artificial colors, artificial flavors, corn syrup, sorbic acid, and polysorbate 60 by forcing manufacturers to find alternative or better sources of subingredients. And these are all ingredients that make the modern Twinkie, as well as all processed food, possible. Late twentieth-century mastery of technology, coupled with the enormous post-World War II consumer demand for convenience and variety as family life became more fractured by demands of the workplace and leisure activities, pushed food scientists and the food companies to even higher levels of creativity that affect almost everything we eat, well beyond a simple snack cake born during the Depression.

This natural evolution led in the early twenty-first century to   9
a highly profitable global processed food market worth $3.2 trillion, one that almost no modern household can do without.

No Cream in the Creme

Shouldn't we be able to admit that we already know that chem-   10
icals have always been in our food, and that food is made of chemicals? In fact, food additives—some as old and simple as

salt and sugar—keep good food from going bad, and thus prevent food from occasionally killing us. In fact, all food is chemicals and all cooking is chemistry ("Cooking is just science that's tasty," the old saying goes). Remember, the chemicals hydrogen oxide, cellulose, hemicellulose, malic acid, dextrose, fructose, pectin, sucrose, amylacetate, and citric acid are found in nature's perfect food: the apple (in fact, that is the apple's complete ingredient list).

11   While there is no reason to be paranoid—these additives have been tested and in use for ages—there is reason to be vigilant. That may be what fuels the very negative reaction to genetically modified foods (GM) in Europe, something that is only beginning here. Now the competing consumer trends of natural or organic foods versus traditional convenience foods are coming into sharper focus and voices on both sides are becoming more shrill.

12   To underscore the confusion around the question of the healthfulness of artificial ingredients, try reflecting on the fact that one of the world's most lethal chemicals, chlorine, and one of the most reactive chemicals, sodium, have an exalted place on every table in the Western world: the salt shaker. Or reduced to the absurd: should the ingredient H_2O scare us because it is often found mixed in with acids and poisons? Shall we sound the alarm? How about those food scientists who manipulate molecules to make new foods? But wait—isn't moving molecules around what you do when you fry an egg or bake a cake or even boil water?

13   In fact, it's not just the commercial bakers who put unpronounceables in their cakes—you do, too, when you add baking powder, enriched, bleached flour, or even shortening to your homemade confections. "It just ain't plain eggs and butter, pal," as one friendly chef once told me. Examining the labels found on supermarket shelves, it becomes obvious that Twinkies are merely an archetype of almost all modern processed foods; so many others share their ingredients and attempts at immortality on the shelf, ranging from Oreos® (which can last six months) to Freihofer's® 100% whole wheat bread. And contrary to the old joke, Twinkies still won't survive a nuclear war. They're just food. One that lots of us like, and have for a good long time.

14   All artificial ingredients, like recipes, reflect the balance of various needs (or our perceptions of needs) such as shelf life (long), taste (sweet), texture (fat), convenience (high), price (low), packaging (airtight), nutrition (sound), and legal requirements—and none would exist if there was no profit in it. All are needs generated by our way of life. It seems that we are, indeed, what we eat.

Back when the original Twinkie was low-tech, it was not 15
good for anyone to find a spoiled cake on a shelf. Before getting on a high horse to decry the excessive pressures of capitalism that force food to be so overwhelmingly engineered,
we need to remember this: no farmer would bring his or her
crops to market without the promise of a reward. Modern food
technology is a growth business. On the retail end, packaged
food and soft drinks generate close to $400 billion in U.S. sales
each year—and their suppliers, whether processors of corn
or colors, are large corporations dependent on growth to survive. They fan the flames of consumer demand to maintain the
marketplace.

Consider the Twinkie

"Good living is an act of intelligence, by which we choose things 16
which have an agreeable taste rather than those which do not,"
said Jean Anthelme Brillat-Savarin in his seminal 1825 book on
gastronomy, *The Physiology of Taste*. Would he have accepted the
Twinkie as a culinary achievement?

Pick up a package. The appealing little finger cake just begs 17
to be eaten. It is an appetizing size. Droplets of lush moisture
cling teasingly to the inside of the perfectly clear wrapper. Rip
it open, feel the softness. Take a bite, not a nibble, and you'll be
hit, all at once, with sweetness, stickiness, and a rapidly dissolving texture.

Then comes a second hit of sweetness. Explore the filling with 18
your tongue. Notice the synergy of flavors that build—butter,
egg, vanilla—then the creamy finish that lingers, sticky, sweet,
and thick. Appreciate the contrast and interplay between the
smooth, cool filling and the delicate cake.

Eat enough of 'em, and you'll be able to suss out the bouquet 19
of fresh, Delaware polysorbate 60, and good Georgian cellulose
gum; a hint of prime Oklahoman calcium sulfate, or that fine,
Midwestern soybean shortening, if not the finest high fructose
corn syrup Nebraska has to offer.

Twinkie, deconstructed. 20
At least now you know what you're eating. 21

James E. McWilliams

From the Golden Age to the Golden Mean of Food Production

James E. McWilliams is an associate professor of history at the Texas State University, where he specializes in the early colonial period of American history. He has also published opinion pieces on food in *The New York Times, Christian Science Monitor,* and *USA Today.* Among his books are *American Pests: The Losing War on Insects from Colonial Times to DDT* (2008), *A Revolution in Eating: How the Quest for Food Shaped America* (2005), and *Just Food: How Locavores are Endangering the Future of Food and How We Can Truly Eat Responsibly* (2009), from which the following excerpt is taken. In this work, McWilliams argues that the locavore movement—which attempts to persuade people to eat only foods produced locally—brings with it potential problems. As you read, you might consider how arguments are not simply "for" or "against" something, but instead include more subtle nuances. Is McWilliams "against" the locavore movement, or is he attempting to revise it in ways that make it more fully aware of the larger picture? Consider also how you might use this type of critical thinking to enter into conversations on sustainable foods in ways that are less confrontational, and more about discussion than—in McWilliams' words—writing "reactionary tracts."

He who has food has many problems.
—Byzantine Proverb

1   Approximately 500 million years ago large clumps of sand and mud formed sedimentary rocks that trapped microscopic plants and animals. This geologic mash eventually decomposed into fossil fuels. For better or worse, these fuels would later serve the endlessly proliferating wants and needs of advanced human civilization. About fifty years ago scientists began to document the environmental problems caused by burning these fuels to power modern life, global warming being the most notable of them. At the turn of the twenty-first century, environmentalists tied this vast history into a tight knot by

showing how conventional food production was responsible for a large portion of the greenhouse gas fouling today's atmosphere. Omnivores, the developed world learned, had a dilemma. We were killing the environment, and thus ourselves and our future, with a diet addicted to fossil fuels.

The most powerful response to this problem has been to pro- 2 duce and consume locally grown food, in other words, to become a "locavore." What has happened since this locavore revolution started has been nothing short of spectacular. Millions of consumers in advanced societies the world over now demand that their food be locally sourced. The phrases "food miles" and "local farmers' market" fall off the environmentalist's tongue as inspired pearls of environmental wisdom. Organizations of environmentally concerned members eating "100-mile diets" have bloomed across North America and Europe. "Slow food" is gaining on fast food as a conventional culinary ethic. In a matter of years, the idea of eating locally produced food has come to seem so indisputably sensible that it's almost a moral obligation to book a seat on the bandwagon headed for the closest sustainable farm.

This revolution—brimming with buzzwords such as "sustain- 3 ability," "agroecology," "foodshed," and "carbon footprint"—has resonated far and wide. Best-selling locavore writers have accomplished the seemingly impossible task of getting Americans to ponder where their food comes from, an achievement that must be celebrated. After all, we recently couldn't have cared less about the source of our food, but today Alice Waters is a household name. Michael Pollan is our unofficial farmer-in-chief. Wendell Berry is the agricultural romantic's poet laureate. Many consumers now turn up their noses at tomatoes that are not heirloom, cows that do not eat native grass, and pigs that do not frolic across a verdant free range. The Golden Arches are the avatar of evil, and chicken nuggets are on par with crack cocaine as a substance to avoid. All in all, it's very real progress. Locavores, and their ceaseless emphasis on fresh, local, sustainable food, are to be thanked for fueling an upsurge in ecological awareness about food and the more hopeful facets of its production.

But for all the deserved accolades, the locavore approach to 4 reforming our broken food system has serious limits—limits that our exuberant acceptance of eating local has obscured. Although these limitations are many, the one I'm particularly concerned with is this: *Eating local is not, in and of itself, a viable answer to sustainable food production on a global level.* In fact, it's a relatively small step toward that critically important goal. As an environmental historian and the author of several books dealing with agriculture, I've become increasingly convinced (somewhat against my will) of this point.

Current popular assessments of our food issues repeatedly and 5 passionately insist that the problem of sustainable production can be solved though a primary emphasis on localism. The underlying premise is that agribusiness has undermined the environmental balance of small-scale food production and all we have to do is restore it by "relocalizing" the food system—that is, taking it back to the way it once was. Most of my friends, as well as many of the writers, thinkers, and activists I most admire, strongly advocate this position.

6   My own research, however, has taught me something different. In the most general terms, it's taught me that "the omnivore's dilemma" is too complicated to be managed through a primary reliance on food grown in proximity to where we live. Such an emphasis, in fact, can in many cases be detrimental to the environment. By no means do I deny that localism has benefits, nor do I deny that agribusiness is generally irresponsible. But I am nonetheless insisting that there are more productive, creative, and global ways to think about the complicated problem of eating an ethical diet. There are alternatives to the local alternative.

7   My goal here is not to write a reactionary tract against the locavore movement. Instead, it is to step back, survey the broader land-scape of food production and consumption, and—with all due respect to the locavore ethos (and I have a lot of it)—grapple honestly with questions that locavores have yet sufficiently to confront: How can we, both collectively and as individual consumers, achieve a sustainable *global* diet? How can the world keep growing in population, feed itself, and at the same time preserve its natural resources for future generations? How can we produce an abundance of safe food while minimizing dangerous environmental costs?

8   Too often environmentalists brush aside such "feed the world" questions as traps intended to promote the productive strengths of factory farming. They point to that infamous agricultural experiment undertaken between 1945 and the 1980s called the Green Revolution and, with justification, highlight the environmental degradation and corporate consolidation that the revolution required to feed the masses a steady diet of rice and wheat. But who ever said that farmers growing food for the world should abandon the quest for—as the agricultural ecologist Gordon Conway puts it—a *doubly* Green Revolution? Who ever said that agribusiness, at least as it currently operates, has a monopoly on the quest to feed the world? For that matter, who ever said local was necessarily equivalent to sustainable, much less the only antidote to the excesses of the Green Revolution?[1]

9   These kinds of questions have driven my research. I've tackled them knowing full well that my answers will inevitably generate controversy. It hasn't taken me long to learn that challenging ideas about food is not unlike challenging ideas about religion. A systematic examination of what's required to produce food responsibly for billions of people necessarily demands that we

confront issues which elicit emotional responses. Regrettably, our current culinary discourse has been pushed to extreme ends of the spectrum. There's agribusiness on the one hand and there's the local farmer on the other. But somewhere in the middle there's a golden mean of producing food that allows the conscientious consumer to eat an ethical diet in a globalizing world. Ambitious as the goal may be, the golden mean is what I'm seeking to pin down in the chapters ahead.

When it comes to food, there are plenty of big issues for   10
environmentally concerned consumers to explore. In addition to the concept of food miles, there are genetically modified foods, farm-raised fish (aquaculture), a reassessment of organic crops, liberalized but regulated trade policies, and sustainable ranching—all key issues that remain central to taking environmentally responsible food production beyond the local context. These issues are thoroughly discussed in the pages ahead and, I hope, productively reconceptualized to offer a vision of global food production that makes sustainability and commercial viability overriding and complementary priorities.

The track record for rationally discussing controversial mat-   11
ters of food and agriculture isn't encouraging. As a rule these issues have been cynically politicized before being explored as legitimate responses to our broken food system. Because the food wars, like any war, need their weapons, these very general ways of thinking about food production and consumption have entered the court of public opinion as cannon shots of contention rather than opportunities to find common ground. Something about food fosters radical dichotomies. We instinctively feel an overwhelming desire to take sides: organic or conventional, fair or free trade, "pure" or genetically engineered food, wild or farm-raised fish. Like most things in life, though, the sensible answer lies somewhere between the extremes, somewhere in that dull but respectable place called the pragmatic center. To be a centrist when it comes to food is, unfortunately, to be a radical.

The fact that we've avoided that center—short-changed com-   12
plexity for extremism—is unfortunate for the cause of sustainable food production and ethical consumption. It's my sincere hope that this book can expand the dialogue about sustainable food without causing yet another tawdry food fight between radicalized perspectives and opposing interest groups, for if there's one thing conspicuously missing from our public discussion of food and the environment, it's nuance.

In the most general terms, then, my mission in the following   13
pages is to transform what have been culinary-ideological weapons into building blocks for a model of sustainable global food production. What emerges will hardly offer a pat or complete answer to one of the twenty-first century's defining challenges. Nevertheless, through a balanced presentation of the

most recent and thoughtful work on food production and the environment, as well as a much-needed historical perspective gutted of myth and nostalgia, I will make a case. This case, if all goes well, will help the omnivore, herbivore, and locavore make food choices that are environmentally just while at the same time reminding us that until we help make basic changes in how the world approaches food, our options are, somewhat tragically, limited in scope.

14   The fact that I aim to offer a balanced account should not imply that my analysis lacks passion or conviction. Underscoring every proposal I highlight in the following pages are precise, and surely controversial, views about nature and agriculture that I should make clear from the start.

15   The more I thought, read, and wrote about such divisive matters as biotechnology, aquaculture, factory farming, and the organic revolution, the more it became clear to me that each issue, in one way or another, has been distorted by a popular misunderstanding of agriculture. This misunderstanding ultimately boils down to the misleading allure of a lost golden age of food production—a golden age of ecological purity, in which the earth was in balance, humans collectively respected the environment, biodiversity flourished, family farms nurtured morality, and ecological harmony prevailed.

16   Thing is, there was no golden age. The perpetuation of this myth is a cheap but very powerful rhetorical strategy to burden the modern environmentalist with a false standard of pastoral innocence. Our contemporary failings as producers and consumers are routinely dramatized as a shameful fall from grace. The problem with this scenario is that we humans have always abused the environment, often without mercy. Romantics can bellow into the wilderness for an enormous shift in human perspective, but the genie of exploitation is out of the bottle. For over 10,000 years humans have systematically manipulated nature to our advantage by making plants and animals do our bidding. I honestly don't believe that this basic relationship will ever change. My proposals will, for better or worse, reflect this opinion.

17   I'm not being cynical on this point, just realistic. Writers who insist otherwise, who believe that achieving truly responsible food production requires rediscovering some long-lost harmonious environmental relationship, are agricultural idealists who do not know their history. These agrarian populists are complicit in what Julie Guthman, the author of the incisive book *Agrarian Dreams*, aptly calls a "stunning erasure" of the past. A hopeless romance with some wilderness of the imagination has shielded them (and us) from the harsh essence that's at the core of agricultural practice. The

inspiring poet Wendell Berry can declare himself bound "for ground of my own where I have planted vines and orchard trees" that in "the heat of the day climbed up into the healing shadow of the woods." But staunch opponents have another take on that healing shadow.[2]

Speaking of agriculture per se—all agriculture—the promi-   18 nent plant geneticist and microbiologist Nina Fedoroff told me that "agriculture is more devastating ecologically than anything else we could do except pouring concrete on the land." Although obviously overstated, her underlying point makes considerable sense. Her thoughts have been echoed by other scientists, who, drawing on the history of how humans have enslaved nature to satisfy hunger, rightly note that "domestication reinvents the rules of nature," that "cultivated plants are nature's misfits," and that farming is, at its historical essence, the art of strategizing against the natural world.[3]

The opinions of another school of prominent agricultural   19 writers similarly counter the agrarian idealists who labor under the misguided assumption that nature is "the supreme farmer." Richard Manning, the author of *Against the Grain: How Agriculture Has Hijacked Civilization,* is refreshingly candid on this matter. Manning, who writes especially well about preindustrial agriculture, argues that "agriculture created poverty," that "agriculture was simply opportunism," and that "grain is the foundation of civilization, and so, by extension, catastrophe." "I have come to think of agriculture," he explains, "not as farming, but as a dangerous and consuming beast of a social system." Again, Manning is writing not about factory farming but of the essence of farming in general. Victor Davis Hanson, an angry but eloquent former raisin farmer in California, quakes in rage at the notion of romantic agrarianism, insisting that "the quaint family farmstead, the focus for such fantasy, is becoming a caricature, not a reality, in the here and now." His advice is advice I've taken to heart: "Any book about farming must not be romantic or naïve, but brutally honest."[4]

As someone whose agricultural experience consists of garden-   20 ing, I prefer to take my cues from voices like Hanson's because not only are their hands dirty with the biology and business of farming, but history bears out their perspective. Indeed, they work and write in the vein of an agricultural history that is shot through with the accounts of hard-bitten men who have yoked their own oxen, dredged their own plows, and balanced their own books, leaving behind not the slightest legacy of romanticism but instead a considerable dose of venom. Frankly, their accounts of agriculture are simply more plausible.

Sober agrarian assessments, perhaps because they're not espe-   21 cially marketable, have gone unappreciated. The new agrarians— those who conceptualize agriculture as a countercultural ideal to industrial modes of production—write often about how we must return to the land and let nature do our farming. But they slight the history underlying their idealism. They ignore those who ran from farming, got out at the first chance, took a job in another sector, never, not for a moment, looked back. The results of sidestepping this bitter view of agriculture would be insignificant if the stakes were not so high. The quest for sustainable methods of global food production cannot wait. What worries me is that well-meaning locavores who have the power to influence thousands of consumers down the primrose path of localism will come to realize that their dreams were unrealistic after it's too late to regroup and pursue more achievable approaches.

22   The history of agriculture provides ample warning against such a perspective. Too often, however, we're asked to erase the actual history of agricultural practice and the relentless press of population and listen to the disembodied wisdom of the ages. But no matter how rhapsodic one waxes about the process of wresting edible plants and tamed animals from the sprawling vagaries of nature, there's a timeless, unwavering truth espoused by those who worked the land for ages: no matter how responsible agriculture is, it is essentially about achieving the lesser of evils. To work the land is to change the land, to shape it to benefit one species over another, and thus necessarily to tame what is wild. Our task should be to deliver our blows gently. Not very sexy, perhaps not very heartwarming, but this is my view.

23   I suppose it would have been a lot more fun to have written a book on the sublime virtues of slow food, Chez Panisse, Berkshire pork, or the gustatory pleasures of an heirloom tomato. For sure, it would have been a pleasure to indulge my research abilities in something sensual and fulfilling. But such concerns, given the challenges we face as socially aware consumers, strike me as overly precious. Such idealization of the luxurious—a staple of food writing today—distracts us from the reality of the concrete. So I've chosen to save the romantic rhetoric for the parlors of hobby farmers and seminar rooms of the chattering culinary class.

24   After all, regular consumers have already been duly flogged, with one sermon after another telling us that we have sinned, that we must repent and restore our agrarian innocence, that we should go back to the land, repair our environmental souls, seek ecological redemption, and do everything but start foraging for nuts and berries and hunting wild boar for sustenance. How else to save humanity? How else to eat a responsible diet? How else to go green? It's an entirely false, if not melodramatic, premise. Real people living and eating in a real world deserve a more sophisticated answer to these myriad questions, all of which make up our shared dilemma.

What follows is in many ways a very personal book. Inten-   25
sifying my interest in sustainable food is the fact that achieving a responsible diet has long been an ongoing quest for me
as an individual. I care deeply about food, and I care even
more deeply about the environment. Indeed, I spent a couple
of very earnest years riding the locavore bandwagon myself.
My conversion to being an emotional and intellectual locavore
was the only activist decision I'd made in my life. As my passion started to stir, I could be found haunting local farmers'
markets around my hometown, Austin, Texas, bashing "big
industrial" and "Frankenfood" at every opportunity, investigating like a Checkpoint Charlie the groceries that crossed the
threshold of my kitchen, becoming a tiresome dinner companion, and once, after teaching two history classes on a
balmy Texas afternoon, slaughtering my own locally raised,
scrap-fed chicken on an oak stump in a friend's backyard.
Sure enough, as my knife scored the chicken's fibrous neck, I
rejoiced that a genuine movement was afoot and that I, with
blood on my oxford shirt, was present at the creation. I had
found my cause: saving the environment through the way I
ate. Empowerment!

Turns out I wasn't much of an acolyte. I'm a skeptic and a prag-   26
matist at heart, so in less enthralled moments my doubts sim-
mered and eventually boiled over. Something about the "eat
local" ethic, heady as it was, began to hit me as not only prag-
matically unachievable but simplistically smug. I started to ask
questions that got me funny looks down on the chicken farm.
Was this all it took to make for an environmentally virtuous diet?
A biweekly bike ride to Boggy Creek—a wonderful farm near my
home—to buy a box of strawberries? A pound of grass-fed beef
handed over the counter by Russ, my butcher at Whole Foods?
A quick jerk of the knife across a chicken's carotid artery?

The problems of global warming and environmental degrada-   27
tion were so widespread and complex—so global—that it felt
mildly disingenuous to believe that my little noble acts of locavore heroism were anything more than symbolic gestures.
Really, wasn't this just checkbook environmentalism (however
well intentioned), with me doing little more than salving my
conscience by buying overpriced tomatoes and cooking with
parsnips when the weather got chilly? The premise of it all
began to feel thin.

It's hard to identify exactly when my skepticism became com-   28
mitted doubt, but several random observations nudged me
down the path of crankiness. Maybe it was watching one too
many times the pretentious woman with the hemp shopping bag
declaring "This bag is not plastic!" make her way to market in
an SUV the size of my house. Or maybe it was the baffling association between buying local food and dressing as if it were

Haight-Ashbury circa 1968 that got me thinking that my sacred farmers' market was a stage set more for posturing than for environmental activism. Maybe it was reading yet another predictable introduction to yet another glossy coffee-table cookbook written by some hotshot chef telling me that I was part of the problem when I purchased food at—gasp—*a supermarket*. Granted, minor disturbances all, but they pushed me to take a closer look at the emperor's clothes.

29   Self-righteousness might have gotten under my skin, but there were also these sobering numbers I kept reading about. When Christopher Columbus landed in Hispaniola, the world's population stood at 450 million. By the late nineteenth century it had grown to 1.5 billion. Today there are almost 7 billion souls on the face of the earth, and frightening as it is to contemplate, by 2050 there will be 9.5 billion. In the past fifty years the world's population has doubled. We all need food. Not only that, but the populations of India and China—the bulk of the world—are on the verge of being able to eat a modern diet regularly consisting of meat, vegetables, and grain. This is an irrepressible component of globalization—one with potentially severe environmental consequences—that we can no longer afford to ignore.

30   Nowhere in the locavore canon has there been a serious discussion about this looming demographic catastrophe. You can reliably hear advocates insist that "organic can feed the world," but there is no blueprint for that transition. The conservation biologists Paul and Anne Ehrlich sum up the current relationship between exploding population and shrinking resources in these terms: "The projected 2.5 billion further increase in the human population will almost certainly have a much greater environmental impact than the last 2.5 billion added since 1975. Our species has already plucked the low-hanging resource fruit and converted the richest land to human uses." This fact is, in essence, the elephant in the locavores' room. The world's productive land has already been turned over to exploitation. The low-hanging fruit is gone. Going local, in light of it all, is akin to making sure that everything is fine in our own neighborhood and then turning ourselves into a gated community.[5]

31   It's little wonder that the manifestos of local production and consumption almost never confront these hard numbers. After all, the figures, so unyielding and alarming, plead with us in their urgency to think beyond an exclusively local perspective. At the least, the diet we strive for must take us beyond the local food activist Vandana Shiva's mantra that "all rules . . . should promote local production by local farmers, using local resources for local production." But is it viable to feed 9 or 10 billion people through local modes of agricultural production, without long-distance trade? And what if, by some crazy miracle, it were?[6]

What would happen to local traffic patterns if every consumer   32
in Austin made daily trips in their SUVs to visit small local farms
to buy locally produced food? What would happen to the nation's
water supply if the entire American Southwest insisted upon
preindustrial, locally produced food? What would happen, for
that matter, in New Delhi, New York, Casablanca, Mexico City, or
Beijing? And how the hell would I get my daily fixes of wine and
coffee? The problem and the solution—local, slow, nonindustrial
food—eventually struck me as fundamentally incompatible with
these logistical (and sensual) concerns. I realize that most locavores are much more flexible when it comes to obeying their
founding premise. But still, it is by taking the ideology to its logical extreme that we make its inherent weaknesses most visible.

When I asked myself the demographic questions, no matter   33
how imaginative my answers, no matter how doggedly I pursued alternative options, I kept slamming into realities—the
reality of 10 billion people scattered across the globe, of declining soil quality, of limited arable land, of shrinking fresh water
supplies, of the Ehrlichs' "already plucked . . . low-hanging
resource fruit." Considering these inescapable global facts, I
remained steadfastly unable to envision anything but a food
dystopia arising from the universalization of the movement
that I had once embraced with religious passion. It might have
worked in 1492, but not today. Not on the eve of 10 billion. We
need bigger systems.

This is not to dash the hopes of the locavore. It's only to point   34
to what's heretofore been hidden in plain sight: there are very
real limits to the locavore vision, limits that cannot realistically
be overcome. When I left the locavore bandwagon, I did not
completely leave behind its ethic. I simply want to place it in a
new perspective, one that acknowledges that there's a world of
consumers out there whose concerns about food have little to
do with anything that Chez Panisse, Berkeley, or the slow-food
movement happens to be celebrating.

Rest assured, I'll control my antielitism. I say this in part   35
because I am pretty much a member of the food elite. For those
of us fortunate enough to spend our leisure time fretting over
heirloom tomatoes, the world is not just our oyster, it's our Mal-
bec, our Blue Point, and our cave-aged Manchego. And good for
us. If you have the leisure time to ponder the subtleties of taste,
and if you can afford to travel the world and eat a diet that hews
to the earthy wonders of *terroir*, well then, be glad and rejoice.
But let's be honest with ourselves: it's a narrow perspective. Most
of the world wants food, just food, and if we don't figure out how
to produce that food in a sensible and sustainable manner, one
that honors future generations, our localized boutique obsessions are going to appear comically misguided (if not downright
tragic) to future historians.

36   And so my journey as a locavore fizzled out on the shoals of common sense and healthy skepticism. Radical locavores continue to brook little deviation from the sacred commandment that local food is virtuous while imported food is irresponsible. But nowadays, the more I talk with advocates of localism, the more I sense their own doubts and frustrations with the idealistic agrarian worldview. Even those located firmly within the locavore movement feel alienated by its expectations. How could they not? The demand that we eat exclusively locally produced, preferably organic food poses an unrealistic hurdle for even the most dedicated, activist-minded foodies. Dreams can be grand, but at some point we must admit their limitations and seek their spirit in more realistic endeavors.

37   What follows is a mass of information delivered with doses of humor, humility, objectivity, and even a little anger, but it's ultimately the story of how I came to terms with the locavore's dilemma. Readers hoping for a journalistic travelogue of eating adventures had best close the book now. Despite my opinion that food miles are the least of our concerns, I did not circumnavigate the globe to investigate the topics that I'm writing about directly. Instead, I settled in behind my desk in Austin, Texas, made the requisite phone calls, sent the critical e-mails, read the relevant reports, learned the scientific lexicons, did the hard research, and threw down my cards when I thought my hand was good. Thus, what follows is my own answer to what I once took to be my own problem. I'd like to think it's a valid, if imperfect, answer based on a rational vision of the future rather than a romantic obsession with the past. I'd also like to think it has relevance for anyone who cares about the environment and the precarious future of food.

38   The first part of an ancient Byzantine proverb reminds us, "He who has food has many problems." And these problems, I would add, are problems for a reason—they're difficult to solve. What follows is thus not a rigid prescription for sustainable eating. Instead, it's a broader framework for developing an environmentally sensible diet. The most general premises I work from are these: first, sustainability means meeting our present-day needs without denying future generations the right to do the same, and second, the key benchmarks of measuring sustainability involve soil quality, water usage, biodiversity, global warming, chemical emissions, and the conservation of natural space.

39   I do not provide a top-ten list on how to eat a green diet. I'm no fan of books that reduce everything to a few pat answers for achieving a goal as elusive and complicated as environmentally sustainable food production. And so, rather than insult readers

with simplistically prescriptive answers, I instead offer a vision of sustainability that assumes that, as socially conscious consumers, we're prepared to take on more complexity in the quest to achieve an environmentally responsible diet.

As nice as it would be to sum up the essence of what follows   40 in a bumper sticker ("Eat Local!"), I pursue a more varied "portfolio solution." Like any portfolio, there will always be room for improvement, some aspects that perform better than others, maybe even a few superior performers and a couple of duds. But ultimately, as immodest as the goal might be, I hope to provide a new baseline from which environmentally conscious consumers can begin as they refine the endlessly complex act we're too often told should be simple: eating responsibly.

Notes

Introduction: From the Golden Age to the Golden Mean of Food Production

1. Gordon Conway, *The Doubly Green Revolution: Food for All in the Twenty-first Century* (Cornell University Press, 1999).
2. Julie Guthman, *Agrarian Dreams: The Paradox of Organic Farming in California* (University of California Press, 2004), 175; Wendell Berry, "A Standing Ground," from *The Selected Poems of Wendell Berry* (Counterpoint, 1999), 73.
3. Interview with Nina Fedoroff, January 8, 2008; "nature's misfits" is from J. G. Hawkes, "The Origins of Agriculture," *Economic Botany* (April 1970): 131.
4. Pamela C. Ronald and Raoul W. Adamchak, *Tomorrow's Table: Organic Farming, Genetics, and the Future of Food* (Oxford University Press, 2008), 32; Richard Manning, *Against the Grain: How Agriculture Has Hijacked Civilization* (North Point, 2004), 8, 24, 29, 119; Victor Davis Hanson, *Fields Without Dreams: Defending the Agrarian Idea* (Free Press, 1996), xi. Not to make too much of this point, but it's hard not to notice that the most vigorous advocates of a romanticized agricultural ideal have never had to make a sustained living from the land. Michael Pollan is a journalist; Wendell Berry is a poet; Alan Chadwick, who started the UC Santa Cruz Farm and Garden Program, was a Shakespearean stage actor before becoming a plant biologist; Jose Bove, the supposedly simple French farmer whose fame comes from having ransacked a McDonald's, is an activist who grew up in Berkeley.
5. Paul H. Ehrlich and Anne H. Ehrlich, "The Biggest Menace?," letter to the editor, *New York Review of Books*, February 14, 2008, 57.
6. Vandana Shiva et al., eds., *Manifestos on the Future of Food and Seed* (South End, 2007), 77.

Steven Sexton

Does Local Production Improve Environmental and Health Outcomes?

Steven Sexton, at the time of publication of this 2009 article, was a Ph.D. student in the Department of Agricultural and Resource Economics at the University of California, Berkeley. This essay was originally published in UC Davis' Agricultural and Resource Economic Update, a publication of the Giannini Foundation of Agricultural Economics, an organization founded to "promote and support research and outreach activities in agricultural economics and rural development relevant to California." In this essay, he suggests that opposition to modern agricultural methods by advocates of local food production—if not handled carefully—could lead to "mass starvation." As you assess his argument, consider how others in this conversation, including authors included in this chapter, might respond to his analyses. What specific stasis points—points of debate—can you identify?

Some critics of industrial agriculture propose the "relocaliza-tion" of food production to reduce environmental damage and improve health outcomes. This article considers the welfare effects of locavorism along these dimensions.

1   Modern agriculture is increasingly under attack by crit-ics who blame the industry's specialization and con-centration for a number of societal problems, from global warming to rising health care costs. The critics contend that today's industrial agriculture is too dependent on fossil fuel, and too eager to ply consumers with cheap but nutrition-ally bankrupt calories. Among the critics, locavores, like best-selling author of *The Omnivore's Dilemma* Michael Pollan, and famed chef Alice Waters, advocate a community-based food production system in which consumers buy goods that have travelled less than 150 miles from farm to fork.

2   The rise of modern farming would seem to be one of the great successes of the last century. Propelled by the Green Revolution, agricultural productivity in the United States grew at an average 1.9% per year from 1948 to 1998, exceeding the rate of growth

in the U.S. manufacturing sector. Similar productivity gains were achieved elsewhere around the world. A doubling of food production in the second half of the 20th century saved the world from mass starvation as its population doubled to six billion. Because of modern agriculture, farmers were able to produce more food per person for more people—without expanding farmland or farm labor demand. In fact, 50 million acres of land were released from farming in the United States over the last half-century, and the percentage of the national workforce employed in agriculture fell from 16% to less than 2%. Norman Borlaug, considered the father of the Green Revolution, credits science with saving from conversion to farming an area of land equal to the U.S. east of the Mississippi River.

Critics of our current food system don't deny these achieve-   3
ments. But they blame the transition to industrial farming for simultaneous increases in the amount of energy embedded in food products and heightened rates of obesity among the American public. The case against industrial agriculture has been articulated in major box-office draws like "Food, Inc.," and "Supersize Me," featured in cover stories for *Time* and the *New York Times Magazine*, and detailed in *New York Times* bestsellers by Pollan.

Amid growing concern about climate change and health care   4
costs, it has become almost conventional wisdom that the federal government's farm program has created a food production and marketing system that poorly serves societal interests and that new policy is needed to coordinate a return to our agricultural roots. Economic theory and empirical evidence suggest, however, that this new conventional wisdom may be quite wrong. This article considers whether a food system based on local production would improve outcomes in the key areas its proponents assert the current system lets us down: human health and environmental preservation.

Climate Change and the Environment

As recently as the 1930s and 1940s, when horses and mules still   5
provided the bulk of power on American farms, food output contained twice the energy consumed in production. But today, ten times more energy is consumed in production than is yielded in food output. Energy has become an important input at every step of the supply chain, from the production of chemical inputs upstream from the farm to the processing of raw material into finished food products downstream. And on the farm, 4.3 million fossil fuel-powered tractors have replaced the 21.6 million work animals that occupied farms in 1900.

As farms became increasingly specialized, reducing the aver-   6
age number of commodities produced per farm from about 5 in

1900 to about 1.5 today, demands for soil enhancements and damage-control agents grew. Specialization and trade also increased demand for energy to transport crops and food products to buyers. It is estimated that today's fresh produce travels an average 1,500 miles from the farm to the consumer. As a consequence of the energy demands throughout the supply chain, agriculture consumes 14% of the national energy budget. Transportation of food products alone consumes 5%.

7   Locavores argue that to accomplish environmental objectives, the food production system must be transformed to one characterized by small farms growing multiple crops and marketing them directly to consumers or local retailers. The "relocalization" of the food system demands a farming landscape that resembles our agricultural past. Farming in the 1930s, in fact, looks a lot like what the critics of industrial agriculture hope to achieve today: 5.7 million farms averaging 147 acres in size and growing an average 5.1 different crops.

8   Implicit in the locavore assertion that local farming is environmentally friendly relative to industrial agriculture is an assumption that altering the scale and location of agricultural production does not alter its efficiency. Holding all else constant, a reduction in food transportation miles and an increase in biological control of pests and soil fertility, necessarily reduces the carbon intensity of food production. However, all else is not likely to be constant under such a transformation.

9   Locavores presume that we can return to a historical form of agriculture without also returning to historical farm yields. The average farmer produced 13 bushels of wheat per acre in 1930 and 20 bushels of corn. In contrast, today's farms, which number only 2.2 million and occupy an average 414 acres, are able to produce an average 44 bushels of wheat and 164.2 bushels of corn per acre.

10   While it is surely true that a small, diverse farm today can improve upon the yields of the early to mid-20th century by employing modern seed varieties and other scale-neutral innovations, it is certainly also true that high yields today reflect modern agriculture's exploitation of two basic principles of economic efficiency that the locavores either ignore or discount: comparative advantage and economies of scale. It is the inability of a local food system to exploit these forces that could render it a net contributor to global warming and environmental damage rather than a net reducer.

11   ***Specialization and Trade:*** Economists have long recognized the welfare gains from specialization and trade. The case for specialization is perhaps nowhere stronger than in agriculture, where the costs of production depend on natural resource endowments such as temperature, rainfall, and sunlight, as well as soil quality, pestilence, and land costs. Because ideal growing

conditions and crop sensitivity to deviations from optimal conditions vary by crop, different regions enjoy comparative advantage in different crops. As a consequence, California, with its relatively mild winters, warm summers, and fertile soil is the leading producer of high-value crops, producing all U.S.-grown almonds and 80% of U.S. grapes and strawberries. Iowa, in contrast, with a less ideal agronomic resource endowment, specializes in corn and soybeans, providing nearly 20% of all U.S. production of these less-valuable crops.

The dramatic change in land-use and input-demand induced   12 by a "relocalization" of the food supply is demonstrated using USDA region-level production cost and return data and state-level data on production, land allocations, and yield. To derive a first-order approximation of locavore effects on production costs and input demands, assume that a local food system must maintain existing levels of per capita production for each crop. Further, assume that each state must produce all the food for its residents. These assumptions reallocate production so that each state produces an average "diet" for each if its residents. Because of data limitations, production is reallocated in this analysis for each crop only over those states for which a complete set of data exists. For instance, yield data for a given crop do not exist for states that are not currently producing that crop, so it is impossible to determine input demands.

Using the regional mean production costs and state-level data   13 on yield, the input-demand under this "proportional" or "pseudo-locavore" production system is determined. This analysis is carried out for four major crops—corn, soybeans, oats, and milk. Results are reported in Table 1. Proportional corn production among current corn producers results in a 22 million acre (26%) increase in area planted to corn, a 35% increase in fertilizer costs, a 23% increase in total input costs. Similar results are reported for the other two field crops considered in this analysis. Notably, however, results for milk suggest that production costs decrease under the "pseudo-locavore" scenario, and purchased feed is substituted for grazing and feed produced in the dairy farm. The changes in feed consumption suggest carbon savings relative to the status quo, but the increased number of cows would induce more carbon emissions. Because of the way data for milk are reported, the change in head of cattle accounts for efficiency differences across states, where as input costs do not.

If a national price for inputs is assumed, these input cost   14 changes can be interpreted as changes in input demand, so that, for instance, fertilizer use in corn grows 35%. Therefore, this analysis suggests that, in general, a transition to a pseudo-locavore production system leads to considerable growth in the use of carbon-intensive inputs, which would lead to increasing carbon emissions and pollution of natural ecosystems.

TABLE 1 Psuedo-Locavore Effects on Input Costs

Change in Millions	Corn	Soybeans	Oats	Change in Millions	Milk
Acres	22.06	13.82	0.95	Head of Cattle	0.64
	26.91%	18.26%	37.36%		7.58%
Fertilizer Costs	$39.01	$30.69	$86.10	Purchased Feed Costs	$-420.26
	35.07%	54.90%	61.88%		0.03%
Chemical Costs	$45.66	$61.64	$-0.46	Homegrown Feed Costs	$7.32
	23.07%	20.04%	−8.71%		0.11%
				Grazed Feed Costs	$33.04
					22.60%
Fuel Costs	$88.60	$32.60	$14.95	Fuel Costs	$25.16
	22.80%	33.92%	27.24%		1.72%
Total Input Costs	$71.62	$35.47	$12.73	Total Input Costs	$-257.74
	29.45%	29.54%	44.77%		−0.93%

15   Availability of cost and return data limits analysis of input cost effects for a broader set of crops. It is possible, though, to estimate the land-use impacts of pseudo-locavore production using state-level production and yield data. Assuming yields are maintained as additional land is brought into production, the increase in demand for land for each crop associated with the pseudo-locavore rule is determined by multiplying the percentage change in state-level production by the state-level area planted. With 500 state-crop observations, covering 40 major field crops and vegetables, it is estimated that localization would require a 60 million-acre increase in land devoted to producing these crops in producing regions—a 23% increase. Table 2 reports the states that gain the most farmland under local production and those

TABLE 2 Change in Cropland by State

State	Thousand Acres
Top 5 Growth States	
California	40,000
Texas	34,600
Florida	26,000
Iowa	22,100
North Dakota	19,900
Bottom 5 Growth States	
New Hampshire	0.54
Vermont	0.65
Connecticut	1.42
Rhode Island	6.99
Oregon	4.68

that lose the most, in absolute terms. Extrapolating this change across the 2.26 billion acres of farmland in the United States, the agricultural land base would grow by 214.8 million acres—an area twice the size of California.

Increased demand for energy-intensive inputs and the expansion of farmland cause carbon emissions that reduce, and may overwhelm, the carbon emissions reductions associated with less transportation and monocropping in "relocalized" food systems. Extrapolating the percentage change in fertilizer and chemical demand from reapportioning corn production among corn producers to all U.S. corn production, for instance, suggests pseudo-locavorism would cause a 2.7 million ton increase in fertilizer applications and a 50 million pound increase in chemical use per year. Conversion of natural land to agricultural uses jeopardizes biodiversity and causes an increase in atmospheric carbon. There are immediate emissions from land-use change as biomass is cleared to make room for crops. And, because natural land sequesters more carbon than cropland, there are emissions associated with foregone annual and ongoing sequestration.

Many of the assumptions made in this simple model will tend to produce a conservative estimate of the carbon costs of locavorism. For instance, this analysis is constrained to consider the reallocation of production to states that are already producing a given crop. Locavores would also reallocate production to states that are not already producers in order to meet the 150-mile constraint on food travel. States that are not among current producers should, on average, be relatively costly producers of a given crop because they would otherwise be growing the crop today. Also, in assuming the persistence of existing yields as land-use expands, this analysis ignores any decline in yields that may result from expansion to marginal lands. Further evidence of the conservatism of this approach is the fact that it shows a net reduction in input costs from localized milk production. Were localized production actually more efficient, we would not be seeing increasing average herd sizes and consolidated production.

18   Because of data limitations, per capita production in producing regions is reallocated among states under the "pseudolocavore" scenario. This will tend to bias upward extrapolations out of sample, producing larger effects.

Economies of Scale: A local food production system would upend long-term trends of growing farm size and increasing concentration in food processing and marketing. Ending the food market dominance of big agribusiness—large monocrop farms and integrated food processors—is a secondary motive of locavorism, which generally views big business as an insincere steward of the environment and a principal cause of the obesity problem in the United States.

19   Local food production would largely eliminate scale economies by dividing a national market for food into local "food-sheds" that can only support smaller farms and food-processing operations. To the extent scale economies exist in farming, food processing, and marketing, they permit larger firms to more efficiently convert inputs to outputs. By forsaking these efficiencies, locavorism causes an increase in the quantity of inputs demanded, which increases carbon intensity, and an increase in the price of commodities and food products.

20   Large monocropped farms are more dependent than small polycrop farms on synthetic fertilizers and tilling operations to restore soil nutrients. They also face heightened pest pressure because they provide a consistent environment for breeding of crop-specific pests. Higher pest pressure increases demand for chemical damage control agents. Disposal of farm residues, like animal waste, also becomes a significant environmental challenge on industrial farms. The direct environmental costs of large-scale agriculture are clearly non-trivial. What is unclear, however, is whether the environmental benefits of small, poly-cropped farms outweigh the loss of efficiencies that are equally well-documented to accompany the increasing scale of production.

21   Recent work presents convincing evidence that economies do exist and that small farms are relatively inefficient. Catherine Morrison Paul and colleagues analyzed farm-level surveys from 1996–2000 and concluded the presence of "significant" scale economies in modern agriculture. They report that small farms are less efficient in both the scale of their operations and the technical aspects of production. They are "high cost" farms that have unexploited scale economies and consequently cannot compete with large farms.

Human Health

Locavores allege that modern agriculture is responsible, in part, 22 for growing rates of obesity and obesity-related illness among Americans. They argue that flawed public policy has fueled the industrialization of agriculture and produced a glut of cheap but nutrient-deficient calories by subsidizing the major commodities like corn and wheat. Locavores are also critics of processed foods and fast food, coining the phrase "slow foods" to encapsulate their ideal of home production of fresh, raw, and unprocessed commodities. Better policy, they argue, would yield better health outcomes.

This argument, however, is also based on a series of assump- 23 tions that seem to belie accepted fact. For instance, agricultural economists have rejected the notion that farm policy is to blame for the obesity epidemic in America. While policy has made grains relatively cheap, it has also made sugar more expensive. Prices for many fruits and vegetables, such as apples, strawberries, tomatoes, and broccoli, have declined over the past 25 or more years, which should increase access to nutrient-dense foods. Where prices for fruits and vegetables have trended upwards, the increases can be attributed to quality improvements, extended availability, and other value-added attributes in processing, such as enhanced product packaging. No identifiable pattern has been found in the price of unhealthy foods relative to healthy foods. Economists have also largely attributed the obesity epidemic to technological innovation that makes labor less strenuous and food products cheaper, meaning people are eating more but burning fewer calories.

Would a local food system improve American diets? In two 24 key respects, the likely answer is no. First, as this analysis has shown, a local food system would greatly increase the costs of food production by imposing constraints on the efficient allocation of resources. The monetary costs of increased input demands from forsaken gains from trade and scale economies will directly bear on consumer welfare by increasing the costs of food. Research shows that as incomes rise, fresh produce as a share of diets increases. Therefore, given that locavorism would effectively make consumers poorer by increasing the cost of food, it is hard to see how local production improves diets or health outcomes.

While it may be beneficial from a health policy perspective to 25 increase the relative cost of grains to reduce the surfeit of cheap calories, it is not clear that locavorism would accomplish this unless cost increases were biased toward grains. Instead the inefficiencies of reallocating food production are likely to be greater for high-value crops like fruits and vegetables so that, if anything, local food production will disproportionately raise the prices of the very foods that should become cheaper from a health policy perspective.

26   Second, taken literally, locavorism would block access to fresh produce for millions of Americans who live in climates that cannot, for many months per year, grow fruits and vegetables outside climate-controlled greenhouses. Greenhouse production is clearly energy-intensive and would impede environmental objectives. Blocking access to fresh produce would impede health objectives.

Conclusion

27   Some critics of modern agriculture have articulated an alternative that they assert would improve environmental and health outcomes. It is unlikely the benefits of locavorism are as substantial as has been asserted, and it is possible they are dwarfed by the costs of less efficient production and reduced access to nutritious foods. With the global population expected to grow to more than nine billion by 2050, today we face a challenge to feed the world, much as we did 60 years ago. The sources of tremendous productivity growth in the past, however, are largely exhausted, at least in the developed world, and the rate of productivity growth has begun to decline. If mass starvation is to be avoided in the current century, then we must either forsake natural land, including tropical forests, or renew our commitment to crop science. The debate about the future of agriculture must weigh the uncertain potential for environmental improvements under local production with the more certain risk to vulnerable populations, if food production doesn't increase, or to precious habitat if productivity doesn't increase.

For further information, the author recommends:

Morrison Paul, C.J. and R. Nehring. "Scale, Diversification and Economic Performance of Agricultural Producers." *ARE Update* 6(4) (Mar/Apr 2003): 5–8.

Gray, A.W. and M.D. Boehlje. "The Industrialization of Agriculture: Implications for Future Policy," Purdue University, (2007), Working Paper 07–10.

Alston, J.M., D.A. Sumner, and S.A. Vosti. "Farm Subsidies and Obesity in the United States." *ARE Update* 11(2) (Nov/Dec 2007): 1–4.

Vasile Stănescu[1]

"Green" Eggs and Ham? The Myth of Sustainable Meat and the Danger of the Local

Vasile Stănescu, at the time he wrote this essay, was a Phd candidate in the Modern Thought and Literature program at Stanford University. This essay first appeared in 2010 in the *Journal for Critical Animal Studies,* a publication established to "eliminate the domination and oppression of animals" through interdisciplinary research. Stănescu is also Senior Editor of the *Critical Animal Studies* book series. Using his background in literary studies and drawing upon rhetorical analyses of writings about the vegetarian and locavore movements, he suggests ways that authors tend to overstate or romanticize the effect of such practices. As you read, you might consider how his critical thinking and analysis skills— as well as his own ethical perspectives—inform the argument he is building. You might also use similar techniques as you read other pieces in this chapter of *Conversations.*

Abstract

In the New York Times bestseller, *The Omnivores Dilemma,*   1
Michael Pollan popularizes the idea of a "local" based diet, which he justifies, in part, in terms of environmental sustainability. In fact, many locavores argue that a local based diet is more environmentally sustainable than a vegan or vegetarian diet and concludes that if vegans and vegetarians truly care about the environment they should instead eat sustainably raised local meat. However locavores are incorrect in their analysis of the sustainability of a local based diet and in its applicability for large scale adaptation. Instead locavores engage in the construction of "a literary pastoral," a desire to return to a nonexistent past, which falsely romanticizes the ideals of a local based lifestyle. They therefore gloss over the issues of sexism, racism, speciesism, homophobia and anti-immigration sentiments which an emphasis only on the local, as opposed to the global, can entail. In this manner the locavorism movement has come to echo many of the same claims that the "Buy American" movement did before it. The conclusion is that a local based diet, while raising many helpful and valid points, needs to be re-understood and rearticulated.[2]

The first thing I ask Salatin when we sit down in his living room is whether he's ever considered becoming a vegetarian. It's not what I had planned to say, but we've been in the hoop houses with the nicely treated hens, all happily pecking and glossy-feathered, and I've held one in my arms. Suddenly it makes little sense that this animal, whose welfare has been of such great concern, will be killed in a matter of days. Naive, I know, and Salatin seems surprised. "Never crossed my mind," he says . . . Salatin is hitting his stride now. "We tried heritage chickens for three years and we couldn't sell 'em. I mean, we could sell a couple. But at the end of the day, altruism doesn't pay our taxes."[3]

- Interview by the *Guardian*
(Sunday 31 January 2010, 44)

I think there is an enormous amount of political power lying around on the food issue, and I am just waiting for the right politician to realize that this is a great family issue. If that politician is on the Right, all the better. I think that would be terrific, and I will support him or her.

- Michael Pollan, Interview with Rod Dreher,
The American Conservative, June 20, 2008

Introduction

2   In 2007 Oxford University Press chose "Locavore" as the word of the year.[4] Such a move, while purely symbolic, at the same time speaks to the movement's growing popularity and emerging significance in any discussion on food policy, environmentalism or animal ethics. The essence of the locavore argument is that because it is harmful to the environment to transport food over long distances (referred to as "food miles") people should instead, for primarily environmental reasons, choose to consume only food which is grown or slaughtered "locally." This idea of "locavorism" has been described and defended by a range of authors; such as Barbara Kingsolver in *Animal, Vegetable, Miracle,* Michael Pollan in his *New York Times* bestselling book *The Omnivore's Dilemma,* as well as enunciated by Joel Salatin, the owner of Polyface farms and a featured personality in both *The Omnivore's Dilemma* and the recent documentary *Food Inc.* However, despite this popularity, there is much I find deeply troubling in each of these texts and their ultimate justification for locavorism. For example part of Pollan's main argument against "organic" meat is that it represents a false pastoral narrative, something produced by the power of well crafted words and images yet lacking ethical consistency, reality, or

ultimately an awareness of animals themselves. He describes these problems, and his own motivation in addressing them, while shopping at Whole Foods:

> This particular dairy's label had a lot to say about the bovine lifestyle: Its Holsteins are provided with "an appropriate environment, including shelter and comfortable resting area . . . sufficient space, proper facilities and the company of its own kind." All this sounded pretty great, until I read the story of another dairy selling raw milk—*completely* unprocessed—whose "cows graze green pastures all year long."
>
> Which made me wonder whether the first dairy's idea of an appropriate environment for a cow included, as I had simply presumed, a pasture. All of a sudden the absence from their story of that word seemed weirdly conspicuous. As the literary critics would say, the writer seemed to be eliding the whole notion of cows and grass. Indeed, the longer I shopped in Whole Foods, the more I thought that this was a place where the skills of a literary critic might come in handy. (2008: 135–136)

However, while I agree with Pollan about the need for literary 3 critics in Whole Foods, I fear many locavore advocates, including Pollan in his own text, suffer from the same flaws of creating an unrealistic literary pastoral, which he attributes to the free-range organic farmer. Hence, as a literary critic, I hope to provide to the locavore movement what they have given to others and to view their work as a text in order to reveal the manner in which they too, create an idealized, unrealistic, and, at times, distressingly sexist and xenophobic literary pastoral which allows them, much as with the first organic dairy farm, to seem to raise the issue of care for actual animals even as they elide the issue of the animal herself. My intention is not to discount the possibility of a more natural, environmentally sustainable food system—a goal I deeply support—but instead to reveal the potential dangers that focusing purely on the "local," at the expense of the global, can contain for both the human and nonhuman animal alike.

Part 1: The Environment

The Vegan Utopia

Tellingly, one of the most forceful rationales for the environ- 4 mental benefits of a "local" food system is expressed by Michael Pollan in a chapter of the *Omnivore's Dilemma* titled "The ethics of eating meat." Under the pejorative subheading "The Vegan Utopia" Pollan writes:

> The vegan utopia would also condemn people in many parts of the country to importing all their food from distant places . . . To give up eating animals is to give up these places as human habitat, unless of course we are willing to make complete our dependence on a highly industrialized national food chain. The food chain would be in turn even more dependent than it already is on fossil fuels and chemical fertilizers, since food would need to travel even farther and fertility—in the form of manures—would be in short supply. Indeed, it is doubtful you can build a genuinely sustainable agriculture without animals to cycle nutrients and support local food production. If our concern is the health of nature—rather than, say, the internal consistency of our moral code or the condition of our souls—then eating animals may sometimes be the most ethical thing to do. (2008: 327)

5   In essence, then, Pollan takes one of the animal rights' movement's most powerful arguments—the significant environmental degradation that the meat industry routinely produces—and inverts it.[5] It is now, according to Pollan, *because* of the environment that one is justified in eating meat, indeed required to do so, since the only alternative given by Pollan is a polluting globalization of large scale food importation. Indeed, the argument, if true, is even more powerful than quoted here. If eating locally slaughtered animals is the only way to prevent global warming, animal ethics itself might well dictate the necessity of eating meat because habitat destruction (in part fuelled by global warming) is already causing mass species extinction at unprecedented rates. Such an argument, therefore, represents a particularly powerful and nuanced refutation to veganism and vegetarianism that I fear few animal rights activist, or animal studies scholars, have yet to adequately address.

6   However, before I engage in a more detailed analysis of Pollan's argument, the main problem with it is that it is simply factually untrue. What is most telling about the passage quoted above is that it lacks any form of citation or footnotes, forms of documentation which *do* pepper Pollan's books in other places of possible controversy. Pollan is far from alone in this omission, for virtually every other locavore claim for environmental supremacy also lacks any form of documentation to back up repeated claims that being vegan is *more* harmful to the environment than eating locally slaughtered animals. Instead locavores, almost universally, rely upon the "commonsense logic" that since transportation harms the environment, the longer something has

been transported, the more harmful, definitionally, it must be to the ecosystem. However, recent studies have brought this common sense wisdom into question. For example, a study conducted at Lincoln University in New Zealand shows that the way apples, lamb, and dairy items are produced in New Zealand makes them more energy-efficient to buy in the U.K. than those same products grown on British soil. The study concludes:

> Food miles are a very simplistic concept relating to the distance food travels as a measure of its impact on the environment. As a concept, food miles has gained some traction with the popular press and certain groups overseas. However, this debate which only includes the distance food travels is spurious as it does not consider total energy use especially in the production of the product.[6]

Indeed, the only study to date to focus on whether a local or   7
vegetarian diet is more helpful in reducing green house gases, conducted by Christopher L. Weber and H. Scott Matthews at Carnegie-Mellon, reached the following conclusion:

> Despite significant recent public concern and media attention to the environmental impacts of food, few studies in the United States have systematically compared the life-cycle greenhouse gas (GHG) emissions associated with food production against long-distance distribution, aka "food-miles." We find that although food is transported long distances in general (1640 km delivery and 6760 km life-cycle supply chain on average) the GHG emissions associated with food are dominated by the production phase, contributing 83% of the average U.S. household's 8.1 t CO2e/yr footprint for food consumption. Transportation as a whole represents only 11% of life-cycle GHG emissions, and final delivery from producer to retail contributes only 4%. Different food groups exhibit a large range in GHG-intensity; on average, red meat is around 150% more GHG intensive than chicken or fish. *Thus, we suggest that dietary shift can be a more effective means of lowering an average household's food-related climate footprint than "buying local." Shifting less than one day per week's worth of calories from red meat and dairy products to chicken, fish, eggs, or a vegetable-based diet achieves more GHG reduction than buying all locally sourced food.*[7]

In other words, shifting from beef to vegetables for even a single day a week would in fact be more helpful in reducing greenhouse gases than shifting the entirety of one's diet to exclusively   8 locally produced sources. This conclusion becomes less surprising when we consider the United Nations Intergovernmental Panel on Climate Change findings that meat production contributes more greenhouse gas emissions than the entire transportation industry, including all automobiles, combined.[8]

9   In fact, recent research suggests that organic free range animals may, in specific cases, be more harmful to the environment than animal raised "conventionally." As the Audubon society recently reported:

> Ironically, data released in 2007 by Adrian Williams of Cranfield University in England show that when all factors are considered, organic, free-range chickens have a 20 percent greater impact on global warming than conventionally raised broiler birds. That's because "sustainable" chickens take longer to raise, and eat more feed. Worse, organic eggs have a 14 percent higher impact on the climate than eggs from caged chickens, according to Williams. "If we want to fight global warming through the food we buy, then one thing's clear: We have to drastically reduce the meat we consume," says Tara Garnett of London's Food Climate Research Network. So while some of us Americans fashionably fret over our food's travel budget and organic content, Garnett says the real question is, "Did it come from an animal or did it not come from an animal?"[9]

Lack of Land

10   Moreover, while locavores imagine all factory farms eventually turning into more sustainable small-scale family farms, that ideal is simply not physically possible given the world's current rate of meat consumption. According the United Nations Food and Agriculture Organization's recent report *Livestock's Long Shadow*, over fifty-five billion land animals are raised and slaughtered every year worldwide for human consumption. This rate of slaughter already consumes thirty percent of the earth's entire land surface (approximately 3,433 billion hectares) and accounts for a staggering eighty percent of the total land utilized by humans (Steinfeld et al, xxi). Even when the land currently used for feed crop production is subtracted, as theoretically it might be in a fully local farm system, the total area *currently* occupied by grazing alone still constitutes, in the words of the report "26 percent of the ice-free terrestrial surface of the planet" (Steinfeld et al, 2006: xxi). And this number is only expected to grow as both human population and human consumption of meat and dairy continue to rise.[10] Therefore, in addition to problems of sustainability, meat consumption also

entails a massive loss of biodiversity which, ironically, would actually be *increased* by a shift to a locally based diet, as even more land would have to be set aside for free-range grazing. According to the UN Food and Agriculture Organization report, "306 of the 825 terrestrial ecoregions identified by the Worldwide Fund for Nature (WWF) . . . reported livestock as one of the current threats" (Steinfeld et al, 2006: xxiii).

Nor would it be possible to keep such farms small, tied to the   11
community, or even "local" in any meaningful sense of that term. As Joel Salatin himself admits to Pollan, in explaining why he primarily uses neighbors coming over to help out to kill the animals he raises: "That's another reason we don't raise a hundred thousand chickens. It's not just the land that couldn't take it, but the community, too. We'd be processing six days a week, so we'd have to do what the industrial folks do, bring in a bunch of migrant workers because no one around here would want to gut chickens every day. *Scale makes all the difference*" (2008: 230, emphasis added). I will return to Salatin's comment about "migrant workers" later, but my point here is that locally based meat, regardless of its level of popularity, can never constitute more than either a rare and occasional novelty item, or food choices for only a few privileged customers, since there simply is not enough arable land left in the entire world to raise large quantities of pasture fed animals necessary to meet the world's meat consumption. And even if such a transition were physically possible, the resulting size of such farms would undo much of their supposed sustainability and community integration and hence their very purpose in existing in the first place. Unfortunately, this simple physical reality is ignored by many in the locavore movement, such as Barbara Kingsolver, who tells her children that they cannot have fresh fruit, during the winter, but instead must consume meat because it is, purportedly, more sustainable (2007: 33).

Belgium Chocolate

Indeed, one is left with the feeling that local food activists them-   12
selves must realize the lack of environmental benefit as many of them fail to follow the practices which they themselves advocate with any version of environmental consistency. For example, in preparing his local based meal on Polyface farms, Pollan admits, "I also need some chocolate for the dessert I had in mind. Fortunately the state of Virginia produces no chocolate to speak of, so I was free to go for the good Belgian stuff, panglessly" (2008: 263). While this line of reasoning might make sense in terms of other arguments for going local, such as preserving local economies, in terms of global warming and green house gases it is clearly not intellectually consistent. Even if, for some unspecified reason,

chocolate was essential for Pollan to have, it is not at all clear why that chocolate would have to come from *Belgium* instead of any of the more local sources of chocolate from within the whole of the United States (which also might be more effective in terms of preserving local economies). Indeed, most of the locavores mentioned continue to enjoy a variety of nonlocal based goods such as coffee, tea, olive oil, and, in my favorite example from Kingsolver, non-locally produced Budweiser (2008: 151).

13   Nor does Joel Salatin, the owner of Polyface farms whom Pollan holds up as a possible model, make much consistent environmental sense. For example, he refuses to fed-ex any of his meat since he says, "I don't believe it's sustainable—or organic, if you will—to FedEx meat all around the country" (2008: 133) and instead tells Pollan that he will have to "drive down here" to Virginia to get it (ibid). But *driving*, in individual cars, particularly from California to Virginia, is a significantly less effective form of transporting goods (think of all the extra steel) than a single fully loaded delivery vehicle. And Salatin is, in fact, proud of how far individual people will drive in order to purchase his food. As he posts on his own website, as a positive review from a customer, "I drive to Polyface 150 miles one way in order to get clean meat for my family."[11] Hence romantic notions of face-to-face contact, perhaps even the great American road trip, seem to play a greater role in the Pollan-Salatin encounter than any environmental logic.

14   Indeed, one of the revealing ironies associated with all of the locavores mentioned is the surprisingly large amount of driving, flying, and transportation they themselves regularly and apparently "panglessly" engage in. For example, Michael Pollan travels all around the country, from Kansas to California just within in the pages of *The Omnivore's Dilemma*; Kingsolver is even more extreme, leaving by car from Arizona so that that she can farm in rural Georgia, then driving all the way to Canada (from Georgia) for a family vacation, which she particularly enjoys because she is now able to consume so many food products which otherwise would have been out of season. As she writes, "Like those jet-setters who fly across the country on New Year's Eve, we were going to cheat time and celebrate the moment more than once. Asparagus season, twice in one year: the dream vacation" (2007: 158). Kingsolver and her family even fly to Europe, in part, to enjoy the local cuisine (2007: 243). And Joel Salatin, who was unwilling to ship his meat to California, recently agreed to fly there himself for a talk at Stanford. Ironically, the talk was, in part, on the environmental benefits of a local economy. Perhaps a certain amount of irony and hypocrisy within the locavore movement can be justified by the argument that while still far from fully realized, it is on the path towards ever greater locavorism. What is distressing is the manner in which violation of even the basic ideas of locally based lifestyle occur "panglessly"

and the manner in which the movement justifies itself via actions <u>more</u> harmful for the environment than the current food system, such as driving to purchase far away local produce, and enjoying out of season food in Canada and Europe.

T-Shirts and DVD's

Moreover, the aspect which most clearly belies all the reasons   15
purportedly given to justify the locavore movement—not just in terms of the environment, but also in terms of protecting local business and protesting against the abuses of globalization—is that it resolutely focuses *only on the question of food*. Neither Pollan, nor Kingsolver, nor even Salatin, is attempting to learn how to weave their own clothing, although cotton, as an agricultural commodity, raises many of the same issues as imported food. For example, the journal *Environmental Health Perspective* recently documented similarities in the environmental effects of the food industry and the fashion industry, in terms of both pollution and worker exploitation. According to the article:

> Cotton, one of the most popular and versatile fibers used in clothing manufacture, also has a significant environmental footprint. This crop accounts for a quarter of all the pesticides used in the United States, the largest exporter of cotton in the world, according to the USDA. The U.S. cotton crop benefits from subsidies that keep prices low and production high. The high production of cotton at subsidized low prices is one of the first spokes in the wheel that drives the globalization of fashion.
>
> Much of the cotton produced in the United States is exported to China and other countries with low labor costs, where the material is milled, woven into fabrics, cut, and assembled according to the fashion industry's specifications. China has emerged as the largest exporter of fast fashion, accounting for 30% of world apparel exports, according to the UN Commodity Trade Statistics database. In her 2005 book *The Travels of a T-Shirt in the Global Economy*, Pietra Rivoli, a professor of international business at the McDonough School of Business of Georgetown University, writes that each year Americans purchase approximately 1 billion garments made in China, the equivalent of four pieces of clothing for every U.S. citizen. (A450)

Hence, at least in terms of "miles," cotton is actually a more   16
egregious example than food. Nor is this the end of the "clothing miles" as the United States purchases so much clothing that

domestic charity outlets simply cannot process it all.[12] So the extra clothing is then shipped *back* to the developing world (where in most cases it was originally manufactured), which for some developing countries actually constitutes the number one import from the United States.[13] A single cotton t-shirt, then, comes from cotton grown in the United States, is sent to the developing world to be manufactured into clothing, then back to the United States to be purchased, and finally shipped to the developing country where the clothing is either donated or purchased. And what is true for cotton is equally true for almost every other product regularly consumed in the United States. Almost every item currently is both produced and consumed in a global marketplace and is therefore part of these exact same systems of production and distribution. In terms of shipping distance it is just as significant to discuss "clothing miles" "computer miles" or even "cell phone miles," many of which are actually transported far longer distances than food and are far more toxic in their results. And in terms of non-environmental concerns, working conditions for many non-agricultural products may well be worse than for the more traditional rural labor of farming (excluding certain products such as coffee and chocolate).[14] My point here is not to criticize locavores unfairly for minor hypocrisy or failures of judgment which do not undermine the logic of the argument itself. Rather, my concern is that a narrow-minded focus on only "food" and "food miles" renders invisible many other environmentally unsound practices, whether they are conscious decisions to drive around in search of the best local food, or unconscious participation in the consumption of non-food goods with an environmental and human cost. For example, in Salatin's online "gift store" in less than four lines he both states that "We do not ship food items, anytime, anywhere, period" and, at the same time, advertises for all nonfood based products, such as tote bags and DVD's,[15] that "All shipping is free! Please allow 2-4 weeks for delivery." There is no discussion of how, where, or by whom any of these other products have been made. Therefore a vegan who drastically decreased her consumption of nonagricultural products, particularly electronic products, wore clothing purchased from second hand shops, and made sure that all of her waste was disposed of in an ethically consistent manner would, in fact, be a far more effective "locavore" even if the entirety of her diet were imported from other countries.

Part II: The Danger of the Local

Blood and Soil

17   If being local is not then "really" about protecting the environment, what is it about? One answer is suggested by Professor Ursula Heise, of Stanford University, in her recent text *Sense of*

Place and Sense of Planet: The Environmental Imagination of the Global. Heise illustrates how the emphasis on "the local" within the broader environmental movement as a whole can possess a deeply disturbing strain of conservatism, provincialism, xenophobia and anti-immigrant sentiment. Indeed, she even goes so far as to excavate genealogically the Nazi's emphasis on *Blut und Boden* (blood and soil), and the bizarre manner in which they interwove calls for environmentalism with a hyper-nationalism based on a romanticized *autochthonous* relationship with both the soil and the local. Of course none of these arguments, by either Professor Heise or me, is meant to suggest the locavore movement, or the local move in environmentalism, possesses any connection with Nazism. It is meant rather to speak to my fear that an outspoken concern for the environment can also contain and support conservatism against those viewed as alien to the speaker's sense of his/her "local" community. Specifically, I believe that many in the locavore movement are moved by a desire for a nonexistent literary pastoral, of a wholly inaccurate nostalgia for a by-gone age. For example, Pollan invokes precisely this image in his description of his first wholly local dinner at Polyface farms "much about dining with the Salatins had, for me, the flavor of a long-ago time and faraway place in America" (2008: 203). However, the danger of this literary pastoral fairytale is not only that it is wholly inaccurate (the Salatins use ATV's daily to move around their cattle) but that it also possesses the potential to mask the darker side of the nostalgic past that an exclusive focus on "the local" likewise elides.

Women in the Kitchen

For example, since locavores choose to focus, unscientifically, only on the question of food, that focus blends over into negative portrayal of women and particularly feminists, who are frequently portrayed as culprits because of their decision, supposedly, to no longer to cook. And, following logically from this first claim, there is tendency to argue for the return of traditional gender roles of heterosexual men farming and ranching while heterosexual women cook and clean. For example, both Michael Pollan and the movie *Food Inc.* specifically hold up Joel Salatin and Polyface farms as a possible template for a local based economy. But what Pollan does not tell us (and may himself have failed to realize) is that Salatin believes so firmly in traditional gender roles that in the past he did not even accept women as workers or interns for the farm labor aspect of his farm although they could work in the kitchen.[16] Salatin's attitude—that the proper place for women is in the kitchen and

18

that their role has somehow been "lost"—surfaced in a recent interview:

> Hey, 40 years ago, every woman in the country—I'll be real sexist here—every woman in the country knew how to cut up a chicken . . . Now 60% of our customers don't even know that a chicken has bones! I'm serious. We have moved to an incredibly ignorant culinary connection.[17]

19   Barbara Kingsolver, too, express explicit gender conservatism; throughout her book, she argues against what she sees as the excesses of feminism which she describes as "the great hood-wink of my generation" (2007: 127) because it wrongly removed the woman from hearth and home, concluding with her complete pride in becoming the type of housewife who finally knows how to make her own cheese (2007: 126-127 and 156). As Jennifer Jeffrey has written in a particularly insightful article "The Feminist in My Kitchen"

> One day during the *Pennywise Eat Local Challenge,* as I was dashing between meetings and wondering how on earth I was going to create an evening meal composed of local ingredients within budget with almost no time to shop, this thought flashed through my head: this whole eat local concept is *so not friendly* for women who work . . .
>
> If eating local is still a challenge for me, what about women who, voluntarily or not, log 8 to 10 hours a day, five or six days a week, in an office or hospital or courtroom? What about women who, in addition to working long hours and commuting back and forth, also have children at home who need love and affection and help with homework? . . .
>
> Can we call ourselves feminists (simply defined here as people who desire the equality of all women, everywhere) and still suggest that an ideal dinner consists of handmade ravioli and slow-simmered marinara from vine-ripened, hand-picked tomatoes and a salad composed of vegetables that (let's be honest) are Not Available at Safeway?

20   An argument she, likewise, specially connects back to Barbara Kingsolver's own book:

> Barbara Kingsolver took a year of her life to grow a garden to feed her family, and proceeded to write a beautiful book about the experience, but what if she had done the same thing twenty-five years ago, near the start of her writing career? My guess is that such a book (if it made it to publication at all,

which is doubtful), might not have had such a receptive audience, but *more importantly*, all of that weeding and watering and meal-planning might have distracted her from the hard, lonely work of learning to write.[18]

All American

Furthermore I am concerned by the criteria that Joel Salatin uses   21
to determine who will receive one of his, now highly, competitive internships on his farm. For example the very first requirement reads that the candidates must be "[b]right eyed, bushy-tailed, self-starter, eager-beaver, situationally aware, go-get-'em, teachable, positive, non-complaining, grateful, rejoicing, get'erdone dependable, faithful, perseverant take-responsibility *clean-cut, all American boy-girl appearance characters. We are very, very, very discriminatory*"[19] (emphasis added). In the first place this list reiterates that same tendency towards gender conservatism as already discussed, since it is hard to imagine that a woman who wears only male clothes would be considered a clean cut all American girl appearance. Nor would, I imagine, a man who wears women's clothes much less a homosexual or a transsexual be considered an all-American boy girl appearance. In fact it is odd to me that "appearance" is such an essential category of who Salatin will, or will not, allow to work on a farm.

There is also a second concern that this litany of traits sug-   22
gests to me, particularly in his use of the phrase "All American." For what does an "all American" appearance even mean in a nation of vast racial and immigrant diversity? I find these comments of particular concern as the college that Salatin chose to attend, Bob Jones University, prohibited African-Americans from attending until 1975 and still prohibited interracial dating in the year 2000 when a media uproar and declining student attendance finally forced the university to overturn its rules.[20] And furthermore, Bob Jones University has throughout its entire history prohibited, as official policy, all acts of homosexuality as perversion condemned by God.[21] Therefore, at least when he was choosing which college to attend, issues of racial inclusion, gay rights, or even social justice were not particularly strong motivating forces in Salatin's life. Nor has Salatin repudiated this relationship with Bob Jones University, which in 2009 recognized Salatin as the "alumus of the year."[22] Salatin has also described the conservative talk show host Glenn Beck, who is both anti-gay marriage and anti-immigration, as "agendaless" and "truth-seeking."[23] And furthermore, as earlier mentioned, Salatin is himself prone to make remarks concerning migrant workers which seem at times to portrary them in a negative or at least a demeaning light. For example, in testimony in front of Congress on how to make a more transparent meat system,

Salatin claimed "Industrialized food and farming became aromatically and aesthetically repugnant, relegated to the offcasts of society C and D students along with their foreign workers."[24] Nor is this tendency limited to Salatin alone. As Kelefa Sanneh writes in the *New Yorker* "Agrarianism, like environmentalism, hasn't always been considered a progressive cause, and there's nothing inherently liberal about artisanal cheese or artisanal bikes . . . Rod Dreher, a *National Review* contributor and the author of 'Crunchy Cons,' is ardently pro-organic and ardently anti-gay marriage. Victor Davis Hanson, the author of 'Fields Without Dreams: Defending the Agrarian Idea,' is also the author of 'Mexifornia,' about the dangers posed by immigration."[25] It is, therefore hard to imagine how Michael Pollan can both, perhaps rightly, indict organic produce harvested by recycled biodiesel tractors as insufficiently progressive because of their unfair treatment of Mexican farm workers and, at the same time, support Joel Salatin as a representative of the future vanguard of a progressive and egalitarian food movement.[26] As the British columnist Yasmin Alibhai-Brown recently argued:

> Should good people be party to a vociferous movement which wants to refuse entry to "alien" foods? Look at the language used and you realize it is a proxy for anti-immigration sentiments: these foods from elsewhere come and take over our diets, reduce national dishes to third-class status, compete unfairly with Scotch broth and haggis, both dying out, excite our senses beyond decorum, contaminate the identity of the country irreversibly.
>
> Turn to the clamour for the west to cut imported foods and a further bitter taste spreads in the mouth. If we decide—as many of my friends have—not to buy foods that have been flown over, it only means further devastation for the poorest. These are the incredibly hard-working farmers in the developing world, already the victims of trade protectionism imposed by the wealthy blocs. It means saying no to Fair-trade producers too, because their products have to travel to our supermarkets. Are we now to say these livelihoods don't matter because we prefer virtue of a more fashionable kind? Shameful are the environmentalists who are able to be this cavalier. They could only believe what they do if those peasant lives do not matter at all.[27]

23   Hence, I fear that the "locavore" movement possesses within it the same potential for anti-immigrant sentiment that the earlier "Buy American" movement displayed. For example as Dana Frank argues in *Buy American: The Untold Story of Economic*

Nationalism, the early 1970's, 1980's and early 1990's were filled with calls to "Buy American" which foreshadowed many of the same reasons now provided to support locavorism including fears of globalization, support for union labor and critiques of exploitive labor practices in other countries, all interwoven with a desire to protect traditional "American" ways of life. However as she documents throughout her book:

> Popular "Buy American" advocates promised, nonetheless, to protect and to serve the American people; but the inward-looking protection of "us" against the threatening "foreigners" spiraled downward into narrower and narrower clubbishness. What began innocently at the border of Orange County, Florida, or the State of Alaska ended less innocently at an economic border drawn by race or citizenship (1999: 243).

This is in turn the basis of my fear that any movement which   24 seeks to prevent the importation of goods from certain countries possesses the danger of justifying nationalistic fears of those nations and groups of peoples. And this worry is perhaps all the more relevant when the product being boycotted is food since an increasing number of both anthropological and sociological texts continue to highlight the deep connection between a culture and the food that it eats.[28] Hence to stigmatize a food, purely because of where it comes from, runs the extreme risk of serving as proxy to stigmatize its people as well as decrease diversity as a whole. As James McWilliams writes:

> A final paradox: in a sense, any community with an activist base seeking to localize the food supply is also a community that's undermining diversity. Although we rarely consider the market influences that make community diversification possible, a moment's reflection reveals a strong tie between cultural diversity and market access. Critics of globalization argue (often with ample evidence) that global forces undermine the world's range of indigenous cultures—wiping out vernacular habits, wisdom, and languages. They overlook, however, how the material manifestations of diversity are brought to us by globalization.
>
> Localization, by contrast, specifies what is and is not acceptable within an arbitrary boundary. In this sense, it delimits diversity. Anyone who doubts this claim should imagine what the culinary map of New York City would look like without open access to globally far-flung producers. It's only because globally sourced distributors are able to provide specialized ingredients that Harlem, Chinatown, and Little Italy are such vibrant emblems of urban, culinary, and cultural diversity.[29]

Saving Souls

25   It is therefore revealing to return to Michael Pollan's earlier claim, made in the context of putting locavore against veganism, that what solely motivates veganism is a desire for absolute moral purity, even to the point of destroying nature, in order to save the vegans' "souls." He continues this theme throughout his text with references to vegetarians as overly self-righteous, indeed to the point of claiming that they are "Puritans" since "A deep current of Puritanism runs through the writing of the animal philosophers, an abiding discomfort not just with our animality, but with the animals' animality too. They would like nothing better than to airlift us out from nature's "intrinsic evil"—and then take the animals with us. You begin to wonder if their quarrel isn't really with nature itself" (2008: 322). However, the irony of this argument is that while Pollan routinely indicts vegans as being metaphorically self-righteous puritans, the only option both he and Kingsolver provide are people who, for religious reasons, feel no complication about killing animals because they lack souls. As Pollan writes, "When I was at the farm I asked Joel how he could bring himself to kill a chicken. 'That's an easy one. People have a soul, animals don't; it's a bedrock belief of mine. Animals are not created in God's image. So when they die, they just die'" (2008: 331). In fact, since they have no souls and are therefore wholly unrelated to people, Joel Salatin encourages even young children to slit the throats of animals:

> Interestingly, we typically have families come—they want to come and see the chicken butchering, for example. Well, Mom and Dad (they're in their late-20s early-30s), they stay out behind in the car, and the 8-, 9-, 10-, 11-year-old children come around to see this. We have not found any child under 10 that's the least bit put off by it. They get right into it. We'll even give them a knife and let them slice some throats.[30]

26   Hence, I wish to suggest, many of the proponents of the locavore movement seek to re-inscribe the very speciesism it first seems to draw into question. Indeed it is hard to imagine how a locavore movement ever could translate into an actual improvement of animals' lives since many of its most famous proponents hold that animals lack souls and furthermore that man's domination and consumption of them is the very definition of our humanity. For example Pollan and Kingsolver claim, with no citations, a laundry list of increasingly esoteric human characteristics which, supposedly, only eating meat has produced in humans including large brains (291), all forms of social interaction including the undefined "pleasures of the table" (272), human free will (297), a variety of children's books (Kingsolver,

2007: 222) and even "civilization" itself (*ibid*). In the most amusing example of this attribution of human traits, Pollan suggests that the reason marijuana works on humans is because it mimics the effects of hunting within human brains. He writes:

> Later it occurred to me that this mental state [while hunting], which I quite liked, in many ways resembled the one induced by smoking marijuana: the way one's senses feel especially acute and the mind seems to forget everything outside the scope of its present focus, including physical discomfort and the passing of time . . . Could it be that the cannabinoid network is precisely the sort of adaption that natural selection would favor in the evolution of a creature who survives by hunting? A brain chemical that sharpens the senses, narrows your mental focus, allows you to forget everything extraneous to the task at hand (including physical discomfort and the passage of time), and makes you hungry would seem to be the perfect pharmacological tool for man the hunter (2008: 342).

Therefore, one of the oddest parts of the locavore literature is   27
that even as its proponents graphically and indeed poetically describe the abuses of the factory farms they, at the same time, remove any reason why anyone should be concerned at all; since animals lack souls, we cannot understand what, or even if, they think or feel, and our domination of them represents the very essence of what defines us as humans. In fact Joel Salatin has, repeatedly, spoken out *against* so called "Prop. 2" ballot initiatives around the country sponsored by the American Humane Society in order to outlaw the worst abuses of factory farming such as battery cages and gestation crates.[31] While Prop. 2 initiatives are themselves controversial within the animal rights community, since they result in larger cages instead of no cages, Salatin's critique is not that they do not go far enough. Instead his claim is that people should be able to, legally, do whatever they want with farm animals. Hence he actually argues for less oversight and control of how farmers raise their livestock. While such a practice may, or may not, as he claims, help small farms who process animals expand their operations, at the same time it would seem to increase the already horrific abuse of all animals that do receive at least some minimal protection under the law currently as well as undercut any other efforts to increase the level of such protection in the future.

I Am A "Locavore" (and a Vegan)

While each of these critiques might seem to suggest that I am   28
opposed to all of the goals espoused by "locavorism" this is in fact not the case. I support urban community gardening, farmers

markets, Community Support Agriculture (CSA's), and organic farms which eschew the use of monoculture crops, pesticides, and treat their workers well. Indeed, perhaps my greatest concern about the manner in which the locavore movement articulates itself is based on its repeated, but largely false, dichotomy between "vegan and vegetarians" on the one hand, and conscious food consumers on the other, as though it were impossible to be concerned about the welfare of animals, the environment, and the broader questions of food policy and food justice all at the same time. Hence, perfectly reasonable arguments against monoculture crops are morphed into unreasonable attacks on vegetarians as though the only two possible options were eating meat or conventional produce from large scale industrial farms. However, the reality is that many vegetarian and vegans, since they have already taken the step to self consciously control and direct their diet, are frequently more aware of the dangers industrial farming practices pose and therefore more likely to seek out ethically grown fruit and vegetables—wherever in the world these may exist. In fact, my opposition to industrial farming practices stems, in part, *from* my life-long commitment to animal rights. Hence as Pollan and others have pointed out, confined animal feeding operations (CAFO's), or "factory farms" are economically feasible only because of the massive subsidies that the government routinely provides to large scale industrial farmers who grow vast acres of soy, wheat, and corn which in turn are sold to factory farms who are the largest consumer of such products in the United States.

29   It is, therefore, not my goal to end the movement for conscious consumption of all food products, including vegan ones, since I believe large-scale industrial agriculture is deeply harmful to the environment, workers, and animals. It is instead meant to suggest that we need a new understanding and new articulation of the manner in which the locavore movements goals are expressed and understood. What matters is not the overly simplistic notion of "food miles" but the total carbon foot print, as well as the total environmental impact of any food purchase—a concern which can only lead to a significant decrease in the amount of meat consumed if not vegetarianism or veganism—and not only food, but the whole array of services, including clothing and electronics, which are marketed in the current global market place. Moreover, it deeply matters how and why these calls for "locavorism" are framed, and the tendency of many in the movement to unfairly and inaccurately criticize feminists and immigrants as corrupting to an idealized, romantic state of a local community is deeply troubling and potentially quite dangerous. As the Buy American movement, originally started by anti-sweat shop unions, demonstrates, originally "progressive" causes which fail to consider the intersections of gender, race, class, and citizenship can devolve into

only nationalistic regionalism. And it is my hope that the false division between vegan and local can be ended, so that both animal rights activists and food policy activists can unite into a shared and, therefore, exponentially more effective movement. It is my hope not to end the growing consensus on the need for a more just diet, including my issues raised by locavors, such as farm subsidies for agribusiness, but instead to expand the struggle to include a consideration for the full panoply of social justice issues that a truly just and therefore truly "green" diet must entail.

Notes

1. Vasile Stänescu is a PhD Candidate in the Program in Modern Thought and Literature at Stanford University. He is also Co-Senior Editor of the *Critical Animal Studies* Book Series published by Rodopi Press and was just named "Tykes Scholar of the Year" by the Institute of Critical Animal Studies. This paper, in an earlier version, won the "Best Graduate Student Paper" at the first annual *Minding Animals* Conference in Australia. He can be contacted at vts@stanford.edu

2. I would like to thank Ursula K. Heise Ph.D., Katherine Downey Ph.D., Carol J. Adams, Adam Rosenblatt, James Stanescu, Pamela Stänescu, and Deborah Stänescu who all read over earlier versions of this paper and provide useful feedback and commentary. I would also like to thank the *Minding Animals* Conference organizers and participants as well as the *Journal of Critical Animal Studies* for their feedback and support. All errors are, of course, my own.

3. Salatin's answer as to why he does not use "heritage" birds (i.e. birds that have not been bred for such traits as abnormally large breasts).

4. "Oxford Word Of The Year: Locavore" *Oxford University Press Blog* http://blog.oup.com/2007/11/locavore/ Last Accessed April 1, 2010.

5. Of course Pollan himself also indicates this same environmental degradation of factory farming and his claim is that small scale local farming will solve the problem. My point here is simply that Pollan inverts one of the most common claims made by animal rights' advocates.

6. Caroline Saunders, Andrew Barber, and Greg Taylor, "Food Miles— Comparative Energy/Emissions Performance of New Zealand's Agriculture Industry" *Research Report* No. 285 Lincoln University, New Zealand, July 2006. 93.

7. Christopher L. Weber, and H. Scott Matthews, "Food-Miles and the Relative Climate Impacts of Food Choices in the United States" *Environ. Sci. Technol.*, 42 (10), April 16, 2008, (3508) Downloaded from http://pubs.acs.org on May 1, 2009. Emphasis added.

8. Richard Black, "Shun meat, says UN climate chief: Livestock production has a bigger climate impact than transport, the UN believes" BBC News, June 7, 2008 http://news.bbc.co.uk/1/hi/sci/tech/7600005.stm. See also the Food and Agricultural Organization of the United States (FAO) report Livestock's Long Shadow.

9. Mike Tidwell, "The Low-Carbon Diet" *AubobonMagizine.org* Last Accessed April 1, 2010.

10. "Growing populations and incomes, along with changing food preferences, are rapidly increasing demand for livestock products, while globalization is boosting trade in livestock inputs and products. Global production of meat is projected to more than double from 229 million

tones in 1999/01 to 465 million tones in 2050, and that of milk to grow from 580 to 1,043 million tones. "(Steinfeld et al, xx) To be fair Pollan has himself, in his most recent work, started to make calls for people to decrease their meat consumption. However these calls are both not stringent enough and not echoed in the wider movement. Given the exponential rate of projected increase for meat consumption, what is needed is a significantly along term and cross the board decrease of the number of animals raised and killed for slaughter.

11. http://www.polyfacefarms.com/story.aspx. Last accessed April 1, 2001.

12. "Only about one-fifth of the clothing donated to charities is directly used or sold in their thrift shops. Says Rivoli, 'There are nowhere near enough people in America to absorb the mountains of castoffs, even if they were given away.'" (A450)

13. "Clothing that is not considered vintage or high-end is baled for export to developing nations. Data from the International Trade Commission indicate that between 1989 and 2003, American exports of used clothing more than tripled, to nearly 7 billion pounds per year. Used clothing is sold in more than 100 countries. For Tanzania, where used clothing is sold at the *mitumba* markets that dot the country, these items are the number one import from the United States." (A452)

14. For example in the case of clothing "According to figures from the U.S. National Labor Committee, some Chinese workers make as little as 12–18 cents per hour working in poor conditions. And with the fierce global competition that demands ever lower production costs, many emerging economies are aiming to get their share of the world's apparel markets, even if it means lower wages and poor conditions for workers." (A450)

15. According to the Environmental Protection Agency, DVD's are a particularly egregious source of e-waste pollution since they derive from rare mined earth materials, are virtually impossible to recycle, leach into water supplies, and produce toxic results for both the environment and human health. Furthermore, as a flyer made by the EPA for school children tries to explain "Once discs are packaged, they are ready to be sent to distribution centers, retail outlets, or other locations. Transportation by plane, truck, or rail requires the use of fossil fuels for energy, which contribute to climate change."

16. http://www.irregulartimes.com/polyface.html, accessed May 1st, 2009. Note: this may be changing due to outside pressure. However it was certainly the case when Pollan attended the farm. Indeed the website, while stating that they will accept six men and two women, still reads at the beginning "An extremely intimate relationship, the apprenticeships offer young *men* the opportunity to live and work with the Salatin's." (emphasis added). It is unclear how many, if any, women have been allowed to serve in the farm labor aspect of the apprenticeship.

17. Interview: Joel Salatin. This article appeared on p. 44 of the *Observer Food Monthly* section of the *Observer* on Sunday, January 31, 2010 http://www.guardian.co.uk/lifeandstyle/2010/jan/31/food-industry-environment. Last accessed April 2010.

18. Jennifer Jeffrey, *The Feminist in My Kitchen,* http://jenniferjeffrey.typepad.com/writer/2007/06/one-day-during-.html. Accessed April 1st, 2010.

19. http://www.polyfacefarms.com/apprentice.aspx. Accessed May 1st, 2009.

20 "Statement about Race at BJU," Bob Jones University. http://www.bju.edu/welcome/who-we-are/race-statement.php. Last accessed April 1, 2010.

21. Student Handbook, Bob Jones University, '05-'06, 29.

22. "Headlines: Giving Due Honor: Accolades for Students and Grades." *BJU Review,* Winter 2009 (Vol. 24 No.3) 2 http://issuu.com/bjureview/docs/ bju_review_winter_2009_vol._24_no.3 Accessed April 1, 2010.
23. Lewis McCrary, "Cultivating Freedom: Joel Salatin practices ethical animal husbandry—no thanks to the feds." *American Conservative,* November 1, 2009. http://www.amconmag.com/. Accessed April 1, 2010.
24. Testimony of Joel Salatin, Polyface Farm, Swoope, Virginia, United States Congress "After the Beef Recall: Exploring Greater Transparency in the Meat Industry" *House Committee on Oversight and Government Reform,* April 17, 2008. While I agree with the view the migrant workers are exploited in factory farming systems it is unclear to be how grouping them intermediately with C and D students and referring to them as social outcasts helps to improve their working conditions. Please see footnote 23 for additional commentary on this point.
25. Kelefa Sanneh, "Fast bikes, slow food, and the workplace wars," *New Yorker Magazine,* June 22, 2009. http://www.newyorker.com/arts/critics/ atlarge/2009/06/22/090622crat_atlarge_sanneh. Last accessed April 1, 2010.
26. While it could be argued that Salatin comments about migrant labor only reflect concern about labor standards Sanneh makes, I believe, an excellent rejoinder: "Proponents of homegrown food and "(very) small business . . . sometimes talk about how artisanalism improves the lives of workers. But the genius of this loosely organized movement is that it's not a labor movement; it's a consumer movement." Although I have searched extensively I can no evidence of where Joel Salatin has been directly working with farm workers unions to improve their labor conditions. And farm worker unions were reportedly kicked out of talks before the screening of *Food Inc.* http://www.ciw-online.org/news.html.
27. "Eat only local produce? I don't like the smell of that: The language in this debate is a proxy for anti-immigration sentiments." *The Independent,* May 12, 2008. http://www.independent.co.uk/opinion/commentators/ yasmin-alibhai-brown/yasmin-alibhaibrown-eat-only-local-produce-i- dont-like-the-smell-of-that-826272.html. Last Accessed April 1, 2010.
28. For a partial list see: Mintz, Sidney W., and Christine M. Du Bois. "The Anthropology of Food and Eating." *Annual Review of Anthropology.* 31 (2002): 99-119.
29. James Mcwilliams "Is Locavorism for Rich People Only?" *New York Times* Blog, October 14, 2009. http://freakonomics.blogs.nytimes.com/ 2009/10/14/is-locavorism-for-rich-people-only/?pagemode=print. Last Accessed April 1, 2010.
30. "Annie Corrigan, Joel Salatin And Polyface Farm: Stewards of Creation" *EarthEats,* March 26, 2010. http://indianapublicmedia.org/eartheats/ joel-salatin-complete-interview/ Accessed April 1 2010.
31. For one example among many see the interview "Joel Salatin - The Pastor of the Pasture" Mandy Henderson, *Columbus Underground,* February 28, 2010. http://www.columbusunderground.com/joel-salatin-the- pastor-of-the-pasture. Last accessed April 1, 2010.

References

Alibhai-Brown, Y. (2008), "Eat only local produce? I don't like the smell of that:: The language in this debate is a proxy for anti-immigration sentiments" *The Independent,* May 12, 2008. www.independent.co.uk/opinion/ commentators/yasmin-alibhai-brown/yasmin-alibhaibrown-eat-only- local-produce-i-dont-like-the-smell-of-that-826272.html (April 1, 2010).

Adams, C. J. (1990), *The Sexual Politics of Meat : A Feminist-Vegetarian Critical Theory,* Continuum : New York.

Ascione, F. R., and Arkow, P. (1999), *Child Abuse, Domestic Violence, and Animal Abuse: Linking the Circles of Compassion for Prevention and Intervention,* Purdue University Press: West Lafayette, Ind.

Black, R. (2008), "Shun meat, says UN climate chief: Livestock production has a bigger climate impact than transport, the UN believes," *BBC News,* June 7 2008, http://news.bbc.co.uk/1/hi/sci/tech/7600005.stm (April 1, 2010).

Claudio, L. (2007), "Waste Couture: Environmental Impact of the Clothing Industry," *Environmental Health Perspectives, vol 115, no 9.*

Cotler, A. (2009), *The Locavore Way: Discover and Enjoy the Pleasures of Locally Grown Food,* Storey Pub: North Adams, MA.

Frank, D. (1999), *Buy American: The Untold Story of Economic Nationalism,* Beacon Press: Boston, Mass.

Haraway, D. J. (2003), *The Companion Species Manifesto: Dogs, People, and Significant Otherness,* Prickly Paradigm; University Presses Marketing: Chicago, Ill.; Bristol

— (1991), *Simians, Cyborgs, and Women: The Reinvention of Nature,* Routledge: New York

— (2008), *When Species Meet,* Vol. 3, University of Minnesota Press: Minneapolis

Heise, U. K. (2008), *Sense of Place and Sense of Planet: The Environmental Imagination of the Global,* Oxford University Press: Oxford.

Jeffrey J. (2010) "*The Feminist in My Kitchen,*" Personal Blog, http://jennifer-jeffrey.typepad.com/writer/2007/06/one-day-during-.html (April 1st, 2010.)

Kenner, R., et al. (2009), *Food, Inc.,* Magnolia Home Entertainment: Los Angeles, CA

Kingsolver, B. (2007), *Animal, Vegetable, Miracle: A Year of Food Life New,* HarperCollins Publishers: New York, N.Y.

Kistler, J. M. (2000), *Animal Rights : A Subject Guide, Bibliography, and Internet Companion,* Greenwood Press: Westport, Conn.

Linzey, A., and Clarke, P. A. B. (2004), *Animal Rights : A Historical Anthology,* Columbia University Press: New York.

Masson, J. M., and McCarthy, S. (1995), *When Elephants Weep : The Emotional Lives of Animals,* Delacorte Press: New York.

McWilliams, J.E. (2009), "*On My Mind: The Locavore Myth,*" Forbes. vol 184, no. 2.

—*Just Food: Where Locavores Get It Wrong and How We Can Truly Eat Responsibly,* Little, Brown and Company: New York.

— (2009), "*Is Locavorism for Rich People Only?*" New York Times Blog October 14, 2009 http://freakonomics.blogs.nytimes.com/2009/10/14/is-locavorism-for-rich-people-only/?pagemode=print (April 1,2010).

Mintz, S. W., and Du Bois, C.M. (2002), "*The Anthropology of Food and Eating,*" Annual Review of Anthropology, 31, pgs.99-119.

Nabhan, G. P. (2002), *Coming Home to Eat: The Pleasures and Politics of Local Food,* W.W. Norton & Company : New York, NY.

Netz, R. (2004), *Barbed Wire: An Ecology of Modernity,* Wesleyan University Press: Middletown, CT.

Nibert, D. A. (2002), *Animal Rights Human Rights: Entanglements of Oppression and Liberation,* Rowman & Littlefield: Lanham, Md.

Patterson, C. (2002), *Eternal Treblinka : Our Treatment of Animals and the Holocaust,* Lantern Books: New York, N.Y.

Pollan, M. (2008), *In Defense of Food: An Eater's Manifesto,* Penguin Press: New York

— (2006), *The Omnivore's Dilemma: A Natural History of Four Meals,* Penguin Books; New York, N.Y.

Richardson, J. (2009), *Recipe for America: Why Our Food System Is Broken and What We Can Do to Fix It*, Ig Pub: Brooklyn, N.Y.

Rifkin, J. (1992), *Beyond Beef: The Rise and Fall of the Cattle Culture*, Dutton: New York, N.Y.

Roberts, M. S. (2008), *The Mark of the Beast: Animality and Human Oppression*, Purdue University Press: West Lafayette, Ind.

Sanneh, K. (2009), *"Fast bikes, slow food, and the workplace wars"* New Yorker Magazine, June 22, 09, www.newyorker.com/arts/critics/atlarge/2009/06/22/090622crat_atlarge_sanneh. (Accessed April 1, 2010).

Saunders, C., Barber, A., and Taylor, G. (2006), "Food Miles—Comparative Energy/Emissions Performance of New Zealand's Agriculture Industry," *Research Report No. 285*, Lincoln University, New Zealand, July 2006

Schlosser, E. (2001), *Fast Food Nation : The Dark Side of the All-American Meal*, Houghton Mifflin: Boston.

Singer, P. (2002), *Animal Liberation*, 1st Ecco paperback ed. Ecco: New York.

— (2006), *In Defense of Animals: The Second Wave*, Blackwell Pub: Malden, Mass.

Steinfeld, Henning, Pierre Gerber, Tom Wassenaar, Vincent Castel, Mauricio Rosales, Cees De Hann. (2006), *Livestock's Long Shadow: Environmental Issues and Options*, Rome, Italy: Food and Agriculture Organization of the United Nations.

Tidwell, M. (2010), *"The Low-Carbon Diet"* Audubon magazine *http://audubonmagazine.org/*(Accessed April 1, 2010).

Turner, D. (1997), *Standing Without Apology: The History of Bob Jones University*, Bob Jones University Press: South Carolina.

Wise, S. M.(2000), *Rattling the Cage: Toward Legal Rights for Animals*, Perseus Books: Cambridge, Mass.

Weber, C. L., and Matthews, H. S. (2008), "Food-Miles and the Relative Climate Impacts of Food Choices in the United States," *Environ. Sci. Technol., 42 (10)*, April 16 2008, 3508-3513.

Weber, K. (2009), *Food, Inc.: How Industrial Food Is Making Us Sicker, Fatter and Poorer—and What You Can Do About It*, Public Affairs: New York.

Michael Pollan

The Industrialization of Eating: What We Do Know

Michael Pollan, probably best known as the author of *The Omnivore's Dilemma (2006)*, is also the author of *The Botany of Desire: A Plant-Eye's View of the World* (2001), *A Place of My Own* (1997), *Second Nature* (1991), and *In Defense of Food: An Eater's Manifesto* (2008), from which the following excerpt is taken. Pollan also serves as Knight Professor of Science and Environmental Journalism at the University of California, Berkeley. His work regularly explores the tension between human actions and natural processes. In this piece, for example, he asks "What would happen if we were to start thinking about food as less of a thing and more of a relationship?" Beginning from that question, Pollan is able to walk his readers through some of those processes, and so to help them see how that shift in perspective might influence their understanding of issues of sustainability. By reading this piece, you cannot only add Pollan's voice to the various others in this chapter who discuss sustainable foods, but also consider how such shifts in perspective can help you, as a writer, invent new ways to approach a topic—and so develop inventive ways of writing about that topic.

1 What would happen if we were to start thinking about food as less of a thing and more of a relationship? In nature, that is of course precisely what eating has always been: relationships among species in systems we call food chains, or food webs, that reach all the way down to the soil. Species coevolve with the other species that they eat, and very often there develops a relationship of interdependence: *I'll feed you if you spread around my genes.* A gradual process of mutual adaptation transforms something like an apple or a squash into a nutritious and tasty food for an animal. Over time and through trial and error, the plant becomes tastier (and often more conspicuous) in order to gratify the animal's needs and desires, while the animal gradually acquires whatever digestive tools (enzymes, for example) it needs to make optimal use of the plant.

2 Similarly, the milk of cows did not start out as a nutritious food for humans; in fact, it made them sick until people who lived around cows evolved the ability to digest milk as adults. The gene for the production of a milk-digesting enzyme called lactase used to switch off in humans shortly after weaning until about five thousand years ago, when a mutation that kept the gene switched on appeared and quickly spread through a population of animal herders in north-central Europe. Why? Because the people possessing the new mutation then had access to a terrifically nutritious new food source and as a consequence were able to produce more offspring than the people who lacked it. This development proved much to the advantage of both the milk drinkers and the cows, whose numbers and habitat (and health) greatly improved as a result of this new symbiotic relationship.

3 Health is, among other things, the product of being in these sorts of relationships in a food chain—a great many such relationships in the case of an omnivorous creature like man. It

follows that when the health of one part of the food chain is disturbed, it can affect all the other creatures in it. If the soil is sick or in some way deficient, so will be the grasses that grow in that soil and the cattle that eat the grasses and the people who drink the milk from them. This is precisely what Weston Price and Sir Howard had in mind when they sought to connect the seemingly distant realms of soil and human health. Our personal health cannot be divorced from the health of the entire food web.

4 In many cases, long familiarity between foods and their eaters leads to elaborate systems of communication up and down the food chain so that a creature's senses come to recognize foods as suitable by their taste and smell and color. Very often these signals are "sent" by the foods themselves, which may have their own reasons for wanting to be eaten. Ripeness in fruit is often signaled by a distinctive smell (an appealing scent that can travel over distances), or color (one that stands out from the general green), or taste (typically sweet). Ripeness, which is the moment when the seeds of the plant are ready to go off and germinate, typically coincides with the greatest concentration of nutrients in a fruit, so the interests of the plant (for transportation) align with those of the plant eater (for nutriment). Our bodies, having received these signals and determined this fruit is good to eat, now produce in anticipation precisely the enzymes and acids needed to break it down. Health depends heavily on knowing how to read these biological signals: *This looks ripe; this smells spoiled; that's one slick-looking cow.* This is much easier to do when you have long experience of a food and much harder when a food has been expressly designed to deceive your senses with, say, artificial flavors or synthetic sweeteners. Foods that lie to our senses are one of the most challenging features of the Western diet.

5 Note that these ecological relationships are, at least in the first instance, between eaters and whole foods, not nutrients or chemicals. Even though the foods in question eventually get broken down in our bodies into simple chemical compounds, as corn is reduced mostly to simple sugars, the qualities of the whole foods are not unimportant. The amount and structure of the fiber in that corn, for example, will determine such things as the speed at which the sugars in it will be released and absorbed, something we've learned is critical to insulin metabolism. The chemist will tell you the starch in corn is on its way to becoming glucose in the blood, but that reductive understanding overlooks the complex and variable process by which that happens. Contrary to the nutrition label, not all carbohydrates are created equal.

6 Put another way, our bodies have a long-standing and sustainable relationship to corn that they do not have to high-fructose corn syrup. Such a relationship with corn syrup might develop

someday (as people evolve superhuman insulin systems to cope with regular floods of pure fructose and glucose[1]), but for now the relationship leads to ill health because our bodies don't know how to handle these biological novelties. In much the same way, human bodies that can cope with chewing coca leaves—a long-standing relationship between native people and the coca plant in parts of South America—cannot cope with cocaine or crack, even though the same active ingredients are present in all three. Reductionism as a way of understanding food or drugs may be harmless, even necessary, but reductionism in practice—reducing food or drug plants to their most salient chemical compounds—can lead to problems.

7   Looking at eating, and food, through this ecological lens opens a whole new perspective on exactly what the Western diet is: a radical and, at least in evolutionary terms, abrupt set of changes over the course of the last 150 years, not just to our foodstuffs but also to our food relationships, all the way from the soil to the meal. The rise of the ideology of nutritionism is itself part of that change. When we think of a species' "environment," we usually think in terms of things like geography, predators and prey, and the weather. But of course one of the most critical components of any creature's environment is the nature of the food available to it and its relationships to the species it eats. Much is at stake when a creature's food environment changes. For us, the first big change came ten thousand years ago with the advent of agriculture. (And it devastated our health, leading to a panoply of deficiencies and infectious diseases that we've only managed to get under control in the last century or so.) The biggest change in our food environment since then? The advent of the modern diet.

8   To get a better grip on the nature of these changes is to begin to understand how we might alter our relationship to food—for the better, for our health. These changes have been numerous and far reaching, but consider as a start these five fundamental transformations to our foods and ways of eating. All of them can be reversed, if not perhaps so easily in the food system as a whole, certainly in the life and diet of any individual eater, and without, I hasten to add, returning to the bush or taking up hunting and gathering.

From Whole Foods to Refined

9   The case of corn points to one of the key features of the modern diet: a shift toward increasingly refined foods, especially carbohydrates. People have been refining cereal grains since at least the Industrial Revolution, favoring white flour and white rice over brown, even at the price of lost nutrients. Part of the reason was prestige: Because for many years only the wealthy could

afford refined grains, they acquired a certain glamour. Refining grains extends their shelf life (precisely because they are less nutritious to the pests that compete with us for their calories) and makes them easier to digest by removing the fiber that ordinarily slows the release of their sugars. Also, the finer that flour is ground, the more surface area is exposed to digestive enzymes, so the quicker the starches turn to glucose. A great deal of modern industrial food can be seen as an extension and intensification of this practice as food processors find ways to deliver glucose—the brain's preferred fuel—ever more swiftly and efficiently. Sometimes this is precisely the point, as when corn is refined into corn syrup; other times, though, it is an unfortunate by-product of processing food for other reasons.

Viewed from this perspective, the history of refining whole   10 foods has been a history of figuring out ways not just to make them more durable and portable, but also how to concentrate their energy and, in a sense, speed them up. This acceleration took a great leap forward with the introduction in Europe around 1870 of rollers (made from iron, steel, or porcelain) for grinding grain. Perhaps more than any other single development, this new technology, which by 1880 had replaced grinding by stone throughout Europe and America, marked the beginning of the industrialization of our food—reducing it to its chemical essence and speeding up its absorption. Refined flour is the first fast food.

Before the roller-milling revolution, wheat was ground   11 between big stone wheels, which could get white flour only so white. That's because while stone grinding removed the bran from the wheat kernel (and therefore the largest portion of the fiber), it couldn't remove the germ, or embryo, which contains volatile oils that are rich in nutrients. The stone wheels merely crushed the germ and released the oil. This had the effect of tinting the flour yellowish gray (the yellow is carotene) and shortening its shelf life, because the oil, once exposed to the air, soon oxidized—turned rancid. That's what people could see and smell, and they didn't like it. What their senses couldn't tell them, however, is that the germ contributed some of the most valuable nutrients to the flour, including much of its protein, folic acid, and other B vitamins; carotenes and other antioxidants; and omega-3 fatty acids, which are especially prone to rancidity.

The advent of rollers that made it possible to remove the germ   12 and then grind the remaining endosperm (the big packet of starch and protein in a seed) exceptionally fine solved the problem of stability and color. Now just about everyone could afford snowy-white flour that could keep on a shelf for many months. No longer did every town need its own mill, because flour could now travel great distances. (Plus it could be ground year-round by large companies in big cities: Heavy stone mills, which typically relied on water power, operated mostly when and where rivers flowed; steam engines could drive the new rollers whenever and wherever.) Thus was one of the main staples of the Western diet cut loose from its moorings in place and time and marketed on the basis of image rather than nutritional value. In this, white flour was a modern industrial food, one of the first.

13   The problem was that this gorgeous white powder was nutritionally worthless, or nearly so. Much the same was now true for corn flour and white rice, the polishing of which (i.e., the removing of its most nutritious parts) was perfected around the same time. Wherever these refining technologies came into widespread use, devastating epidemics of pellagra and beriberi soon followed. Both are diseases caused by deficiencies in the B vitamins that the germ had contributed to the diet. But the sudden absence from bread of several other micronutrients, as well as omega-3 fatty acids, probably also took its toll on public health, particularly among the urban poor of Europe, many of whom ate little but bread.

14   In the 1930s, with the discovery of vitamins, scientists figured out what had happened, and millers began fortifying refined grain with B vitamins. This took care of the most obvious deficiency diseases. More recently, scientists recognized that many of us also had a deficiency of folic acid in our diet, and in 1996 public health authorities ordered millers to start adding folic acid to flour as well. But it would take longer still for science to realize that this "Wonder Bread" strategy of supplementation, as one nutritionist has called it, might not solve all the problems caused by the refining of grain. Deficiency diseases are much easier to trace and treat (indeed, medicine's success in curing deficiency diseases is an important source of nutritionism's prestige) than chronic diseases, and it turns out that the practice of refining carbohydrates is implicated in several of these chronic diseases as well—diabetes, heart disease, and certain cancers.

15   The story of refined grain stands as a parable about the limits of reductionist science when applied to something as complex as food. For years now nutritionists have known that a diet high in whole grains reduces one's risk for diabetes, heart disease, and cancer. (This seems to be true even after you correct for the fact that the kind of people who eat lots of whole grains today probably have lifestyles healthier in other ways as well.) Different nutritionists have given the credit for the benefits of whole grain to different nutrients: the fiber in the bran, the folic acid and other B vitamins in the germ, or the antioxidants or the various minerals. In 2003 the *American Journal of Clinical Nutrition*[2] published an unusually nonreductionist study demonstrating that no one of those nutrients alone can explain the benefits of whole-grain foods: The typical reductive analysis of isolated nutrients could not explain the improved health of the whole-grain eaters.

For the study, University of Minnesota epidemiologists David   16
R. Jacobs and Lyn M. Steffen reviewed the relevant research and
found a large body of evidence that a diet rich in whole grains
did in fact reduce mortality from all causes. But what was surprising was that even after adjusting for levels of dietary fiber,
vitamin E, folic acid, phytic acid, iron, zinc, magnesium, and
manganese in the diet (all the good things we know are in whole
grains), they found an additional health benefit to eating whole
grains that none of the nutrients alone or even together could
explain. That is, subjects getting the same amounts of these
nutrients from other sources were not as healthy as the whole-
grain eaters. "This analysis suggests that something else in the
whole grain protects against death." The authors concluded,
somewhat vaguely but suggestively, that "the various grains and
their parts act synergistically" and suggested that their colleagues begin paying attention to the concept of "food synergy."
Here, then, is support for an idea revolutionary by the standards
of nutritionism: A whole food might be more than the sum of its
nutrient parts.

Suffice it to say, this proposition has not been enthusiastically   17
embraced by the food industry, and probably won't be any time
soon. As I write, Coca-Cola is introducing vitamin-fortified
sodas, extending the Wonder Bread strategy of supplementation
to junk food in its purest form. (Wonder Soda?) The big money
has always been in processing foods, not selling them whole,
and the industry's investment in the reductionist approach to
food is probably safe. The fact is, there is something in us that
loves a refined carbohydrate, and that something is the human
brain. The human brain craves carbohydrates reduced to their
energy essence, which is to say pure glucose. Once industry figured out how to transform the seeds of grasses into the chemical equivalent of sugar, there was probably no turning back.

And then of course there is sugar itself, the ultimate refined   18
carbohydrate, which began flooding the marketplace and the
human metabolism around the same time as refined flour. In
1874, England lifted its tariffs on imported sugar, the price
dropped by half, and by the end of the nineteenth century fully
a sixth of the calories in the English diet were coming from
sugar, with much of the rest coming from refined flour.

With the general availability of cheap pure sugar, the human   19
metabolism now had to contend not only with a constant flood
of glucose, but also with more fructose than it had ever before
encountered, because sugar—sucrose—is half fructose.[3] (Per
capita fructose consumption has increased 25 percent in the
past thirty years.) In the natural world, fructose is a rare and
precious thing, typically encountered seasonally in ripe fruit,
when it comes packaged in a whole food full of fiber (which
slows its absorption) and valuable micronutrients. It's no

wonder we've been hardwired by natural selection to prize sweet foods: Sugar as it is ordinarily found in nature—in fruits and some vegetables—gives us a slow-release form of energy accompanied by minerals and all sorts of crucial micronutrients we can get nowhere else. (Even in honey, the purest form of sugar found in nature, you find some valuable micronutrients.)

20   One of the most momentous changes in the American diet since 1909 (when the USDA first began keeping track) has been the increase in the percentage of calories coming from sugars, from 13 percent to 20 percent. Add to that the percentage of calories coming from carbohydrates (roughly 40 percent, or ten servings, nine of which are refined) and Americans are consuming a diet that is at least half sugars in one form or another—calories providing virtually nothing but energy. The energy density of these refined carbohydrates contributes to obesity in two ways. First, we consume many more calories per unit of food; the fiber that's been removed from these foods is precisely what would have made us feel full and stop eating. Also, the flash flood of glucose causes insulin levels to spike and then, once the cells have taken all that glucose out of circulation, drop precipitously, making us think we need to eat again.

21   While the widespread acceleration of the Western diet has given us the instant gratification of sugar, in many people—especially those newly exposed to it—the speediness of this food overwhelms the ability of insulin to process it, leading to type 2 diabetes and all the other chronic diseases associated with metabolic syndrome. As one nutrition expert put it to me, "We're in the middle of a national experiment in the mainlining of glucose." And don't forget the flood of fructose, which may represent an even greater evolutionary novelty, and therefore challenge to the human metabolism, than all that glucose.

22   It is probably no accident that rates of type 2 diabetes are lower among ethnic Europeans, who have had longer than other groups to accustom their metabolisms to fast-release refined carbohydrates: Their food environment changed first.[4] To encounter such a diet for the first time, as when people accustomed to a more traditional diet come to America or when fast food comes to them, delivers a shock to the system. This shock is what public health experts mean by the nutrition transition, and it can be deadly.

23   So here, then, is the first momentous change in the Western diet that may help to explain why it makes some people so sick: Supplanting tested relationships to the whole foods with which we coevolved over many thousands of years, it asks our bodies now to relate to, and deal with, a very small handful of efficiently delivered nutrients that have been torn from their food context. Our ancient evolutionary relationship with the seeds of grasses and fruit of plants has given way, abruptly, to a rocky marriage with glucose and fructose.

Notes

1. Glucose is a sugar molecule that is the body's main source of energy: most carbohydrates are broken down to glucose during digestion. Fructose is a different form of sugar, commonly found in fruit. Sucrose, or table sugar, is a disaccharide consisting of a molecule of glucose joined to a molecule of fructose.
2. David R. Jacobs and Lyn M. Steffen, "Nutrients, Foods, and Dietary Patterns as Exposures in Research: A Framework for Food Synergy," *American Journal of Clinical Nutrition,* 2003; 78 (suppl): 508S–13S.
3. Fructose is metabolized differently from glucose; the body doesn't respond to it by producing insulin to convey it into cells to be used as energy. Rather, it is metabolized in the liver, which turns it first into glucose and then, if there is no call for glucose, into triglycerides—fat.
4. In the past, changes in the food environment have led to measurable changes in human biology over time. A recent study found that populations eating a high-starch diet have more copies of a gene coding for amylase, the enzyme needed to break down starch. The authors of the study suggest that natural selection has favored the gene in those populations that began eating cereal grains after the birth of agriculture. George H. Perry, et al., "Diet and the Evolution of Human Amylase Gene Copy Number Variation," *Nature Genetics* published online September 9, 2007; doi:10.1038/ng2123.

Paul Roberts

Food Fight

Paul Roberts is a journalist who has written for the *Los Angeles Times,* the *Washington Post,* the (UK) *Guardian, Slate, USA Today,* the *New Republic, and Newsweek.* He gained further notoriety for his 2004 book about the peak in oil production, and the coming decline, *The End of Oil.* In 2008, he published *The End of Food,* which explores the ability of the current food industry to feed the growing world population, and from which the following excerpt is taken. As you read this piece, you might consider how the economics of food is a driving force in whether efforts at sustainability can succeed. Taking this approach will also help you think in interdisciplinary ways, considering not only the ethical and behavioral facets of the sustainability issue, but also the ways in which business and economics play a role. As you read other pieces in this chapter, try to see each argument through a number of disciplinary lenses.

1   A few hours northeast of Rod Van Graff's feedlots, near the town of Reardon, Washington, wheat farmer Fred Fleming swings his pickup truck off the highway and onto a farm field to show me his plan to save the world. It's early March, and the field is already showing the green blades of a crop of winter wheat, a hard white variety that bakers prefer and that, with the ripple effects of the ethanol boom, looks to be a money maker for the first time in decades. What makes this field special, however, isn't what Fleming planted but *how*. Where most of his neighbors till their fields after harvest, making the dirt clean and neat for the next planting, Fleming leaves the stubble and other plant matter from the previous crop and, with a machine known as a direct seeder, pokes his seeds through the sod and into the soil beneath. The results of this "no-till" farming aren't pretty: the fields look so bedraggled and unkempt that when Fleming, a tall, gregarious fifty-nine-year-old whose family has grown wheat here since the 1920s, switched to no-till in 2000, his neighbors "would drive by and assume I was having marital problems."

2   But looks can be deceiving. Because no-till farming leaves the dirt largely intact, the topsoil in Fleming's fields has been able to knit together into a thick mat of roots, rhizomes, bugs, worms, and decaying organic matter—a living layer that retains nutrients and moisture, helps keep yields high, and protects the soil from erosion, much as the sod did when these fields were all in native prairie grass. This seemingly minor difference from conventional farming becomes glaringly apparent a few minutes later when we drive to another farmer's fields some miles away. Because this farmer uses conventional methods, the field has been tilled so regularly—as many as a dozen different times a year—that the soil is almost inert; when I reach down and dig out a handful, it crumbles on my palm like a moist brown talc with a cakelike texture, no bugs, and not much of a smell. Of course, with enough of what Fleming calls "farm chemistry"—mainly, synthetic fertilizers—this sorry dirt will still produce big yields, but not without a substantial cost. Because these overworked soils have lost their structure, they're highly vulnerable to erosion; dust storms here still shut down airports, and a heavy winter rain can be a disaster: three weeks before I showed up, a downpour cut huge gullies across the field, taking tons of soil with it. "And all that soil, and all that farm chemistry, ends up in the Spokane River," says Fleming, who often tells visitors that erosion has cost this region thousands of tons of topsoil over the last century. The claim is hard to believe until Fleming points to the ridge top where this farmer's land butts up against land that has been idle for decades in a federal conservation program: even from a distance, I can see that the ground level in the conservation area is more than two feet above the surface of the farm field.

Fleming isn't the only one touting the benefits of no-till wheat 3
farming. Soil scientists from nearby Washington State University say the layer of sod that builds up after several years of no-till not only minimizes erosion but substantially reduces the amount of nitrogen leaching from the soil. As important, the method is also economically sustainable: even before the current grain boom, Fleming discovered that socially concerned commercial buyers, especially urban bakeries catering to upscale "correct" consumers, would pay a premium for "sustainably grown" wheat flour. In 2002, Fleming and a few like-minded farmers formed Shepherd's Grain, a marketing co-op that bypasses big commodity traders and sells directly to bakeries and other commercial customers. Their pitch was simple: not only is Shepherd's Grain flour cheaper than organic, but because it is grown with no-till methods, it actually disrupts the soil less than organic does. It's an argument that is gaining traction: in the four years since its launch, Shepherd's Grain's sales have jumped from ten thousand to nearly half a million bushels a year—and all, crows Fleming, "while finding a way to protect an ecosystem."

Advocates of sustainable food production point to Shepherd's 4
Grain as proof that the trend toward commodity food production can be reversed or at least redirected: by taking their grain directly to consumers rather than selling to a middleman, Fleming and his partners have transformed wheat from a low-cost commodity into a upscale consumer product whose premium price allows it to be produced in a much more ecologically sustainable fashion. As important, however, is the way this venture has allowed midsize producers to compete in a food market increasingly ruled by very large players. By working in a cooperative organization, Fleming and his fifteen partners have sufficient scale and market power to strike favorable deals with buyers and other players in a supply chain that has historically squeezed such midsize producers to the point of bankruptcy or consolidation. "Individually, we're tiny," says Fleming. "But collectively, no one else even comes close."

Shepherd's Grain's success highlights a second stress point in 5
the evolving food economy: the battle over scale. Just as greater crop diversity can reduce externalities at the farm level, greater size diversity could allow producers to balance the economic demands of their particular market with the agronomic and ecological capacities of their landscape.

In practice, of course, the trends in production scales are moving the other way. In the industrialized world and, increasingly, in 6
many emerging economies as well, the farm sector is morphing into a two-tier system, with a small number of very large producers and a very large number of very small producers—neither of which has much capacity for sustainable food production.

7   The downsides of large producers are quite familiar: although they are exceptional at generating huge volumes of cheap food (in the United States, for example, just 163,000 mega-farms, representing a third of the agricultural land base, generate 60 percent of our food),[1] the need for continuous cost reductions leaves these large-scale, low-cost operations structurally disinclined to incorporate, or even acknowledge, external costs—a disinclination that will grow stronger as they face competition from foreign low-cost producers. (There are important exceptions; companies like AgriNorthwest, a massive grain and produce grower in Washington State, recently shifted to direct seeding as a means of cutting operating costs.)

8   What is often surprising, however, is that *small* farmers and producers are also challenged as long-term contributors of sustainable food. To be sure, small farmers can (and often do) produce food in a sustainable fashion. Small farmers have also been critical in bringing the ideas of sustainability into the mainstream and in linking rural and urban communities, thus reminding consumers that food is, or can be, something made by a person. For all that, the small-farm sector lacks the structural capacity to generate the volumes of food that will be necessary in coming decades. Few small farmers have time or the skills to develop a Furuno kind of out-put; in the United States, for example, most of the nation's 1.3 million small farms are part-timers or even hobbyists, relying on off-farm income to support what is less a profession than an avocation. And even if small farmers were somehow able to raise their output substantially, the nation no longer has a distribution system to transfer the yields of hundreds of thousands of small producers to retailers and consumers. All told, small farms, though they are the fastest-growing segment in the United States, generate less than 10 percent of the food supply. "We tend to lionize the small producers," says Scott Exo, executive director of the Food Alliance, a Portland, Oregon-based nonprofit that acts as a third-party certifier for sustainable producers. "There are undeniably opportunities for small farmers to deal directly with consumers in farmers' markets, restaurants, and other new markets, but in terms of actual food production and consumption, it's a real drop in the bucket."

9   It's for these reasons that many sustainable food advocates are looking to the area *between* large and small producers—and specifically, to midsize farmers, whose scale (between fifty and five hundred acres) and numbers (half a million in the United State alone) theoretically make them the ideals basis of sustainable food production. Many of these farms and ranches are large enough to generate sizable volumes at a reasonable cost. But they are not so large that farmers can't work each acre with some degree of knowledge and deliberateness—a critical distinction,

according to sustainability advocates like Wendell Berry, who famously argues that sustainable production can't happen unless farmers "know and love" their land. And, as agricultural economist John Ikerd puts it, "Each farmer can only know and love so much land."[2] Most midsize family farmers and ranchers might not put it in exactly those terms, but many would likely agree that any kind of sustainable production is a lot more plausible when farmers and ranchers are actually familiar with soil qualities, hydrology patterns, and other strengths and weaknesses of their land. Thus we can understand why sustainability advocates are so excited by the success of Shepherd's Grain and other ventures that have been structured to give midsize producers the necessary marketing clout while preserving their capacity for stewardship.

Despite the apparently huge potential for this model of mid-   10 size food production, defending the middle ground is no easy feat. Half a century of falling commodity prices has left many midsize farmers unable to compete with their large-scale rivals; so many have sold out (often to those same low-cost rivals) that, since the 1970s, even as large and small farms have grown, midsize operations have declined markedly[3]—a trend agricultural experts bemoan as the "hollowing of the middle." Even with today's higher commodity prices, large producers continue to reap advantages from their scale economies and market power; and, of course, large commodity operations also benefit enormously from government programs that compensate growers by the acre or the bushel but pay little or nothing to ranchers and farmers who produce in ways that actually conserve their land and other natural resources.

Further, although some successful midsize producers have   11 managed to convert the easier manageability of their lands into a sustainable practice that can justify a price premium, the process has added significantly to the complexity of their work. When Fleming switched from commodity wheat to a premium-priced sustainable flour, he expected the hardest part would be mastering the new production methods. In fact, the more challenging task was to learn how to sell to consumers, a task Fleming, like most commodity producers, had been content to leave to the big grain buyers and food processors. Fleming now had to understand the entire supply chain, study grocery retailing, develop a brand and a product story, and familiarize himself with something he'd never bothered with before: consumers. As a result, this fourth-generation rural conservative found himself spending long days in upscale urban supermarkets, trying to discern how left-of-center, socially concerned shoppers made their flour-buying decisions. "We had to learn a new language," says Fleming. "It was a hard mind shift to make, and I still have flashbacks to my commodity side of life."

12   Being a pioneer has other costs, as well. Some of Fleming's neighbors regard his alternative methods as a thousand-acre rebuke to their own faith in industrial farming, and some alternative farming advocates aren't much happier. Because tilling helps keep weeds under control, no-till farmers such as Fleming must compensate with "judicious" applications of synthetic herbicide (usually Roundup); they must also apply some synthetic nitrogen. As a result, not only is Fleming's wheat excluded from the organic market, but his methods earn the scorn of some in the alternative farming movement. Invited recently to address a statewide meeting of alternative producers, Fleming, a Republican from a very conservative town, found himself in a room filled with flute music, odd clothing, and organic "purists." "They were polite," he recalls. "But some of them definitely gave me the cold shoulder."

13   There are other penalties for those seeking payment for producing food sustainability. Because value-adding producers like Fleming are essentially maintaining ownership of their product as it moves down the supply chain—not just handing it off to an intermediary as soon as it leaves the "farm gate," as conventional commodity producers do—they get to keep a larger share of the value being added. For example, members of an Oregon-based cooperative ranching venture, Country Natural Beef, whose cattle are raised on chemically untreated pasture that is allowed to fully recover naturally between each season and who carefully trace each animal as it moves from pasture to slaughterhouse to grocery display case, receive 96 percent of the wholesale price—substantially more than conventional producers get. But in so doing, these new producers expose themselves to a new set of risks. Where ranchers and farmers once dealt only with rapacious middlemen, now they must work in a retail market that is often far more competitive. Big grocery chains will gladly appropriate new value-adding ideas, like "organic," which they then will seek to produce more cheaply using conventional, large-scale producers. Further, the rapid consolidation of the natural-food retail market (in 2007, Whole Foods, the largest natural-food chain, announced a half-billion-dollar buyout of its nearest competitor, Wild Oats)[4] will give these socially correct retailers even more price leverage over their suppliers.

14   Finally, if traditional producers thought that commodity markets could be unpredictable, with wild price swings, that is nothing compared to the fickleness of consumers. "Today's value added is tomorrow's commodity," says Doc Hatfield, who, as a cofounder of Country Natural Beef, knows how quickly a consumer trend can change. Country Natural Beef spent years finding a way to compete with traditional organic beef by offering consumers a different value proposition—beef that was ecologically sustainable—only to watch consumer preferences shift

from environmentally correct food to food produced locally. And while Hatfield is all for local food, it's a challenging criterion for grass-fed beef. In order to sell fresh beef year-round to progressive consumers in a key urban market like Portland, Oregon, Country Natural Beef must source its cattle not only from in-state ranches but occasionally from northern California, because that's the nearest place where pasture grass grows all winter and, thus, the nearest place where cattle can be grazed sustainably. Yet conveying this geographically complex reality to the "well-intentioned, moderate-income consumer" hasn't always been easy. "Local is the new organic," says a mildly exasperated Hatfield, echoing what has become the lament of the alternative food universe. "But you have to be at least a hundred miles from Portland before you can find an environmentally friendly place to raise cattle."

In the tiny mountain village of Sambucano, Italy, just a few   15
miles south of the Swiss border, I'm sitting in a restaurant above an enormous alpine meadow, chewing on a piece of locally raised lamb and learning, between sips of red wine, how gourmet food can reconnect consumers to the countryside. My hosts are all associates of Slow Food, an international organization that began as a jocose response to McDonaldization but has since become the elite guard of the eat-local movement. Just now, agronomist Antonio Brignone, a diminutive, elfish man with bright green eyes and silver hair, is explaining how the flavor of the Sambucano lamb, a breed that was nearly extinct ten years ago, cannot be found anywhere else on earth because it feeds on nothing but local grass, which is the product of local soils, local weather conditions, and even the local angle of the sun. "You can't find Sambucano lamb in New York," Brignone tells me. "If you want it, you have to come here." Brignone's point is that when it comes to real food a particular taste is inseparable from its place of origin, and if consumers wish to preserve that taste, they must preserve the countryside from which it springs. "Once you start to understand how gastronomic food is produced," says Renato Sardo, a former Slow Food official, "you realize you have to do something to protect the ecology of the place where it is produced."

Granted, the endangered Sambucano lamb may not be the   16
linchpin of the next food economy. But the move toward local food, for all its trendiness (the more adamant adherents, known as "localvores," strive to buy products that have traveled the least "food miles"),[5] highlights one of the problematic pieces of the modern food economy: the increasing reliance on foods shipped halfway round the world. Because long-distance food shipments promote profligate fuel use and the exploitation of cheap labor (which compensates for the profligate fuel use), shifting back to a more locally sourced food economy is often

touted as a fairly straightforward way to cut externalities, restore some measure of equity between producers and consumers, and put the food economy on a more sustainable footing. "Such a shift would bring back diversity to land that has been all but destroyed by chemical-intensive mono-cropping, provide much-needed jobs at a local level, and help to rebuild community," argues the UK-based International Society for Ecology and Culture, one of the leading lights in the localvore movement. "Moreover, it would allow farmers to make a decent living while giving consumers access to healthy, fresh food at affordable prices."[6]

17   While localvorism sounds superb in theory, it is proving quite difficult in practice. To begin with, there are dozens of different definitions as to what local is, with some advocates arguing for political boundaries (as in Texas-grown, for example), others using quasi-geographic terms like food sheds, and still others laying out somewhat arbitrarily drawn food circles with radii of 100 or 150 or 500 miles. Further, whereas some areas might find it fairly easy to eat locally (in Washington State, for example, I'm less than fifty miles from industrial quantities of fresh produce, corn, wheat, beef, and milk), people in other parts of the country and the world would have to look farther afield. And what counts as local? Does food need to be purchased directly from the producer? Does it still count when it's distributed through a mass marketer, as with Wal-Mart's Salute to America's Farmer program," which is now periodically showcasing local growers?[7]

18   The larger problem is that although decentralized food systems function well in decentralized societies—like the United States was a century ago, or like many developing nations still are—they're a poor fit in modern urbanized societies. The same economic forces that helped food production become centralized and regionalized did the same thing to our population: in the United States, 80 percent of us live in large, densely populated urban areas,[8] usually on the coast, and typically hundreds of miles, often thousands of miles, from the major centers of food production.

19   Some agricultural economists have advocated the wholesale shifting of our food centers closer to urban centers, as is happening by default in many fast-growing Asian countries. Such an arrangement would impose far fewer costs in terms of transportation energy but poses extraordinary technical and economic challenges. In developing countries, the intermingling of food production and dense urban populations is now seen as a driver for flu outbreaks. As well, even in mature economies such as the United States, where biosecurity is much higher, the high cost of urban land precludes all but the most high-value food production. This is one reason so much of the farmland in the rapidly urbanizing Salinas Valley has shifted from low-value

pursuits, such as ranching, to high-value crops, such as spinach and tomatoes; it's also why most low-value crops, like corn and soybeans, can be grown economically only on relatively cheap rural acres. Even in regions where farmlands still exist near cities, the roads, rails, and short-haul supply chains that once linked farms to nearby urban markets has been largely usurped by national and global supply chains, managed by retailers and distributors who prefer sourcing from large suppliers, not from hundreds or even thousands of local producers. These are powerful economic forces that would work against any large-scale shift to local food production.

The more practical advocates of local food insist that they   20
aren't asking for wholesale localization. "I know perfectly well that every product cannot be made on a small farm," says Sardo, formerly with Slow Food. "But we have to start somewhere." Indeed, the more nuanced view of localism doesn't seek to completely do away with nonlocal foods—at least, not right away—but to recover some degree of geographic diversity in food sources, based on region, food type, and season, while striving to moderate the more egregious impacts of globalization—soy protein from China, for example, or planeloads of year-round fresh produce from South America.

But here, too, the benefits of going local aren't always clear.   21
Although reducing the distance traveled by a food product would seem to be an automatic gain for sustainability, this isn't always the case. A semi driving several tons of produce 312 miles from a mega-farm in the Salinas Valley to a Wal-Mart in Reno may seem an egregious waste of energy, but it actually burns less fuel than would the dozens of pickup trucks needed to haul the same quantity of produce to a farmers' market in Reno from local farms just twenty miles away. One advantage of the centralized industrialized food system, with its carefully scheduled deliveries and obsessive focus on efficiency, is that it can keep food-transportation energy costs down.

The more fundamental problem with the food-mile concept   22
is the same one that plagues organic: it's a simplistic solution to an extraordinarily complex problem. In the same way a pesticide-free head of lettuce may still not be environmentally friendly, distance isn't always the most important determinant in a particular food product's sustainability. Organic food produced in Chile and flown to the United States may represent massive food miles, but it also represents a shift in farming practices in Chile—fewer pesticides and synthetic fertilizers—which might be beneficial to the Chilean environment and people.

Even if we omit such fuzzy, hard-to-quantify social benefits   23
and focus strictly on tangible costs, such as energy savings, climate impact, or water use, "local" doesn't always represent a win. According to researchers at the University of Wales Institute,

the shipping of food from the farm to the grocery accounts for, on average, just 2 percent of that product's total environmental impact. Far more significant contributors are the way the food is processed, packaged, and especially the way it is farmed, because modern agriculture and livestock methods rely so heavily on energy-intensive and ecologically dubious fertilizers, irrigated water, and imported grain.[9]

24   To capture this complexity, many sustainability advocates want to replace food miles with the more detailed ecological footprint concept, which tries to account for *all* of the costs of a particular food product—usually expressed in the number of theoretical acres needed to generate all the materials, energy, plant matter, and other inputs necessary for making and moving a particular food product. "I'm a bit worried about the food miles [debate] because it is educating the consumer in the wrong way," Ruth Fairchild, one of the authors of the University of Wales study, told *The Guardian* newspaper. "It is such an insignificant point . . . If you just take food miles, it is the tiny bit on the end."[10]

25   This point was made succinctly when local-food advocates in the United Kingdom complained about the practice of importing meat and dairy products from New Zealand. In response, researchers at Lincoln University in New Zealand showed that because New Zealand farmers use far less fertilizer than their counterparts in the United Kingdom do and because New Zealand sheep feed almost entirely on grass whereas UK livestock are mainly grain-fed, consumers in the UK importing New Zealand mutton and dairy products actually cut energy use and climate impacts by 75 and 50 percent, respectively, over locally produced items.[11]

26   This isn't to dismiss distance as an important factor in gauging the sustainability of a particular product or practice or to reject the idea that local food might be worth promoting for other, less quantifiable values. Reconnecting consumers with producers, and helping those consumers become more aware of the specific place where their food is grown, or with specific traditions, would seem to offer an important counterweight to a food system characterized by increasing uniformity and separation. As well, a robust local-food movement might help revitalize an environmental movement that has become almost bloodless. As Sardo puts it, "The gourmet needs to be an ecologist, because without the right ecology, you will lose the flavor. But we also know that the ecologist needs to be a gourmet, in order to be less sad, less apocalyptic."

27   Nor is it to suggest that just because global sourcing of some foods is cost-effective and perhaps even sustainable today, this will always be the case. A sharp rise in energy prices or tough new regulations on carbon emissions, to say nothing of new

revelations about food safety in places like China, could rapidly shift that balance, rendering some or most of our system of global sourcing obsolete and making it far more economically viable to grow apples and potatoes in places like Iowa and Nebraska again.

What is true, however, is that for all the benefits of local food, 28 the realities of the local-food debate are far more complex than they often appear—and certainly will not be resolved by a single number or definition. "The emphasis on speed and convenience has seduced a lot of us into thinking that we can boil down the implications of our decisions into a single word, and that if we embrace the word, then we can go merrily on our way and feel good about it," says Food Alliance's Exo. In the next food economy, Exo says, consumers will "still have to think."

Not surprisingly, most strategies for reforming the food system 29 rely heavily on "thinking" consumers. Many of the groups advocating a more sustainable food system, improved nutrition, or related issues have created elaborate education campaigns to tell consumers about their food, the idea being that the more one knows about what is wrong with food, the more likely one is to take steps to make it right. This is the rationale behind the numerous efforts to force companies to label their products with information not just about the ingredients used but also where the ingredients originated and whether the conditions of production were sustainable or equitable. "Food consumption is an area where individual decisions can make a difference—supply will follow demand," declares the Sierra Club on its website "The True Cost of Food," which invites readers to take a pledge: "We, the consumers, through our food choices, can stop the practices that harm our health, our planet, and our quality of life."[12]

Notes

1. U.S. Department of Agriculture, "American Farms," *Agriculture Fact Book, 2001–2002*, http://www.usda.gov/factbook/chapter3.htm.
2. John Ikerd, "Why Do Small Farmers Farm?" *Small Farm Today* magazine (September-October 2003), archived at http://web.missouri.edu/~ikerdj//papers/SFT-WhyFarm.htm.
3. USDA, *Agriculture Fact Book, American Farms, 2001–2002*.
4. Allison Linn, "Grocer merger raises unique legal questions: Will Whole Foods, Wild Oats merger hurt consumers, or help them?" *MSNBC*, June 12, 2007, http://www.msnbc.msn.com/id/19120095/.
5. *The Economist*, "Voting with your trolley," December 7, 2006, http://www.economist.com/business/displaystory.cfm?story_id=8380592.
6. International Society for Ecology and Culture, "Local Food Bringing the Food Economy Home," group website, http://www.isec.org.uk/pages/local food.html.
7. Wal-Mart, "Maine's Ricker Hill Farm Teams with Wal-Mart to Celebrate America's Farmers," press release, November 6, 2006, http://www.walmart facts.com/articles/4594.aspx.

8. The Rural Institute, "Ruralfacts: Update on the Demography of Rural Disability, Part One: Rural and Urban," http://rtc.ruralinstitute.umt.edu/RuDis/DescribeFigure2.htm.

9. James Randerson, "Focus on Distance Is Too Narrow, Say Researchers," *Guardian*, June 4, 2007, http://www.guardian.co.uk/uk_news/story/0,,2094651,000.html.

10. Ibid.

11. Caroline Saunders et al., "Food Miles: Comparative Energy/Emissions Performance of New Zealand's Agriculture Industry," Research Report No. 285, University in New Zealand, Christchurch, July 2006, http://www.lincoln.ac.nz/story_images/2328_RR285_s6508.pdf.

12. See http://www.truecostoffood.org/leaders.asp.

Victoria Moran

Veg and the City: My Beef with Locavores

Victoria Moran, who holds a degree in Comparative Religion, is a journalist, radio host, and holistic health advocate who writes for publications such as *Yoga Journal, Body and Soul, Woman's Day, Mothering, Natural Health, Vegetarian Times,* and the *Huffington Post,* where this piece was first published in 2010. In this essay, she uses a personal experience to illustrate why the world "needs us vegans." As you read, you might consider how her background in religious studies seems to influence the argument she makes. You might also consider how the scientific and economic arguments made in other pieces in this section might intersect with the more personal, ethical arguments here. Is one discipline more authoritative than the other? Is there a way to promote dialogue among people with such differing perspectives, backgrounds, and contexts?

1   The ally relationship can be an odd one. I remember my shock in third grade, learning that the Soviets had been our ally in World War II. "How could this be?" I wondered. "Our arch-enemies, the reason we have to crawl under our desks and prepare for The Bomb, were once our *friends*?"

2   I'm having similar feelings now, as I contemplate the locavore movement. As a vegan, and someone who believes in organic

growing methods and family farms, I thought we were allies. I'm also a realist: I know the world isn't going vegetarian overnight. Our numbers are growing, certainly, but the global demand for meat is greater than it's ever been. Amid all this, I was happy to see a substantial group of small farmers, given a voice by authors and commentators such as Michael Pollan and Barbara Kingsolver, take a stand for better farming, including more humane methods of animal husbandry than the factory-farming norm. We didn't have the same ultimate goal, but both theirs (replacing corporate agriculture with small, conscientious farms) and ours (a vegan planet) are so lofty that none of us will live to see either one. But for now we were, I thought, allies.

I'd go to the farmers' market at Union Square—it's every bit 3 as gorgeous as anybody's Eiffel Tower or Grand Canyon—and if the farmer selling goat cheese also had glorious spring greens, I'd buy her greens. It was totally friendly. I never said, "Shame on you for stealing the milk God meant for goat babies!" and she never said, "Damn you, veg-head: buy some cheese or you don't deserve arugula!" And the couple that provide the provisions for my CSA (Community-Supported Agriculture: you buy a share in a small farm for a season) always knew that I wouldn't be getting eggs. I didn't ask for anything to make up for that, but they often put in some extra potatoes or apples or a bottle of herb-flavored vinegar. It was nice. We were allies.

And, in terms of individuals like that woman, that couple, and 4 me, we still are. I fear, however, that a strong anti-vegetarian sentiment has grown up in the locavorism movement as a whole. Several recent documentaries suggest this. The first I saw, *Food, Inc.*, was an impeccably researched indictment of the corporations that want to take over all food production and apparently don't care how thoroughly we're poisoned and "genetically modified" in the process. It showed small, organic farmers weighing in on the issue while doing what they do, in one case, cutting the heads off chickens. "This is hard to watch," my husband whispered. "I know," I said, "but he's the good guy."

The next film we saw was *Food Fight*. It went into detail about 5 providing whole food in school cafeterias, rather the way chef Jamie Oliver did on his reality show, *Jamie Oliver's Food Revolution*. No one could fault the sincerity of these people, but it did cross my mind that the vegan option—getting our nutrition firsthand rather than cycling it through animals who are, even in the best of circumstances, slaughtered in their youthful prime—was never mentioned.

My final cinematic foray into the locavores' way of seeing 6 things was a film called *Fresh*, screened at a yoga studio here in Manhattan. It featured *The Omnivore's Dilemma* author Michael Pollan; Joel Salatin (the guy who beheaded the chickens in *Food, Inc.*, and referred to himself in this doc as "a caretaker of creation"); and Will Allen, an urban farmer in Milwaukee, quoted in *Fresh* saying, "Food is the foundation, but it's really about life." Yes. I think so, too. Everybody's life.

7   After that showing of *Fresh*, there was a group discussion led by two erudite young men, one of whom claimed to be a vegetarian but who joined his cohort in ripping to shreds the concept of a plant-based lifestyle. "A vegan diet is totally unsustainable in this part of the country," somebody said. "That's nuts," I was thinking, remembering my grandmother and how she "put by" so much food with drying and canning, her pantry was overstuffed, even (according to my mom) during the Great Depression. My grandparents had a small farm in northern Missouri, and although they did raise animals, the produce alone could have gotten them through the winter. Hardy vegetables like cabbage and kale stayed in the garden, where Gramma built little coverings to protect them. "Now your kale is always sweeter after a frost," she'd say.

8   Apples, potatoes, yams and winter squash went into the root cellar and were good till spring. Black walnuts, hazelnuts, and pecans joined them there. Tomatoes, string beans, peaches and pears were canned, along with all sorts of preserves and jams and marmalades. Beans and peas were dried, as was some of the fruit. Nobody in Missouri had heard the word "vegan" in those days, but if such a person had wandered by, he'd have been well-fed.

9   I didn't pipe up with my opinion during the Q&A after that film, however, because I'd rather be an ally than an adversary. Besides, my message is to the farmers and their spokespeople, not a bunch of New Yorkers who think Long Island is "the country." I want to tell them they need us vegans: There aren't nearly enough low-intensity farmers growing animals to meet the demand. For them to make a dent in the marketplace, there will need to be millions of people not eating animal products. I'd tell them that I admire their commitment and believe there are ways we can work together, but that the vegetarian ethic didn't come into being with modern factory farming. Some of us don't like the idea of taking a life, even if that life wasn't nonstop horrific, as on factory farms.

10   My vegetarian predecessors from Pythagoras to Einstein made two conclusions: First, the killing of a sentient being for anything less than self-preservation or to save another is wrong; and secondly, it is close to impossible to raise animals for food and keep the process consistently humane. My grandparents, on their little farm, did the things the locavores say farmers should be doing now. Their chickens lived in a coop, had access to the outside, and nobody seared off their beaks. Roosters were pretty much dispatched with, however, because one was enough. And come Sunday, a hen whose laying was waning a bit, had her neck

wrung and she showed up on a platter. The pigs gave birth and nursed their young without the hideous confinement of farrowing crates, but each one was destined for slaughter and the runt of every litter was killed as an infant.

It wasn't that my grandparents were bad people. They were   11 simply trying to make a living and, in terms of animal agriculture, they—and the modern proponents of family farming—do it in the best way possible. This is why I want to be their ally. I know that as a vegan, I'm in a minority. People love their meat. It's up there with sugar and TV and maybe even coffee on the list of inalienable American rights. As long as people demand the product, of course I champion anyone who's willing to produce it with the least amount of suffering to the creatures involved, *but that is still a great deal of suffering.*

Former Michigan beef farmer Harold Brown put it this way   12 on the site http://www.humanemyth.org/: "In my experience, there is no such thing as humane animal products, humane farming practices, humane transport, or humane slaughter." I realize that in quoting him, I'm bringing out one of the "big guns" from "my side," just as the locavores have theirs. But I myself spent a day in a slaughterhouse once, and those sights and smells and screams will never leave me. With what I know and what I've experienced, I gladly I support anyone working to make things better. But, ultimately, "better" isn't good enough.

Conversations 2.0: Is Local Always Better for Food Production?

In the current environment, many public conversations take place   13 in a virtual, online space. And while calling these conversations "virtual conversations" might make them seem less real or less important, that is not the case. In fact, online conversations have become one of the central locations for public debate on key issues, including the issues that are included in this book. To enrich your understanding of public conversations, you can make use of the array of online discussion boards, listservs, blogs, Facebook pages, and Twitter sites that are available via the web. The Conversations 2.0 pages in this book suggest some possible ways to do so, and point out some particularly useful and credible online conversations; you of course can use your own online forums and communities to add to these suggestions—or even to start your own.

As should be evident from the pieces included in this chapter,   14 the "local foods" movement is not uncontested; nor is it a simple "agree" or "disagree" proposition. More accurately, the debate about food production involves a great many facets, including but not limited to questions like:

1. Is eating meat environmentally sustainable?
2. Can focusing on local foods harm the food production system, and so cause more hunger and starvation?
3. Are factory farms destroying the American tradition of the family farm?
4. Is a vegan diet the healthiest way to eat?
5. Does the marketing of food lead to obesity?
6. Are current farming practices depleting the soil?
7. Is the use of pesticide an environmental danger or an important part of sustaining our ability to feed our citizens?

15   Questions like these, as well as many others, continue to breed many virtual conversations on the web—conversations, to which you might listen or into which you'd like to join. There are numerous blogs, discussion boards, listservs, and interactive websites (with visuals and video as well as text) that will help you to learn the nature of the conversation. And even if you'd like to then move on to more reliable and academic sources, lurking a bit on these sites can help you to find the stasis points in those debates.

16   The problem with these online communications, of course, is that each particular site or blog tends to attract only like-minded individuals, leaving the conversation somewhat one-sided. Here's where you can practice your rhetorical skills and also experience the nature of online conversation. Try this:

1. First, choose a facet of the conversation that most interests you; the list above might get you started.
2. Do some research on this topic, attempting to find the most reliable, well-evidenced information you can find. As you find various sources, use techniques of source evaluation discussed in this book and in your course.
3. Find a site that seems to disagree with your own perspectives on this issue, or that doesn't seem to provide serious evidence or reasoning for its arguments among the participants. Using some of the most reliable information you can find, join in to an online discussion or blog, adding the information that you have found to the conversation.
4. Gauge the reactions you get from the other participants: Are they willing to listen to your perspective? Do they tend to react with their own information or is their reaction based more on emotions? Were you able to convince any of the participants of your informed perspectives? To what degree? Were your own perspectives changed by the responses you received?

Doing this exerices can not only help you learn more about 17 this topic, but can help you to assess the nature of Web 2.0 conversations. You might even write an analysis or narrative about your experiences in this virtual conversation space.

getting into the conversation ••• 9

Feeding the World: Toward Sustainable Foods

1. Eric Schlosser's bestselling *Fast Food Nation* set off a great many conversations about the ways that America's fast-food mentality has affected not only our physical health, but also the societal health of our culture more generally. As you can see by the many recent pieces included in this chapter, that conversation has continued. Amidst that conversation, the suggestion that we should regulate food and the food industry—or even the concept that the culture, not the individual, is responsible for guiding our food choices—has led some to question whether this represents an infringement upon our personal freedoms. Look back through the various arguments that are made by authors in this chapter, and try to identify each writer's stance on the relationship between individual rights and our responsibility to more "communitarian" ideals—ideals that put the good of the group ahead of the good of each individual. Select specific arguments made by each author that illustrate where they seem to stand on this, and try to construct an essay that articulates the various perspectives in this debate.

2. One of the sites of debate about food surrounds vegetarianism. While vegetarianism is for some a choice of diet, for others it represents a larger set of issues. That is, people choose to be vegetarian for a wide array of reasons. Some choose not to eat meat because of animal cruelty issues. Some make this choice for religious or spiritual reasons. Others consider the environmental impact of meat production and so forth. Look back at the various pieces in this section that address the vegetarian lifestyle, and perhaps seek other arguments that you might find about vegetarianism. Then, write an analysis of the various arguments made for vegetarianism, evaluating the strength of those arguments and their implications for the individual and the culture.

3. The debate about food spans a number of fields of disciplines. In fact, sustainability issues are a naturally interdisciplinary topic; even college curricula in environmental studies or sustainability generally include courses from many departments or majors, often including chemistry, biology, ethics, literature, art, and business, among others. For this reason, the debate about sustainability is especially rich. In order to better understand the various perspectives that are at work as our culture debates issues of sustainability, locate in this chapter's readings specific arguments that seem to draw upon a particular discipline's concepts and methods. Where does an author seem to be articulating the view from business? Where are there perspectives that might interest a psychologist or social scientist? Where does the evidence seem to be drawn from scientific studies or literature? Then,

develop an interdisciplinary look at the issue of sustainability, providing your readers with a sense of the complexity of this issue. As an alternative, you might also focus on one of those perspectives, giving particular attention to the field you are studying.

4. Another key site of debate about food production and consumption involves what has been called the "locavore" or "local foods" movement. This movement has as its central tenet that our culture would benefit if we largely (or even wholly) consume foods that are grown and/or produced within a limited geographic distance. There are many arguments for such movements, including the desire to support small, local agriculture, the advantage of avoiding long-distance transportation of foods, the health gains of encouraging people to eat fresher foods and those not treated to survive transport, and so forth. Others in this section, however, see this movement as shortsighted and perhaps even dangerous to the well-established network of food production that feeds our citizens and supports our economy. Examine the various arguments that support or critique this movement, and try to formulate your own position on this topic. Remember that you need not be wholly "for" or "against" the locavore ideals; feel free to find some middle ground that may—as you see it—represent a reasonable compromise.

The Past and Future of Nuclear Energy

I. The Context

For those who remember the Russian nuclear disaster at Chernobyl, the near-nuclear disaster at Three Mile Island in Pennsylvania, and the protests (and protest films like the 1979 *The China Syndrome*) against nuclear energy, the idea that somehow nuclear energy might be part of a sustainable energy future, or even be considered a "green" technology, might seem baffling. But as our country and the world attends to growing energy needs in the context of sustainability movements and fears of global climate change, nuclear energy has again started to emerge as one potential solution. To understand the context of this new discussion, we first must consider earlier moments in the history of nuclear power and how they might influence our present and future.

At 4:00 A.M. on March 24, 1979, a partial meltdown occurred in the now infamous Reactor 2 at the Three Mile Island Nuclear Power Plant, just outside the state capital of Harrisburg, Pennsylvania. In the days that followed, the governor of Pennsylvania, Dick Thornburgh, and his staff struggled to balance between panic and safety; conflicting stories abounded, including a newscast by CBS' well-trusted news anchor, Walter Cronkite, who reported that there was a "remote but very real possibility of a nuclear meltdown at Three Mile Island." By the next day, there were also false reports (now known as the "bubble scare") that a hydrogen bubble could explode, causing a major disaster; many citizens voluntarily evacuated. To squelch that rumor, President Jimmy Carter visited the plant. By day 10, it was reported that the situation was finally under control. But although disaster was averted, this event left a lasting impression on public opinion about nuclear power in America.

Seven years later, in Chernobyl, Russia, the outcome was not as positive. When Chernobyl's Reactor 4 suffered a steam explosion and fire, releasing 5 percent of the nuclear reactor core into the atmosphere, two operators were killed immediately, followed by 28 other workers and several emergency workers who died of radiation poisoning soon afterward. The effects continued longer term as well: 19 more people died of cancers linked to the disaster, and between 1987 and 2004, a large number of childhood thyroid cancers in the area were also attributed to residual radiation. The surrounding area was badly contaminated as well. In 2005, a panel of experts at the Chernobyl Forum issued a report that concluded that, "apart from the [thyroid cancer] increase, there was no evidence of a major public health impact attributable to radiation exposure. There is no scientific evidence of increases in overall cancer incidence or mortality or in non-malignant disorders that could be related to radiation exposure." However, they also noted that people in the area did suffer psychologically, calling the effects a "paralyzing fatalism."

These two incidents, although somewhat faded from memory (and less impactful upon those who did not live through them), still provide a context for current discussions of a possible return to a reliance upon nuclear power. But there are other contexts as well: The growing concern about our reliance upon foreign oil, about the deleterious effects of coal-burning plants upon the environment (along with the many coal mining disasters and environmental impact of mining coal), and the growing energy needs of a country that is also increasingly committed to finding sustainable energy sources. These contexts have caused some to revisit to nuclear energy as a source of clean, efficient fuel. As such, among the many discussions of sustainability now being conducted in the United States, conversations about nuclear power is a particularly exigent one.

Another key point to keep in mind is that public support is crucial for any innovation. That is, even if nuclear power is clean and safe (and that argument is itself far from settled), without the support of American citizens and their representatives, it is unlikely that this large investment will be made. After all, much of the cost of nuclear power is upfront—the cost of building the plant that then can produce relatively inexpensive electricity. Of course, it is impossible to hear "nuclear" without also thinking about nuclear weaponry. For that reason, the context of this conversation—both past and present—is particularly important and involves emotional and reason-based issues.

This is also a particularly visual argument. Photographs of disasters and potential disasters, of protests by activists, and so forth, all add to the deep fear that many Americans have of this energy source. That is not to say that the fear is not justified or based in reasonable information. But as many of the excerpts below suggest, the context, too, is a determining factor, and so we need to consider the arguments that pictures make.

Below, you will find brief arguments that can help you consider the stasis points in this debate. As you read, note the way that each argument is developed within a different context—the country's energy future, the green movement, and the failed history of nuclear power. After reading these three brief pieces, and the excerpts and images from other citizens that follow, you will then have some context for developing your own thoughts on this topic.

Considering Contexts: Steven Chu, Small Modular Reactors will Expand the Ways We Use Atomic Power

Steven Chu is President Obama's Secretary of Energy. He is a physicist whose research area involves the trapping and cooling of atoms, research for which he was awarded a Nobel Prize. While this background makes his writings upon the topic of nuclear power particularly credible, his argument is also based upon his political role in the President's cabinet. How does he balance those two within this piece?

Small Modular Reactors will Expand
the Ways We Use Atomic Power

Steven Chu

America is on the cusp of reviving its nuclear power industry. Last month President Obama pledged more than $8 billion in conditional loan guarantees for what will be the first U.S. nuclear power plant to break ground in nearly three decades. And with the new authority granted by the president's 2011 budget request, the Department of Energy will be able to support between six and nine new reactors.

What does all of this mean for the country? This investment will provide enough clean energy to power more than six million American homes. It will also create tens of thousands of jobs in the years ahead.

Perhaps most importantly, investing in nuclear energy will position America to lead in a growing industry. World-wide electricity generation is projected to rise 77 percent by 2030. If we are serious about cutting carbon pollution, then nuclear power must be part of the solution. Countries such as China, South Korea, and India have recognized this and are making investments in nuclear power that are driving demand for nuclear technologies. Our choice is clear: Develop these technologies today or import them tomorrow.

That is why, even as we build a new generation of clean and safe nuclear plants, we are constantly looking ahead to the future of nuclear power. As this paper recently reported, one of the most promising areas is small modular reactors (SMRs). If we can develop this technology in the United States and build these reactors with American workers, we will have a key competitive edge.

Small modular reactors would be less than one-third the size of current plants. They have compact designs and could be made in factories and transported to sites by truck or rail. SMRs would be ready to "plug and play" upon arrival.

If commercially successful, SMRs would significantly expand the options for nuclear power and its applications. Their small size makes them suitable to small electric grids so they are a good option for locations that cannot accommodate large-scale plants. The modular construction process would make them more affordable by reducing capital costs and construction times.

Their size would also increase flexibility for utilities because they could add units as demand changes or use them for on-site replacement of aging fossil fuel plants. Some of the designs for SMRs use little or no water for cooling, which would reduce their environmental impact. Finally, some advanced concepts could potentially burn used fuel or nuclear waste, eliminating the plutonium that critics say could be used for nuclear weapons.

In his 2011 budget request, President Obama requested $39 million for a new program specifically for small modular reactors. Although the Department of Energy has supported advanced reactor technologies for years, this is the first time funding has been requested to help get SMR designs licensed for widespread commercial use.

Right now we are exploring a partnership with industry to obtain design certification from the Nuclear Regulatory Commission for one or two designs. These SMRs are based on proven light-water reactor technologies and could be deployed in about 10 years.

We are also accelerating our R&D efforts into other innovative reactor technologies. This includes developing high-temperature gas reactors that can provide carbon-free heat for industrial applications and advanced reactor designs that will harness much more of the energy from uranium.

Just as advanced computer modeling has revolutionized aircraft design—predicting how any slight adjustment to a wing design will affect the overall performance of the airplane, for example—we are working to apply modeling and simulation technologies to accelerate nuclear R&D. Scientists and engineers will be able to stand in the center of a virtual reactor, observing coolant flow, nuclear fuel performance, and even the reactor's response to changes in operating conditions. To achieve this potential, we are bringing together some of our nation's brightest minds to work under one roof in a new research center called the Nuclear Energy Modeling and Simulation Hub.

These efforts are restarting the nuclear power industry in the United States. But to truly promote nuclear power and other forms of carbon-free electricity, we need long-term incentives. The single most effective step we could take is to put a price on carbon by passing comprehensive energy and climate legislation. Requiring a gradual reduction in carbon emissions will make clean energy profitable and will fuel investment in nuclear power.

Considering Contexts: Patrick Moore, "Going Nuclear: A Green Makes the Case"

> Patrick Moore is an environmental activist who was an early member of Greenpeace and who now has his own organization called Greenspirit. For more information on Moore's relationship with the environmentalist community, see the headnotes to the two other selections he authored in this section of Conversations. Here, Moore argues for nuclear power as part of the "green" movement. What methods does he use to refute the arguments of those who oppose a renewed interest in this energy source?

Going Nuclear: A Green Makes the Case

Patrick Moore

In the early 1970s when I helped found Greenpeace, I believed that nuclear energy was synonymous with nuclear holocaust, as did most of my compatriots. That's the conviction that inspired Greenpeace's first voyage up the spectacular rocky northwest coast to protest the

conversations in context ⋯5

testing of U.S. hydrogen bombs in Alaska's Aleutian Islands. Thirty years on, my views have changed, and the rest of the environmental movement needs to update its views, too, because nuclear energy may be just the energy source that can save our planet from another possible disaster: catastrophic climate change.

Look at it this way: More than 600 coal-fired electric plants in the United States produce 36 percent of U.S. emissions—or nearly 10 percent of global emissions—of CO_2, the primary greenhouse gas responsible for climate change. Nuclear energy is the only large-scale, cost-effective energy source that can reduce these emissions while continuing to satisfy a growing demand for power. And these days it can do so safely.

I say that guardedly, of course, just days after Iranian President Mahmoud Ahmadinejad announced that his country had enriched uranium. "The nuclear technology is only for the purpose of peace and nothing else," he said. But there is widespread speculation that, even though the process is ostensibly dedicated to producing electricity, it is in fact a cover for building nuclear weapons.

And although I don't want to underestimate the very real dangers of nuclear technology in the hands of rogue states, we cannot simply ban every technology that is dangerous. That was the all-or-nothing mentality at the height of the Cold War, when anything nuclear seemed to spell doom for humanity and the environment. In 1979, Jane Fonda and Jack Lemmon produced a frisson of fear with their starring roles in *The China Syndrome,* a fictional evocation of nuclear disaster in which a reactor meltdown threatens a city's survival. Less than two weeks after the blockbuster film opened, a reactor core meltdown at Pennsylvania's Three Mile Island nuclear power plant sent shivers of very real anguish throughout the country.

What nobody noticed at the time, though, was that Three Mile Island was in fact a success story: The concrete containment structure did just what it was designed to do—prevent radiation from escaping into the environment. And although the reactor itself was crippled, there was no injury or death among nuclear workers or nearby residents. Three Mile Island was the only serious accident in the history of nuclear energy generation in the United States, but it was enough to scare us away from further developing the technology: There hasn't been a nuclear plant ordered up since then.

Today, there are 103 nuclear reactors quietly delivering just 20 percent of America's electricity. Eighty percent of the people living within 10 miles of these plants approve of them (that's not including the nuclear workers). Although I don't live near a nuclear plant, I am now squarely in their camp.

And I am not alone among seasoned environmental activists in changing my mind on this subject. British atmospheric scientist James Lovelock, father of the Gaia theory, believes that nuclear energy is the only way to avoid catastrophic climate change. Stewart Brand, founder of the "Whole Earth Catalog," says the environmental movement must embrace nuclear energy to wean ourselves from fossil fuels.

On occasion, such opinions have been met with excommunication from the anti-nuclear priesthood: The late British Bishop Hugh Montefiore, founder and director of Friends of the Earth, was forced to resign from the group's board after he wrote a pro-nuclear article in a church newsletter.

There are signs of a new willingness to listen, though, even among the staunchest anti-nuclear campaigners. When I attended the Kyoto climate meeting in Montreal last December, I spoke to a packed house on the question of a sustainable energy future. I argued that the only way to reduce fossil fuel emissions from electrical production is through an aggressive program of renewable energy sources (hydro-electric, geothermal heat pumps, wind, etc.) plus nuclear. The Greenpeace spokesperson was first at the mike for the question period, and I expected a tongue-lashing. Instead, he began by saying he agreed with much of what I said—not the nuclear bit, of course, but there was a clear feeling that all options must be explored.

Here's why: Wind and solar power have their place, but because they are intermittent and unpredictable they simply can't replace big baseload plants such as coal, nuclear, and hydroelectric. Natural gas, a fossil fuel, is too expensive already, and its price is too volatile to risk building big baseload plants. Given that hydroelectric resources are built pretty much to capacity, nuclear is, by elimination, the only viable substitute for coal. It's that simple.

That's not to say that there aren't real problems—as well as various myths—associated with nuclear energy. Each concern deserves care-ful consideration:

- *Nuclear energy is expensive.* It is in fact one of the least expen-sive energy sources. In 2004, the average cost of producing nuclear energy in the United States was less than two cents per kilowatt-hour, comparable with coal and hydroelectric. Advances in technology will bring the cost down further in the future.
- *Nuclear plants are not safe.* Although Three Mile Island was a suc-cess story, the accident at Chernobyl, 20 years ago this month, was not. But Chernobyl was an accident waiting to happen. This early model of Soviet reactor had no containment vessel, was an inher-ently bad design and its operators literally blew it up. The multi-agency U.N. Chernobyl Forum reported last year that 56 deaths could be directly attributed to the accident, most of those from radi-ation or burns suffered while fighting the fire. Tragic as those deaths were, they pale in comparison to the more than 5,000 coal-mining deaths that occur worldwide every year. No one has died of a radi-ation-related accident in the history of the U.S. civilian nuclear reac-tor program. (And although hundreds of uranium mine workers did died from radiation exposure underground in the early years of that industry, that problem was long ago corrected.)
- *Nuclear waste will be dangerous for thousands of years.* Within 40 years, used fuel has less than one-thousandth of the radioactivity

it had when it was removed from the reactor. And it is incorrect to call it waste, because 95 percent of the potential energy is still contained in the used fuel after the first cycle. Now that the United States has removed the ban on recycling used fuel, it will be possible to use that energy and to greatly reduce the amount of waste that needs treatment and disposal. Last month, Japan joined France, Britain and Russia in the nuclear-fuel-recycling business. The United States will not be far behind.

- *Nuclear reactors are vulnerable to terrorist attack.* The six-feet-thick reinforced concrete containment vessel protects the contents from the outside as well as the inside. And even if a jumbo jet did crash into a reactor and breach the containment, the reactor would not explode. There are many types of facilities that are far more vulnerable, including liquid natural gas plants, chemical plants and numerous political targets.

- *Nuclear fuel can be diverted to make nuclear weapons.* This is the most serious issue associated with nuclear energy and the most difficult to address, as the example of Iran shows. But just because nuclear technology can be put to evil purposes is not an argument to ban its use.

Over the past 20 years, one of the simplest tools—the machete—has been used to kill more than a million people in Africa, far more than were killed in the Hiroshima and Nagasaki nuclear bombings combined. What are car bombs made of? Diesel oil, fertilizer and cars. If we banned everything that can be used to kill people, we would never have harnessed fire.

The only practical approach to the issue of nuclear weapons proliferation is to put it higher on the international agenda and to use diplomacy and, where necessary, force to prevent countries or terrorists from using nuclear materials for destructive ends. And new technologies such as the reprocessing system recently introduced in Japan (in which the plutonium is never separated from the uranium) can make it much more difficult for terrorists or rogue states to use civilian materials to manufacture weapons.

The 600-plus coal-fired plants emit nearly 2 billion tons of CO_2 annually—the equivalent of the exhaust from about 300 million automobiles. In addition, the Clean Air Council reports that coal plants are responsible for 64 percent of sulfur dioxide emissions, 26 percent of nitrous oxides and 33 percent of mercury emissions. These pollutants are eroding the health of our environment, producing acid rain, smog, respiratory illness and mercury contamination.

Meanwhile, the 103 nuclear plants operating in the United States effectively avoid the release of 700 million tons of CO_2 emissions annually—the equivalent of the exhaust from more than 100 million automobiles. Imagine if the ratio of coal to nuclear were reversed so that only 20 percent of our electricity was generated from coal and 60 percent from nuclear. This would go a long way toward cleaning the air and reducing greenhouse gas emissions. Every responsible environmentalist should support a move in that direction.

Considering Contexts: Steven Cohen, "Nuclear Power is Complicated, Dangerous, and Definitely Not the Answer"

Steven Cohen is the director of the Master of Public Administration Program in Environmental Science and Policy at Columbia University's School of International and Public Affairs and the Earth Institute, and executive director of Columbia University's Earth Institute. The essay that follows was first published in 2006 on the environmental news site, Grist. This site claims to "dishing out environmental news and commentary with a wry twist since 1999— which, to be frank, was way before most people cared about such things." It also claims to go beyond the overused ideals of "going green" to deliver more credible information. As you read this piece, then, you should consider the reliability of the argument presented here and the implied dialogue with the previous two authors.

Nuclear Power is Complicated, Dangerous, and Definitely Not the Answer

Steven Cohen

If the media and the *New York Times* editorial page are any guide, nuclear power is the new green-energy option being embraced by environmentalists. This is not a new idea. The first mainstream statement of the "nuclear option" came from a 2003 report by MIT professors John Deutch and Ernest Moniz, "The Future of Nuclear Power."

As the duo's press release put it: "The nuclear option should be retained precisely because it is an important carbon-free source of power . . . Taking nuclear power off the table as a viable alternative will prevent the global community from achieving long-term gains in the control of carbon dioxide emissions."

While I share their alarm at our failure to address the problem of overabundant greenhouse-gas emissions, I am equally alarmed by their willingness to accept this dangerous, complicated, and politically controversial technology as a fix for our looming climate crisis.

Let's begin with dangerous, setting aside the obvious problems raised by Three Mile Island and Chernobyl. In the past few years, we have seen the horror that suicide bombers set loose in restaurants from Tel Aviv to Baghdad, and the danger of jets flying into skyscrapers. Do we really want to see what happens if a terrorist attacks a nuclear power plant? Are we so arrogant as to believe that these facilities are not already tempting, and vulnerable, targets?

Let's move on to complicated. The primary waste product of nuclear power, spent fuel rods, remains toxic for thousands of years. We do not yet know how to detoxify these waste products and, despite

20-some years of trying, we have not yet been able to establish a long-term repository anywhere in the United States.

Money is not the issue. We have the resources to build a nuclear-waste storage facility—under the Nuclear Waste Policy Act, customers of nuclear-generated electricity have been paying a $0.001 per kilo-watt-hour fee on their electric bills since 1983. Utilities pass the money into an account that has generated $24 billion over the years. Despite assurances that the proposed repository at Yucca Mountain in Nevada will last longer than the waste will be toxic, serious failings in storage technology and the risks of transportation have resulted in widespread opposition. Today, our nuclear waste goes into "spent fuel pools" at nuclear power plants like the one at Indian Point, just 35 miles north of New York City.

If the problem of detoxifying waste is beyond current technology—which is why we need to store it for thousands of years—what about the technology of power generation? The MIT study acknowledges that no power plant can be made risk-free. In reality, all technology carries risks. When we drive on an interstate highway, we face the risk of a crash. We accept the risk because it is relatively low, and because the effect of the risk is localized. A mistake in a nuclear power plant, however, can cause long-standing, widespread damage to people and ecosystems. Just ask the people who survived Chernobyl. The risk may be low, but the potential impact is high.

That leads to the politics. No one wants to host the nuclear-waste repository. No one wants a nuclear power plant next door. This is not an engineering or economic issue, but one of politics. In an increasingly crowded and interdependent world, people have grown more sensitive about questions of land-use development. Environmental justice has also reached the political stage, because the rich are better able to defend themselves against environmental insults than the poor. In the United States, local politics in many places has become the politics of land use and development. If we can't site Wal-Marts without a lengthy battle, why does anyone seriously think that we will be able to site the hundreds of new nuclear power plants that may be necessary to meet our energy needs without increasing greenhouse-gas emissions?

Moreover, why waste our time and effort on a so-called solution to climate change and high oil prices that has no real chance of gaining political traction? The largest impacts of global warming lie in the future, and are global in scope. But the problem of a nuclear accident would be comparatively local, and would potentially last for decades or centuries. The American political process is designed to respond to intense, local issues—that is why constructing even one nuclear power plant is a non-starter.

I agree that the answer to reducing carbon-dioxide emissions and reducing energy costs is to develop new technology. I agree that the need for a technological fix is urgent. The problem of energy prices and global climate change is real, and reaching crisis proportions.

conversations in context ...5

The American government should start a major research and development effort to create new power sources that are small-scale, decentralized, environmentally safe, and feasible in the political climate of the U.S. in the first decade of the 21st century.

Despite the promises of a previous generation, nuclear power never became "too cheap to meter." Rather, it became a discredited, mid-20th century mistake. Raising this issue is a distraction from the real work we need to undertake. We need to put our brain power to work on a way of reducing energy prices and emissions that can actually be implemented here in the United States—and very, very soon.

II. The Conversation

The conversation among the previous three authors reveals how the context within which each writer frames his argument can influence his stance. Chu writes as a physicist and Secretary of Energy; Moore writes as the founder of an organization devoted to helping industry and environmentalists work together (and for critics, an organization that has lost some of the ideals of the environmental movement); and Cohen writes as a public affairs specialist who warns against accepting too quickly the claims of those who forward nuclear energy as a green option. Consider the ways that each uses his own context to build his essay.

The words and images that follow widen the contexts even further, giving you a sample of the ongoing discussion about the future of nuclear power in America. Each snippet of this conversation offers alternative perspectives on this issue, and so opens upon areas for further research. As you read and view these pieces, look for stasis points among them that might help you do further research, and thus enter this conversation in informed ways.

It is a travesty that the nation that first harnessed nuclear energy has neglected it so long because of fads about supposed "green energy" and superstitions about nuclear power's dangers.

George Will, syndicated columnist

SOURCE: Newsweek, April 9, 2010 [http://www.newsweek.com/id/236177]

We conclude that, over at least the next 50 years, the best choice to meet these challenges is the open, once-through fuel cycle. We judge that there are adequate uranium resources available at reasonable cost to support this choice under a global growth scenario. Public acceptance will also be critical to expansion of nuclear power. Our survey results show that the public does not yet see nuclear power as a way to address global warming, suggesting that further public education may be necessary.

The Future of Nuclear Energy, An Interdisciplinary MIT Study

SOURCE: http://web.mit.edu/nuclearpower/pdf/nuclearpower-summary.pdf

---

In my mind, that's one of the most important numbers in the debate over whether to expand nuclear power in the U.S. The country currently has 104 commercial nuclear plants and these plants provide approximately 20 percent of the electricity for the nation. (The navy also has 103 nuclear reactors).

That's a plant-to-power ratio that's tough to beat. By contrast, the U.S. gets around 49 percent of its electricity from around 614 coal plants, and these coal plants belch carbon dioxide and particulate matter into the atmosphere. Coal mining and burning can also be linked to thousands of deaths annually around the world and shortened life spans.

And, despite all of the rooftops covered in solar panels you see today, solar right now only accounts for around 0.03 percent of power in the U.S. (That's three hundredths of a percent if you don't feel like counting the zeros." Although pro nuke factoids might sound a little weird coming from someone who works at a research firm dedicated to green technologies, it is difficult to look at America's energy needs for a long time without warming to nuclear. Simply put, nuclear remains one of the most feasible ways right now to produce large amounts of power consistently without generating carbon emissions.

Michael Kanellos, "Should the U.S. Expand Nuclear Power?", The Green Eye, CBS News

SOURCE: http://www.cbsnews.com/8301-504466162-6087612-504466.html

How does the image above of the cooling plants of a nuclear power plant help build the argument made by Kanellos? How is this iconic image of the cooling tower used in the photos below to send very different messages?

How is this image likely to affect viewers emotionally? Could a similar pathos appeal be used in words rather than images? How might you phrase that appeal in words? SOURCE: http://www.virginiawestern.edu/faculty/vwhansd/HIS122/Test4.html

What messages do the images on this cooling tower portray? Do the images relate directly to the context, or is this just a canvas for the painters? How is the image of a cooling tower changed when it becomes a mural? SOURCE: http://legalplanet.wordpress.com/2009/05/29/the-nuclear-option/

conversations in context ...5

In the modern era, the discovery of the potential energy that is stored within the structure of the atomic nucleus led to the usage of a new form of energy, that is nuclear energy. The concept of nuclear physics is constantly developing, as an independent discipline of science. The usage of nuclear energy often sounds incredible and every advantageous, but the use of this technology results into disaster if proper precautions are not taken.

Scholasticus K, blog post to The Buzzle by a "student of commerce, corporate law, and economics."

SOURCE: http://www.buzzle.com/articles/
    nuclear-energy-problems-and-dangers.html

The potential impact on the public from safety or waste management failure and the link to nuclear explosives technology are unique to nuclear energy among energy supply options. These characteristics and the fact that nuclear is more costly, make it impossible today to make a credible case for the immediate expanded use of nuclear power.

– The Future of Nuclear Power, MIT (2003)

SOURCE: quoted in: http:/
    /www.ieer.org/reports/
    insurmountablerisks/
    summary.pdf

The large number of reactors required for nuclear power to play any meaningful role in reducing greenhouse gas emissions greatly complicates the efforts required to deal with its unique vulnerabilities, including the potential for the nuclear fuel cycle to enable nuclear weapons proliferation, the risks from catastrophic reactor accidents, and the difficulties of managing long-lived and highly radiotoxic nuclear waste. The rapid rate of nuclear construction required to meet the global or steady-state growth scenarios would also put great pressures on the nuclear industry and on regulatory bodies and make it more difficult to achieve or sustain the substantial improvements in cost that have been envisioned by nuclear proponents.
Brice Smith, "Insurmountable Risks: The Dangers of Using Nuclear Power to Combat Global Climate Change," A Report by the Institute for Energy and Environmental Research

SOURCE: http://www.ieer.org/reports/insurmountablerisks/summary.pdf

conversations in context ...5

It's commonly believed that nuclear power plants are unsafe, unstable, frightening. This perception can be blamed primarily on a few movies and the public revulsion at Hiroshima. But the truth is, nuclear power is surprisingly safe, with hardly any deaths and hardly any pollution. Consider the following:

In 2006, 47 American miners died in coal mining accidents; many others were killed by mining-related diseases like black lung and cancer. Add to this untold deaths from the sooty pollution put out by coal, and you have a fairly large number.

Many more people each year die from oil-related accidents, primarily on ocean-based drilling rigs. In addition, with oil there's always the risk of a terrible leak that can lead to poisoning of the ocean and the death of a wide swath of marine life. Oil is also associated with greenhouse gases, refinery fires, and deaths from pollution—not clean energy.

Hydroelectric power, which is perhaps the cleanest bulk power available, has a rate of approximately $2\frac{1}{2}$; times the deaths related to coal in accidents—so over a hundred deaths a year related to hydroelectric power in the US.

But in the United States, there has never been a death related to a nuclear power accident—not at a plant, not due to a leak, not due to the disposal of nuclear waste.

Put it another way; worldwide, for the electricity gained, per billion megawatt-hours, there have been:

- 101 hydroelectric deaths.
- 39 coal-related deaths.
- 10 gas-related deaths.
- Less than one nuclear-related death— and that's in spite of the Chernobyl accident.

Jamie K. Wilson, "Nuclear Power Has an Undeserved Bad Reputation."

SOURCE: http://www.associatedcontent.com/ article/361189/relative_dangers_of_ nuclear_ power.html?cat=27

By the end of the century, climate change and its impacts may be the dominant direct driver of biodiversity loss and changes in ecosystem services globally . . . The balance of scientific evidence suggests that there will be a significant net harmful impact on ecosystem services worldwide if global mean surface temperature increases more than 2° Celsius above preindustrial levels or at rates greater than 0.2° Celsius per decade (medium certainty).—United Nations Millennium Ecosystem Assessment (2005)

SOURCE: quoted in: http:/ /www.ieer.org/reports/ insurmountablerisks/ summary.pdf

conversations in context ...5

"The ability to repair damage and replace cells, we discovered in the last 50 years, show how radiation doesn't cause damage except under extreme circumstances," he says. "The radiation that a patient gets in one day from a course of radiotherapy treatment, it would take a million hours of exposure for someone standing in the radioactive <u>waste</u> hall of Sellafield. And, if you have radiotherapy, it goes on for several weeks."

Wade Allison, Oxford University

SOURCE: http://www.guardian.co.uk/environment/ 2010/jan/10/nuclear-power-irrational-fears

This photograph of nuclear energy protestors accompanied the Guardian article, "Irrational Fears Give Nuclear Power a Bad Name, Says Oxford Scientist." How does that context, and the previous quotation from Wade Alison, affect our view of the visual? SOURCE: http://www. guardian.co.uk/environment/2010/jan/10/ nuclear-power-irrational-fears

I do not find [Allison's] these arguments particularly convincing. I have to say, when I've reviewed the evidence, it is very difficult to detect the adverse effects of radiation at low levels because the predicted excess risk of cancer is small and is easily hidden in the noise of other factors like smoking and diet and drinking. All of the people who hang on to these arguments are missing the point. If you take the evidence as a whole from radiation epidemiology, there's probably a risk from cancer arising from small doses of radiation [and] they're around about what you get from a linear no-threshold dose response.

Susan Short, clinical senior lecturer in oncology at University College London

SOURCE: http://www.guardian.co. uk/environment/2010/jan/10/ nuclear-power-irrational-fears:

conversations in context ...5

This newspaper story appeared in a county paper nearby to Three Mile Island. How do the headlines and photograph work together? How does it compare to the image of the Chernobyl site below? Looked at in retrospect, is the photo journalistic or argumentative—or somewhere in between?

SOURCE: http://www.yorkblog.com/yorktownsquare/2007/03/

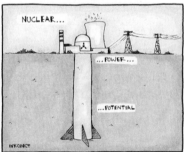

Though cartoons work through humor, the message is often serious. What is the argument made by this cartoon? Does it have a "thesis," and if so, what is it?

SOURCE: http://www.inkcinct.com.au/web/australian/political/2006—political.htm

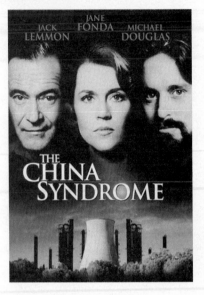

The China Syndrome was a fictional film about the potential dangers of nuclear power which debuted eerily just twelve days before the Three Mile Island incident. Does this movie poster itself make an argument? What can you find out about the politics beyond the making of this film? Can fiction have real effects?

SOURCE: http://history.sandiego.edu/gen/ filmnotes/chinasyndrome.html

III. Entering the Conversation

As the various perspectives expressed in words and images in this section indicate, the conversation about whether the U.S. should renew its attention to nuclear power as part of a sustainable, environmentally sound policy has many facets. As a researcher and writer, as well as a stakeholder in this debate (as all U.S. citizens are), there are many ways into this dialogue. After all, this issue has implications for all fields of study; as such, it is a topic that you can approach through your own disciplinary lens.

For example, businesspeople have a large stake here, because sustainable energy is important for both those directly engaged in providing energy and for those who consume energy for their endeavors. How might nuclear energy play a role in the growth of specific businesses? What marketing opportunities does it provide? How can government and industry collaborate in the future of this resource? For those interested in political science and public policy, the history of nuclear energy can form a fine area of analysis. For those involved in philosophy, the ethical implications of moving in this direction may be worth examining, whereas for social scientists, the psychological effects on the individual and community of a nearby nuclear power plant are worth examining. Of course, for scientists, there are multiple research areas on the processes of nuclear energy production, how it has advanced, and its effect upon natural habitats. All of these areas and many more provide possible points of entry into the conversation.

Your entry into the conversation, of course, will begin from the questions you ask about nuclear energy (or other energy sources on the horizon, if you choose to focus upon another alternative). Some of those questions include

- Whether recent scientific advances have made the process of producing nuclear energy safer, more efficient, and more environmentally sound

- Whether there are any potential solutions to one of the thorniest issues surrounding nuclear power—the disposal of nuclear waste

- Whether the public seems ready to support the return to nuclear energy

- Whether businesses are likely to make the huge upfront investment that is required in order to build and outfit a nuclear power plant

- Whether regulatory agencies are effective enough to protect the public safety

- Whether the environmental community is likely to support this energy source and/or what it would take to gain their support

- Whether your local community would be willing to accept a nuclear power plant in its environs

- Whether current nuclear power plants remain safe, or whether they pose an imminent or long-term threat

conversations in context ...5

- Whether the existence of a nuclear power plant in a community causes undue anxiety for that community

- Whether other alternative energy sources are a more feasible or more sustainable choice

The list, of course, could go on; indeed, you would find many other conversations on this topic if you do more research. In any case, as you weigh in on this topic, be sure to consider the larger contexts here and decide what other information you may need to write in informed ways. The following are a few suggestions to get you started. You can use them as jumping-off points for further reading and research. Feel free to take them in whatever directions your interests and your research take you, or to develop related topics on your own.

1. One of the questions surrounding a possible renewal of our commitment to nuclear energy centers on whether events at Three Mile Island and Chernobyl, or the connection between nuclear energy and nuclear weaponry, still make this option untenable in public opinion. In order to research this question, you might do a combination of secondary and primary researches. You could begin by better understanding the events themselves and the public reaction to them in more detail, taking into account both the facts of the cases and the responses on the part of government and citizens. There are many first-hand accounts, news stories, and retrospectives that can help you better understand the full historical context. Then, you can build on that context by doing some primary research to see whether those perspectives on nuclear energy linger. There are a number of ways that you might do so. You could use surveys, interviews, and/or focus groups to gather opinions about nuclear energy. You could look at public opinion polling across generations on the topic. Or you could set up a wiki or blog to gather opinions, collecting demographic information as well that would help you note differences in public opinion across generations, educational level, or other factors. This will help you reach some conclusions and write about the ways opinions may have changed (or not) across time. It might also help you predict the likelihood of public support for nuclear power.

2. Informed publics usually make better decisions than publics that base their decisions upon second-hand or sketchy information. In order to help educate the public about nuclear energy, you could create a paper or informational campaign in some other medium (website, video, public service announcements) that helps the public better understand the facts—as far as we know them—about the risks and benefits on nuclear energy. To do so, of course, you will need to first inform yourself, which means turning to the most reliable sources you can find and studying the work of those who understand the science behind this technology—and who do not have a specific agenda. That will likely lead you to articles from peer-reviewed journals, which follow careful scientific protocols in their methods. Your job will be to then provide information in ways that are at once accurate and

understandable by a general audience. Learning to do so can also help you hone your writing skills, giving you experience with writing clearly about complex topics.

3. As the images surrounding the disaster at Chernobyl and the near-disaster at Three Mile Island make clear, much of the argument about nuclear energy has been waged in pictures and in other visual media like the news and film. This fact gives you the opportunity to analyze not just the issue itself, but also the ways that the public can be influenced by visual rhetoric. Collect a variety of arguments that rely upon these alternative forms of arguments—films (both fiction and documentaries), television and Internet news sources, bumper stickers, t-shirts, and so forth—upon which the campaigns for and/or against nuclear energy have been made. Then, using the skills of rhetorical analysis, weigh the impact of these visual forms of argument upon the emotions of the audiences, the credibility of the sources, and the reasoning that they imply. Write an analysis that draws some conclusions about the place of visual argument in the debate about nuclear power; consider also what your analysis suggests about how public policy issues like this one are influenced by visual media.

conversations in context ...5

CHAPTER **10**

Sustaining Our Environment: Who Are the Best Guardians?

Patrick Moore

Hard Choices for the Environmental Movement

In the case of Patrick Moore, not only his views, but also his biography, have become the topic of a good deal of conversation. While Moore claims publicly and in this piece to be "one of a dozen or so activists who founded Greenpeace," one of the most well-known environmental activist groups, current leadership of Greenpeace has denied this foundational role of Moore. They suggest that, though he was for a time one of its leaders, he was not among those who first imagined and created the organization. This dispute, and this rift, has come about because Moore has separated himself from what he now calls the "extremist" practices of many environmental groups. In 1991, Moore founded Greenspirit, an organization whose mission reflects Moore's interest in sustainability through consensus-building among all of the stakeholders in environmental protection, including industrial corporations. As you will read in the Greenpeace statement on Patrick Moore, Greenpeace views this shift not so much as consensus building, as a selling-out to corporate interests. So as you read this dialogue between Moore and representatives of Greenpeace, your task will be to sort out the various parts of this dispute and to consider which arguments seem to you to be most compelling. To do so effectively, you may need to do some fact-checking of your own.

More than twenty years ago I was one of a dozen or so 1 activists who founded Greenpeace in the basement of the Unitarian Church in Vancouver. The Vietnam War was raging and nuclear holocaust seemed closer every day. We linked peace, ecology, and a talent for media communications and went on to build the world's largest environmental activist organization. By 1986 Greenpeace was established in 26 countries and had an income of over $100 million per year.

In 1986 the mainstream of western society was busy adopting 2 the environmental agenda that was considered radical only fifteen years earlier. By 1989 the combined impact of Chernobyl, the Exxon Valdez, the threat of global warming and the ozone hole clinched the debate. All but a handful of reactionaries joined the call for sustainable development and environmental protection.

Whereas previously the leaders of the environmental move- 3 ment found themselves on the outside railing at the gates of power, they were now invited to the table in boardrooms and caucuses around the world. For environmentalists, accustomed to the politics of confrontation, this new era of acceptance posed a challenge as great as any campaign to save the planet.

For me, Greenpeace is about ringing an ecological fire alarm, 4 waking mass consciousness to the true dimensions of our global predicament, pointing out the problems and defining their nature. Greenpeace doesn't necessarily have the solutions to those problems and certainly isn't equipped to put them into practice. That requires the combined efforts of governments, corporations, public institutions and environmentalists. This demands a high degree of cooperation and collaboration. The politics of blame and shame must be replaced with the politics of working together and win-win.

Collaboration versus Confrontation

It was no coincidence that the round-table, consensus-based 5 negotiation process was adopted by thousands of environmental leaders. It is the logical tool for working in the new spirit of green cooperation. It may not be a perfect system for decision-making, but like Churchill said about democracy, "It's the worst form of government except for all the others." A collaborative approach promises to give environmental issues their fair consideration in relation to the traditional economic and social priorities.

Some environmentalists didn't see it that way. Indeed, there 6 had always been a minority of extremists who took a "No Compromise in Defense of Mother Nature" position. They were the monkey-wrenchers, tree-spikers and boat scuttlers of the Earth

First! and Paul Watson variety. Considered totally uncool by the largely pacifist, intellectual mainstream of the movement, they were a colorful but renegade element.

7   Since its founding in the late 60's the modern environmental movement had created a vision that was international in scope and had room for people of all political persuasions. We prided ourselves in subscribing to a philosophy that was "trans-political, trans-ideological, and trans-national" in character. For Greenpeace, the Creed legend "Warriors of the Rainbow" referred to people of all colors and creeds, working together for a greener planet. The traditional sharp division between left and right was rendered meaningless by the common desire to protect our life support systems. Violence against people and property were the only taboos. Non-violent direct action and peaceful civil disobedience were the hallmarks of the movement. Truth mattered and science was respected for the knowledge it brought to the debate.

8   Now this broad-based vision is challenged by a new philosophy of radical environmentalism. In the name of "deep ecology" many environmentalists have taken a sharp turn to the ultra-left, ushering in a mood of extremism and intolerance. As a clear signal of this new agenda, in 1990 Greenpeace called for a "grassroots revolution against pragmatism and compromise."

9   As an environmentalist in the political center I now find myself branded a traitor and a sellout by this new breed of saviors. My name appears in Greenpeace's "Guide to Anti-Environmental Organizations." Even fellow Greenpeace founder and campaign comrade, Bob Hunter, refers to me as the "eco-Judas." Yes, I am trying to help the Canadian forest industry improve its performance so we might be proud of it again. As chair of the Forest Practices Committee of the Forest Alliance of B.C. I have lead the process of drafting and implementing the Principles of Sustainable Forestry that have been adopted by a majority of the industry. These Principles establish goals for environmental protection, forest management and public involvement. They are providing a framework for dialogue and action towards improvements in forest practices. Why shouldn't I make a contribution to environmental reform in the industry my grandfather and father have worked in for over 90 years?

10   It's not that I don't think the environment is in deep trouble. The hole in the ozone is real and we are overpopulating and overexploiting many of the earth's most productive ecosystems. I believe this is all the more reason to hang on to ideas like freedom, democracy, internationalism, and one-human-family. Our species is probably in for a pretty rough ride during the coming decades. It would be nice to think we could maintain a semblance of civilization while we work through these difficult times.

The Rise of Eco-Extremism

Two profound events triggered the split between those advocat-   11
ing a pragmatic or "liberal" approach to ecology and the new
"zero-tolerance" attitude of the extremists. The first event, mentioned previously, was the widespread adoption of the environmental agenda by the mainstream of business and government.
This left environmentalists with the choice of either being drawn
into collaboration with their former "enemies" or of taking ever
more extreme positions. Many environmentalists chose the latter route. They rejected the concept of "sustainable development" and took a strong "anti-development" stance.

Surprisingly enough the second event that caused the envi-   12
ronmental movement to veer to the left was the fall of the Berlin
Wall. Suddenly the international peace movement had a lot less
to do. Pro-Soviet groups in the West were discredited. Many of
their members moved into the environmental movement bringing with them their eco-Marxism and pro-Sandinista sentiments.

These factors have contributed to a new variant of the envi-   13
ronmental movement that is so extreme that many people,
including myself, believe its agenda is a greater threat to the
global environment than that posed by mainstream society.
Some of the features of eco-extremism are:

- It is anti-human. The human species is characterized as a
  "cancer" on the face of the earth. The extremists perpetuate the belief that all human activity is negative whereas
  the rest of nature is good. This results in alienation from
  nature and subverts the most important lesson of ecology;
  that we are all part of nature and interdependent with it.
  This aspect of environmental extremism leads to disdain
  and disrespect for fellow humans and the belief that it
  would be "good" if a disease such as AIDS were to wipe
  out most of the population.
- It is anti-technology and anti-science. Eco-extremists
  dream of returning to some kind of technologically primitive society. Horse-logging is the only kind of forestry
  they can support. All large machines are seen as inherently
  destructive and "unnatural." The Sierra Club's recent
  book, "Clearcut: the Tragedy of Industrial Forestry", is an
  excellent example of this perspective. "Western industrial
  society" is rejected in its entirety as is nearly every known
  forestry system including shelterwood, seed tree and
  small group selection. The word "Nature" is capitalized
  every time it is used and we are encouraged to "find our
  place" in the world through "shamanic journeying" and
  "swaying with the trees." Science is invoked only as a

means of justifying the adoption of beliefs that have no basis in science to begin with.

- It is anti-organization. Environmental extremists tend to expect the whole world to adopt anarchism as the model for individual behavior. This is expressed in their dislike of national governments, multinational corporations, and large institutions of all kinds. It would seem that this critique applies to all organizations except the environmental movement itself. Corporations are criticized for taking profits made in one country and investing them in other countries, this being proof that they have no "allegiance" to local communities. Where is the international environmental movements allegiance to local communities? How much of the money raised in the name of aboriginal peoples has been distributed to them? How much is dedicated to helping loggers thrown out of work by environmental campaigns? How much to research silvicultural systems that are environmentally and economically superior?

- It is anti-trade. Eco-extremists are not only opposed to "free trade" but to international trade in general. This is based on the belief that each "bioregion" should be self-sufficient in all its material needs. If it's too cold to grow bananas—too bad. Certainly anyone who studies ecology comes to realize the importance of natural geographic units such as watersheds, islands, and estuaries. As foolish as it is to ignore ecosystems it is absurd to put fences around them as if they were independent of their neighbors. In its extreme version, bio-regionalism is just another form of ultra-nationalism and gives rise to the same excesses of intolerance and xenophobia.

- It is anti-free enterprise. Despite the fact that communism and state socialism has failed, eco-extremists are basically anti-business. They dislike "competition" and are definitely opposed to profits. Anyone engaging in private business, particularly if they are successful, is characterized as greedy and lacking in morality. The extremists do not seem to find it necessary to put forward an alternative system of organization that would prove efficient at meeting the material needs of society. They are content to set themselves up as the critics of international free enterprise while offering nothing but idealistic platitudes in its place.

- It is anti-democratic. This is perhaps the most dangerous aspect of radical environmentalism. The very foundation of our society, liberal representative democracy, is rejected as being too "human-centered." In the name of "speaking for the trees and other species" we are faced with a movement that would usher in an era of eco-fascism. The "planetary police" would "answer to no one but Mother Earth herself."

- It is basically anti-civilization. In its essence, eco-extremism rejects virtually everything about modern life. We are told that nothing short of returning to primitive tribal society can save the earth from ecological collapse. No more cities, no more airplanes, no more polyester suits. It is a naive vision of a return to the Garden of Eden.

As a result of the rise of environmental extremism it has   14
become difficult for the public, government agencies and industry to determine which demands are reasonable and which are not. It's almost as if the person or group that makes the most outrageous accusations and demands is automatically called "the environmentalist" in the news story. Industry, no matter how sincere in its efforts to satisfy legitimate environmental concerns, is branded "the threat to the environment." Let me give you a few brief examples.

The Brent Spar

In 1995, Shell Oil was granted permission by the British Environ-   15
ment Ministry to dispose of the oil rig "Brent Spar" in deep water in the North Sea. Greenpeace immediately accused Shell of using the sea as a "dustbin." Greenpeace campaigners maintained that there were hundreds of tons of petroleum wastes on board the Brent Spar and that some of these were radioactive. They organized a consumer boycott of Shell service stations, costing the company millions in sales. German Chancellor Helmut Kohl denounced the British government's decision to allow the dumping. Caught completely off guard, Shell ordered the tug that was already towing the rig to its burial site to turn back. They then announced they had abandoned the plan for deep-sea disposal. This angered British Prime Minister, John Major.

The Brent Spar was towed into a Norwegian fjord where it   16
remains to this day. Independent investigation revealed that the rig had been properly cleaned and did not contain the toxic and radioactive waste claimed by Greenpeace. Greenpeace wrote to Shell apologizing for the factual error. But they did not change their position on deep-sea disposal despite the fact that on-land disposal will cause far greater environmental impact.

During all the public outrage directed against Shell for daring   17
to sink a large piece of steel and concrete it was never noted that Greenpeace had purposely sunk its own ship off the coast of New Zealand in 1986. When the French government bombed

and sunk the Rainbow Warrior in Auckland Harbor in 1985, the vessel was permanently disabled. It was later re-floated, patched up, cleaned and towed to a marine park where it was sunk in shallow water as a dive site. Greenpeace said the ship would be an artificial reef and would support increased marine life.

18   The Brent Spar and the Rainbow Warrior are in no way fundamentally different from one another. The sinking of the Brent Spar could also be rationalized as providing habitat for marine creatures. It's just that the public relations people at Shell are not as clever as those at Greenpeace. And in this case Greenpeace got away with using misinformation even though they had to admit their error after the fact.

WWF and Species Extinction

19   In March 1996, the International Panel on Forests of the United Nations held its first meeting in Geneva. The media paid little attention to what appeared to be one more ponderous assemblage of delegates speaking in unintelligible UN-ese. As it turned out, the big story to emerge from the meeting had nothing to do with the Panel on Forests itself. In what has become a common practice, The World Wide Fund for Nature (WWF) chose to use the occasion of the UN meeting as a platform for its own news release.

20   The WWF news release, which was widely picked up by the international media, made three basic points. They claimed that species were going extinct at a faster rate now than at any time since the dinosaurs disappeared 65 million years ago. They said that 50,000 species were now becoming extinct each year due to human activity. But of most significance to the subject of forests, WWF claimed that the main cause of species extinction was "commercial logging," that is, the forest industry. They provided absolutely no evidence for this so-called fact about logging and the media asked no hard questions. The next day newspapers around the world proclaimed the forest industry to be the main destroyer of species.

21   Since that announcement I have asked on numerous occasions for the name of a single species that has been rendered extinct due to forestry, particularly in my home country, Canada. Not one Latin name has been provided. It is widely known that human activity has been responsible for the extinction of many species down through history. These extinctions have been caused by hunting, the conversion of forest and grassland to farming and human settlement, and the introduction of exotic diseases and predators. Today, the main cause of species extinction is deforestation, over 90% of which is caused by agriculture and urban development. Why is WWF telling the public that logging is the main cause of species extinction?

While I do not wish to guess at the WWF's motivation, it is   22
instructional to consider the question from a different angle. That
is, if forestry does not generally cause species extinction, what
other compelling reason is there to be against it? Surely the fact
that logging is unsightly for a few years after the trees are cut is
not sufficient reason to curtail Canada's most important industry.

Despite the WWF's failure to support its accusations, the myth   23
that forestry causes widespread species extinction lives on. How
can a largely urban public be convinced that this is not the case?
The challenge is a daunting one for an industry that has been
cast in the role of Darth Vader when it should be recognized for
growing trees and providing wood, the most renewable material
used in human civilization.

Chlorine in Manufacturing

I don't mean to pick on Greenpeace but they are close to my   24
heart and have strayed farther from the truth than I can toler-
ate. In this case the issue is chlorine, an element that is used in
a wide variety of industrial, medical, and agricultural applications. In 1985 Greenpeace took up the campaign to eliminate
chlorine from all industrial processes, to essentially remove it
from human use despite its enormous benefits to society.

The basis of the campaign was the discovery that the use of   25
chlorine as a bleaching agent in the pulp and paper industry
resulted in the production of minute quantities of dioxin, some
of which ended up in waste water. The industry responded
quickly and within five years of the discovery had virtually eliminated dioxins by switching to a different form of chlorine or
eliminating chlorine altogether. The addition of secondary treatment resulted in further improvements. Independent scientists
demonstrated that after these measures were taken, pulp mills
using chlorine had no more environmental impact than those
that used no chlorine. Did Greenpeace accept the science? No,
they tried to discredit the scientists and to this day continue a
campaign that is based more on fear than fact. It's as if chlorine
should be banned from the periodic table of elements altogether so future generations won't know it exists.

Forestry

This critique of radical environmentalism is nowhere more   26
appropriate than in the present debate over managing our
forests and manufacturing forest products. Human management of forests is portrayed as somehow "unnatural." As mentioned before, horse-logging appeals to the extremists because
it uses less technology. My response to this idea is that it would

make more sense for the city people to use horses to get their 150 pound bodies to work in the morning and let the loggers have the engines from their cars so they can move the heavy loads in the forest. I suppose this is a result of my twisted country perspective.

27   For Greenpeace the zero chlorine campaign was just the beginning. Now Greenpeace Germany is leading a campaign for a global ban on clearcutting in any forest. They want lumber and paper manufacturers to use a label that states their product is "clearcut-free." Canada has been chosen as the target for consumer boycotts because it uses clearcutting in forestry. It doesn't matter that the world's most knowledgeable silviculturists believe that clearcutting is the most appropriate form of harvesting in many types of forest. It doesn't matter that most forestry in Germany is by the clearcut method, they want to boycott us anyway. What matters is that it makes a good fundraising campaign in Europe.

28   The public is unaware of the basic flaws in the Greenpeace campaign to end clearcutting worldwide. They do not realize that there is no clear definition of the term "clearcutting" and that Greenpeace refuses to engage in a dialogue to determine the precise nature of what it is they are opposed to. It is also not widely realized that there is no such thing as a supply of pulp and paper that is "clearcut-free." The practice of clearcutting is so widespread that it would be impossible to obtain a supply of wood chips that came from forests where only single-tree selection forestry is practiced.

29   Perhaps the most cynical aspect of the Greenpeace campaign is their assertion that forests are clearcut in British Columbia to make tissue paper and toilet paper for Europeans. They use the slogan "When you blow your nose in Europe you are blowing away the ancient forests of Canada" to imply that Europeans could save Canadian forests if they would stop buying tissue made from Canadian pulp. Everyone who has studied Canadian forestry, including Greenpeace, knows that the pulp and paper industry in British Columbia is based entirely on the waste products of the saw milling industry. The forests are harvested to supply high value solid wood for furniture, interior woodwork and construction. Only the wastes from making lumber and those logs that are unsuitable for saw milling are made into pulp. If we did not make pulp from these wastes they would have to be burned or left to rot as was the case in the past.

30   Rather than promoting unilateral boycotts that are based on misinformation and coercion, organizations like Greenpeace should recognize the need for internationally accepted criteria for sustainable forestry and forest products manufacturing. Through dialogue and international cooperation it would be possible to achieve agreement and end the unfair practice of

singling out an individual nation for sanctions. Unfortunately they have now joined in the effort to spoil an International Convention on Forests. Their reasons for opposing a convention are not valid and amount to a transparent front for a strong anti-forestry attitude.

Conclusion

It is not reasonable to expect the environmental movement to   31
drop its extremist agenda overnight. The rise of extremism is a major feature of the movement's evolution and is now deeply embedded in its political structure. We can hope that as time passes the movement will be retaken by more politically centrist, science-based leaders and that the extreme wing will be marginalized. At the same time, we must remember that most of the larger environmental groups such as the World Wildlife Fund, Greenpeace, the Sierra Club, the Natural Resources Defense Council etc. do have many members and campaign teams that are reasonable and based on good science. It's just that for the time being, major elements of their organizations have been hi-jacked by people who are politically motivated, lack science, and are often using the rhetoric of environmentalism to promote other causes such as class struggle and anti-corporatism.

The only way industry can successfully help to promote a   32
more pragmatic and reasonable environmental movement is to prove that it is willing and able to avoid future damage to the environment and to correct past abuses. In other words, if your house is in order, there will be little or nothing for extremists to use as a reason for taking an essentially "anti-industry" position.

The challenge for environmental leaders is to resist the path   33
of ever increasing extremism and to know when to talk rather than fight. To remain credible and effective they must reject the anti-human, anarchistic approach. This is made difficult by the fact that many individuals and their messengers, the media, are naturally attracted to confrontation and sensation. It isn't easy to get excited about a committee meeting when you could be bringing the state to its knees at a blockade.

The best approach to our present predicament is to recognize   34
the validity of both the bio-regional and the global visions for social and environmental sustainability. Issues such as overpopulation and sustainable forest practices require international agreements. Composting of food wastes and bicycle repairs are best accomplished locally. We must think and act both globally and locally, always cognizant of impacts at one level abused by actions at another. Extremism that rejects this approach will only bring disaster to all species, including humans.

Greenpeace International

Statement on Patrick Moore

Greenpeace International is an NGO (non-governmental organization) that evolved from the peace movements of the 1960s and 1970s, and which has since become nearly synonymous with environmental advocacy. This group has been on the forefront of issues related to global warming, deforestation, the dangers of oil drilling and transportation, commercial overfishing and whaling, and many other issues that concern the environmental movement. Some describe its methods as confrontational and extreme, others as reasoned, well-planned, and necessary. It is in that space between the two views that the dispute between former Greenpeace member Patrick Moore and the current organization exists. This piece attempts to discredit Moore, his claims to be a founder of Greenpeace, and what they see as his corporate interests. As you read, consider how this organizational statement uses the occasion to support and defend its own positions. A response by Moore follows in this chapter.

1   WASHINGTON—Patrick Moore often misrepresents himself in the media as an environmental "expert" or even an "environmentalist," while offering anti-environmental opinions on a wide range of issues and taking a distinctly anti-environmental stance. He also exploits long-gone ties with Greenpeace to sell himself as a speaker and pro-corporate spokesperson, usually taking positions that Greenpeace opposes.

2   While it is true that Patrick Moore was a member of Green-peace in the 1970s, in 1986 he abruptly turned his back on the very issues he once passionately defended. He claims he "saw the light" but what Moore really saw was an opportunity for financial gain. Since then he has gone from defender of the planet to a paid representative of corporate polluters.

3   Patrick Moore promotes such anti-environmental positions as clearcut logging, nuclear power, farmed salmon, PVC (vinyl) production, genetically engineered crops, and mining. Clients for his consulting services are a veritable Who's Who of companies that Greenpeace has exposed for environmental misdeeds, including Monsanto, Weyerhaeuser, and BHP Minerals.

4   Moore's claims run from the exaggerated to the outrageous to the downright false, including that "clear-cutting is good for

forests" and Three Mile Island was actually "a success story" because the radiation from the partially melted core was contained. That is akin to saying "my car crash was a success because I only cracked my skull and didn't die."

By exploiting his former ties to Greenpeace, Moore portrays 5 himself as a prodigal son who has seen the error of his ways. Unfortunately, the media—especially conservative media—give him a platform for his views, and often do so without mentioning the fact that he is a paid spokesperson for polluting companies.

The following provides a brief overview of Patrick Moore's 6 positions and his history of working for corporate polluters.

Truth V. Fiction on Patrick Moore

Patrick Moore claims he is an environmentalist and represents 7 an independent scientific perspective on forest issues.

TRUTH: Moore was paid by the British Columbia Forest 8 Alliance, an industry-front group set up by the public relations firm Burson-Marsteller (the same PR firm that represented Exxon after the Valdez oil spill and Union Carbide after the Bhopal chemical disaster). The BC Forest Alliance is funded primarily by the logging industry. He also has ties to other corporations including Monsanto and Weyerhaeuser.

According to Moore, logging is good for forests causing refor- 9 estation, not deforestation.

TRUTH: Webster's Dictionary defines deforestation as "the 10 action or process of clearing of forests."

The argument advanced by forest industry spin-doctors that 11 clear-cutting "causes reforestation, not deforestation" is without basis in fact. It is like arguing that having a heart attack improves your health because of the medical treatment you receive afterwards.

According to Moore: "Forward-thinking environmentalists 12 and scientists have made clear, technology has now progressed to the point where the activist fear mongering about the safety of nuclear energy bears no resemblance to reality."

TRUTH: The Nuclear Regulatory Commission's Advisory 13 Committee on Reactor Safeguards (ACRS) concluded years ago that the lack of containment on Department of Energy (DOE) sponsored advanced nuclear reactor designs constituted a "major safety trade-off."

Patrick Moore has recently begun touting the "safety" of 14 nuclear energy at the behest of the Nuclear Energy Institute (NEI), which is being bankrolled by the nuclear industry to promote nuclear energy as clean and safe energy. The public relations firm Hill & Knowlton has been hired to roll out a multi-million dollar campaign to repackage Moore's propaganda to convince congressional leaders of public support for the building of new nuclear plants.

15   Hill and Knowlton are most well known for their public relations work defending the tobacco industry. The PR firm has also worked for industry interests to stall action to protect the ozone layer by executing "a carefully designed campaign attacking the science behind the ozone depletion and delaying government action for two years. This was enough time for DuPont to bring new, ozone-friendly chemicals to market." Austin American Statesman, Cox News Service Jeff Nesmith June 26, 2005 http://www.statesman.com/search/content/insight/stories/06/26doubt.html

16   More information on Hill and Knowlton can be found at: http://www.sourcewatch.org/index.php?title=Hill_%26_Knowlton

17   Moore's recent call that the U.S. should generate 60 percent of U.S. electricity from nuclear power is ludicrous. These plants are acknowledged by the federal government's own National Commission on Terrorist Attacks Upon the United States—commonly referred to as the 9/11 Commission—as terrorist targets. An accident or terrorist attack at a nuclear plant could result in thousands of near-term deaths from radiation exposure and hundreds of thousands of long-term deaths from cancer among individuals within only fifty miles of a nuclear plant.

18   His proposal not only fails to address the risk posed to the American public by our existing plants, but also fails to address the urgent issue of global warming. According to Dr. Bill Keepin, a physicist and energy consultant in the U.S., "given business-as-usual growth in energy demand, it appears that even an infeasibly massive global nuclear power programme could not reduce future emissions of carbon dioxide. To displace coal alone would require the construction of a new nuclear plant every two or three days for nearly four decades . . . in the United States, each dollar invested in efficiency displaces nearly seven times more carbon than a dollar invested in new nuclear power."

19   According to Moore, "Three Mile Island was actually a success story in that the radiation from the partially melted core was contained."

20   TRUTH: The U.S. Nuclear Regulatory Commission (NRC) estimates that 10 million curies of radiation were released into the environment by the Three Mile Island Meltdown. Expert witnesses in the TMI law suits estimated that 150 million curies escaped, because the containment at Three Mile Island was not leak tight and the NRC ignored many of the potential escape routes for the radiation.

Patrick Moore

How Sick Is That? Environmental Movement Has Lost Its Way

This article, first published in *The Miami Herald* in 2005, represents one of Patrick Moore's responses to what he considers the "sharp turn to the political left" of Greenpeace. He also outlines the reasons why he believes his own version of environmentalism—which moves from "confrontation to consensus"—squares better with the sustainability movement. As you read, you might compare his arguments with those in the statement on Moore made by administrators of Greenpeace, considering the stance of each and deciding which holds more validity for you. (For more information about Patrick Moore and his dispute with Greenpeace, see the headnote to "Hard Choices for the Environmental Movement," included earlier in this chapter.)

I am often asked why I broke ranks with Greenpeace after 1 fifteen years as a founder and full-time environmental activist. While I had my personal reasons—spending more time with a growing family rather than living out of a suitcase most of the year—it was on issues of policy that I found it necessary to move on.

Beginning in the mid-1980s, Greenpeace, and much of the envi- 2 ronmental movement, made a sharp turn to the political left and began adopting extreme agendas that abandoned science and logic in favor of emotion and sensationalism. I became aware of the emerging concept of sustainable development—the idea that environmental, social, and economic priorities could be balanced. I became a convert to the idea that win-win solutions could be found by bringing all interests together around the same table. I made the move from confrontation to consensus.

Since then, I have worked under the banner of Greenspirit to 3 develop an environmental policy platform based on science, logic, and the recognition that more than six billion people need to survive and prosper, every day of the year. The environmental movement has lost its way, favoring political correctness over factual accuracy, stooping to scare tactics to garner support. Many campaigns now waged in the name of the environment would result in increased harm to both the environment and human welfare if they were to succeed.

4   So we're faced with environmental policies that ignore science and result in increased risk to human health and ecology. To borrow from the vernacular, how sick is that?

Genetic Enhancement

5   Activists persist in their zero-tolerance campaign against genetically enhanced varieties of food crops when there is zero evidence of harm to human health or the environment, and the benefits are measurable and significant. Genetically enhanced (GE) food crops result in reduced chemical pesticides, higher yield, and reduced soil erosion. Golden Rice, for example, could prevent blindness in 500,000 children per year in Asia and Africa if activists would stop blocking its introduction. Other varieties of food crops will contain iron, Vitamin E, enhanced protein and better oils. No other technology can match the potential of GE to address the nutritional deficiencies of billions of people. The anti-GE campaign seeks to deny these environmental and nutritional advances by using "Frankenfood" scare tactics and misinformation campaigns.

Salmon Farming

6   The campaign against salmon farming, based on erroneous and exaggerated claims of environmental damage and chemical contamination, is scaring us into avoiding one of the most nutritious, heart-friendly foods available today. Activists persist in this campaign, yet the World Health Organization, the American Heart Association and the US Food and Drug Administration say eating salmon reduces the risk of heart disease and fatal heart attack. Salmon farming has the added benefit of taking pressure off wild salmon stocks. Activists respond by telling us to eat only wild fish. Is this how we save them, by eating more?

Vinyl

7   Greenpeace wants to ban the use of chlorine in all industrial processes, yet the addition of chlorine to drinking water has been the single greatest public health advance in history, and 75% of our medicines are based on chlorine chemistry. My old Greenpeace colleagues also call for a ban on polyvinyl chloride (PVC or vinyl), claiming it is the "poison plastic". There is not a shred of evidence that vinyl damages human health or the environment. In addition to its cost-effectiveness in construction, and ability to deliver safe drinking water, vinyl's ease of maintenance

and its ability to incorporate antimicrobial properties is critical to fighting germs in hospitals. Banning vinyl would further raise the cost of an already struggling health care system, ultimately denying health care to those who can least afford it.

Hydroelectricity

International activists boast they have blocked more than 200 8
hydroelectric dams in the developing world and are campaigning to tear down existing dams. Hydro is the largest source of renewable electricity, providing about 12% of global supply. Do activists prefer coal plants? Would they rather ignore the needs of billions of people?

Wind Power

Wind power is commercially feasible, yet activists argue the tur- 9
bines kill birds and ruin landscapes. A million times more birds are killed by cats, windows and cars than by all the windmills in the world. As for aesthetics, wind turbines are works of art compared to some of our urban environments.

Nuclear Power

A significant reduction in greenhouse gas emissions seems unlike- 10
ly given our continued heavy reliance on fossil fuel consumption. Even UK environmentalist James Lovelock, who posited the Gaia theory that the Earth operates as a giant, self-regulating super-organism, now sees nuclear energy as key to our planet's future health. Lovelock says the first world behaves like an addicted smoker, distracted by short-term benefits and ignorant of long-term risk. "Civilization is in imminent danger," he warns, "and has to use nuclear—the one safe, available energy source—or suffer the pain soon to be inflicted by our outraged planet."

Yet environmental activists, notably Greenpeace and Friends 11
of the Earth, continue to lobby against clean nuclear energy, and in favour of the band-aid Kyoto Treaty. We can agree renewable energies, such as wind, geothermal and hydro are part of the solution. But nuclear energy is the only non-greenhouse gas-emitting power source that can effectively replace fossil fuels and satisfy global demand.

Forestry

Anti-forestry activists are telling us to stop cutting trees and 12
to reduce our use of wood. Forest loss, or deforestation, is nearly all caused by clearing forests for farms and cities. Forestry

operations, on the other hand, are geared towards reforestation and the maintenance of forest cover. Forests are stable and growing where people use the most wood, and are diminishing where they use less. When we use wood, we send a signal to the marketplace to plant more trees and produce more wood. North Americans use more wood per capita than any other continent, yet there is about the same forest area in North America today as there was 100 years ago.

13   Trees, and the materials they produce, are by far the most abundant, renewable and biodegradable resource in the world. If we want to retain healthy forests, we should be growing more trees and using more wood, not less. This seems lost on activists who use chilling rhetoric and apocalyptic images to drive us in the wrong direction.

The Prognosis

14   Environmentalism has turned into anti-globalization and anti-industry. Activists have abandoned science in favour of sensationalism. Their zero-tolerance, fear-mongering campaigns would ultimately prevent a cure for Vitamin A deficiency blindness, increase pesticide use, increase heart disease, deplete wild salmon stocks, raise the cost and reduce the safety of health care, raise construction costs, deprive developing nations of clean electricity, stop renewable wind energy, block a solution to global warming, and contribute to deforestation. How sick is that?

Emma Marris

In the Name of Nature

Emma Marris is a reporter for *Nature* magazine. She has a Master's Degree in science writing from Johns Hopkins University and a Bachelor's Degree in English from the University of Texas–Austin. She writes largely on biological issues. In this piece, she explores a key question of this chapter of *Conversations*—how far is too far for activists to go "in the name of nature." You might also find blog entries debating this issue in direct response to Marris's article at Nature.com's site.

One day in June 1998, three young environmental activists 1 of a radical bent drove from Eugene, Oregon, to Olympia, Washington. Their route took them through some of the loveliest country in the Pacific Northwest: up Interstate 5, through the Willamette Valley, between dark green forested mountains and misty hillside vineyards. Their van shared the road with logging trucks carrying immense trees hung with lichens and mosses.

According to the Federal Bureau of Investigation (FBI), the 2 three were on their way to take part in fire-bombing two research facilities. Things, however, didn't go according to plan. They picked up one friend and lost another to a shoplifting bust. They lost contact with their second vehicle. But something compelled them to set fire to their target anyway.

On the night of 21 June, they drove down quiet Blomberg Road 3 in Olympia, past a dairy and a few houses. They stashed 5-gallon buckets of fuel around a wooden one-storey building, then lit them with barbecue lighter sticks. A national wildlife research facility, run by the federal government's Animal and Plant Health Inspection Service, was utterly destroyed. It served as lab and office space for government scientists who study animals that eat trees and invent ways to keep them from doing so. At the time of the arson, the lab was working on chemical repellents for beavers and a long-term study of what induces bears to dine on Douglas fir bark.

The attack wouldn't be the last, or the largest, on a scientific 4 facility. Seven years later, in December 2005, the US government indicted 11 men and women on charges of conspiracy and arson for 17 fire-bombings whose results included $12 million in damage at a ski resort in Colorado as well as the destruction of the Olympia lab. The 11 had come together loosely under the banner of the Earth Liberation Front (ELF) and the Animal Liberation Front (ALF). Their trial, for those not dead, fled or pled out, will be held in Eugene.

For a certain segment of the radical environmental move- 5 ment, science is seen as both useful and oppressive. Activists sometimes use scientific findings to support their arguments but often view science, and especially technology, with deep distrust. To them, science is a string of proclamations issued by men in white coats and does not respect their deeply felt connection to individual places, animals and trees. Researchers, particularly environmental scientists, should be aware of such thoughts—not least because to some of these activists, science is a legitimate target in a war in which the very future of Earth is at stake.

Terror list

Although it is impossible to know how large such pockets of rad- 6 icalism are, the FBI considers them a serious threat. Spokesman Bill Carter says, "From January 1990 to June 2004, animal and environmental rights extremists have claimed credit for more than 1,200 criminal incidents, resulting in millions of dollars in damage and monetary loss." The bureau has officially labelled both groups terrorists—a word freighted with emotion, rhetoric and law-enforcement response.

7   Dale Nolte, who ran the Olympia facility at the time of the arson, remembers an ELF communiqué claiming credit. "They said they had targeted us because of work we had done with beaver traps and cougars," says Nolte, now mammals programme manager at the National Wildlife Research Center headquarters in Fort Collins, Colorado. "I don't know where they got their information, because we had never worked with cougars and we were working with repellents, not traps."

8   Nolte has never understood the arsonists' motives. He lost a personal library in the fire, as well as several crates' worth of original data and observations about the mountain beaver going back decades. "Our goal was to establish a better understanding of the relationships between the animals and forest, and to enhance the establishment of trees," he says. "I have a strong sense of protecting the environment."

9   To the activists, a lab that served the interests of lumber companies was fair game. Many of them came from the anti-logging community in Eugene.

Among the outsiders

10   Quiet, pretty and populated with anti-establishment characters, Eugene is a magnet for the kind of activists who end up in the ELF. On a fine day at the downtown Eugene market, one might see the following clues that one has stumbled deep into the heart of a west-coast radical paradise: people bristling with clipboard petitions on a range of left and anarchist issues; others wearing fairy wings; kids in home-made nappies being toted behind bicycles; tie dye, drum circles and the sweet reek of marijuana.

11   The taxonomy of subcultures here is nearly impenetrable to an outsider. There are anarchists, feminists, Marxists, primitivists, old-school hippies, libertarians and socialists. The groups tend to spend their time debating with each other, more or less ignoring the mainstream.

12   In June, friends and sympathizers of the Eugene-based eco-prisoners held a benefit at a local bar. The night was mellow, the band good, the beer organic—just the sort of ideological cocoon that can make radical ideas seem pedestrian. Primitivist writer Derrick Jensen gave a lecture on the futility of working within any system to save Earth. For those in the room, his contention that humanity is in "the thrashing endgame of civilization" seemed obvious. A man in a cowboy hat and black

overalls, smoking a cigarette on the back porch, said he was ready to give up civilization completely: "Everything, man, the whole gig."

Jensen, a middle-aged man in a T-shirt reading "Better dead   13 than domesticated," proved a good rhetorician. Unlike many radical speakers, he was also very funny. But the logic of his arguments sometimes fell apart, and he displayed a strong anti-science streak. He referred to "the myths of science" and said it doesn't take a rocket scientist to see that industrial civilization is not sustainable. "In fact," he continued, "it probably takes everybody but a rocket scientist."

Jensen's attitudes are not unusual among ELF-sympathizing   14 eco-activists. These people are deeply sceptical of anything having to do with that entity variously known as 'the dominant culture', 'the white supremacist capitalist imperialist patriarchy,' 'the man' or 'the machine.' Science is part of 'the machine,' based, in their view, on hard rationalism and cold technology.

Philosophers of science have produced reasonable arguments   15 against science as the pure, objective, single road to truth. But something bad happens when you mix half-baked versions of these critiques with a soul-shaking environmental fervour. What you get is anti-intellectual spasms of violence. This approach is a long way from the earlier tradition of direct action in favour of the environment, pioneered by the group Earth First!

Many scientists were among the first members of that group,   16 formed in 1980 in the US southwest. As Susan Zakin describes them in *Coyotes and Town Dogs*, her 1993 book on the movement, they were boozing, redneck 'desert rats'—men who had seen the mesas mined, the Colorado River dammed and the great American West becoming tamed. They stressed ecosystems over scenery, unlike many environmentalists of the time. They never resorted to arson: rather, they dismantled construction equipment, trashed billboards and spiked trees with nails to break chain-saws—but they generally told loggers where they had done this to avoid nasty accidents.

Later in the 1980s, a schism opened between the ecologists in   17 the group and those who were more interested in "monkey-wrenching"—sabotage or other forms of troublemaking. The scientists began to drift off. "By the time we began sitting in redwood trees in northern California, the pagan vegan pacifists outnumbered the biologists ten to one," says founding member Mike Roselle.

The non-scientists that were left, he says, spawned the ELF.   18 They were radical and committed. "These folks are often the unsung heroes, the true foot soldiers of the movement," he says. "The ones in jail were among our best, some of the most skilled and committed members of our movement. Their incarceration is a tragic loss for all of us."

19   Earth First! co-founder Dave Foreman doesn't quite agree. "We wanted to use the science of ecology to guide us," he says. "The current group of people I don't consider conservationists, but part of the international anarchist animal-rights movement. It becomes sort of an inarticulate yowl against the establishment— revolution for the hell of it."

20   The yowl often starts young. Chelsea Gerlach, one of the recent indictees, was a 16-year-old high-school student in Eugene when she was arrested at an Earth First! logging blockade in Idaho, according to her support website. At school, she ran an environmental club, and, according to Seattle's alternative weekly, *The Stranger,* was quoted in the yearbook as saying, "Our generation was born to save the Earth. If we wait until we're out of school it might be too late." She was 23 when, the FBI indictment alleges, she helped set fire to the Jefferson Poplar Farms in Clatskanie, Oregon, spray-painting "ELF" and "You cannot control what is wild."

21   That was 21 May 2001. For maximum effect, the FBI says, on the same night three others—William Rodgers, Stanislas Meyerhoff and Briana Waters—torched the University of Washington's centre for urban horticulture, about 230 kilometres away in Seattle. They took time to remove some cages for pet snakes from the building, Merrill Hall, before setting it aflame.

The Merrill fire

22 The hall housed lab space for botanists and ecologists, and served as a meeting place for Seattle's horticulturalists. Assistant professor Sarah Reichard, a specialist in rare plants, remembers the day well. "It was a beautiful morning," she says, until she got the message that her lab was on fire. She rushed to the hall, which sits just down the hill from the main University of Washington campus and is surrounded by demonstration gardens, meadows, and a grove of native trees.

23 "There was Merrill Hall with flames leaping 30 or 40 feet into the air," she remembers. The young academic lost everything, including a tissue culture lab where she was growing the highly endangered showy stickweed, a blue-white flowering plant in the forget-me-not family. Losses of specimens, along with irreplaceable books and slides, put her career back at least a year, she estimates.

24 It wasn't just the blow to her road to tenure that worries her. That morning, standing by the blazing building, she feared that someone had been killed. "Academic units are not nine-to-five places," she says. "In fact, it was very unusual that there was no one there at three in the morning. One graduate student told me that the only reason he wasn't there was because I gave an

extension on an assignment." No one was hurt in the blaze, but
the building was a total loss.

Reichard may have been the hardest hit but she wasn't the tar-   25
get of the arson. "We could see Toby's office was black—a big
black hole," she says. "Everyone realized immediately that it was
not an accident."

Toby is Toby Bradshaw, a plant geneticist who at the time ran   26
the Poplar Molecular Genetics Cooperative, a group working
on finding genes in hybrid poplars that code for traits useful in
a crop tree—fast-growing, disease-resistant and straight. The
team used traditional breeding techniques, ultimately aiming to
make productive tree farms more attractive than logging big
trees from old-growth forests. Somehow, however, the radical
greens got the idea that Bradshaw was genetically engineering
trees.

Bradshaw says he has never done so, although his colleagues   27
have. He'd been a target before. Someone had tried to overturn
his potted seedlings during the protest against the World Trade
Organization meeting in Seattle in 1999. And two weeks after
the Merrill Hall fire, a communiqué was issued through Craig
Rosebraugh, a former spokesman for the ELF who has not been
indicted. It reads, in part, "Bradshaw, the driving force in G.E.
tree research, continues to unleash mutant genes into the environment that is certain to cause irreversible harm to forest
ecosystems. As long as universities continue to pursue this reckless 'science,' they run the risk of suffering severe losses. Our
message remains clear, we are determined to stop genetic engineering."

Bradshaw likes to joke that the fire actually helped his career.   28
He got tenure and a new lab shortly afterwards, and has since
moved on to unrelated work. But the attitudes behind the crime
trouble him. "As social commentary, these kinds of arsons are
ineffective because they are so misguided," he says. "Science at
its heart is a rational enterprise and, at its heart, this kind of terror tactics with fire-bombing is an irrational enterprise."

The Crackdown

The FBI last interviewed Bradshaw at the time of the arson, and   29
he was surprised last December when the arrests were
announced. In fact, the FBI had spent years putting together
information for the indictment; the most recent of the 17 arsons
listed in the charges dated to October 2001, at a Bureau of Land
Management wild-horse facility in Litchfield, California. The
small group that had acted under the ELF banner seems to have
more or less broken up after that, scattering to Virginia, Arizona,
and around the Pacific Northwest. Reportedly, the FBI laid the
groundwork for the charges by getting activist and heavy-metal

guitarist Jake Ferguson to call his old pals for some nostalgic, and wire-tapped, conversations.

30   The bust was important enough to bring out the top law-enforcement brass. On 20 January, FBI director Robert Mueller gave a press conference on the indictments in Washington DC. "Terrorism is terrorism, no matter the motive," he said. "The FBI becomes involved, as it did in this case, only when volatile talk crosses the line into violence and criminal activity." Terrorism, however, is not defined as a crime in the United States; the group was charged with arson and associated crimes.

31   Most of the indictees are now in jails in Oregon, with some under house arrest or out on bail. Lauren Regan, head of the Civil Liberties Defense Center in Eugene, calls the arrests the 'green scare', a play on the 'red scare' of the 1950s in which US citizens with communist ties were persecuted.

32   Regan says that many of the indictees don't deserve the sentences they are facing—life several times over for each. "A lot of these people were at the time very young," she points out. "You are easily swayed, you've got a lot of passion. You hold a radio while some genetically modified trees are burned down. Chances are that they were not thinking, in that pre-9/11 time, that they were looking at life in jail."

Repentance and Escape

33   Many of those arrested have since pleaded guilty and are cooperating with the authorities. Gerlach made a public statement at the time of her plea, saying, "These acts were motivated by a deep sense of despair and anger at the deteriorating state of the global environment and the escalating inequities within society. But I realized years ago that this was not an effective or appropriate way to effect positive change."

34   Those outside jail have reacted harshly to those cooperating with the government. In Eugene, Jensen began his speech with a message: "What you are doing is wrong, and I plan on seeing you brought to justice. And fuck you." Ferguson, who never faced charges, is known in some activist circles as "Jake the Snake."

35   A few of the indictees are still at large. Their wanted posters reveal a bit about them. Justine Overaker's, for example, paints a portrait of her as a seeker; it mentions that she may seek work as a "firefighter, a midwife, a sheep tender or a masseuse" and that she can speak Spanish and has been known to use narcotics. She has a tattoo of a bird across her back.

36   Rodgers, also known as Avalon, was arrested at his bookstore in Prescott, Arizona. He suffocated himself to death with a plastic bag in his jail cell. He left a note that said, "Human cultures have been waging war against the Earth for millennia. I chose

to fight on the side of bears, mountain lions, skunks, bats, saguaros cliff rose and all things wild. I am just the most recent casualty in that war. But tonight I have made a jail break—I am returning home, to the Earth, to the place of my origins."

At 41, Rodgers was the oldest of the indictees and by some 37
reports the ringleader. His lover, Katie Rose Nelson, says, "Life mattered to him—and that meant all life." She and Rodgers both felt the environmental cause was urgent—too urgent to spend time on research. "In our hearts we can all see what is happening around us," she says.

With most indictees not talking, missing or dead, they can't 38
explain the motivations and justifications for their alleged crimes. But a rare glimpse of three of the activists, including Ferguson and Rodgers, can be seen in the 1999 documentary film *Pickaxe*, which chronicles an 11-month battle in the mid-1990s to keep an area in Oregon called Warner Creek from being logged. Here, they engage in legal protests, such as hunger strikes, and the kind of non-violent illegal protest that many condone, such as blockading the road into the area.

And they won. At least that one patch of forest is still there, 39
old and moist and green. So why were these same people drawn to anonymous arson attacks late at night—and why target scientists?

"Science does not have a lock on truth," says David Agranoff, 40
an animal-rights and veganism activist in San Diego, California, who knows some of the defendants. He says he is sure they considered their actions carefully: "I would guess they had a pretty good reason." Rosebraugh, the former ELF spokesman, notes that each would have had their own motives. "For all the people involved," he says, "you would probably give a different answer."

The "Pure Ones"

Donna Haraway, who studies feminism and science at the Uni- 41
versity of California, Santa Cruz, met some of the radical-activist set in Eugene when she went to speak there in 2001. Because Haraway, author of *Simians, Cyborgs and Women: The Reinvention of Nature,* embraces technology as an agent for positive change, the group saw her as an enemy. Their protest included flyers that she found distinctly threatening. "At least one felt that the rape of nature justified the rape of anyone who supported it," she says. "These people don't go for complexity; they believe that they are the only pure ones who can defend nature."

The ELF indictees are by no means the last of the self-anointed 42
environmental "pure ones." Jeffrey Luers of Eugene is appealing a 22-year sentence for setting fire to sports utility vehicles as a protest. Activist Trey Arrow is fighting extradition from

Canada to the United States, where he faces charges of having burned logging and mining trucks. In January, three people were arrested in the parking lot of a Kmart while buying supplies, allegedly to bomb a forest genetics lab in Placerville, California: they are charged with conspiracy, and two have pleaded guilty, although many activists blame an FBI agent provocateur for the plot. In Canada, a group of eco-saboteurs are currently on a fire-bombing tour of construction sites across Ontario. By its nature, the movement is decentralized, non-hierarchical and open. Anyone can be an environmental arsonist.

43   From jail, Luers publishes a magazine called *Heartcheck*, with an estimated circulation of 1,000. For the latest issue, he has penned an essay called "Time's up" in which he summarizes recent facts and figures on species extinction in various ecosystems, glacier melt rates in Alaska and carbon dioxide levels. He ends: "I could go on, but you get the point. Or do you? We are not running out of time, we are out of time! We have to act now just so it doesn't get any worse. Smash it, break it, block it, lock down to it. I don't care what you do or how you do it. Just stop it. Get out there and stop it."

Margery Kraus and Michael Brune

Are Businesses Better Equipped Than Governments to Address 21st-Century Environmental Challenges? A Dialogue

The question of who is most equipped to address our environmental challenges is debated here by two expert voices from very different areas of expertise. Margery Kraus is the CEO for APCO Worldwide, a public relations firm that represents some of the world's largest corporations. Michael Brune is an environmentalist and the Executive Director of the Rainforest Action Network. Published in *CQ Researcher* in 2006, this dialogue reveals many of the key points of debate that inform the pieces throughout this section. As you read, consider how each writer's profession informs both their opinions and their rhetorical strategies.

Margery Kraus

There is no doubt the environment is on people's minds: Used   1
hybrid cars can fetch more than the original sticker price at
resale; the *Oxford American Dictionary*'s word of the year for
2006 is "carbon neutral." However hip it may be, environmental responsibility is more than just the "flavor of the month," it
is our future. And businesses not only can be the most efficient
catalyst for creating a more sustainable planet but they also are
increasingly expected to play that role.

A recent study conducted by APCO Worldwide reveals that   2
the American public holds businesses to a higher standard on
environmental issues than it does the U.S. government. There
is a belief that business is less encumbered by politics and
bureaucracy and has more resources to act and influence others
to do so.

Today's progressive companies already know they have this   3
responsibility and embrace it. Big corporations are larger than
many nations. Major companies' global reach and standards
allow them to directly impact environments beyond the boundaries of any one country. As they expand globally, businesses are
able to build factories with proven technologies that often
exceed the requirements of local governments.

Corporations have a tremendous opportunity to influence   4
individual behavior. Employees can be offered incentives to
use public transportation, recycle and contribute time to community environmental efforts. More broadly, businesses can
sway consumer bases to adopt environmentally responsible
behavior.

Finally, an increased number of businesses see sustainable   5
products as a new part of their business. They are engineering
or re-engineering those products to be recyclable and to incorporate recycled materials; they are employing clean production
processes to create less waste and pollution.

Down the road, these forward-looking businesses will have a   6
healthy, sustainable work force, clean water and quality of life
that will enable them to have good employees and more consumers. Their ultimate incentive: You can't run a successful
business in a failed world.

Obviously, safeguarding our environment is best accom-   7
plished by governments, businesses and individuals working
together. However, businesses, especially multinational corporations, are well-positioned to take decisive leadership and have
the infrastructure and resources to achieve measurable results—
and consumers are expecting nothing less.

Michael Brune

8   Businesses and governments both have a vital role to play in addressing environmental challenges. We are beginning to see strong policies from a select number of high-profile businesses on issues such as forest protection and climate change. Meanwhile, state and local governments are responding to widespread public support for environmental protection, compensating for a disturbing lack of leadership in the White House and Congress.

9   One test for either businesses or governments is to determine to which constituency they are the most loyal. Most companies are guided by the old business axiom, "The customer is always right." These businesses realize that not only do consumers want to do business with companies that exhibit strong environmental values but also their own employees want to feel good about their employer's environmental record. Indeed, it is this view that has helped Home Depot, Lowe's, FedEx Kinko's and others to work with Rainforest Action Network to help protect endangered forests, and for Citigroup, Bank of America, JP Morgan Chase and Goldman Sachs to take principled stands on climate change and forest protection.

10   Conversely, many officials in Washington are stuck in the past, guarding the status quo. Within the last few years, the federal government has failed to enact, protect or enforce strong environmental policies, as evidenced by the attempted rollback of the Forest Service's "Roadless Rule" and the gutting of the Clean Water Act. Our politicians have fallen into the trap of believing they must choose between prosperity and the environment. Consequently, neither political party has stood up to the corporations whose policies are destabilizing and devastating our environment.

11   By leveraging public opinion and consumer choice to publicly stigmatize companies that refuse to adopt responsible environmental policies, environmental organizations are able to positively influence corporations' policies. This tactic strengthens marketplace democracy and empowers the consumer. It also has created significant progress and dramatic successes for environmental preservation. It gives consumers the ability to influence companies, stepping in where government has failed.

12   The reality is there is a new voice of business that shows how it is possible to do well by doing good, earning profits while upholding environmental principles. These businesses have shown a strong interest in working with government to meet the pressing environmental challenges of the 21st century. It's time for officials in Congress and the White House to listen and get to work.

Marc Gunther, Doris Burke, and Jia Lynn Yang

The Green Machine

Marc Gunther is a senior writer at *Fortune Magazine,* a well-respected popular business publication. His work examines the impact of business policy on society. He is the author of *Faith and Fortune: How Compassionate Capitalism is Transforming American Business* (2004). The piece below was co-written by Gunther and two other *Fortune* writers, senior reporter Doris Burke and general assignment reporter Jia Lynn Yang. This essay explores the potential for Wal-Mart, one of the world's largest companies, to transform the environmental movement, and the skepticism some have about anything that has to do with this retail behemoth. Consider whether that skepticism is warranted or if, indeed, the solution to our environmental crises might be in actions of large corporations.

L ee Scott is no tree-hugger. But Wal-Mart's CEO says he 1
wants to turn the world's largest retailer into the greenest.
The company is so big, so powerful, it could force an
army of suppliers to clean up their acts too. Is he serious?

"DOESN'T IT FEEL GOOD to have this kind of commitment 2
made by the company that you are part of? Don't you feel
proud?"

The 800 Wal-Mart Stores employees gathered in the home 3
office for an all-day meeting were used to this kind of rah-rah
talk. Top executives from Fortune 500 companies regularly trek
to Bentonville, Ark., to pay homage to one of the world's most
powerful companies and to shout out the Wal-Mart cheer. This
time, though, the cheerleading was coming from an unlikely
source: Al Gore.

Wal-Mart had invited America's most famous environmental- 4
ist to show his movie, *An Inconvenient Truth.* "Having the former Democratic Vice President was a shock" to some people at
the company, chief executive Lee Scott told the crowd. "At least
based on a couple of my e-mails."

But as the credits rolled, Gore strutted onto the stage to a 5
standing ovation. Dressed in a blue suit and cowboy boots, he
joked with the audience, answered questions in his best Southern drawl, and coyly denied that he had any plans to run for
President again. (This wasn't exactly his base: He took just 32%

of the vote in Benton County in 2000.) Before heading off to dinner with Wal-Mart chairman Rob Walton and Scott, Gore delivered a parting thought: As Wal-Mart embarks on a far-reaching plan to adopt business practices that are better for the environment, he said, the world will learn that "there need not be any conflict between the environment and the economy."

6   Wal-Mart, you see, has decided to help save the earth.

7   Just listen to Scott. "To me," he says, "there can't be anything good about putting all these chemicals in the air. There can't be anything good about the smog you see in cities. There can't be anything good about putting chemicals in these rivers in Third World countries so that somebody can buy an item for less money in a developed country. Those things are just inherently wrong, whether you are an environmentalist or not."

8   In a speech broadcast to all of Wal-Mart's facilities last November, Scott set several ambitious goals: Increase the efficiency of its vehicle fleet by 25% over the next three years, and double efficiency in ten years. Eliminate 30% of the energy used in stores. Reduce solid waste from U.S. stores by 25% in three years. Wal-Mart says it will invest $500 million in sustainability projects, and the company has done a lot more than draw up targets. It has quickly become, for instance, the biggest seller of organic milk and the biggest buyer of organic cotton in the world. It is working with suppliers to figure out ways to cut down on packaging and energy costs. It has opened two "green" supercenters.

9   Plenty of people won't buy it—or anything else from Wal-Mart. To labor leaders, left-wing elites, and the small-is-beautiful crowd, the $312-billion-a-year retailer stands for everything that's wrong with big business. They see the company in a race to pave the planet and turn it into a giant emporium of cheap goods built on the back of cheap labor. The union-funded website walmartwatch.com dismisses Wal-Mart's environmental push as a "high-priced green-washing campaign."

10   Wal-Mart, though, has a whole lot more to worry about than convincing a few ideological critics that its eco-intentions are pure. Its business, for starters. Its same-store sales growth has slowed down, trailing Target's and Costco's. Its stock price is another big concern. After rising 1,205% during the 1990s, the stock has fallen by 30% since Scott took over as CEO in January 2000.

11   It's no wonder that inside Wal-Mart some veteran executives grouse that Scott's green crusade will be a costly distraction. Many remember the last time Wal-Mart set out an initiative this broad: founder Sam Walton's 1985 "Made in the U.S.A." campaign. That move burnished Wal-Mart's red-white-and-blue image, but it wasn't long before critics noted that Wal-Mart continued to seek out goods from the absolute lowest-cost supplier—and typically that meant "Made Anywhere but America."

Indeed, Wal-Mart's single-minded desire to save its customers   12
money has been its raison d'être for 44 years. Which raises two
questions: Why is the world's largest retailer so determined to
become the greenest? And how green can a company that operates 6,600 big-box stores really get?

Rob Walton, his son Ben, Pearl Jam guitarist Stone Gossard,   13
and conservationist Peter Seligmann were scuba-diving off Coco
Island, a lush, uninhabited Costa Rican national park populated
by manta rays, dolphins, and sharks. During a ten-day trip in
February 2004, Seligmann, co-founder and CEO of Conservation International, a big Washington, D.C., environmental
organization whose mission is to protect the world's biologically
rich habitats, had been pointing out fleets of fishing boats that
were destroying the delicate Costa Rican marine habitat.
Toward the end of the trip, Seligmann looked Walton in the eye:
"We need to change the way industry works. And you can have
an influence."

Like all Sam Walton's children, S. Robson "Rob" Walton, 60,   14
grew up in the Ozarks with a love of the outdoors. "All our family vacations were camping trips," he says in a rare interview.
His younger brother John, who died last year in a private plane
crash, was a conservationist. And his son Sam, who worked as
a Colorado River guide, sits on the board of Environmental
Defense, a nonprofit group. About four years ago, after a trip to
Africa, Rob Walton began to think about ways his family could
help preserve wilderness areas through its foundation, which
has assets of about $1 billion. (The Walton family's 40% stake in
Wal-Mart is worth about $80 billion.)

A mutual friend then introduced Walton to Seligmann. Over   15
the next two years the preppy ex-biologist guided Rob and his
two sons on a series of adventures. They hiked in Madagascar.
They took a boat trip through the world's largest freshwater wetland, in Brazil. They went diving in the Galápagos Islands. "We
spent a lot of time diving and talking," says Seligmann. The family foundation eventually made a $21 million grant to CI for
ocean-protection programs, and Walton joined the group's board.

But Seligmann had another agenda, one that he finally put on   16
the table in Costa Rica. Whatever money the foundation could
contribute would pale in comparison to what Wal-Mart the corporation could do. "I suggested to Rob that Wal-Mart could be
a driver of tremendous change," Seligmann says.

He wasn't exaggerating. The company is the biggest private   17
user of electricity in the U.S.; each of its 2,074 supercenters uses
an average of 1.5 million kilowatts annually, enough as a group
to power all of Namibia. Wal-Mart has the nation's second-
largest fleet of trucks, and its vehicles travel a billion miles a
year. If each customer who visited Wal-Mart in a week bought one
long-lasting compact fluorescent (CF) light bulb, the company

estimates, that would reduce electric bills by $3 billion, conserve 50 billion tons of coal, and keep one billion incandescent light bulbs out of landfills over the life of the bulb. If Wal-Mart influenced the behavior of a fraction of its 1.8 million employees or the 176 million customers that shop there every week, the impact would be huge. And because of the extraordinary clout Wal-Mart wields with its 60,000 suppliers, it could make even more of a difference by influencing their practices.

18   Walton was intrigued, but he had taken himself out of an operational role at Wal-Mart years ago. He didn't want to overstep his bounds. "We are really, really careful about mixing personal interests and the business," he says. Still, he agreed to introduce Seligmann to Lee Scott.

19   The timing was fortuitous. Scott had just undertaken a review of Wal-Mart's legal and PR woes—and it wasn't a short list. A lawsuit alleging that Wal-Mart discriminated against its female employees had been certified as a federal class action. Opponents blocked new stores in the suburbs of Los Angeles, San Francisco, and Chicago. A study found that Wal-Mart's average spending on health benefits for its employees was 30% less than the average of its retail peers. The company's environmental record was nothing to boast about either: It had paid millions of dollars to state and federal regulators for violating air- and water-pollution laws.

20   For years Wal-Mart simply brushed off such criticism. "We would put up the sandbags and get out the machine guns," Scott recalls. After all, business was good. They were saving their customers billions, fighting for the little guy. But as the upstart rural retailer grew into one of America's biggest companies and clashed with unionized competitors, it made powerful enemies. Expectations of business were rising, and Wal-Mart was failing to meet them. A McKinsey & Co. study leaked to the press by walmartwatch.com found that up to 8% of shoppers had stopped patronizing the chain because of its reputation.

21   Scott wondered, "If we had known ten years ago what we know now, what would we have done differently that might have kept us out of some of these issues or would have enhanced our reputation? It seemed to me that ultimately many of the issues that had to do with the environment were going to wind up with people feeling like we had a greater responsibility than we were, at the time, accepting."

22   In a drab Bentonville conference room, Scott, Rob Walton, Seligmann and Glenn Prickett of Conservation International, and a friend of Seligmann's named Jib Ellison, a river-rafting guide turned management consultant, convened a pivotal meeting in June 2004. For a presentation to the man who is arguably the most powerful CEO in the world and the man who is inarguably one of the richest, the pitch was surprisingly informal.

The five men chatted about the environment and about   23
ways Wal-Mart could improve its practices. Seligmann and
Prickett talked about their work with Starbucks, which developed coffee-buying methods to protect tropical regions, and
about McDonald's, which was helping to promote sustainable
agriculture and fishing.

Their argument was simple: Wal-Mart could improve its   24
image, motivate employees, and save money by going green.

If there was any group that could deliver such a message to   25
Scott, it was CI, whose board members include former Intel
chairman Gordon Moore, BP chief executive John Browne, and
former Starbucks CEO Orin Smith. CI works closely with corporations, and about $7 million of its $93 million in 2005 revenues came from such consulting arrangements.

Scott hired CI and Ellison's management consulting firm,   26
called BluSkye, and asked them to measure Wal-Mart's environmental impact. The assessment would include not just Wal-
Mart's operations, but the impact of growing or producing all
the products it sells and shipping them to stores. Wal-Mart was
defining its responsibility broadly, in a way that would bring its
vast supply chain—where its environmental impact is greatest—
into the picture.

About a dozen people from BluSkye, CI, and Wal-Mart spent   27
nearly a year measuring the company's impact. Fairly quickly,
the environmentalists spotted waste that Wal-Mart's legendary
cost cutters had overlooked. On Kid Connection, its private-label
line of toys, for instance, Wal-Mart found that by eliminating
excessive packaging, it could save $2.4 million a year in shipping
costs, 3,800 trees, and one million barrels of oil. On its fleet of
7,200 trucks Wal-Mart determined it could save $26 million a
year in fuel costs merely by installing auxiliary power units that
enable the drivers to keep their cabs warm or cool during mandatory ten-hour breaks from the road. Before that, they'd let the
truck engine idle all night, wasting fuel. Yet another example:
Wal-Mart installed machines called sandwich balers in its stores
to recycle and sell plastic that it used to throw away. Company-
wide, the balers have added $28 million to the bottom line.

"Think about it," Scott said in his big speech to employees last   28
fall. "If we throw it away, we had to buy it first. So we pay
twice—once to get it, once to have it taken away. What if we
reverse that? What if our suppliers send us less, and everything
they send us has value as a recycled product? No waste, and we
get paid instead."

That was talk any Wal-Mart executive could understand, even   29
if few knew it came straight from the pages of *Natural Capitalism*, an influential book by Paul Hawken, Amory Lovins, and
Hunter Lovins that lays out a blueprint for a new green economy
in which nothing goes to waste. Not coincidentally, Lovins and

his Rocky Mountain Institute were also hired as consultants by Wal-Mart to study a radical revamp of its trucking fleet.

30   Wal-Mart was pulling ideas from everywhere—consultants, NGOs, suppliers, and eco-friendly competitors such as Patagonia and Whole Foods. This open-source approach worked so well that the company decided to form "sustainable value networks" made up of Wal-Mart executives, suppliers, environmental groups, and regulators; they would meet every few months to share ideas, set goals, and monitor progress.

31   Today there are 14 networks, each with a focus: facilities, internal operations, logistics, alternative fuels, packaging, chemicals, food and agriculture, electronics, textiles, forest products, jewelry, seafood, climate change, and China. Experts from the World Wildlife Federation, the Natural Resources Defense Council, and even Greenpeace have made the pilgrimage to Bentonville. "I can honestly say I never expected to be at Wal-Mart's headquarters watching people do the Wal-Mart cheer," says John Hocevar, a Greenpeace campaigner. Environmental Defense announced plans to open a satellite office in Bentonville.

32   Though hundreds of people are in the networks, only five Wal-Mart employees, led by corporate strategist Andy Ruben, work full-time on the initiative. Key decisions are decentralized. "If you are a buyer, sustainability is going to be your business," says Scott. Some environmentalists who are part of the networks worry the initiative is understaffed. They say that the Wal-Mart people responsible for keeping the networks going, all of whom already had full-time jobs like running truck fleets or buying jewelry, are stretched thin.

33   Still, getting tree-huggers and Wal-Mart lifers in the same room led to some unexpected benefits. "Sustainability helped us develop the skills to listen to people who criticize us and to change where it's appropriate," Scott says. His managers are learning "not to be so afraid of venturing out there, thinking that if people see our warts, they're just going to castigate us." It also gives them another reason to feel good about Wal-Mart, a sense of working for a "higher purpose," he says.

34   Scott, too, was filled with the zeal of the newly converted. "I had an intellectual interest when we started," he says. "I have a passion today." As a lifelong angler from Baxter Springs, Kan., Scott, who is 57, was particularly worried about pollution in the world's rivers and oceans. He visited Mount Washington in New Hampshire, where he chatted with a maple-sugar producer about the impact of global warming. And he traded in his Volkswagen Beetle for a hybrid Lexus SUV. Hurricane Katrina, after which Wal-Mart employees mobilized to deliver vital supplies to victims, deepened Scott's resolve. "We stepped back from that and asked one simple question: How can Wal-Mart be that company—the one we were during Katrina—all the time?"

The environmental campaign that Scott admits started out as a   35
"defensive strategy" was, in his view, "turning out to be precisely
the opposite." His people were feeling better about the company.
They were saving their customers money. That was one of
Wal-Mart's strengths. Another was twisting the arms of suppliers—
who would soon learn all about Wal-Mart's new crusade.

In the cold waters off Kodiak Island, Alaska, where the sockeye   36
salmon are running in early June, a 45-year-old third-generation
fishing-boat captain named Mitch Keplinger is having a disap-
pointing day. Operating under Alaska's strict regulatory regime,
Keplinger and his crew labor for more than 12 hours to haul in
about 1,000 pounds of sockeye, which they sell for 70 cents a
pound to Ocean Beauty, a Seattle-based processor and Wal-Mart
supplier. They catch another 500 pounds of pink salmon, which
sells for 35 cents a pound. That's $1,050 before expenses, to be
shared by the four of them—barely worth the effort.

What does that have to do with Wal-Mart? Keplinger—and   37
fisherman like him who play by the rules—are getting killed by
competition from unregulated fisheries and farmed salmon. In
February, Wal-Mart announced that over the next three to five
years it would purchase all its wild-caught seafood from fisheries that, like Alaska's salmon fishery, have been certified as
sustainable by an independent nonprofit called the Marine
Stewardship Council (MSC). The company is working on a similar certification system for farmed fish, and it hopes consumers
will come to value "brands" like MSC-certified as they do the
organic label. Says Rupert Howes, chief executive of the MSC:
"It's supply-chain pressure of the best kind."

Keplinger and his buyers at Ocean Beauty are watching Wal-   38
Mart closely. Says Tom Sutherland, Ocean Beauty's vice president of marketing: "When Wal-Mart hiccups, it's all we can talk
about."

It's not just Alaskan fishermen who are talking. So are corn   39
farmers in Iowa (who want to sell more ethanol throughWal-
Mart), coffee growers in Brazil (who are being promised higher
prices for their beans), and factory bosses in China (who are
being told to cut their energy and fuel costs). Wal-Mart's campaign has already turned the small world of organic cotton
upside down, thanks in part to Coral Rose, a ladies' apparel
buyer for Sam's Club. In spring 2004—just before Wal-Mart held
its first meeting with CI—Rose ordered a yoga outfit made of
organic cotton for Sam's Club; the tops sold for about $14, the
loose-fitting pants for $10. The 190,000 units sold out in ten
weeks.

That got Scott's attention. Sales of organic food had grown at   40
Wal-Mart; he wondered if organic cotton could do as well. With
Scott's encouragement, Wal-Mart's buyers visited organic cotton
farms. They learned about the environmental risks posed by

conventional cotton farming, which uses more chemical pesticides and synthetic fertilizer than any other crop. Wal-Mart's purchases of organic cotton have eliminated millions of tons of chemicals, Scott says. Today, Wal-Mart and Sam's Club stock a range of organic-cotton products—baby clothes under the Baby George brand, teenage fashion, and a line of bed sheets and towels.

41   The organic-cotton industry had found its best customer. Five years ago global production of organic cotton amounted to about 6.4 million metric tons, and some farmers who converted to organic methods, which can cost more, could not find buyers willing to pay a premium. In 2006, Wal-Mart and Sam's Club alone will use between eight million and ten million metric tons, and they've made a verbal commitment to buy organic cotton for five years, giving farmers an assurance that there will be a market for their crops.

42   Wal-Mart is also increasing the amount of organic food it sells, but some even find fault with this, assuming that it buys only from massive corporate organic farms. Not true. Wal-Mart buys locally in two dozen states, striving to reduce "food miles" to save shipping costs and increase freshness.

43   Scott, meanwhile, is personally pushing his cause with Fortune 500 CEOs. He has talked with Jeff Immelt at GE about LED lighting for Wal-Mart's buildings. He's talked with Tom Faulk, the CEO of Kimberly-Clark, about "compressed toilet paper," which squeezes three rolls into one. Steve Reinemund, Pepsi-Co's CEO, just sold Wal-Mart on a massive recycling contest involving Aquafina water.

44   Wait a minute. Recycling's great. But why consume Aquafina in the first place? Bottled water is bad for the environment, period. But neither PepsiCo nor Wal-Mart will stop selling it as long as consumers want to buy it. This is one place where tensions arise between what's good for business and what's good for the planet.

45   Packaging is another thorny issue. On my grocer's shelf are a bulky, 100-fluid-ounce, orange plastic jug of Procter & Gamble's bestselling Tide and a slim 32-ounce aqua plastic bottle of Unilever's "small and mighty" All. Both contain enough detergent for 32 loads of wash, but the smaller package, made possible by condensing All, saves energy, shipping costs, and shelf space—a big win all around, right? Not quite. Bigger packages command more shelf space, provide more surface area for advertising, and suggest to consumers that they're getting more for their money. Unilever executives voiced all those worries when they went to see Scott. He agreed to make "small and mighty" All a VPI (that's Wal-Mart code for "volume-producing item," and it means that Wal-Mart will promote it heavily). "That helps to increase their confidence," he says. You can now find "small and mighty" All in supermarkets everywhere.

And guess what? This fall Procter & Gamble will replace the   46
bulky plastic jugs with condensed, slimmed-down versions of all
its liquid laundry detergents—Tide, Cheer, Gain, Era, and
Dreft—in a test in Cedar Rapids, Iowa, to prepare for a likely
national rollout. We wondered if Wal-Mart had anything to do
with that. "We've been doing sustainability for quite some time,"
replied a P&G spokeswoman. "And we're pleased to work with
all our distributors, including Wal-Mart." You figure it out.

This is why Wal-Mart's eco-initiative is potentially more   47
world-changing than, say, GE's. GE sells fuel-efficient aircraft
engines and billion-dollar power plants to a few customers. Wal-
Mart sells organic cotton, laundry soap, and light bulbs to millions. When shoppers see a display promoting "the bulb that
pays for itself, again and again and again," they'll be reminded
of their own environmental impact. By buying CF bulbs they'll
also save money on their utility bills, leaving them more money
to spend at, you guessed it, Wal-Mart. The bigger idea here is
that poor and middle-income Americans are every bit as interested in buying green products as are the well-to-do, so long as
they are affordable. Plenty of places sell fair-trade coffee, for
example. Only Wal-Mart sells it for $4.71 a pound. "The poten-
tial here is to democratize the whole sustainability idea—not
make it something that just the elites on the coasts do but something that small-town and middle America also embrace," says
CI's Glenn Prickett. "It's a Nixon-to-China moment."

Several weeks ago a dozen Japanese supermarket industry   48
executives flew halfway around the world to visit a store in a suburb of Denver that is unlike any they had ever seen. They snapped
pictures of wind turbines and solar cells and listened as a tour
guide explained how dirty cooking oil from the deli and used
motor oil from the lube department are recycled to heat the
store. They ran their fingers across jewelry cases built of renewable bamboo and peered into the dairy case at the superefficient
light-emitting diodes that illuminate rows of organic milk.   49

The visitors wandered among shelves stocked with tuna certified by the Marine Stewardship Council and coffee endorsed
by the Rainforest Alliance. They learned that spoiled food was
composted into fertilizer and resold. They walked on sidewalks
that are—no joke—made of recycled airport runways.

This is Wal-Mart Store No. 5334, which opened last winter. It's   50
one of two experimental stores the company built to test ways
to cut energy and reduce waste. It sounds terribly futuristic, but
this isn't totally new ground. In 1993 the company debuted a Bill
McDonough-designed eco-store in Lawrence, Kan., with great
fanfare. Two more stores followed, but the concept quietly died.

Wal-Mart's more serious now, but skeptics remain. Jeffrey   51
Hollender is president of Seventh Generation, a Burlington, Vt.,
maker of nontoxic household products. Though Scott met with

Hollender in Bentonville and offered to carry some of his line, Hollender declined. "We might sell a lot more products in giant mass-market outlets, but we're not living up to our own values and helping the world get to a better place if we sell our soul to do it," he says.

52   Scott understands there are some critics he will never win over. He knows that not everyone at Wal-Mart shares his vision. But he's quite certain that one person would. Midway through the daylong sustainability summit, the one where Al Gore showed his movie, Scott did what Wal-Mart executives always do when they want to get people's attention: He invoked the name of Sam Walton.

53   "Some people say this is foreign to what Sam Walton believed, that Sam Walton focused solely on the customers, driving prices down so the average person can have a higher standard of value," Scott said. "What people forget is that there was nobody more willing to change. Sam Walton did what was right for his time. Sam loved the outdoors. And he loved the idea of building a company that would endure. I think Sam Walton would, in fact, embrace Wal-Mart's efforts to improve the quality of life for our customers and our associates by doing what we need to do in sustainability."

54   Then he posed a challenge to the audience: "What other company in the world could do this? This company is uniquely positioned. But we will not be measured by our aspirations. We will be measured by our actions." Of that there's no doubt. This is Wal-Mart, after all. The whole world will be watching.

Gregg Easterbrook

Some Convenient Truths

Playing on the title of Al Gore's influential book and film, *An Inconvenient Truth,* Gregg Easterbrook suggests that global warming can be a "convenient truth" once we find the will to stop it—and once we stop believing that the disaster is inevitable. Easterbrook is a contributing editor at the *Atlantic Monthly,* where this piece was published in 2006, as well as at the *Washington Monthly* and *New Republic.* He has served as a fellow at the Brookings Institute. Consider how this piece frames the issue of global warming amidst those who see the media debate as counterproductive and those who believe that public awareness must be raised in support of a sustainable future.

I f there is now a scientific consensus that global warming   1
must be taken seriously, there is also a related political consensus: that the issue is Gloom City. In *An Inconvenient
Truth*, Al Gore warns of sea levels rising to engulf New York and
San Francisco and implies that only wrenching lifestyle sacrifice can save us. The opposing view is just as glum. Even mild
restrictions on greenhouse gases could "cripple our economy,"
Republican Senator Kit Bond of Missouri said in 2003. Other
conservatives suggest that greenhouse-gas rules for Americans
would be pointless anyway, owing to increased fossil-fuel use in
China and India. When commentators hash this issue out, it's
often a contest to see which side can sound more pessimistic.

Here's a different way of thinking about the greenhouse effect: 2
that action to prevent runaway global warming may prove
cheap, practical, effective, and totally consistent with economic
growth. Which makes a body wonder: Why is such environmental optimism absent from American political debate?

Greenhouse gases are an air-pollution problem—and all previ-   3
ous air-pollution problems have been reduced faster and more
cheaply than predicted, without economic harm. Some of these
problems once seemed scary and intractable, just as greenhouse
gases seem today. About forty years ago urban smog was increasing so fast that President Lyndon Johnson warned, "Either we
stop poisoning our air or we become a nation [in] gas masks
groping our way through dying cities." During Ronald Reagan's
presidency, emissions of chlorofluorocarbons, or CFCs, threatened to deplete the stratospheric ozone layer. As recently as George
H. W. Bush's administration, acid rain was said to threaten a "new
silent spring" of dead Appalachian forests.

But in each case, strong regulations were enacted, and what   4
happened? Since 1970, smog-forming air pollution has declined
by a third to a half. Emissions of CFCs have been nearly eliminated, and studies suggest that ozone-layer replenishment is
beginning. Acid rain, meanwhile, has declined by a third since
1990, while Appalachian forest health has improved sharply.

Most progress against air pollution has been cheaper than   5
expected. Smog controls on automobiles, for example, were predicted to cost thousands of dollars for each vehicle. Today's new
cars emit less than 2 percent as much smog-forming pollution
as the cars of 1970, and the cars are still as affordable today as
they were then. Acid-rain control has cost about 10 percent of
what was predicted in 1990, when Congress enacted new rules.
At that time, opponents said the regulations would cause a
"clean-air recession"; instead, the economy boomed.

Greenhouse gases, being global, are the biggest air-pollution   6
problem ever faced. And because widespread fossil-fuel use is
inevitable for some time to come, the best-case scenario for the
next few decades may be a slowing of the rate of greenhouse-gas

buildup, to prevent runaway climate change. Still, the basic pattern observed in all other forms of air-pollution control—rapid progress at low cost—should repeat for greenhouse-gas controls.

7   Yet a paralyzing negativism dominates global-warming politics. Environmentalists depict climate change as nearly unstoppable; skeptics speak of the problem as either imaginary (the "greatest hoax ever perpetrated," in the words of Senator James Inhofe, chairman of the Senate's environment committee) or ruinously expensive to address.

8   Even conscientious politicians may struggle for views that aren't dismal. Mandy Grunwald, a Democratic political consultant, says, "When political candidates talk about new energy sources, they use a positive, can-do vocabulary. Voters have personal experience with energy use, so they can relate to discussion of solutions. If you say a car can use a new kind of fuel, this makes intuitive sense to people. But global warming is of such scale and magnitude, people don't have any commonsense way to grasp what the solutions would be. So political candidates tend to talk about the greenhouse effect in a depressing way."

9   One reason the global-warming problem seems so daunting is that the success of previous antipollution efforts remains something of a secret. Polls show that Americans think the air is getting dirtier, not cleaner, perhaps because media coverage of the environment rarely if ever mentions improvements. For instance, did you know that smog and acid rain have continued to diminish throughout George W. Bush's presidency?

10   One might expect Democrats to trumpet the decline of air pollution, which stands as one of government's leading postwar achievements. But just as Republicans have found they can bash Democrats by falsely accusing them of being soft on defense, Democrats have found they can bash Republicans by falsely accusing them of destroying the environment. If that's your argument, you might skip over the evidence that many environmental trends are positive. One might also expect Republicans to trumpet the reduction of air pollution, since it signifies responsible behavior by industry. But to acknowledge that air pollution has declined would require Republicans to say the words, "The regulations worked."

11   Does it matter that so many in politics seem so pessimistic about the prospect of addressing global warming? Absolutely. Making the problem appear unsolvable encourages a sort of listless fatalism, blunting the drive to take first steps toward a solution. Historically, first steps against air pollution have often led to pleasant surprises. When Congress, in 1970, mandated major reductions in smog caused by automobiles, even many supporters of the rule feared it would be hugely expensive. But the catalytic converter was not practical then; soon it was perfected, and suddenly, major reductions in smog became affordable.

Even a small step by the United States against greenhouse gases could lead to a similar breakthrough.

And to those who worry that any greenhouse-gas reductions   12
in the United States will be swamped by new emissions from China and India, here's a final reason to be optimistic: technology can move across borders with considerable speed. Today it's not clear that American inventors or entrepreneurs can make money by reducing greenhouse gases, so relatively few are trying. But suppose the United States regulated greenhouse gases, using its own domestic program, not the cumbersome Kyoto Protocol; then America's formidable entrepreneurial and engineering communities would fully engage the problem. Innovations pioneered here could spread throughout the world, and suddenly rapid global warming would not seem inevitable.

The two big technical advances against smog—the catalytic   13
converter and the chemical engineering that removes pollutants from gasoline at the refinery stage—were invented in the United States. The big economic advance against acid rain—a credit-trading system that gives power-plant managers a profit incentive to reduce pollution—was pioneered here as well. These advances are now spreading globally. Smog and acid rain are still increasing in some parts of the world, but the trend lines suggest that both will decline fairly soon, even in developing nations. For instance, two decades ago urban smog was rising at a dangerous rate in Mexico; today it is diminishing there, though the country's population continues to grow. A short time ago declining smog and acid rain in developing nations seemed an impossibility; today declining greenhouse gases seem an impossibility. The history of air-pollution control says otherwise.

Americans love challenges, and preventing artificial climate   14
change is just the sort of technological and economic challenge at which this nation excels. It only remains for the right politician to recast the challenge in practical, optimistic tones. Gore seldom has, and Bush seems to have no interest in trying. But cheap and fast improvement is not a pipe dream; it is the pattern of previous efforts against air pollution. The only reason runaway global warming seems unstoppable is that we have not yet tried to stop it.

Heather Rogers

Green by Any Means

Heather Rogers is a journalist who has written for the *New York Times Magazine, Mother Jones,* and *The Nation.* She is the author of *Gone Tomorrow: The Hidden Life of Garbage (2006),* from which this excerpt is taken. She also has created a documentary film of the same name and a later book entitled *Green Gone Wrong: How Our Economy Is Undermining the Environmental Revolution.* In this piece, Rogers explores some of the ways that the sustainability movement has attempted to overcome the large environmental issues surrounding our throw-it-away culture. As you read, consider how Rogers focuses upon the ways in which individual citizens might use their own awareness to drive reform. Do you feel that the practices that she describes might become common practice and are themselves sustainable?

"I find that everything I see is garbage . . . I went to a new restaurant last week, nice new place, you know, and I find myself looking at scraps of food on people's plates. Leftovers. I see butts in ashtrays. And when we get outside."

"You see it everywhere because it is everywhere."

"But I didn't see it before."

"You're enlightened now. Be grateful," I said.

Don Delillo, *Underworld*

1   Just up the Batcave's inclined concrete driveway lies a compact back-yard. The rear garden of this dwelling in Oakland, California, is no longer a patch of fertilized, clipped sod, but has been transformed into a thriving vegetable garden with squash, potatoes, strawberry plants, lettuce, flowers, beehives and a handmade solar oven. Surrounded by neighboring single-family bungalow style homes, the Batcave, as its denizens refer to it, is a low-waste abode created and occupied by a crew of political and environmental activists. The Batcave's garden is not only where the group grows a sizable portion of its food, but in this quiet oasis they process much of their waste.

2   A retooled plumbing system channels all the house's "graywater"—wastewater that flows down sinks and shower drains—into a homemade wetland system. A series of cascading pools filters out impurities as the wastewater passes through rocks,

sand, cattails and water hyacinths, rendering a prolific supply
for garden irrigation. A few short steps from the back door sits
a series of organic waste composting bins. One has active red
worms that process carrot tops, onion skins and moldy bread
into a rich soil amendment in a matter of days.

"We only throw out one small bag of garbage for the whole   3
house of eight adults each week," explains Tim Krupnik, Batcave resident. Krupnik and his housemates practice a "strict
conservation ethic," growing much of their own food, dumpster
diving and buying almost nothing new to maximize their use of
resources. The house even boasts a compost toilet, where
human excrement can be collected for processing into fertilizer.[1]

While this may not be enticing or realistic for the average   4
ecofriendly American, the Batcave proves that a low-waste
lifestyle is possible. Small-scale, individual rubbish reduction
and reuse efforts like the Batcave's are important visionary projects that demonstrate the viability of reconfiguring production,
commodity circulation, consumption and wasting. By now it is
commonly recognized among mainstream and radical environmental groups alike that discards should not be treated *after*
they get made, but instead society should generate less waste.
Advocates for addressing the root causes of rubbish vary widely
in their approaches and implementation of alternatives.

A plethora of waste solutions are available, other than those   5
offered by industry today. In addition to changes made based on
individual choice, the concept of "green capitalism" aims to keep
mass consumption chugging along while business and industry
take up more costly environmentally sound measures on their
own, without government involvement. An effort at reducing
discards using state intervention to influence changes in production is called "extended producer responsibility." In this
system, manufacturers are held financially accountable for the
consumer wastes their products generate. Some activists and
policy analysts advocate a return to refillable beverage containers as a low-cost way of reducing a huge category of discards.
The goal of "zero waste," another alternative, is to create mandated garbage reduction quotas, indirectly limiting production
with the aim of eliminating waste altogether. All of these
approaches stem from a common recognition that something is
dangerously off-kilter, but these solutions differ in crucial ways
that warrant closer scrutiny.

Refuseniks

People unwilling to wait for official solutions have always made   6
meaningful contributions to imagining different ways of living.
The following admirable yet Lilliputian efforts help point the
way forward in the realm of garbage.

7   Working as a free agent. San Francisco resident Caycee Cullen encourages people to stop consuming all those to-go cups and reuse empty food jars to drink from instead. (So many cafes and restaurants have switched to disposable dishware that, even if one doesn't order takeout, reusable ceramic cups and plates are increasingly scarce.) Americans consume more than 125 million disposable cups every day.[2] Cullen distributes clean, empty jars along with an illustrated instruction 'zine that notes the importance of keeping the container's original lid, to prevent leaking. The last page features a drawing of discarded paper cups piled high juxtaposed to the lone glass vessel with the lines: "The Jar keeps my daily contribution to the landfill low. One jar, not this waste."[3]

8   On a larger scale, the grassroots practice of "freecycling" is gaining momentum in towns across the globe. Started in 2003 by Tucson resident Deron Beal, freecycling matches people trying to purge with those in need of objects ranging from telephone poles to personal computers. These unions take place on local branches of the main freecycling website with the primary stipulation that everything must be given for free, the goal being to keep materials out of the landfill.[4] More immediate than classified ads, the Internet facilitates the quick linking of people and goods for reuse, eliminating time and communication delays that often lead to wasting.

9   Old-fashioned salvaging can also put a serious dent in trash production, as the owners of Berkeley's Urban Ore have learned. Thanks to an unusual municipal contract, Urban Ore has a license to glean discards from the city's dump. The for-profit business sells its haul at a depot it calls "Eco Park," a former factory surrounded by a giant outdoor lot. Countless rows of old white, pink and yellow toilets, sinks and bathtubs line the yard's western quadrant. Nearby, delicately paneled doors ripped from remodeled Victorians stand vertical and neat in a series of aisles. Near the back of the massive grey building are several clusters of upright windows leaning against each other, translucent and glinting in the sun. Inside, a wall of file cabinets butt up against a mound of precariously stacked chairs and everything from building materials, tools and old light fixtures to spatulas, desks and electronics are for sale.

10   Established in 1980, Urban Ore is dedicated to rerouting discarded goods away from the landfill and back into circulation. Mary Lou Van Deventer, co-owner of the enterprise, explains: "When we salvage for reuse and we save something in its already manufactured form, we conserve the material, the cultural value, and the energy that went into producing that object. Now, if the same object is shredded up and bashed and remanufactured into something new, it's good for it to be recycled, but it isn't nearly as good as if that value had been conserved in the

first place by using the object as is."[5] Urban Ore is the kind of operation that could be duplicated everywhere. Municipalities could be required by law to contract with salvaging companies, creating an improved version of common nineteenth-century scavenging and reuse practices.

These attempts at reducing and reusing, and the countless 11 others not mentioned here, reveal the wide range of grassroots alternatives to burning, burying and official forms of recycling.

Having It Both Ways

Green capitalism is a waste-cutting solution currently gaining 12 popularity among environmentalists, policy wonks, enlightened entrepreneurs, yuppies and New Agers alike. A product of the early 1990s and a kindred spirit to "socially responsible" business, green capitalism forges environmentally sound approaches to production that keep business and industry from poisoning and killing the planet. Central to this "new industrial revolution," as its proponents call it, is no government intervention and a belief that with the right tweaking, high consumption levels can continue unabated. While green capitalism's goal of taking care of nature is commendable, and while it rightly asserts that production processes need to change, the means by which it aims to achieve these goals must be interrogated to ascertain their viability.

Some of green capitalism's most vigorous promoters are the 13 upscale gardening chain-store owner Paul Hawken and the eco-minded architect William McDonough. Both have published books outlining their ideas and strategies for creating greener business, at the center of which lies design. Capitalism is not the root of environmental decline, green capitalists proclaim. The real problem stems from poor product and manufacturing design, which inevitably leads to huge amounts of wasted natural resources. Shunning government intervention, green capitalism's goal is for individual companies to voluntarily back-engineer manufacturing so that wastes are designed out of the process; castoffs would either break down harmlessly into the natural environment or be recycled infinitely in a nontoxic manner. It's a seductively simple idea. But there's a catch: how will this industrial transformation take place with no reduction in consumption and on a purely voluntary basis?

Continued high consumption levels are possible under green 14 capitalism if companies redesign their products to be endlessly reincarnated or to harmlessly disintegrate (a new twist on disposability). Under this system, markets can theoretically continue expanding, bypassing the perceived threat to business of reduced consumption that is so often associated with a pro-environmental agenda. The problem here is that ongoing mass production and its accompanying waste will persist.

15   This outcome is apparent with new forms of plastics. Current iterations of "bioplastics" (endorsed by McDonough and others) like those made from starch, soy and hemp may require huge amounts of water and energy to manufacture. They are also likely to promote monocropping and increased use of chemical fertilizers to ensure a uniform and reliable feedstock. This would further wipe out biodiversity and pollute water and soil. Additionally, increased demand and higher prices for crops to feed the plastics sector could impact the food supply, since those with the strongest purchasing power get the goods. Journalist George Monbiot argues: "Those who worry about the scale and intensity of today's agriculture should consider what farming will look like when it is run by the oil industry."[6]

16   According to environmental writer Daniel Imhoff, vegetable-based polymers are in theory better than the old resins, but "bioplastics are fundamentally a techno-fix to support our existing habits without changing the lifestyles of our convenience/consumer society."[7] And as we've seen with dumping, burning and recycling, although techno-fixes may appear to work in the short run, they are inadequate as long-term solutions because they leave intact the underlying structures that produce so much waste.

17   Green capitalism's other major weakness, a strident rejection of state intervention and regulatory laws, means that companies must make these changes because they believe it is the right thing to do. Furthermore, since going green often involves increasing expenses, business leaders must not only feel a sense of moral obligation, they must be willing and able to take actions that will reduce profits.

18   Addressing this issue in his book *Cradle to Cradle*, McDonough explains that he first establishes whether or not a potential client can become what he calls "eco-effective." "If they are firmly entrenched in . . . the grip of an ism (pure capitalism)—they might consider moving production to a place where labor and transportation are as cheap as possible, and [we] end the discussion there. If they are committed to a more stable approach, however, we press on."[8] In other words, if individual producers and businesses are able to incur greater costs, then they can go green. But if a company simply must compete in the marketplace, McDonough and his co-author Michael Braungart cut them loose. Since capitalism is bound by competition's coercive powers—after all, getting an edge on the competition by producing commodities at ever-lower prices is the root of so much resource extraction and wasting—McDonough and Braungart drop the ball at the most crucial moment.

19   When individual companies assume the added costs of going green, they risk losing business to rivals not saddled with the extra expenses. For the eco-friendly manufacturer, production

can easily result in more expensive commodities that can't hold their own in the marketplace.

In reality, business and industry must have unfettered access 20 to natural resources to compete effectively. In an amoral assessment, the market's sole purpose is accumulation for accumulation's sake, meaning that its only relation to nature is accumulation.⁹ To transform the relationship of business and manufacturing to nature requires the transformation of capitalism. Green capitalism's aversion to legally mandated controls on production is a reactionary tendency that may buffer its environmental agenda in the eyes of oldline industry but ultimately precludes meaningful change. As has been proven unequivocally over the last thirty years, corporate self-restraint does not work, especially when it comes to preserving the health of natural systems.

Without regulatory oversight, companies can adopt an eco- 21 logically responsible façade without making real systemic changes. Over the last several years, many companies have appeared to go green, but beneath the surface the exploitative apparatus churns away. Just because Ford hired McDonough to rebuild one of its River Rouge factories—where he famously installed grass on the roof—doesn't hinder the automaker from turning out some of the least fuel-efficient vehicles on the road, like its F-150 trucks and Expedition SUVs. Ford now exploits the "eco-effective" River Rouge plant as a tool to greenwash its image while continuing to market its gas-guzzling, carbon-dioxide-spewing hulks.

The same is true of corporate self-governance in the realm of 22 garbage. Coca-Cola pledged a 25 percent recycling target in the early 1990s when much public attention was concentrated on the issue. As political pressure and consumer focus shifted, without any government accountability and no restrictions on the use of the recycling symbol, Coke found that it didn't need to actually recycle to maintain its green image among consumers. In this permissive climate, Coke stopped using recycled plastic in its bottles altogether in 1994 and suffered few consequences, none of them legal or lasting. In 2001 the company was faced with renewed public calls for more recycling, but feeling little pressure to aim high, it promised to use a meager 2.5 percent reprocessed resin.¹⁰ In addition, Coca-Cola's biggest plastic PET bottle supplier, South Eastern Container, recently upgraded two factories that now output 60,000 brand-new half-liter soda bottles every hour, "which the company is claiming as a world first."¹¹ So much for the moral imperative.

The state has always been central not only in managing pop- 23 ulations in times of rebellion, disease, and economic or natural disaster, but also in stimulating capitalist expansion. No major developments in U.S. industry have taken shape without direct or indirect government assistance—from nineteenth-century railroad construction and the massive reorganization and streamlining of industry during World War II to today's corporate welfare and the ongoing subsidy of waste management. Since anti-environmental free marketeers have relied so extensively on the state and public funding, why should the government not intervene to responsibly steward ecological resources? If it can muster its armies, police, massive budgets and political power on behalf of U.S. industry, why should the state not gather those forces to protect the environment?

24   Just as the U.S. government has acted to promote industry, it has also been forced by social movements to make structural reforms that business hates (even if these changes benefit business in the long run) yet that are good for average people—reforms such as social security, welfare and food and drug inspection. Programs such as these prove that the state can effectively enforce restructuring that serves the public good.

Waste Not . . .

25   In a striking move, the conservative German government of Helmut Kohl passed the landmark 1991 Packaging Ordinance, a law that shifted the burden of collecting, sorting, recycling and disposing of packaging wastes away from taxpayers and onto manufacturers. A version of "extended producer responsibility," the ordinance forced industry to administer and bankroll a separate refuse handling system just for packaging. Amid fierce resistance from business and cheers from environmentalists, the Packaging Ordinance marked a serious intervention by government in the decisions of production, disallowing industry's full externalization of commodity waste costs. Not without its limits and flaws, Germany's still-active law has served as a model program for addressing the single largest component of the discard stream—packaging.

26   The mandatory nationwide ordinance allowed the manufacturing sector to formulate its own methods for handling trashed wrappers and containers; the result was what came to be known as the "green dot" system. Still in operation, the program is overseen by the environmental ministry and administered by an industry-led entity called Duales System Deutschland (DSD). The procedure is simple: After consumers make their purchases, they can discard the wrapping at the store, or, once home, they can place all their spent packaging into a yellow bin or bag that gets collected at the curbside by DSD.[12]

27   DSD financing comes from the country's private producers, who are required to pay a licensing fee proportionate to the cost of handling their specific packaging material based on weight and type. To signal payment, these manufacturers get to stamp

their cellophane, boxes, bottles and cans with the green dot symbol—two arrows swirling together—an image that not only helps consumers sort their discards, but also, like the recycling symbol in the United States, generates excellent eco-PR.

Germany's program was the first successful large-scale public implementation of extended producer responsibility (EPR). A new spin on waste reduction strategies proposed in the 1970s, EPR has gained popularity in the past decade and aims to shift from the public to manufacturers the duties of managing discarded commodities like packaging and the mushrooming piles of e-waste. The underlying idea is to persuade companies to generate less from the start. If they have to pay to handle and treat these wastes, the logic goes, producers will ultimately choose to create fewer disposables.   28

According to economist Frank Ackerman, the 1991 ordinance "jump-started producer responsibility—it was proof of possibility." Ackerman also explains that in the face of the German program's indisputable success, government's active role in curtailing waste production could no longer be discredited: "It was such a striking example of going from nothing to accomplishing this complex task. The government decided to do it and did it, proving that producer responsibility could actually be implemented."[13]   29

The green dot system invalidated opponents' predictions of economic cataclysm and claims that the state could not successfully regulate industry for environmental protection. Hailed a success, the program significantly cut packaging consumption, boosted recycling, and sustained the use of refillable bottles. In the ordinance's first half-decade, manufacturers used 7 percent less packaging; by contrast during that same period, U.S. container consumption grew by 13 percent.[14] Obligatory recycling targets under the Packaging Ordinance, which increased incrementally over time, have kept DSD on track. As a result, recycling for packaging has surged by 65 percent since 1991.[15] And the ordinance's requirement that at least 72 percent of the country's beverage containers be refillable has guaranteed reduced consumption by requiring reuse.[16] The program has proven so beneficial that, since the mid-1990s, fifteen European Union countries as well as Korea, Taiwan and Japan all enacted variations on Germany's Packaging Ordinance.[17]   30

Unfortunately, the German system has its downsides. In more recent years packaging production in the country has increased, despite the green dot program.[18] As of 2003, Germany was the largest single market for packaging throughout Europe.[19] So, while producers may be financing the handling of their packaging wastes, they are not deterred from producing these discards in ever-greater amounts. This reveals the system's limits; mere encouragement of rubbish reduction is not enough.   31

While Germany's system forces manufacturers to internalize some refuse treatment fees, more accurately distributing production costs, it has not brought changes that directly cut waste.

32   Among its other shortcomings, the green dot signals only that a producer has paid its fees to DSD, guaranteeing neither that a package was made from recycled materials nor that it will be reprocessed. What's more, recycling is defined so broadly under the green dot system that it includes the channeling of used plastics to the steel, petrochemical and oil industries for burning as "fuel." And since recycling in Germany is just as susceptible to market fluctuations as in the United States, materials that get collected by DSD might easily end up incinerated or landfilled instead.[20]

33   Despite these weaknesses, the daily sifting of one's discards contributes to more widespread popular consciousness of the value of trashed materials. The German green dot is but one element in a nationwide household trash-sorting culture. In addition to segregating most packaging wastes, residents separate recyclable paper, glass and metal, while they store food castoffs in special brown bins. Consumers return empty milk and beer bottles to the supermarket and whatever is left over (not much) gets deposited into a black refuse can.[21] In the United States, such setups are not entirely unheard of. San Francisco's recently revamped municipal system calls for extensive household segregation of castoffs—sending bottles, cans and paper to recycling centers and food scraps to a compost facility, with the much reduced remainder going to the landfill.[22] San Francisco's new program is a sharp improvement on previous methods and, like the German system, it fosters and awareness of discards as useful, not just spent and dirty waste.

34   In their own way, these comprehensive programs address the significance of individual choice in the creation of waste. While the underlying structures that enforce garbage are paramount, individual practices are not entirely irrelevant. In the last century the majority of Americans have gleefully accepted, even embraced, a high-waste lifestyle. And in some ways it's understandable. There are real conveniences offered by disposable products like paper cups and disapers, while seductive packaging and entrancing new commodities are hard to resist for many shoppers. There's no doubt that bulk bins, canvas shopping totes and used plastic bags drying in the dish rack can seem like part of a more pinched, less spontaneous lifestyle. Consuming sexy packaging and the latest styles is, for large parts of the population, an intensely fun and gratifying experience. And, while people might feel bad about throwing things away, they may also get a type of pleasure from tossing out the old and bringing in the new.[23]

These realities, constantly reinforced in mainstream society, 35
can present cultural and political obstacles to change. Creating
an atmosphere where expanded reforms protecting human and
environmental safety and health seem normal and even hip—
witness programs like those in Germany and San Francisco—
can foster a shift in thinking about consumption that counters
the dominant line. Recycling unleashes various forms of imag-
inings; rather than just the misperception that it actually works
as a long-term solution, recycling—crucially—also opens the
political and cultural imagination to other creative possibilities.

. . . Want Not

A more sustainable solution to the flood of trash is the refillable 36
bottle. Cast aside by major U.S. manufacturers in the 1970s and
1980s, this method of reusing packaging is profitably employed
in parts of Western Europe, Latin America and Canada today,
often by the same North American firms that reject using it at
home. Stimulating local and regional economies, refillable bottling plants create more jobs while massively reducing packaging wastes.

The way the refillable system works might still be familiar to 37
some: the thick bottles usually require a deposit and are
returned to stores once they're empty. From there, beverage
makers take them to a washing and refilling facility. After bottles are sanitized and an electronic "sniffer" has weeded out any
contaminated units, the containers are filled on an assembly line
at a pace equal to that in factories using brand-new packaging.
Once refilled, the bottles are shipped to retailers and the cycle
begins anew. Today refillables are used on average twenty times
before getting tossed.[24]

Refillables have stuck around in other countries for two rea- 38
sons: regulatory laws and economics. Once ubiquitous in the
United States, refillables still hold the vast majority of bottle
markets in Denmark, the Netherlands, Germany and Finland,
and in Ontario, Quebec, and Prince Edward Island in Canada
because their governments have enacted measures that require
and promote reusable containers. Many of these laws were
passed in the 1970s to prevent throwaways from needlessly clog-
ging disposal sites. Beverage makers have also continued using
refillables in Latin American countries like Mexico, Brazil and
Argentina because these bottles cost markedly less than disposable packaging. And producing drinks that sell at a lower price
opens more markets to buyers with lower incomes.[25]

Coming typically in glass or thick PET, this washable, reusable 39
form of packaging has slashed garbage output by an estimated
380,000 tons annually in Denmark, while in Finland garbage has

been reduced by an estimated 390,000 tons.[26] As of 1998, the annual per capita output of packaging wastes in Finland was half that of other European Union countries, most of which don't mandate the use of refillables.[27] The larger environmental impact of recirculating packaging includes dramatic reductions in greenhouse gas and carbon monoxide emissions, and reduced consumption of water and energy.[28] The positive effects extend into the creation of jobs; more workers are needed when companies use refillables than when they use one-way containers. If Germany switched entirely to reusable bottles, 27,000 new jobs would be created.[29] Refillables also stimulate local economies, because the system requires processing in decentralized bottling plants.

40   And, contrary to the dominant cultural narrative in countries like the United States over the last thirty years, people still like bringing back their empties. According to a recent Gallup poll, Finnish consumers preferred buying beer in returnable bottles by a margin of almost 80 percent, while 94 percent favored soda in reusable containers.[30] The majority of Germans— 69 percent—want to buy their refreshments in returnable vessels. But it's not just consumers who like less packaging; the Quebec Brewers Association says its members' loyalty to the reusable stems from its unbeatable low cost and high customer participation. A group of regional Canadian beer makers prefer the returnable system so much that they joined in a formal agreement to continue using refillables.[31]

41   Despite all the upsides, the reusable is under assault from government and business in many European and Latin American countries. The European Union has challenged Denmark's and Germany's laws as obstacles to free trade. The outcome of this offensive appears to be a gradual eroding of each country's refillable system.[32] Many drink makers are also antagonistic toward refillables, constantly angling to ditch the practice so they can centralize bottling and distribution and market the higher-priced disposables. But another culprit is supermarket chain stores like Aldi and Wal-Mart. These companies often refuse to stock refillables because of the extra space and labour that handling them requires. As these retailers take over markets formerly served by small local shops, they exercise their colossal market power over the future of refillables. If there are no laws regulating and promoting bottle reuse, then such mega-retailers can extinguish the practice with relative ease. This outcome serves neither customers nor the environment, but instead benefits producers and sellers.[33]

Beyond Waste

42   Another approach gaining momentum among environmentalists over the past decade is called "zero waste." Zero waste refers to eliminating refuse before it gets made, at the front end, instead of

the current norm of treating trash only after it already exists, at the back end. Some advocates explain that zero waste sprang from the inadequacies of recycling, since the latter does not directly curb waste production.[34] This new method is more comprehensive than reprocessing alone: "Zero waste maximizes recycling, minimizes waste, reduces consumption and ensures that products are made to be reused, repaired or recycled back into nature or the market-place."[35] Similar to green capitalism's program to redesign industrial production, and a further development of past reuse and recycling practices like 1970s source reduction, zero waste works through grassroots activism and policy-level advocacy to foster deep structural reforms.

According to the GrassRoots Recycling Network, zero waste   43
centers on "corporate responsibility for wastes, government policies for resource conservation, and sustainable jobs from discards."[36] Although they share many aims, zero waste differs from green capitalism in that the state plays a key role in regulating discard levels and natural resources. Zero-waste proponents Bill Sheehan and Daniel Knapp explain that government intervention is warranted if asking business to change is not effective. Federal, state and local officials should step in to "change rules and laws to reward resource conserving behavior and penalize resource wasting behavior."[37]

Enforcing production modifications is an important aspect of   44
zero waste because so much refuse is the result of commodity packaging and built-in obsolescence, and most castoffs are actually created during manufacturing. A zero-waste system would require manufacturers to use nontoxic biodegradable materials that could be safely returned to the earth; maximum recirculation would be mandatory for any hazardous nonrenewable inputs that were absolutely necessary. According to some nowasters, whatever does not fit into those two categories should be banned. Zero waste thus aims to retool industry so that it relies only on resources that are easily reusable.[38]

This anti-trash system also seeks to incorporate environmen-   45
tal costs into the price of a commodity, ending the long-time industry practice of externalizing these costs. As a result, that bottle of water for sale at the corner store would carry a higher price tag and might even list ingredients that more accurately reflect the product's contents—like waste from drilling for the natural gas used to make resin for the container.

But these changes are impossible according to pro-waste lob-   46
byists and their industry clients. Those opposed to transformations like zero waste use the old chimera of mass layoffs and ensuing poverty. This assertion is as baseless today as it was in the 1970s when the same bogeyman was enlisted against beverage container deposit laws. Arguments that reusing discards would eliminate manufacturing jobs are vague and as yet unproven,

while recycling actually increases the demand for labor, creating ten times more jobs per ton than landfilling or incineration.[39] What's more, per-ton, recycling-based manufacturers can employ up to sixty times more workers than do landfills.[40] In 2000, North Carolina had almost 9,000 employees in the recycling trades while a much smaller proportion were displaced from old jobs—ninety waste handlers and three timber harvesters.[41] Zero waste promises to generate opportunities for small businesses, boost the need for skilled labor, and enrich local economies rather than siphon off revenues and jobs.[42]

47   Zero-waste advocates have the goal of shutting down landfills and incinerators altogether. While this might sound implausible, it is important to note there are still cultures that have yet to formulate a word for garbage because it is incomprehensible that any object could be useless.[43] Zero-waste programs have already been implemented in places like Toronto; Canberra Territory, Australia; and Halifax, Nova Scotia; and almost half of New Zealand's local authorities have committed to eliminate landfilled waste by 2015.[44] Zero waste poses the idea of garbage as an option, not some inevitable outcome of a natural system. In other words, discarded materials do not have to be wasted.

Garbage In, Garbage Out

48   To truly confront the issue of garbage and its impact on the environment two fundamental shifts must take place. First, trash needs to be addressed in terms of production instead of consumption. Pinning responsibility for the ever-growing swells of packaging and broken, outmoded commodities on individual consumers has only facilitated manufacturing's expanded and intensified wasting. Additionally, while consumers making choices with the environment in mind is a good thing, it is in no way a real solution to our trash woes. Second, industry's inability to regulate itself must be acknowledged and replaced with enforceable environmental measures. Failing to remake production and sidestepping legislatively mandated protections will only bring further environmental degradation.

49   In encouraging waste reduction before garbage gets produced, Germany's system and zero-waste programs do not operate just in the spheres of circulation and consumption, they begin to reach back into the realm of production. This profoundly distinguishes them from other strategies that focus on the acts of the consumer and aim to manage wastes only after they're already made. Extended producer responsibility and zero waste programs broach a more active role for the public as stewards of human and ecological health by influencing the production process. However, in the United States and many other capitalist countries, manufacturing has remained largely untouched,

allowing business to operate on its own terms, in what Marx called "the hidden abode of production."[45]

Over the last thirty years, when individual towns, states 50 and countries have passed laws restricting the disposal of certain materials—closing a dump site or prohibiting toxic substances—without limiting the *creation* of those wastes, companies have continued making the stuff. And when the resulting trash can't be treated locally, it just gets exported elsewhere. Likewise, when recycling and recycled content in commodities is not mandated, U.S. firms have shown they will not implement the practice in a meaningful way. Anything short of government enforcement of production regulations to protect human and environmental health will ultimately end in failure.

And if these measures are to successfully govern and protect 51 natural systems, then the state must act in the public interest and not as an agent of business. It is not enough simply to turn over regulatory control to governments without addressing the injustice so often inherent in the state. Currently, the EU is pursuing a legal case against container laws in Denmark and Germany, arguing that these countries' packaging regulations violate free trade. Likewise, U.S. courts consistently support the export of garbage on the grounds that restricting it would illegally hinder interstate commerce. Putting the well-being of commerce above the health of the environment that everyone depends on reveals a profound lack of real democracy. As sociologist Joel Kovel writes, "The struggle for an ecologically rational world must include a struggle for the state, and since the state is the repository of many democratic hopes, it is a struggle for the *democratization* of the state."[46] There must be democratic decision-making in the regulation of industry and the use of natural resources.

When the public has no say in manufacturing—which mate- 52 rials get used; how they are extracted from nature; what kind of production process is employed; and levels of toxicity in manufacturing, use, and disposal of materials—the democratic utilization of our common natural resources is fundamentally undermined. Just as the airwaves belong to the people, so too is the rest of the natural world part of the public commons. It is only fair that since we share the responsibility for and consequences of wastes, we should also participate in the choices made during production, the real source of trash. U.S. industry's largely unfettered access to natural resources is the mark of a deeply undemocratic system.[47]

Industry and government justify ever-more disposable com- 53 modities, growing mountains of trash, and environmental destruction from unchecked production as necessary for a healthy economy that provides jobs and a high standard of living. However, according to the U.S. Census, the country has grown more economically polarized over the last thirty years. Today there is greater income inequality than any time since World War II. This disparity increased throughout the 1990s as the middle class shrank even in the midst of the longest period of economic expansion in fifty years.[48] And, as of 2000, the poorest 20 percent of households received just 3.6 percent of the country's total household income, while the richest 20 percent took home 49.7 percent.[49] Today, layoff rates are higher than they have been since the deep recession of the early 1980s.[50] Under the current U.S. market system, since the year 2000 more than 2 million jobs have left the country due to outsourcing, replaced by half as many low-wage, unprotected service-sector jobs.

54   This means that all those trashed appliances, cars, clothes, and the mountains of wasted packaging are actually not the product of an economy that delivers its benefits to the most people. On the contrary, the biggest beneficiaries of a trash-rich marketplace are those at the top. Garbage is the detritus of a system that unscrupulously exploits not only nature, but also human life and labor. Why should Americans risk their health and the survival of natural systems to enrich the nation's elite? Though the benefits of trash are unequally distributed, pollution threatens the natural systems that affect everyone.

55   Since the 1970s predictions of an environmental apocalypse have abounded, but today's supply of food, manufactured goods, fossil fuels and clean water seems to indicate that the natural world is just fine. This is because in the market economy deeper environmental destruction is kept hidden, cloaked by the commodity form. Since consumers find the finished product in the store and don't see the piles of mining slag, clear-cut forests, and air and water pollution resulting from the item's production and disposal, they more easily believe that waste is manageable, while the devastation of nature remains an abstraction. This destruction is further obscured by the pro-waste bloc, which consistently generates messages minimizing the effects of industrial production on nature. As sociologist Leslie Sklair argues, these interests aim to "deflect attention from the idea of a singular ecological crisis and to build up the credibility of the idea that what we face is a series of manageable environmental problems."[51] But, in reality, ecological cataclysm has been unfolding unevenly across the globe over the last several decades.

56   Garbage, the miniature version of production's destructive after-math, inevitably ends up in each person's hands, and it is proof that all is not well. Trash therefore has the power to unmask the exploitation of nature that is crystallized in all commodities. Garbage reveals the market's relation to nature; it teases out the environmental politics hidden inside manufactured goods. Because of this, transforming the way our society

conceives of and treats the everyday substance of garbage would have profound effects in other areas of ecological crisis, such as dying oceans, ozone depletion, global warming, and the proliferation of toxic chemicals throughout our food, water, and air.

Notes

1. Based on visits to the Batcave and multiple interviews with Tim Krupnick, 2001-2002. Also see Tim Krupnick, "The Urban Wilds Project," *Permaculture Activist* 6, no. 45 (March 2001), pp. 63–65.
2. Daniel Imhoff, "Thinking Outside of the Box," *Whole Earth* (Winter 2002), p. 9.
3. Caycee Cullen, "The Jar," instruction 'zine, 2003.
4. Tina Kelley, "One Sock, with Hole? I'll Take It," *New York Times*, March 16, 2004. Also see Freecycle website, www.freecycle.org.
5. From the documentary film *Gone Tomorrow*.
6. George Monbiot, "Fuel for Nought," *Guardian Weekly*, Dec. 3, 2004. It would be naïve to think the petroleum sector would give up the booming plastics trade just because new synthetics weren't made with petrochemicals.
7. Imhoff, "Thinking Outside of the Box."
8. McDonough and Braungart, *Cradle to Cradle*, p. 151.
9. According to urban geographer Richard Walker, "Capital's only relation to nature is ultimately its relation to accumulation. But the technological power is so great now that the law of accumulation can mean a law of destruction of the earth and of life on earth at a scale never before seen . . . Social regulation is an inherent part, a necessary part of social life under modern production." From the documentary film *Gone Tomorrow*.
10. "Setting the Record Straight," available from the Container Recycling Institute website, www.container-recycling.org/plasfact/PETstraight.htm.
11. Des King, "Calling the Shots," *Packaging Today International* 25, no. 9 (Sept. 2003).
12. Sara Bloom, "How Is Germany Dealing with Its Packaging Waste?" *Whole Earth* (Winter 2002), pp. 23–25.
13. From an interview with Frank Ackerman, April 22, 2004.
14. Imhoff, "Thinking Outside of the Box," p. 14; Jim Motavalli, "Zero Waste," *E the Environmental Magazine* 12, no. 2 (March/April 2001), electronic version.
15. "Germany's Green Dot System Challenged," *UK: Environment News*, March 30, 2004; "Packaging Recycling for a Better Climate," *The OECD Observer*, Dec. 2002.
16. Thanks to this guideline, the government was able to rein in producers who in recent years marketed almost twice as many single-use containers as was allowed. Otto Pohl, "Sales Slow as Germans Pile Up Empties," *New York Times*, March 5, 2003.
17. Motavalli, "Zero Waste."
18. Bloom, "How Is Germany Dealing?" p. 24.
19. As of 2003, the annual per capita consumption for packaging in Germany was €319, in the United Kingdom it was €234, and in Russia (whose population exceeds Germany's by 77 percent) the figure was a miniscule €19. See King, "Calling the Shots."
20. All green dot packaging that does not go to recycling plants is burned or buried outright. See Rob Edwards, "Waste Not, Want Not: Outside

Every German Home Stands a Multicolored Set of Dustbins," *New Scientist* (Dec. 23, 1995), electronic version.

21. Ibid.

22. San Francisco's program is dubbed "Fantastic Three" and is operated by the refuse company Norcal. See Kim A. O'Connell, "San Francisco Giant," *Waste Age* 34, no. 12 (Dec. 1, 2003).

23. This point came out of a correspondence with my editor, Liza Featherstone.

24. Brenda Platt and Doug Rowe, *Reduce, Reuse, Refill* (Washington, D.C.: Institute for Local Self-Reliance, April 2002), produced under a joint project with the Grass-Roots Recycling Network, p. 27.

25. Ibid., pp. 1-2.

26. Ibid., p. 1.

27. Ibid., p. 33.

28. Ibid., pp. 5-9.

29. Ibid., pp. 14-15.

30. Ibid., p. 33.

31. If companies are not trying to centralize production and distribution, as the giant first like Coca-Cola have done, then refillables can actually lower costs. See ibid., p. 25.

32. Paul Millbank, "Aluminum Recycling Vital to Global Supply Chain," *Aluminum International Today* 16, no. 5 (Sept. 1, 2004); "Bottle Battle," *Economist Intelligence Unit—Country Monitor* (Nov. 3, 2003).

33. Platt and Rowe, *Reduce, Reuse, Refill*! pp. 27–29, 40–41.

34. Eric Lombardi, "Beyond Recycling! Zero Waste . . . Or Darn Near"; see Grass-Roots Recycling Network website, www.grrn.org/zerowaste/articles/biocycle-_zw_commentary.html.

35. GrassRoots Recycling Network website, www.grrn.org/zerowaste/zerowaste_faq.html.

36. Ibid.

37. Bill Sheehan and Daniel Knapp, "Zeroing In on Zero Waste," see Grass-Roots Recycling Network website, www.grrn.org/zerowaste/articles/zeroing_in.html.

38. Kate Soper, "Waste Matters," *Capitalism Nature Socialism* 14 (2), no. 54 (June 2003), pp. 131-32. As noted in previous chapters, for every ton of household waste, more than 70 tons of manufacturing wastes are produced. See GrassRoots Recycling Network, *Wasting and Recycling in the United States 2000*, p. 13.

39. According to the GrassRoots Recycling Network, *Wasting and Recycling in the United States 2000*: "On a per-ton basis, sorting and processing recyclables alone sustains ten times more jobs than landfilling or incineration." Cited in Eric Lombardi, "Beyond Recycling! Zero Waste . . . Or Darn Near."

40. GrassRoots Recycling Network, *Wasting and Recycling in the United States 2000*, p. 27.

41. Ibid., p. 28.

42. Gary Liss, "Zero Waste?" GrassRoots Recycling Network website, www.grrn.org/zerowaste/articles/whatiszw.html. For more on jobs, see Paula DiPerna, "Mean Green Job Machine," *Nation* 278, no. 20 (May 24, 2004), p. 7.

43. One example: Gabriela Zamorano explained in a November 2003 conversation that she worked with in Oaxaca, Mexico, has no word for garbage in their native language.

44. "Drowning in a Tide of Discarded Packaging," *Guardian* (London), March 9, 2002.

46. Joel Kovel, *The Enemy of Nature: The End of Capitalism or The End of The World?* (London: Zed Press, 2002), p. 155.

47. On the undemocratic nature of the use of natural resources, see Soper, "Waste Matters"; Commoner, *Making Peace with the Planet*.

48. "The U.S. Labor Force in the New Economy," *Social Education* 68, no. 2 (March 1, 2004), electronic version.

49. "USA Risk: Macroeconomic Risk," *Economist Intelligence Unit— Riskwire*, no. 101 (July 7, 2003), electronic version.

50. Statistical evidence shows that layoffs are more frequent now, whether the economy is on the upswing or in the trough of a downturn. See Louis Uchitelle, "Layoff Rate at 8.7%, Highest Since 80's," *New York Times*, Aug. 2, 2004.

51. Leslie Sklair, *The Transnational Capitalist Class* (Oxford: Blackwell, 2001), p. 207.

getting into the conversation ···10

Sustaining Our Environment: Who Are the Best Guardians?

1. Before taking on the title question of this section, it is important to settle on some definitions: What do we mean by "sustainability"? What does it mean to act as a "guardian" of the environment? As is discussed in the introduction to this section, there are many stakeholders in our nation's attempts to sustain our natural environment. After all, no one wants the destruction of the environment. The debate is really about the details: What does a sustainable environment look like? Who is best equipped to bring that about? What methods might be used to do so? What is the best balance of sustaining our environment and other competing interests such as the economy? Debates on these and related questions are carried out in this chapter through the dialogue between Patrick Moore, one of the early members of Greenpeace, and representatives of the current Greenpeace administration. How is each author's perspective on those questions similar or different? How do their perspectives interact with definitions offered or implied by some of the other pieces in this section? Develop a range of possible definitions of sustainability, guardianship, and activism to see what points seem to extend across all of them, and where they differ. You might also offer, based on these pieces, your own definitions.

2. In many protest movements, businesses and industry are cast into the role of the enemy—as organizations that put profit motive ahead of the larger good of individuals and the society. But Patrick Moore, Margery Kraus, Michael Brune, and Marc Gunther illustrate some ways that businesses can be great advocates for the sustainability movement. Are you convinced by these arguments? Can businesses, considering their profit motives, be trusted as guardians of the environment? Do they have a stake in a sustainable environment? Or should we be suspicious of their motives? Based upon your reading of these pieces and those about the work of activist groups that suggest that businesses are more of the problem than a source of the solution, where do you stand on this?

3. Are violence and destruction of property ever justified in activism? That is the question that many of the pieces in this section explore. Emma Marris' essay, in particular, asks how far we should go "in the name of nature," asking us to consider whether, and when, extremist measures are called for in order to counteract the inaction of government and business on important matters—matters that they believe themselves will cause even more widespread damage. After listening in to these various arguments (including the dialogue between Patrick Moore and his critics), see whether you can formulate your own position on "extremist" behavior. How far can/should we go in the

name of nature? As you do, consider some of those who have, in the past, been called *extremists* (including Martin Luther King Jr. and bell hooks, whose work is included in Chapter 6). How does one find the line?

4. One of the goals of the environmental and sustainability movements has been to put into the public eye the practices that may be harming our environment, and thus make us more conscious of the choices that we make as individuals and as a society. For example, Heather Rogers' book *Gone Tomorrow* (from which the chapter, "Green by Any Means" is excerpted), is subtitled *The Hidden Life of Garbage*; that is, her book tries to show us places and practices that are often hidden from us when we simply place our trashcan out on the curb. As you look back at the readings in this chapter, consider how they attempt to bring the hidden facets of our culture's practices into the public eye. Then, you might do some further research on the kinds of public campaigns that have or might advance these arguments. You might even try to formulate a public relations campaign that helps particular audiences better understand why an environmental issue is worth our consideration—and how to best get that message across to specific audiences.

extending the conversation ...5

Opportunities for Reading, Writing, and Research

Although the readings in *Conversations* are organized into specific topic areas, they can also be used to start your research into other related areas of interest. The following writing opportunities suggested can help you extend the conversations across the various subjects discussed in the book—and beyond the book into research areas you might explore on your own. These examples demonstrate how you might develop the readings from this book into larger projects; you can come up with many more on your own. As you do so, think especially about how your major field of study or other interests you have can inform your research.

1. The first Earth Day took place in 1970 and was modeled after the activism that surrounded the Vietnam war protests. Hence, from the start, the environmental movement has carried with it some of the power and some of the stigma of grassroots activism. For some, that is considered its strength. For others, the connection between sustainability movements and the turbulent protests of the 1960s and 1970s has continued to label those interested in environmentalism "extremists" (or to quote Rush Limbaugh, "wackos"). In order to better understand the aura surrounding the contemporary environmental movement, you might do some research on the history and reputation of environmentalists. You could do this in a number of ways. You might study a particular figure in this movement (say, Rachel Carson or Wallace Stegner) or a particular organization (Greenpeace or the World Wildlife Federation). Or you could try to piece together a history of key moments in the movement from Earth Day 1970 to the present, showing how changes in the approach to this societal issue have changed with the times, taken on new dimensions due to other social contexts, or been passed down from one generation to the next. You also might do a visually based study, showing us a pictorial history of the environmental movement or some moment in it. As you study these individuals, movements, and approaches, you might also be able to discover what key principles or beliefs are at the heart of these movements as well and how the tactics to support those principles have changed over time.

2. While there are many facets to sustainability efforts, our attention to creating sustainable foods has been among the most pressing in recent public conversations. These conversations have forced us to be more conscious of what we eat, where it comes from, and how food production networks function. In order to extend the conversation about sustainable foods conducted through the readings in Chapter 9 and to connect it to larger issues of environmental sustainability in Chapter 10, you might do further research on the ways that foods are produced in this country. There are many models for this approach in this

section of *Conversations*; whether it be asking us to think about "green eggs and ham," the "hidden life of garbage," or the ingredients that comprise that tasty little snack food, many of the authors help widen our perspective on food by asking us to see its origin. Choose a particular food or food type, and do some research on that topic, constructing an essay that tells us the truth about its production. For example, you might write about what makes something a certified "organic" product. Or you might investigate how vegetables are transported from foreign countries. Or you might look at the preservation techniques of a particular food or the practices that are used by large or small manufacturers (and their suppliers) to provide us with a particular product—Hershey's chocolate, Campbell's soups, Kashi foods, Uncle Ben's rice, and so forth. Tell the story of that food and the specific benefits and problems that the cycle of food production provides.

3. It is difficult to pass a single hour, let alone a day, without being confronted with some "Going Green" message. Companies are touting their environmental efforts, rebranding themselves in ways that foreground their efforts at advancing a more sustainable world. (B.P., British Petroleum, has reinvented itself as "Beyond Petroleum," and General Electric has used a successful Ecomagination campaign, for example.) So is this a sincere effort at pushing environmental awareness and practices, or is it just new packaging—what some have called "greenwashing"? In order to reach some conclusions about this, you might first choose a particular advertising campaign that is built upon the "go green" movement, and then go on to research the actual environmental record and changes made by that company, writing a report that shows how a specific company or industry ("clean coal," for example) is, or is not, living up to its public face.

A Guide to Incorporating Sources and Avoiding Plagiarism

B ecause the conversation model of reading and writing necessarily involves your bringing together your own ideas with those of others, incorporating the words and ideas of others both effectively and ethically is crucial. As you situate yourself in the conversation, do so in ways that make clear the line between your thoughts and those of others. This is important both to help build a credible argument and to avoid plagiarism.

Plagiarism is using someone else's work—published or unpublished—without giving the creator of that work sufficient credit. This can include words, ideas, or illustrations. A serious breach of scholarly ethics, plagiarism can have severe consequences. Students risk a failing grade or disciplinary action ranging from suspension to expulsion. Plagiarism can occur both intentionally and unintentionally.

Documentation: The Key to Avoiding Unintentional Plagiarism

It can be difficult to tell when you have unintentionally plagiarized something. Writers are free to use a limited amount of another's work in their own papers and books. However, to make sure that they are not plagiarizing that work, they need to take care to credit the source accurately and clearly for every use. Documentation is the method that writers use to give credit to the creators of material they use. It involves providing essential information about the source of the material, which enables readers to find the material for themselves. Documentation requires two elements: (1) a list of sources used in the paper and (2) citations in the text that point readers to items in that list. To use documentation and avoid unintentionally plagiarizing from a source, you need to know how to

- Identify sources and information that need to be documented

- Document sources in a Works Cited list (MLA) or Reference list (APA); in some classes, you may be asked to use other documentation styles such as Chicago, Turabian, or CBE, depending upon the discipline
- Use material gathered from sources: in summary, paraphrase, and quotation
- Create in-text references
- Use correct grammar and punctuation to blend quotations into a paper

Identifying Sources and Information that Need to Be Documented

Whenever you use information from outside sources, you need to identify the source of that material. Major outside sources include books, newspapers, magazines, government sources, radio and television programs, material from electronic databases, correspondence, films, plays, interviews, speeches, and information from websites. Virtually all of the information you find in outside sources requires documentation. The one major exception to this guideline is that you do not have to document common knowledge. Common knowledge is widely known information about current events, famous people, geographical facts, or familiar history. However, when in doubt, the safest strategy is to provide documentation.

Documenting Sources in a Works Cited List

You need to choose the documentation style that is dominant in your field or required by your instructor. Take care to use only one documentation style in any one paper and to follow its documentation formats consistently. In English classes, the most widely used style manual is the *MLA Handbook for Writers of Research Papers,* published by the *Modern Language Association (MLA),* which is the style shown in this guide. No matter the style you use, it is important that you refer to a reliable handbook to help you properly use the documentation method; what follows is meant as a brief introduction to MLA style.

Constructing a Works Cited List in MLA Style

MLA lists are alphabetized by authors' last names. When no author is given, an item can be alphabetized by title, by editor, or by the name of the sponsoring organization. MLA style spells out names in full, inverts only the first author's name, and separates elements with a period. In the following MLA Works Cited list, note the use of punctuation such as commas and colons to separate and introduce material within elements. Note that in the most recent edition of the MLA Guide, the medium (Print, Web, etc.) is also listed, indicating the form of the source that you used. Note also that URLs are now rarely used; they are suggested only in the case of obscure or hard-to-locate sources. Another change from past versions of MLA style is that italics are preferred over underlining.

Periodicals

"Living on Borrowed Time." *Economist* 25 Feb. 3 Mar. 2006: 34–37. Print.

Spinello, Richard A. "The End of Privacy." *America* 4 Jan. 1997: 9–13. Print.

Williams, N. R., M. Davey, and K. Klock-Powell. "Rising from the Ashes: Stories of Recovery, Adaptation, and Resiliency in Burn Survivors." *Social Work Health Care* 36.4 (2003): 53–77. Print.

Zobenica, Jon. "You Might As Well Live." Rev. of *A Long Way Down* by Nick Hornby. *Atlantic* July–Aug. 2005: 148. Print.

Electronic Sources

Glanz, William. "Colleges Offer Students Music Downloads." *Washington Times* 25 Aug. 2004. Web. 17 Oct. 2004.

Human Rights Watch. *Libya: A Threat to Society? Arbitrary Detention of Women and Girls for "Social Rehabilitation."* Feb. 2006. Index No. E1802. Human Rights Watch. Web. 4 Mar. 2006.

McNichol, Elizabeth C., and Iris J. Lav. "State Revenues and Services Remain below Pre-Recession Levels." *Center on Budget Policy Priorites.* 6 Dec. 2005. Web. 10 Mar. 2006.

Books

Bidart, Frank. Introduction. *Collected Poems.* By Robert Lowell. Ed. Frank Bidart and David Gewanter. New York: Farrar, Strauss and Giroux, 2003. vii–xvi. Print.

Conant, Jennet. *109 East Palace: Robert Oppenheimer and the Secret City of Los Alamos.* New York: Simon, 2005.

—. *Tuxedo Park: A Wall Street Tycoon and the Secret Palace of Science That Changed the Course of World War II.* New York: Simon, 2002. Print.

Using Material Gathered from Sources: Summary, Paraphrase, Quotation

You can integrate material into your paper in three ways—by summarizing, paraphrasing, and quoting. A quotation, paraphrase, or summary must be used in a manner that accurately conveys the meaning of the source.

A *summary* is a brief restatement in your own words of the source's main ideas. Summary is used to convey the general meaning of the ideas in a source as a whole, without giving specific details or examples that may appear in the original. A summary is always much shorter than the work it treats. Take care to give the essential information as clearly and succinctly as possible in your own language.

A *paraphrase* is a restatement, in your own words and using your own sentence structure, of specific ideas or information from a source. The chief purpose of a paraphrase is *to maintain your own writing style* throughout your paper. A paraphrase can be about as long as the original passage.

A *quotation* reproduces an actual part of a source, word for word, to support a statement or idea, to provide an example, to advance an argument, or to add interest or color to a discussion. Often, a writer will use a quotation to show not only the information in a source, but also to capture the tone of the original author. The length of a quotation can range from a word or a phrase to several paragraphs. In general, quote the least amount possible that gets your point across to the reader.

Creating In-Text References in MLA Style

In-text references need to supply enough information to enable a reader to find the correct source listing in the Works Cited list. To cite a source properly in the text of your report when using MLA style, you generally need to provide some or all of the following information for each use of the source:

- Name of the person or organization that authored the source
- Title of the source (if there is more than one source by the same author or if no author is given)
- Page, paragraph, or line number, if the source has one (In APA style, you provide the year of publication and only include the page number if you are using a direct quotation.)

These items can appear as an attribution in the text ("According to Smith . . .") or in a parenthetical reference placed directly after the summary, paraphrase, or quotation.

Using an Introductory Attribution and a Parenthetical Reference

The author, the publication, or a generalized reference can introduce source material. Remaining identifiers (title, page number) can go in the parenthetical reference at the end, as in the first sentence of the example below. If a source, such as a website, does not have page numbers, it may be possible to put all of the necessary information into the in-text attribution, as in the second sentence of the following example.

> *The Economist* noted that since 2004, "state tax revenues have come roaring back across the country" ("Living" 34). However, McNichol and Lav, writing for the Center on Budget and Policy Priorities, claim that recent gains are not sufficient to make up for the losses suffered.

Identifying Material by an Author of More Than One Work Used in Your Paper

The attribution and the parenthetical reference combined must provide the title of the work, the author, and the page number of the citation.

> Describing the testing of the first atom bomb, Jennet Conant says, "The test had originally been scheduled for 4:00 A.M. on July 16, when most of the surrounding population would be sound asleep and there would be the least number of witnesses" (*109 East Palace* 304–05).

Identifying Material that the Source is Quoting   To use material that has been quoted in your cited source, add *qtd. in*, for "quoted in." Here, only one source by Conant is given in the Works Cited list.

> The weather was worrisome, but procrastination was even more problematic. General Groves was concerned that "every hour of delay would increase the possibility of someone's attempting to sabotage the tests" (qtd. in Conant 305).

Using Correct Grammar and Punctuation to Blend Quotations into a Paper

Quotations must blend seamlessly into the writer's original sentence, with the proper punctuation, so that the resulting sentence is neither ungrammatical nor awkward.

Using a Full-Sentence Quotation of Fewer Than Four Lines

A quotation of one or more complete sentences can be enclosed in double quotation marks and introduced with a verb, usually in the present tense and followed by a comma. Omit a period at the close of a quoted sentence, but keep any question mark or exclamation mark. Insert the parenthetical reference, then a period.

> "The test had originally been scheduled for 4:00 A.M. on July 16," Jennet Conant writes, "when most of the surrounding population would be sound asleep" (*109 East Palace* 304–05).

Introducing a Quotation with a Full Sentence

Use a colon after a full sentence that introduces a quotation.

> Spinello asks an important question:
> "What accounts for the government's ineptitude in safeguarding our privacy rights?" (9).

Introducing a Quotation with "That"

A single complete sentence can be introduced with a *that* construction.

> Chernow suggests that "the creation of New York's first bank was a formative moment in the city's rise as a world financial center" (199–200).

Quoting Part of a Sentence

Make sure that quoted material blends grammatically into the new sentence.

> McNichol and Lav assert that during that period, state governments were helped by "an array of fiscal gimmicks."

Using a Quotation That Contains Another Quotation

Replace the internal double quotation marks with single quotation marks.

> Lowell was "famous as a 'confessional' writer, but he scorned the term," according to Bidart (vii).

Adding Information to a Quotation

Any addition for clarity or any change for grammatical reasons should be placed in square brackets.

In *109 East Palace,* Conant notes the timing of the first atom bomb test: "The test had originally been scheduled for 4:00 A.M. on July 16, [1945,] when most of the surrounding population would be sound asleep" (304–05).

Omitting Information from Source Sentences

Indicate an omission from the original source with ellipsis marks (three spaced dots).

In *109 East Palace,* Conant says, "The test had originally been scheduled for 4:00 A.M. on July 16, when . . . there would be the least number of witnesses" (304–05).

Using a Quotation of More Than Four Lines

Begin a long quotation on a new line and set off the quotation by indenting it one inch from the left margin and double spacing it throughout. Do not enclose it in quotation marks. Put the parenthetical reference *after* the period at the end of the quotation.

> One international organization recently documented the repression of women's rights in Libya: The government of Libya is arbitrarily detaining women and girls in "social rehabilitation" facilities, . . . locking them up indefinitely without due process. Portrayed as "protective" homes for wayward women and girls, . . . these facilities are de facto prisons . . . [where] the government routinely violates women's and girls' human rights, including those to due process, liberty, freedom of movement, personal dignity, and privacy. (Human)

Evaluating Sources

It's very important to evaluate critically every source you consult, especially sources on the Internet, where it can be difficult to separate reliable sources from questionable ones. Ask these questions to help evaluate your sources:

- Is the material relevant to your topic?
- Is the source well respected?
- Is the material accurate?
- Is the information current?
- Is the material from a primary source or a secondary source?

In the end, although you will need to consult a reference book to properly cite sources, it is important that you begin from the spirit of why we cite sources. No matter the citation style, the purpose is to give credit where it is due and to incorporate respectfully the words and ideas of others as a way of showing the relationship of others' words and ideas to your own thesis or argument.

Linda Stern
Publishing School of Continuing
and Professional Studies
New York University

Credits

Author / Title Index